The Politics of the Urban Poor in Early Twentieth-Century India

In an area which has previously been neglected by the scholarly literature, Nandini Gooptu's magisterial history of the labouring poor in urban India represents a tour de force. By focusing on the role of the urban poor in caste, religious and nationalist politics, the author demonstrates how they emerged as a major social and political factor in South Asia during the interwar period. She explores their central importance in the economy through a discussion of the patterns of urbanisation, migration and employment and the development of a casual, 'informal' labour market. The empirical material, drawn from towns in Uttar Pradesh, provides compelling insights into what it meant to be poor in the urban environment: the insecurity and exploitation of the workplace; the problems of finding housing and the lack of access to the basic amenities of life; harassment and coercion by the police; and social and political exclusion by the elite, who regarded the impoverished with suspicion as undesirable and potentially dangerous. The author illuminates the processes of cultural transformation among the poor and their construction of social identities by concentrating on their modes of political action and perceptions. In this way, she takes issue with current interpretations of sectarian and nationalist politics that argue the salience of community identity and the irrelevance of class in political analysis. The book will be of interest to all those concerned with urban social history and with the comparative history and politics of poverty, labour and class relations, ethnic and sectarian conflict, and nationalist movements.

NANDINI GOOPTU is University Lecturer in South Asian Studies at the University of Oxford and Fellow of St Antony's College, Oxford.

Cambridge Studies in Indian History and Society 8

Cambridge Studies in Indian History and Society publishes monographs on the history and anthropology of modern India. In addition to its primary scholarly focus, the series also includes work of an interdisciplinary nature which contributes to contemporary social and cultural debates about Indian history and society. In this way, the series furthers the general development of historical and anthropological knowledge to attract a wider readership than that concerned with India alone.

A list of titles which have been published in the series is featured at the end of the book

The Politics of the Urban Poor in Early Twentieth-Century India

Nandini Gooptu

University of Oxford

CAMBRIDGE
UNIVERSITY PRESS

PUBLISHED BY THE PRESS SYNDICATE OF THE UNIVERSITY OF CAMBRIDGE
The Pitt Building, Trumpington Street, Cambridge, United Kingdom

CAMBRIDGE UNIVERSITY PRESS
The Edinburgh Building, Cambridge CB2 2RU, UK
40 West 20th Street, New York NY 10011–4211, USA
477 Williamstown Road, Port Melbourne, VIC 3207, Australia
Ruiz de Alarcón 13, 28014 Madrid, Spain
Dock House, The Waterfront, Cape Town 8001, South Africa

http://www.cambridge.org

First published 2001
First paperback edition 2004

Typeset in 10/12pt Plantin   System 3b2   [CE]

A catalogue record for this book is available from the British Library

Library of Congress Cataloguing in Publication data

Gooptu, Nandini.
   The politics of the urban poor in early twentieth-century India /
Nandini Gooptu.
      p.   cm. (Cambridge studies in Indian history and society; 8)
   Includes bibliographical references and index.
   ISBN 0 521 44366 0 hardback
   1. Urban poor – India.   2. Rural–urban migration – India.   I. Series.

HV4138.I4 G66 2001   305.569´0954–dc21   00–050239

ISBN 0 521 44366 0 hardback
ISBN 0 521 61713 8 paperback

To
my mother, Mukti,
and
my daughter, Sreya,
through whom I trace my spiritual genealogy

To
my father, Naranarayan,
who inspired my interest in political struggles

Contents

Tables

Acknowledgements

This book, which started as a doctoral dissertation, has taken many years to be completed and has, in the process, expanded to more than twice its length as a thesis. My foremost gratitude is to all those at Cambridge University Press, especially the editors of this series and Marigold Acland, who agreed to publish the vastly extended version with only limited truncation. It would be a most ungrateful act now if I proceed to write a long acknowledgement, and thus add even more words to this book. So, much as I would like to thank at length everyone to whom I have become indebted over the many years of writing this book, I shall have to take recourse to listing names of institutions and individuals in most cases.

I thank the librarians, custodians and staff of the archives and libraries where much of this research was done: Centre of South Asian Studies, Cambridge (I owe special thanks to Lionel Carter, the former Secretary-Librarian); Cambridge University Library; Indian Institute Library and Bodleian Library, Oxford; Queen Elizabeth House Library, Oxford; India Office Library and Records, London; National Archives of India, New Delhi; Nehru Memorial Museum and Library, New Delhi; Uttar Pradesh State Archives, Lucknow; Uttar Pradesh State Assembly Library, Lucknow; Uttar Pradesh Secretariat Library, Lucknow; Criminal Investigation Department Office, Uttar Pradesh Police, Lucknow; Commissioner's Office Record Rooms at Allahabad and Varanasi; District Collectorate, English Record Rooms in Allahabad, Kanpur, Lucknow and Varanasi; Nagar Mahapalika (Municipal Corporation) Record Rooms in Allahabad, Kanpur, Lucknow and Varanasi; Urban Development Authority Record Rooms in Allahabad, Kanpur and Lucknow; Northern India Employers' Association Record Room, Kanpur; Upper India Chamber of Commerce Library, Kanpur; Gaya Prasad Library, Kanpur; Marwari Pustakalaya and Vachanalaya, Kanpur; Kashi Nagri Pracharani Sabha Library, Varanasi; Archives of *Aj* newspaper, Varanasi; Bharati Bhavan Library, Allahabad.

This research was substantially done in Allahabad, Kanpur, Lucknow and Varanasi, where I received generous help from many people. I am deeply indebted to Kalyan Bakshi, IAS (formerly Home Secretary, Uttar Pradesh), who made it possible for me to surmount formidable bureaucratic hurdles and to have remarkably easy entry to district, municipal and police offices for access to vital primary sources. Kalyan and Jayati Bakshi, Abu and Gora always welcomed me warmly to their home in Lucknow. I have greatly benefited from the insight and knowledge of Dr Z. A. Ahmad and Hajra Begum; I am no less grateful to them for their enduring enthusiasm for my research and their affection towards me. Had I not met Anwarullah Khan in Allahabad, I would never have believed that someone could bestow such unstinting help and kindness on a complete stranger. I was also most fortunate to be able to draw upon his seemingly limitless knowledge of local politics and people. The presence of Robert and Lucy Ruxton in Lucknow during one of my field-trips made it a particularly enjoyable one. I am deeply indebted to all those who have directed me to unexplored sources, allowed me to use their private libraries, given generously of their time, offered me home and hospitality, and helped me in innumerable other ways: Nasir Abid, Ram Advani, Nuruddin Ahmed, Shakha Bandyopadhyay, Amaresh Banerjee, Ashish Banerjee, Sudarshan Chakr, Sunil Das Gupta, Naresh Dayal, Zahid Fakhri, Suhaib Faruqi, Asra Khatun, J. A. Matin (Matin Mian), S. P. Mehra (Citizen Press, Kanpur), Mukti Kumar Misra, Prof. A. K. Mukherjee and Minati Mukherjee, Amitabha and Sumita Mukherjee, Amrit Lal Nagar and family (especially Diksha), S. A. Naqvi, Safia Naqvi, Khalid Newani, Munishwar Nigam, Mohd. Nizamuddin, Jameel Akhtar Nomani, Chandra Pant, Habib-ur-Rehman 'Betab', Mata Prasad Sagar 'Vaid', C. S. Saran and Sadiqa Saran, R. K. Sen and Shyamali Sen, Arijit and Abhijit Sen, Shakeel Siddiqi, and Harimohan Das Tandon. Ram Sumiran Yadav and Kallan Hussain spared no effort to ensure my well-being at the Hostel of the Department of Public Administration in Lucknow, where I spent many months. Noor Mohammed in Calcutta provided most valuable help with reading Urdu texts.

I am grateful for generous grants in support of this research from the Inlaks Foundation, Cambridge Commonwealth Trust, Edward Boyle Memorial Trust, Harold Hyam Wingate Foundation, Smuts Memorial Fund (Cambridge), and Churchill and St John's Colleges, Cambridge.

I have been most fortunate in having particularly congenial and supportive academic homes: Churchill College and St John's College, Cambridge; Centre of South Asian Studies, Cambridge; St Antony's College, Oxford; Queen Elizabeth House, Oxford. To everyone at these institutions who immeasurably enhanced the quality of my life and provided intellectual stimulation, I am most grateful. In particular, I would like to mention Dick (my tutor) and Margaret Whittaker at Churchill and the bed-makers and porters. I have greatly valued the friendship, good humour and efficiency of the library and non-academic staff at Queen Elizabeth House.

Friends have sustained me through the writing of the thesis and then the book. I shared the pleasures and trials of graduate life in Cambridge with Frederic, Terry, Dilip, Anu, David (Lambourne), David (Lawunmi), Rehana, Aparna, Ajay, Charu, Shantanu and Mitali. Francesca Fremantle, Pradip Banerjee, I. G. Patel and Alaknanda Patel provided much-needed shelter and kept up my spirits with warm hospitality during my stints of archival work in London. Raj Chandavarkar supervised the thesis of this book. He drove me to despondency with his relentless scepticism about my abilities as a historian, and by instituting a regime of terror, albeit tempered with his inimitable wit and humour, to ensure not only that I submitted a passable thesis but that I also successfully secured research fellowships and finally a lectureship. His fierce determination to reform me (which, he will argue, I resisted equally fiercely, thus driving him to distraction) may not have enhanced the quality of my scholarship to meet his standards, but it must have affected the quantity of academic output in the form of this very long book. I remain grateful to Raj for his unremitting support, wise counsel and concern for my welfare over so many years. Polly O'Hanlon read numerous drafts of my work from my first year at Cambridge until the completion of this book, and fortified me with her abiding interest in my research. Chris Bayly has encouraged and supported me in every conceivable way from my early days at Cambridge. He and David Arnold gave me invaluable comments as the examiners of my thesis. At Oxford, Barbara Harriss-White has been the friend and ally everyone must hope for, as well as a source of inspiration and encouragement. David Washbrook has been a pillar of strength in negotiating the pressures and peculiarities of Oxford; on occasion he has even cheerfully stepped in to do my work, despite being chronically over-worked himself, to help tide me over personal or family illnesses. In the final stages of writing this book, Rangan Chakravarty's friendship was most valuable. I am grateful to him for producing the cover illustration for this book. Judith Brown, Judith Heyer, Gordon Johnson, George Peters, Frances Stewart, Megan Vaughan and Gavin Williams have been most supportive. I would like to mention here Rajat Ray and Rudrangshu Mukherjee, my teachers at Presidency College, Calcutta, for generating my interest in historical research as an undergraduate.

I cannot thank Margaret Shade adequately for knocking into shape a very long and messy manuscript with no standardised style and chaotic footnoting, and still graciously expressing her enjoyment at reading it. Alaine Low provided valuable editorial help to reduce the length of the manuscript. I greatly appreciate the care and understanding with which Liz Paton copyedited this book.

Parts of chapters 3, 5 and 6 have been published in Peter Robb (ed.), *Dalit Movements and Meanings of Labour in India* (Oxford University Press, Delhi, 1993), *Oxford Development Studies*, 24, 3 (1996), *Economic and Political Weekly*, 31, 50 (14 December 1996), and *Modern Asian Studies*, 31, 4 (1997). I am grateful to the editors and publishers of the above for permitting me to incorporate material from those previous publications in this book.

To acknowledge the contribution of one's family and closest friends, and to express gratitude formally, is a contrived exercise, but I must mention my parents, my brother and sister and their families, and my friend Nandinee in Calcutta, who have stood by me in all things. The very fact that they are there has been a source of profound comfort, without which this book would never have been possible. This book must be a reminder to my parents that this is the research that first brought me to England, not temporarily as we then expected, but permanently. I hope they see the book not only as a mark of my uprooting from home, but as the product of a journey that has enabled me to understand and appreciate my roots and history better. My husband, Mark, shared my excitement for my research, and has in recent years patiently endured my anxieties at the glacial progress of the book through the many distractions of university teaching and administration. Sreya's birth delayed the completion of the book, but for that I am truly glad. To her and to my parents, this book is dedicated.

Abbreviations

AICC	All India Congress Committee
AIT	Allahabad Improvement Trust
AMB	Allahabad Municipal Board
BEC	*Report of the United Provinces Provincial Banking Enquiry Committee, 1929–30*
BMB	Benares Municipal Board
CID	Criminal Investigation Department, UP Police
CPI	Communist Party of India
CSP	Congress Socialist Party
DIG	Deputy Inspector General of Police
DM	District Magistrate
EPW	*Economic and Political Weekly*
ERR	English Record Room in District Collectorates
FR	*Fortnightly Report for the United Provinces*
GAD	General Administration Department
GOI	Government of India
GUP	Government of UP
Home Poll.	Home Department, Political Branch
ICS	Indian Civil Service
IESHR	*Indian Economic and Social History Review*
IGP	Inspector General of Police
IOR	India Office Records, London
KIT	Kanpur Improvement Trust
KLIC	Kanpur Labour Inquiry Committee (Committee of Inquiry into Wages and Conditions of Labour in Cawnpore, 1938)
KMB	Kanpur Municipal Board
KRIC	Kanpur Riots Inquiry Commission (Commission of Inquiry into the Communal Outbreak at Cawnpore, 1931)
LIT	Lucknow Improvement Trust
LMB	Lucknow Municipal Board

MAS	*Modern Asian Studies*
NAI	National Archives of India, New Delhi
NML	Nehru Memorial Library, New Delhi
NNR	*Native Newspaper Reports*
PAI	*Police Abstracts of Intelligence* (Weekly)
RAPUP	*Report on the Administration of the Police of the United Provinces*
RCLI	*Royal Commission on Labour in India,* 1931
RDIUP	*Report of the Director (or Department) of Industries, UP*
RTITC	*Report of the Town Improvement Trusts Committee*
SP	Superintendent of Police
UICC	Upper India Chamber of Commerce
UP	Uttar Pradesh, or the United Provinces of Agra and Oudh (before 1947)
UPPCC	Uttar Pradesh Provincial Congress Committee
UPSA	Uttar Pradesh State Archives, Lucknow

Select glossary

acchutoddhar	uplift of untouchables
ahata	complex of small houses in walled compound
ahir or yadav	a Hindu pastoral and agricultural caste, often associated with cattle-rearing
akhara	gymnasium; wrestling den; centre of physical culture; the spatial organisation or the site of activities and training of any specialised group
alim (*pl.* ulema)	Islamic learned person
anjuman	an organisation
ansari	Muslim caste of weavers
arti *or* arti puja	Hindu ceremony of worship
ashraf	Muslim upper classes
auqaf (*pl.* Waqf)	Islamic religious endowment
azadi	independence, freedom
azan	Islamic call to prayers
badelog	literally 'big people', refers to the upper classes
badli	substitute
badmash	thug or roguish person; miscreant
bandha	tied or bonded
bania	trader or moneylender
baqidari	a system of deferred payment of wages for workers
Barawafat	Islamic festival
Basant Panchami	Hindu festival
basti/busti	slum
bazar	marketplace
beer/bir	brave, courageous; also refers to deified heroic martyrs
begar	unpaid labour
bhagat	devotee
bhakti	Hindu devotionalism

bhangi	an untouchable caste group; sweeper
bidi/biri	Indian cigarettes
Biraha	a genre of folk song
bisati	general merchant; lower-caste pedlar
brahmin	upper-caste Hindu, usually associated with scholarly or priestly functions
chamar	an untouchable caste group; leather worker
charkha	spinning wheel
chaudhuri	headman of a caste panchayat or council of elders
chaukidar	neighbourhood watchman or guard
chehlum	Islamic festival
chikan	hand embroidery on cloth
chowkie/chauki	police outpost
Dadhkando	Hindu festival
daira	Islamic sufi shrine; tomb of sufi saint
dal	corps, party or group
dalit	term used to refer to untouchables
dangal	tournament or competition
dar-ul-harb	territory considered by Muslims to be that ruled by non-believers or infidels
darzi	tailor
dasa	servant or slave
dasata	servitude, bondage
deshdrohi	traitor to the country
dharma	religion or religious duty
dhobi	Hindu caste of washermen
diksha	Hindu religious initiation
Diwali	Hindu festival of light
dom	an untouchable caste group
Dusserah	Hindu festival
ekka	horse-drawn hackney carriage
ekkawala	driver of horse-drawn hackney carriage
faqir/fakir	Islamic mendicant or holy man
fizulkharch	unnecessary expenditure
garha	coarse handwoven cloth
garib janata	poor common people
garibi	poverty
gariwan	vehicle driver; coachman
ghat	bathing or washing place on the bank of a river, usually paved
ghazi	Muslim warrior

goonda	thug; tough
goondashahi	rule of thugs
gujar	Hindu agricultural and pastoral caste
gulam/ghulam	servant
gulami/ghulami	servitude
guru	preceptor; teacher
halwai	Hindu caste of confectioners
harijan	term used to refer to untouchables
hartal	strike; stoppage of work
Holi	Hindu festival
Id-milad-ul-nabi	Islamic festival
Idgah	compound for Id prayers
jamadar	labour contractor; overseer
janata	common people
Janmastami	Hindu festival
jihad	Islamic holy war
julaha	Muslim caste of weavers
Kabirpanthi	followers of the devotional saint Kabir
kahar	carrier of load; Hindu caste of water-carriers
kalwar	Hindu caste of alcohol distillers
kamdani	embroidery on cloth
kanta	a weapon like a battle-axe
kanthi	sacred necklace of beads usually worn by followers of Hindu devotional sects
karkhana	artisanal or manufacturing workshop
karkhanadar	owner or proprietor or organiser of Karkhana
karmchari	employee
kasai/qasai	Muslim butcher
katha	reading and exposition of Hindu religious texts
khadi	handwoven cloth from homespun yarn
khatkana	residential neighbourhood of khatiks
khatik	Hindu caste of greengrocers and rearers of pigs and poultry
khattri	Hindu administrative and commercial caste
khayal *or* khayal-lavni	a genre of folk song
khonchawala	street-vendor
kirtan	devotional song
kotwal	law and order official of a town
kranti	revolution
kshatriya	Hindu upper caste associated with a martial or royal history
kuccha	temporary; raw

kunjra	Muslim caste of greengrocers
kurmi	Hindu agricultural caste
lathi	a wooden staff, pole or baton
lavni *or* khayal-lavni	a genre of folk song
Loriki	oral epic of north Indian pastoral and agricultural castes, especially of the ahirs
madrassa	Islamic educational institution
mahajan	moneylender
mahasabha	conference or meeting; organisation or association
majlis	Islamic religious meeting or gathering, especially during Mohurram
maktab/maqtab	Islamic school
mallah	Hindu caste of boatmen
mandi	wholesale market
Manusmriti	corpus of Hindu religious laws
marsiya	elegiac poetry recited during Mohurram
matam	mourning
Maulud Sharif/Milad	recitation of verses in praise of the Prophet
mazdur	labourer
mehtar	untouchable caste group; sweeper
mela	fair
Meraj Sharif	Islamic festival
mochi	untouchable caste group; leather worker; cobbler
mohalla	neighbourhood
mohallawala	resident of a mohalla
Mohurram	Islamic festival
momin	Muslim caste of weavers
naukar	servant
naukri	work as servant
nautanki	genre of folk play or popular theatre
nirguna bhakti	Hindu devotionalism in which god is believed to be formless or without attributes
nishad	Hindu caste of boatmen
pahalwan	strong, muscular person; wrestler
pahalwani	wrestling; body-building
palledar	manual labourer or porter working in markets
panchayat	caste council or council of elders
panth	Hindu religious sect
pasi	Hindu agricultural and pastoral caste

pir	sufi saint or spiritual guide
prabhat pheries	morning processions usually associated with the Congress nationalist movement
pucca	permanent
puja	Hindu worship
qasbah	small town
qassab, qasai, *or* kasai	Muslim butcher
qawwali	genre of religious songs, usually sung at sufi shrines
qist	instalment
qistbandi	loans extended on an instalment basis
qistia *or* qistwala	moneylender who extends loans on an instalment basis
Quran	Islamic scripture
Rajbi Sharif	Islamic festival
Ramdol	Hindu festival
Ramlila	Hindu festival
Ramrajya	kingdom or regime of Lord Ram; connotes ideal polity
Ravidas/Raidas	followers of the devotional saint Ravidas
rozai	loan of money taken and repaid on the same day
sabha	association; society; council; assembly
sabzi mandi	vegetable market
sadhu	Hindu ascetic or mendicant
saguna bhakti	Hindu devotionalism in which god is believed to be with form or attributes
sahukar	banker; moneylender
sajjada nashin	head of a sufi shrine
samyavadi	socialist
Sanatana Dharma	orthodox Hinduism
sangathan	political movement to promote Hindu religious unity and organisation
sangit	genre of folk play or popular theatre
sant	Hindu ascetic; preacher of Hindu devotionalism
sant-mat	the ideology of sants; Hindu devotionalism
sarraf	moneylender; bullion merchant
satsang	literally 'keeping good company'; congregational prayers and religious meetings for the reading and discussion of Hindu devotional ideas of sants

satyagraha	'truth-force' or 'soul-force'; non-violent, passive resistance to injustice
satyagrahi	person offering satyagraha
sewa/seva	service
Shab-i-Barat	Islamic festival
shahi	rule or regime
shahid	martyr
shaikh	sufi spiritual guide
Shaivaite	follower of Shaivism
Shaivism	Hindu devotional sect
shaktishali	powerful
shariat	Islamic law
Shivaratri	Hindu festival
Shivnarayani	followers of the devotional preacher Swami Shivnarayan
shuddhi	literally 'purification'; religious movement for the reconversion of Muslims to Hinduism or for the incorporation of lower castes into the Hindu caste hierarchy
shudra	Hindu low-caste groups
sipahi	subordinate policeman
swadeshi	nationalist; home industry
swadhinta	freedom
swang, svang	genre of folk play or popular theatre
swaraj	independent rule; self-rule
swatantrata	independence; autonomy
tabligh	religious movement for the propagation of Islam
taluqdar	landowner
tanzeem	religious movement for the unity and organisation of Muslims
tazia	model of a tomb of Imam Hussain carried in procession by Muslims during the festival of Mohurram
thela	hand-pulled cart
thelawala	operator of hand-pulled cart
tonga	horse-drawn hackney carriage
tongawala	driver of horse-drawn hackney carriage
ulema (s. alim)	Islamic learned men
Upanishads	Hindu religious texts
urs	sufi religious ceremony
ushr	Islamic religious tax

Vaishnavism	Hindu devotionalism
Vaishnavite	follower of Vaishnavism
vaishya	Hindu upper caste, usually associated with trading and commercial activities
varnashrama dharma	religious duty pertaining to Hindu classification of society into four orders and lifespan into four stages
Vedas	Hindu religious texts
vyamshala	gymnasium
waqf (*s.* auqaf)	Islamic religious endowments
yadav or ahir	Hindu agricultural and pastoral caste, often associated with cattle-rearing
zakat	Islamic religious tax
zamindar	landlord; landowner
zulm	tyranny; oppression

1 The study and its perspectives

I

The simultaneous and unprecedented expansion of the politics of class, community and nationalism marked a decisive transition in the history of the Indian subcontinent in the years between the two world wars. At the heart of this political transformation lay the emergence of 'mass' movements and widespread popular political action, the nature and terms of which form the central theme of this book. It illuminates how the popular classes inscribed their own space in, and thus also determined the direction of, caste, communal and nationalist movements. The focus is on the poor in towns, who have received little attention from historians compared with their rural counterparts. Yet, in the interwar years, various parts of the subcontinent underwent extensive urbanisation and urban demographic expansion,[1] and towns became central to political developments in the country, with the poor coming to play a pivotal role. Arguably, the urban poor contributed substantially to the transformation of Indian politics in this period, and our understanding of the nature of mass politics and political conflict in late-colonial India might be significantly modified by approaching the subject from this perspective.

The politics of the urban working classes have not, of course, been entirely ignored in Indian historiography.[2] Most works, however, give

---

[1] For patterns of interwar urbanisation in southern India, see C. J. Baker, *An Indian Rural Economy, 1880–1955: The Tamilnad Countryside*, Oxford, 1984.

[2] For example, M. D. Morris, *The Emergence of an Industrial Labour Force in India: A Study of the Bombay Cotton Mills, 1854–1947*, Berkeley, 1965; V. B. Karnik, *Indian Trade Unions: A Survey*, Bombay, 1966; V. B. Karnik, *Strikes in India*, Bombay, 1967; S. M. Pandey, *As Labour Organises: A Study of Unionism in the Kanpur Cotton Textile Industry*, Delhi, 1970; R. Newman, *Workers and Unions in Bombay, 1918–29: A Study of Organisation in the Cotton Mills*, Canberra, 1981; M. Holmstrom, *Industry and Inequality: The Social Anthropology of Indian Labour*, Cambridge, 1984; Dipesh Chakrabarty, *Rethinking Working Class History: Bengal, 1890–1940*, Princeton, 1989; R. S. Chandavarkar, *The Origins of Industrial Capitalism in India: Business Strategies and the Working Classes in Bombay, 1900–1940*, Cambridge, 1994; Subho Basu, 'Workers Politics in Bengal, 1890–1929: Mill Towns, Strikes and Nationalist Agitations' Ph.D. thesis, University of Cambridge, 1994.

only a partial picture. Studies usually concentrate on factory workers, and they deal largely with politics arising from the experience of work or workplace relations. However, urban workforces are not clearly differentiated between formal or organised sector factory-hands and the rest: casual, unorganised labour in the informal sector.[3] Workers move from one kind of work to another, and straddle both the so-called informal and formal sectors, as well as industry, trade, transport and construction. The various sectors are, thus, not rigidly compartmentalised, and the labour market is characterised by interchangeability and mobility of workers between sectors. Scholars have also realised that it is historically inaccurate to assume that the informal sector is merely a transitional stage for new urban migrant labour biding its time to graduate to skilled employment in the formal manufacturing sector. Instead, the informal sector has proved to be the overwhelming and enduring reality of Indian urban economies, both past and present.[4] In such a context, only a restricted vignette of the politics of the urban labouring poor is revealed when the politics of factory labour in the formal sector are isolated for analysis. This approach is even less adequate when workers' politics are considered to emanate largely, if not wholly, from the imperatives of workplace relations. This remains a problem even if studies of workers' political action is not confined to 'labour' unrest or trade unionism alone, but includes nationalist or caste and religious movements. Some recent studies have sought to surmount these lacunae by emphasising the need to step outside the workplace to understand working-class politics. These have drawn attention variously to the importance of the state, the social organisation of urban neighbourhoods, and a range of non-economic relations in shaping working-class politics. They have also pointed to forms of political action other than workplace-based politics.[5]

In tune with this emerging body of work, this book sketches urban popular politics on a broad canvas. It does not concentrate on labour in factories, but draws in manual workers in the *bazars* (market areas) and in a whole host of small-scale manufacturing units; artisans and crafts-

---

[3] Jan Breman, 'A Dualistic Labour System? A Critique of the "Informal Sector" Concept', *EPW*, Part I: XI, 48, 27 November 1976, pp. 1870–6; Part II: XI, 49, 4 December 1976, pp. 1905–8; Part III: XI, 50, 11 December 1976, pp. 1939–44; Chandavarkar, *Origins of Industrial Capitalism*, pp. 72–123; Holmstrom, *Industry and Inequality*, pp. 76–9, 319–21.

[4] Jan Breman, *Footloose Labour: Working in India's Informal Economy*, Cambridge, 1996, pp. 5–7.

[5] Chandavarkar, *Origins of Industrial Capitalism*. For working-class politics elsewhere, see G. Stedman Jones, *Languages of Class: Studies in English Working Class History, 1832–1982*, Cambridge, 1983; P. Joyce, *Visions of the People: Industrial England and the Question of Class, 1848–1914*, Cambridge, 1991.

people; transport and construction workers; hawkers, street-vendors and pedlars; and service groups such as sweepers and municipal workers. These groups constituted the bulk of the urban labour force in most Indian towns, especially in those with few or no large industries, as was, and still is, often the case. The labouring population in these towns also clearly included occupational groups who were not permanently engaged in wage labour, for they were often involved in petty trade and service occupations. For many workers, wage labour thus coexisted with 'self-employment'. The appellation 'poor', rather than the 'working classes' or 'labour', is used to refer to all these groups, for the latter terms have connotations mainly of organised, formal sector industrial workers. The epithet 'poor' also avoids the suggestion of the existence of urban workers or labour as a distinct social class arising from a particular set of production relations, as the term 'working class' often implies. 'Poor' here also does not refer to any particular economic measure of poverty nor does it denote only the 'casual poor' or a residual under-class, supposedly existing on the margins of the industrial labour force, which has been the common use of the term in many other contexts, especially when discussing Victorian Britain. The term 'poor' then is deployed in a largely descriptive sense to encompass various urban occupational groups and to highlight the diversity and plurality of their employment relations and working conditions. The use of the term, however, does not arise from any assumption that the diverse groups of the poor were conscious of being a cohesive class with shared interests and plight. Indeed, this study makes the construction of their complex social identities the very subject of enquiry. Furthermore, by referring to the 'poor' instead of the 'working classes', this book seeks to draw attention to vital aspects of urban experience, other than work, that determined the nature of politics. Economic relations, conditions of labour or experience at the workplace alone did not constitute the entire universe of the urban poor. Non-economic modes of domination, exclusion and oppression, based on caste or religion for instance, contributed to the nature and forms of poverty. Municipal government and the regime of law and discipline were equally important in moulding the politics of the poor, as were the initiatives of urban elites to reform, improve and control them, or to harness them to projects of nation-building or construction of caste and religious community.

The term 'poor' is invoked in this book as an analytical category for another significant reason, which has to do with the emerging discursive practices and political rhetoric of the time. Administrative or state policies and middle-class perceptions in the interwar period increasingly tended to identify the labouring classes of the towns as a homogenised category of the 'poor'. In contrast to the rural masses, the urban poor were often seen as a distinct social segment, sharing undesirable traits and posing a threat to moral and social order, public health and political stability. At the same time, the expansion of representative and mass politics after the First World War encouraged a rhetorical reference to the 'poor' as the wider normative political constituency whom all parties or political formations claimed to represent. The development of the concept 'poor' as an elite construct lends further relevance to the use of this term in analysing urban social contradictions in the interwar period.

Central to this study is the nature of the political consciousness and identity of the labouring poor. It is now widely accepted that, among the labouring classes, the development of class consciousness, narrowly conceived in terms of material relations or economic exploitation alone, is not inevitable. Nor is it the only or primary form of political identity of the working classes. Class, in this limited sense, is only one of the many ways in which the social order is understood and interpreted.[6] Instead, the labouring classes variously interrogate or seek to subvert the relations of power as well as contend with rivalries within their own ranks, through a range of political action, organisation, ideologies and identities, including nationalism or ethnicity. The prevalence of non-economic forms of domination also ensures that political identity does not take the form of class consciousness based only on economic relations. It is evident from recent studies that class awareness is expressed in languages other than that of economic antagonism. Conceptions of class refer, for instance, to political exclusion or to a social identity defined as 'the people' against unrepresentative and corrupt systems.[7] Moreover, it has been recognised that classes develop by inflecting other languages of politics, such as nationalism or ethnicity, with their own meaning. It has also been argued, based on Bakhtin's dialogic analysis of language, that 'class is revealed [in] . . . the ways in which working people seek to create an oppositional vocabulary within

---

[6] For discussions on 'class' as an analytical category, see P. Joyce (ed.), *Class: Oxford Reader*, Oxford, 1995. For recent debates on the question of class, see L. R. Berlanstein (ed.), *Rethinking Labour History*, Urbana, 1993; H. J. Kaye and K. McClelland (eds.), *E. P. Thompson: Critical Perspectives*, Cambridge, 1990. For a critique of the narrow conceptualisation of class formation in the African context, see Frederick Cooper, 'Work, Class and Empire: An African Historian's Retrospective on E. P. Thompson', *Social History*, 20, 2, 1995, pp. 235–41.

[7] Joyce, *Visions*; Stedman Jones, *Languages of Class*; W. H. Sewell, *Work and Revolution in France: The Language of Labour from the Old Regime to 1848*, Cambridge, 1980; R. McKibbin, *The Ideologies of Class: Social Relations in Britain, 1880–1950*, Oxford, 1990; C. Calhoun, *The Question of Class Struggle: Social Foundations of Popular Radicalism during the Industrial Revolution*, Oxford, 1982; Paul Lubeck, *Islam and Urban Labor in Northern Nigeria: The Making of a Muslim Working Class*, Cambridge, 1986.

the language of their oppressors'.[8] In other words, class struggle is understood to be conducted between opposing or contested visions and discourses *within* a shared political code.[9] Drawing upon these various analytical perspectives, this study examines the interaction and overlap of diverse forms of political action and social identities of the poor based on class, labour, caste, religion or nation. It concentrates, in particular, on the alternative or contested interpretations by the poor of the wider, elite-generated political ideologies and movements of nationalism, caste and religion.

Popular or subaltern politics in India have usually been approached in terms of the history of particular kinds of political movements, whether in the name of nation, caste or communalism. This in itself is not a problem, but becomes so when the emphasis on one kind of politics conveys the impression that a particular variety of politics and identity was paramount for the poor. A recent study of communalism, for instance, imparts a particular trajectory to popular politics, which appear inexorably to develop towards communal or religious consciousness. The study ultimately gives the impression that the social identity of the north Indian popular classes in the early twentieth century came to be overdetermined by conceptions of religious community.[10] Not only do such approaches subsume the history of the poor under histories of nationalism or communalism, they also obscure the interconnections between various forms of politics and identities of the poor by privileging only one form, and therefore produce a partial picture of popular politics. In contrast, this book simultaneously engages with various kinds of politics of the poor and highlights their interplay, in order to draw out the frequently acknowledged, but rarely investigated, point that no single identity is salient, that identities are multiple and interlinked, and that the politics of the poor, as indeed of other social groups, take varied and diverse, but overlapping and interconnected forms.

Four of the largest towns in the United Provinces (UP) – Allahabad, Benares, Kanpur and Lucknow – are covered in the discussions. These towns were the sites of concerted and pervasive political agitation and conflict in the interwar period. Widespread mass support for the nationalist movement in these towns made them the strongholds of the Congress. Some of the most ferocious communal riots occurred here and political, religious and social reform movements intensified among

---

[8] Marc W. Steinberg, 'Culturally Speaking: Finding a Commons between Post-structuralism and the Thompsonian Perspective', *Social History*, 21, 2, 1996, p. 206.

[9] Joyce, *Visions*, pp. 332–3.

[10] S. B. Freitag, *Collective Action and Community: Public Arenas and the Emergence of Communalism in North India*, Berkeley, 1989.

low caste groups in these towns in the 1920s and 1930s. The political ferment in UP towns makes them an ideal focus for the study of popular politics and for the exploration of interconnections between various political movements. In addition, it was from this period onwards that political developments in UP gradually came to exercise a decisive influence in all-India politics – an influence that continues to this day.

II

The growing importance of urban mass politics in interwar north India as well as the central role of the poor in urban politics were underpinned by momentous changes in the towns themselves. The interwar years were significant for extensive urbanisation, with towns developing rapidly in north India, away from the colonial, industrial port cities or the presidency towns of Bombay, Madras and Calcutta, which had experienced earlier growth spurts from the later nineteenth century. Urban development in the two decades after the First World War was stimulated by growth in manufacturing industries and the substantial migration from rural areas that took place as a result of both increasing demographic pressures in the countryside from the 1920s onwards and agrarian depression in the 1930s. Migration radically altered the demographic profile of the towns, with a large expansion in the ranks of the poor and their consequent emergence as a crucial social force. Their growing importance in urban society and polity, however, did not arise only from their more numerous presence in the towns. This was also a consequence of the transformation of the economy and shifts in the matrix of social relations in the towns after the First World War and during the depression, which, together, gave rise to an intensification of social conflict involving the poor. The organisation of production, the investment preferences of the commercial and mercantile classes, and the nature of trade, manufacturing, and employment patterns, all underwent substantial change and adjustment, and all had implications for the network of social and economic relations of the growing numbers of the urban poor. They faced new insecurities and vulnerabilities in employment and everyday urban life, but without the mitigation of patronage reciprocities in social relations, for these could not be sustained or instituted under the scale of the demographic pressure and the migration that was taking place. Most importantly, the development of urban trade and industry in the interwar period was characterised by the primacy of small-scale enterprise, which was to generate a fluid, shifting and fiercely (often violently) competitive labour market with high turnover and the proliferation of casual, and usually unskilled, work.

This largely explains why the urban poor would be perceived by the propertied and middle classes as a footloose and volatile mass, threatening the moral and social well-being of 'respectable' people and undermining political progress. To contend with this perceived problem, numerous policy and administrative measures were adopted in the towns variously by the government, local authorities and the police. The policy-makers dealt with scarce municipal resources and infrastructure, public health, housing, law and order, and crime control – all of which were seen to be jeopardised by population growth in general, and more particularly by the increasingly prominent 'floating' population of the poor. The consequent administrative measures made the poor the major targets of governance and ensured a far greater presence of an interventionist state and local authorities in the lives of the poor than ever before. State and local policies further aggravated social conflict in the towns, sharpened class tensions, generated antagonisms among the poor against the state and local institutions, and deepened or created extensive divisions and rivalries among various groups of the poor themselves. Some of these rivalries overlapped with, reinforced or even precipitated caste or religious differences among the poor and gave such divisions new contextual significance and immediacy, further expanding the arena and forms of conflict and political action. The urban poor in the interwar period, therefore, came to inhabit a more bitterly divided and conflictual world; there were now larger numbers of them in the towns and under greater pressure than ever before. Ironically, the administrative policies and forms of political control employed, while generating internal rifts among the poor, at the same time discursively created a homogenised category of the 'poor', laden with negative connotations. It was in response to both the conflict-ridden urban milieu and the negative characterisation faced by the poor that their political initiatives were to emerge. All these developments formed the background and the material context of popular politics in the interwar period, and underpinned the emergence of urban mass politics, helping to fuel caste, religious and nationalist movements. The overtly conflictual world in which the poor found themselves also often drove them towards fierce strife, thus precipitating urban mass violence.

The fact of the emergence of the urban poor as a major social force and their deepening experience of deprivation, conflict or fragmentation did not, however, automatically catapult them into political action. The context for their political action was also crucially set, first of all, by the significant reconfiguration of the institutions and organisations of politics in the interwar period, and, secondly, by the development or further elaboration of a multiplicity of political 'languages' and ideologies, referring variously to nation, class or community. The First World War was a landmark in Indian politics.[11] Although the British government had gradually devolved power from the 1880s, decisive steps in this direction were taken during and after the war. The consequent expansion of representative politics and its flip-side, the need for popular political mobilisation, changed the entire nature of Indian politics.[12] This is a familiar story and the implications of these developments for the elite – who had access to political institutions and a stake in constitutional negotiations – have been amply documented. This well-known story, however, requires recapitulation here in order to highlight the fact that the significant reconfiguration of politics in this period not only transformed elite politics, but also had considerable significance for popular politics. The imperatives of representative politics necessitated effective mass mobilisation, which, in turn, meant that 'politics' penetrated the lives of far wider social groups than ever before. As the elites galvanised themselves into action to compete for office and influence, they needed to make those whom they sought to represent a part of the political process. This, in turn, spurred on the formation of new organisations and the evolution of new modes of political action and discourse. It led to the expansion of the 'public sphere' and the innovation of political rituals and practices to forge political collectivities.[13] All these trends had already begun to emerge in the closing years of the nineteenth century, but their scale and pace accelerated immeasurably in the interwar years, and inevitably informed the development of the politics of the poor. The latter found new arenas and forms of action which they could inflect with their own political meaning and purpose. This is not to say that the 'passive' poor were 'mobilised' at the behest of the elites, but rather that the emerging forms of action and organisation opened up vast new avenues and terrain for the politics of the poor. In the process, the 'public sphere' itself became an increasingly contested domain, with the popular classes seeking either to appropriate it or to

---

[11] B. R. Tomlinson, *The Indian National Congress and the Raj, 1929–1942: The Penultimate Phase*, London, 1976, pp. 9–15; J. M. Brown, 'War and the Colonial Relationship: Britain, India and the War of 1914–18', in M. R. D. Foot (ed.), *War and Society: Historical Essays in Honour and Memory of J. R. Western, 1928–71*, London, 1973, pp. 85–106.

[12] A. Seal, 'Imperialism and Nationalism in India', in J. Gallagher, G. Johnson and A. Seal (eds.), *Locality, Province and Nation: Essays on Indian Politics, 1870–1940*, Cambridge, 1973, pp. 1–27, reprinted from *MAS*, 7, 3, 1973.

[13] On the 'public sphere' and aspects of the 'public' in colonial India, see *South Asia*, 14, 1, 1991: Special Issue edited by S. B. Freitag. See also, D. Haynes, *Rhetoric and Ritual in Colonial India: The Shaping of a Public Culture in Surat City, 1852–1928*, Delhi, 1992; first published Berkeley, 1991.

develop alternative or oppositional arenas.[14] Insight into these processes of contestation lies at the heart of this book.

The wider institutional context of politics had another crucial implication for popular politics. While the colonial government extended representation and devolved power in the interwar period, it was also concerned to tighten the reins of state control through other means, especially through policing and the repression of collective political action. These attempts at political control were further elaborated as the colonial state increasingly faced a crisis of legitimacy and authority, with the growth of nationalism and other forms of political protest from the 1920s onwards.[15] The extensive measures for control, discipline and repression affected the poorer sections of society more directly than ever before. They became the focus of policing as their increasing prominence in urban society unleashed fears of public disorder and social anomie, and because they were imagined to be ideal raw material for crafting into explosive political actors by rabble-rousers. All this made the state a more concrete and intrusive presence in the everyday lives of the poor. Inevitably, this shaped their perceptions of the state and conditioned their political ideas and agenda.[16]

The historians of the 'Subaltern' school, in their efforts to rescue the autonomy of the subaltern classes, have often tended to underplay, although not altogether deny, the analytical significance of these wider developments in the realm of state institutions and elite practices in informing popular politics or imparting particular directions and forms.[17] The present study takes the view that subaltern autonomy, self-determination and agency are not completely isolated or independent from elite politics or state structures, or untainted by supposedly 'bourgeois' ideologies of democracy, citizenship or individualism. Subaltern politics do not spring entirely from their own 'pure' culture and subjectivity. This book interprets the autonomy of subaltern politics in terms of their 'distinctiveness of practice',[18] that is, their ability to appropriate, refashion and mould, for their own purpose, the organisations, institutions and ideologies of elite politics. It deals with this interface between the emerging forms of elite institutional and

---

[14] For the 'proletarian public sphere' in the European context, see Geoff Eley, 'Edward Thompson, Social History and Political Culture: The Making of a Working-class Public, 1780–1850', in Kaye and McClelland (eds.), *E. P. Thompson*, pp. 12–49.

[15] G. Kudaisya, 'State Power and the Erosion of Colonial Authority in Uttar Pradesh, India, 1930–42', Ph.D. thesis, University of Cambridge, 1992.

[16] Chandavarkar, *Origins of Industrial Capitalism*, pp. 410–11.

[17] For the writings of the 'Subaltern' historians, see the various volumes of essays entitled, *Subaltern Studies: Writings on South Asian History and Society*.

[18] R. O'Hanlon, 'Recovering the Subject: *Subaltern Studies* and the histories of Resistance in Colonial South Asia', *MAS*, 22, 1, 1988, p. 197.

organisational politics, on the one hand, and the initiatives of the poor on the other, and concentrates on their differential perceptions, oppositional practices and contested self-constructions.

The transformation of political institutions and organisations in the interwar period was not the only wider development that influenced the politics of the poor. Equally crucial were a vast range of political ideologies and new political 'vocabularies' that emerged out of the imperatives of representative and mobilisational politics early in the twentieth century. These too proved to be highly significant in popular politics. Manifestly, social experience does not directly translate into political action, but the nature and forms of the latter are mediated through various ideologies and 'languages' or 'discourses' of politics which help to order, interrogate and understand social experiences. Prevalent discursive practices thus influence the nature of engagement in political action, as stressed in recent historiography. The poor hardly ever adopt the political discourses of the elite without modification; they interpret and deploy them in the light of their own social contexts, traditions and histories. This study emphasises the plural interpretations and contested meanings given by the poor to the political discourses which they shared with, or even derived from, the elites. It should be clarified here that political discourses and 'languages' in this book are seen to be embedded in social structures and power relations. The 'linguistic turn' in social history has stressed the valid point that social identities cannot be reduced to material contexts and should not be taken to derive directly from the structural position of individuals or groups in the economy and society. There has, however, been an accompanying tendency to interpret the construction of social identities *entirely* in terms of discursive practices or the 'social imaginary', leading to an overwhelming emphasis on 'self-constitution, randomness and the reflexivity of subjects'.[19] Identities are considered to have little or no external social referent, and to be subjective products of discursive and linguistic constructions. This perspective fails to explain why a particular identity or ideology becomes important out of a range of discursive formations available at any particular time, unless it is acknowledged that the dominant form has some bearing on reality. The social context is thus not only relevant, but also crucially influences the adoption or popularity of particular discourses. This study is informed by a recognition of the 'reciprocal relations of conceptual systems and social relations in a given historical moment'.[20]

In interwar north India, a range of ideologies and languages of politics

[19] P. Joyce, 'The End of Social History?', *Social History*, 20, 1, 1995, p. 90.
[20] R. Chartier, *Cultural History: Between Practices and Representations*, Oxford, 1988, p. 45.

arose out of various forms of elite politics – caste, nationalist and religious. These were available to the poor to draw upon, to engage with and to elaborate. The politics of representation and mobilisation precipitated political rhetoric of at least two kinds that were relevant for popular politics: one set arose from the need of elite politicians and leaders to negotiate with the British government for political representation or the allocation of jobs and resources; the other related to the imperatives of mass mobilisation, but the two overlapped. Although these interconnected political discourses were not always immediately concerned with the poor, the political vocabulary and ideas were relevant to them. Underpinning much of this political rhetoric was a notion of deprivation, not just or even primarily in its material sense of economic impoverishment, but also encapsulating the lack of social or political power and rights. Thus, in demanding special representation or privileged access to jobs and resources from the government, be it for lower-caste groups or for religious minorities like the Muslims, the political leaders and propagandists invoked arguments about the historical deprivation of their communities, although they identified the sources and nature of deprivation in different ways. The Congress too, with its pan-Indian nationalism, both in seeking a place in the government of the country and in its subsequent quest for full independence, referred to the lack of power and rights of Indians as well as to the economic degradation of the country. Moreover, to shore up and bolster their legitimacy to represent the constituencies they claimed, whether the entire Indian people or particular caste or religious communities, the leaders and publicists took refuge in a vocabulary that could reach out to those beyond their own ranks and help to forge wider political collectivities. This they did by invoking the deprived and the poor of their communities: the 'poor common people', referred to increasingly in Hindi as *garib janata* – a 'populist' metaphor which continues to dominate Indian politics today. These two different but overlapping vocabularies of deprivation and of the 'common people' had the great potential of being appropriated by the poor. The poor could inflect with their own meaning these discourses, which they came to share with the political elites. This study is concerned precisely with this interface. It examines how the poor understood these emerging languages of politics, and how and to what extent they imparted to them new meaning and significance in order to forge their own political initiatives. It is also necessary to discern whether or how far these discourses placed limits on the politics of the poor.

There was another related set of political discourses in the interwar period that affected the urban poor, not so much for the possibility of creative appropriation, as from the urgency to contest the negative

stereotypes of the poor envisioned and projected through these discourses. These dealt with the urban poor directly, rather than metaphorically raising the issue of deprivation. Foremost amongst these was
the discourse of local administration and state policy. The emergence of
a seemingly 'floating' population of the urban poor as a significant
presence triggered fears over the possible adverse political and social
outcome. In administrative and political circles – including British
officials and Indian personnel, provincial legislators or local councillors
– the urban poor, far more than the rural poor, came to be viewed as a
potential threat to political order and stability, as well as to public health
and to the social or moral fabric of 'respectable' urban society. The
genealogy of such ideas about the urban poor, prevalent in British
official circles, may be traced partly to the history of the ideological and
intellectual transformation of nineteenth-century Europe, where the
emerging liberal projects of property, wealth, citizenship and political
rights found poverty to be a social problem and sought to institute 'a
disciplinary pedagogy' for the poor and a programme of behavioural
reform through the promotion of 'association, education, savings, mutu-
alism and hygiene'.[21] The official perception of the poor in Indian towns
as a social threat came more directly from Victorian Britain. Here, a
moral imagination had underpinned ideological constructions of
poverty and the urban casual poor or a residual underclass had come to
be seen as the repository of a deviant culture needing moral and
behavioural transformation, either by philanthropic persuasion or, if
necessary, by administrative fiat or state coercion.[22] These various ideas
found a specific orientation and configuration in interwar north India,
with the moralising impulse and disciplining urge riveted increasingly on
the burgeoning and seemingly threatening body of the poor, specifically
in the towns and not in the countryside.

Negative images of the urban poor were reinforced by the growing
political disturbances of the interwar years, when nationalist agitation
and communal riots both escalated, and labour unrest became prominent in towns and cities of India, especially from the war years. The
consequent fear of political disorder and riots emanating from the lower
orders fixed the administrative gaze on the entire mass of the urban
poor, without distinguishing between the casual and the respectable
poor, as was the case in Victorian England. It was not the 'respectable'

---

[21] G. Proccaci, 'Governing Poverty: Sources of the Social Question in Nineteenth-century
France', in Jan Goldstein (ed.), *Foucault and the Writing of History*, Oxford, 1994,
pp. 206–19.
[22] For Victorian ideas of poverty, see G. Stedman Jones, *Outcast London: A Study in the
Relationship between Classes in Victorian Society*, Oxford, 1971; G. Himmelfarb, *The Idea
of Poverty: England in the Early Industrial Age*, London, 1984.

or 'industrious' working classes of Manchester, Lancashire or the West Riding but the threatening underclass of 'outcast London' that provided the image in which the north Indian urban poor came to be conceived. In Britain, the tendency to isolate the casual poor of London as the main source of social malaise or political tumult had emanated from the fear that they could hinder industrial and social development and impair national efficiency. It was also anticipated that they might corrupt and contaminate the 'industrious' and productive working classes, in whom liberal middle-class Britain placed its faith in achieving industrial development and 'rational' modernisation.[23] The absence in India of a similar project of industrial modernisation by the colonial state, as well as the blurring of the social lines between an industrial workforce and a casual residuum, may explain why all sections of the labouring poor were tarred with the same brush. Moreover, the policy emphasis to deal with the supposed problem of the seemingly undifferentiated mass of the poor was on punitive measures and on their segregation. Interestingly, in Britain, by the early twentieth century, the solution to poverty was sought through an emerging state welfare regime and the middle classes gradually incorporated working classes in institutional and representative politics. Only an indigent fringe, seen to be suffering from a 'culture of poverty' and resisting the ministrations of the welfare state, continued to be the target of punitive and segregative measures, often informed by Social Darwinist views.[24] In India, however, a welfarist approach was entirely absent under a colonial government, which not only faced ever-increasing financial constraints in the early twentieth century, but was also, in any case, scarcely interested in wooing the poor as collaborators of the Raj. The policy measures, therefore, remained oriented largely towards discipline, regulation and segregation, often in alliance with Indian elites. These tendencies were most clearly reflected in local policies and policing, which encompassed attempts to control the behaviour of the poor, clear their slum settlements and regulate their collective activities. These policies were based on the assumption that the undisciplined poor were impediments to order and stability. The impact of these various developments was contradictory, as the first part of this book will show. On the one hand, the various measures to control and discipline the poor deepened scarcity and thus served to divide the poor and caused conflict among them. On the other hand, these policy measures discursively homogenised the poor as a uniform social category sharing undesirable and dangerous traits, and thus, at times, opened up the possibility of political unity among the poor against the

---

[23] Stedman Jones, *Outcast London*, pp. 7–16.
[24] Ibid., pp. 322–36; Himmelfarb, *Idea of Poverty*, pp. 531–2.

government and the state. The policy discourses, moreover, crucially influenced the politics of the poor as they sought to contest adverse characterisations or strove to establish their own respectability.

Another cognate and overlapping corpus of ideas – mainly the province of Indian reformers and politicians – harboured similar stereotypes of the urban poor as volatile and violent or prone to undesirable practices and habits. As will be seen in chapter 3, the urban poor were frequently seen as erstwhile rural folk uprooted from their simple, 'traditional' country life – their supposed natural habitat – and succumbing to moral and material degeneration in the towns. Morever, the casual and impermanent nature of jobs available to the poor in the towns and the consequent 'floating' nature of their work enhanced the image of instability, volatility and rootlessness, which was, in turn, seen to be the primary source of urban moral decay, social anomie and political disorder. Thus, unlike the rural poor, who were often idealised and romanticised, especially under a Gandhian influence, their urban counterparts were regarded as corrupted misfits in the towns, culpable for thwarting progress, development or national regeneration. The solution to these putative problems posed by the urban poor was sought not simply through control or repression, as in the case of the colonial state, but also through the uplift and improvement of the lower classes. Indeed, the mission of social and moral reform was a central element in the relation of the Indian elites to those whom they identified as the poor and the lower classes. The targets of reform and uplift were those suffering from poverty, ignorance and moral deficit, who were identified in terms of both economic deprivation and social backwardness, the two being seen to be integrally related. Nineteenth-century ideologies of social reform, religious revival and moral discourses of improvement were the background to the development of these ideas, which were directed at a range of groups, including the lower castes, who were seen to be underprivileged and backward. These reform movements had developed as a form of expression of power and as an aspect of self-definition of the ascendant commercial classes and their allies in the professions and government services – the newly emerging middle classes of north India. For the commercial communities in particular, piety, patronage of religion, charity, philanthropy and promotion of reform were important constituents of their identity and markers of their newly found social prominence in the towns.[25] Ranajit Guha has

---

[25] C. A. Bayly, 'Patrons and Politics in Northern India', *MAS*, 7, 3, 1973, 349–388; C. A. Bayly, *The Local Roots of Indian Politics: Allahabad 1880–1920*, Oxford, 1975, pp. 104–17; Vasudha Dalmia, *The Nationalization of Hindu Traditions: Bharatendu Harishchandra and Nineteenth-century Banaras*, Delhi, 1997, pp. 50–145.

argued that the 'urge for improvement' originated in Britain as the 'big thrust of an optimistic and ascendant bourgeoisie to prove itself adequate to its own historic project'.[26] The mission of improvement was then deployed in India by the Raj as a strategy 'of persuasion to make imperial dominance acceptable, even desirable, to Indians'.[27] Indian nationalists soon adopted this project of improvement for themselves and further fleshed it out with the Hindu conception of duty and 'obligation to protect, foster, support and promote the subordinate', in order to elicit the obedience of the lower orders and to earn the right to rule.[28] In this way, 'improvement' and reformism developed as a potent and key ideology of both the state and the indigenous elites.

In the interwar period, the reformist and 'improvement' ideas, as directed towards the lower classes and castes, gained a new and vigorous lease of life and reinforcement from a range of emerging forces, especially in the urban milieu. The expansion of the arena of representative politics and the consequent need for effective mass mobilisation had several significant implications. First, political publicists, ideologues and leaders elaborated visions of ideal community and the nation in a variety of ways with greater vigour. Ideas about national character and notions of development for a future democratic polity were all articulated. In these concepts of the nation and national community, considerations of the role of the vast mass of the Indian people – rhetorically the poor common people – inevitably came to occupy a significant place. Secondly, the devolution of power in this period, most importantly, took the form of the expansion of the franchise to incorporate a far larger section of local propertied classes and middle-class rate-payers in institutions of municipal government. These local institutions were also accorded greater autonomy and powers than in the past. Within this context, an urban-based civic vision developed among the newly enfranchised middle classes, in which they saw urban local institutions and towns as centres of modernisation and progress.[29] The blossoming of civic ideals, coupled with the elaboration of visions of community and nation, inevitably put the spotlight on the poor in the towns, who had to be moulded as fit and proper members of the community and made to conform to projects of civic development and nationalism, or else simply marginalised and excluded. Moreover, industrialisation was assuming

[26] R. Guha, 'Dominance without Hegemony and Its Historiography', in R. Guha (ed.), *Subaltern Studies VI: Writings on South Asian History and Society*, Delhi, 1989, pp. 240–1.
[27] Ibid., pp. 242–3.   [28] Ibid.
[29] See chapter 3 below. For the evolution of civic ideals from an earlier period in Gujarat, see Haynes, *Rhetoric and Ritual*, pp. 108–44; for the centrality of cities in the conception of nationalist modernisation, see Sunil Khilnani, *The Idea of India*, London, 1997, pp. 107–49.

ever greater significance as an issue in nationalist politics and in conceptions of national development.[30] It is probable that this concern served
to focus further attention on reforming and controlling the urban
labouring classes for national development, efficiency and production.

The focus on the poor in the interwar years and a reformist interest in
them also came from the accelerating caste uplift movements, militant
religious politics and the emerging nationalist discourse of moral and
social regeneration. Central to these was the growing need for both
ideological construction and political mobilisation of communities.
Religious and social reformers tried to moralise and uplift the lower
castes and classes by purging their supposed aberrant practices or
behavioural defects and purifying their habits. Such rescue attempts
were geared, in no small measure, to making the lower orders better and
fit members of the religious, caste or national community, which they
were now called upon to join. This attitude towards the poor was shared
by Hindu and Islamic reformers alike. Carey Watt has recently shown
that, in the decades immediately before the First World War, a movement for national efficiency and constructive nationalism gradually
gathered momentum in north India; it aimed to enhance the material,
physical and intellectual efficiency of the Hindu community.[31] The urge
for national efficiency was partially influenced by international cross-
currents of racial competition and eugenics, which motivated Hindu
nationalist leaders to achieve a leading place for India in the hierarchy of
races and nations.[32] The movement was also partly a product of
representative politics and the need to consolidate and augment the
number of Hindus.[33] Watt shows that education and social reform were
the central pillars of the movement, and were particularly directed at the
'depressed classes' and poorer sections among the Hindus, upon whom
social anxiety came to focus, both to maintain the numerical strength of
the community and to make them more productive and efficient. As
Watt comments: 'It was not all a matter of charity and pity for destitute
and marginalized Hindus since the ideology of national efficiency
promoted an organically-ordered society in which every component
played a productive part.'[34]

The ideology of reform of the poor was also effectively expanded from
the 1920s by the emerging Gandhian nationalist rhetoric. Ranajit Guha
has argued that, in seeking to achieve mass mobilisation and political

[30] D. Rothermund, *An Economic History of India: From Pre-colonial Times to 1991*, London,
      1988; 2nd edn, 1993, pp. 91–3; S. Sarkar, *Modern India, 1885–1947*, Delhi, 1983,
      pp. 170–8.
[31] Carey A. Watt, 'Education for National Efficiency: Constructive Nationalism in North
      India, 1909–16', *MAS*, 31, 2, 1997, pp. 339–74.
[32] Ibid., pp. 340–1.   [33] Ibid., pp. 364–5.   [34] Ibid., p. 365.

hegemony for the Congress from the 1920s, Gandhi had had recourse to persuasion and the projection of the moral legitimacy of the party to lead Indian politics, in conscious opposition to the coercive practices of the colonial state. Reformism played an important role in emphasising the moral superiority and legitimacy of the Congress. Reformism was also expected to help in the self-representation of a middle-class nationalist leadership in its quest for acceptance by the mass of its targeted constituents. Guha further argues that this strategy was not entirely successful and the Congress increasingly turned to 'disciplining' the masses in its mobilisational drives.[35] Thus, in Gandhian nationalist ideology, the lower classes were seen as insufficiently enlightened to grasp the noble concepts of self-restraint, self-sacrifice and self-discipline – the pivots of the Gandhian philosophy of political and social transformation. In this view, the poor were either childlike, needing reform and moral and spiritual guidance, or misguided and violent, needing discipline and a strong, paternalistic, even coercive, hand of control and direction. These various discourses of reform, religious revival and nationalism were ambivalent, and ran in two registers. On the one hand, they attempted the acculturation and incorporation of the 'reformed' poor in the new purified communities defined by religion, caste or nation. On the other hand, they were dismissive of, even opposed to, the popular classes and their culture; they excluded and censured the poor as being unworthy elements of a community, unless improved or properly 'reformed'. The consequent exclusion and distancing of the poor, *inter alia*, took the form of a withdrawal of elite patronage from various forms of urban popular culture and attempts to purify these.[36]

Reformism in public life and vigorous activism to uplift the lower orders, which accelerated in the interwar years, were thus undoubtedly grounded both in nationalist efforts to mould worthy and upright citizens and in religious and social movements to forge unified communities of either Hindus or Muslims. Yet, arguably, the timing of the intensification of reformism, spearheaded largely by an urban-based middle-class leadership, suggests that it had more than a little to do with the perceived threat from an urban 'underclass' during a period of mounting social tensions and the emergence of the poor as a prominent urban social presence. If reformism was about sculpting the nation and religious communities, it equally well met the need to impose order,

---

[35] R. Guha, 'Discipline and Mobilize', in P. Chatterjee and G. Pandey (eds.), *Subaltern Studies VII: Writings on South Asian History and Society*, Delhi, 1992, pp. 69–120.
[36] For a discussion on this theme, see, for example, N. Kumar, *The Artisans of Banaras: Popular Culture and Identity, 1880–1986*, Princeton, 1988, pp. 190–5.

discipline and social conformity in the towns, and to establish the cultural and moral superiority and authority of the middle classes. Reformism harboured the urge to affirm power over the conduct and behaviour of the poor. It encompassed efforts to contain potential social threats from the lower classes and castes, as evident from nationalist preoccupations with caste uplift in the early twentieth century.[37] More overt expressions of these imperatives to establish order and stability lay in the changing patterns of urban policing as well as in the extensive measures taken to sanitise the poor and to promote their hygiene through public health measures and town planning or urban improvement projects. The coincidence of timing and context of all these interrelated endeavours in the interwar period strongly suggests that they sprang, in no small measure, from the growing urban class distinctions and the urgency of the middle classes to achieve social control over the burgeoning numbers of the poor. The unifying motif underpinning all these diverse, even conflicting, endeavours to reform or control the swelling ranks of the urban poor was, of course, a negative conception of their character and a conviction of their culpability in undermining social development and political stability. These negative discourses about the poor, as well as the class tensions and social distinctions on which they were grounded, came to assume central importance in the evolving politics of the poor in the interwar period. It was largely with reference to and in dialogue with these discourses that the poor forged their political practices and social identities through contested self-constructions.

III

Part I of this book examines the changing conditions and experiences of the poor in the interwar period: the social and economic relations in which they were involved; their changing experience of power, subordination, dominance and social control; and their experience of the state and governance. Central themes include the stereotypical negative characterisations that the poor faced as well as their relations with each other and divisions within their own ranks, arising both from the social organisation of work or labour processes and from the nature of local and state policies. In Part II, the discussion moves on to an exploration of the political identities and action of the poor as part of the process of their rapidly changing experiences in the early twentieth century. Each chapter explores the interplay of diverse forms of emerging identities of

---

[37] Sumit Sarkar, *Writing Social History*, Delhi, 1998, ch. 9.

the poor based variously on caste, class, religion, nation or labour, bearing in mind the fluidity and plasticity of these identities. The chapters examine how social identities were constituted through political practice. Such identities are not assumed to be pre-existing and prior to politics, emerging directly from experience; they are understood to be shaped by and forged through the very processes of political action and 'power plays'. Moreover, politics are not conceived in narrow terms, limited either to institutions, organisations and state structures or to overt 'political' acts and agitations, but are taken to include cultural, ritual and religious innovations.

An analytical concern here is to avoid essentialising the nature of the political consciousness of the poor. Some Subaltern historians, for instance, tend to ascribe an inherently oppositional and resistant, even insurgent, mentality or consciousness to the subaltern classes.[38] This oppositional mentality is assumed to flow naturally and inevitably from their social situation and experience of 'subalternity', subordination and domination, which often unite the subaltern classes politically. Although this study does not proceed with the liberal political assumption of plurality in social structures or of functional consensus in shared cultures, and does accord analytical centrality to relations of power and domination in the experience of the subaltern classes, it is, none the less, sceptical of the proposition that resistance and protest form the corner-stone of the politics of the poor. Resistance – collective, everyday forms or any other – is considered to be just one aspect, albeit an important one, of the political response of the subaltern classes to their social conditions.[39] Their vast armoury of responses also includes attempts at self-expression and cultural assertion, or negotiation and contestation of power through other means such as ritual and symbolic struggles, as well as directing their wrath towards each other. The politics of the poor, even when they seek to assert themselves or to contest power, may ultimately produce ambiguous outcomes and undermine their emancipatory or radical possibilities. An apt example would be the subalterns' emulation or appropriation of symbols of power and dominance, such as their claims to higher ritual status or adoption of the 'respectable' social

[38] For a critique of this perspective, see O'Hanlon, 'Recovering the Subject', pp. 189–224.
[39] For arguments along these lines, see, for instance, Sumit Sarkar, 'The Conditions and Nature of Subaltern Militancy: Bengal from Swadeshi to Non-Cooperation, c. 1905–22', in R. Guha (ed.), *Subaltern Studies III: Writings on South Asian History and Society*, Delhi, 1984, p. 274; D. Haynes and G. Prakash, 'Introduction: The Entanglement of Power and Resistance', in D. Haynes and G. Prakash (eds.), *Contesting Power: Resistance and Everyday Social Relations in South Asia*, Oxford, 1991; 1st edn of the University of California Press, Berkeley, 1992, pp. 1–22.

and cultural practices of the upper castes and classes. These inclinations, however, do not necessarily betoken their submission to or acceptance of the existing social order. Still, these leanings may well circumscribe their political action and set the terms and boundaries of possible aspirations. The subalterns may thus also become implicated in hegemonic projects of others to buttress the social status quo by perpetuating the importance of the symbols of power and thereby prove themselves incapable of evolving alternative conceptions of the social order. It is, therefore, necessary to probe the limits of their politics, rather than drawing attention solely to resistance. The crucial point is not radical resistance, but the repertoire of action and ideas of diverse kinds through which the poor negotiate their condition.

The implicit or explicit assumption of an oppositional and resistant subaltern consciousness has another problem which this study seeks to avoid. Many studies of popular politics focus on outstanding, even tumultuous, events, chiefly because that is when the popular classes become 'visible' in historical documents. While this is undoubtedly a useful ploy to capture the history of the popular classes, it also has its problems.[40] Concentration on one particular event, and the nexus of developments around that moment, tends to reveal one type of consciousness or identity, usually a particularly militant, radical or insurgent one. The attempts to rectify the problem of the absence of subaltern classes from history-writing thus unwittingly conjure up much too forceful and unidimensional a presence. This approach also fails to capture more sustained and abiding forms of popular politics and culture, and the varied and complex processes of construction of identities.[41] In view of these problems, this book eschews an event-based approach and, on the whole, does not engage in detailed analyses of riots or nationalist events, which might privilege either an insurgent or a community consciousness, and reify them. The subaltern classes are neither insurgent nor conservative nor religious *inherently or in essence*; it is the politics and the contingencies of the context that make them one or the other or a mixture of some of these. Because this book focuses on the multiplicity of identities and their interlacing, a less episodic account has been preferred, relying less on events and more significantly on forms of change of social and cultural practices. Thus, the book engages in analysing, in varying degrees, the public rituals, religious ideas and practices of the poor, their dramatic or musical culture and performative traditions, their myths, folklore, iconography

---

[40] O'Hanlon, 'Recovering the Subject', pp. 189–224.
[41] For similar arguments, see O'Hanlon, 'Recovering the Subject'; Haynes and Prakash, 'Introduction: The Entanglement of Power and Resistance', pp. 1–22.

of heroes, martyrs or revered figures, and their narratives of the past. As important modes of self-expression of the poor, especially in periods when 'insurgency' is not in the forefront of politics, these cultural forms and practices act as the media through which the subaltern might 'speak' to the historian. These changing cultural practices are also situated within the social context of the early twentieth century and in a history of social change, in order to tease out how the perceptions and attitudes of the poor evolved in this period. More importantly, changes in popular cultural practices in this period, as well as their divergence from elite versions of history or social relations, are identified in order to capture the shifting self-perceptions, conceptions of the polity or social visions of the poor, and their contested world-views or constructions of the self.

In recent years, the study of culture, rituals and public rites of community has engaged many South Asianists. A preoccupation underlying some of this work has been to demonstrate how shared cultural practices in the public arena enabled the construction and constitution of community.[42] Ritual culture in these accounts is often presented as possessing some unifying motifs, even when differing motivations for the participation of diverse actors are recognised. The shared participation of many diverse, even conflicting, groups in the same ritual arena is argued to provide the basis for the formation of larger, more cohesive collectivities of caste or religion. The spirit of these studies, possibly coloured by functionalist interpretations of rituals as the site of reproduction of social integration, has been to demonstrate collective engagement and unity, as well as the affirmation of community identity. In contrast, rituals in the present study are dissected for their polysemic and multi-vocal nature, which reveal them to be arenas of contest and negotiation, where rival self-expressions of various social groups are acted out. Rituals are seen both as theatres of self-representation or affirmation of power of the dominant classes, and as vehicles of contestation from below. The contest for ritual supremacy and struggles over control of symbols of power and community are interpreted here as forms of political conflict between the poor and the dominant classes. Nicholas Dirk has pointed out the limitations of a conventional view of ritual 'as productive of social solidarity', and commented that 'ritual has always been a crucial site of struggle, involving both claims about authority and struggles against it'. He argues that, 'while rituals provide critical moments for the definition of collectivities and the articulation

---

[42] For instance, Freitag, *Collective Action*; P. Van der Veer, *Religious Nationalism: Hindus and Muslims in India*, Berkeley, 1994.

of rank and power, they often occasion more conflict than consensus'.[43] From such a perspective, collectivities look less cohesive than they are portrayed in some recent work based on ritual. Evidently the study of rituals must also be accompanied by an analysis of the social contexts of conflict and antagonism which underlie them. This would reveal the diversity of meanings accorded to rituals by various political actors within a community, and thus also illuminate how class is often imbricated in relations of community.

This study pays considerable attention to religion as an important dimension of the politics of the poor. It does not agree, however, with a prominent view in some history writing, which projects religion as a necessary component of the world-vision of the popular classes.[44] This view comes from two overlapping angles of approach. One arises from the concern to resurrect the autonomy and agency of the subaltern classes. The attempt to salvage subaltern subjectivity has often led to the quest for an 'authentic' subaltern mentality, central to which are believed to be conceptions of community, frequently defined by religion.[45] This approach is buttressed by post-Orientalist and post-Colonial denunciations of 'enlightenment' rationality, which is said to accord normative primacy to the secular over the sacred, and to reduce politics to material considerations and 'rational' calculations alone, denying the analytical autonomy of 'culture', including religious faith and belief. The implications of these interconnected approaches often get perilously close to a 'primordialist' view of the religion of the poor as a set of norms and beliefs with immanent and durable meaning and relevance.[46] The emphasis in this book is on the social construction of the meaning of religion in changing historical circumstances, and its contextual significance for the adherents. I analyse why, how and which particular forms of religion became important to the poor in the interwar period. The aim is to explain and discern the dynamics of religious change, and to reveal its evolving importance for the poor in coming to terms with the rapidly transforming urban milieu and its new social conflicts.

In exploring the politics of the poor, it is important to take into account how the poor were divided among themselves, and when and why they united. In their economic activities as well as in their caste, religious, neighbourhood and other affiliations, the poor were scarcely a unified or uniform social group. Notwithstanding elite tendencies to

---

[43] Nicholas B. Dirks, 'Ritual and Resistance: Subversion as a Social Fact', in Haynes and Prakash (eds.), *Contesting Power*, pp. 219–20.

[44] For instance, Chakrabarty, *Rethinking*, pp. 213–17.

[45] For a critique of this view, see C. A. Bayly, 'Rallying around the Subaltern', *Journal of Peasant Studies*, 16, 1, 1988, pp. 110–20.

[46] Sarkar, *Writing Social History*, pp. 82–108.

view them as a homogeneous entity defined by common character traits or habits, internally the poor remained divided. Political unity in action was rarely achieved by all groups of the poor. The book discusses the nature of the differences amongst the poor and their political conflicts, arising both from diverse constructions of social identity and from material rivalries. Despite this, however, the question of class as a form of social identity is addressed in this book. Given that discursive formations in the interwar period stressed notions of the poor, the 'common people' and deprivation, it becomes particularly relevant to ask whether some conceptions of class did, in fact, emerge. Although a notion of class identity based on economic antagonisms and invariably productive of political solidarity now seems to be analytically restrictive, this does not justify the jettisoning of class altogether as a subject of enquiry. It remains a valid exercise to identify the possible parameters of class identity and its relation to domination, power, inequality or exploitation in complex articulation with caste, religious or national identities. If ideas of class did emerge in the interwar period and were not primarily defined by economic relations, to what then did they refer: power, social distances, political rights? If conceptions of class did develop, how was internal fragmentation amongst the poor accommodated or explained? How far and in what ways were such ideas of class expressed in the politics of caste, nation or religion? To tackle these questions, it is first necessary to explore the specific context of the towns of UP. The next three chapters are devoted to this task. The modes of political action and perception of the poor are addressed in Part II.

Part I

Changing conditions and experiences in interwar north India

2   The poor in the urban setting

In the economy and society of north India, the function of towns as well as the relation of social groups within urban areas had been slowly, but decisively, changing from the late eighteenth century. As Christopher Bayly's study of north India in the eighteenth and nineteenth centuries has shown, successive reorientations in state power and the accompanying reconfiguration of social forces wrought profound transformations in urban forms.[1] From the middle of the eighteenth century, the gradual decline of the Mughal empire, the rise of regional 'successor' states, and the decentralisation of royal power accelerated the development of towns primarily as centres of elite consumption and trade and as the seats of a 'rooted service gentry' and of 'a homogeneous merchant class', to use Bayly's terms. The growth of trade and towns in this period was partly stimulated by the rise in agrarian production and commerce in response to the more rigorous extraction of land revenue by the regional regimes. This was coupled with an accelerating export trade in products such as cotton, indigo and opium. Urbanisation was also partly related to the expanding consumption demands of both the increasing number of town-based service elites involved in revenue administration and the aristocracies of the regional polities. Consumption demands boosted the intermediate economies of transport services, local trade and artisanal production. Increasingly active and buoyant merchant communities came to provide the infrastructure for this economic transition and the growth of towns.

While these various processes improved the fortunes of many towns, trades and merchants in the late eighteenth century, there was a setback during the early expansion of British political power in the first half of the nineteenth century. The ascendance of a centralising state, favouring low levels of government expenditure, slowed down the dynamic expansion of towns. The economic depression from the 1830s to the 1850s

---

[1] The account here of the evolution of towns in the eighteenth and nineteenth centuries is based on C. A. Bayly, *Rulers, Townsmen and Bazaars: North Indian Society in the Age of British Expansion, 1770–1870*, Cambridge, 1983; first paperback edn, 1988.

accentuated the downward trend. Attempts at the standardisation of the revenue system and the vigorous promotion of a cash economy destabilised existing systems of production and taxation, perturbed local power structures and hierarchies, interrupted the expansion in elite consumption, and thus further hindered the growth of towns. This disruption, however, proved to be short lived.

From the mid-nineteenth century, the nature of the state changed again with the consolidation of colonial rule after the uprising of 1857. The process of urbanisation gradually regained its dynamism, reaping the harvest of a number of interconnected developments under *Pax Britannica*. Government expenditure was stepped up considerably for the construction of canals and railways and for the reconstitution of centres of civil and military administration. Agrarian production and internal trade along the new railway routes, especially in grain, grew, albeit at an uneven pace and with regional variations. Consumption, too, expanded again as the population slowly rose and as urban culture gradually altered to generate new lifestyles and social mores.

As an integral part of these developments, by the early part of the twentieth century urban centres in north India were relocated and redistributed. Some of the erstwhile seats of regional courts or service elites declined, as did those commercial and market centres that were bypassed by the rail network. Other towns, however, developed primarily as centres of colonial administration, as commercial entrepots for local and long-distance trade and as nodal railhead points for processing, bulking and redistribution of goods. The nature of towns was, thus, significantly modified, as were social relations in them. Most notable was the expansion of the urbanised English-educated professional and scribal groups under British rule as well as the further enhancement of the fortunes and influence of the town-based merchant communities who came to control the reins of trade and production. These groups also gradually eclipsed the aristocratic classes and land-based service gentry, who had hitherto been located at the heart of local power structures.

The process of urbanisation was to undergo yet another shift in the interwar years. The aftermath of the First World War and the years of the economic depression are well known to have transformed the nature of trade, industry and urban centres throughout South Asia.[2] Demographic boom, agricultural decline and large migration flows into towns,

---

[2] C. J. Baker, 'Economic Reorganisation and the Slump in South and Southeast Asia', *Comparative Studies in Society and History*, 23, 3, 1981, pp. 325–49; D. Rothermund, *India in the Great Depression, 1929–39*, Delhi, 1992; C. J. Baker, *An Indian Rural Economy, 1880–1955: The Tamilnad Countryside*, Oxford, 1984.

as well as an expansion of urban-based manufacturing industries, were important developments seen in various parts of the Indian subcontinent. It is within such a context of urban development and shifting social relations in Uttar Pradesh that political developments would unfold in the interwar years.

Profile of the towns at the beginning of the twentieth century

At the turn of the century, Uttar Pradesh (UP) was dotted with a variety of urban centres.[3] At the top of the urban hierarchy were the commercial and administrative towns of varying sizes. The largest of these, which included Kanpur, Allahabad, Benares and Lucknow, had a population of over 100,000. The development of these large towns from the latter half of the nineteenth century was influenced to a great extent by two prominent factors: first, the consolidation of British rule in north India after the suppression of the uprising of 1857, and the reconstruction and elaboration of civil and military administration in the towns; and, second, the proliferation of the railway network, coupled with the growth of local and long-distance trade.[4] The aftermath of 1857, however, affected the towns unevenly; while Kanpur and Allahabad developed rapidly, the pace of growth in Lucknow and Benares was slower.

Benares was the oldest of these towns in origin, its antiquity as a Hindu pilgrim centre supposedly dating back to the Vedic age. During Mughal times it was a centre for the production of silk fabrics, muslin and perfume oil. In the eighteenth century, Benares prospered as a prominent political and commercial centre, under its merchant-bankers and trading corporations of ascetic religious orders.[5] Benares at this time fell within the territory of the Nawab Wazirs of Awadh, but the town received political patronage from the Rajas of Benares, who held sway in the locality. The Benares division was ceded to the East India Company by the Nawab of Awadh in 1775. Soon afterwards, in 1794, Benares came under the direct administration of the Company and the

---

[3] For a discussion on various kinds of small towns, see C. A. Bayly, 'The Small Town and Islamic Gentry in North India: The Case of Kara', in K. Ballhatchet and J. Harrison (eds.), *The City in South Asia: Pre-modern and Modern*, London, 1980, pp. 20–4.

[4] Ian D. Derbyshire, 'Opening up the Interior: The Impact of Railways on the North Indian Economy and Society, 1860–1914', Ph.D. thesis, University of Cambridge, 1985.

[5] S. B. Freitag (ed.), *Culture and Power in Banaras: Community, Performance, and Environment, 1800–1980*, Berkeley, 1989, pp. 3–8; H. R. Nevill, *Benares: A Gazetteer: vol. XXVI of the District Gazetteers of the United Provinces of Agra and Oudh*, Allahabad, 1909, p. 56.

town became the Company's headquarters for the eponymous administrative division. After 1857, Benares remained the British divisional and district capital. The trade of the town also benefited from new road and railway links, especially with the establishment of the various branches of the Eastern, Northern and Northeastern railway lines, connecting Benares with Gorakhpur, Faizabad, Lucknow, Calcutta, Bombay and Patna. The importance of Benares as a prominent commercial entrepot in the province was, however, gradually eclipsed by the growth of Kanpur and other towns benefiting from rail-borne trade. Nevertheless the city remained a centre of local retail trade, a redistribution point for agricultural produce to its hinterland, and a marketing centre for locally produced silk fabrics, artistic brassware and brass utensils, of which there were substantial and prominent artisan industries in the city.[6]

Allahabad was a regional capital and fort town of the Mughals from the time of Akbar. However, by the end of Mughal rule, it had been reduced to an ordinary township. In 1801, the Nawab of Awadh, who had by then gained control over Allahabad, ceded it to the East India Company. Thereafter, in the years before the 1857 rebellion, Allahabad began to experience slow and limited development as the British headquarters of the district, with a military garrison posted there. After 1857, Allahabad was selected as the provincial capital by the British. The district law courts and the High Court of the United Provinces were also located in the town. Allahabad embarked on a rapid phase of development as a political and administrative centre. Like Benares, Allahabad was not a major trading centre in the late nineteenth century; but after the advent of the railways it functioned as a distribution centre for its environs and on the upper India trade routes, and became the home of a powerful merchant class.

Lucknow was the seat of the Mughal government of the Suba of Awadh from 1590. After Mughal decline, Asaf-ud-daulah, the Shia Nawab of Awadh, founded Lucknow as his capital city in 1775. Under Nawabi court patronage, Lucknow became one of the most flourishing towns of north India in the late eighteenth and early nineteenth centuries, famous as a literary, commercial and cultural centre, with its majestic Nawabi buildings and the artisan industries of *chikan, kamdani, zardozi* (embroidered lace, silver and gold-thread work), silver ornaments, calico printing, bleaching, dyeing, shoe-making and ivory work. The rebellion of 1857 brought about the final demise of the Nawabi culture and polity of Lucknow. The casualties included the largely Muslim courtly classes, who depended on Nawabi patronage. With their

---

[6] R. L. Singh, *Banaras: A Study in Urban Geography*, Banaras, 1955, p. 12; Nevill, *Benares: A Gazetteer*, pp. 58–64.

decline, Hindu and Jain bankers and merchants gained social prominence in the town as moneylenders to the indigent *wasiqadars* or royal
pensioners and as financiers of artisan industries and trade. With the
emergence of nearby Kanpur as the chief trading entrepot in UP, the
importance of Lucknow as a provincial commercial centre diminished.
Lucknow, however, remained the centre of grain trade in Awadh. It was
also a railway junction, with large workshops connected to it. Many of
its artisan industries, however, received a serious setback with the loss of
royal and courtly patronage. The city housed the provincial legislative
council and was maintained as an administrative centre by the British.[7]

Kanpur, compared with Allahabad, Benares and Lucknow, was a
town of more recent origin. It acquired a place on the urban map of
north India after the arrival of the British forces in 1778. Under the
protective presence of the army, the commercial activities of the East
India Company began to develop in Kanpur from the late eighteenth
century. During the uprising of 1857, the city witnessed some of the
most ferocious battles and much of it was reduced to rubble. Reconstruction and British consolidation after 1857 involved the stationing of
the British Indian Army and the establishment of an expanded cantonment, new civil lines and district administration offices. The main
impetus for the phenomenal growth of the town, however, came from
the development of commerce and manufacturing industries. A tannery
was established in 1863, followed by the government leather factory to
supply the military demand for harness, saddlery and other leather
products. The Kanpur cotton committee was formed in 1860 and
several cotton mills were set up between 1861 and 1885, along with a
woollen mill and an army clothing factory. Kanpur emerged as the only
important manufacturing centre in the province, largely servicing
British military demands and meeting the requirements of local weavers
in upper India for cotton twist and yarn.[8] With the arrival of the railways
in Kanpur in the 1860s, the city also became a centre of retail trade with
its hinterland, as well as the chief trading entrepot and distribution point
in UP for cotton yarn and textiles, piece goods, grain, sugar, oil,
oilseeds, animal hides and skins. Though a number of textile and leather
mills were owned by British industrialists, indigenous bankers and
merchants came to the town to provide the entrepreneurial backbone

---

[7] D. A. Thomas, 'Lucknow and Kanpur, 1880–1920: Stagnation and Development
under the Raj', *South Asia*, 5, 2 (New Series), 1982, pp. 68–80; H. R. Nevill, *Lucknow:
A Gazetteer: vol. XXXVII of the District Gazetteers of the United Provinces of Agra and
Oudh*, Allahabad, 1909, pp. 39–45, 50–3; V. T. Oldenburg, *The Making of Colonial
Lucknow, 1856–1877*, Princeton, 1984, pp. 3–26, 145–51.
[8] Bayly, *Rulers, Townsmen*, p. 443.

for commercial and industrial growth in the city. Rural labourers also gradually began to migrate to Kanpur. The city expanded in size, with new markets, industrial areas and residential zones.[9]

Kanpur, Benares, Allahabad and Lucknow were, thus, by the turn of the twentieth century important urban centres, developing at diverse paces and with somewhat different functions, but all owing their growth primarily to trade and administration, and, in the case of Kanpur, to nascent manufacturing industries as well. With the development of administration and commerce, as well as the growing concentration of financial and legal services and educational institutions in these towns, from the late nineteenth century Indian professional and administrative groups, Hindu and Jain bankers, traders and merchants, and British civil servants and military personnel settled in all these towns in ever larger numbers.[10] This brought about a significant territorial extension of the town areas and vigorous construction activities for residential settlements or to accommodate the government offices and law courts.[11] Along with these, municipal services and sanitary infrastructure expanded considerably.[12] Local retail trade developed to meet the consumption demands of urban mercantile, professional and administrative groups.[13] Growth of administration, settlement and rail-borne trade in these larger towns gave them a steady base for development by the first two decades of the twentieth century.

Apart from economic, infrastructural and territorial expansion, the consolidation of the merchant classes was an especially significant

[9] H. R. Nevill, *Cawnpore: A Gazetteer: vol. XIX of the District Gazetteers of the United Provinces of Agra and Oudh*, Allahabad, 1909, pp. 74–84; D. N. Mazumdar, *Social Contours of an Industrial City: Social Survey of Kanpur, 1954–56*, Westport, Conn., 1960, pp. 9–25; Bayly, *Rulers, Townsmen*, pp. 443–4; Derbyshire, 'Opening up the Interior', pp. 380–90; C. S. Chandrasekhara, 'Kanpur: An Industrial Metropolis', in R. P. Misra (ed.), *Million Cities of India*, New Delhi, 1978, pp. 273–303.

[10] C. A. Bayly, *The Local Roots of Indian Politics: Allahabad, 1880–1920*, Oxford, 1975, pp. 19–46.

[11] Between 1865 and 1901, total built-up areas increased from 5.02 km^2 to 13.8 km^2 in Kanpur, from 7.25 km^2 to 14.44 km^2 in Benares, from 6.48 km^2 to 15.23 km^2 in Allahabad, and from 6.73 km^2 to 9.97 km^2 in Lucknow. Cited in K. K. Dube, 'Use and Misuse of Land in the KAVAL Towns (Uttar Pradesh)', Ph.D. thesis, Benares Hindu University, 1966, p. 10.

[12] This was reflected, for instance, in the increase of municipal expenditure on conservancy services. In Allahabad: from Rs 67,917 in 1890–1 to Rs 1,10,201 in 1907–8; in Lucknow: from Rs 77,738 in 1890–1 to Rs 1,17,841 in 1907–8; in Kanpur: from Rs 50,171 in 1890–1 to Rs 78,496 in 1907–8, with the highest expenditure in this period recorded at Rs 2,03,331 in 1902–3; and in Benares: from Rs 44,290 in 1890–1 to Rs 83,211 in 1906–7. Cited in Appendix, Table XVI of *Lucknow: A Gazetteer; Allahabad: A Gazetteer; Benares: A Gazetteer; Cawnpore: A Gazetteer*. The development of municipal services in Lucknow in the years after the 1857 uprising has been described in Oldenburg, *Making of Colonial Lucknow*, chs. 2, 4.

[13] Bayly, *Rulers, Townsmen*, pp. 429–30.

feature of urban growth.[14] By the early twentieth century, the landed
service gentry and aristocracies of the successor states were gradually
overshadowed by commercial people in the locality in social and political
importance. A vibrant commercial culture came to dominate north
Indian towns. Traders and merchants, a majority of whom were Hindu
or Jain, came to constitute a cohesive social group, despite the diversity
of mercantile functions and caste distinctions. Their credit and market
institutions or trading organisations, as well as their shared activities of
religious piety and associations for charity and philanthropy, provided
the cement of social cohesion and transcended business rivalries 'to
create a corporate culture of great vitality' in the towns.[15] This has led
Bayly to characterise these urban centres where the commercial communities entrenched themselves as 'Hindu corporate towns'.[16] Vasudha
Dalmia has further argued, based on her study of Benares, that the
social and commercial organisations of the merchant communities,
including caste associations, and the 'mutual code of honour' that
bound them and made efficient 'commercial transactions over time and
place possible', 'amounted to a virtual civic government'.[17] Moreover,
from the early twentieth century, the commercial people developed
extensive social and political links with the emerging professional and
service classes under British rule. Together, Bayly holds, they laid 'the
foundations for a more cohesive middle class opinion' in these towns.[18]
The shared Hindu religious and charitable institutions as well as emerging political associations of merchants and professional people made
them 'a recognisable social group'.[19] 'The strengths and limitations of
these binding institutions', Bayly has argued, 'were also carried over into
the era of public politics to form the ligaments of the emerging Indian
middle class.' Such institutions were also 'particularly important in
linking together "the respectable part of Hindu society"'.[20] The merchant groups, often in alliance with professional people, also emerged as
the driving force behind the increasingly 'purist', 'revivalist' or 'reformist' Hindu religious and social initiatives.[21] It was this 'middle class
opinion' and 'respectable' Hindu society that would, in the interwar
period, come to face the poor as a major social force in the towns. This
would provide the basis for a central social contradiction that henceforth
increasingly shaped urban politics.

---

[14] Ibid., pp. 449–57.   [15] Ibid., p. 451.   [16] Ibid., p. 456.
[17] Vasudha Dalmia, *The Nationalization of Hindu Traditions: Bharatendu Harishchandra
and Nineteenth-century Banaras*, Delhi, 1997, pp. 87–8.
[18] Bayly, *Rulers, Townsmen*, p. 452.
[19] Ibid., p. 453.   [20] Ibid., p. 453.
[21] C. A. Bayly, 'Patrons and Politics in Northern India', *MAS*, 7, 3, 1973, pp. 349–88.

Urban development in the interwar period

Growth of industries

The pace of urban growth was to quicken considerably after the First World War, with a remarkable population increase and the extensive development of small-scale manufacturing industries producing a wide variety of goods, catering both to local urban demands and to the rural hinterland. While industries began to flourish in Allahabad, Benares and Lucknow, Kanpur, which was already an important manufacturing centre for cotton textiles and leather products, saw the growth of new kinds of industries. A significant impetus behind the development of industries from the 1920s came from processes of mercantile accumulation and the changing investment pattern and business priorities of urban *sarrafs* – moneylenders or bankers, who also financed trade.

Sarrafi business in the early twentieth century gradually underwent a decisive change. Private banking had become less lucrative, largely owing to the competition of joint-stock banks, and the sarrafs turned to investment in real estate and small-scale industries.[22] In the early 1920s, there was local demand in the towns and adjacent rural areas for both consumption goods and intermediate products, such as machine parts or processed raw materials, required by larger industries and farm production in the countryside. Demand existed for engineering goods, hardware, hosiery, ready-made clothing and carpentry products, to name a few items, which were not produced in sufficient quantity locally.[23] An unprecedented expansion of the population in the province from the 1920s also undoubtedly increased consumption demand and encouraged sarrafi investment in manufactured goods. The slowing down of the flow of consumption goods into the province during the war and general scarcity further stimulated the demand for locally produced commodities. The moneylender-merchants responded to the changing trends of demand and gradually began to finance the manufacture of these products locally, as lucrative avenues for investment. Many of them had also made speculative profits during the First World War, which augmented their ability and willingness to invest in industries.[24]

---

[22] *Report of the United Provinces Provincial Banking Enquiry Committee, 1929–30* (hereafter *BEC*), Allahabad, 1930, vol. I, pp. 63–4; *BEC*, II, pp. 48, 96; *BEC*, IV, pp. 42, 50; L. C. Jain, *Indigenous Banking in India*, London, 1929, p. 44; *Report of the Industrial Finance Committee, U.P. 1934* (Chairman, S. N. Pochkhanawala), Allahabad, 1935, mentioned that small-scale urban industries were financed almost entirely by urban moneylenders and dealers.

[23] *Report of the Director of Industries, U.P.* (hereafter *RDIUP*), 1922–23, p. 23.

[24] Derbyshire, 'Opening up the Interior', p. 387.

The Upper India Chamber of Commerce (UICC) reported to the UP Provincial Banking Enquiry Committee of 1929–30 that 'latterly many sarrafs are becoming industrialists and in some cases this activity is superseding their original function' of banking.[25] With expanding sarrafi funding, urban manufacturing units began to develop rapidly after the war. Back streets and pavements in the bazar areas in the towns became more and more crowded with working people engaged in artisanal and manufacturing workshops (*karkhanas*) or working for merchants and dealers.[26] Urban industries included chemical and dye factories, oil and flour mills, printing presses and bookbinding workshops, iron and steel-rolling mills, and numerous small workshops, producing metal utensils, copper and brassware, iron implements, carpentry products, furniture, shoes, hosiery goods, ready-made garments and engineering and electrical goods.[27]

The most significant consequence of sarrafi investment on the pattern of industrial development in the UP towns was the growth of small-scale[28] manufacturing units, for which the term 'bazar industrialisation' is often used. Only a handful of industries in UP in the interwar years were organised with substantial use of mechanical power and with the employment of large permanent workforces, financed by joint-stock companies or government funds. The norm was those termed 'minor industries' and 'cottage industries' in contemporary industrial reports and surveys.[29] 'Minor industries', which accounted for the largest number of industrial units, were defined as smaller factories using simple mechanically powered machines, while 'cottage industries' rarely used power-driven machinery. Both types of industries were substantially funded by sarrafs, merchants, bankers and dealers in finished products. 'Minor industries' usually employed small numbers of un-

[25] *BEC*, IV, pp. 42–3, Reply of the UICC to the questionnaire of the UP Banking Enquiry Committee.

[26] The UP trade directory of 1935 listed innumerable workshops and manufacturing units located in the bazar areas of the towns. *The Trade and Industries Directory of the United Provinces, 1935*, Kanpur, 1935, pp. 67–87, 134–54, 176–216, 298–323.

[27] *BEC*, II, pp. 392–411, 'Extracts from a survey of the small urban industries of Lucknow' by A. Bhattacharya; pp. 371–91, 'Extracts from a survey of the small urban industries of Benares' by S. N. Majumdar Choudhury; pp. 418–23, 'Survey of small urban industries of Allahabad city' by Shanti Prasad Shukla; *RDIUP* 1921–22 to 1922–23; *Report of the Department of Industries, U.P.* (hereafter *RDIUP*), 1923–24 to 1930–31.

[28] The term 'small-scale' is used here in a descriptive sense to refer to the size or scale of operation of the manufacturing units, which usually employed fewer than 20 workers and used little mechanical power.

[29] For discussions on 'major', 'minor' and 'cottage' industries, see *Report of the Industries Reorganisation Committee U.P. 1932* (Chairman, J. P. Srivastava), Allahabad, 1934; *Memoranda of the U.P. Government Submitted to the All India National Planning Committee, 1939*, Allahabad, 1940, ch. II, MSS, Eur, E 251/10, IOR.

skilled hands on a casual basis, except when a core of skilled operatives was necessary. Many such 'minor' and 'cottage' industries were frequently not enumerated in compiling official factory statistics under the amended Factories Act of 1921, which took into account units employing twenty or more workers and utilised mechanical power.[30] Figures and statistics are, therefore, scarcely available to gauge accurately the spread and extent of small-scale industries. However, it is now widely recognised that throughout India until at least the Second World War (and indeed afterwards, until the present, in many parts) small-scale ventures were favoured by investors – 'mercantile capitalists' in Breman's characterisation.[31] The UP towns were no exception. Indeed the UP government's memorandum to the Royal Commission on Labour recorded that twenty-five times more workers were employed in cottage industries in UP, than in large-scale factories.[32] The memorandum added that 'perhaps in no other province of India do cottage industries still occupy such a relatively important position as they do in the United Provinces.[33] Moreover, compared with the presidency towns of Bombay or Calcutta, where both large and small industries existed together, the towns of the interior, including those in UP, had far fewer large factories and were almost entirely based on small-scale units. The evidence given to the Royal Commission, for instance, noted their dominance in Allahabad, Lucknow and Benares.[34] Large factories remained few in number and were largely concentrated in Kanpur. However, even in Kanpur, apart from the textile and leather factories, most other industrial units were of the 'minor' variety, organised on a small scale.[35]

The banker-merchant investors preferred the small-scale operations of 'minor industries' for a number of now well-known reasons. These small units could avoid the restrictive regulatory regime of factory legislation, did not require extensive management and, as Baker comments in his study of Tamilnadu, the small-scale ventures helped 'to

---

[30] R. K. Das, *Principles and Problems of Indian Labour Legislation*, Calcutta, 1938, pp. 14–16.
[31] See Baker, *An Indian Rural Economy*, pp. 378–80; R. S. Chandavarkar, *The Origins of Industrial Capitalism in India: Business Strategies and the Working Classes in Bombay, 1900–1940*, Cambridge, 1994, pp. 76–87; M. Holmstrom, *Industry and Inequality: The Social Anthropology of Indian Labour*, Cambridge, 1984, p. 52; J. Breman, *Footloose Labour: Working in India's Informal Economy*, Cambridge, 1996, p. 159.
[32] *Royal Commission on Labour in India*, London, 1931 (hereafter *RCLI*), Evidence, vol. III (United Provinces and Central Provinces), Part I, p. 134, Memorandum of the Government of U.P.
[33] Ibid.   [34] Ibid., pp. 135–6.
[35] C. Joshi, 'Kanpur Textile Labour: Some Structural Features of Formative Years', *EPW*, XVI, 44–46, Special Number, November 1981, p. 1824.

minimize the problems of raising capital and finding managerial talent from beyond the original family'.[36] For these same reasons, Sarrafi investment in UP took the form of financing intermediaries to organise workshops or karkhanas and of directly advancing money to workmen and artisans on a 'putting-out' basis. Demand for consumption and intermediate goods, which the sarraf-financed industries produced, was prone to seasonal fluctuation. In such circumstances, the organisation of manufacturing units on a small scale, with limited mechanisation, low management costs and high turnover of unskilled labour, ensured that they had low fixed costs, thus permitting the suspension of production during periods of low demand without incurring any losses. The restricted scale of operations and low capital costs also permitted the investors to diversify and spread their investment over a range of products to match the variable market demands and preferences, without tying down their capital to any particular product. This was particularly helpful to the sarrafs, who usually had less access to large pools of capital than joint-stock enterprises, and thus found it especially important to maintain flexibility in their investments.

In the early 1930s, during and after the agrarian depression, the 1920s' trend of the development of small-scale industries based on merchant enterprise was further reinforced, probably owing in part to the redirection of capital from depression-hit agricultural production and agrarian trade to urban investments.[37] Among urban industries, the small units were often more resilient than larger factories in weathering the pressures of the depression. The slump in prices and the dumping of cheap factory products from Japan, China and Europe placed formidable constraints on industrial activity in the UP towns.[38] In response, investment in joint-stock companies, which financed large industrial concerns, slowed down considerably, as is evident from table 2.1.

Industrial reports from this period, however, indicate that smaller workshops to an extent continued to hold their own, though many were forced to curtail production. Their greater adaptability to market conditions made them better equipped to respond effectively to the pressures of the depression. Low capital costs, the consequent ability to produce goods at cheaper rates and flexibility in diversifying products allowed a range of smaller workshops to withstand competition from foreign products and to continue production in spite of the prevailing low prices. The small hosiery workshops, for instance, were reported to have

---

[36] Baker, *An Indian Rural Economy*, p. 380.
[37] For similar developments in southern India, see Baker, *An Indian Rural Economy*, pp. 379–80.
[38] *RDIUP*, 1929–30, 1930–31, 1931–32.

Table 2.1. *Paid-up capital of joint-stock companies in Uttar Pradesh, 1929/30–1934/5*

Year	Paid-up capital (Rs)
1929–30	12,93,97,834
1930–31	11,47,75,655
1931–32	11,57,05,428
1932–33	7,77,95,336
1933–34	8,45,51,841
1934–35	9,42,56,844

Source: R. C. Pande, 'Growth of Factories in U.P.', *Department of Economics and Statistics, U.P., Bulletin*, No. 21, 1951.

been competing well with foreign products in prices and design and, in 1929–30, UP hosiery products were being exported to the Punjab.[39] Smaller engineering and hardware workshops also fared better compared with the larger factories, such as the Empire Engineering Company in Kanpur, which collapsed during the depression. In contrast, smaller concerns, such as the Singh Engineering Works in Kanpur, remained afloat by manufacturing bolts and rivets at low prices, replacing European products in the market, while other engineering units in the town produced luggage carriers for bicycles.[40] The large-scale leather footwear industry was one of the worst affected by falling demand and competition from Canadian, Czech and Japanese leather and rubber shoes. Yet local small firms in the towns were able to remain in business by producing cheap shoes and harnesses and saddlery for use with horse-drawn hackney carriages.[41]

The effects of the depression on urban industry began to ease from early 1934. The UP Department of Industries reported in that year that the industrial 'tone and feeling are those of buoyancy'.[42] The artisan industries, which had been adversely affected during the depression, recovered from the mid-1930s. The handloom silk weavers in Benares, for instance, who had faced falling demand and competition from low-priced Japanese and Chinese artificial silk during the depression, gradually switched to cheaper imported silk yarn and thus were able to produce fabrics at lower prices. Moreover, demand for specialised Benares silk, used for social and religious ceremonies, also began to pick up and the silk industry revived quickly.[43] In addition to artisan

[39] Ibid., 1927–28, Appendix A, p. 15; 1929–30, p. 3.
[40] Ibid., 1928–29, p. 5; 1929–30, p. 6.
[41] Ibid., for the 21 months ending 31 March 1934, p. 9.
[42] Ibid., p. 3.
[43] Ibid., for the year ending 31 March 1935, p. 7.

industries, the manufacturing workshops producing consumer and intermediate goods, set up in the 1920s, which had cut back production during the depression, began to recover and advance rapidly from 1934, to some extent owing to the introduction of some tariff protection against cheap foreign imports in the years after the depression.[44]

The post-depression years, however, were characterised not only by industrial recovery but also by a substantial expansion and a further diversification of urban industries, as import substitution in consumer products gradually emerged to be an important feature of Indian manufacturing in this period.[45] In UP, the products of urban manufacturing industries, especially consumer goods, began to replace imports from other provinces and abroad, and were often exported outside the province. Moreover, many of the crop-processing industries, which had been spread over the countryside, gradually came to be concentrated in the towns and their production increased manifold in their new urban setting. Mills that processed agricultural products such as rice, oil and flour, and workshops manufacturing hosiery, ready-made garments, soap, engineering goods, hardware, metal utensils and various other consumer and intermediate products, all flourished during this period. The hosiery industry, for example, met burgeoning local urban and rural demand in UP and also exported goods to the Punjab, Delhi and Calcutta.[46] Between 1933–4 and 1937–8 the annual production of hosiery goods in UP increased from 144,908 lbs to 800,136 lbs.[47] Oil mills began to be concentrated in the towns from the 1920s, replacing rural oil crushers, and produced oil for urban and rural domestic use and machinery lubrication. With easy access to a variety of oil-seeds local to the province, UP also effectively penetrated the oil markets of the Punjab, Bengal, Bihar, Central India and Rajputana.[48] Between 1934 and 1939, annual mustard oil production in UP increased by 63 per cent, from 748,000 maunds to 1,218,000 maunds.[49] The production in groundnut oil crushing mills in Kanpur alone increased nearly fifty-fold from 2,000 maunds in 1934–5 to 95,000 maunds in

[44] B. R. Tomlinson, *The Political Economy of the Raj, 1914–47: The Economics of Decolonization in India*, London, 1979, pp. 31, 34, 46; B. R. Tomlinson, *The Economy of Modern India, 1860–1970: New Cambridge History of India, III:3*, Cambridge, 1993, pp. 133–5.

[45] Ibid.

[46] *Department of Industries and Commerce, U.P., Bulletin*, No. 2 (New Series), 1939, R. C. Srivastava, 'Survey of the Hosiery Industry in U.P.'.

[47] *RDIUP*, for the year ending 31 March 1936, p. 4; for the year ending 31 March 1938, p. 6.

[48] *Report of the Industries Reorganisation Committee U.P. 1932.*

[49] *Memoranda of the U.P. Government Submitted to the All India National Planning Committee, 1939.*

1937–8.[50] The soap industry, entirely urban based and a recent introduction in UP in the early 1930s, was also reported to have registered rapid development, with 7 large factories and 122 small units in the province by 1939.[51] Soap factories in Kanpur proliferated primarily in response to growing government and military demand for local products and to high import duties on foreign soap.[52] The engineering workshops and iron and steel-rolling mills began to meet local demand for building fittings, metal bars, castings and bearings and replaced imports of these products. The boom in building construction in the interwar period also gave a major boost to the engineering industry. General engineering works received an impetus from the increasing demand for machinery in the new sugar factories and hydro-electric schemes, both of which expanded in the province in the 1930s. The development of motor transport opened up a market for vehicle spare parts and spurred on the growth of repair workshops.[53]

A large majority of all these industries, of course, continued to be based in small-scale units. Thus, the UP trade directory of 1935, which listed all industrial and commercial establishments regardless of their size, mentioned twenty hosiery dealers and manufacturers in Lucknow, eighteen in Kanpur, eight in Allahabad and four in Benares.[54] Yet, for the entire province, only seven large hosiery factories were listed in the factory statistics of 1938, which took into account units employing twenty or more workers and using mechanical power.[55] Similarly, the 1938 factory statistics enumerated a total of twenty-seven registered engineering units, metal and hardware workshops and iron and steel-rolling mills in the whole of UP.[56] In contrast, the UP trade directory of 1935 listed seventy such firms of dealers and manufacturers in Lucknow, seventy-four in Allahabad, twenty-two in Benares and seventy-eight in Kanpur.[57]

---

[50] *RDIUP,* for the year ending 31 March 1938, p. 12.
[51] *Memoranda of the U.P. Government Submitted to the All India National Planning Committee, 1939; RDIUP,* 1929–30, p. 5; 1930–31, p. 7; 1931–32, p. 5; for the 21 months ending 31 March 1934, p. 9; for the year ending 31 March 1935, p. 9; 1937, p. 7; for the year ending 31 March 1938, p. 12.
[52] *RDIUP,* 1931–32, p. 3; for the 21 months ending 31 March 1934, p. 9.
[53] *Report of the Industries Reorganisation Committee U.P. 1932; RDIUP,* for the year ending 31 March 1939, p. 10; *Memoranda of the U.P. Government Submitted to the All India Planning Committee, 1939.*
[54] *The Trade and Industries Directory of the United Provinces, 1935,* pp. 78, 143–4, 198–9, 309–10.
[55] *Statistics of Factories Subject to the Indian Factories Act. For the Year Ending December 31, 1938,* Delhi, 1940, Statement number II: Enumeration of Factories, p. 7.
[56] Ibid., pp. 13–14.
[57] *The Trade and Industries Directory of the United Provinces, 1935,* pp. 67–87, 134–54, 176–216, 298–323.

With the development of manufacturing industries from the 1920s, the nature of urban development clearly changed. Until the First World War, the large towns studied here had been primarily administrative and commercial centres, with some artisan industries and, in Kanpur, some large mills. From the 1920s, the towns also became centres for the production of manufacturing goods for local urban and rural markets and processing centres for agrarian produce. This function of the towns in the economy became even more pronounced in the 1930s, with further advance in 'bazar industrialisation'. The towns, thus, began to generate new occupational opportunities in the workshops and factories, attracting rural migrants in turn. The growth of urban industries, together with their concentration in small-scale units, was to have significant implications both for the nature of population growth and for the occupational pattern and economic relations in the towns in the interwar period. The social composition of the townspeople was to undergo a significant shift. Before 1920, merchants and professional people had formed a majority of those who settled in the towns.[58] In the interwar years, poorer cultivators and agrarian labourers formed the bulk of the migrants who began to come to the towns in larger numbers in search of jobs promised by the expansion of manufacturing industries.

Migration and population expansion: The demographic driver of urban transformation

Population growth and in-migration until 1920 had been slow and uneven in Allahabad, Lucknow, Benares and Kanpur. Agricultural prosperity in the early decades of the twentieth century, low rates of population growth in the province in general, the stagnation or slow advance of industries in the towns, except in Kanpur, as well as poor urban health conditions militated against steady population expansion.[59] Between 1901 and 1921, the populations of Allahabad, Benares and Lucknow in fact registered a decline (see table 2.2).

It was from the early 1920s that existing demographic trends were radically reversed. Census reports noted that between 1921 and 1931 urban population grew twice as fast as that of rural areas, whereas between 1881 and 1921 population in the towns had grown only about half as fast as rural population.[60] The 1931 census further recorded an

---

[58] Bayly, *Local Roots*, ch. 2.
[59] *Census of India, 1921*, vol. XVI (United Provinces) (hereafter *Census 1921*), Part I, Report, Allahabad, 1923, pp. 34–6, 161–3; *Census of India, 1931*, vol. XVIII (United Provinces) (hereafter *Census 1931*), Part I, Report, Allahabad, 1933, pp. 141–2.
[60] *Census 1931*, p. 126.

Table 2.2. *Population change in the towns, 1901–1921*

Town	Population change
Lucknow	−23,483
Kanpur	+13,639
Benares	−14,632
Allahabad	−23,483

Source: Census of India, 1921, vol. XVI (United Provinces), Part I, Report, Allahabad, 1923, p. 36.

Table 2.3. *Population increase and migration gain in the towns, 1921–1931*

Town	Actual increase	Percentage increase	Migration gain	Total population in 1931
Lucknow	33,930	15.6	32,956	251,097
Kanpur	24,104	12.4	40,953	219,189
Benares	5,664	2.9	14,486	201,137
Allahabad	28,290	19.4	16,670	173,895

Source: Census of India, 1931, vol. XVIII (UP), Part I, Report, Allahabad, 1933, pp. 141–2.

unprecedented demographic increase in the 'large' towns of the province, defined as those with populations over 100,000, with Kanpur, Lucknow, Benares and Allahabad falling within this category (see table 2.3).

Even Kanpur, where population had, in fact, increased before 1921, albeit irregularly, registered a comparatively far larger growth from the 1920s. Here, as tables 2.2 and 2.3 show, in comparison with an increase by only 13,639 in the previous two decades, in the single decade between 1921 and 1931 the increase was 40,953. Between 1931 and 1941, there was an even more dramatic population increase in all four towns, as indicated in table 2.4.[61]

Apart from the hitherto unseen pace of the population increase from 1921, even more significant was the fact that demographic expansion in this period, although partially helped by the general improvement in urban morbidity and mortality rates, was mainly due to the influx of migrants from the countryside, as is evident from the figures in table 2.3. The 1931 census deduced the importance of migration from the fact that the actual number of people enumerated far exceeded the

[61] The 1941 population figures are taken from the 1951 census and I have calculated the percentage population increase between 1931 and 1941 on the basis of the 1931 census figures cited in table 2.3.

Table 2.4. *Population increase in the towns, 1931–1941*

Towns	Percentage increase	Total population in 1941
Lucknow	54.1	387,117
Kanpur	122.3	487,324
Benares	30.8	263,100
Allahabad	49.8	260,630

Source: *Census of India, 1951,* vol. II (UP), Part I-A, Report, Allahabad, 1953, p. 169.

reported natural increase in population, the latter being calculated from birth and death rates.[62] The 1951 census confirmed that 'the drift from rural to the urban areas continued' between 1931 and 1941, and reported that in this period, for all UP towns, migration gain was higher than natural increase, the respective figures being 12.3 per cent and 10.8 per cent.[63] In keeping with these census findings, the evidence recorded by the Royal Commission on Labour in 1931 suggested that about half the population of Kanpur city in 1921 were migrants.[64] A survey of 300 families of mill workers in Kanpur, conducted in 1939–40, also found that 219 of them came to Kanpur between 1920 and 1940, 31 had lived in the town since birth and only 49 had migrated between 1904 and 1920.[65]

Migration from the countryside in the interwar period was stimulated by the galloping pace of general population growth in the province from 1921. In the four decades between 1881 and 1921, the total population of UP had increased by 1.6 million, whereas in a single decade after 1921 provincial population grew by 3.1 million, followed by an increase of over 6.7 million between 1931 and 1941.[66] The pressure of population on land in the countryside and the growing scarcity of rural sources

[62] *Census 1931,* p. 127.
[63] *Census of India, 1951,* vol. II (United Provinces) (hereafter *Census 1951*), Part I-A, Report, Allahabad, 1953, pp. 164, 198.
[64] *RCLI,* III:I, p. 140, Memorandum of the Government of U.P.
[65] The date of migration of one family was not available. 'Preliminary Draft of the Pro Forma Report on the Enquiry into Family Budgets and Housing Conditions of the Mill Workers at Cawnpore, 1939–40, p. 9, prepared by the Bureau of Economic Intelligence, UP, manuscript held at the Record Room of the Northern India Employers' Association, Kanpur.
[66] Between 1881 and 1921, the total population of UP increased from 45,034,574 to 46,669,865 or by 1,635,291, whereas between 1921 and 1931 the population grew to 49,776,754, or by 3,106,889. Between 1931 and 1941, the population increased to 56,531,848, involving an increase of 6,755,094. *Census 1951,* p. 25.

of livelihood propelled people towards the towns.[67] Tiwari, in a study in 1938–9, showed that, from 1921–2, average real income declined in rural areas, while urban income rose in comparison.[68] Declining trends in rural incomes and agrarian depression in the late 1920s and early 1930s further accentuated the march of rural populations to the towns.[69] While economic difficulties propelled the migrants away from the villages, they came mainly to the larger towns in the province, including Kanpur, Benares, Lucknow and Allahabad, where the growth of industries had been concentrated, generating employment opportunities. The 1931 census report commented that, 'due to the extension of industrial and commercial activities in the larger cities', which had populations of 50,000–100,000 or over at the time of the 1921 census, they attracted most of the rural migrants.[70] According to the census, smaller towns, (with a population below 50,000), lacking an upturn in industrial or commercial activity, not only failed to attract migrants but also lost some of their poorer population, who departed for the larger towns in quest of work.[71] The census reported that 'labour', 'artisans, clerks and servants' were leaving for the 'larger and more prosperous towns' from the smaller towns such as Shahjahanpur, Hathras, Amroha, Mirzapur and Sambhal.[72] The census of 1951 confirmed the continuation of this trend of growth of larger towns in the 1930s and 1940s. It was reported that towns with a population of over 100,000 increased at a rate of 22.3 per cent between 1921 and 1931,[73] and that the pace of growth accelerated further, with a provincial average rate of increase of 71.3 per cent, between 1931 and 1941.[74]

Rural migrants who came to the towns were poorer cultivators and agrarian labourers, often from lower and intermediate agricultural castes,[75] who were pushed to the towns by economic difficulties in the

---

[67] Eric Stokes, *The Peasant and the Raj: Studies in Agrarian Society and Peasant Rebellion in Colonial India*, Cambridge, 1978, first paperback edn, 1980, ch. 9, esp. pp. 207, 221, 235; *RCLI*, III:I, pp. 138–43, Memorandum of the Government of U.P.; *Census 1931*, p. 127; *Report of the Committee of Inquiry into Wages and Conditions of Labour in Cawnpore* (Chairman, Dr Rajendra Prasad), 1938 (hereafter *KLIC Report*), included in V. Chaudhary (ed.), *Dr Rajendra Prasad: Correspondence and Select Documents, Volume Two: 1938*, Delhi, 1984, pp. 342–3.

[68] S. G. Tiwari, *The Economic Prosperity of the United Provinces: A Study in the Provincial Income and Its Distribution and Working Conditions, 1921–1939*, Bombay, 1951, pp. 272–3; the population 'pull' factor of relatively high urban wages is also mentioned in *Census 1931*, p. 40.

[69] *Census 1931*, p. 61.   [70] Ibid., pp. 127–8.

[71] Ibid., p. 127.   [72] Ibid., pp. 127, 146.

[73] *Census 1951*, p. 164.   [74] Ibid.

[75] A study on Kanpur, for instance, mentions that migrants to the town before the Second World War were mostly unskilled labourers belonging to the lower castes. Mazumdar, *Social Contours of an Industrial City*, p. viii.

countryside.[76] The survey of 1939–40 in Kanpur, mentioned above, indicated that 173 workers' families, out of a total of 260 families surveyed, migrated from villages on account of 'poverty or lack of subsistence, uneconomic fragmentation of holdings, increased pressure on holdings of surplus labour, ejectment from holdings, indebtedness and economic calamities'. The reason for the migration of the remaining 87 families was stated to be 'economic ambition or adventure'.[77] The Upper India Chamber of Commerce (UICC) further reported in 1929 that these migrant workers, 'to a large and increasing extent, severed their connections with their villages',[78] suggesting the declining importance of rural livelihoods for them and their more permanent, rather than seasonal, migration to the towns. In the 1920s and 1930s, therefore, poorer labourers and agriculturists, who were losing their sources of subsistence in the countryside, were coming in large numbers to the towns and looking to depend increasingly on urban jobs. These migrants, even if they continued to maintain their village social connections, appeared to have largely ceased to draw economic sustenance from the countryside. Evidence given to the Royal Commission on Labour by the representatives of the UICC suggested not only that the labour supply from rural areas was now relatively more stable and abundant than in the past, but also that the continuing tendency of labour to return to the countryside for seasonal work was, in fact, partly due to the uncertainty of urban employment rather than the positive pull of rural jobs or income.[79] This point was confirmed by the Director of Public Health of the government of UP, who stated that, in the past:

[Kanpur millowners] drew all their labour from the agricultural tracts. The labourers came for a period and went back home. They were in no sense an industrial population. This phase has been gradually passing away and there is now an established industrial population which forms a very large percentage of general labourers.[80]

Other witnesses to the Royal Commission remarked that when the Kanpur mills periodically needed surplus labour from the 'city', referring to the stock of casual general labourers, they were readily available.[81] One witness reiterated that additional labour for the factories

---

[76] *Census 1931*, p. 127.
[77] 'Preliminary Draft of the Pro Forma Report on the Enquiry into Family Budgets and Housing Conditions of the Mill Workers at Cawnpore, 1939–40', p. 10.
[78] *RCLI*, III:I, p. 256, Evidence of the UICC. Elsewhere in its evidence, the UICC reiterated that 'of late years there is far less contact with villages than formerly' (ibid., p. 249).
[79] *RCLI*, III:II, p. 161, Oral Evidence of the Representatives of the UICC.
[80] Ibid., p. 147, Oral Evidence of Lt. Col. C. L. Dunn, Director of Public Health, UP.
[81] Ibid., p. 164, Oral Evidence of Mr Ryan, Secretary representing the UICC.

came, not from the villages, but from among those 'employed in local bazars', especially in 'loading and unloading' jobs, including as coolies at railway stations. 'It is a floating population in Kanpur', this witness concluded.[82] These comments clearly suggest the growing and abundant supply of more permanent labour in the city by the late 1920s, which was confirmed some years later by an official committee enquiring into the conditions of labour in Kanpur in 1938. In the view of this Committee:

In India it is often said that . . . the so-called industrial worker was really an agriculturist. . . . [But the rural labourer] is now coming to stay and not to run away back to his village home. . . . City populations are now in increasing proportions being composed of 'native-born' people.[83]

All these various statements point to the fact that the large towns were becoming the homes, or at least the main site of work and livelihood, of an increasing number of poorer people and labourers from the countryside, although they may have had to revert to whatever rural work was available during periods of urban unemployment.

Many of these migrants also sought to settle permanently in the towns with their families whenever possible,[84] although the scarcity of housing and urban residential land often deterred them and ensured that they maintained at least social and family contacts with their villages. A study of urbanisation in Kanpur observes, 'it was seen that entire families moved into the city as the earnings from agriculture were greatly reduced due to the downward trend in agricultural prices'.[85] However, despite this tendency, migration with families remained difficult and the working population in the towns was overwhelmingly male. Women earners and working dependants were remarkably few. In 1931, the percentage of women in the total population of urban earners and working dependants was 21.8 in Allahabad, 9.2 in Kanpur, 17.7 in Benares and 8.5 in Lucknow.[86] Most of the women earners were, however, not part of the manual labouring population, but were concentrated in domestic service, in municipal sweeping work and in some

---

[82] Ibid., p. 125, Oral Evidence of Lt. Col. L.C. Larmour, Superintendent, Harness and Saddlery Factory, Kanpur.

[83] *KLIC Report*, pp. 342–3.

[84] UICC in its evidence to the *RCLI* reported that 'about 80 to 90 per cent of the workers have their families with them', *RCLI*, III:I, p. 250, Evidence of the UICC. This is likely to be either an overestimate, as housing was scarce in the towns, or a comment about the core of permanent labourers employed by the mills who had some provision of housing from the mills. *Census 1931*, p. 191, in contrast, states that 'at least half of the males who go to Cawnpore to find work leave their family behind'.

[85] Chandrasekhara, 'Kanpur: An Industrial Metropolis', p. 283.

[86] *Census 1931*, Part II, Tables, Table No. X, Part III, p. 382.

artisanal industries, such as the Indian cigarette (*bidi*) industry in Allahabad or the handloom silk-weaving industry in Benares, in which women took part in spinning and dyeing. According to factory statistics in the early 1930s, 95 per cent of the industrial labour force was male.[87] The world of urban labour was thus clearly predominantly male. This would have important political implications, especially in the prominence of a martial, masculine political culture of the poor, which will be discussed in the second part of this book.

Urban occupations of the poor and economic relations

Employment in manufacturing industry

In the interwar period, then, Kanpur, Allahabad, Lucknow and Benares, in varying degrees, experienced the increasing specialisation and concentration of manufacturing and commercial functions, and attracted a large number of job seekers, swelling the ranks of the poor who were already there. Low-paid employment opportunities had gradually opened up by the first two decades of the twentieth century as a result of urban territorial extension, vigorous building construction, the expansion of municipal services and the development of trade. With the growth of industries in the interwar period, factories and workshops began to offer new employment opportunities and absorbed a significant proportion of urban job seekers. In 1921 and 1931, 25.1 and 27 per cent of the working population in the towns, respectively, were employed in industries.[88] Industry in the interwar years, being driven by merchant capital, was based mainly on small-scale units. Employment came to be concentrated here, with, of course, the notable exception of the large factories of Kanpur.

The exact numbers employed in the smaller units are difficult, even impossible, to gauge, as these units were rarely systematically surveyed in reports on industries and were excluded from the factory statistics. Their importance can, however, be well surmised from indirect evidence. In Benares, 32 per cent of total urban workers were recorded to be engaged in industries in the 1931 census,[89] even though there was no large factory at all in the town, except a 'medium sized weaving and spinning mill', according to the Royal Commission on Labour.[90] Many

---

[87] *Annual Report on the Working of Indian Factories Act XII of 1911, as modified up to June 1, 1926, in U.P.* 1933.
[88] *Census 1931*, p. 393.   [89] Ibid.
[90] *RCLI*, III:I, p. 136, Memorandum of the Government of U.P.

of those identified in the census as 'industrial' workers in Benares were engaged instead in the extensive artisanal silk-weaving industry and in the production of metal and brassware in small workshops. The over-whelming importance of small-scale industries is also evident from a comparison of the figures of overall industrial employment with the numbers employed in the large factories, which involved over twenty workers and were enumerated under the Factories Act. According to the census returns of 1931, the total number of people employed in industries in all UP towns was 258,988,[91] while the provincial average daily factory employment in that year accounted for 93,223 workers,[92] which included workers in larger enumerated factories in both urban and rural areas, though a substantial majority of these 93,223 workers can be expected to have been concentrated in the towns, especially in Kanpur. These figures indicate that in 1931 not more than 36 per cent of urban industrial workers were absorbed by large factories and the other 64 per cent were engaged in small manufacturing units and in artisan industries.

An important feature of industrial employment in interwar urban UP was its largely unskilled and casual nature. Small-scale units, which dominated the industrial scene, relied on low levels of mechanisation and flexibility of production, thus allowing easy adaptability to market fluctuations. Employment in them, as a result, could not be based substantially on permanent skilled workforces, but depended mainly on general, manual labour. Demand for labour was shifting and variable, creating a casual labour market. This was, however, not a characteristic feature of smaller units alone. Chandavarkar has persuasively argued for Bombay that 'patterns of labour use, intensive yet flexible and casual in deployment, were common to both the formal and informal sectors'.[93] This was equally the case in the large mills of UP. Like the smaller industrial units, the larger factories of the so-called organised or formal sector, with greater mechanisation and bigger workforces, relied only on a core of skilled workers and employed a large proportion of casual, temporary or substitute labour.[94] Tiwari noted for the period 1921–39 that a large number of unskilled workers were employed by organised industries. Large-scale cotton gins, oil presses and rice or flour mills relied almost entirely on unskilled labour, and even in the Allahabad

---

[91] *Census 1931*, p. 372.
[92] *Statistics of Factories Subject to the Indian Factories Act. For the Year Ending 31 December, 1931*, Calcutta, 1932, Statement Number IV: Average Daily Number of Workers Employed in Factories, p. 30.
[93] R. S. Chandavarkar, 'Industrialization in India before 1947: Conventional Approaches and Alternative Perspectives', *MAS*, 19, 3, 1985, p. 638.
[94] Joshi, 'Kanpur Textile Labour', p. 1833.

Ordnance Factory 70 per cent of workers were unskilled.[95] The Memorandum of the Government of UP to the Royal Commission on Labour similarly noted that 'the number of persons employed in [large-scale] factories is still a small fraction of total population and the number of skilled workers is smaller still'.[96]

Kanpur was, of course, an exception to the general pattern of industrial employment in the towns of UP. Although smaller workshops were numerous in Kanpur, especially from the 1920s, large factories employed over 30,000 workers in the 1930s.[97] Many of these workers in the Kanpur mills, enumerated under the Factories Act, were, however, neither skilled operatives nor permanently employed by the mills.[98] For carting and loading of consignments and stocking of goods, workshops and industrial establishments did not employ permanent workers, but temporarily hired unskilled manual labourers, often through labour contractors. Some mill workers were thus temporary porters and coolies. Moreover, the mills relied on a large reserve of *badli* or substitute workers for recruitment to periodic vacancies.[99] All these workers alternated between employment in the large mills and jobs in smaller workshops or casual, manual labour in the urban markets as carters or porters.[100] The number of such people is difficult to estimate for lack of statistics. However, a rather extreme indication of the shifting nature of unskilled employment in the larger factories was given by the Superintendent of the Government Harness and Saddlery Factory in Kanpur, in his oral evidence to the Royal Commission on Labour. The Superintendent stated that, owing to seasonal variation in employment, 100 per cent of the unskilled workers employed by the factory left each year at various times and worked in the bazars or other workshops, though some returned to the factory when demand for labour increased again.[101] Achchha Singh, an employee in the Harness Factory, in his evidence to the Royal Commission also mentioned that during periods

[95] Tiwari, *Economic Prosperity*, p. 153. The industrial census of 1921 indicated the predominance of unskilled labourers in flour, rice and sugar mills. *Census 1921*, p. 185, Industrial Subsidiary Table I (Distribution of industries and persons employed).

[96] *RCLI*, III:I, pp. 145–6, Memorandum of the Government of U.P.

[97] Cited in Joshi, 'Kanpur Textile Labour', p. 1825. About 37% of those engaged in large industries in the entire province were concentrated in Kanpur. *RCLI*, III:I, p. 135, Memorandum of the Government of U.P.

[98] From Labour Officer, Kanpur, to Secretary, Industries Department, UODO, Letter No. 1934, dated 11 January 1939, File no. 6/1938–9 (Labour Correspondences), Department XXX, Industries, Kanpur Collectorate, ERR; *RCLI*, III:I, p. 146, Memorandum of the Government of U.P.

[99] Joshi, 'Kanpur Textile Labour', pp. 1831–3.

[100] *RCLI*, III:II, p. 164, Oral Evidence of Mr Ryan, Secretary representing the UICC.

[101] Ibid., p. 125, Oral Evidence of the Superintendent, Harness and Saddlery Factory, Kanpur.

of unemployment workers found jobs in 'other factories . . . not necessarily leather factories' and stated that 'we can do all sorts of work'.[102]

As a result of such high labour turnover across a variety of large and small industrial establishments, the supply of labour was not rigidly demarcated along the lines of organised, formal sector, permanent workers on the one hand, and the informal, unorganised sector, casual labourers on the other. The urban labour market was, in fact, largely integrated, and the strategies of labour deployment by employers did not vary significantly between the so-called formal and informal sectors. Both tended to rely on casual labour whenever possible. Apart from a small core of skilled, permanent labour employed by the mills, the pool of labour supply for the two sectors was, to a large extent, unified.[103] Large and small industries, as well as manual work in the trade and transport sectors, drew from the same stock of largely casual labour. The difference between the workforces of large mills and others was thus blurred and scarcely conformed to that envisaged by a dualistic model of the labour market.[104] It would, however, be misleading to over-stress this case to argue that the entire labour market was casual and unskilled. There were, of course, enclaves of skilled workers, especially in the artisan crafts, as well as nuclei of more permanently employed skilled hands in large textile and other factories. Nevertheless, the nature of work in the towns was primarily shifting, casual and mobile, with labourers forced to move from job to job, spanning the industrial and trading sectors. It should not, however, be imagined that the labour market was thus characterised by infinite mobility, with workers freely able to move from one employment to another and to choose work as they pleased. On the contrary, the very overcrowding and fluidity of the labour market in the interwar years ensured that various sections of workers sought to maintain their jobs in particular occupations, often trying fiercely to prevent the incursion of outsiders. If

---

[102] Ibid., p. 246, Oral Evidence of Achchha Singh of the Deputation of Workers from the Harness and Saddlery Factory. A survey of labour conditions in the leather industry in Kanpur in 1946 mentioned that, in a sample taken from six tanneries, out of a total of 774 workers, 500 were employed for less than a year. *Labour Investigation Committee*, 'Report on an Enquiry into the Conditions of Labour in Tanneries and Leather Goods Factories', Delhi, 1946.

[103] The dualistic model of labour markets has been critically assessed, among others, by Breman and Chandavarkar. Their arguments are also applicable to the UP towns studied here. Jan Breman, 'A Dualistic Labour System? A Critique of the "Informal Sector" Concept', *EPW*, Part I: XI, 48, 27 November 1976, pp. 1870–6; Part II: XI, 49, 4 December 1976, pp. 1905–8; Part III: XI, 50, 11 December 1976, pp. 1939–44; Jan Breman, *Footloose Labour: Working in India's Informal Economy*, Cambridge, 1996, pp. 5–11, 67–71; Chandavarkar, *Origins of Industrial Capitalism*, pp. 72–123.

[104] Ibid.; Holmstrom, *Industry and Inequality*, pp. 76–9, 319–21.

necessary, they entered into unfavourable labour arrangements with employers, most notably by acquiescing in a system of partial payment of their wages by the employers as a form of job security.[105] Similarly, in some cases, workers relied on caste and kin connections to gain and maintain a foothold in particular areas of employment and thus ensured the segmentation of the labour market along the lines of caste or religious community. The labour market, then, was fragmented in diverse ways and there were various impediments to free entry and access into particular segments, despite imperfect differentiation along the formal–informal sector axis or between industry and trade or transport. The overall consequence was a highly unstable and competitive job market with severe difficulties in finding work and little security of employment.

What was the nature and condition of employment and economic relations in the manufacturing establishments, mostly 'minor' or 'cottage' units, that employed the vast majority of urban industrial workers? Such small units ranged from artisanal units to small factories or workshops, a few of them utilising power-driven machinery. Production in them was organised either directly by the sarrafs or by intermediaries and middlemen such as master artisans, contractors and *karkhanadars*, who employed labourers on piece or time wage and worked with borrowed capital from merchant-financiers or moneylenders.[106] In the latter case, the financiers advanced capital on credit to the workshop owners to organise production and for procuring equipment, tools and raw materials and for paying workers' wages. The dealers and merchants who supplied credit also bought the finished products for marketing. The entrepreneurs sold their products either to their creditor-merchants or to wholesale dealers, and in the former case repayment of credit was adjusted against the price of the finished product.[107] At times, individual workmen or artisans also directly worked for the dealers, who supplied them with raw materials and procured their products for marketing.[108]

Where the investors themselves organised production, workers were directly employed by the merchant-moneylenders. A variety of forms and sources of labour recruitment prevailed in these cases. Labour contractors were at times engaged by the employers to select, supervise and manage labour. However, jobbers were less significant in small-scale industries than in the recruitment and control of labour in the

---

[105] This system of withholding of wages, usually called *baqidari*, will be discussed later in this chapter.
[106] *BEC*, II, pp. 392–411, 371–91, 418–23.
[107] Ibid.   [108] Ibid.

larger establishments, such as the Kanpur cotton mills[109] or railway workshops. In most cases, workers in small industries were hired from the regular pool of job seekers who congregated at some known fixed points in the towns each day. Of course, bazar contacts and networks frequently served as sources of labour supply for the employers. When the manufacturing units were somewhat larger and known to employ labour regularly, the workers often presented themselves at the gates.[110]

Employment in the small-scale and artisanal industries was not only casual, but also prone to seasonal fluctuations. A survey of artisan industries in Lucknow mentioned that these were characterised by 'exaggerated alternation of over-work and unemployment due to the fact that they satisfy occasional or seasonal needs'.[111] Such seasonal variation of employment was also common in other small-scale industries. In the hosiery industry, for instance, demand for products was brisk between September and February. During the period of low demand, many workers were out of work or were employed only part time. The number of workers was reduced during this period by 53.8 per cent in Lucknow, 50 per cent in Allahabad and 40 per cent in Benares. Kanpur, being a centre for the export of hosiery products to other provinces, enjoyed somewhat more steady demand, and production was maintained on a more even keel throughout the year, with a comparatively smaller reduction in the number of workers during the slack season.[112] Similarly, in the ready-made clothing industry in Kanpur, the busy season was confined to the period between October and December, which accounted for 40 per cent of the annual sale of products. For the rest of the year, production was drastically reduced.[113] The small-scale garment industry in Kanpur was, thus, characterised by high demand for workers during the 'boom' period and the existence of a large surplus labour force of *darzis* (tailors) during slack periods, who were either partially or entirely unemployed and were forced to find supplementary work in other industries or as manual labourers in the bazars.[114]

While seasonal variation in employment in hosiery or garment industries arose from fluctuations in demand, in factories processing

[109] Ibid.; Joshi, 'Kanpur Textile Labour', pp. 1829–30.
[110] *RCLI*, III:I, p. 144, Memorandum of the Government of U.P.; p. 225, Evidence of Mr W. G. Mackay, Chief Inspector of Factories and Boilers, U.P.
[111] *BEC*, II, p. 119, 'Memorandum on the Small Industries of Lucknow' by Dr Radhakamal Mukherjee.
[112] Srivastava, 'Survey of the Hosiery Industry in U.P.'.
[113] *Bureau of Economic Intelligence, U.P., Bulletin*, No. 1, 1938, C. Ackroyd and Devaraj, 'The Cawnpore Wholesale Clothing Trade'.
[114] Ibid.

agricultural products, such as oil, rice, sugar or flour mills, employment was reduced during periods when the raw material supply was low. Most mills closed down for two or three months in the year. Moreover, employment was not regular even when the supply of raw material was abundant. This was because the mills worked in response to particular orders for products as they were received and curtailed production when orders were not forthcoming.[115] Fluctuation in production also affected such industries as hardware, engineering, furniture, soap and printing presses, all of which had seasonal variations in demand. These industries employed a large number of unskilled labourers on a temporary basis during busy periods, while at other times employment plummeted. Workers in the small-scale urban industries and artisans thus faced an unstable job market and periods of under-employment. Loss of work and arbitrary dismissals were key elements in their experience of work, and labour unrest against such dismissals was frequently reported in the 1930s.[116] Scarce and temporary industrial employment was, moreover, particularly prominent during the depression of the early 1930s, when demand for many industrial products remained low or unsteady for an extended period. The seasonal curtailment of production and decrease in employment arose largely from the small-scale nature of workshops and their pattern of financing. Whether managed by the financiers themselves or run by middlemen workshop owners, the industrial units operated on limited amounts of capital. The sarrafs or dealers slowed down production at periods of low demand, and redirected their capital to other industries or trade to maintain a steady return on their capital. The workshop owners, who depended on borrowed capital, were forced to suspend production when the pace of sale of goods dwindled, for they were unable to repay their existing loans and mobilise more capital.[117] This pattern of fluctuating production and demand for labour in the UP towns matches the scenario sketched by Chandavarkar for Bombay, where 'the patterns of investment and business strategies which tailored production to the short-term fluctuations of the market'[118] generated a labour market with high turnover and instability, exposing large numbers of job seekers to the vagaries of the casual labour market.[119]

Related to seasonality and impermanence of employment was the

---

[115] From Labour Officer, Kanpur to Secretary, Industries Department, UODO, Letter No. 1934.
[116] Workers' agitations will be discussed in chapter 9 below.
[117] Ackroyd and Devaraj, 'The Cawnpore Wholesale Clothing Trade'.
[118] Chandavarkar, *Origins of Industrial Capitalism*, p. 120.
[119] Ibid., pp. 72–123; Chandavarkar, 'Industrialization in India before 1947', p. 643. Chandavarkar stresses that such strategies of flexible labour use were characteristic of large industries too, and not simply of small units.

indebtedness of workers. Indeed, indebtedness was arguably the single most important feature of the experience of urban labour. In artisan industries, such as metalware, woodwork, silk weaving and cloth embroidery, during periods of under-employment workers often took advances against future wages from the merchants or dealers to whom they supplied their finished products or from workshop owners for whom they worked. Such advances were, however, considered to be loans and future wages were withheld partially as security for the loans. This system of payment was usually called *baqidari*, or deferred payment. The artisans remained indebted and received only part of their wages until the loans were repaid. Underpayment of wages and periods of lack of work forced artisans to take further loans and the cycle perpetuated itself.[120] In a report by the government of UP, indebtedness of this nature among artisans was stated to be 'so common as to be one of the characteristic features of the system on which cottage industries employing hired labour are carried on.'[121]

Small-scale workshops, especially those that employed skilled and semi-skilled labour, also often operated on the basis of baqidari. In the ready-made clothing industry, for instance, darzis were paid only half their wages in cash, while the rest was kept by the workshop owner.[122] A survey of small urban industries in Benares reported that, in steel trunk workshops, 'the labourers are paid daily up to half the amount of their dues for their maintenance, the balance [being paid] after a week, a fortnight or a month. A portion of the wages is thus withheld by the dealer so that the labourers might not leave the work whenever they like'.[123] As in the case of artisans, while a part of the workers' wages was usually withheld, they were allowed to take advances on arrears, which were treated as loans. Until the loans were repaid, the workers remained indebted, could not recover arrears in wages and continued to receive only part of their wages in the future. The written evidence of the UP government submitted to the Royal Commission on Labour cited this as one of the chief forms of indebtedness of workers in small industries, which was built into the prevalent system of wage payment. It was stated that the creditor of workers was 'the employer who makes a loan or a payment of wages in advance, the distinction between wages paid in advance and loans often being blurred'.[124] Baqidari, with indebtedness as its key feature, was the most usual face of 'bonded labour' and

---

[120] *BEC*, II, pp. 119, 372, 397, 403–5.
[121] *RCLI*, III:I, p. 182, Memorandum of the Government of U.P.
[122] Ackroyd and Devaraj, 'The Cawnpore Wholesale Clothing Trade'.
[123] *BEC*, II, p. 384, 'Survey of Small Urban Industries of Benares'.
[124] *RCLI*, III:I, p. 182, Memorandum of the Government of U.P.

'patronage' relations at the workplace in a surplus labour market. Workers – both skilled and unskilled – conformed to this restrictive system of deferred payment and advance loans and to this nearly 'bonded' labour arrangement, for, crucially, it provided them with the vital security of relatively stable, though often seasonal, employment in an overcrowded labour market with limited opportunity of spatial mobility in search of jobs owing to lack of cheap public transport. Moreover, it enabled them to solve the perennial problem of access to credit, and in particular they could take advances or loans to tide them over idle periods, emergencies and social ceremonies.

From the perspective of the employers, the withholding of wages in the baqidari system enabled them to tie down skilled labourers and to ensure that they would return during busy periods. Even when the workers were unskilled, partial payment, of course, also served as a useful means of discipline and control, and especially to prevent workplace unrest. Moreover, and crucially, as a survey of Benares silk weaving pointed out, 'the weaver can not claim higher wages notwithstanding the rise in general prices unless and until he repays the money in full', which rarely happened, as the workers tended to remain indebted over long periods.[125] The system thus helped the employers in the recruitment and management of labour and wage fixing. Delaying payments to workers may also have been useful to the employers, financiers and intermediaries alike, in coping with their own periodic shortage of capital. While many workers were indebted to their employers, others took loans from a variety of moneylenders during periods of unemployment or for social and religious celebrations, emergencies and illnesses. Indebtedness was indeed a ubiquitous element in the experience of the workers, often being coupled with coercive pressure and extortion by the creditors and debt-collectors. The problems of indebtedness worsened at times when earnings declined, as they did for almost all sections of workers during the depression. For many, wage levels remained low throughout the 1930s and did not recover to the 1921–2 level.[126]

---

[125] *BEC*, II, p. 372, 'Survey of Small Urban Industries of Benares'.
[126] Tiwari, *Economic Prosperity*, pp. 197, 199, 201; S. P. Saxena, 'Wages and labour conditions in Kanpur', *Department of Economics and Statistics, U.P., Bulletin* No. 3, 1937, ch. II. Real wages also declined for textile workers in Kanpur in the years after the depression as the mills undertook rationalisation and intensification measures, forcing workers at times to work for reduced hours. *KLIC Report*, pp. 344–61; Memorandum Submitted by the Executive Committee of the Mazdur Sabha, Kanpur, pp. 14–31, Proceedings of Meetings of Labour Inquiry Committee (Kanpur), 15 November 1937 to 31 January 1938 (hereafter KLIC Proceedings), File No. 1145/ 1937, Box No. 418, Industries Department, GUP, UPSA.

Employment in trade, transport and construction

Industry was a significant employer in the interwar period, but it none the less failed to support the burgeoning numbers of the poor. Even though urban industrial employment increased in this period, it did not keep pace with population growth.[127] Fluctuations in employment in industries and high labour turnover meant that workers frequently had to find alternative jobs.[128] Most job seekers tended to fall back on the trading and transport sectors, either as street-vendors, hawkers (*khonch-awalas*), and *ekka* and *tonga* (horse-drawn hackney carriages) drivers, or as manual labourers and coolies in the bazars and railway stations.[129] Thus, while urban industries employed a substantial number of people, trade and transport absorbed nearly as many, and also supported out-of-work employees of industries. In 1931, compared with 27 per cent of urban earners employed in industries, there were 23.9 per cent engaged in trade and transport.[130] Even in the industrial centre of Kanpur, while 34.1 per cent of the working population were engaged in industries in 1931, both large and small scale, 25 per cent were in trade and transport.[131] Interestingly, compared with the period before 1921, a proportionately larger number of urban people were supported by trade and transport than by industry, even at a time when industrial work expanded. Thus, whereas, in 1911, 31.1 per cent of people derived their livelihood from industry and 19.9 per cent relied on trade and transport, the corresponding figures for 1921 were 25.1 and 19.6 per cent, and, for 1931, 27.0 and 23.9 per cent.[132] Clearly, rural people flocked into the towns irrespective of the demand for labour in industry and then turned to both trade or transport and industrial work. A substantial section of the urban labouring classes evidently could not depend on industry for employment, either wholly or partly. Thus, alongside workshops and factories, bazars and *mandis* (wholesale markets) were important work-places for the poor, both as manual labourers and as peripatetic or sedentary street-vendors and hawkers.

127 Percentage increases in population between 1921 and 1931 were 15.6% in Lucknow, 12.4% in Kanpur, 2.9% in Benares, and 19.4% in Allahabad. In the same period, provincial industrial employment in urban areas increased from 251 to 270 per 1,000 people, amounting to a 7.6% increase in 1931 over the 1921 figures. *Census 1931*, pp. 141–2, 393.
128 A report by the UICC stated: 'The mills find little difficulty in obtaining their full requirements of labour, even at times of extra pressure. Extra staff readily revert to other methods of employment when such pressure ceases,' *RCLI*, III:I, p. 250, Evidence of the UICC.
129 *RCLI*, III:II, pp. 125–6, Oral Evidence of the Superintendent, Harness and Saddlery Factory, Cawnpore; p. 164, Oral Evidence of Mr J. G. Ryan, Secretary Representing the UICC.
130 *Census 1931*, p. 393.   131 Ibid.   132 Ibid.

In the interwar period, local urban trading activities appear to have increased, notwithstanding the general trade depression of the early 1930s. The census operations of 1931, conducted during the depression, reported a remarkable increase in the proportion of people deriving their livelihood from trade in urban areas. Between 1921 and 1931, the numbers engaged in trade in the towns increased from 140 to 173 per 1,000 people, or by 23.6 per cent.[133] The explanation for this phenomenon perhaps lies in the fact that urban population growth had given a boost to local retail trading in the towns, including petty trade. A study on Lucknow shows that, in the 1930s, the growth of urban retail trade was indicated by a significant increase in population density in such wards as Yehiaganj, where some of the main markets were located.[134] Trade in food was particularly buoyant, catering for the increasing numbers of townspeople. The 1931 census report noted a marked increase in the number of owners, managers and employees in cafes, restaurants and shops for cooked food, and also indicated that 75 per cent of those engaged in urban trade were concerned with foodstuffs.[135] Many among those searching for occupational opportunities in the towns were taking up the hawking and vending of vegetables, fruits, betel nuts, milk, cooked food items or snacks, tea and drinks. The possibilities for hawking and vending were, however, limited, and such activities served often as a supplementary or secondary occupation, with job seekers tending to fall back on petty trade from time to time because of the absence of other work. They usually combined these activities and supplemented their incomes with temporary industrial employment or casual manual labour as carters or coolies in the bazars. An interesting illustration of this trend was the development of a particular kind of dairy business in Allahabad. A number of milkmen (gwalas) congregated daily at one place, where a businessman bought milk from them and organised marketing in the city to sweetmeat makers (halwais) or private households. These gwalas usually kept a couple of milch cows, but they also worked as ekka or tonga drivers, fruit sellers or manual labourers.[136] Alongside petty trade, transport plying provided employment to a section of the job seekers. The number of ekka-tonga drivers increased in the towns in the 1930s, even though this was a time when motor transport was becoming more widespread.[137] In Allahabad, for

---

133 Ibid.
134 R. Mukerjee and B. Singh, *Social Profiles of a Metropolis: Social and Economic Structure of Lucknow, Capital of Uttar Pradesh, 1954–56*, London, 1961, p. 32.
135 *Census 1931*, p. 402.   136 *BEC*, II, p. 421.
137 In Benares, for instance, the number of licences issued to hackney carriage drivers was 1,183 in 1930–1, whereas in 1938–9 the number had increased to 1,835. Benares Municipal Board Annual Report, 1931–32, p. 5; 1938–39, p. 5.

instance, between 1922 and 1936 urban vehicular traffic increased rapidly, giving a boost to the number of ekkas and tongas, which increased by 92 per cent.[138] Increased production and trade in the towns in the interwar years provided employment opportunities to the operators of hand-pulled or bullock-driven carts for the movement of goods. Another area of employment was in the building trade. The interwar period witnessed a boom in construction activities as well as an expansion in urban improvement projects undertaken by the local authorities.[139] This opened up work opportunities for carpenters, masons, bricklayers, metal smiths and general labourers, as well as for workers in establishments producing building materials, such as brick kilns.[140]

The general poverty or lack of capital of those employed in trade, transport and construction, either as a full-time or a temporary occupation, frequently forced them to depend on loans from urban money-lenders. Carpenters, metal smiths and masons required money for the purchase and maintenance of the tools of their trade and also needed money during periods of unemployment. *Ekka-tonga walas* (drivers) had to borrow money to buy or rent vehicles and animals, to feed animals and to pay municipal licence fees. Street-vendors and hawkers needed small sums of capital to purchase goods for sale and often to pay the municipal *tehbazari* (ground rent for shop or stall space in the markets) dues. Some of them could procure goods for retailing from wholesale merchants and shopkeepers on credit, to be paid back at the end of a day. Most of these groups relied on the urban merchant or money-lenders for loans.[141] Moneylenders such as *qistwalas* or *qistias, mahajans* and *sahukars* specialised in advancing loans of small sums, either on a daily or *rozai* basis or on a system of instalments *(qistbandi)*. Surveys of money-lending, conducted for the Banking Enquiry Committee in the late 1920s, reported that, under the daily loan system, 'in the morning money is advanced to the hawkers, those who sell *kachauries, jallebees* [cooked snacks and sweets], *mungphallies* [peanuts] and so on. These men take a rupee in the morning, work all day and make a profit of eight or ten annas and pay back in the evening', both principal and interest.[142] From the moneylenders' point of view, rozai loans could be risky and difficult to recover. The rates of interest in the rozai system were, thus,

---

[138] Allahabad Improvement Trust (hereafter AIT) Annual Report, 1935–36, pp. 17–18.

[139] This will be discussed in chapter 3.

[140] AIT Annual Report, 1937–38.

[141] *BEC*, III, pp. 297–9, 'A Monograph on Qist Business in the United Provinces' by Lala Babu Lal Vaish, Income tax officer; *BEC*, III, p. 289, Oral Evidence of Lala Babu Lal Vaish; *BEC*, I, pp. 64, 278, 280.

[142] *BEC*, IV, p. 474, Oral Evidence of B. G. Bhatnagar.

high.[143] Qistbandi instalment loans on weekly, fortnightly or monthly bases were taken by petty shopkeepers, hawkers, sweetmeat sellers, vegetable and fruit vendors, betel nut sellers, milkmen and hackney carriage drivers. These people would borrow a certain sum for several months, and the interest was paid back in daily, weekly or monthly instalments. Since they could not offer any security for their loans, the rates of interest, as in the case of rozai loans, were very high. Moreover, the moneylenders could expect the principal to be paid back only after several months. This further tended to push up the rates of interest.[144] A monograph on the *qist* (instalment loan) business, included in the evidence recorded by the Banking Enquiry Committee of 1929–30, stated that the qist money-lending business 'is showing a great tendency towards increase',[145] which suggests that, notwithstanding high interest rates, an increasing number of people took recourse to qistbandi loans in this period for petty trade or transport plying.

Carting, loading, storage, warehousing and transportation provided employment in the bazars to a large number of manual labourers, such as *palledars* (packers, loaders), *taulas* or *dandidars* (weighmen), *thelawalas* (pushcart pliers), *gariwans* (bullock-cart drivers), porters and coolies.[146] Demand for these functions had been gradually increasing from the middle of the nineteenth century with the expansion of urban-based commerce, especially with the advent of the railways and bulk trading. Now in the interwar period, need for labour of this nature had a major boost, as processing and manufacturing operations expanded in the towns and consumption demand expanded with population growth, contributing to the flow of larger volumes of goods. Estimating the numbers involved in such activities is difficult, for the census categorised them under various different heads, including 'insufficiently described occupations'. Some indication of the significance of such work can be gained from figures showing that 14 per cent of urban earners in Kanpur were returned under the head 'insufficiently described occupations' in the 1931 census, out of whom 88 per cent were 'general labourers'.[147] Evidence of a somewhat different nature comes from elsewhere. For instance, the number of hand-pulled carts, or *thelas*, which provided the key mode of transportation of goods, increased by 106 per cent between

---

[143] *BEC*, II, pp. 49, 58, 'Monograph on the Indigenous Banking System in the United Provinces' by Mohan Lal Sah; *BEC*, II, pp. 123–4, 'Memorandum on Indigenous Banking' by Dr L. C. Jain.

[144] *BEC*, II, p. 52; *BEC*, III, pp. 297–9, 304.

[145] *BEC*, III, pp. 297–9, 'A Monograph on Qist Business in the United Provinces'.

[146] *Department of Economics and Statistics, Bulletin*, No. 20, undated, 'Directory of certain wholesale agricultural markets of U.P.'.

[147] *Census 1931*, pp. 393–4.

1922 and 1936 in Allahabad.[148] This increase was attributed to the growing need for the movement of goods in bulk, as a result of the burgeoning urban population. Some of these carters, porters and weighmen in the bazars were employed by shops and firms on a regular basis (*bandha* or tied down), with fixed wages. The mode of payment of bandha workers was similar to the baqidari system. Wages were partially withheld by the employers, while loans were extended on arrears, and the workers were often indebted to their employers – the merchants and businessmen. Although these bandha workers were relatively permanently employed, arbitrary dismissals were nevertheless not ruled out owing to the abundant availability of manual labourers.[149] Being tied to the employers, bandha workers were also at times required to perform unpaid or *begar* work, often domestic manual duties at the homes of their employers. The labourers often courted the bandha status, for it provided them much-coveted job security in an increasingly competitive casual labour market, yet their conditions of employment, involving begar, were often worse than those of casual employees. Most bazar workers were indeed employed temporarily as casual labourers. In each town, labourers congregated daily at one or two fixed places, from where they were recruited for manual labour in the bazars, as well as for construction work. Every morning they gathered, for instance, at Moolganj in Kanpur, Nakkhas Kohna in Allahabad, Chowk in Benares and Aminabad in Lucknow. Although employers often recruited the workers directly, labour contractors were at times deployed by the employers to recruit and manage labour for carting and loading assignments or in building construction. Contractors were also frequently responsible for recruitment and employment of coolies at railway stations. The manual labourers in the towns moved from one job to another, often alternating between the bazars and industrial workshops for carting and loading work, while also falling back on street-vending occasionally.

Political implications

The interwar period was a period of major transformation in the history of large towns. Their role in the rural hinterland and their function in the north Indian economy underwent a decisive shift. Urban centres, especially the largest ones of 100,000 people and over, increasingly supplied the rural environs with their own services and manufactures,

---

[148] AIT Annual Report, 1935–6, pp. 17–18.
[149] Interviews in the Kanpur wholesale markets of Generalganj, Naughara and Collectorganj, with shop employees: Ram Kripal Yadav, Ramfer Khalifa, Ram Shankar Shukla and Dutti Ram Yadav.

propelled by a provincial demographic boom that drove up consumption. Processing functions, trade and the production of consumption and intermediate goods were increasingly centralised and concentrated in the towns. The composition of urban populations, the contours of the occupational structure and the organisation of trade and production registered commensurate transitions. Most importantly, the towns came to attract large numbers of rural migrants, contributing to a substantial expansion of the labouring poor in the towns. If, until the early twentieth century, the history of north Indian towns and their politics could be narrated in terms of the 'rulers, townsmen and bazars' and the rise of commercial classes, by the 1920s the story became inescapably one in which the 'poor and bazars' were central.

For these poor people, insecurity of employment, indebtedness and dependence on moneylenders and merchants were economic experiences shared by all in varying, but increasing, degrees. The poor did not, however, form a unified group. They were differentiated in terms of their work and economic conditions, and they were involved in networks of employment and credit relations with moneylenders and merchants in diverse ways. The uncertain and vulnerable condition of urban labour was not mitigated by patronage and obligation on the part of the employers or creditors. The baqidari system, with the workers relying on their employers, could potentially operate as a kind of patronage system. However, baqidari in this period appears largely to have taken the form of debt bondage and labour control, with the terms increasingly set by the employers unilaterally.[150] The labourers had little bargaining power to elicit obligations from the employers, threatened as they were with the possibility of dismissal and replacement in a context of labour abundance. Employers were hardly solicitous of labour, and hence disinclined to extend patronage of a paternalistic kind, which might have been instituted in a context of scarce labour. In any case, patronage relations could never be of an entirely benevolent nature serving the interest of workers, though scarcity of labour could at least have provided them greater leverage to negotiate favourable terms. Demographic expansion ensured that the need to tie down labour, except for skilled workers, was not an overwhelmingly important consideration for the employers. So long as workers did not cause trouble, employers found that the baqidari system variously enabled them to retain workers, to enhance workplace discipline, to hold down wages or to minimise the high cost of recruitment of labour that could arise from the employment

---

[150] For comparative discussions on labour bondage and patronage in other contexts, see J. Breman, *Beyond Patronage and Exploitation: Changing Agrarian Relations in South Gujarat*, Delhi, 1993, pp. 297–316; Breman, *Footloose Labour*, pp. 162–9.

of casual workers with high turnover. However, if workers did fall out of line and new recruits could be easily found and trained, then, to wrest compliance from the workers and to impose discipline, the employers had the effective weapon of dismissal and did not need to rely on patronage. The workers, therefore, usually had little choice but to submit to debt relations on the terms set by the employers, both because of overcrowding of the labour market and for easy access to credit. Demographic growth and the expansion of the labour supply thus tended to exercise a corrosive influence on the possibility of patronage benefits at work, while perpetuating debt dependence. Moreover, the extension of benefits in kind by many sections of urban employers, such as gifts of clothes during festivals for workers and their families, or provision of blankets in the winter season, became gradually rarer from this period, although such practices were thought to have existed at the turn of the century.[151] Historians have also noted an increasing tendency among the merchant classes from this period to withdraw patronage from forms of popular culture and festivals.[152]

While all this suggests growing contradictions at workplaces, it does not imply that the employers came to exercise absolute power and dominance over their employees, and that the workers were locked in abject dependence on the employers. The power that the employers were able to wield over the workers would be circumscribed by the censure and bargaining strategies of labour, howsoever limited. Chitra Joshi has argued that workplace norms and practices in the large mills of Kanpur were products of negotiations and contestation between employers and employees, and that the workers did play a determining role.[153] None the less, the available evidence for the smaller industries and bazar employment in UP suggests that the options of manoeuvre for labour were severely restricted in the interwar period, and that urban workplace and occupational relations were not governed, in any significant measure, by the norms of reciprocity, paternalist obligations or moral community. Inevitably this served to sharpen economic contradictions, without patronage relations to smooth at least some of the rough edges. In addition to these trends, the employers and merchants had little sustained contact with or authority as patrons over the vast mass of urban workers in shifting occupations. All these developments

---

[151] Interviews in the Kanpur wholesale markets of Generalganj, Naughara and Collectorganj, with shop employees: Ram Kripal Yadav, Ramfer Khalifa, Ram Shankar Shukla and Dutti Ram Yadav.

[152] N. Kumar, *The Artisans of Banaras: Popular Culture and Identity, 1880–1986*, Princeton, 1988, pp. 195, 233; Freitag (ed.), *Culture and Power*, p. 223.

[153] C. Joshi, 'The Formation of Work Culture: Industrial Labour in a North Indian City (1890s–1940s)', *Purusartha*, 14, 1991, pp. 155–72.

had significant political implications, in particular in contributing to a weakening of social control. The erosion of networks of urban local control based on notables, merchants or community leaders and the decline of the influence of so-called 'natural leaders', which Bayly and Freitag have described,[154] were in part related to these changing relations in the labour market and the workplace. As Bayly points out, these poorer sections of the urban population, who were imperfectly integrated into local patronage structures, were increasingly to step forward as important participants in mass politics and urban riots.[155] It will be seen that the issue of control over the burgeoning number of the poor in the interwar period came to constitute an important determinant of political developments.

There were a number of other significant political implications of the changing occupational structure and relations. While there is no direct or straightforward link between economic conditions and political action or perception, economic circumstances and occupational relations do, however, form the material context within which politics take shape. It is, therefore, appropriate here to indicate a few of the more important political implications, as a pointer toward some of the themes that will emerge later in this book.

First, for the rural migrants who flocked to the towns, agriculture had largely ceased to provide a significant source of economic sustenance. Urban occupations became central to the livelihood of the poor, rather than being supplementary employment outside the agricultural season. Many migrants continued to maintain their rural social and family links or were even forced to fall back on rural work during periods when urban employment was impossible to find. Despite this, the workers were largely severed from their rural economic bases. As a result, it was increasingly the context of work or living in the towns, as well as their position in urban society and their relations with other urban groups, that came to shape the political preoccupations of urban workers.

Secondly, as a result of the specific nature of urban development and the evolution of the occupational structure in the interwar period, urban commercial classes and merchant-financiers emerged as the chief employers and creditors of the poor. These merchants classes not only dominated the urban economy, but also were the moving force behind

---

[154] Bayly, *Local Roots*, pp. 87–91; Bayly, 'Local Control in Indian Towns: The Case of Allahabad, 1880–1920', *MAS*, 5, 4, 1971, pp. 289–311; S. B. Freitag, *Collective Action and Community: Public Arenas and the Emergence of Communalism in North India*, Berkeley, 1989, pp. 70–8; S. B. Freitag, '"Natural Leaders", Administrators and Social Control: Communal Riots in the United Provinces, 1870–1925', *South Asia*, 1, 2 (New Series), 1978, pp. 27–41.

[155] Bayly, 'Local Control in Indian Towns', pp. 299–302.

many of the urban social and religious reform activities in the early twentieth century, and key players in the evolution of the 'middle class opinion' of 'respectable Hindu society'.[156] This ensured that the economic subordination of the poor to the commercial communities was reinforced by the latter's social and cultural domination of the towns. Not surprisingly, the relation of the poor to the merchant classes came to be of key significance in their politics.

Thirdly, political developments were influenced by the fact that the labour market was largely casual, unskilled and manual in nature, with the lines blurred between formal and informal sector employment as well as between industrial labour and work in transport, construction and urban markets. The mobility and impermanence of work as well as the fluidity of the labour market meant that political action, arising from employment relations and the context of work, at times found generalised expression through wider political movements of nationalism or religion, rather than being directed at particular employers or based on specific work-related issues.

Conflict in the interwar period not only developed between the poor and their employers or creditors, but also crucially arose among the poor themselves over scarce jobs in an overcrowded and casual labour market. Conflict and competition centred around control over segments of the labour market. Fierce rivalries – often violent confrontations – thus characterised the unstable job market. Casual labour, especially the single male migrant job seeker, is frequently associated with a predisposition to lawlessness and volatility. Of course, violence and strife were frequently the characteristics of urban labour in UP in the interwar period, but not because of the inherently undisciplined propensities of a casual 'underclass'. Instead, violence and conflict were bred by the very instability of the labour market, which, in turn, arose from the employers' preference for casual and temporary workforces. Competition in the job market was one of the factors that came to shape the political alliances and rivalries of the urban poor, and, in particular, exercised a significant influence in caste and communal politics. Although urban employment was characterised by the mobility of workers from one kind of occupation to another, such mobility was subject to the segmentation of the labour market along the lines of caste or religion. Kin and community connections were important resources of the poor to gain or maintain a foothold in both the urban labour and housing markets. This not only contributed to caste and religious differentiation in occupational and residential settlement patterns in the towns, but also gave rise

[156] Bayly, 'Patrons and Politics', pp. 349–88; Freitag (ed.), *Culture and Power*, pp. 19–22; Dalmia, *Nationalization of Hindu Traditions*, pp. 50–145.

to rivalries shaped by such community affiliations. In turn, such conflicts frequently influenced the nature of caste and communal politics and identities in the towns, as later chapters of this book will show.

Finally, the shifting nature of jobs to which the vast majority of the workforce were exposed and the proliferation of casual labour generated anxieties among the propertied classes about the supposed threat of social and political disruption emanating from a footloose population of the poor. The inadequacy of workplace patronage relations and the related absence of integration of the poor into networks of local control further aggravated concerns about maintaining or enforcing social control over them. To contend with such perceived dangers, a range of measures was introduced to discipline them, to regulate their living and working habits, and to control their cultural expressions, public conduct and political behaviour. This was a major repercussion of the changing demography and occupational relations in the towns and had crucial implications for urban politics and the very nature and experience of poverty. Material deprivation now went hand in hand with more overt forms of discipline and social subordination. Among other measures, the policies of the urban local authorities and the government were specifically geared to dealing with what was perceived as the emerging 'problem' of the poor. The following two chapters turn to this theme.

3   Urban local policies and the poor

The vast expansion in the ranks of the labouring poor in the towns in the interwar period generated grave concern amongst the urban propertied classes and local administrators alike. Terms such as 'poor class people', 'inferior classes' or the 'lower classes' featured as a focus of social anxiety in both official parlance and non-official vocabulary, and pointed to the mass of the poor in an undifferentiated way. Unlike in Victorian England,[1] distinctions between the casual poor and respectable industrial labour were difficult to discern in interwar north India, given the fluid and shifting nature of urban work. Indeed, this very fluidity seemed to have engendered worries about a 'floating', footloose, rootless population living in penury, who were seen to disturb the social and cultural stability of the 'better class' or 'decent' people. The aversion of the Indian upper castes to physical work or manual labour as demeaning is also likely to have tainted all the labouring poor, not just a casual fringe, and probably partly explains the universal stigmatisation of the poor.[2] Apprehension and fear about the disruption of the social, moral and political fabric of the city caused by the poor were evidently becoming so prevalent in the interwar years that one witness in his written evidence to the Provincial Banking Enquiry Commission (1929–30), observed that 'it is *surely needless to mention* that an ill-fed, ill-housed and ill-clothed population is a *menace to the peace, health and prosperity of the city*' (emphasis added). To many like him, the relation between poverty and urban decay was self-evident and axiomatic. He added: 'It would be superfluous to dilate upon the social and moral evils that progressive impoverishment would lead to.'[3]

Such negative stereotypical images of the poor and of the problems

---

[1] G. Stedman Jones, *Outcast London: A Study in the Relationship between Classes in Victorian Society*, Oxford, 1971; G. Himmelfarb, *The Idea of Poverty: England in the Early Industrial Age*, London, 1984.

[2] For middle-class attitudes towards industrial labour in Bengal, see S. Basu, 'Workers Politics in Bengal, 1890–1929: Mill Towns, Strikes and Nationalist Agitations', Ph.D. thesis, University of Cambridge, 1994, ch. 3.

[3] *BEC*, II, p. 407, Written evidence of Ardhendu Bhattacharya.

they supposedly posed were gradually magnified during the interwar years and were shared by British officials and the Indian middle classes.[4] At its most benign, perceptions of the urban poor denigrated them as rural migrants in the towns, nursing immutable, insular, tradition-bound rustic mindsets that perpetuated backwardness and fatalism on their part and acted as a stumbling block on the way to progress and development. Opinions about the labouring poor such as the following were not untypical:

The average Indian [urban] labourer, uneducated, uncultured, superstitious and conservative that he is, has got his own prejudices, social customs and habits, to which he clings tenaciously.[5]

The labourer's outlook is extremely narrow and produces in him an attitude to look upon his lot as one ordained by the fates and therefore not capable of much improvement by his personal exertion. Such a cramped outlook on life and fatalism help to perpetuate in industrial centres the conditions which obtain in rural areas and seriously handicap the reforming efforts of Government, the employers and private organizations.[6]

Unable to adapt to urban life, these supposed socially and psychologically maladjusted people were seen to become immoral and deviant, especially prone to the lure of crime, gambling, prostitution and, in particular, the 'liquor-shop', which seemed to emerge as a key metaphor representing the dangers and deficiencies of the poor. Both official and non-official commentators would thus argue:

leading an unnatural existence [being uprooted from the village], . . . the overworked, ill-paid labourer, living hundreds of miles away from his family, finds the liquor-shop, the only place where he can forget the toils and worry of the day . . . The bazar girl or the prostitute is his sole recreation and luxury.

---

[4] Comments in government documents and by middle-class people about the problems posed by the poor virtually echoed each other. Interesting parallels can be seen, for instance, in the evidence gathered by the Royal Commission on Labour in India (RCLI) in the late 1920s from both official and non-official sources. Comments by Raj Bahadur Gupta in his *Labour and Housing in India* (Calcutta, 1930) also illuminate the views of Indian middle-class society in UP. Gupta was a lecturer in economics and sociology at the Lucknow University when he wrote this book. This department, under the headship of Professor Radhakamal Mukherjee, was especially important in both moulding and reflecting middle-class opinion. The members of this department conducted numerous studies and surveys of urbanisation, industrialisation and banking as well as of the conditions of the urban poor, the findings of which were widely publicised. Academic staff and research scholars of the department also gave evidence to and produced commissioned reports for several official enquiry committees, including the UP Provincial Banking Enquiry Committee and the Royal Commission on Labour. The views expressed in Gupta's book are arguably typical not only of ideas held by other members of his department but also of middle-class opinion in general.

[5] Gupta, *Labour and Housing*, p. 217.

[6] *RCLI*, III:I, p. 139, Memorandum of the Government of UP. Similar views about the poor as resistant to change and thus hindering general improvement were also expressed in Gupta, *Labour and Housing*, p. 42.

Under the influence of raw country liquor, he plays the hooligan and sets about doing mischief.[7]

Denied the comforts of a regular family life, the temptation to him to seek diversion after the day's work by resorting to drinks or drugs or the bazar is greater.[8]

Clearly, the burgeoning numbers of the poor were expected to unleash depravity and degeneracy on urban society and were considered a threat to the body civic, although often a degree of remorse for their miserable condition and an urge to uplift them from their predicament accompanied such characterisations of the poor. The urgency to counter the social and moral dangers posed by the poor, both to improve the general conditions of urban life and to save the poor from their own flaws and drawbacks, came to inform a vast array of diverse social or political initiatives and policy measures in the interwar period. These ranged from attempts to reform religious and social practices, to intensive policing and to cleansing and sanitising the habitat of the poor. In reports and studies on urban labour in the 1930s much emphasis was laid on socialising the poor into new urban ways, while at the same time attempting to preserve forms of 'traditional' community life based on caste or kinship, with the hope that this would help to nurture social stability and inculcate moral values. The process of urban socialisation was to be aided by welfare work on the part of both the employers of labour and the state. The aim would be to promote literacy, sanitation, hygiene and public health awareness. It was also intended to sponsor and encourage edifying and well-structured recreational activities in the place of 'bazar' entertainment, and to instil habits of thrift and temperance.[9] It will be seen in later chapters that nationalist and religious reformers also stepped into the battle to improve and uplift the poor. They variously cajoled or exhorted the lower castes and classes to conform to 'purified', respectable or 'sanskritised' modes of behaviour and practices, and to purge their 'bad', 'immoral' or 'vulgar' habits. Historians have also noted that, in the early twentieth century, local elites withdrew their patronage from popular cultural practices in an attempt to curb or control supposed unwholesome forms of self-expression by the poor in festivals or public cultural performances.[10]

---

[7] Gupta, *Labour and Housing*, p. 51.

[8] *RCLI*, III:I, p. 144, Memorandum of the Government of UP.

[9] Gupta, *Labour and Housing*, pp. 170–87; *KLIC Report*, pp. 420–3; *RCLI*, III:I, pp. 159–61, Memorandum of the Government of UP.

[10] These themes will be discussed below. N. Kumar, *The Artisans of Banaras: Popular Culture and Identity, 1880–1986*, Princeton, 1988, pp. 190–5; S. B. Freitag, 'State and Community: Symbolic Protest in Banaras's Public Arenas', in S. B. Freitag (ed.), *Culture and Power in Banaras: Community, Performance and Environment, 1800–1980*,

Social reformers were not without philanthropic and benevolent motivation in their attempts to rescue the poor from what was seen as their
miserable condition, squalid environment, vice and moral degradation.
However, the poor as they existed, until reformed, remained the repository of negative attributes and the targets of a moralising impulse, of a
'civilising mission', of policing and discipline, and of general improvement, cleansing and sanitising.

While all these initiatives were informed by the perception of the poor
as a potential source of disorder, crime, moral lassitude and social
anomie, or as a retarding influence on development, the urban propertied classes at the same time saw the poor as the chief impediment to
orderly and clean urban development and as a serious threat to their
own health and well-being. Urgent concern about the decline of urban
public health not only arose as a result of the pressure of population on
urban infrastructure and municipal resources caused by an increase in
the number of the labouring poor in the towns, but also, and more
importantly, emanated from the middle-class belief that the poor were
inherently insanitary in their habits. Thus, the rustic misfits in the
towns, which the poor were supposed to be, were claimed to be
'accustomed to open spaces, scrub, fields, ravines and banks of tanks
and streams in their villages', which predisposed them to 'preserve the
same habits in an [urban] environment lacking such facilities', as a
consequence of which, 'all round the labour *bastis* [slums] filth and dirt
accumulate'.[11] The poor were seen to be particularly afflicted with a
deficiency 'in the matter of disposal of refuse and rubbish . . . [which]
they throw all over the area where they live', just as they were supposed
to be especially zealous in damaging and defacing the walls of their
accommodation.[12] Above all, they were considered guilty of taking to
any 'open space for answering calls of nature, *even though municipal
latrines have been provided*',[13] glossing over the numerical inadequacy
and the lack of maintenance of these public toilets which prevented
most potential users from proper access to this facility. In addition to
anxieties about public health, the nature of the living conditions and
physical surroundings of the poor was thought to have a causal relation
to their deficient culture, character and public behaviour and their
moral destitution. Habitat and habit were closely linked. 'Humanity is
dehumanised in these slums', one scholar affirmed in his doctoral work

---

Berkeley, 1989, p. 223; K. Hansen, 'The Birth of Hindi Drama in Banaras,
1868–1885', in Freitag (ed.), *Culture and Power*, pp. 85–91.
[11] *RCLI*, III:I, p. 158, Memorandum of the Government of UP.
[12] *RCLI*, III:I, p. 220, Evidence of S. P. Shaha, Director of Industries, UP.
[13] Ibid., emphasis added.

in the 1940s based on his study of the housing conditions of the poor in Kanpur in the previous few decades. Describing urban slums, he commented, 'These pits are even unfit for animal habitation. . . . No wonder then if these people take resort to ale-houses and brothels . . . Drunkenness and sex immorality are rampant.'[14] Views of this nature were already becoming entrenched in the 1920s. One commentator identified the insalubrious living environs of the poor not only as a threat to public health, but also as the factor that 'lie[s] at the root of the characteristic inefficiency, slothfulness and other short-comings' of the poor.[15] An official report in the later 1930s similarly commented, 'the only relief available to the worker from the dirt and squalor of his house and its surroundings . . . is the liquor shop or the grog shop'.[16] Not surprisingly, the transformation of the physical environment of the poor came to assume a central importance in attacking the 'problem' of the poor and precipitated hitherto unprecedented changes in the policies of the urban local bodies in the interwar period.

Dipesh Chakrabarty and Sudipta Kaviraj note that the interlocking colonial and Indian middle-class projects of the imposition of 'modernity' and of social reform and 'improvement' entailed an attack, simultaneously, on dirt, disease and disorder.[17] As the supposed source of these evils, the poor naturally became the major targets of civic governance and local administration. Kaviraj has pointed out that the control and regulation of urban space and eliciting the conformity of the poor to the use of public spaces in accordance with the emerging 'bourgeois' notions of hygiene and order were central to the assertion of middle-class social supremacy in the city.[18] He holds that 'the obedience of the poor had to be secured to a sovereign conception of what the city was like'.[19] The poor were thus a central concern of urban administrative policies in the interwar period, as they were expected to threaten or erode middle-class social dominance. For all these reasons, local policies came to affect far larger numbers and wider sections of the poor, and impinged upon their work and housing in direct and interventionist ways. Urban local policy would thus contribute to the creation of the 'problem' of the urban poor, both materially by intervening in their

---

[14] P.C. Banerjee, 'Labour and Industrial Housing in Cawnpore', D.Phil. thesis, Allahabad University, 1948, p. 142.

[15] Gupta, *Labour and Housing*, p. 64.

[16] *KLIC Report*, p. 420.

[17] D. Chakrabarty, 'Open Space/Public Place: Garbage, Modernity and India', *South Asia*, 14, 1, 1991, pp. 18–19; Sudipta Kaviraj, 'Filth and the "Public Sphere"', *Österreichische Zeitschrift für Soziologie*, 21 2, 1996, pp. 36–8.

[18] Kaviraj, 'Filth and the "Public Sphere"', pp. 36–8.

[19] Ibid., p. 37.

housing patterns or economic activities and discursively by categorising them as a distinct social group defined by their undesirable habits and practices. The second part of this book shows that shifts in urban local policies were significant in shaping the political preoccupations of various sections of the poor, and influenced the nature of their involvement in caste, communal or nationalist politics. To sketch out the context of political action in this particular respect, this chapter examines the changes in local policies in the 1920s and 1930s.

New departures in the interwar period

Municipal administration in UP under British rule was systematically organised in the wake of the pacification of the uprising of 1857. Municipal councils were established in the 1860s, manned largely by British officials, with the gradual induction of a few nominated representatives of Indian commercial or landowning interests. In their initial years, these institutions had at least three primary considerations. The first and central preoccupation was the improvement of sanitary and public health conditions. This arose mainly from the findings and recommendations of the Royal Commission on the Sanitary State of the Army in India in 1863. The Commission attributed the high incidence of mortality and morbidity of British troops stationed in urban areas to the prevailing insanitary conditions as well as to the absence of a sanitary administration, and prescribed that improved sanitary infrastructure should be established.[20] Municipal councils, during the first three decades after their inception, thus concentrated on erecting infrastructure for drainage, sewerage and water supply as well as on cleaning and paving some congested and insanitary bazar areas.[21] A second related aim of early municipal work was to enable the British, and occasionally Indian, personnel of civil and military administrations and some affluent Indian professional groups and notables to move away from the disease-prone central areas of the towns to the protected havens of newly developed zones.[22] The towns were envisaged in terms of a social duality, with segregation occurring largely along the axes of race and administrative seats of power and governance, between the so-called

---

[20] Parliamentary Papers, East India (Sanitary State of the Army), *Royal Commission on the Sanitary State of the Army in India*, vol. 7, Part I, Report, Session: 5 February to 28 July 1863, vol. XIX, pp. xxvi, lxxvii.

[21] J. B. Harrison, 'Allahabad: A Sanitary History', in K. Ballhatchet and J. Harrison (eds.), *The City in South Asia: Pre-modern and Modern*, London, 1980, pp. 167–95; Veena Talwar Oldenburg, *The Making of Colonial Lucknow, 1856–1877*, Princeton, 1984, chs. 2, 4.

[22] Harrison, 'Allahabad: A Sanitary History', p. 188.

'native', older parts and the new cantonments and civil and police lines. Finally, with memories of the 1857 uprising still fresh in their minds, colonial local administrators were concerned to protect the towns from tumult, riots or large-scale outbreaks of disorder. To achieve this, they needed to alter the landscape of the towns by laying down broad and straight thoroughfares for the easy and speedy movement of troops, arms and the police.[23]

In order to achieve these various aims, municipal institutions undertook a range of interventionist policies in the post-1857 period.[24] Disruptive and penetrating though they were, these early policies were far less extensive in their scope and reach than the ones that followed in the interwar years. The measures in the later nineteenth century to render the towns sanitary and healthy for British civil and military personnel remained limited in their geographical compass, for they concentrated largely on the creation of secluded new enclaves, away from the older parts of the towns. Somewhat greater intervention in the 'native' parts of towns was required for those measures of sanitary or security improvement that entailed the re-laying of bazar areas or constructing drainage and sewerage infrastructure, as well as building broad thoroughfares for military manoeuvres.[25] These changes were, however, concentrated in particular areas of towns, rather than involving wholesale urban re-planning, as the policy-makers of the interwar period would aspire to do. They sought to carve out residential areas for the Indian middle classes, with the town populations gradually segregating along the lines of class rather than race. In contrast, sanitary policies in the UP towns until the 1920s had remained concentrated on what were envisaged to be circumspect and cautious 'measures of permanent preventive effect' against the spread of disease epidemics.[26] There was one powerfully persuasive reason for adopting such a policy of caution. Haunted by the spectre of the 1857 uprising in north India and to avoid a re-enactment, the authorities eschewed extensive intervention beyond what was seen to be essential to make the cities adequately safe and orderly. Moreover, during this early period, sanitary measures were not directed towards any particular urban group, since

---

[23] Oldenburg, *Making of Colonial Lucknow*, pp. 29–42.

[24] Ibid., passim.

[25] These measures were carried out initially by the Municipal Boards and subsequently, from the 1910s, by special Town Improvement Trust Committees of the Boards. These Committees were formed after the UP Sanitary Conference at Nainital in 1908 advocated the formation of separate committees for town improvement, to which the provincial government granted Rs 2.5 lakhs every year specifically for constructing roads and parks and for town extension.

[26] Extracts from proceedings of the meeting of the Plague Committee, 25 August 1907; cited in File No. 596D, Box No. 506, Municipal Department (Block), GUP, UPSA.

unhealthy conditions were thought to emanate from heat or miasma and from the general lack of sanitary administration and infrastructure in Indian towns. Besides, the local administrators were eager above all to avoid 'friction between the government and many of the poorer towns-people, perhaps the most dangerous and most easily excited class', who were 'much more insubordinate and unruly than the peasantry and containing a strong infusion of a criminal or semi-criminal element'.[27] Significantly, the policies of the later era ceased to be so cautious and targeted the poor specifically.

The characterisation of the poor as the breeders of disease was not new as a guiding principle of local policies in the 1920s and 1930s. In the 1890s, the plague hit many Indian towns, and it was believed to be a disease of filth and squalor. There emerged widespread concern at that time among British officials about those whom they singled out as the main inhabitants of insanitary and overcrowded areas – the poorer sections in the towns. These views, often inspired by the concern about the urban underclass in Victorian England, were, however, more pre-valent in the administrative circles of the presidency towns of Bombay or Calcutta. Not only were these cities worst affected by the plague, but they also had large labouring populations and working-class neighbour-hoods in the late nineteenth century because of the presence of major industries. In contrast, the concern with the poor in the municipal administration of UP was much less pronounced, except in the indus-trial centre of Kanpur with its workers in the textile and other mills. Even in Kanpur, however, vigorous plague control measures had been eschewed and attempts to sanitise the poor had been reined in, following an initial, short-lived outburst of zeal in 1900 which had provoked riots in the city.[28] Besides, the plague reached UP later than the presidency towns, by which time the government of India had tempered or abandoned draconian plague control measures, in view of the serious disturbances precipitated by such interventions in the 1890s.[29] In the UP towns, by and large, measures to deal with the poor had remained limited until the First World War, because the British feared political unrest. As a consequence, discussions about the habits and traits of the

[27] Note by A. L. Saunders, Commissioner, Lucknow Division, dated 22 August 1907, File No. 596D, Box No. 506, Municipal Department (Block), GUP, UPSA.

[28] For the plague riot in Kanpur, see C. Joshi, 'Bonds of Community, Ties of Religion: Kanpur Textile Workers in the Early Twentieth Century', *IESHR*, 22, 3, 1985, pp. 265–8.

[29] The gradual abandonment of draconian plague measures all over India by the end of the 1890s is discussed in D. Arnold, 'Touching the Body: Perspectives on the Indian Plague, 1896–1900', in R. Guha (ed.), *Subaltern Studies V: Writings on South Asian History and Society*, Delhi, 1987, pp. 55–90; I. Klein, 'Plague Policy and Popular Unrest in British India', *MAS*, 22, 4, 1988, pp. 723–55.

poor, and overt or active policy prescriptions concerning them, were not very prominent until the early twentieth century. The policy of caution was reversed only in the early 1920s. It was from this period that the identification of the poor as the creators of insanitary 'plague spots' came into play in framing local policies, now primarily geared to ending congestion and overcrowding in the settlements of the poor. Reconfiguration of the physical environment of cities and the imposition of control and order through the appropriation and regulation of urban space had, of course, begun in the nineteenth century under the British administrators of the Municipal Boards.[30] The change in the interwar period was, first, that control over space was now designed increasingly to facilitate control over the habits and practices of the poor, and, second, that local policies to this end became far more activist and extensive. The contrast would throw into sharp relief the emerging interventionist role of local institutions in regulating the living conditions and settlement patterns of the poor in the interwar period and came to generate new tensions over local policies.

The sea-change in the orientation of local policies from the 1920s came about primarily because of the perception that the swelling ranks of the poor were the cause of worsening overcrowding and insanitary conditions, as well as of the attendant moral and social deterioration and political instability. The policy shifts were also significantly impelled by the fact that the British government largely withdrew its official presence from local institutions after the First World War. More local power than in the past was devolved to the Indian elites, and the franchise was extended to incorporate a larger section of the Indian middle classes in the municipal electorate. The latter were less apprehensive of the threat to state power arising from a popular uprising and more concerned to deal with what they perceived to be a direct threat to their own health and well-being posed by the influx of the poor. From the point of view of the British officials, a degree of interventionist policies by the local elites, now at the helm of affairs, could be permitted from the 1920s, as any possible popular discontent could be expected to remain focused on local Indian administrators and less likely to become generalised and be directed towards the colonial state.

The enfranchisement of an increased number of rate-payers was one of the most significant developments that marked the changes in local government from the 1920s. To facilitate this process, the UP Municipalities Act of 1916 was amended in 1922, electoral rolls were revised and, in March 1923, municipal elections were held under the amended

---

[30] Oldenburg, *Making of Colonial Lucknow.*

Act with a far larger electorate. In Kanpur, for instance, the number of registered voters increased by 300 per cent on the previous voter list.[31] This extension of the municipal franchise inevitably influenced the nature of municipal policies in significant ways. A larger number of rate-payers, who became municipal electors, were now in a position to exert greater pressure than had hitherto been possible on the elected Indian members of the Municipal Boards to formulate policies which would be favourable to various propertied rate-paying interests. The Benares Municipal Board Enquiry Committee noted this trend in 1933: 'For the security of their seats in the Boards, members were open to importunate overtures of the taxpayer – the prospective voters.'[32] One consequence of these developments was the adverse effect on those sections of the urban population who were not enfranchised. The municipal electors included only the propertied groups in the towns: those who were assessees of municipal direct taxes or rates, such as house or water tax, tax on property and circumstances and tax on trade and professions, as well as those who paid land revenue or income tax on a minimum stipulated annual income, tenants paying rent over a specified sum, and university graduates.[33] The electors thus constituted a small proportion of the total urban population. In Kanpur, for instance, only 8 per cent of the population was enfranchised in 1923, even after a 300 per cent increase in the electorate on the previous voter rolls.[34] In the subsequent triennial municipal elections in Kanpur, between 1925 and 1935, the total proportion of the urban population eligible to vote varied between 12 and 16 per cent.[35]

[31] Kanpur Municipal Board (hereafter KMB) Annual Report, for the year ending 31 March 1923, p. 3.

[32] *Report of the Benares Municipal Board Enquiry Committee, 1933* (hereafter *BMB Enquiry Committee*), Allahabad, 1933 p. 18.

[33] *The Municipal Manual: Laws, Rules and Instructions Relating to Municipal Administration in the United Provinces*, 1st edn, 4th reprint, corrected up to 31 December 1925, Allahabad, 1926, vol. I, Part II, p. 192; Part III, pp. 371–2; *The United Provinces Municipalities Act, 1916* (Act No. II of 1916), ch. II, section 14: 'Qualification of Electors'.

[34] The number eligible to vote in the 1923 election was 19,395, out of a total population of 216,436, enumerated by the 1921 census, KMB Annual Report, for the year ending 31 March 1923, p. 3.

[35] Calculated from the number of eligible voters cited in the annual reports of the Kanpur municipality and the population of the town enumerated by the censuses of 1921 and 1931. The census figures have been used, since the exact population of Kanpur for the years of the elections is not known. The calculations are, therefore, rough estimates. KMB Annual Reports, for the year ending 31 March 1926, pp. 1–2 (number of eligible voters 33,061 for elections held in December 1925); for the year ending 31 March 1929, p. 1 (number of eligible voters 31,218 for elections held in February 1929); for the year ending 31 March 1933, p. 2 (number of eligible voters 33,620 for elections held in December 1932); for the year ending 31 March 1936, p. 1 (number of eligible voters 37,342 for elections held in December 1935). To calculate the ratio of voters to

The Improvement Trusts, which came into existence after 1919 as the motor of large-scale urban re-planning, were also the focus of influence and interest of urban propertied and commercial groups. Each Trust was composed of seven members, of whom two were nominated to the Trust by the Municipal Board from among its own members, and the third was the chairman of the Municipal Board, who was an *ex officio* member of the Trust. The remaining four members, including the chairman of the Trust, were nominated by the provincial government. One of these four government nominees was by convention the District Magistrate (DM). The other three were often appointed with a view to ensuring the representation of commercial interests in the towns. In Kanpur, for instance, from the time of the inception of the Trust in 1919, the government's policy was to nominate at least two members from the commercial and industrial community, drawn from the European-dominated Upper India Chamber of Commerce (UICC) and the UP Chamber of Commerce, representing Indian business interests.[36] A similar trend was noticeable in Allahabad, where leading commercial magnates of the town and members of mercantile families, such as Babu Man Mohan Das and Baldev Ram Dave, were nominated to the Trust.[37] Affluent local notables and professional men, especially prominent lawyers of the towns, such as Anand and Brijendra Swarup in Kanpur or Kamta Prasad Kacker in Allahabad, were also well represented on the Trusts.[38] Given the propertied and commercial social character of the trustees, it is not surprising that Improvement Trust policies, like the municipal administration, to a large extent would come to reflect the needs and preoccupations of these groups.

Town planning and urban improvement

History and philosophy of urban renewal

From the first decade of the twentieth century, British administrators in India had begun to advocate the efficacy of town planning as the best

---

total population for the elections of 1923 and 1925, the population of 1921 has been taken into account; for the elections of 1929, 1932 and 1935, the population of 1931 has been taken into account. The population was 216,436 in 1921 and 243,755 in 1931; cited in *Census of India, 1941*, Simla, 1942, vol. V, p. 26.
[36] Cited in Notes and Orders, dated 19.2.41, File No. 30 I.T./1935, Box No. 27, Public Health Department, GUP, UPSA.
[37] AIT Annual Reports, various years.
[38] C. A. Bayly, *The Local Roots of Indian Politics: Allahabad, 1880–1920*, Oxford, 1975, p. 232.

means of dealing with insanitary conditions. They were influenced by the vigorous town planning movement in Britain, which had been developing from the turn of the century and had culminated in the passing of the Housing and Town Planning Act in 1909. The mood of some officials in India in the early twentieth century was reflected in a memorandum submitted by Mr L. C. Porter, a member of the Indian Civil Service (ICS), to the government of India, for discussion at the first All India Sanitary Conference in Bombay in 1911. Porter emphasised that 'in no direction is there room for substantial advance in dealing with the problem of sanitation comparable with this [i.e. town improvement and planning]'.[39] At the second All Indian Sanitary Conference, held in 1912 in Madras, the 'introduction on modern lines of town planning schemes' was declared to be among 'the most urgently required sanitary needs in India'.[40]

During the First World War, Patrick Geddes, one of the leading figures of the British town planning movement, toured India and promoted his ideas with evangelical zeal. With Geddes' visit, the concept of town planning gained a determined following well beyond official circles and seized the imagination of Indian urban notables and the propertied, who would soon be at the helm of local affairs.[41] Town planning emerged as a new orthodoxy of civic governance, and Geddes' role in this was instrumental.[42] Between 1916 and 1918, Geddes visited a number of Indian cities, including Allahabad, Lucknow, Kanpur and Benares. He mounted town planning exhibitions in several of these and produced town planning reports for some, including Lucknow. His exhibition laid out his philosophy underlying the movement for urban renewal, or 'Revivance of Cities'.[43]

Geddes' vision was grounded in the idea of a civilisational transition from what he termed the Paleotechnic to the Neotechnic city. Paleo-

[39] Note by L. C. Porter, ICS, addressed to the Secretary to the Government of India, Department of Education. Appendix 6 to the Proceedings of the All India Sanitary Conference, Bombay, 13–14 November 1911, p. 150. Cited in Parliamentary Papers, East India (Sanitary Measures), *Progress of Sanitary Measures in India*, Session: 1912–13, vol. LXII, Cd. 6538.

[40] Resolution passed at the All Indian Sanitary Conference, Madras, 11–16 November 1912, cited in Parliamentary Papers, East India (Sanitary Measures), *Report on Sanitary Measures in India*, Session: 1911–12, Vol. LXIII, Cd. 7113, p. 73. For the development of town planning in India, see H. E. Meller, 'Urbanization and the Introduction of Modern Town Planning Ideas in India, 1900–1925', in K. N. Chaudhuri and C. J. Dewey (eds.), *Economy and Society: Essays in Indian Economic and Social History*, Delhi, 1979, pp. 330–50.

[41] Jaqueline Tyrwhitt (ed.), *Patrick Geddes in India*, London, 1947.

[42] Meller, 'Urbanization and the Introduction of Modern Town Planning', p. 342.

[43] Patrick Geddes, *Cities in Evolution*, 2nd edn, London, 1949, (first published 1915), p. 161.

technic towns were modern industrial cities, with squalid slums as their defining feature, which Geddes saw not simply as an inferior form of housing but as a debased way of life. He deeply abhorred, and declared war against, the 'noxious squalor',[44] chaos and confusion of these slums.[45] The Neotechnic town of the future, to be achieved through town planning, would inaugurate a new age of health, hygiene and order, and would be instrumental in character-building and the reform of society.[46] Geddes thus projected town planning as nothing less than the key to the transformation of society. The way forward in realising the ideal physical, social and moral environment of the Neotechnic town would be to 'penetrate into the older existing town, and with energies Herculean indeed – cleansing its Augean stables'.[47] Urban regeneration, he believed, would rescue workers from their 'deteriorative labour conditions'.[48]

To prove this point, he argued against the 'eugenist' belief in the inherent inferiority of some races and social groups. Geddes stated instead that 'many of those whom eugenists are apt to think of and to tabulate as "degenerates" in type and stock are really but deteriorates, and this in correspondence with their depressive environment'.[49] He further asserted that 'such types and stocks', who had been most prone to the evil and corrupting influences of Paleotechnic slum culture, would 'respond to better conditions, and thus, rise above average, as they now fall below'.[50]

He buttressed his argument for providing a better living environment for workers with the pithy comment: 'It has long been known that to get the best work out of a horse, one must not put the worst in it.'[51] The centre-piece of his town planning vision, as with those of most of his British colleagues and contemporaries, was the normative value of the 'open space' and the 'garden': 'It is primarily for lack of this touch of first hand rustic-experience that we have forced young energy into hooliganism,' he argued.[52] Indeed, it was the ideal of the 'Garden City' – 'smokeless and slumless', with large open spaces[53] – that came to consume the energies of architects, philanthropists and town planners in interwar Britain.

Geddes helped to generate considerable enthusiasm and determination for town planning among Indian city fathers and opinion builders because his ideas struck a resonant cord with middle-class hopes and

[44] Ibid., p. 84.
[45] Geddes, *Cities in Evolution* (1915), ch. 6.
[46] Geddes, *Cities in Evolution* (1949), p. 54 and passim.
[47] Ibid., p. 55.   [48] Ibid., p. 153.
[49] Ibid., p. 152.   [50] Ibid., p. 152.
[51] Ibid., p. 49.   [52] Ibid., p. 54.   [53] Ibid., p. 190.

fears. Geddes' vision presented solutions to what the middle classes saw as the interconnected problems of squalor, overcrowding, urban decay, moral degeneracy and social disruption, which accosted them with great urgency in this period. Moreover, Geddes outlined the model of a citizens' dream of civic order and hygiene, rather than sketching a template for cities as majestic imperial monuments. 'The great city', Geddes said, 'is not that which shows the palace of government at the origin and climax of every radiating avenue: the true city . . . is that of a burgher people, governing themselves from their own town hall and yet expressing also the spiritual ideal which governs their lives.'[54]

This glorification of the spirit of the town hall, as the centre of public life with a soul, fitted rather neatly with the history of institutional evolution and the nationalist ideas of local politics in India in the aftermath of the First World War. An urban-based 'constructive'[55] civic nationalist vision was gradually emerging in the interwar years among the newly enfranchised middle classes. They increasingly saw civic institutions, town governance and urban development as the motors of modernisation, progress and national efficiency. Helen Meller notes that the further development of local self-government in the interwar period placed the towns themselves 'in a new light as the centres for moder-nizing Indian society'.[56] The Geddesian vision of urban renewal was highly attractive to the local elites, who saw themselves as the instru-ments of political progress and nationalist construction based on their recently expanded powers in the local seats of governance.[57] Geddes' town planning reports were, implicitly or explicitly, celebrations and expositions of civic virtue and social responsibility.[58] This appealed to the Indian middle classes in their endeavour to define a superior role and identity for themselves through local government, both in opposi-tion to colonial rule and in contrast to the seemingly undisciplined mass of the poor.

Geddes' vision of achieving urban regeneration also had a philan-thropic orientation. The new city of the future would evolve at the initiative of high-minded, enlightened and altruistic pioneers.[59] This corresponded well with the self-image of the Indian nationalist and social reformers as the harbingers of a new age and a better society. A

[54] Ibid., p. 80.
[55] C. A. Watt, 'Education for National Efficiency: Constructive Nationalism in North India', *MAS*, 31, 2, 1997, pp. 348–50.
[56] Meller, 'Urbanization and the Introduction of Modern Town Planning', p. 332.
[57] Helen Meller, *Patrick Geddes: Social evolutionist and city planner* (London, 1990), p. 207.
[58] Tyrwhitt (ed.), *Geddes*, p. 12.
[59] Geddes, *Cities in Evolution* (1949), pp. 146–53.

specific brand of civic nationalism developed in this context, with town governance and urban development as its rallying focus, rather than notions of political enfranchisement or democratic rights for all citizens encompassing both the propertied and the impoverished. The major enthusiasts of Geddesian town planning came from Indian elites and middle classes, for most of his ideas were presented in a 'nationalist' or indigenist idiom, attuned to contemporary nationalist cross-currents of thought and in keeping with the predilections of middle-class reformers, policy-makers and intellectuals.[60] Geddes was highly critical of colonial policies of urban improvement, which he denounced as disruptive of indigenous ways of life and as an imposition of western imperial cultural ideas, not to mention being uncoordinated and interventionist.[61] Influenced by Swami Vivekananda, he visited several temple-towns in southern India, which he saw as the embodiment of the inherent spirituality of Indian life. He then came to advocate the religious architectural form of the temple-towns as the appropriate guiding principle of modern town planning in India.[62] His passion for Hindu spiritualism as well as his eulogies on ancient Indian urban forms and housing endeared him to many of the reformers and revivalists of the period. He was even invited to deliver the inaugural address at the ceremony to lay the foundation stone of the Benares Hindu University and was considered a possible architect for the university campus.[63]

Geddes was at his best in linking the town improvement project of eradicating filth with the reformist ideal of restoring health, hygiene and moral fibre, which would together, in his view, contribute to prosperity and the building of the ideal national character. He excelled himself in conveying his message through existing ritual and religious forms. He advocated the marriage of the rites of spring, renewal and rebirth with the mission of civic reconstruction in order to anchor the physical endeavours to cleanse dirt in 'traditional', cultural ideas of moral and spiritual regeneration. He selected *Diwali*, the festival of Light, for a spectacular and inspired expression of the ideal of urban renewal through ritual pageantry. The pageant was staged in Indore in 1917 as a dramatised lesson in civics. However, the event gained widespread

[60] Raj Bahadur Gupta, for instance, the author of *Labour and Housing* cited above and whose views have been discussed earlier, laid down his plans of housing and town improvement in ways that clearly suggest the powerful influence of Geddes. Gupta, *Labour and Housing*, pp. 217–20.
[61] P. Mairet, *Pioneer of Sociology: The Life and Letters of Patrick Geddes*, London, 1957, p. 162; P. Boardman, *The Worlds of Patrick Geddes: Biologist, Town Planner, Re-educator, Peace-warrior*, London, 1978, p. 255; Meller, *Geddes*, pp. 205, 208–9, 257, 285n; Oldenburg, *Making of Colonial Lucknow*, pp. 41–2, 122–3.
[62] Meller, *Geddes*, pp. 217–20, 238.
[63] Mairet, *Pioneer of Sociology*, pp. 172–3.

publicity outside that princely state through the 600 delegates from all over India, who were attending the Eighth All India Hindi Language Conference in Indore at the time, and whose enthusiastic help Geddes enlisted in organising a processional masque for Diwali.[64] With the consent and cooperation of the Maharaja of Indore, Geddes planned Diwali as a festival of civic renovation, where the annihilation of the evil figure of Ravana by Ram would serve as the metaphor for the conquest of filth and disease by the people of the city.[65] To achieve this, Geddes made a number of innovations. He announced that the Diwali festival procession would deviate from its traditional route to traverse the neighbourhoods which were best cleansed and tidied by the local inhabitants, including the repair and renovation of houses, in the days leading up to Diwali. It was recorded that this inspired the removal of 6,000 cartloads of dirt and rubbish from the city.[66]

On the day of Diwali, the festival procession that Geddes organised was led by the image of the Goddess of Wealth, Lakshmi, mounted on an elephant, painted white, representing the ideals of purity, prosperity and chaste well-being. This was followed by the various evil and disruptive forces impeding the realisation of prosperity: first, 'weird figures dressed as tigers, demons and disease danced and mocked at the crowd', accompanied by 'melancholy, wailing and discordant instruments'; then came 'swordsmen and raiders representing the ugly aspects of war'; behind these were models of slum dwellings, ramshackle, dilapidated and with accumulated refuse, exuding 'a general air of misery and dirt'; finally came a towering effigy of Ravana arrayed as the fierce Lord of Dirt, along with a gigantic model of a mosquito crawling with malarial microbes[67] and 'a colossal rat of the kind it is necessary to exterminate, which was covered with quivering insect forms representing the fleas which were carriers of plague-germs'.[68] These depictions of evil were followed by representations of the forces that would conquer them. The music changed to cheerful tunes from discordant notes. First came all the town's sweepers in an orderly march, dressed 'in spotless white raiment', carrying new brooms and wearing flower garlands, accompanied by their bullock carts for the removal of rubbish, beautifully cleaned and painted, and the animals bedecked with orna-

---

[64] Meller, *Geddes*, p. 254.
[65] This festival is fully described by Geddes' biographer: P. Boardman, *Patrick Geddes: Maker of the Future*, Chapel Hill, 1944, pp. 386–90; Boardman, *The Worlds of Patrick Geddes*, pp. 294–7.
[66] Meller, *Geddes*, p. 254.
[67] P. Kitchen, *A Most Unsettling Person: An Introduction to the Ideas and Life of Patrick Geddes*, London, 1975, p. 280.
[68] Mairet, *Pioneer of Sociology*, p.179.

ments, flowers and vermilion. Geddes wrote in a letter on this subject, 'every sweeper too was wearing a new turban, and of the town's colour – as were all the employees and higher officers of Indore, as well as the mayor and myself: this had been arranged with his warm approval as symbol of the democracy of civic service'.[69] After the sweepers and the municipal functionaries came the image of a newly created goddess of Indore City, holding aloft a banner with the new city plan, followed by floats carrying models of the proposals laid down in the plans, including new housing. The procession ended with floats representing craftsmen such as masons, potters and ironmongers as the mainstay of the rebuilding project. Finally came carts full of fruits and flowers, signifying natural abundance and beauty, and thousands of pots of Tulsi plant saplings were distributed to bystanders and audience, Tulsi being the emblem of the well-kept Hindu home and hearth.

This magnificent procession was, of course, a display of Geddes' own interpretation of the ideas of urban regeneration and civic service in the Indian context, but this could very well have been a pageant organised by any city Congress committee in India at the time. It resonated most poignantly with a range of central themes and iconography of contemporary nationalism and reformism, including civic governance, expression of 'Indianness' and uplift of the lower castes. Most importantly, in a brilliant move, all of these were linked with the ideal of town planning and sanitation.

It is hardly surprising then that the newly enfranchised Indian propertied classes of the UP towns would eagerly embrace the promise and plan of urban renewal, with its manifold ramifications, that Geddes, in particular, and other town planners offered to them. It is perhaps not a coincidence that the stalwarts of some of the Improvement Trusts in UP and the enthusiasts of town planning were also prominent nationalists and 'reformers', such as the Congress leader P. D. Tandon in Allahabad[70] or Anand and Brijendra Swarup, who consecutively chaired the Kanpur Improvement Trust and were two of the most important leaders of the Arya Samaj in UP, well known for their philanthropy and caste uplift work. Geddes' presence in India and his missionary dissemination of town planning were, thus, instrumental in generating extensive enthusiasm for the idea. He played an extraordinarily successful role in bringing about a wider consensus about the need for town planning, so paving the way for the extensive reordering of the towns in the interwar period.

---

[69] Cited in Kitchen, *A Most Unsettling Person*, p. 280.
[70] B. N. Pande, *Allahabad: Retrospect and Prospect*, Allahabad, 1955, pp. 338–9.

However, in the actual framing of policies and implementation, Geddes' ideas proved to be far less decisive.[71] He did not stay in India for long. It fell to his colleagues and successors such as H. V. Lanchester[72] and Linton Bogle,[73] as well as the local institutions, to propel forward the practical task of town improvement in UP. While Geddes was more concerned with projecting town improvement in terms of a grand vision of civilisational transition and civic nationalism, Lanchester and the members of the local institutions had to contend with practical difficulties, circumvent financial constraints[74] and address the urgent problems. They were thus far less visionary and more pragmatic in their approach.[75] Besides, in the circles of British officialdom, to whose views and policies of town planning Geddes clearly posed a challenge, his ideas of reconstruction were considered too radical, a trifle dangerous and impractical.[76] Moreover, as Lanchester pointed out, the chief consideration in Indian town planning was the 'treatment of congested areas',[77] to which all other goals were secondary. Geddes' evolutionary strategy of 'conservative surgery' and gradual eradication of slums, as opposed to 'drastic surgery',[78] had little practical value in achieving this aim, quite apart from being protracted and expensive. Those who were responsible for the implementation of town improvement programmes preferred more decisive measures to clean out and sanitise the towns by the wholesale and speedy demolition of congested areas. If this entailed the loss of housing for the poor, and financial constraints prevented the provision of alternatives, then that outcome had to be endured. Among the Indian city-fathers, although Geddes' ideas provided the rationale and vision for their zeal for town improvement, his concrete suggestions often went unheeded and Lanchester's more practical ideas found greater acceptance.[79] Similarly, the Indian middle classes, with their nationalist and reformist orientation, would in theory go along with Geddes' ideas,[80] but in practice they were more keen to see the towns modernised and expanded into clean new zones for their own use, the squalor-ridden slums eradicated, and the poor kept at bay and under

[71] Meller, 'Urbanization and the Introduction of Modern Town Planning', pp. 345–8.
[72] For Lanchester's ideas on town planning, see H. V. Lanchester, *The Art of Town Planning*, London, 1925; H. V. Lanchester, *Talks on Town Planning*, London, 1924.
[73] Meller, *Geddes*, p. 247; Linton Bogle, *Town Planning in India*, London, 1929.
[74] Meller, 'Urbanization and the Introduction of Modern Town Planning', pp. 345–6.
[75] Ibid., pp. 346–7.
[76] Meller, *Geddes*, p. 204; Meller, 'Urbanization and the Introduction of Modern Town Planning', p. 346.
[77] Lanchester, *Art of Town Planning*, pp. 201–2.
[78] Tyrwhitt (ed.), *Geddes*, pp. 40–59.
[79] See Pande, *Allahabad*, pp. 303–23.
[80] Gupta, *Labour and Housing*, pp. 217–45.

control.[81] Indeed, as town improvement ventures began and increasingly met with the resistance of the poor, who faced problems of scarcity or loss of housing, the local councils became even more determined and coercive in forging ahead with their policies and increasingly enlisted the help of the police to overcome resistance. Their chief concern, after all, was to reclaim the towns for the middle classes from the threat of the poor and to ensure the universal enforcement and acceptance of the civic ideal of a planned, orderly, safe and hygienic environment.

Of course, there were many critics and detractors who opposed particular projects that were excessively disruptive and interventionist. Some even championed the case of the poor against wholesale demolition and clearance of overcrowded areas. However, such criticism was lodged within a wider framework of consensus over the need and principles of town planning. Criticisms thus had little effect on the overall thrust of policies, but were only levelled at, and often achieved alterations in, particular schemes.

Ultimately, the grand conception of urban transformation was whittled down and domesticated to meet the immediate interests of the propertied classes. Instead of unfolding as idealistic projects of social regeneration, the town planning schemes evolved as avenues to further the interests and aspirations of the propertied and the instrument of the growing marginalisation of the poor. The war against slums came dangerously close to being a battle to control the settlement and habitation of the poor, and indeed an offensive against the poor themselves. Rather than developing as the sites of national self-expression and social idyll of Geddes' Neotechnic place, the towns became the arena of fierce conflict over scarce housing and land for the poor and their dispossession.

Protecting the 'decent people' and the 'better classes'

Already during the First World War, partly stimulated by the excitement generated by Geddes' tour and exhibition, the Municipal Boards in the major UP towns had commissioned town planning experts to suggest schemes for urban improvement. Such schemes were outlined in a number of reports on town planning. The first report was prepared by Geddes himself for Lucknow, in 1916. As the idea caught on, Geddes' report was followed by one for Allahabad by Stanley Jevons in 1919, produced in consultation with Lanchester,[82] and one for Kanpur in 1917 by the Kanpur Expansion Committee, headed first by Henry

[81] Meller, *Geddes*, pp. 220–1.
[82] Pande, *Allahabad*, p. 339.

Ledgard, the Chairman of the Upper India Chamber of Commerce, and subsequently by Lanchester in 1918. The urban improvement schemes proposed in these reports were far-reaching and entailed the extensive acquisition of land and re-planning of insanitary and congested areas, as well as urban territorial expansion through the reclamation of undeveloped land within and on the periphery of the towns. While the notion of urban improvement was not new, the idea of 'planning' and the strategy of such extensive reorganisation were unprecedented.

The execution of such far-reaching schemes was beyond the administrative power or the financial capacity of the Town Improvement Committees of the Municipal Boards, which had so far been responsible for urban improvement schemes.[83] The government considered it necessary to form separate and independent bodies for town planning, with minimum direct or obvious involvement of British officials, the government being disinclined to be overtly implicated in town planning activities for fear of facing the popular discontent that was likely to arise. Accordingly, to expedite the implementation of town improvement and planning schemes, at the end of the war the provincial government passed the UP Town Improvement Trusts Act (No. VIII) in 1919. Improvement Trusts were formed in Lucknow and Kanpur in December 1919 and in Allahabad in 1920. According to the Trusts Act, the new Improvement Trusts were to have greater powers than the Town Improvement Committees of the Municipal Boards with regard to compulsory land acquisition and re-planning of townscapes. The government also extended initial grants to the Trusts in order to finance their schemes.[84]

With the creation of the institutional authority of the Trusts with extended powers, projects for the clearance of insanitary areas began on a more systematic and hitherto unprecedented scale. H. V. Lanchester had pointed out that town planning in India 'arose out of health measures' and sanitary concerns.[85] A more recent commentator noted not only the preoccupation with public health, but a decisive shift of focus in the early twentieth century: 'The original conception of public health was fairly simple: the improvement of drainage and sewerage, the provision of adequate and satisfactory water supply, and the scavenging and isolation of cases of infectious diseases. Then came the supervision of housing conditions, the clearance of slums, the provision of open

[83] Note by Awadh Behari Lal, Land Valuation Officer of the Kanpur Improvement Trust (undated), Kanpur Improvement Trust (hereafter KIT), File No. 1 (IT).
[84] *Report of the Town Improvement Trusts Committee* [hereafter *RTITC*], *1924* (Chairman: S. H. Fremantle), Allahabad, 1924, pp. 4–5.
[85] Lanchester, *Art of Town Planning*, pp. 201–2.

spaces and the efforts to provide a cleaner atmosphere.'[86] It was for the latter purpose that Improvement Trusts came into being.[87] As a consequence, the acquisition, demolition and clearance of overcrowded and insanitary areas constituted a chief activity of the Trusts. As could be expected, the main targets of such Trust schemes were the poorer sections in the towns, which were identified as the perpetrators of 'plague spots'. Indeed the term 'plague spot' developed as a metaphor to signify the undesirable and unhygienic habitat of the poor, rather than as the epicentre of the disease itself. This notion that the poor were chiefly responsible for insanitary conditions was now overtly deployed in the 'clearance' drives, and the main strategy was clearly enunciated in a number of reports and policy documents on town improvement. The Ledgard Committee for the improvement of Kanpur in 1917 stated:

The treatment of congested areas in the existing city will be a very essential branch of the work of the Trust. The first step necessary is the removal of the superfluous population. . . . But it is not expected that people, especially the poorer classes in those areas, where congestion is the worst, will migrate themselves; they must be made to go; the worst mohallas [neighbourhoods] must be taken in hand and systematically cleared.[88]

This view was echoed by the various provincial Town Improvement Trusts Committees, which reviewed the activities of the Trusts every five years and framed guidelines for the future. The Committee of 1929 declared:

A primary duty of the Trusts is the clearing of insanitary and congested areas. It is ordinarily inevitable, therefore, that the process of improvement mainly affects the poorer portion of the population, whose habitations are generally both insanitary and congested.[89]

The report of the same Committee was also unequivocal that 'the transference of these labourers to places outside the heart of the city is the first step necessary for the relief of the present congested and insanitary condition'.[90] The Committee of 1935 stressed the need to continue this policy towards the houses and settlements of the poor, which 'occupy the spaces in between the *better residential and commercial areas*' (emphasis added) and which 'are regular breeding grounds of disease and are the main factors in the prevailing high rate of infantile mortality'. The Committee endorsed the policy to clear the congested neighbourhoods of the poor and 'to transfer the greater part of their present occupants to sites outside the city'.[91] Evidently, the most

---

[86] Pande, *Allahabad*, p. 318.   [87] Ibid., p. 337.
[88] Cited in S. P. Mehra, *Cawnpore Civic Problems*, Kanpur, 1952, p. 47.
[89] *RTITC, 1929* (Chairman, H. J. Crosthwaite), Allahabad, 1929, p. 11.
[90] Ibid., p. 13.
[91] *RTITC, 1935* (Chairman, J. F. Sale), Lucknow, 1936, p. 41.

important solution to urban sanitary and health problems was considered to be the removal and segregation of the poor to urban outskirts, in order to keep them away from the 'better residential and commercial areas'. The principle of spatial 'zoning' to demarcate various areas for designated functions emerged as a pivot of town planning partly in response to the urge to confine the poor to particular parts of the town. The imperfect implementation of zoning was thought to jeopardise the isolation of middle-class areas. A municipal report, discussing the problems in some newly laid out housing areas in Allahabad, commented: 'As no care was given to zoning in this area [Katra and Colonelganj in Allahabad], it is traversed in its interior by menial quarters', which caused the area to be marred by 'the most insanitary houses adjacent to comparatively better houses of middle class men'.[92]

The increasing urgency of the local authorities to segregate the poor was clearly revealed in the course of controversies over the neighbourhood of Khalasi Lines in Kanpur. Mill workers, hawkers and casual labourers lived in shanties and huts in this area, located on the periphery of the British civil lines and the bungalow complex of officials of local textile mills and other factories.[93] The inhabitants of Khalasi Lines had repeatedly complained to the Municipal Board about the lack of water supply and public latrines in the area.[94] On their failure to persuade the municipality to provide these facilities, in 1932 some of them deliberately invaded a vacant plot of land between the civil lines' bungalows and the Khalasi Lines settlement, and began to use it as an outdoor latrine. This caused severe consternation among the bungalow residents, who urged the Chairman of the Improvement Trust to 'stop this nuisance', on the argument that the area was 'surrounded on all sides by superior residences'.[95] The Municipal Board then persuaded the district authorities to post policemen in the area to prevent the invasion of the field near the bungalows and ordered them to arrest and prosecute 'offenders'. This led to skirmishes between the Khalasi Lines people and the policemen. Well before 1932, the Khalasi Lines settlement had already caused much soul-searching among Improvement Trust authorities about the 'advisability of developing this area [i.e. Khalasi Lines]

[92] Allahabad Municipal Board (hereafter AMB) Annual Report, 1936–7; cited in Pande, *Allahabad*, pp. 351, 376.
[93] Note No. 834, dated 2 August 1920, addressed to the Chairman, Improvement Trust, from the Land Valuation Officer, KIT File No. 23(IT), Khalasi Lines Scheme (No. III A).
[94] Cited in a letter to the Chairman, Improvement Trust, dated 19 April 1932, signed by the Residents of Khalasi Lines, ibid.
[95] Letter (undated) from Mr Williamson, Director, Begg, Sutherland and Co. Ltd, to Chairman, Improvement Trust (date of receipt of letter at the Improvement Trust, 12 February 1932), ibid.

for workmen's quarters, seeing that opposite there are Civil Lines bungalows'.[96] Lanchester, while framing town improvement schemes for Kanpur, was also reported to have said that 'he could not tolerate the continuance of this insanitary hamlet in the midst of the bungalow area'.[97] The tensions in the Khalasi Lines in 1932 eventually prompted the Trust to adopt an unequivocal decision to remove the huts from the area.[98] This controversy is a typical example of the perception of the local authorities that proximity to the habitations of the poor threatened the public health conditions of 'superior residences', which, in turn, justified attempts to remove them from the vicinity of the residential areas of the 'decent people'.

The urge to distance the settlements of the poor arose as much from the fear of moral and social degeneracy, as from the need to eradicate dirt and disease. Immorality was considered just as much a part of the landscape of the slums as filth. In particular, the bazars in the congested central areas, where many of the poor worked and lived, were seen as dens of vice. In middle-class minds, bazars and streets had the connotation of licence and even tumult. The culture of the bazars stood for sexual promiscuity, intoxication, hooliganism and crime. For instance, the use of the term 'bazar women' for prostitutes not only referred to the market and economic transaction involved in prostitution, but also pointed to bazars as places of immoral activities. Naturally, the bazars were prime targets of clearance drives, not only for their overcrowding and sanitary problems, but also as sites of moral decay and social deviance. As Dipesh Chakrabarty writes of urban Bengal, the bazar was seen as 'a place against which one needs protection' and which 'harbours qualities that threaten ones well being';[99] accordingly, bazars were sought to be turned into 'benign regulated places, clean and healthy, incapable of producing either disease or disorder'.[100]

Within the bazars, the houses of prostitutes were sought to be removed with particular alacrity, for they epitomised the immoral temptation to which the poor succumbed. In Kanpur, the area called Moolganj, located at the junction of several major roads at the heart of the vast *bazar-mandi* zone, was a central place for workers and labourers to congregate every day. Here they assembled to be recruited for casual work, and the porters and transport pliers waited with their carts and

---

[96] Note on Khalasi Lines by the Acting Chairman, Improvement Trust, dated 28 November 1928, ibid.
[97] Cited in Note No. 834, dated 2 August 1920, addressed to the Chairman, Improvement Trust by the Land Valuation Officer, ibid.
[98] 'Khalasi Lines Quarters' – Note by Chairman, Improvement Trust (undated), ibid.
[99] D. Chakrabarty, 'Open Space/Public Place', p. 25.
[100] Ibid., p. 28.

vehicles for customers from the bazars. Moolganj, not surprisingly, was considered an especially dangerous place, with milling crowds of the poor. The menacing nature of the area was believed to be aggravated since drinking and gambling opportunities and prostitutes' quarters were close at hand. The area inevitably developed as an important site to control the poor. From the 1930s, the police concentrated much of their patrolling and armed pickets here to prevent the supposedly 'volatile' population from erupting into violence.[101] The local authorities were not far behind. As the site of prostitute quarters, Moolganj was seen as the rendezvous of 'bad characters'. The removal of prostitutes to a secluded area elsewhere in the town was, therefore, greatly favoured. The Improvement Trust stepped in to remove the prostitutes from Moolganj, with the hope that it would improve public behaviour and moral conduct, and thus also minimise the possibility of violence.[102] In Allahabad too, from the 1920s, the expulsion of prostitutes from some of the busy bazars was seen as an integral component of urban improvement, and was initiated during the municipal chairmanship of the nationalist leader P. D. Tandon.[103]

While moral, social and sanitary concerns generated sufficient consensus among the urban middle classes over town improvement projects and the segregation of the poor, in some quarters there was also growing concern about the adverse effects of these policies on the poor. The annual report of the Allahabad Municipal Board in 1941–42, for instance, vigorously advocated the cause of the poor, and even verged on a denouncement of the policies of the Trust and emphatically argued the need to lay out proper housing areas for the poor. However, this report, too, betrayed the view that separate sites for the poor were necessary not simply because they needed housing, but also because they created 'plague spots' in the midst of the residential areas of those identified as 'decent people':

The areas that have been well planned and good schemes [for middle class housing] have come into existence, suffer from great insanitary features due to the entrance of *poor class men* . . . [who] made the dwellings not what they would otherwise have been . . . By the time the full scheme comes into play and the houses are occupied by *decent people*, the scheme will be traversed by *poor class men* . . . This has led to the growth of *plague spots* even in those areas that

[101] District Magistrate, Kanpur, to Chief Secretary, UP, Letter No. 94–B/32, dated 6 April 1932, File No. 12/1931, Department XX, Police, Allahabad Commissioner's Office Records.
[102] 'Removal of Prostitutes from the Central Localities of Cawnpore City'. File No. 43 (I.T.)/1931, Box No. 51, Bundle 16, Municipal Department, GUP, UPSA; KIT Annual Report, 1931–2, p. 7.
[103] Pande, *Allahabad*, pp. 459–60.

are improved. A well conceived scheme for housing of various classes of poor in different parts of the town is long overdue.[104]

The advocacy of the case of the poor here seems to owe more to instincts of self-preservation of the 'decent people' than to humane concerns for the 'poor class people' living in their 'plague spots'. Precisely a view of this kind had been expressed several years earlier by Ganesh Shankar Vidyarthi, a prominent Congressman of Kanpur, in 1917, when he stated that 'if the opening up of congested areas is decided upon, adequate accommodation should be provided for the poorer classes in other quarters at cheap rates, for otherwise the *evil* would be shifted from one portion of the city to another' (emphasis added).[105] Here Vidyarthi's concern for the poor scarcely disguised his view of them as 'evil' blots on the face of the town.

Many politicians and local notables in the 1920s and 1930s, in particular the town Congress committees,[106] led campaigns against the municipalities and Trusts for displacing and dispossessing the poor, often forcing changes in particular schemes.[107] However, as in the case of Vidyarthi, these leaders, belonging as they did to the urban middle classes, harboured beliefs about the habitual degradation of the poor, albeit with an aim to rescue and reform them. In this respect the fundamental principles and intrinsic efficacy of urban improvement were not doubted by the nationalist reformers. Even while they disagreed with particular projects, they never saw town planning and improvement as anything other than worthy ideals in essence, imbued as many were with a nationalistic civic vision. Thus, the basic premises of local policies or their overall logic and aim were never challenged in public discourse. Campaigns against local policies concentrated largely on the question of 'dehousing' and 'rehousing', or the provision of proper sanitary facilities for the poor, all of which had to do with the specific nature and detail of implementation of policies. In all of this, the broad conception of local policies was hardly contested or the negative characterisation of the poor ever questioned.

It is, however, possible to discern two somewhat different broad perspectives within a largely consensual framework. One approach, which was mainly the one reflected in Trust policies, was primarily concerned with the segregation of the poor, possibly in the belief that their conduct and circumstances were beyond redemption. Another

---

[104] AMB Annual Report, 1941–42, pp. 34, 36, emphases added.
[105] *NNR*, No. 50/1917, pp. 875–6, cites an article by Ganesh Shankar Vidyarthi in *The Cawnpore Samachar*, 9 December 1917.
[106] See chapter 7 below.
[107] Some of these cases will be discussed in chapters 6 and 7.

view, critical of local policies and with faith in the reform of the poor, seemed to favour segregation as a desirable way to alleviate the problems of health and housing of the poor. These differences ultimately had little decisive impact on the overall contour of policies. In both cases, the poor were associated with filth, grime and vice, even if in one case the poor were seen as 'degenerate' lost causes and in the other as 'deteriorates' awaiting betterment, to invoke Geddes' distinctions.

Housing and 'class' differentiation in urban social geography

With the twin aims of clearing urban congestion and protecting the so-called 'superior residences' or 'better residential and commercial areas' from insanitary conditions, the Municipal Boards and Improvement Trusts in the interwar period acquired and demolished overcrowded settlements of the poor and evicted the residents. Obviously the poor could not be forcibly shifted and isolated *en masse*, not least because of the resistance that the Trusts encountered from the poor, which will be discussed in the second part of this book. Attempts were made, however, to clear many of their residential buildings and slum areas in the centre of the towns through the 'internal' schemes of the Trust and by enforcing municipal sanitary by-laws. Armed with powers to acquire land on a compulsory basis, the Trusts, immediately after their inception in the early 1920s, began large-scale acquisition of insanitary or congested land. The Town Improvement Trusts Committee of 1924 reported that the Trusts deliberately acquired large areas of land 'as quickly as possible' to avoid 'speculation in land and the consequent rise in its price'.[108]

The *kuccha*, or temporary, hutments of the poor and their dilapidated, insanitary or overcrowded houses were naturally the first targets of acquisition and demolition. This was also partly because these houses, being either temporary or in conditions of disrepair, had low demolition costs and cheap rates of compensation for acquisition.[109] The Trusts also took the view that the construction of buildings constituted the most valuable use of land and considered the occupation of land by the kuccha hutments of the poor to be a waste of vital urban land, as well as being insanitary, and such areas were usually acquired and cleared in preparation for building construction. The Town Improvement Trusts Committee of 1929 acknowledged that the 'poorer classes of the population in these areas [i.e. schemes areas] come in for the major share of demolition'.[110]

---

[108] *RTITC, 1924*, p. 11.   [109] *RTITC, 1935*, p. 9.
[110] *RTITC, 1929*, p. 11.

The schemes for clearing congested and insanitary areas began to displace large numbers of the poor from their existing dwellings. The annual report of the Lucknow Improvement Trust in 1922 admitted that 'dehousing' was a new, but unavoidable, problem arising from Trust activities.[111] The Town Improvement Trusts Committees in 1924 and 1929 also confirmed that 'dehousing' was extensive.[112] The actual extent of loss of housing is difficult to estimate. Exact figures, available for one case in Kanpur, give an indication of its magnitude. In 1929, a census was taken of those who would be 'dehoused' as a consequence of Trust schemes in twenty-seven slums. The census showed that 9,351 people living in 2,400 houses would be dislodged, of whom 3,200 were mill workers, 4,191 general labourers, 376 *ekka-tonga* drivers (drivers of horse-drawn hackney carriages), and the remaining 1,584 petty shop-keepers, domestic workers and others, possibly casual manual labourers and such self-employed groups as milkmen, carpenters or metal smiths.[113]

The loss of housing in the central areas of the towns was often coupled with a threat to the sources of livelihood of the affected groups, since the places of employment of the poor were usually located near their previous dwellings, especially in the case of labourers and petty traders in centrally located bazars. In 1926, for instance, a scheme to clear overcrowding in the Nachghar-Birhana area in Kanpur, situated in the bazar-mandi heartland of the city, displaced the community of *lodhas* (pulse grinders), who lived in the area and worked in the adjacent pulse-grinding workshops in Dalmandi (pulses market). Moved away from the bazar zone to urban outskirts and without cheap forms of public transport, the lodhas' access to their place of work was seriously impeded.[114] The town improvement policies thus adversely affected both the housing conditions and the economic activities of the poor.

Whilst the policies of the Improvement Trusts and the municipalities caused extensive loss of housing of the poor, the provision of alternatives was entirely inadequate. In theory, the 'internal' schemes of the Trusts to clear congestion and overcrowding within the city were to be supple-mented by simultaneous 'external' schemes of town expansion, in order to accommodate the 'dehoused'. The 'external' schemes of development and reclamation of land were adopted to open up new areas for settlement in certain undeveloped pockets within the towns and in

---

[111] Lucknow Improvement Trust (hereafter LIT) Annual Report, 1922, p. 1.
[112] *RTITC, 1924*, p. 12; *RTITC, 1929*, p. 40.
[113] *RTITC, 1929*, p. 40.
[114] Statement of objections to Scheme No. XVIII, KIT File No. 104/IT Part (1926), Nachghar Birhana Scheme (No. XVIII).

urban outskirts. However, the annual report of the Allahabad Municipal Board for 1937–8 stated that such 'external' schemes had 'simply afforded opportunities for the well-to-do middle class men to expand themselves in these areas . . . They [the poor] have not found, in the Improvement Trust Schemes, suitable quarters for their housing.'[115] The problem was not so much that the Trusts failed to lay out new sites, but that the poor had little access to these areas and the beneficiaries were the middle classes. A priority of the Trusts from the outset had been to cater to the demand for land for the construction of buildings. The 1942 annual report of the Lucknow Improvement Trust mentioned that the Trusts, in the previous two decades, had tried to meet two specific kinds of demand for land for construction. The first kind of demand cited was for residential homes for urban professional and administrative groups and affluent business people. The policy of the Trust was to open up land on the periphery of the city and sell it at relatively low prices for the construction of residential buildings. To counter the low profits accruing from these sales, the Trusts tried to meet a second kind of demand for land by commercial investors or property developers. They acquired and redeveloped land in the central areas of the town, and sold these for high prices at auctions to property developers, who constructed buildings for letting to shops and commercial establishments.[116] As a result of the policy of the Trusts to sell newly developed, reclaimed or acquired land either to capitalist investors or to the middle classes, increasing areas of urban land were being built over for commercial purposes or for middle-class residential use. This, in addition to the consequent escalation of land prices, created a scarcity of land for the settlement of the poor. The Kanpur Improvement Trust admitted this fact with remarkable candour and a touch of worldly philosophy: 'It is not the rule of the Trust, but of the world, that it is the rich that get served first.'[117]

The disinclination of the Trusts to provide land for the housing of the poor along with their eagerness to cater to property developers and real estate investors to meet the residential needs of the middle classes undoubtedly arose from the fact that the trustees represented the propertied and commercial classes in towns. Indeed, the trustees and their associates were often themselves interested in investing in land and building construction. However, a financial consideration was cited by the Trusts to account for their inability to allocate land for the poor. From their point of view, selling developed land at prices affordable by

---

[115] AMB Annual Report, 1937–38, pp. 38, 42.
[116] LIT Annual Report, 1942, pp. 22–3.
[117] KIT Annual Report, 1921–22, p. 5.

the poor, or constructing houses to be sold or rented to them at low rates, would not yield substantial returns. The Trusts, therefore, considered it financially non-viable to adopt such 'unremunerative schemes', 'without a sufficient recurring income'.[118] The Trusts did not have any such source of recurring income. The initial grants available from the provincial government for town improvement were spent on paying compensation for acquisitions and were locked up in development expenses. To ensure a subsequent flow of income and to remain financially solvent, the Trusts sold their developed land to capitalist investors or to affluent people, who could pay high prices for Trust land. The Kanpur Trust, for instance, arrived at the firm decision, early in its life in 1921–2, that 'it is not economic [for the Trust] to put up low rented buildings on [Trust] land' to house the poor.[119] The Trusts, therefore, chose to operate as commercial ventures, rather than as public service institutions intending to subsidise housing for the poor. They had the option of utilising their incomes either to provide housing for the poor or to open up further areas for middle-class residences. Financial logic, buttressed by the powerful concern to create safe and sanitary havens for the middle classes, free and far from the threat of the 'insanitary' poor, clearly clinched the issue in favour of the middle classes.

The scarcity of housing land for the poor, precipitated by the policies of the Improvement Trusts, intensified in the early 1930s as the demand for building sites by the propertied classes increased substantially from the time of the depression.[120] From the late 1920s, indigenous bankers in the UP towns had begun to invest in urban land, owing to the declining profitability of their banking business when faced with competition from joint-stock banks.[121] The economic depression of the early 1930s further stimulated investments in urban real estate. The Town Improvement Trusts Committee of 1935 attributed it to 'the prevailing cheapness of money which makes the purchase of land and construction of houses more profitable than other forms of investment'.[122] Moreover, the crisis in the agrarian sector during the depression redirected capital to the towns away from rural land-ownership or agricultural production. In Allahabad, for instance, some landlords disposed of their rural holdings, because they were faced with difficulties in the collection of rents from their tenants. As an alternative form of investment, they

[118] *RTITC, 1929*, pp. 11–12.
[119] KIT Annual Report, 1921–22, pp. 6–7.
[120] *RTITC, 1935*, p. 5.
[121] *BEC*, II, p. 48; Bayly, *Local Roots*, pp. 229–31.
[122] *RTITC, 1935*, p. 5.

bought urban land to develop housing schemes for the middle classes, to earn rental returns.[123] Affluent lawyers and government officials also invested in land and the construction of buildings for rental income. Lucknow was reported to have become 'a paradise for contractors and retired officials, who come and settle here and build houses'.[124] Some such investors seemed to have found places for themselves in local institutions with the aim of furthering their own interest in real estate and related ventures. One witness giving evidence to the Lucknow Municipal Board Enquiry Committee stated that 'members of the Board are generally contractors in disguise and some of them having entered the Board as men living in ordinary houses have since built palatial buildings'. Several other witnesses echoed this view.[125]

The marked increase in house rents from the time of the First World War gave a fillip to investment in housing as a lucrative source of return on capital. Between 1914 and 1922, house rents had increased by 100 per cent in Lucknow and by 200 per cent in Kanpur between 1914 and 1923.[126] The UP government as a matter of policy did not introduce rent ceiling regulations. In the opinion of the government, the problem of scarcity of housing with increasing population in the towns would be exacerbated by rent ceiling measures, since 'landlords will be encouraged to build more houses, if rents are unrestricted, but will assuredly be discouraged if rents are artificially depressed'.[127] The Allahabad Improvement Trust reported, in 1935–6, very high returns on capital to owners of completed buildings, constructed for middle-class housing or commercial use on land cleared and improved by the Trust.[128] Owing to increased house rents, coupled with low rates of house tax,[129] banking

---

[123] Chairman of the Allahabad Improvement Trust to the Secretary, Municipal Department, Government of UP, Letter dated 4 April 1938, AIT File No. 17/19, Sultanpur Bhava Scheme, Department III. At a later stage in 1936–7, the AIT Annual Report noted that rural zamindars were 'still on the look out for an opportunity to exchange their village land with house property in the city'.

[124] *Report of the Lucknow Municipal Board Enquiry Committee, 1942*, Allahabad, 1942 (hereafter *LMB Enquiry Committee*), p. 7.

[125] Ibid., p. 6.

[126] Secretary, Lucknow Improvement Trust, to Secretary, Municipal Department, UP (through Commissioner, Lucknow Division), Letter No. 401/7118, dated 18 September 1922; District Magistrate, Kanpur, to Commissioner, Allahabad Division, Letter No. 1674, dated 5 February 1923, File No. 90/1922, Box No. 124, Municipal Department, GUP, UPSA.

[127] Note by G. B. F. Muir, Secretary to the Government of UP, dated 4 May 1923, ibid.

[128] AIT Annual Report, 1935–36, p. 6. Between 1922 and 1926, the greatest increase in house rents was for middle-class residential accommodation, according to an Allahabad Civic Survey, cited in the AIT Annual Report, 1936–37.

[129] In the 1930s, the rate of assessment of house tax in Kanpur was only 3.25% of the annual rental value of a property; in Benares it was 4.5%, in Lucknow, 2.5%, and in Allahabad, 4.06%. Cited in *LMB Enquiry Committee*, p. 7.

or commercial groups, district landlords, lawyers and government servants found it worthwhile to invest in private housing schemes and in real estate development for commercial renting. The Lucknow Municipal Board Enquiry Committee reiterated this fact and reported: 'Not only is the rate [of house tax] low but it seems to have no reference to the high rents prevailing in Lucknow. Comparatively with the cost of land and construction, house owning is a good investment.'[130] The magnitude and consequence of developments of this nature were noted in the Allahabad Improvement Trust Annual Report of 1936–7:

The demand for land for construction of houses and shops in the city remains unabated and people are even prepared to advance money on undeveloped lands of the Improvement Trust . . . The rapidity with which buildings are springing up and multiplying these days in the Municipality and Trust areas is amazing.[131]

The ever-increasing use of urban land for building construction in the interwar period as well as the rise in house rents and land prices immeasurably aggravated the scarcity of vacant sites for the poor to settle on, at the same time as they were being evicted from congested areas that were being acquired, cleared and redeveloped by the Trusts. The annual report of the Allahabad Municipal Board commented in 1941–2 that:

The Improvement Trust and *zamindars* [urban landlords] have been floating scheme after scheme for the housing of middle class men and whenever these schemes have come into play, the original inhabitants of the place, the poor class people, have been ousted and made to seek new houses in newer surroundings. Thus the poor toss about from place to place and where they go they have to live in an uncongenial atmosphere.[132]

Because of the inadequate compensation they received for the acquisition of their old houses, they could not afford better housing or the high rents in the houses constructed in the newly developed residential settlements,[133] and 'after an intervening period of considerable discomfort . . . provide[d] themselves with similar undesirable quarters elsewhere'.[134] In most cases, of course, they did not receive any compensation at all, being tenants rather than owners of the acquired property. The poorer sections of the population in the towns, therefore, had to house themselves in whatever sites and buildings were available and affordable. The Allahabad Municipal Board reported in 1942 that

[130] Ibid., p. 7.
[131] AIT Annual Report, 1936–37.
[132] AMB Annual Report, 1941–42, p. 34.
[133] *RTITC, 1929*, pp. 11–12; *RTITC, 1935*, p. 9.
[134] *RTITC, 1929*, p. 11.

'on the whole [the] town seems to have very much expanded as far as
the houses for the middle class men are concerned', while the poor 'have
to content themselves with the space and surroundings that may fall to
their lot'.[135] They crowded into insanitary buildings and neighbourhoods which were yet to become targets of Trust schemes and were
unattractive to the middle classes, who had the option of shifting to
newly developed residential areas. The poor had to fall back on unreclaimed and insanitary plots inside and on the periphery of the towns,
which were unsuitable for construction.

As a result of these developments, from the interwar period, the
pattern of residential settlements and urban social geography increasingly mirrored class differences in the towns. The Allahabad Municipal
Board annual reports for 1937–8 and 1941–2 gave detailed descriptions
of what were called 'poor houses'.[136] These descriptions clearly indicate
the way in which the poor had been adversely affected by town planning
policies with the emergence of separate concentrations of 'poor houses'.
Large settlements of kuccha hutments and temporary shanties had
sprouted on low-lying marshy tracts, undrained ditches and swampy
river fronts, which could not be built over. Bungalows and cottages had
been constructed at the higher level of the street, while labourers had
built their huts in the adjacent undrained deep ditches. These areas,
according to the municipal reports, were 'sadly deprived of sanitary
conveniences' and remained waterlogged throughout the monsoon.
Labourers, odd job men and hawkers, who needed to live in the central
areas of the town near their places of work, housed themselves in the old
part of Allahabad in buildings which were insanitary and overcrowded
and, hence, had low rents, as these were deemed unfit for middle-class
residence. These premises, already overcrowded, became more so, as
those who were displaced from their original residences in the course of
Trust schemes in the central areas were forced to flock to the decreasing
number of low-rent houses available in the neighbourhood. Bazar
workers, vegetable vendors and hawkers also lived in and around the
mandi (wholesale market) areas in hutments with thatched roofs or in
temporary shelters, often within the walled compounds of the markets.
These mandis were frequently visited by 'animals of load' which were
generally tethered for long hours during the unloading period. Here
mandi owners were known to 'make practically no arrangement for the
removal of rubbish or clearing of open spaces. These areas become
invariably plague spots specially during the rains and bad seasons.'[137]

135 AMB Annual Report, 1941–42, p. 34.
136 Ibid., 1937–38, pp. 38–42; 1941–42, pp. 34–6.
137 Ibid., 1941–42, pp. 34–6.

Clearly, the policies of the Allahabad Trust contributed to worsening the living conditions of the poor, as they were being 'ghettoised' in particular areas. This was, moreover, in marked contrast to the new housing schemes in reclaimed and developed areas, which provided better and planned residential sites for the middle classes.

Despite the obvious escalation of the problem of housing the poor, the provision of public housing by the municipalities or the Trusts was never seriously considered. Deliberations on the subject of public housing that took place a decade earlier had by the interwar period come to form the basis of future policies regarding the housing of the poor. Following the recommendations of the Plague Committee of 1905 to solve the problem of insanitary 'plague spots', the UP government had proposed that the Municipal Boards should construct low-priced, sanitary 'model' houses to resettle those who lived in insanitary and congested areas – the poor.[138] The proposal was vehemently opposed by local British officials such as A. L. Saunders, Commissioner of Lucknow, who strongly objected to the plan of 'model' housing in 1907, on the twin grounds of political inexpediency and lack of municipal funds. The former he regarded to be the 'most important consideration of all', since attempts at resettlement by the municipal authorities and inspection and regulation of living conditions in the 'model' houses would be 'a source of future friction' between the government and the poor, who were seen to be 'the most dangerous and most easily excited class', and whom the government was not inclined to provoke into political unrest.[139] He emphasised that the government would be the object of discontent of 'the poorer townspeople', for the British district officials were also the administrators in the Municipal Boards.[140] By 1910–11, the UP government abandoned the model housing plans, possibly because of such strong political misgivings of district officials and financial constraints. Instead the government decided that the Municipal Boards would lay out sanitary sites for the construction of quarters for the poorer sections of the population. However, houses on these sites were not to be built by the municipal authorities or maintained by them. Land was to be sold to private builders 'on favourable terms' to encourage them to construct houses for the poor. The government also decided that the builders would be allowed to construct these houses 'in their own way with cheap material and rough workmanship, subject only to the most elementary sanitary rules' of drainage, water

---

138 Cited in *RTITC, 1924*, p. 2.
139 Note by A. L. Saunders, Commissioner, Lucknow Division, dated 22 August 1907, File No. 596 D, Box No. 506, Municipal Department (Block), GUP, UPSA.
140 Ibid.

supply, adequate ventilation and *pucca* (permanent, masonry) walls.[141] The municipal authorities from then onwards abandoned all direct responsibility for housing the poor, except for occasionally providing sites where, they hoped, houses for the poor would be constructed. The implications of this policy for the poor is best illustrated by the case of Kanpur.

The situation of housing for the poor was somewhat different in Kanpur from that in Allahabad or Lucknow. In the latter two towns, the Improvement Trusts were the focus of interest of various propertied groups seeking to invest in urban land and buildings. In comparison, the Trust in Kanpur, as noted earlier in this chapter, was dominated by members of the Upper India Chamber of Commerce and the UP Chamber of Commerce, who were the chief employers of labour in the local mills and factories. They therefore had the additional concern of providing housing for the urban workforce in order to ensure an adequate supply of labour. Moreover, the employers were conscious of the need for better housing, for they subscribed to the view that a healthy habitat bred better and more efficient workers.[142] Although the employers were, by their own admission, thus 'universally sympathetic' to the housing problems of their workers, for 'on the health of the worker rests their usefulness to employers',[143] yet they maintained the position that the provision or improvement of housing was not the responsibility or function of employers, but 'essentially the duty of the government or the corporate authority [e.g. Municipal Boards or Improvement Trusts]'.[144] With this attitude, the employers of labour who were involved in the activities of the Kanpur Trust eagerly embraced the institution as the key vehicle for the betterment of workers' living and sanitary conditions. However, the view that the construction of houses for the labouring population was 'unremunerative', and possibly 'dangerous', dissuaded the trustees from undertaking such projects directly. Instead, they decided to open up new areas of land, where houses were to be constructed by private investors and constructors as commercial ventures. In order to attract private investment in housing for the poor, the Trust extended generous incentives and concessions to potential builders. First, to encourage private owners of unused land to undertake housing schemes for the poor, the Trust exempted the owners from compulsory acquisition of their vacant and unbuilt-up land, provided they devoted such land to houses for labourers. The Trust undertook to

---

[141] Parliamentary Papers, East India (Sanitary Measures), *Report on Sanitary Measures in India*, Session: 1912–13, vol. LXII, Cd. 6373, p. 62.
[142] *RCLI*, III:I, p. 152, Memorandum of the Government of UP.
[143] Ibid., p. 251, Evidence of the UICC.   [144] Ibid.

develop these plots by providing drainage and sewerage, for which the landowners were to pay 'betterment' charges.[145] As 'betterment' charges were considerably lower than the expected rental returns, landowners willingly accepted the 'betterment' package. Secondly, in the new areas developed by the Trust, such as in Sisamau, plots were sold at concessional prices to prospective builders, on condition that they constructed houses for mill workers. Thirdly, in certain cases, the Trust advanced loans at low rates of interest to building contractors who undertook to build residences for the poor.[146]

The incentives extended by the Trust had the desired effect of stimulating the construction of houses or *ahatas* (complexes of small houses in walled compounds) for the labouring population in Kanpur. Between 1920, when the Trust was inaugurated, and 1935, the total number of houses built on Trust land, which mainly accommodated the poor, was 8,430, accounting for an estimated 42,000 people.[147] In 1935–6 alone, 2,000 workers' quarters had been built on Trust land, which housed 10,000 people.[148] In Kanpur, therefore, unlike in Allahabad or Lucknow, the Improvement Trust took the initiative to provide land to house the poor. This did not, however, mean that the poor in Kanpur thus came to enjoy abundant, attractive and cheap housing. Instead, as pointed out by trade union leaders in Kanpur in 1944, 'the areas developed by the Improvement Trust, as far as the labour areas are concerned, quickly degenerated into slums'.[149] This was primarily because the Trust did not subject the house builders and owners to stringent sanitary regulations or rent ceilings, since these would have discouraged the private investors from providing quarters for the poor. If the Trust itself had tried to provide housing, being a public body it would have had to avoid overcrowding and high rents as well as arrange for public latrines, water supply, drainage and conservancy services, the cost of which was considered to be prohibitive. However, in the case of private builders and house-owners, the Trust could simply turn a blind eye to such conditions, and in fact acknowledged and anticipated, in 1921–2, that houses for the poor, built by contractors or private landlords, 'would not pass the test of any public building'.[150] The underlying

---

[145] *RTITC, 1924*, p. 20.   [146] Ibid., pp. 25–6.

[147] KIT Annual Report, 1934–35, p. 13.

[148] Ibid., 1935–36, p. 11.

[149] *Recommendations of the Kanpur Improvement Committee, 1944* (Chairman, Edward Souter), Allahabad, 1945, vol. II: Comments on the Recommendations of the Committee, pp. 39–41, Serial No. K, Letter from Arjun Arora and Suraj Prasad Awasthi, Secretaries of the Provincial Trade Union Congress, dated 20 November 1944.

[150] KIT Annual Report, 1921–22, pp. 6–7.

assumption here was that, even if new housing had to be created for the
working classes, none the less they did not need or deserve the standards
appropriate for a 'public building', presumably because they were used
to and content with sub-standard housing, in contrast to the middle
classes. The perception that the poor were intrinsically prone to filth and
squalor could fortify the view that they required and were entitled to
only the minimum of a roof and four walls, and not much more by way
of spacious surroundings or sanitary facilities, so long as general urban
public health conditions were not jeopardised.

On paper and in theory, the Kanpur Trust, of course, had to stipulate
certain conditions for the builders of private houses or ahatas. Ahata
owners were required to adhere to specific regulations, such as fewer
than a certain stipulated number of houses per acre; houses were to be
constructed according to sanctioned plans to ensure adequate space and
ventilation; rents were to be charged at rates approved by the Trust; and
conservancy and water supply facilities were to be provided.[151] In
practice, however, neither the Trust nor the Municipal Board felt the
need to enforce any of these regulations, not only because it would
discourage private investment in working-class housing, but also
because the poor were expected to make do with minimum standards.
In consequence, working-class housing emerged as overcrowded
'wretched low hovels of one tiny room and verandah, badly built and
most insanitary', yet let out at very high rents.[152] Not surprisingly, the
ultimate beneficiaries of Trust schemes to provide land for housing the
poor in Kanpur were the house builders. They reaped large profits by
building sub-standard houses on Trust land, with few sanitary facilities,
in which they packed large numbers of the poor, who were forced to
share accommodation owing to high rents.

Thus, in Kanpur, as elsewhere, the grand venture of town improvement and reduction of squalor and congestion paradoxically served only
to worsen the housing conditions of the poor, and divided the town
spatially more and more into areas for the rich or the middle classes and
for the poor. The poor were forced to crowd into undeveloped and
insanitary areas, which lacked conservancy and other municipal services.
Sanitary conditions were further impaired in these neighbourhoods
owing to the uneven allocation of available municipal services – a
disproportionately large part of the funds and resources was directed to
the sanitary maintenance and improvement of the residential localities
of the municipal electorate and the propertied rate-payers.

---

[151] *RTITC, 1924*, p. 20.
[152] Ibid., pp. 25–6; *KLIC Report*, pp. 413–14.

Regulation of the economic activities of the poor

Local taxation

Local policy initiatives to sanitise the surroundings of the poor did not remain confined to their residential settlements but also attempted to encompass their economic activities and working habits. Endeavours in this direction were boosted in the interwar period by the changing taxation policies of the municipalities. One of the most significant developments in local administration after the First World War was a shift in the municipal taxation structure. Municipal Boards sought to minimise the tax bill of their constituency of the propertied rate-paying electorate – the payers of direct tax – by reducing the assessment as well as by tempering the rigour and effectiveness of the collection of direct taxes (house tax, tax on property and circumstances, and tax on trades and professions).[153] Instead, indirect taxes and 'non-tax' or 'productive' sources of revenue were exploited more fully, these being collected from a much wider range of town dwellers.[154] An official of the municipal department of the provincial government, who reviewed the structure of municipal finances, documented that in 1935–6 the total income from indirect taxes (octroi, terminal tax and toll) of all UP municipalities was Rs 74,84,776, while total income from direct taxes was only Rs 14,52,120.[155]

The Municipal Boards in the interwar period increasingly concentrated on raising revenue from market rates, rent for the use of municipal land, licensing and the taxation of trades and economic activities, including those of hawkers and labourers. Manual labourers in the bazars, such as *palledars* (porters) and weighmen, were required to obtain licences and pay fees.[156] *Ekkawalas* and *tongawalas* (drivers of horse-drawn hackney carriages) were charged a wheel tax and needed animal and vehicle licences.[157] Bullock-cart pliers and hand-cart pullers were similarly subject to a licence fee and licensing regulations.[158] Both cartmen and carriage drivers were often charged a ground rent (*tehbazari*) for parking their vehicles or carts on public streets,[159] and were

[153] Hugh Tinker, *The Foundations of Local Self-Government in India, Pakistan and Burma*, London, 1954, pp. 164, 317, 322.
[154] Ibid., p. 317; the declining importance of direct taxes and the preponderance of indirect taxes in UP municipalities is well documented in Note, dated 2 November 1939, File No. 243/1939, Box No. 213, Municipal Department, GUP, UPSA.
[155] Note, dated 2 November 1939.
[156] *The Municipal Manual*, 1925, vol. I, Part III, pp. 342–3, p. 396.
[157] Ibid., Part III, pp. 350–1, Part IV, pp. 474–83.
[158] Ibid., Part III, pp. 374–8.
[159] Ibid., Part III, pp. 379–80.

prosecuted for violating traffic rules by causing an obstruction on roads or pavements.[160] In 1928, the police administration report of UP noted that in Lucknow alone in one year 13,000 cases of obstruction of traffic had been prosecuted under municipal by-laws.[161]

This range of regulations covering various occupational groups was not, of course, new in the 1920s and 1930s. However, these measures were implemented more vigorously, stringently and effectively than ever before, with fines imposed on those who contravened the rules. The Benares Municipal Board, for instance, decided in 1928 to locate *chowkies* (outposts) of inspectors at the two ekka-tonga stands in the town to register complaints by passengers against high fares and to detect cases of violation of licensing regulations. Offences were reported to the municipal licensing officer, who initiated proceedings for prosecutions and fines.[162] In addition to labourers and transport pliers, petty traders, hawkers and vendors who set up their shops or stalls on pavements and roadsides or in the bazar areas were charged tehbazari ground rent for the occupation of public land.[163] Vendors of foodstuffs, vegetables and fruits, tea and cooked snacks were required to comply with certain sanitary and public hygiene regulations.[164] Butchers, milkmen and keepers of animals or poultry needed special licences to carry on their trades.[165] Hawkers of foodstuffs, in addition, came under the purview of the Prevention of Adulteration Act (VI) of 1912.[166] Municipal superintendents and inspectors tended to concentrate their inspection and prosecution on petty traders and hawkers, while more affluent merchants, who often had influential friends and associates on the Municipal Boards, were left undisturbed. In 1936, the *Tahsildar* of Kanpur, who undertook investigations into the nature of enforcement of sanitary by-laws and the Prevention of Adulteration Act in the town, found that about 80 per cent of prosecutions involved 'petty hawkers and poor shopkeepers'.[167]

---

[160] Ibid., Part III, p. 374.
[161] *Report on the Administration of Police of the United Provinces*, 1928, p. 2.
[162] Copy of resolution number 120, dated 5 June 1928, of the Benares Municipal Board, cited in File No. 88/1928–33, Department XXIII, Municipal, Benares Collectorate, ERR.
[163] *The Municipal Manual*, 1925, vol. I, Part III, pp. 379–80.
[164] Ibid., Part III, pp. 382, 431–2 (foodstalls), 397 (tea shops).
[165] Ibid., Part III, pp. 383–7 (dairy and cattleshed by-laws), 382–3, 391–5 (by-laws for sale of meat and slaughter houses).
[166] *The Municipal Manual*, 1st edn, 9th reprint, corrected up to 30 June 1933, Allahabad, 1941, Part IV, p. 555.
[167] Note by the *Tahsildar*, Kanpur, dated 10 January 1936, addressed to the Collector, Kanpur, File No. 16/1934–35, Department XIII, Revenue and Scarcity, Kanpur Collectorate, ERR.

The changing trends in the fiscal policies of the municipalities in the interwar period, and the attempt of the Municipal Boards to reduce the burden of direct taxes on the rate-paying electorate, had the effect of subjecting these various occupational groups among the poor to more rigorous enforcement of municipal regulations and fines for default. One set of figures, indicating the increase in collection of fines by the municipalities between the 1910s and the 1920s, illustrates the extent to which the poor were affected by these changing municipal fiscal preferences in the interwar period. In the financial year 1917–18, the income of the Kanpur Municipality from fines was Rs 6,603 rupees, but by 1927–8 this had increased to Rs 25,237. Corresponding figures for Lucknow were Rs 12,674 and Rs 26,662; for Benares, Rs 6,776 and Rs 20,537; and for Allahabad, Rs 8,725 and Rs 16,206.[168] The enforcement of licensing regulations, the collection of rents and fees or the imposition of fines for violation of municipal rules did not constitute the chief sources of municipal income but, in a period when the municipal authorities were concerned to reduce direct taxation and maximise income from all other possible sources, they could ill brook the evasion of dues and fees. They were also eager to rake in revenue from fines whenever possible.

Ever larger numbers of the poor thus came under the purview of municipal regulations and their economic activities were affected more directly by local policies. They were exposed to growing harassment and constant inspection by municipal superintendents, who either enforced the municipal regulations and collected fines or accepted bribes to connive at the violation of rules. The shift in municipal taxation policies thus ultimately placed serious constraints on the economic activities of various groups of the poor. In a period when occupational opportunities were already scarce, these developments served to intensify competition and rivalries among the poor themselves, quite apart from inevitably generating tensions and antagonisms against the local authorities. The fiscal measures of the local bodies to regulate economic activities went hand in hand with a discourse of administration which increasingly and vocally condemned the poor and their activities as defiling and ugly blots on the urban landscape, and in need of monitoring and control.

---

[168] Figures taken from the Annual Report on *Municipal Administration and Finances in the United Provinces*, 1917–18 and 1927–8, Statement II, showing the income of the municipalities from different sources.

Drives against encroachment on public land

Campaigns against encroachment on public, government-owned (*nazul*) land emerged as one of the chief preoccupations of the local authorities from the 1920s, both as part of the grand plan to reduce insanitary conditions and overcrowding and as a new aspect of municipal tax policies. For the anti-encroachment campaigns, extensive surveys of nazul land were undertaken by all Municipal Boards in the 1920s. By the early 1930s, it was widely recognised by the Municipal Boards that fines for encroachment were an important source of revenue.[169] The prime targets of anti-encroachment measures were hawkers, vendors, transport pliers and carters, as well as artisans or workmen who worked at the roadside. 'The great insanitary features of roads' that the municipal authorities had specially identified in Allahabad, for instance, were 'small cabins of such shop keepers as betel leaf sellers, *chat* [cooked snacks] sellers, vendors'.[170] Similarly, 'tradesmen and craftsmen as iron smiths and carpenters' were held culpable for insanitary conditions, for 'the roadside *patris* [pavements] are, as a matter of fact, godowns [storage area] for their shops and working-tables for their workshops'. Another 'insanitary feature' singled out was 'the parking of hackney carriages and hackney carriage animals'. According to the municipal authorities, all of these were special impediments to ensuring sanitation, for they caused 'a complete blockage to the movement of pedestrians and much obstruction in cleaning the *patris* and drains'.[171] The view of the municipal authorities was clearly that the hawkers, vendors, carters and workmen were intrinsically insanitary, disorderly and undisciplined in their habits and practices; they were blamed for laying out their wares chaotically and setting down to work wherever and whenever they could find the opportunity, without any high-minded civic spirit to keep the towns tidy and orderly. Of course, in addition to these temporary shops and stalls, squatting on public land for dwelling purposes was a prime target. Nothing violated the emerging civic ideal of planned development and urban renewal more than these 'disorderly' encroachments and obstructions.

One remedy against such 'insanitary' activities and encroachment was to enhance the collection of tehbazari dues or ground rent from roadside hawkers and to impose fines for encroachment at exorbitant rates, 'which would be out of most pockets, the purpose being to prohibit petty shopkeepers and vendors to occupy roadsides'.[172] The usual

---

[169] *Report on Municipal Administration and Finances*, 1930–31, p. 9.
[170] AMB Annual Report, 1940–41, p. 31.
[171] Ibid.   [172] Ibid.

policy pursued also included the demolition of huts or shelters and shops, the confiscation and removal of goods or vehicles and animals, and the prosecution and fining of 'offenders'.[173] By the 1930s, such drives against encroachment were especially stepped up, as many more temporary shops or stalls and shanties began to appear with the growth of population in the towns.[174] There were also attempts to make the system of prosecution more effective, often in alliance with the district authorities. The Kanpur Municipal Board had recourse to 'moving courts' of City Magistrates, who would prosecute and fine the encroachers on the spot.[175] This was aimed at ensuring that vendors would not be able to flee and so evade prosecution and fines. The municipal authorities expected this measure to exercise a strong deterrent effect against future encroachments elsewhere.[176] Moreover, the District Magistrate of Kanpur advised the City Magistrates 'to adopt ruthless measures'.[177] If all these measures failed, which they frequently did, even greater force was brought to bear by calling in the police. Not surprisingly, removals of encroachment in this manner gradually elicited severe resistance and were reported to have 'become dangerous' – 'the Demolition Overseers often face great difficulties'.[178] Coercion and violence thus became an integral feature of the experience of displacement and dispossession of the poor.

The implementation of these vigorous anti-encroachment measures, in conjunction with the enforcement of a range of other municipal regulations seen above, severely hindered the work of those sections of the poor who were targeted, and often jeopardised their sources of livelihood and prospect of employment. In particular, such measures deepened the scarcity of shop space faced by hawkers and vendors. As discussed above, petty trading activities increased in the towns in the

173 Note from the District Magistrate, Kanpur, to City Magistrates, 10 June 1937, File (not numbered) on miscellaneous correspondences of the District Magistrate, 1937–38, Kanpur Collectorate, ERR.
174 Vigorous and intensified anti-encroachment drives mentioned in ibid.; District Magistrate, Kanpur, to Chairman, Kanpur Municipal Board, Letter No. 1266, dated 9 December 1938, File No. 1–35/1938, Department XXIII, Municipal, Kanpur Collectorate, ERR; Benares Municipal Board Annual Reports, 1928–29, p. 8; 1934–35, p. 13; 1935–36, p. 14; LIT Annual Report, 1929, pp. 21–2; KMB Annual Report, for the year ending 31 March 1939, pp. 16–17.
175 From District Magistrate, Kanpur, to City Magistrates, dated 10 June 1937, File on miscellaneous correspondence of the DM, 1937, Kanpur Collectorate, ERR.
176 KMB Annual Reports, for the year ending 31 March 1939, pp. 16–17; for the year ending 31 March 1942, pp. 13–14.
177 From District Magistrate, Kanpur, to City Magistrates, dated 10 June 1937.
178 Chairman, Municipal Board, to District Magistrate, Kanpur, Letter No. 2415/E, dated 19 November 1938; District Magistrate, Kanpur, to Chairman, Kanpur Municipal Board, Letter No. 1266, dated 9 December 1938, File No. 1–35/1938, Department XXIII, Municipal, Kanpur Collectorate, ERR.

interwar period amongst the poor, either as a permanent source of livelihood or to supplement income from manual labour, especially during periods of lack of employment. As a result, competition among street-hawkers and vendors for access to shop space intensified in the central trading districts in the towns. Gaining a foothold in the bazar areas was the first step to securing business and customers. It was especially difficult for hawkers and vendors to find shop space in these areas. Renting shop space from private owners at the prevailing high commercial rates was beyond their means. The provision of shop space by the Municipal Boards was inadequate, as municipal markets were few in number. Besides, the Boards frequently leased out shop space through auctions, where petty traders were outbid by richer merchants. Moreover, large municipal markets were usually leased out to contractors, who then let out individual shops or stalls. Rents in such cases tended to be high, as the lessees charged high rates to earn profits after covering their initial outlay. The lack of cheap shop space meant that vendors and hawkers set up temporary shops or stalls at the roadside. However, the zealous anti-encroachment drives of the local authorities in the interwar period rendered this option increasingly difficult.

In contrast to the treatment meted out by the municipal authorities to the encroachments of the hawkers, the richer shopkeepers, with permanent shops in buildings in the bazars, had a far better deal. They, too, were frequently guilty of encroaching on public land through extensions of their shops on to the pavements, in the form of *pucca* or permanent *chhajjas* (canopies) and *chabutras* (platforms). However, the municipalities were not inclined to demolish these permanent extensions, on the ground that 'they cannot be in all conscience claimed after the superstructure is raised',[179] and because demolition costs would be prohibitive. Besides, such permanent or pucca additions to shops were allowed to stand because the Boards could either sell or charge rents on the encroached area of land.[180] The lenient attitude towards the more affluent shopkeepers arose because it was the poorer hawkers, not the better-off traders, who were thought to be culpable for causing insanitary conditions. The difference in municipal policy towards the encroachments of richer merchants on the one hand and hawkers and vendors on the other tended to bias urban trading activities in the towns in favour of the former. Municipal evictions and demolition of encroachments by petty traders in the bazar areas played into the hands of richer merchants, who were often concerned to reduce the competition from smaller shopkeepers in central commercial areas, since the latter could

[179] *LMB Enquiry Committee*, p. 28.
[180] *BMB Enquiry Committee*, p. 116.

offer goods at cheaper prices owing to the low establishment costs of their temporary shops and stalls. In seeking to keep hawkers away from the central bazars, the bigger shopkeepers deployed the argument of encroachment and congestion.

Controversies in the 1920s and 1930s involving hawkers' pavement shops and stalls at Aminabad in Lucknow and at Moolganj, Halsey Road, Couperganj and Bansmandi in Kanpur illustrate the growing conflict. The obstruction of roads by vendors and hawkers in Aminabad engaged the attention of the Lucknow Municipal Board from 1932. The Municipal Board tried to remove some obstructions in 1933, but the 'police and the merchants kept complaining of [continued] nuisance caused by hawkers'.[181] The merchants complained that the Board did not prevent hawkers from setting up stalls in front of the shops in buildings. According to the Lucknow Municipal Board Enquiry Committee, the hawkers' stalls caused a 'nuisance before the sites of their shops', and the Municipal Board had 'failed to secure to the shop-keepers of Aminabad their right to proper approach'.[182] The owners of shops in the area argued that the view and access to their shops were being obstructed, resulting in financial loss, presumably because their clientele was decreasing. After innumerable complaints from shop-owners, the Board cancelled the trading licences of some pavement hawkers.[183] By the late 1930s, the complaints of richer merchants in Aminabad grew even more vocal and the Executive Officer of the Board reported to the Lucknow Municipal Board Enquiry Committee that 'quite a number of unauthorised shops are being removed almost daily by seizing their goods and putting them to auction in case they refuse to pay removal charges'.[184] In the bazar areas of Moolganj, Halsey Road, Couperganj and Bansmandi in Kanpur, the Municipal Board similarly tried to minimise the number of hawkers through repeated and vigorous clearance drives. The reasons for this were cited to be the restricted access to shops and warehouses of wholesale merchants, as well as the insanitary conditions, congestion and obstruction of traffic caused by the hawkers.[185] However, the ultimate impact of municipal policies was to render petty trading activities in the towns more and more difficult, especially by restricting access to the vital central business districts, thus accentuating the problem of sources of livelihood for the poor who sought employment as hawkers and vendors. Moreover, measures against encroachment and congestion directed towards the carters and

[181] *LMB Enquiry Committee*, p. 31.
[182] Ibid., p. 33.   [183] Ibid., p. 32.   [184] Ibid.
[185] KMB Annual Report, for the year ending 31 March 1926, p. 15; KMB Proceedings, 19 July 1926, 20 April 1927, 17 June 1931.

porters, as well as the enforcement of licensing regulations for them, similarly threatened their economic activities.

Political implications

In the UP towns in the interwar years, deprivation and dispossession of the poor worsened owing to the decisive shifts in local policies, and class differences were sharpened. Even if not all sections of the poor directly faced loss of housing or prosecution for encroachment, urban living became more conflictual and unstable, and all experienced greater vulnerability and insecurity. The vigorous town improvement measures and local taxation policies impinged more directly and extensively on the economic activities and housing and settlement patterns of the poor. They served to aggravate the scarcity of housing or occupational opportunities during a period of rapid population growth and intensified conflict and competition in the towns. Local policies thus came to assume hitherto unseen prominence in the lives of the poor. In addition, the growing residential segregation of the poor came to represent class differences and social distances graphically. Most importantly, local policies were central to the discursive definition of the poor as a social problem and as a separate social class, sharing undesirable habits and practices and suffering from moral deficit and 'backwardness'. Ironically, the deterioration and instability of residential settlement, which arose from Improvement Trust policies themselves, went a long way to reinforcing the negative stereotypical image of the poor as rootless and underdeveloped.

All these developments were to have significant implications for the political action and perceptions of the urban poor, which will be explored in Part II of this book. It became imperative for diverse sections among the poor to contend with the impact of municipal policies in the urban locality, either in the context of work or in their residential neighbourhoods. Serious opposition and hostility developed among the poor against the urban authorities, and at times against the propertied classes, who were the usual beneficiaries of municipal policies. Moreover, the fact that various groups of the poor were the objects of municipal regulations and interventionist policies, while they had no voice in local administration, drew attention to the unrepresentative nature of the political system and the exclusion of the poor from power or rights. The political tensions that were generated as a result of all this came to influence the course of political protests and agitations, often informing nationalist politics and caste or communal conflict. Crucially, a significant motive force in the politics of the poor came from their need to reverse the negative characterisations that they faced and the urgency of undermining discipline, censure and the imposition of control, all of which accompanied the conception and implementation of local policies and urban improvement campaigns.

Despite the discursive homogenisation of the poor as a distinct social group with shared traits, local policies did not affect all groups of the poor equally, and they served in many cases to create schisms among them. Greater scarcity of housing and rivalry over economic opportunities exercised a divisive influence and contributed to competition and antagonism among the poor themselves. While their resistance against the local authorities could engender a sense of shared deprivation at the hands of municipal institutions, the differential impact of local policies on various groups of the poor also divided them. The divisive consequences of local policies reinforced the conflict over jobs, and both played decisive roles in sectarian riots.

Finally, the force and coercion employed by the local authorities, with the aid of the police, contributed in an important way to extensive political unrest and violence in urban north India in the interwar period. Confrontations between the police and the poor frequently arose in the course of dispute and conflict over local policies. This magnified the image of the poor as lawless, disorderly, violent and criminal, and provided justification for their control and discipline through policing, which is examined in the next chapter.

4   Urban policing and the poor

If urban local policies were increasingly geared to regulate the habitat and working environment of the poor in the interwar period, policing was to be directed at controlling their collective action and political behaviour in the public arena. While shifts in local policies often related to the fears about the lower orders in the minds of the propertied classes, policing additionally registered official preoccupation with the so-called 'dangerous classes'. Until the early part of the century, the chief concern of urban policing to enforce and maintain public order was addressed through three key measures. These included a physical reconfiguration of the towns for greater and swifter mobility of arms and men, organisation of a centralised constabulary force, and the institution of a system of criminal justice and laws, which empowered the police to deal especially effectively with 'offences' that were seen to affect public order adversely.[1] In the interwar period, the escalation of political unrest in the province led to significant reorientations in policing strategies. In particular, policing involved increasing armed intervention to curb or suppress political disturbances.[2] The emerging policies to control political unrest and collective action were also crucially concerned with the poor. In official perception, even well before the interwar period, the urban lower classes were unruly, violent and the worst perpetrators of disorder. The Divisional Commissioner of Lucknow in 1907 was not untypical in pronouncing that the 'poorer townspeople' were 'the most dangerous and easily excited class'.[3] However, this anxiety about potential disorder and lawlessness emanating from the poor, often associated with the particular volatility of a 'floating' population, had not played a decisive role in shaping policing policies until the 1920s. In comparison,

[1] Gyanesh Kudaisya, 'State Power and the Erosion of Colonial Authority in Uttar Pradesh, India, 1930–42', Ph.D. thesis, University of Cambridge, 1992, pp. 10–51.

[2] D. A. Low, '"Civil Martial Law": The Government of India and the Civil Disobedience Movements, 1930–34', in D. A. Low (ed.), *Congress and the Raj: Facets of the Indian Struggle, 1917–47*, New Delhi, 1977, pp. 165–98.

[3] Note by A. L. Sanders, Commissioner, Lucknow Division, dated 22 August 1907, File No. 596D, Box No. 506, Municipal Department (Block), GUP, UPSA.

in the context of the expansion of mass politics in the interwar years, worries about the public conduct and political behaviour of the poor came to be vastly magnified. Particularly alarming was the fact there were far larger numbers of them in the towns, forming a shifting, casual workforce, and often homeless too. Believed to be especially prone to the exhortation and rabble-rousing of politicians, this supposedly rootless, 'floating' population was viewed as a prime source of political disturbances and violent outbreaks. The ways in which these perceptions of the poor determined policing strategies, as well as the impact of these changing policies on the poor, are considered in this chapter.

In the 1920s and 1930s, attacks on policemen and police stations and defiance of the authority of the police came to form a recurrent pattern in the political action of the poor, either through the nationalist movement or through caste and religious politics. A large number of volunteer corps developed among the poor, which engaged in regular drills, exercises, neighbourhood patrols and parades, often with *lathis* (wooden staffs) and other weapons. They 'model[led] themselves on the pattern of the military and police forces'[4] and at times attempted 'to override law and authority' or 'to usurp the functions of the police'.[5] Indeed, the cultivation of a martial culture and the adoption of quasi-military practices were among the key motifs in the politics of the poor, suggesting a significant determining influence of policing. These political developments will be explored later but, to provide the context, this chapter investigates urban policing in the interwar years. It seeks to postulate how policing could shape the views of the poor on political power and authority, and influence their attitudes toward the state and the elites.

Structure and function of the colonial urban police force

Under British rule, urban policing in UP was organised on a regular basis shortly after the uprising of 1857, as part of the measures undertaken to consolidate civil administration. The police force was constituted as a centralised, paramilitary constabulary. The structure and functions of the urban police were governed by the broader framework of the policing policy of the government of India. While the government stipulated that the police should form a civilian force, it was also emphasised that they would replace the army in suppressing civil

---

[4] Volunteer Movement in India III, File No. 4/2/1939, Home Poll., GOI, NAI.
[5] Note on the Volunteer Movement in the United Provinces, by T. A. L. Scott O'Connor, Criminal Investigation Department, UP, dated 27 May 1922, File No. 604/1920, Box No. 132, GAD, GUP, UPSA.

disturbances. This was a major reason why the police were organised as a constabulary, with a military character.[6] As Jeffries, a former colonial officer, pointed out, the colonial police were 'organised mainly with a view to suppression of crimes of violence and mass outbreaks against the peace', and, hence, the police retained 'certain continuing supplementary functions of a military character . . . for the preservation of internal security', and reliance was 'placed upon the police to deal with any emergency calling for armed action'.[7] The primary concern of policing, then, was the maintenance of public order rather than the control of crime, other than 'crimes of violence', and the police consequently assumed an overtly military character.

In the north Indian towns, the new constabulary police system marked a departure from the pre-colonial structure of policing. The system of urban policing here had continued more or less unchanged from the Mughal times until the nineteenth century. The urban police consisted of ward *chaukidars* or watchmen and a force of city guards under the town *kotwal. Mohalla Chaukidari* or neighbourhood patrol was organised by the *panchayat* (committee or council of elders) of each ward. The kotwal, a civilian official, was responsible for the overall maintenance of law and order and the prevention and detection of crime, along with certain duties of urban local administration, such as controlling markets, slaughter houses and cemeteries; supervising weights and measures; monitoring prices and levying local taxes, market dues and tolls.[8]

Under British administration, the watch and ward duties of the *chaukidari* police and the crime control functions of the kotwal's city guards were combined and brought under the purview of an urban constabulary, with the additional function of suppression of civil disorders. Municipal administration was excluded from the duties of the police, though the constabulary force was made responsible for the enforcement of municipal regulations and by-laws. The process of the creation of a centralised constabulary police force had begun with the passing of the Police Act (V) of 1861, which divested mohalla panchayats of all responsibility for neighbourhood patrols and the power to organise watch and ward was transferred to the municipal councils, manned largely by British officials at this stage. Alongside the municipal

---

[6] For the introduction of a constabulary police force in southern India, see D. Arnold, *Police Power and Colonial Rule: Madras, 1859–1947*, Delhi, 1986, pp. 26–9.

[7] C. Jeffries, *The Colonial Police*, London, 1952, pp. 32–3. The 'military' role of the colonial police was also mentioned by another imperial official: P. Griffiths, *To Guard My People: The History of the Indian Police*, London, 1971, pp. 77, 89.

[8] H. Tinker, *The Foundations of Local Self-Government in India, Pakistan and Burma*, London, 1954, p. 17.

police, a partially armed constabulary force of town police was created under the District Superintendent of Police. The proposals of the Police Committee of 1890 paved the way for the fusion of these two branches. The Committee stipulated that Municipal Boards were to continue appointing their own watch and ward policemen, but the latter were to be enlisted under the Police Act of 1861 and placed under the control of the Superintendent of Police.[9] From the late nineteenth century, the British government gradually began to devolve the powers of municipal administration to the Indian elites. Simultaneously, however, to retain control over the police, the government entirely excluded policing functions from the purview of municipal administration and also decided to meet the entire cost of the police from the provincial revenue, replacing the hitherto prevalent system of paying the chaukidari force from municipal funds. Ward patrol under local bodies was finally abolished and the urban constabulary became responsible for watch and ward and the enforcement of municipal regulations.[10] The constabulary police were placed under the centralised control of an inspectorate, with a Superintendent of Police as the head of the urban force. The strategy of policing, the internal organisation of the police force and the extent of expenditure on it were determined by the inspectorate under the authority of the provincial government. The urban constabulary was centrally recruited and was divided into armed, civil and mounted branches. The civil police were responsible for watch and ward, municipal duties and investigation and detection of crime. The functions of the armed police included the suppression or prevention of disorder and escort duties. The mounted police were engaged in road patrol and breaking up unlawful assemblies. However, the civil and mounted branches were also deployed to deal with outbreaks of disorder.[11]

A significant change in the nature of urban policing under British administration was, thus, the creation of a centralised constabulary police force, responsible not only for watch and ward, municipal duties and the suppression of crime, but also for the control of internal disturbances, replacing the army. The consolidation of these various functions under a single force was crucial in changing the nature of the interaction between the police and the general population of the towns. The police authorities considered that 'branches of the work of the

---

[9] Cited in *Report of the Police Reorganisation Committee U.P., 1947–48* (Chairman, Sita Ram), Allahabad, 1948, vol. I, pp. 42–3.
[10] Ibid.
[11] Note on the strength and distribution of the police force, submitted to the UP Retrenchment Committee, 1931, File No. 667/1931, Box No. 208, Police Department, GUP, UPSA.

Police, which at first sight may appear to be entirely separate and distinct, are in reality interrelated and connected'.[12] The policy of policing adopted for crime control or watch and ward overlapped with, and was envisaged as an extension of, a strategy to prevent and repress political disturbances.[13] Since the same police force, though not necessarily the same personnel, came to perform all these functions, day-to-day encounters between the police and members of the public over watch and ward, the enforcement of municipal regulations and crime control could not remain isolated from more general confrontations with the police during outbreaks of disorder and armed suppression. The conduct of the police in dealing with the latter and their consequent overall image increasingly came to colour public responses to daily encounters. The new system of policing created a situation in which the role of the police in its watch and ward and municipal duties could be perceived as being integrally linked with the imposition of discipline and authority during the suppression of disorder. The police appeared primarily to be the instrument of government to impose order on local populations. The figure of the police constable also came to be associated with petty tyranny and exertions. The coercive image of the police was greatly magnified in the interwar period, evoking greater fear of oppression and *zulm* (tyranny and atrocities), because their role in suppressing disorder became increasingly overt and ubiquitous with the intensification of political disturbances and communal discord.

Urban policing between the two wars

The guiding principle: Economy versus emergency

In the interwar period, the policy of the provincial government with regard to policing was governed by two primary considerations: 'emergency situations' and 'economy'. The government was confronted with communal conflicts and nationalist agitations on a hitherto unprecedented scale, defined in official parlance as 'abnormal conditions' and 'emergencies'. Having largely replaced the army in suppressing internal disorders, the police had to play a key role in contending with communal riots, political disturbances and the disruption of law and order. Moreover, the police became far more important in maintaining urban order from the 1920s as the colonial authorities gradually lost confidence in the already imperfect mode of enforcing local control through the

[12] J. C. Curry, *The Indian Police*, London, 1932, p. 183.
[13] Arnold, *Police Power and Colonial Rule*, pp. 3, 131.

mediation of urban notables and so-called 'natural leaders'.[14] By the 1920s, new entrants to the political arena – professional politicians – staked out their claims to community leadership and displaced the 'natural leaders'.[15] The new leaders were less concerned with maintaining order, and more interested in challenging the government or in expanding their own constituency of support through agitational politics and mass mobilisation. This, coupled with the fact that the strategy of local control based on 'natural leaders' had been of limited and uneven effectiveness in the past, eroded official faith in this particular mode of control. The government now emphasised a formalised system of public order through policing. This approach, however, was not free of problems. During and after the First World War, the government found itself in severe financial straits, which were exacerbated by the economic depression of the early 1930s.[16] This necessitated measures of economy in all administrative departments. The police were no exception. The government was unable to increase expenditure on the police in order to augment the numbers and strength of the police force to match the needs of 'emergencies'. The police authorities were, therefore, required to tackle escalating political unrest and disorder with a limited force. It was this dilemma of 'economy' versus 'emergency' that gave rise to a specific strategy of policing in the interwar period, with increasing reliance placed on the armed police.

Immediately after the First World War, the UP government appointed a Civil Police Committee and a Police Decentralisation Committee, which submitted proposals for the reorganisation of the police force in 1919–20 and 1922 respectively, 'with a view to bringing the expenditure on the police to the irreducible minimum'.[17] Accordingly, the numerical strength of the provincial police force was decreased from 87,903 in 1922 to 51,885 in 1923, with a concomitant reduction in the total expenditure on the police from Rs 1,38,60,400 to Rs 1,34,29,175 (see table 4.1).[18] Another substantial curtailment of expenditure was undertaken during the depression. Between 1931 and 1933, police

---

[14] C. A. Bayly, 'Local Control in Indian Towns: The Case of Allahabad, 1880–1920', *MAS*, 5, 4, 1971, pp. 303–11; S. B. Freitag, *Collective Action and Community: Public Arenas and the Emergence of Communalism in North India*, Berkeley, 1989, pp. 70–8; S. B. Freitag, '"Natural Leaders", Administrators and Social Control: Communal riots in the United Provinces, 1870–1925', *South Asia*, 1, 2,(New Series), 1978, pp. 27–41.
[15] Ibid.
[16] B. R. Tomlinson, *The Political Economy of the Raj, 1914–1947: The Economics of Decolonization in India*, London, 1979, ch. 4.
[17] *Report on the Administration of the Police of the Uttar Provinces* (hereafter *RAPUP*), 1922, p. 39.
[18] Ibid., 1923, pp. 25, 28.

Table 4.1. *Expenditure on the UP police between the wars*

Financial year	Expenditure (Rs)
1919–20	1,31,92,000
1920–21	1,36,87,100
1921–22	1,38,60,400
1922–23	1,34,29,175
1923–24	1,34,81,800
1924–25	1,35,71,633
1925–26	1,34,94,971
1926–27	1,40,43,948
1927–28	1,42,26,803
1928–29	1,44,37,299
1929–30	1,51,98,039
1930–31	1,78,61,841
1931–32	1,71,49,706
1932–33	1,58,05,088
1933–34	1,61,92,283
1934–35	1,63,53,003
1935–36	1,62,78,533
1936–37	1,65,04,327
1937–38	1,66,10,426

Source: *Report on the Administration of the police of the United Provinces,* relevant years

expenditure declined from Rs 1,78,61,841 to Rs 1,58,05,088.[19] In 1935, the government directed that further economies were necessary, and the cost of the police was decreased to Rs 1,62,78,533 in 1935–6, from Rs 1,63,53,003 in 1934–5.[20]

Even though actual reductions in police expenditure were undertaken only in the early 1920s and again in the early 1930s, budgets remained severely restricted throughout the 1920s and 1930s. Between 1921 and 1939, overall expenditure on the police increased by less than 10 per cent, which was well below the rate of inflation.[21] Throughout the interwar period, the police authorities considered that the restricted police budget was not commensurate with requirements to meet the 'emergencies'. Successive Inspectors General of Police (IGP) repeatedly complained to the government that, owing to financial constraints and the resultant inadequacy in police numbers, they found it difficult to prevent outbreaks of disorder. In 1924, A. D. Ashdown drew the

[19] Resolution no. 2199–1/VIII–126, dated 1 October 1932, Police Department, p. 6, in *RAPUP,* 1931; *RAPUP,* 1932, p. 27.
[20] *RAPUP,* 1934, p. 18; 1935, pp. 18, 26.
[21] Kudaisya, 'State Power and the Erosion of Colonial Authority', p. 109.

attention of the government to the fact that the 'strength of the force has been fixed on the exact requirements . . . in normal conditions', when in fact, 'conditions are not normal all the time – quite the reverse' and hence 'reductions have gone too far'.[22] His successor, R. J. S. Dodd, reiterated Ashdown's view in almost identical words in 1929, even though expenditure on the police had increased between 1924 and 1929. Summing up the situation of policing in the 1920s, Dodd commented, 'looking back on the last decade I can find hardly one [year] in which conditions for the police have been normal'. He added, 'the time is ripe for a further review of the allocation and conditions of service in the police'.[23] In particular, he reported the acute shortage of city police constables.[24] In 1932, S. T. Hollins, the then IGP, expressed his own dissatisfaction with the state of affairs: 'the demand for economy has foreshadowed all other considerations, and we have been required to make sacrifices that have seriously impaired the efficiency of the force.'[25] R. Horton, the IGP in 1937, had much the same to say.[26] The continuous shortage of regular policemen, especially in the towns, from 1923 was emphasised at a later stage by the Police Reorganisation Committee of 1945:

An examination of existing strengths of Watch and Ward Police shows that these fall far below the accepted standards. There has been no revision of police strengths since 1923 except by way of reductions, and there has been no attempt to maintain Watch and Ward Police on a scale commensurate with increased demands brought about by a substantial increase in population . . . in the past 20 years.[27]

The consternation of the police authorities with a restricted budget arose because they attributed the widespread outbreak of disorder to under-policing. The official argument ran as follows: urban disturbances had their origin in the spirit of lawlessness and contempt of authority that political agitators were instilling among the masses; this lawlessness was turning into actual violation of public order, since policemen were not present in sufficient numbers to act as a disciplining force or intimidating deterrent. The District Magistrate of Kanpur, when discussing the City Police Reorganisation Scheme in 1936, specifically emphasised that the paucity of policemen in Kanpur and elsewhere had always been a difficulty in maintaining order and in controlling riots and disturbances. He argued that widespread rioting usually occurred after a series of localised affrays, each of little importance in itself, but together

---

[22] *RAPUP,* 1924, pp. 27, 32.
[23] Ibid., 1929, p. 39.   [24] Ibid., 1925, p. 42.
[25] Ibid., 1932, p. 41.   [26] Ibid., 1937, p. 20.
[27] *Report on the Reorganisation of the U.P. Police Force, 1945* (Chairman, G. A. Pearce), Lucknow, 1945, p. 12.

engendering lawlessness and ultimately full-scale riots. He contended that effective and sustained policing was indispensable to strike terror in the hearts of potentially 'lawless' elements and to prevent localised disturbances from igniting larger conflagrations. This could be achieved only with adequate numbers of regular watch and ward civil police. He reminded the government that the communal riots in March 1931 in Kanpur had got out of control because of long-term under-policing.[28] The provincial government, during periods of heightened political unrest, also appeared to agree with the local officials about the need for sustained stricter policing in preventing disorders. The Governor of UP after a tour of the province during the Civil Disobedience movement in 1930 remarked that, 'where district authorities have taken a firm attitude from the outset, the movement has been very definitely checked . . . Further, in places where it has been necessary to apply force, the situation is better than elsewhere.'[29]

The armed police

While the general official preference was clearly for stricter, more effective and extensive policing, it was also evident that this could not be achieved because of financial constraints. The total numerical strength of permanent police and manpower in UP remained more or less constant in the interwar years,[30] despite phenomenal demographic expansion and the escalation of political unrest. The solution had to be sought in concentrating available resources in selected areas to achieve maximum deterrent or preventive effect against outbreaks of disorder. The conse-quent strategy of policing that developed during the interwar period involved a strong reliance on the armed police.[31] S. T. Hollins, the IGP between 1931 and 1936, later wrote in his memoirs that 'the armed police were in fact the back-bone of the whole Civil Administration'.[32]

A widely held opinion in official circles was that, in the absence of

---

[28] District Magistrate (DM), Kanpur to Commissioner, Allahabad Division, Letter No. 2514, dated 18/19 February 1936, File No. 10/1936, Department XX, Police, Allahabad Commissioner's Office Records.

[29] Tour Report of the Governor of UP, File No. 249/1930 & K.W. Home Poll., GOI, NAI.

[30] Kudaisya, 'State Power and the Erosion of Colonial Authority', p. 108.

[31] The expansion of the armed police from the time of the First World War was not peculiar to UP. For the Madras presidency, see D. Arnold, 'The Armed Police and Colonial Rule in South India, 1914–1947', *MAS*, 11, 1, 1977, pp. 101–25. Arnold has argued that the expansion of the armed police was partly 'a direct response to the enlargement of political activity' and partly because the involvement of the army in controlling civil disorders had been substantially reduced after the First World War.

[32] S. T. Hollins, *No Ten Commandments: Life in the Indian Police*, London, 1954, p. 139.

adequate numbers of policemen, a show of armed force was the only deterrent that would effectively curb lawlessness. After a communal riot in March 1931 in Kanpur, the District Magistrate reporting his success in maintaining peace amidst continued communal tensions, argued that 'it is only the presence of 24 pickets of armed police and the knowledge that these have orders to take immediate action if riot begins, that are maintaining peace in the city now'.[33] In 1932, he argued that a large civil police force was required in the city at all times to maintain order, but the number of policemen being limited, 'it is perfectly clear that armed police in large numbers must remain [in the city] unless replaced by others [non-armed police] on a permanent basis'.[34] The Commissioner of the Allahabad Division, in a letter to the Chief Secretary of UP, endorsed this view on the ground that in Allahabad and Kanpur the deployment of the armed police had helped to contain impending outbreaks of disorder during the Civil Disobedience movement.[35]

An incident recounted in a lecture for police training by G. Waddell, a member of the UP Police, amply illustrates the workings of the official mind. The incident he described occurred in 1927 in a district town to which Waddell was posted at the time. Waddell anticipated communal clashes during a religious festival in 1927, but he did not have sufficient numbers of policemen, nor did he expect reinforcements. He therefore enlisted the help of a man from the European Mounted Volunteer Corps, who happened to be visiting the town. The man, decked out in uniform and an impressive array of firearms, menacingly paraded the street on horseback, while word was spread around that armed reinforcements were waiting just outside the town, and that the man on horseback headed the force. After describing this incident, Waddell triumphantly concluded that, as a result of this subterfuge, violence was averted and the festival passed peacefully.[36] Waddell's lecture demonstrates that police officials thought riots and disturbances could be effectively prevented only by projecting the police as an armed, disciplining and coercive agency, especially when policemen were not available in large numbers. The outcome of this strategy of policing was paradoxical. Though the police were in fact numerically weak and

---

[33] DM, Kanpur, to Commissioner, Allahabad Division, Letter No. 165, dated 8 October 1931, File No. 12/1931, Department XX, Police, Allahabad Commissioner's Office Records.

[34] DM, Kanpur, to Chief Secretary, UP, Letter No. 47B/32, dated 25 February 1932, ibid.

[35] Commissioner, Allahabad Division, to Chief Secretary, UP (Letter No. and date illegible), ibid.

[36] Transcript of a lecture delivered by G. Waddell on 'Police Action in Riots', pp. 14–15, Waddell Papers, Box No. 1, Item No. 11, MSS. Eur. F 161, Indian Police Collection. IOR.

beleaguered, their image as an armed repressive force was vigorously developed.

The armed police were deployed with increasing frequency in the towns from the 1920s, whenever disruption of public order was anticipated or actually occurred. Simultaneously, available financial resources were directed to augment the numerical strength and efficiency of the armed branch of the police. In contrast, economy drives were concentrated on the civil watch and ward branch. It was felt that the civil police could not be used as a deterrent against public disorder, unless their numbers were substantially increased, which was impossible given the financial circumstances. The trend of deploying the armed police force and developing it as a favoured branch began soon after the First World War, when reductions in police numbers were first undertaken, precisely at the time of growing nationalist agitation and communal riots. In 1922, the IGP reported that, during the latter part of the Non-Cooperation movement, the police authorities had to draft additional armed police to 'prevent or quell' disturbances, since regular police were decreasing.[37] In the circumstances, the provincial government considered it expedient to concentrate further economy measures and re-trenchment solely on the civil watch and ward police.[38] At the same time, in 1922 the government found it necessary to sanction a temporary increase of 220 officers and men in the armed branch of the police to deal with political unrest. These policemen were recruited from ex-soldiers returning from the war, equipped with service rifles and ammunition, and they received special rates of remuneration.[39] This temporary force was, however, disbanded after four months at the end of the Non-Cooperation movement.[40] When the Non-Cooperation movement was followed by an escalation in communal tensions, the government decided to form a permanent military police battalion to be called in during disturbances.[41] A policy of deputing armed policemen to accompany religious processions and to patrol during festivals was introduced on a regular basis in the towns from 1925–6, following communal riots in Allahabad and Lucknow in 1924–5.[42] In 1927, a further major expansion of the armed police was approved by the government, to meet the demands of local Superintendents of Police. It was decided to constitute an armed emergency reserve force, to be deployed during riots and disorders as well as to escort religious or

[37] *RAPUP*, 1922, p. 42.
[38] Cited in *Report on the Reorganisation of the U.P. Police Force, 1945*, p. 11.
[39] *RAPUP*, 1922, p. 42.
[40] Ibid.   [41] Ibid., p. 39.
[42] File No. 72/1925–6, Department XVIII, Judicial (Civil), Lucknow Collectorate, ERR.

political processions and to maintain order at meetings and demonstrations. For this purpose, 32 head constables, 90 *naiks* or captains and 715 constables were newly recruited.[43] Police administration reports throughout the 1920s referred to the regular deployment of the armed police in the towns.[44] In 1925, it was reported that in Lucknow every armed policeman was on duty for 327 out of 365 days in the year.[45] To increase the efficiency of the armed police, from April 1930 rearmament of the police force was also undertaken by replacing the old Martini-Henry guns with the 'far more efficient' .410 Muskets.[46] The armed police, emerging by the late 1920s as an elite corps favoured by the police authorities, enjoyed better conditions of service than the civil branch. The police administration reports of 1928 and 1929 happily noted 'improved conditions of service' in the armed police and the consequent decline in resignations from the force and requests by men from the civil police for transfer to the armed branch.[47]

The armed police were further strengthened in the 1930s. Although the economic depression in the early 1930s necessitated drastic reductions in the police budget, the government had to deal with the Civil Disobedience movement as well as with the communal riots and labour agitation that gripped the province in the 1930s. In such a situation, the police authorities had no choice but to call in the armed police more readily, even in the face of growing nationalist protests against repressive policing. Moreover, at the height of the Civil Disobedience movement, the government instituted a regime of what D. A. Low has termed 'Civil Martial Law',[48] which the police were called upon to implement. Special ordinances in this period gave the armed police a central role and extensive powers in enforcing order.[49] The government sanctioned the formation of special armed reserve forces, usually at the cost of the civil police. In 1931, it created a temporary armed reserve force of 700 men and officers.[50] In 1935–6, a permanent increase of 691 men in the strength of the armed police was ordered, with funds to be released by abolishing the Civil Emergency Reserve Force and by a reduction in the number of civil constables.[51] Moreover, in 1936–7, to 'increase the

---

[43] *RAPUP*, 1926, p. 42; 1927, pp. 43, 48.
[44] Ibid., 1924, p. 27; 1926, p. 42; 1927, p. 58; 1929, p. 30.
[45] Ibid., 1925, p. 35.   [46] Ibid., 1929, p. 30.
[47] Ibid., 1928, p. 40; 1929, p. 30.   [48] Low, 'Civil Martial Law', pp. 165–98.
[49] Ibid.; Kudaisya, 'State Power and the Erosion of Colonial Authority', pp. 149–50.
[50] D.O, Letter No. 179–8, dated 21 April 1931, addressed to the Assistant IGP, UP, File No. 1263/1931, Box No. 211, Police Department, GUP, UPSA; Resolution No. 2873/VIII-64, dated 29 September 1931, Police Department, p. 7, in *RAPUP*, 1930.
[51] *RAPUP*, 1936, pp. 14, 19. Between 1935 and 1937, the number of armed police constables increased from 6,510 to 7,101, while civil constables decreased from 20,257 to 19,421. Ibid., 1935, p. 17; 1937, p. 12.

striking power of the Force' the armed police in urban areas were equipped with motor transport, telephones and other facilities for fast communication and mobility.[52] The cost was met by a reduction in the watch and ward staff to two-thirds of its prevailing strength under the City Police Reorganisation Scheme.[53]

The Congress Ministry in the province between 1937 and 1939 continued the policy of strengthening and deploying the armed police, notwithstanding the party's own strident complaints against the police throughout the 1920s and early 1930s. The Ministry, faced with communal riots and labour agitation, decided to sanction an increase of 500 armed policemen 'in view of the urgency',[54] to be deployed specifically in the towns affected most by political unrest, including Kanpur, Lucknow, Benares and Allahabad.[55] The cost was to be met primarily by the curtailment of the watch and ward staff.[56] It was also decided to raise a permanent Armed Emergency Reserve of 600 officers and men, which would be 'specifically trained for dealing with riotous mobs and should be equipped for that purpose with the necessary motor transport, tear gas requisites and any other apparatus'.[57] In 1939, the IGP welcomed these accretions to the strength of the armed police, for they met 'the necessity . . . for the formation of a striking force to deal with emergent situations'.[58]

Thus, from the early 1920s, the armed police were strengthened and expanded in order to deal with 'emergency situations'. There were, however, constraints on the frequent and indiscriminate deployment of the armed police, owing to the political opposition it elicited. The armed intervention of the police in political agitations or communal conflicts and their actual or alleged brutalities were taken up by political parties in their campaigns against the government. In spite of the danger of provoking opposition against the government, local police authorities remained in favour of deploying the armed police whenever they felt it was necessary, having failed to devise alternative strategies. Often, they deliberately exaggerated and advertised the presence and strength of the armed police by posting pickets at prominent places and by organising route marches of armed battalions. Because they were in the midst of the so-called 'emergency situations' and responsible for maintaining

[52] Ibid., 1936, p. 19; 1937, p. 20.
[53] Cited in *Report on the Reorganisation of the U.P. Police Force, 1945*, p. 12.
[54] Note by G. B. Pant, Premier of UP, dated 30 January 1939, File No. 176/1938, Box No. 287, Police Department, GUP, UPSA.
[55] Note by S. H. Zaheer, dated 5 January 1938., ibid.
[56] Ibid.
[57] Note by R. Horton, IGP, dated 5 January 1938., ibid.
[58] *RAPUP*, 1939, p. 26.

order, political considerations took second place in their priorities. At the time of the Civil Disobedience movement in early 1932, for instance, the UP government had ordered the local police officials to refrain from armed intervention in political demonstrations, in order to avoid intensifying Congress agitations. The Superintendent of Police in Kanpur openly expressed his dissatisfaction at the government's directives, on the argument that 'if reliance is to be placed only on prosecutions and arrests, there is no possible hope of putting a stop to this continuing series of disturbances of peace'. He argued strongly that lathi charges, firing and the posting of armed police pickets were necessary.[59] P. Mason, a civil servant posted to UP in the 1930s, in a later historical work described the frame of mind of the local British officials in dealing with the political disturbances of the period. In Lucknow in 1933, Mason deployed the armed forces to prevent sectarian tensions from developing into a riot. Explaining his action, he noted that 'a temporary solution had been imposed by a threat of force', for it was 'hard to see the long term aim and easy to take the quickest way of dealing with an immediate crisis'.[60] For this reason, notwithstanding political constraints, the armed police were used frequently and their presence was made elaborately visible as a measure of deterrence. It is not, therefore, surprising that the Commissioner of the Allahabad Division could comment in 1946 that 'it is a widely believed popular misconception that the police are a heavily armed force because firearms are used in quelling disturbances'. [61]

Additional punitive police

The image of the police as a powerful and armed force of repression was further reinforced by the frequent deployment of additional police in the towns. While on occasions the government raised additional forces at its own expense, in a period of financial stringency additional police were often financed by imposing a punitive police tax, on the populations of localities affected by political disturbances, under Section 15 of the Police Act. Indeed, this measure enabled significant increases in police presence, despite an overall squeeze on police budgets. Punitive policing

[59] A note on Congress rowdyism in the Generalganj area since 1 April 1932, by the Superintendent of Police (SP), Kanpur, dated 5 April 1932, File no. 12/1931, Department XX, Police, Allahabad Commissioner's Office Records.

[60] P. Mason, *The Men Who Ruled India*, London, 1985, pp. 289–90. In this incident described by Mason, the army had also been called in.

[61] Commissioner, Allahabad Division, to Deputy Inspector General of Police (DIG), HQ, Letter No. 2376/XX-2 dated 2 April 1946, File No. 2/1946, Department XX, Police, Allahabad Commissioner's Office Records.

was not only a measure of chastisement and discipline, but also a convenient expedient to draft extra policemen in the face of a shortage of government funds. Residents of disturbed areas were asked to pay the tax either for their own protection during riots and disorders, or as a punishment for their violent misdeeds.[62]

Additional punitive police had been deployed occasionally before the First World War, but from the mid-1920s this became a regular feature of policing, especially in urban areas. In police reports, the first reference to the quartering of punitive police on a large scale appeared in 1926. In that year of serious communal rioting, punitive police were imposed in Allahabad, Bijnor and Etah.[63] The cost of these police, recovered from local residents, was the remarkably substantial sum of Rs 93,725-10-0, in comparison with the total provincial expenditure of Rs 1,34,94,971 on the police in that year.[64] In connection with communal conflicts in the late 1920s, additional punitive police were imposed in Allahabad between July 1926 and October 1928, in Lucknow in 1926 and October 1927, and in Kanpur in 1927 and 1929.[65] As nationalist agitation intensified in the early 1930s and communal conflicts continued to proliferate throughout the 1930s, the imposition of additional punitive police became a semi-permanent feature of urban policing. During the Civil Disobedience movement of 1930–2, and at the time of the communal riots of 1931 in Benares and Kanpur, punitive police were imposed in all the towns at various times. In Kanpur, for instance, punitive armed police were present for a whole year between 31 March 1931 and 31 March 1932, and intermittently before and after that period.[66] When the situations in 1921–2 and 1930–1 are compared, it becomes evident that, over the years, the government was increasingly raising additional forces at public cost, rather than from provincial revenues. Whereas in 1921–2 the number of punitive police imposed under Section 15 of the Police Act was only 136, it was 1,250 in 1930 and 1,803 in 1931.[67]

---

[62] The principle behind punitive policing has been discussed in Curry, *The Indian Police*, pp. 111–12.

[63] *PAI*, No. 26, 10 July 1926, mentions the imposition of punitive police in Allahabad.

[64] *RAPUP*, 1926, pp. 9, 38.

[65] Ibid., 1927, p. 44; 1928, p. 38; Commissioner, Allahabad Division, to Assistant IGP, UP, Letter No. 16, dated 10 May 1929, File No. 29/1928, Department XX, Police, Allahabad Commissioner's Office Records.

[66] Commissioner, Allahabad Division, to Chief Secretary, Government of UP, Letter No. 2353, dated 25 April 1932, File No. 12/1931, Department XX, Police, Allahabad Commissioner's Office Records.

[67] Resolution No. 2873/VIII-64, dated 29 September 1931, Police Department, p. 7, in *RAPUP*, 1930; Resolution No. 2199-1/VIII-126, dated 1 October 1932, Police Department, p. 6, in *RAPUP*, 1931.

The years 1936 to 1939 were characterised by a renewed outbreak of communal rioting as well as by widespread unrest and strikes among urban workers. During this period, as mentioned above, the provincial government and, during its tenure between 1937 and 1939, the Congress Ministry had undertaken the expansion of the armed police. However, additional police continued to be imposed on the basis of the punitive tax. Between March 1937 and September 1938, the total numbers of additional police stationed at various times in Kanpur, Lucknow, Allahabad and Benares were 2,197, 510, 882 and 164, respectively.[68] In 1938, 1147 additional police officers and men were enlisted, and 1,202 in 1939, along with 1,000 ex-army reservists and 400 ex-soldiers in 1938, though not entirely under Section 15 of the Police Act.[69] Benares, Allahabad, Kanpur and Lucknow were reported to have accounted for a substantial proportion of this additional force.[70]

As a result of the frequent deployment of additional policemen, the actual police presence in the towns was often much greater than the usual number of policemen sanctioned by the government. This accentuated the perception of the police as a vast, numerous and intimidating force. Throughout the 1920s and 1930s, while regular watch and ward policing could not be intensive owing to financial constraints, armed and additional punitive police were prominent in the towns. Armed policemen escorted processions, patrolled religious festivals and political demonstrations, formed pickets in areas where rioting or violence was anticipated, and engaged in route and flag marches as a demonstration of their strength. Through these measures, the police authorities deliberately projected the police as a coercive force. Against this background of the changing strategy and image of the police in the interwar period, the following section explores the nature of encounters between the police and various groups of the poor.

Control of collective action and policing the poor

The police authorities, in diagnosing the cause of growing communal conflicts and political disturbances in the towns from the 1920s, had singled out the poorer sections of the population as the main perpetrators. The Inspector General of Police unequivocally stated in 1929 that 'the poorer classes are usually the most active participants in trouble'.[71]

---

[68] Ibid., 1938 p. 4; Statement Showing Additional Police Deployed, File No. 176/1938, Box No. 287, Police Department, GUP, UPSA.

[69] *RAPUP*, 1939, p. 18; 1940, p. 18.   [70] Ibid., 1939, p. 3.

[71] IGP, UP, to the Deputy Secretary, UP, Letter No. VI-44–29, dated 25 June 1929, Serial No. 3, Proceedings No. 1 to 28 September 1930, p. 2, File No. 478/1929, Box No. 192, Police Department. GUP, UPSA.

Large urban centres with a 'shifting population, many without any settled ties', who were 'always ready for mischief',[72] were considered to be particularly vulnerable. After a serious communal riot in Kanpur in 1931, the Commission inquiring into it concluded, referring to the working population, that 'the existence of turbulent elements contributed to the spread, continuance and intensity of the trouble'.[73] The Commissioner of the Allahabad Division, in his evidence to the Commission, highlighted the 'distinct weakening of . . . the general respect for law and order', owing to the presence in the town of mill hands and casual labourers, who 'are not a very tractable lot'.[74] Similar views were aired by other British officials. The Superintendent of Police, Kanpur, expressed his alarm in 1930, that 'there is a large floating population with more or less no fixed abode'. He argued that 'a large proportion of them are bad characters', and claimed that 'gradually large bands of these lawless folk have come into existence'.[75] The Commissioner of the Allahabad Division attributed the deterioration in law and order to 'vagabonds' of 'desperate and dangerous character', who had 'no ostensible means of livelihood'.[76] The impermanent and casual nature of work for large sections of the urban labouring population as well as their shifting housing ensured that vast numbers of the poor precisely fitted these official descriptions. This served to reinforce the characterisation of the mass of the poor as 'turbulent' and 'dangerous'. This stereotype did not, of course, originate in the 1920s and 1930s. However, in this period, the growing prominence of the poor in the towns and the conflictual environment of their work and housing, coupled with mounting political disturbances, generated far greater concern about the role of the poor in political unrest and communal conflict. Colonial officials thus perceived the need for more concerted and active attempts to control the involvement of the poor in political agitation.

Even though the authorities identified the 'poorer classes' as 'the most active participants in trouble', it was not possible to subject them to stricter or intensive policing on a regular basis with a limited number of watch and ward policemen. As the poor could not be targetted

[72] Parliamentary Papers, East India (Cawnpore Riots), *Report of the Commission of Inquiry into the Communal Outbreak at Cawnpore and the Resolution of the Government of U.P.*, Session: 1930–31, vol. XII, Cmd. 3891, pp. 12–13.
[73] Ibid.
[74] Reported in *The Pioneer* (Lucknow), 27 April 1931.
[75] Extracts from a note by the SP, Kanpur, dated 3 April 1930, cited in File No. 412/1931, Box No. 206, Police Department, GUP, UPSA.
[76] A Note on the Goonda Act for the UP (N-236 P) by the Commissioner, Allahabad Division, ibid.

effectively in everyday policing, the authorities adopted a policy of concentrating on stricter policing of public events in which the poor participated, such as political demonstrations, meetings, processions and religious festivals. Crowds and public gatherings were seen by colonial officials both as prime sources of disorder and as a challenge to state authority.[77] Moreover, crowded meetings or processions were believed to be the main arenas where poorer sections of the urban population – the most disorderly elements in the official view – participated most actively, and supposedly contributed to the outbreak of disorder. As such, crowds and collective action were the key foci of colonial policing. The Indian Penal Code and the Criminal Procedure Code, as well as a range of special regulations introduced during periods of intensified political disturbances, provided the coercive instruments to deal with the menace of tumult associated with crowds and collective action.[78] The behaviour and conduct of crowds of onlookers, supporters and participants at demonstrations, pickets and processions were sought to be governed and regulated by an elaborate set of rules, backed up by a concentrated, and usually armed, police force, who frequently took recourse to baton charges or firing. The aim of such intervention in collective activities was to impose restrictions and discipline on the 'turbulent' and 'lawless elements'.

For the first time in UP, from the mid-1920s onwards, in the wake of several communal riots in various towns, the police authorities decided to depute armed police during religious ceremonies and festivals on a regular basis. Moreover, during periods of communal tension, to prevent crowd gatherings, armed policemen patrolled the streets at short intervals, staged route marches and were posted at pickets in areas considered to be 'dangerous points'.[79] Armed police accompanied religious processions and were given orders to fire at any sign of disorder.[80] The extent of the police presence during the Hindu *Dadhkando* festival of 1926 in Allahabad gives an indication of the nature of policing policy. The route of the Dadhkando procession was guarded by 200 armed policemen and all available civil policemen who could be

---

[77] S. B. Freitag, 'Collective Crime and Authority in North India', in A. Yang (ed.), *Crime and Criminality in British India*, Tuscon, 1985, pp. 141–2.

[78] Kudaisya, 'State Power and the Erosion of Colonial Authority', pp. 42–6.

[79] *PAI*, No. 26, 10 July 1926, mentions armed patrols and route marches by armed, civil and mounted police in Lucknow during a period of communal tensions.

[80] File No. 72/1925–6, Department XVIII, Judicial (Civil), Lucknow Collectorate, ERR; also cited in duplicate copy of letter from the Allahabad Municipal Tax Payers Association to the Premier, UP, Letter No. 25/XI–1R, dated 9/20 April 1928, File No. 47/1938, Department XV, GAD, Allahabad Commissioner's Office Records.

spared from regular duties; 50 armed policemen were posted at a mosque to be passed by the procession.[81] S. T. Hollins, the Superintendent of Police at that time, reported to the Deputy Inspector General that 'the police had orders not to be gentle with anyone who was out to make a disturbance, and they carried out their orders'.[82] In cases where communal clashes occurred in spite of extensive police presence, so-called 'dangerous' persons were arrested and rounded up to prevent further disturbances. In Kanpur during a communal riot in 1927, 1,000 men were arrested in a day, which included, according to the Superintendent of Police, those who were 'caught rioting' or were 'going to riot' and 'who looked dangerous'.[83] The Superintendent also reported that he had no legal difficulty in arresting these supposedly potential rioters, for he 'ran them in' for 'bad livelihood'.[84] This suggests that the targets of arrests were those who did not have permanent occupations and were, therefore, understood to have a 'bad livelihood'. This certainly included those with shifting jobs, who formed a substantial section of the urban poor. Evidently, casual labour was automatically equated with 'bad livelihood', crime and violence. This *a priori* characterisation of the poor as having 'bad livelihood' appears to have done away with the need for any evidence or onus of proof to 'run in' suspects. It is reasonable to surmise that such indiscriminate and arbitrary arrests and prosecutions caused resentment among the poor and a fear of becoming victims of police action. Not surprisingly, the Police Reorganisation Committee reported in 1947–8 that 'he [the policeman] was looked upon as a terror to be avoided at all costs'.[85]

During periods of communal tension during festivals, police authorities also often imposed curfews or issued orders under Section 144 of the Criminal Procedure Code to prohibit public gatherings or the carrying of arms. The enforcement of these orders was obviously undertaken with excessive vigour, for complaints about the conduct of the police swamped government files. In 1939, after a riot in Benares, Sampurnanand, a local Congress leader, wrote to the Congress Premier

---

[81] Cited in a letter from DM, Allahabad, to Commissioner, Allahabad Division, Letter No. 6203/S.T., dated 16 August 1937, File No. 429/1937, Box No. 589, GAD, GUP, UPSA.
[82] True copy of letter from SP, Allahabad, to DIG, UP, Range III, D.O, Letter No. 406, dated 13 September 1926, File No. 612/1926, Box No. 473, GAD, GUP, UPSA.
[83] Evidence of Mr G. A. Anderson, DIG, Allahabad (he was the SP of Kanpur at the time of the riot in 1927), given to the Kanpur Riots Inquiry Commission (KRIC), 1931; reported in *The Pioneer*, 3 May 1931.
[84] Evidence of Mr G. A. Anderson, given to the KRIC, 1931, cited in File No. 412/1931, Box No. 206, Police Department, GUP, UPSA.
[85] *Report of the Police Reorganisation Committee, 1947–48*, vol. I, p. 23.

of UP that, during the curfew period, people in poorer neighbourhoods, going to public latrines or to fetch water from municipal taps were arbitrarily arrested for 'loitering' and in certain areas inhabitants of houses were beaten up for keeping their front doors and windows open.[86] Such incidents would have added to the general hostility towards the police.

Police intervention was not confined to religious festivals and processions, but encompassed nationalist action. In the case of nationalist demonstrations, the view of police officials was that nationalist meetings, processions or pickets degenerated into 'violence' because of the participation of 'disorderly mobs' and 'crowds'. During the Civil Disobedience movement, the dispersal of crowds and 'unlawful assemblies' by force and fire-power was a common feature of policing.[87] The District Magistrate of Kanpur argued that Congress activists and demonstrators were less of a threat to public order than the 'huge riotous crowds [which] gather up [during pickets] . . . and pour forth abuse and provocative slogans. The mobs soon after take to violence, throwing stones . . . and beating people'.[88] The Commissioner of the Allahabad Division reported to the provincial government that during Congress demonstrations in the early 1930s 'by far the most dangerous element is that provided by the large crowds collected'.[89] In Kanpur, at Congress pickets of foreign cloth shops in the Generalganj market, the District Magistrate had decided not to attempt to remove the Congress volunteers, but only forcibly to disperse 'crowds of mohallawalas [neighbourhood people]', who collected there.[90] The reference to *mohallawalas* in the market suggests that labourers and hawkers, who worked and usually lived in the neighbourhood, had formed the crowds and were dispersed by lathi charges. This strategy of dispersing crowds was intended to deter the bazar poor from joining in political agitations. For the same purpose, pickets of armed policemen were posted at Moolganj in the heart of the commercial area in Kanpur. Since a large number of labourers and petty traders lived and congregated daily at Moolganj and the adjacent bazars, the area was regarded as being particularly 'turbulent'. The District

[86] Sampurnanand to the Premier, UP, Letter dated 12 May 1939, File No. 67(3)/1939 & K.W., Box Nos. 603 and 604, GAD, GUP, UPSA.
[87] Low, 'Civil Martial Law', pp. 165–98.
[88] Draft of a letter by the DM, Kanpur, to the President of the Upper India Chamber of Commerce, File No. 12/1931, Department XX, Police, Allahabad Commissioner's Office Records.
[89] Commissioner, Allahabad Division, to Chief Secretary, UP, undated, ibid.
[90] Collector, Kanpur, to Commissioner, Allahabad Division, Letter No. 387B/30, Confidential, dated 8 July 1930, File No. 151/1930, Box No. 89, Police Department, GUP, UPSA.

Magistrate of Kanpur considered the stationing of armed guards at Moolganj to be 'the pivot on which the whole scheme of policing in the city rests'. The police picket there was maintained on a regular basis, even when political agitations were not intense.[91] The urban bazars therefore constituted a chief focus of policing, which was also partly because the local merchants clamoured for protection against outbreaks of disorder.[92] As a result of the policy of dispersing crowds as well as of the location of permanent police pickets in the market areas, confrontations were frequent between the policemen and their targets, the poorer sections of the bazar population. Even a merchant in the Kanpur cloth market complained during the Civil Disobedience movement that the exertions of the police and the indiscriminate beating of local labourers in the area served to aggravate tensions and confrontations.[93]

Another police method of attenuating the supposed lawlessness of the poorer classes was the imposition of the punitive police tax. This tax, it has been seen, was a convenient expedient for the government to raise funds to draft additional policemen. It was also envisaged that 'lawless elements' would be 'chastened by this taxation'.[94] The tax was not, of course, imposed only on the poor. For the propertied classes, however, it was intended not as a punitive measure, but as a tax that citizens paid for extra police arrangements for their own protection and security.[95] The attitude of the authorities was that 'the poorer classes who are usually the most active participants in trouble, as far as possible, should be made to pay',[96] and it was officially acknowledged that 'the tax fell mainly on the poor'.[97] The District Magistrate of Lucknow argued in support of the punitive police tax in 1939 that 'the illiterate masses really understand only two things', namely, 'bodily hurt' or physical force and beating, and 'inroads on private purses' or financial penalities.[98]

---

[91] DM, Kanpur, to Chief Secretary, UP, Letter No. 94–B/32, dated 6 April 1932, File No. 12/1931, Department XX, Police, Allahabad Commissioner's Office Records.

[92] DM, Kanpur, to Chief Secretary, Government of UP, Letter No. 48–B/32, dated 26 February 1932, ibid.

[93] Copy of a letter (not signed) addressed to the President of the Upper India Chamber of Commerce, dated 8 April 1932, ibid.

[94] DM, Kanpur, to Chief Secretary, UP, Letter No. 48–B/32, dated 26 February 1932, ibid.

[95] Ibid.; *The Leader* (Allahabad), 3 January 1932, p. 15.

[96] IGP, UP, to Deputy Secretary, UP, Letter No. VI-44–29, dated 25 June 1929, Serial No. 3, Proceedings Nos. 1 to 28, September 1930, p. 2, File No. 478/1929, Box No. 192, Police Department, GUP, UPSA.

[97] Extracts from Council Proceedings of 7 March 1929, cited in Serial No. 1 of Notes and Orders, ibid.

[98] Deputy Commissioner [and DM], Lucknow, to Commissioner, Lucknow Division, Letter No. D.O. 205 C.R., dated 10 April 1939, File No. 65/1939, Box No. 602, GAD, GUP, UPSA.

Evidently, punitive policing was to supplement the armed interventionist initiatives in disciplining the poor.

Some attempts were made by the police to identify especially 'bad characters', who were considered to be prone to habitual offences against the law. A system had been in existence for some time to maintain 'history sheets' or records of activities of both known and suspected offenders and their associates, who were then subjected to police surveillance.[99] However, the dearth of watch and ward civil policemen had impaired the regular compilation of such records and the surveillance of those included in the 'history sheets'. The system was not considered to be particularly effective in controlling crime and violence.[100] Nevertheless, 'history sheets' were not abolished, for the police authorities felt that 'the fact that history sheets are maintained must exercise a restraining influence over many men'.[101] Thus, although the officials regarded the 'history sheet' system to be of limited effectiveness, its persistence was envisaged to exert a generalised measure of deterrence against 'lawlessness' by unleashing fear of surveillance, discipline and coercion. The impact of the 'history sheet' system is difficult to gauge, since details are not available of those brought under surveillance. It is possible that, although the system of surveillance may not have affected large numbers directly or was ineffective, still it may have generated fear and hostility even among those not on 'history sheets', as many were afraid of being brought under surveillance by false reporting of subordinate policemen. Indeed, the Report of the Police Surveillance Committee of 1934 acknowledged that false reporting occurred.[102] The 'history sheet' system therefore added to the intimidating and coercive image of the police.

The repressive role that the police gradually assumed in controlling political unrest and riots, as well as the deliberate projection of a tough and coercive image, gave rise to increasing confrontation between the police and various groups among the poor and contributed to hostility and resentment against the police. This, in turn, influenced the responses of the poor to day-to-day encounters with the police in other spheres, especially with regard to the implementation of sanitary measures, municipal regulations and other local policies of town improvement.

---

99 Report of the Police Surveillance Committee, 1934, File No. 251/1934 & K.W., Box Nos. 245–6, Police Department, GUP, UPSA.
100 Ibid.; Resolution No. 6971/VIII-360, dated 11 November 1930, Police Department, p. 3, in *RAPUP*, 1929.
101 Ibid.
102 Report of the Police Surveillance Committee, 1934.

Policing, discipline and municipal affairs

The urban police force was responsible for the enforcement of municipal regulations and by-laws, infringements of which could expose 'offenders' to police action and prosecutions.[103] Municipal regulations governed the plying of hackney carriages, general vending and hawking activities, the selling of food materials, the disposal of waste material and litter, the stabling and tethering of animals, public nuisance and similar other activities which had implications for urban public hygiene and sanitation. As seen in the previous chapter, the growing concern of the local authorities with the cleansing of towns as well as the tendency to discipline and control the public conduct of the poor had led to more extensive attempts to enforce the sanitary regime. Consequently, the role of the police as the guardians of such municipal regulations also became more visible, intrusive and direct. From the mid-1920s, a traffic police branch of the watch and ward civil police force was introduced in the towns as an extension of municipal policing.[104] The traffic police monitored the location of the shops and stalls of hawkers or vendors, enforced road rules for the plying of vehicles and prevented obstructions on public roads by shopkeepers, cartmen and carriage drivers.

It was in these areas that the day-to-day encounters between the police and groups of the poor were most frequent. The police were responsible for enforcing municipal regulations, but they often permitted the violation or evasion of such rules on payment of fees and bribes. In their municipal functions, moreover, the subordinate police were widely known to be guilty of 'abuse of authority and contravention of law and procedure'.[105] The Anti-Corruption Committee of 1938 confirmed the common knowledge that bribery and extortion by the subordinate police were rampant.[106] A witness to the Police Reorganisation Committee of 1947–8 similarly pointed to the magnitude of this problem: 'That corruption is widely – if not universally – prevalent in the police is a fact so well known and accepted that no argument or evidence is needed to prove it.'[107] While subordinate policemen concentrated their attention on various sections of the bazar poor, they did not normally harass the affluent and influential members of the trading

---

[103] *Report of the Local Self-Government Committee, 1938* (Chairman, A. G. Kher), Allahabad, 1939, Part II, ch. I.

[104] *Report of the Police Reorganisation Committee, 1947–48*, vol. I, p. 56.

[105] Ibid., vol. I, p. 23.

[106] Report of the Anti-Corruption Committee, 1938, pp. 3–4, File No. 70/1938, Box No. 594, GAD, GUP, UPSA.

[107] *Report of the Police Reorganisation Committee, 1947–48*, vol. II, Part II (Oral Evidence), p. 14, Evidence of a Member of the Legislative Council from Benares.

community, for fear of reprisals from their own superiors. Many were also known to be on the payroll of urban merchants, often helping to discipline their workers. With regard to the exertions of the subordinate police, the police authorities 'were in most cases unconcerned by complaints against them [i.e. subordinate police] so long as no serious trouble occurred'.[108] The officials clearly gave free rein to the subordinate police in their extortion and petty harassment. This was perhaps because it was felt that such coercion served to tyrannise and intimidate the poor in the bazars and could help to discipline them, albeit indirectly, in much the same way as the history sheet system and punitive taxation were expected to do.

In the course of their municipal or traffic duties, policemen exacted obligatory fees or *mamuli* payments from hawkers, carriage drivers and cartmen, on the threat of falsely implicating them in police cases.[109] Workers in the bazars also often fell victim to the traffic police. A complaint against one such incident at Moolganj in Kanpur was voiced in 1938 in a local newspaper by a person who called himself 'a *mazdur*' (labourer). At Moolganj, casual labourers congregated daily for recruitment to temporary jobs. The 'mazdur' complained that two policemen on fixed point traffic duty at Moolganj regularly drove away the assembled labourers by caning them, on the ground that they caused disorder and traffic obstructions. In protest, the labourers had organised a meeting at the adjacent Shera Babu Park, where the police lathi charged and dispersed them.[110] Labourers, hawkers or transport workers had to devise ways and means of contending with such exertions of the subordinate police by entering into networks of bribery, regular payments and patronage with them, whenever possible. This, of course, accentuated conflicts between rival traders, hawkers, cartmen or labourers, for some could gain advantage over others by bribing policemen. However, the main impact of bribery was to intensify hostility toward the police. For, despite the informal patronage and protection that the subordinate police provided, their relationship with bazar workers and hawkers was essentially unequal, because they derived their authority from the state. The workers and vendors clearly entered into a nexus of bribery with the police not out of choice, but from compulsion to avoid the rigorous imposition of municipal rules or to prevent harassment. Importantly, in the 1930s, interaction and contact between local people and the police, beyond the official duties of the police, were decreasing. Policemen were recruited through a centra-

---

[108] *Report of the Police Reorganisation Committee, 1947–48*, vol. I, p. 23.
[109] Ibid.
[110] *Pratap* (Kanpur), 31 July 1938, p. 6.

lised system from all over the province and seldom from local neighbourhoods. There was also a significant trend towards concentrating
policemen in centrally located police stations and outposts, where
housing conditions were better, and from where the limited forces could
be effectively deployed. This entailed 'the removal of police units to
places distant from the areas in which they were required to patrol'.[111]
Such residential and social distance reinforced the image of the police as
a disciplining, coercive agency imposed from outside by the state.

The police played an increasingly prominent role in the growing
conflicts over town improvement and clearance drives in the 1920s and
1930s. As shown in the previous chapter, the Municipal Boards and
Improvement Trusts sought to remove and demolish encroachments or
unauthorised constructions on public land and to acquire congested and
insanitary areas of habitation. Naturally those who were affected by
these measures did not submit to such dispossession passively, and
resistance against the municipal authorities increased. The latter therefore called for police help more frequently to deal with these conflicts.
Police authorities considered it necessary to intervene in such municipal
disputes as potential sources of unrest and disorder. This was also a way
of curbing recalcitrance and protest among diverse groups of the poor,
which could serve the wider purpose of deterring their 'lawlessness' and
imposing discipline. In 1938, the District Magistrate of Kanpur informed the Chairman of the Municipal Board that 'the SP [Super-
intendent of Police] has ordered all his station officers to give the
Municipal Board every assistance in demolishing unauthorised structures'. He also reported that the encroachers 'obstruct the officers in the
performance of their duties or abuse or assault them', as a result of
which the offenders were being subjected to criminal prosecution.[112]

Such intervention of the police in municipal affairs opened up
another area of confrontation between the police and various groups of
the poor. In these cases of removal of encroachments or enforcement of
eviction orders, police action affected increasingly larger numbers of the
poor in the 1920s and 1930s. Furthermore, the intervention of the
police was usually decisive in bringing about eviction or removal, thus
augmenting the constraints that the poor faced in securing trading
opportunities or land for housing and shop space. The police could thus
be seen by the poor as a significant element in reinforcing their
dispossession and hardship, quite apart from being a disciplining,

---

[111] *Report on the Reorganisation of the U.P. Police Force, 1945*, p. 12.
[112] DM, Kanpur, to Chairman, Municipal Board, Letter No. 1266, dated 9 November
1938, File No. 1–35/1938, Department XXIII, Municipal. Kanpur Collectorate,
ERR.

intimidating force. Not surprisingly, clashes between the poor and the police regularly featured in the press and police files.[113] Inhabitants of poorer localities who were targets of forcible eviction by the police as well as occupational groups such as transport pliers, carters, bazar labourers and hawkers resolutely protested against police high-handedness, arrest and prosecution.

The importance of the police in municipal and local affairs was enhanced at a time when the government was presenting the police as a powerful armed force and deploying them to exercise greater coercive power and repression over the urban masses. At the same time, municipal policing sought to discipline and control the poor. The roles of the police in enforcing municipal regulations and in imposing political control increasingly overlapped. Encounters in the bazars arising from the enforcement of local policies ran alongside the general policy of intensive, often armed, policing of crowds and collective action in these areas. Within this context, the petty tyrannies and high-handedness of the police in day-to-day encounters assumed more menacing proportions. Together these various developments reinforced the overall repressive and tyrannical image of the police and elicited both fear and hatred of their regime of coercion and atrocity (zulm).

Political implications

What conclusions can be drawn about the possible impact of the changing strategy of policing in the interwar period on the political actions and perceptions of the poor? Policing from the 1920s onwards emphasised the suppression of disorder, with the poor as major targets, while at the same time the authorities upheld a deliberate policy of projecting the police as a disciplining and intimidating force. This was clearly aimed at presenting the police as the mailed fist of the government, and, indeed, this was largely achieved in practice. The police were the most visible public face of a repressive state in everyday life. The state appeared to be primarily a coercive institution, imposing itself illegitimately upon the population. Discipline and control were manifest as its main functions. Public perception of this role of the police and the related repressive character of the state was further fortified by the demonisation of the government by nationalist politicians, who ceaselessly cited the police as the chief manifestation of the coercive power of

---

[113] *Police Abstracts of Intelligence* and local newspapers frequently reported such incidents. For example, *PAI*, No. 23, 19 June 1937; No. 32, 21 August 1937; No. 17, 30 April 1938; No. 25, 25 June 1938; No. 32, 13 August 1938; No. 44, 5 November 1938. These incidents are discussed in chapters 8 and 9 below.

the colonial state. For the poor, their actual experience of increasing confrontation with the police lent credence to this projected image of the police as the strong arm of the state. This elicited antagonism not only against the police directly, but also crucially against the colonial state. Within this context, various groups of the poor could attribute the petty tyrannies and extortion of the subordinate police in daily encounters to the power and authority that the police derived from the state. Escalating day-to-day exertions could thus be seen as an aspect of the increasing coercive intent of the state. That the harassment and extortion of the police in the course of their municipal or traffic duties would breed hostility is only to be expected. However, from the 1920s, as a consequence of the prominence of the coercive image of the police and the colonial state, resisting both the police and the state assumed a greater political relevance among the poor, and found expression through nationalist agitations and other forms of protest.

The nature of policing in the interwar period not only shaped the attitudes of the poor towards the state, but, in specific situations, also influenced their perception of various sections of urban elites. In certain cases, the police acted or appeared to be acting at the behest of employers or the urban local authorities, such as when they assisted in anti-encroachment drives or broke up pickets and demonstrations during labour or nationalist agitations or when subordinate policemen intervened in local disputes on behalf of employers, creditors or landlords.[114] At other times, such as during Civil Disobedience demonstrations in the Kanpur bazars, urban merchants, in order to ensure the unimpeded flow of business and trading activities, openly and actively lent their support to the police authorities in suppressing political unrest and in preventing the participation of bazar employees in nationalist agitations. The local merchants demanded stricter and more extensive police arrangements and, at times, showed a willingness to make financial contributions to the cost of drafting additional policemen.[115] In these cases, the urban authorities and employers could be seen to be enlisting the help of the police to strengthen their own position. As the police clearly emerged to be an intimidating force, instances of their action on behalf of urban elites and local authorities created or reinforced a coercive image of the latter two in the minds of the poor. For example, when the police fired at pickets of striking labourers of the

[114] The embroilment of subordinate policemen in local disputes is particularly highlighted in Police Administration Report of the Allahabad Division, 1927, File No. 11/1927–28, Department XX, Police, Allahabad Commissioner's Office Records.

[115] DM, Kanpur, to Chief Secretary, UP, Letter No. 48–B/1932, dated 26 February 1932, File No. 12/1931, Department XX, Police, Allahabad Commissioner's Office Records; *PAI*, No. 14, 9 April 1932.

Cawnpore Cotton Mills in 1924, killing six workers, the mill authorities were branded as the 'killers' owing to the manner in which the police had acted on their behalf, and the mill came to be known as the 'Murderous Cotton Mill' among Kanpur labourers.[116] Similarly, many sections of urban workers turned against the Congress leadership in the province in the period of provincial autonomy in 1937–9, on the grounds that police action against striking workers had been extensively sanctioned by the Congress Ministry, and therefore the Congress Party was acting in the interests of employers and following in the footsteps of the colonial state in unleashing a reign of police oppression.[117]

There was another somewhat different, but related and important implication of policing on the politics of the poor. Policing strategies and official concern with law and order, in effect, 'criminalised' and 'outlawed' the poor as the prime culprits in violence and political unrest. This characterisation of the poor, in turn, invigorated the middle-class preoccupation with the improvement and discipline of the poor, be it through urban renewal or social reformism. All these various discourses of reform and control reinforced each other and all portrayed the poor in negative terms as needing either discipline or uplift and betterment. Not surprisingly, the politics of the poor would, to a significant extent, come to be driven by the urgency to overcome the stigma attached to them, not least through policing principles and practice, and to reverse the consequent social exclusion and marginalisation that they came to face.

For all these reasons, as the following chapters will show, defying or attacking the police emerged as a recurrent motif in the political action of the poor, not simply to contend with direct police repression or petty tyrannies, but also to contest the power of the state or the elites. In this context, the formation of volunteer corps, along with martial and quasi-military activities, would come to assume central significance in the politics of the poor as the means to undermine or symbolically usurp the power of the police. The relevance of the volunteer activities to the poor lay in their significance as acts of defiance against the imposition of authority and discipline. Replicating or imitating the actions and forms of organisation of the police in this way could be seen by various groups of the poor as a form of empowerment. At the same time, orderly martial activities could help the poor to portray and express themselves

---

[116] *Report of the Non-Official Enquiry Committee Regarding the Shooting of Mill Hands at the Cawnpore Cotton Mills Company, 1924*, Kanpur, 1924. N. P. Arora Collection, Printed Material, Serial No. 10, NML; Sudarshan Chakr, *Kanpur Mazdur Andolan Ka Itihas*, Kanpur, 1986, pp. 22–4.
[117] This point is fully discussed in chapter 9 below.

as heroic warriors and thus to overcome the image of being a violent and fractious underclass. Not surprisingly, as it will be illustrated later, religious, caste and nationalist politics in the interwar period all involved volunteer units and nurtured a martial culture in varying degrees. In turn, these developments ultimately contributed to the extensive eruption of violence. Interventionist, armed and coercive policing in themselves often met the counter-violence of the poor, thus further augmenting the extent of urban violence. Indeed, the escalation of violence in the interwar years related very significantly to the changing patterns of policing. The shifts in policing in this period clearly emerged as a significant factor in shaping the politics of the poor.

Part II

Modes of political action and perception

5   Untouchable assertion

Urban transformation in the early twentieth century profoundly affected the social and political experience of the poor, and shaped the ways in which they came to understand the world and their place in it. At the heart of this process was their quest for new identities and the search for new cognitive frameworks to conceptualise the nature of change. These ontological endeavours to imagine the self and its relation to the world and others in rapidly evolving settings provided the central dynamic behind the construction and reformulation of religious, class, caste and nationalist ideologies among the poor. The forging of new identities and political vocabularies constituted the responses of the poor to changing relations of power, inequality and domination, and encapsulated variously their resistance to, negotiation with or contestation of power. By constructing new forms of identity, the poor redefined their subjectivity as political actors and reconceptualised their own capabilities and potentials as human agents. This defined the nature of their political endeavours and collective action, aimed to interrogate extant norms of hierarchy and power. With this analytical perspective, and against a backdrop of the extensive social transformation of the early twentieth century, discussed in the first part of this book, the second part now turns to the changing political identity and action of diverse groups of the poor. This chapter concentrates on the untouchable poor and explores their experience of caste distinctions in the towns, their fashioning of new forms of caste identities and the nature and significance of caste and religion based social movements among them. In particular, the inter-connections and symbiosis between their identities based on caste, religion, status, labour, deprivation, inequality and domination are examined.

In an article entitled *Chhote aur Bade ka Sawal* ('The Question of the Big and the Small People'), written in 1938, Kashi Baba, a Kanpur mill worker, while discussing the nature of deprivation, identified caste status as a significant element.[1] He introduced the 'big person' as

[1] *Samyavad* (Kanpur), 27 November 1938, p. 6.

Shoshak Chand. A 'shoshak' is an exploiter and 'Chand' is the colloquial version of *Chandra*, a name prevalent among the higher castes. The 'small person' he called *Dalit Ram*. 'Ram' is a second name widely used by untouchables, while the term *dalit* (literally the downtrodden), had gradually come to denote the untouchables in the early twentieth century. Kashi Baba described *Shoshak Chand* as a wealthy person, capable of *chori*, or stealing, not in the sense of thieving, but as one who appropriates social resources and deprives people like Dalit Ram and thus becomes rich. Shoshak Chand was also educated and therefore, *shaktishali*, or powerful, for he was able to deceive and dominate Dalit Ram by dint of his education. Kashi Baba also presented *Sita Ram Bajpaye*, a high-caste person, to whom *Maikulal* was always forced to be subservient, the latter being an untouchable and considered to be low in status. In identifying the differences between the 'big' and the 'small' people in this way, Kashi Baba indicated low-caste status as a significant determinant of being poor, illiterate and powerless. Thus, he postulated a specific perspective from which the nature of caste relations and its implications were perceived in the 1930s.

This view, expressed in Kashi Baba's exposition,[2] was noticeable in religious and social movements which developed among poorer untouchables in the early twentieth century in the towns of UP. They attacked caste inequalities through an assertion of *bhakti* devotionalism, a rejection of vedic Hinduism and the construction of a pre-Aryan identity of the untouchables as the original inhabitants – Adi Hindu – of India. Significantly, a well-known trend of twentieth-century caste movements, which involved a claim to higher status within the caste hierarchy and which occurred among upwardly mobile untouchables in UP,[3] was less noticeable among the poorer sections of the community. With a focus on bhakti revival and on the assertion of Adi Hindu identity, this chapter discusses the nature and significance of caste-based social movements from the perspective of the untouchable poor in a rapidly changing urban milieu. The forms of caste-based politics among the untouchable poor are also investigated within the context of wider political developments. In particular, attention is paid to the efforts of Hindu reformist and revivalist groups to incorporate the untouchables into the caste hierarchy, and to Gandhian nationalist initiatives to uplift *harijans* ('children of god' – Gandhi's coinage to refer to untouchables).

---

[2] Kashi Baba himself may not have belonged to an untouchable caste.
[3] Lynch discusses movements for upward mobility within the caste hierarchy among untouchable Jatavs in Agra city. Owen Lynch, *The Politics of Untouchability: Social Mobility and Social Change in a City of India*, New York, London, 1969, pp. 67–85 and passim.

The untouchable poor in the urban milieu and bhakti resurgence

From the late nineteenth century, untouchable caste groups from rural areas had begun to migrate to Allahabad, Benares, Kanpur and Lucknow, where demand for the menial services they performed was expanding. As noted in previous chapters, after the uprising of 1857, British military and civil administrations were consolidated in the towns and army cantonments and civil stations were reconstituted on a larger scale. To accommodate these, as well as the settlement of Indian professional groups and government servants who converged on the towns, urban built-up areas extended very substantially. Urban territorial growth was coupled with the extensive expansion of sanitary infrastructure and municipal services, which created a demand for scavengers, sweepers and conservancy workers. Moreover, British bureaucrats, civil servants and military personnel, who settled in the towns, required domestic servants and retainers. Untouchable groups, such as *mehtars*, *bhangis*, *chamars* and *doms*, found jobs in cantonments and civil lines and with the municipalities. Caste Hindus were usually disinclined to perform work of this nature owing to notions of ritual pollution or loss of status associated with cleansing and menial work, leaving employment in these areas open for the untouchables. In Kanpur, chamars and *mochis*, who were often skinners of dead animals or leather workers in the countryside, were also employed in the newly developing leather factories and tanneries set up by the government and British industrialists.[4]

The nature of incorporation of untouchable rural migrants in the urban labour force marked a change from their past economic and social relations of work in the countryside. In the towns, the untouchables ceased to be servile labourers of the higher castes, and worked instead as paid municipal employees or domestic servants of the British, and at times in factories.[5] This did not necessarily bring them affluence or economic self-sufficiency, but the nature of the urban occupations of untouchables came to undermine their direct caste subordination at work. Though wage employment was not free from economic conflict and exploitation, it could give rise to a sense of liberation among dominated caste groups, for whom caste subordination had been the

---

[4] *RCLI*, III:I, p. 241, Evidence of the Superintendent, Harness and Leather Factory, Cawnpore; H. R. Nevill, *Cawnpore: A Gazetteer: vol. XIX of the District Gazetteers of the United Provinces of Agra and Oudh*, Allahabad, 1909, pp. 104, 117.

[5] The *District Gazetteer* of Kanpur in 1909, for instance, commented about the chamars that, while in the fields 'formerly their position was that of mere serfs', in Kanpur city 'they are well off [as] is evident from the state of the labour market'. Ibid., p. 104.

prominent social experience in rural areas. The sense of relaxation of caste domination in the towns was likely to have been especially significant in the context of a recent rural history of tightening caste controls and a rigidification of the ritual hierarchy in the nineteenth century, which had occurred in the course of the expansion of settled agriculture and the pacification of the countryside under British rule.[6] The altered circumstances of the untouchables in the towns did not, however, mean that social distinctions based on caste dissolved.

The experiences of segregation and exclusion of the untouchables in rural life were not reversed in the urban context. Colonial sociology and British classification of caste groups on the basis of occupation tended to 'fix' the untouchables in particular kinds of urban jobs, especially as sweepers, scavengers and skinners or handlers of dead animals. The untouchables were absorbed almost entirely in ill-paid, menial service jobs or in work connected with handling leather, in keeping with their 'traditional' 'low' or 'impure' occupations. While this did create protected enclaves of employment for the untouchables in the urban labour market, it prevented occupational mobility, and with time even produced a glut in employment opportunities. Alternative avenues of employment were virtually non-existent. Touchable Hindu low-caste *shudra* groups had a near-monopoly over unskilled manual work in the trading sector and manufacturing, for the high-caste Hindu employers there seldom recruited untouchables.[7] Nor were the untouchables able to venture into trades and occupations, other than 'impure' ones such as leather work. This was, however, not entirely because of their low status, but also the result of their general poverty and lack of capital, even to undertake petty trading. The untouchables also had very little opportunity to enter educational institutions, both because of the expense and because these institutions were usually unwilling to accept untouchable students. Being mostly illiterate, they were seldom employed in the lower government services in clerical posts. Before 1934 they were not recruited to the subordinate ranks of the police force.[8] Occupational divisions along the lines of caste, often prevalent in the rural situation, were thus being replicated in urban areas, notwithstanding the relaxation of direct caste domination in employment relations. This could generate or accentuate a sense of ritual discrimina-

[6] C. A. Bayly, *Indian Society and the Making of the British Empire: New Cambridge History of India: II.1*, Cambridge, 1987, pp. 136–68.
[7] Mentioned in Ram Shankar Shukla, 'Karmchari Sangathan aur Andolan Kyun?', in *Kanpur Bazar Karmchari Federation: Rajat Jayanti Smarika* (Kanpur Market Employees' Federation: Silver Jubilee Souvenir), Kanpur, 1977, editorial article (pages not numbered).
[8] *Report on the Administration of the Police of the United Provinces*, 1935.

tion among the untouchables, especially when juxtaposed against a new experience of relative independence at work. Occupational distinctions were coupled with spatial segregation in terms of the untouchables' residential settlement patterns. The untouchables had lived on the village periphery; in the towns, they similarly had no access to the residential areas of higher castes. Untouchable settlements were concentrated in secluded pockets on urban outskirts or in unreclaimed, insanitary areas, almost invariably devoid of water supply and conservancy facilities, or in the isolated niche of servants' quarters in cantonments and civil stations.[9] In the rare cases when they lived in urban slum complexes along with people of other castes, their houses formed separate blocks.[10] Caste distribution in urban neighbourhoods thus also provided ample expression of caste distinctions. Both occupational and residential segregation thus tended to ossify the low status and social subordination of the urban untouchables.

In the late nineteenth and early twentieth centuries, therefore, the untouchable migrants to the towns were exposed to two contrary trends. On the one hand, caste domination to a large extent ceased to be a feature of occupational relations. It would be reasonable to surmise that this was also likely to have created expectations and aspirations for economic advancement, improved living conditions and education. On the other hand, continued caste distinctions in employment or educational opportunities and settlement patterns, as well as their general poverty, thwarted economic or social improvement. Moreover, the way in which the higher castes viewed the untouchables had clearly not changed. The two simultaneous processes together appear to have created an urgency among untouchables to assert themselves and to undermine caste barriers, for it was in the early twentieth century in the towns that heterodox bhakti devotionalism gained a large following among urban untouchables.[11] That the idiom of their self-assertion took this form is not surprising, for bhakti encapsulated a message of social

[9] Allahabad Municipal Board Annual Report, 1937–38, pp. 38–42; R. Mukerjee and B. Singh, *Social Profiles of a Metropolis: Social and Economic Structure of Lucknow, Capital of Uttar Pradesh, 1954–56*, London, 1961, pp. 4–5.; Vidyadhar Agnihotri, *Housing Condition of Factory Workers in Kanpur*, Lucknow, 1954, pp. 32–3; A. Singh, 'Varanasi: A Study in Urban Sociology', Ph.D. thesis, Benares Hindu University, 1971, pp. 81–2; B. N. Pande, *Allahabad: Retrospect and Prospect*, Allahabad, 1955, pp. 345–58.

[10] C. Joshi, 'Bonds of Community, Ties of Religion: Kanpur Textile Workers in the Early Twentieth Century', *IESHR*, 22, 3, 1985, p. 254.

[11] The revival of bhakti and the emergence of the new religion of Ad Dharm in the towns of the Punjab in the early twentieth century had a different social origin. Here, a relatively affluent section of untouchable entrepreneurs had emerged, for whom bhakti and Ad Dharm provided the 'symbols of identity and ethical standards for a new species of lower caste entrepreneur'. Mark Juergensmeyer, *Religion as Social Vision: The Movement against Untouchability in 20th-century Punjab*, Berkeley, 1982, pp. 115–23.

equality.[12] Bhakti was a way of worshipping god through devotion and personal communion, in which one's caste could be eliminated or could become irrelevant, as all were considered to be equal in the eyes of god.

Devotionalism or bhakti had been the dominant form of Hindu worship in medieval north India for several centuries. From the latter part of the fifteenth century, bhakti became broadly bifurcated into the *saguna* and *nirguna* traditions.[13] Followers of saguna bhakti believe the divine being to be 'with form' or 'attribute', and hence they worship anthropomorphic manifestations of gods, usually Vishnu or Shiva, relating respectively to the *Vaishnavite* and *Shaivaite* traditions of devotionalism. Believers of nirguna bhakti, in contrast, worship a formless universal god, but have, at the same time, faith in the partial embodiment of god in the person and words of poet-saints (*guru* or *sant*), such as Ravidas or Kabir, who are considered figures of veneration. Historically, saguna bhakti, with its most important north Indian literary expression in the works of Tulsidas and Surdas, had been a powerful religious force, followed by a diverse range of caste groups. Saguna bhakti provided a socially integrative message to unify all castes through devotional worship, but affirmed a framework of belief based on the *varnashrama dharma* and the caste system. While saguna bhakti represents the dominant version of north Indian devotional Hinduism, nirguna bhakti developed partly in opposition to it among lower castes as a heterodox devotional alternative, and partly to resist hierarchical, brahmanical Hinduism through an egalitarian religious message.[14] It was this version of nirguna bhakti or *sant-mat* (ideology of the sants) which found widespread following among urban untouchables in the early twentieth century.

Although nirguna bhakti, propounded by sants or gurus (teachers or preceptors) such as Kabir and Ravidas, had developed gradually in north India from the fifteenth century onwards amongst lower-caste groups, this tradition remained a 'subordinate, minority tradition', subject to the

---

[12] D. N. Lorenzen (ed.), *Bhakti Religion in North India: Community, Identity and Political Action*, New York, 1995, pp. 1–32; Joseph Schaller, 'Sanskritization, Caste Uplift and Social Dissidence in the Sant Ravidas Panth', in ibid., pp. 105–16; K. Schomer and W. H. McLeod (eds.), *The Sants: Studies in a Devotional Tradition in India*, Delhi, 1987, pp. 1–17; David Lorenzen, 'The Kabir Panth and Social Protest', in ibid., pp. 281–303; Jayant Lele (ed.), *Tradition and Modernity in Bhakti Movements*, Leiden, 1981, pp. 1–15.

[13] C. Vaudeville, '*Sant Mat*: Santism as the Universal Path to Sanctity', in Schomer and McLeod (eds.), *The Sants*, pp. 21–40.

[14] Lorenzen (ed.), *Bhakti Religion*, pp. 1–32; Schaller, 'Sanskritization, Caste Uplift and Social Dissidence in the Sant Ravidas Panth', pp. 105–16; Schomer and McLeod (eds.), *The Sants*, pp. 1–17; Lorenzen, 'The Kabir Panth and Social Protest', pp. 281–303; Lele (ed.), *Tradition and Modernity*, pp. 1–15.

'hegemony of the saguni tradition'.[15] Moreover, some bhakti cults, such as the Kabirpanth, after their heyday in the fifteenth to the seventeenth centuries during the so-called *bhakti-kal*, or the age of bhakti, had either become absorbed within mainstream Hinduism or gradually grown more exclusive and often survived primarily among orders of *sadhus* or ascetic mendicants.[16] At the end of the nineteenth century, the British ethnographer-administrator William Crooke reported that many bhakti sects in rural areas, especially in the case of heterodox bhakti sects of lower castes, were closed groups, which practised secrecy in their activities and followed strict rites of initiation.[17]

In the early twentieth century, however, adherence to bhakti religion and the veneration of Kabir, Ravidas and other lower-caste sants became much more widespread among urban untouchable migrants in UP.[18] From the turn of the century, many untouchables in the towns began to call themselves *bhagats*, a term which denoted lay practitioners of bhakti cults, who were not ascetics of insular religious sects. They also often added the terms *Kabirpanthi*, *Shivnarayani* or *Ravidas/Raidas* after their names to indicate the gurus whom they revered. They projected themselves as adherents of bhakti by wearing necklaces of beads, called *kanthis*, which were distinctive marks of bhakti sects, in self-conscious rejection of the brahmanical sacred thread or *janeyu*.[19] When the untouchable migrants settled in the towns, they reconstituted their caste *panchayats* (councils of elders) in urban neighbourhoods, which dealt with internal disputes among members of caste groups and stipulated the religious and social practices to be observed. Many of these panchayats were named after bhakti gurus, such as the Ravidas Chamar Panchayats in all the towns.

Temples dedicated to bhakti sants were also refurbished or newly constructed in the early twentieth century. These temples were neighbourhood shrines, established gradually over extended periods on the initiative of local priests or the panchayats, financed by small donations from members of the local community of untouchables. Funds for temple-building were raised from voluntary donations at religious congregations or at the meetings of panchayats, which were attended by many caste members, and each person or family contributed small sums

---

[15] Lorenzen (ed.), *Bhakti Religion*, p. 13.
[16] J. T. F. Jordens, 'Medieval Hindu Devotionalism', in A. L. Basham (ed.), *A Cultural History of India*, Oxford, 1975, p. 275.
[17] W. Crooke, *The Tribes and Castes of the North-Western Provinces and Oudh*, Calcutta, 1896, vol. II, pp. 184–8.
[18] G. W. Briggs, *The Chamars*, London, 1920, p. 210.
[19] It was mentioned in several interviews that I conducted in the towns that at the turn of the century 'everyone' became bhagat and kanthidhari (wearer of kanthi).

of money. The consequent slow accumulation of funds was the reason temple construction was often a gradual process. Individual untouchables in the towns were usually not affluent enough to be able to finance temple-building, and hence these had to be community efforts.[20] A Shivnarayani Sant Sampradaya, or a congregation of disciples of the saint Swami Shivnarayan, was initiated in Allahabad by the untouchable chamars, who came to the towns to work in the British cantonment as horse-keepers, gardeners and domestic servants.[21] The religious head or *mahant* of this congregation was called the *Brigade Mahant*. The term 'Brigade' in this case indicates the roots of the Shivnarayanis in urban military cantonments, and suggests that the worship of Swami Shivnarayan was either initiated or re-emerged in the towns, rather than being a continuity of rural cults. In Benares, an old Shivnarayani temple was repaired for worship by the growing number of devotees. Regular readings of *Gyan Dipak*, a book authored by Swami Shivnarayan, were organised at the temple.[22] In Kanpur, a Shivnarayani temple had been set up in a low-caste neighbourhood in Colonelganj. Two Kabirpanthi temples had also been erected in Kanpur at the chamar mohallas (neighbourhoods) of Benajhaber Idgah Colony and Collectorganj.[23] In Lucknow, a Ravidas temple was gradually constructed between the mid-1920s and mid-1930s, as contributions trickled in from worshippers. In a dom mohalla (neighbourhood of untouchable doms) in Benares, by 1929, a panchayat headman established a temple dedicated to Lord Shiva, regarded as a deity personifying bhakti and religious heterodoxy. On the four corners of the temple, busts of well-known bhakti saints had been placed.[24] Neighbourhood celebrations and town-wide processions on the occasion of the birth anniversaries of bhakti gurus had also begun to be organised by the 1920s.[25] Regular sessions of devotional singing – *bhajans* and *kirtans* – as well as religious meetings called *satsangs* (keeping 'good company' or associating with sants and imbibing their teachings) for the discussion of bhakti ideology and the messages of the sants were held in untouchable neighbourhoods and at temples dedicated to bhakti saints.

In this way, bhakti devotionalism came to be practised more exten-

---

[20] Interview with D. C. Dinkar (untouchable politician) in Lucknow.
[21] Interview with the present head priest or mahant of the Shivnarayanis in Allahabad in 1987.
[22] Interviews with the mahant of the temple and with Ram Narayan, a member of the governing body of the temple.
[23] Interview in Kanpur with Hanuman Prasad Kureel, an untouchable politician.
[24] Interview in Benares with Gopi Dom (a leading member of the local dom panchayat) and my own visit to the temple.
[25] Interviews with untouchable politicians: Hanuman Prasad Kureel in Kanpur and Sita Ram Visharad in Benares.

sively by the urban untouchables from the early twentieth century. For the untouchable poor in the towns, the message of caste equality and the denial of ritual hierarchy in bhakti gave them a means to question the discriminations, disabilities and deprivation that they continued to face. This was in contrast to those upwardly mobile sections of untouchables who, as counter-elite aspirants, sought to find a niche in caste Hindu society, and claimed higher status and respectability through 'sanskritisation' within the caste hierarchy rather than stepping outside it.[26] However, for the poorer untouchables, lacking the economic affluence or political bargaining power of their more successful counterparts, 'sanskritised' behaviour or claims to high-caste ranking were likely to have been disregarded by the upper classes and castes. Such attempts at ritual ascendance within the caste system were unlikely either to bring about any substantive change in the material condition of the urban untouchable poor or to reverse their social subordination and marginalisation.[27] Instead, a more radical approach of denying caste distinctions was appropriate to their quest for dignity and the assertion of their rights. Their social location and life experience in the changing urban milieu of the interwar years were, thus, important determinants in their espousal of bhakti devotionalism. In his study of untouchables in Lucknow a few decades later, Khare has also noted a variety of social and religious action among them and commented that they 'demonstrated a generally patterned response . . . , depending both on where they stood socially, and on their practical experiences, needs and expectations'.[28]

It is significant that, in the resurgence of heterodox devotionalism among the poorer untouchables, bhakti was conceived explicitly and primarily as an egalitarian ideology which opposed the caste hierarchy. While medieval bhakti had provided the possibility of salvation for all and thus implicitly promised social equality, its radical social message, as Fuller points out, was fleshed out largely in the course of the social and religious reform movements of the last couple of centuries. Through these more recent movements, Fuller argues, 'devotionalist ethic come[s] to be widely reinterpreted as a charter of egalitarianism'.[29]

[26] Lynch, Politics of Untouchability, pp. 67–85.
[27] M. N. Srinivas, who formulated the notion of 'sanskritisation' through the emulation of higher-caste practices, himself recognised that 'sanskritisation results only in positional changes in the [caste] system and does not lead to any structural change'. M. N. Srinivas, Social Change in Modern India, Berkeley, 1968; Indian edn, Delhi, 1972, p. 7.
[28] R. S. Khare, The Untouchable as Himself: Ideology, Identity and Pragmatism among the Lucknow Chamars, Cambridge, 1984, p. 87.
[29] C. J. Fuller, The Camphor Flame: Popular Hinduism and Society in India, Princeton, 1992, p. 158.

At the same time, this particular resurgence of twentieth-century egalitarian bhakti of nirguna origin among the untouchables was projected as a caste-based religious expression which was their exclusive preserve. This version of bhakti, with its distinctive content of egalitarianism, was self-consciously construed as a specifically lower-caste and heterodox sant tradition, in contrast to both saguna bhakti and the devotional piety and renunciation of other social groups, such as the commercial or professional middle classes. Moreover, this egalitarian bhakti tradition was believed to have a spiritual genealogy stretching back to the pre-Aryan period before the advent of vedic Hinduism, and subsequently developed by heterodox thinkers such as Mahavir, Buddha, Kabir, Ravidas, Dadu, Paltu and Sattakop.[30] To explain away the prominence of devotionalism of various kinds in mainstream Hinduism, some of the new untouchable preachers of the twentieth century would argue that even the upholders of vedic Hinduism had to acknowledge the philosophical and theological superiority of pre-Aryan bhakti and thus incorporated it in their religious corpus, albeit in distorted forms. They asserted, however, that the true, superior, ancient version of bhakti had been kept alive by secret cults and a distinguished lineage of heterodox sants, which they now sought to resurrect in the twentieth century.[31] This idea of the pre-Aryan origin of bhakti devotionalism, along with the exclusive claim of the untouchables over egalitarian, heterodox bhakti, lent fuel to an emerging belief that the untouchables were the original Indians or Adi Hindus, and, in turn, developed into a social movement in the early 1920s – the Adi Hindu movement. According to the ideology of Adi Hinduism, bhakti was the religion of the ancient, pre-Aryan inhabitants and rulers of India, the Adi Hindus, from whom the untouchables were supposed to have descended. Underlying the argument of Adi Hindu ancestry was the central assertion that the social division of labour based on caste status was forced on Indian society by the Aryan conquerors, who had subjugated the Adi Hindus as servile labourers. While bhakti posited caste equality, the emerging Adi Hindu ideology constructed a theory of ancient racial origin of untouchables in order to claim back their supposed original rights and power.

Emergence of the Adi Hindu movement

Whereas urban heterodox bhakti had re-emerged in the context of the changing social experience of the untouchables at the turn of the

---

[30] Chandrika Prasad Jijnasu, *Adi Hindu Andolan ka Prabartak Sri 108 Swami Acchutanand Harihar* (hereafter *Acchutanand biography*), Lucknow 1968, 2nd edn, p. 106.
[31] *Acchutanand biography*, p. 52.

century, Adi Hinduism evolved against a background of new social and political developments that affected the untouchables from the 1920s. With population growth in the towns in the interwar period, there was an increasing scarcity of jobs. The rapid expansion of cantonments and civil stations as well as the building of municipal sanitary infrastructure that occurred in the latter half of the nineteenth century had also slowed down by the 1920s, and would have been unable to absorb all untouchable job seekers, especially the second generation in the towns, forcing them to turn to work outside the confines of menial work and trades. Very few avenues were, however, open to them. Caste constraints on securing jobs became more perceptible to the generation of untouchables who reached adulthood in the second and third decades of the twentieth century. Shifts in urban local policies after the First World War began to place increasing restrictions on the economic activities of a large number of untouchables and accentuated their occupational problems. Chamars, doms and bhangis, for instance, who handled dead animals, hides and skins or engaged in pig rearing and came under the purview of municipal sanitary by-laws and licensing regulations, encountered stricter enforcement of these rules.[32] Sweepers and scavengers as municipal employees were directly affected by local administration. Local policies also caused the displacement and dispossession of untouchable groups from their residential areas. From the 1920s, the new schemes of the Improvement Trusts for sanitary improvement and development of unreclaimed land for the expansion of urban areas especially affected the untouchables, for they almost invariably lived on urban outskirts and in insanitary areas. Moreover, for them, it was doubly difficult to identify alternative residential sites owing to caste segregation in the towns. The educational policies of the local authorities also had a bearing on the access of the untouchables to municipal schools. The second generation of urban untouchables, therefore, increasingly began to seek means to get better jobs and education, as well as to find avenues for engagement with institutional politics and to organise themselves to contend with local policies. This was the backdrop against which bhakti resurgence evolved into the Adi Hindu movement. The latter developed as a vehicle to assert the rights and demands of the untouchables and to challenge the disabilities and exclusions they faced in the towns on account of their low ritual status.

The material context of urban life did not provide the sole, or even the primary, impetus behind the development of Adi Hinduism. The changing context of politics and ideological discourse of the interwar years

---

[32] See chapter 3 above.

proved to be crucial in the metamorphosis of bhakti into Adi Hinduism. Rethinking about the caste system had been catalysed by political and intellectual cross-currents of the late nineteenth and early twentieth centuries, when caste uplift endeavours of upper-caste social reformers and various theories about the caste system developed and lent themselves to elaboration and reinterpretation by untouchable ideologues. The growing familiarity of the untouchables, especially of a newly literate section among them, with the ideas preached by religious reformist groups such as the Arya Samaj or by Christian missionaries, as well as deliberations about the representation of caste and religious communities in government and political institutions, accelerated the development of urban low-caste social movements from the 1920s.

The Adi Hindu ideology was formulated in the 1920s by a new generation of literate untouchables. Their growing interest in bhakti religion had generated among the untouchables a need for literacy, in order to acquaint themselves with religious scriptures and the writings of the gurus. Attempts to gain literacy were also prompted by the teachings of medieval bhakti saints, who had preached the need for knowledge as a way to religious salvation.[33] Moreover, bhakti revivalism among the untouchables went hand in hand with efforts to improve their social and economic conditions, for which literacy was considered to be a prerequisite. Education was a highly valued qualification, for a prevalent notion was that illiteracy was a cause both of their social domination by the educated higher castes and of their exclusion from better jobs and opportunities.[34] Some untouchables had acquired elementary literacy from Christian missionaries in the cantonments or civil stations. Others, born in the 1880s and 1890s to untouchable parents who had migrated to the towns, were sent to municipal schools, insofar as their parents could afford the expenses. Bhakti resurgence thus gradually produced a group, albeit a small one, of literate untouchables, who emerged to be the leaders and ideologues of the Adi Hindu movement.[35] Swami Acchutanand (1879–1933), one of the most prominent Adi Hindu leaders in the 1920s and 1930s, was brought up at a military

[33] Dr Rampravesh Singh, 'Neeche se Upar ki Aur ki Gatishilata', *Ravidas* (Benares), *Praveshank* (Introductory issue), 1, 24 February, 1986, pp. 21–6.

[34] D. C. Dinkar, *Swatantrata Sangram mein Acchuton ka Yogdan*, Lucknow, 1986, p. 89.

[35] Provincial literacy figures of untouchable castes cited in the various census reports from 1901 onwards suggest an increase in literacy rates, especially in the towns, although the increase was remarkably slow and small, indicating the spread of literacy to a handful of untouchables only. *Census of India, 1901*, vol. XVI (Northwestern Provinces and Oudh), Part I, Report, Allahabad, 1902, p. 170; *Census of India, 1911*, vol. XV (United Provinces of Agra and Oudh), Part I, Report, Allahabad, 1912, p. 255; *Census of India, 1921*, vol. XVI (UP), Part I, Report, p. 126; *Census of India, 1931*, vol. XVIII (UP), Part I, Report, p. 480.

cantonment, where his father worked, and later settled in Kanpur. He had been taught by missionaries and had gained an extensive knowledge of religious texts.[36] Ram Charan (1888–1938), an Adi Hindu leader of Lucknow, was born in a slum at Gwaltoli in Kanpur. His parents were casual labourers, but sent him to school despite economic hardship. Later, he went to Lucknow, where he worked in the Railway Audit Office to earn money to attend night-school for higher education and eventually took a degree in law.[37] By the 1910s, a group of literate, but usually not wealthy, men like Acchutanand and Ram Charan had begun to emerge among the second generation of urban untouchables, who became concerned with the issue of caste uplift. Some among them had joined the Arya Samaj, which promised to facilitate the social uplift of lower castes, set up schools and hostels for them, offered scholarships to untouchable students, and presented the hope of surmounting caste divisions by allowing untouchables to enter the Hindu caste hierarchy through 'purification' or *shuddhi*.[38] In the early 1920s, however, the literate Arya Samajist untouchables broke away from the Samaj and put forward the argument that the untouchables were Adi Hindus. While the new material needs of their generation set the backdrop for the genesis of Adi Hinduism, the immediate impetus behind this development came from shifts in the activities of the Arya Samaj.

From the early 1920s, in the aftermath of the Khilafat movement to oppose western intervention in the Ottoman empire and in response to the religious ferment it generated among Muslims, the Arya Samaj stepped up its shuddhi or reclamation activities for the inclusion of lower castes and Hindu converts to Islam into the Hindu fold, in an attempt to expand and strengthen the Hindu community.[39] The Samaj, in this period, increasingly found itself drawn into political action in defence of Hinduism and attempted to highlight certain religious symbols to unite Hindus. One important rallying point for the Samaj was found in the Vedas, which were projected as the ultimate repository of religious truths.[40] The growing emphasis on the Vedas by the Arya Samaj, however, implied the fortification of the caste distinctions on which the Vedas were based. Of course, the Arya Samaj also upheld the

---

[36] *Acchutanand biography*, pp. 9–10.

[37] A. P. Chaudhury, *Picchre tatha Dalit Barg ke Mahan Neta Rai Ram Charan ka Jivan Charit tatha Unke Sanshipta Karya* (hereafter *Ram Charan biography*), Lucknow, 1973, pp. 1–2.

[38] *Acchutanand biography*, pp. 10–11, 98–9; *Ram Charan biography*, p 3.

[39] P. Hardy, *The Muslims of British India*, Cambridge, 1972, p. 208; G. Minault, *The Khilafat Movement: Religious Symbolism and Political Mobilization in India*, New York, 1982, pp. 192–3.

[40] K. W. Jones, *Socio-religious Reform Movements in British India: The New Cambridge History of India: III.1*, Cambridge, 1989, pp. 217–18.

hierarchical varnashrama dharma. This gradually disillusioned the untouchables who had joined it, especially because the Samaj did not
accord them equality of status, even though it admitted lower castes to
the Hindu hierarchy through shuddhi. The distinction between high-
caste Hindus and the 'purified' low castes had remained, in spite of the
Samaj's shuddhi initiative.[41] Even the religious recitations (*mantras*) that
the 'purified' lower castes were allowed to perform upon the bestowal of
sacred thread, in many cases, remained restricted in nature, omitting,
for instance, the crucial '*Om*', which continued to be the monopoly of
the higher castes. Moreover, in the 1920s, in order to sculpt a cohesive
pan-Hindu community, the Arya Samaj along with the Hindu Sabha, as
a part of the shuddhi initiative, increasingly committed themselves to
reform the social and cultural practices of the lower castes and to make
them conform to a more uniform and puritanical version of Hinduism,
usually akin to higher-caste beliefs and practices.[42] These endeavours,
while infused with a zeal to uplift the untouchables and imbued with
social reformist enthusiasm, both condemned lower-caste practices as
'immoral or indecent' and attempted to enforce restraint in social
behaviour and practices in the interest of 'purity and sobriety'.[43] The
attempts to achieve orderly homogeneity in the Hindu community, and
the attendant denigration of lower-caste practices, in effect amounted to
a perpetuation of the prejudices against pollution and inferiority in ritual
status that the Arya Samaj was supposed to undo. Indeed, the Arya
Samajist ceremony of shuddhi or purification, designed primarily for the
reconversion of Hindu converts to Islam but also at times applied to the
untouchables, evolved from the ritual of *prayaschit*, or atonement for
sins, thus implicitly suggesting that the condition of the untouchables
prior to being purified was sinful.[44] These various trends, not surprisingly, began to alienate many of the untouchables who had joined the
Arya Samaj as well as the mass of the untouchables who had increasingly
become the targets of caste uplift initiatives from the turn of the century.
The untouchable leaders associated with the Arya Samaj gradually
became convinced that the Samaj acted as the 'army of high caste
Hindus', whose only intention was to rally the Hindu community

[41] J. T. F. Jordens, 'Hindu Religious and Social Reform in British India', in Basham (ed.),
A Cultural History of India, p. 380.
[42] K. W. Jones, *Arya Dharm: Hindu Consciousness in Nineteenth-century Punjab*, Delhi,
1976, pp. 95–6.
[43] Ibid.; Gangaprasad Upadhyaya (ed.), *Dalitoddhar*, Arya Samaj, Chowk, Prayag, 1941,
p. 11 and passim.
[44] Jones, *Arya Dharm*, pp. 132–3; R. K. Ghai, *Shuddhi Movement in India*, Delhi, 1990,
pp. 48–9. The shuddhi rituals included the ceremonies of tonsure (*mundan*), fire
sacrifice (*hom*), investiture of the sacred thread, and instruction in the sacred *gayatri
mantra*.

against the Muslims, and that the Samaj's attempt to uplift the lower castes was merely a part of this strategy. They argued that the Samaj did not aim to eradicate untouchability and that shuddhi was a cunning ploy to perpetuate the hold of the higher castes over the untouchables.[45] Swami Acchutanand claimed in a speech that the Samaj 'aim[ed] to make all Hindus slaves of the Vedas and the brahmins'.[46]

It was also from this period that the political reforms of 1919, introduced by the British government, brought into sharper focus the issue of the relative numerical strength of various religious groups, as the principle of communal representation was fully recognised. This further prompted the untouchables of the Arya Samaj, not unreasonably, to conclude that the intensification of shuddhi and the caste uplift programmes of the Samaj were motivated by intentions to increase the number of Hindus. Ram Charan argued that 'in 1919 reforms came . . . and representation was given according to population; those religious groups who are more numerous get more places; and then what else but *acchutoddhar* [uplift of untouchables] conferences everywhere to uplift untouchables'.[47] In the early 1920s, therefore, many of the literate untouchables arrived at the conclusion that an alliance with the Arya Samaj and attempts to gain entry into the Hindu caste hierarchy would not further the interests of the untouchables and they dissociated themselves from the Samaj.[48] In search of a new ideology to repudiate vedic Hinduism and the caste system, they drew upon bhakti and formulated the ideology of Adi Hinduism.

Based on the notion of bhakti as the exclusive religion of the untouchables, the leaders developed their own interpretation of the history of Indian religions and of the historical roots of untouchability. For their reconstruction of the history of untouchables, the ideologues referred to sources other than bhakti religion. The various intellectual influences on Acchutanand, one of the chief Adi Hindu preachers, described by his biographer, indicate how the Adi Hindu ideology was formulated.[49] An important influence was naturally that of the Arya Samaj and the Samaj's vigorous propagation of shuddhi or reconversion in Hinduism.[50] One of the arguments underlying shuddhi was that Hindus had been forcibly converted to Islam by the Muslim conquerors and rulers in medieval India and that these converts were to be reclaimed to

---

[45] *Acchutanand biography*, pp. 11–12, 31; *Ram Charan biography*, pp. 8–9.
[46] Extracts from speeches in *Acchutanand biography*, p. 11.
[47] Extracts from speeches in *Ram Charan biography*, pp. 8–9.
[48] *Acchutanand biography*, pp. 9–10; *Ram Charan biography*, p. 4.
[49] *Acchutanand biography*, p. 12.
[50] Jones, *Arya Dharm*, pp. 129, 134.

Hinduism.[51] Acchutanand adopted this central explanatory concept of forcible imposition of a religion. He projected it backwards to the vedic age to argue that the Aryan invaders had subjugated and imposed vedic Hinduism on the original Indians, the Adi Hindus, and deprived them of their bhakti religion, which they had supposedly practised prior to the advent of the Aryans. According to his biographer, Acchutanand had also read R. C. Dutt's Bengali translation of the *Rig Vedas*, and had discussed religious issues with the missionaries of the Theosophical Society and with Jain and Buddhist sadhus. The biographer stated that, from these various sources, Acchutanand had become aware of the racial and religious differences between the Aryans and the pre-Aryans. He had concluded from accounts of warfare in Hindu religious texts between *dasyus* (bandits or plunderers) or *asuras* (demons) and Aryan gods that these were references to the conquest of ancient pre-Aryan races in India by the Aryan invaders. It is possible that Acchutanand and other Adi Hindu leaders in UP may have been aware of the Adi Dravida movement in southern India or the Ad Dharm movement in the Punjab around the same time, with whom the idea of an original race could have been shared. However, there is no evidence to suggest any links between these various 'Adi' movements in their initial stages. It is more likely that the theory of a separate racial origin of untouchables in the various simultaneous 'Adi' movements was derived from British ethnographic classifications and a notion that the caste system originated through encounters between Dravidian and Aryan races.[52] These racial theories had gained widespread publicity, especially with the various censuses. Acquaintance of the urban untouchables with Christian missionaries, who were propagating the concept of the original races of India and the theory of the genesis of the caste system among an Aryan minority, was another significant source of these ideas.[53]

Soon after their rift with the Arya Samaj in the early 1920s, the untouchable leaders began to propagate the concept of an Adi Hindu original race and bhakti as their separate, pre-Aryan religion. A book

---

[51] Ibid., pp. 150–1.

[52] For the British view of 'caste as race' and its incorporation in the census, see R. Inden, *Imagining India*, Oxford, 1990, pp. 56–66. For a different perspective on the symbiosis between ideas of race and caste, see Susan Bayly, 'Caste and "Race" in the Colonial Ethnography of India', in P. Robb (ed.), *The Concept of Race in South Asia*, Delhi, 1995, pp. 164–218. For the notion of Aryan races in India, see R. Thapar, 'The Theory of Aryan Race and India: History and Politics', *Social Scientist*, 24, 1–3, 1996, pp. 3–29.

[53] An argument about the ancient racial origin of the untouchables, as distinct from the Aryan races, was mentioned by G. W. Briggs in his history of the chamars, written in 1920 as part of a series of monographs published by the Young Men's Christian Association, which reflected the ideas that the missionaries were preaching among the untouchables. Briggs, *The Chamars*, pp. 11–15.

entitled *Mool Bharatbasi aur Arya* ('Original inhabitants of India and the Aryans') was published, written by Swami Bodhanand. The *Kumbh Mela* or fair at Allahabad of 1928–9 saw the most strident proclamation of Adi Hinduism. At the mela, a *Mahotsav* or great festival of all Adi Hindu bhakti sant *panths* (devotional sects) was held, in which Kabirpanthi, Ravidas and Shivnarayani groups participated.[54] By 1924, local Adi Hindu *sabhas* (associations) had been organised in Kanpur, Lucknow, Benares and Allahabad to spread the message of Adi Hinduism, the initiative being taken by literate untouchables and bhakti religious preachers.[55] Each Sabha had its *pracharaks* and *upadeshaks*, modelled on Christian missionaries and Arya Samajist preachers, who regularly visited untouchable neighbourhoods. The emphasis of the Adi Hindu movement was not, however, on formal organisation, but on a shared religious and ideological perspective between the Adi Hindu preachers and local untouchable groups who practised bhakti. Various panchayats and caste groups in their neighbourhoods were informally associated with the Adi Hindu sabhas of the towns or with individual leaders. Adi Hindu preachers were regularly invited to address meetings of local caste panchayats and bhakti religious congregations. The meetings of panchayats were occasions for discussions about Adi Hinduism. The Ravidas chamar panchayats in Kanpur, for instance, acknowledged Acchutanand as the leader of their community in the 1920s, and chamars in Kanpur in large numbers attended meetings convened by the Adi Hindu Sabha and addressed by Acchutanand.[56] Sweepers in Kanpur, on a number of occasions in 1925, were also reported to have organised meetings for social uplift, at some of which Acchutanand was invited to preside in his capacity as an Adi Hindu leader.[57] In Allahabad, the chamars of the cantonment had declared themselves to be a 'self-contained' community, having broken away from high-caste Hindus, and celebrated their festivals separately in 1926.[58] Similarly, in Lucknow, in April 1927, various chamar panchayats held a joint meeting, where they pledged their support to the Adi Hindu movement and resolved to form a volunteer corps.[59] The informal nature of links between apex Adi Hindu organisations in the towns and local caste

---

[54] *Acchutanand biography*, pp. 72–4.
[55] An Adi Hindu Samaj was formed in Lucknow in 1919; the Adi Hindu Mahasabha in Kanpur in 1923; a similar organisation in Allahabad in the 1920s. *Acchutanand biography*, pp. 24–25.
[56] Interview with Hanuman Prasad Kureel, untouchable politician of Kanpur. Acchutanand lived for some time in the house of Hanuman Prasad's father.
[57] *PAI*, No. 16, 2 May 1925; No. 30, 8 August 1925.
[58] *PAI*, No. 35, 11 September 1926; No. 45, 26 November 1927.
[59] *PAI*, No. 14, 9 April 1927.

groups in urban neighbourhoods contributed to the strength and breadth of the movement. A police report in 1922 referred to a 'spirit of revolt' among untouchables, which appears to be an allusion to bhakti resurgence and the development of the Adi Hindu movement.[60]

Why did Adi Hinduism, spearheaded by a literate group, gain popularity among the mass of the untouchable poor? One reason was the social character of the leadership and the role they played within the untouchable community by virtue of their literacy. Although the leaders were literate and, therefore, in some ways stood apart from the rest of urban untouchables, none the less the leaders had risen from the ranks of the untouchable poor. Even though their literacy distinguished them from the vast majority of the urban untouchables, their common social origin enabled the leaders to enjoy the allegiance and trust of the untouchable poor, for the latter could identify with the leaders socially and culturally. Moreover, those who had assumed leadership could do so by virtue of their literacy. It is equally true, though, that it was precisely because of their literacy that they were accepted as leaders and spokesmen by the untouchables. Literacy was a highly valued qualification among untouchables, for a prevalent notion was that illiteracy was a cause of their social domination by the educated higher castes, who knew how to manipulate the administrative and judicial systems to their own advantage.[61] It was, therefore, natural that the literate were accorded the status of leaders by the untouchable poor. Ram Charan initially gained popularity as an untouchable leader in 1919–20, when, as a lawyer, he challenged in court and prevented the acquisition by the local authorities of a vast area of land in Lucknow on which untouchable groups lived. He was also well known and respected for defending and securing the acquittal of a chamar labourer, who was accused of murdering a merchant.[62] The intervention of literate leaders in local disputes between individuals or groups of untouchables and the urban authorities or employers, on behalf of the former, also enabled the leaders to gain support for the Adi Hindu movement.

The spread of the Adi Hindu movement was not, however, due simply to the lure of practical benefits accrued from supporting its leaders or the role of 'patron' that the leaders played in the local community. It was primarily caused by the message that the Adi Hindu leaders put forward. The Adi Hindu ideology was particularly attractive to the mass of the untouchables and was espoused by them because it provided them with a historical explanation for their own poverty and

[60] *PAI*, No. 13, 1 April 1922.
[61] Dinkar, *Swatantrata Sangram*, p. 89.
[62] *Ram Charan biography*, pp. 2–3.

deprivation, and presented them not only with a vision of their past power and rights, but also with hopes of regaining their lost rights. The Adi Hindu leaders were in fact providing an ideology to a receptive audience that was already seeking means to claim rights and privileges in urban society.

The Adi Hindu ideology: A statement of rights against exclusion

The message of Adi Hinduism was primarily twofold.[63] First, it attempted to dissociate low-caste status from menial occupations. Adi Hinduism challenged the imposition of specific 'low' social roles on untouchables based on their ritual status. In this, Adi Hinduism was a direct response to the exclusions that untouchables encountered in urban society, especially in the sphere of work and labour. Its emphasis was less on caste oppression or exploitation, which might have been the chief concern if the movement had emerged in rural areas, and more on ritual exclusion, which was directly relevant to the urban untouchables. To challenge the exclusion of untouchables, the Adi Hindu leaders not only argued for caste equality, but also highlighted a view that the untouchables had been deprived of their original rights through force and political machinations by the higher castes, and that their rights should be restored. Arising from this, the second focus of Adi Hinduism was the notion that the untouchables were the past rulers of India. Through this generalised assertion, Adi Hindu leaders also attempted to fortify the claims of the untouchables to rights and opportunities.

Bhakti is based on the idea of direct and personal communion with God, through devotion, meditation and spiritual introspection. Adi Hindu ideologues, such as Acchutanand, emphatically highlighted the introspective dimension of bhakti (*atmavad*) and gave this religious concept a new social significance. Spiritual introspection (*atmaanubhav*) was accorded supreme importance as the only way to arrive at true knowledge or *sadgyan* and to evolve one's own world-view. Introspection, it was held, would lead to self-realisation or self-knowledge (*atmagyan*). This would, in turn, facilitate the articulation of an autonomous value system that was not derived from or imposed by the higher castes. The concept of introspective self-realisation (atmavad) was, thus, propounded not simply as a way of worshipping but more importantly to stimulate 'thinking-for-oneself' without reference to received notions and religious prescriptions from higher castes. Acchutanand thus urged:

---

[63] For a detailed account of the Adi Hindu ideology, see Khare, *Untouchable as Himself*, pp. 83–5.

Do not follow any ideology *[mat]* because you have been hearing it for a long time, or because it is held by some great [*bade*, literally big, implies a socially superior person of upper class or caste] person or because it is the view held by any cult or sect. Accept only an ideology that you have arrived at yourself.[64]

This cultivation of atmagyan would finally enable one to express an independent self-identity – *swatantra satta*. By deploying the concept of introspective spiritualism and atmavad, therefore, Acchutanand proclaimed an autonomous identity for the untouchables.

The realisation of true knowledge and independent thinking through atmavad was above all seen as the key which would help to discern the difference between truth and falsity. It would then crucially reveal the irrelevance and falsity of one's 'low' status in society. Acchutanand, at a session of religious catechism with an audience of untouchables, in reply to the question 'what is atma-anubhav?', said:

Real knowledge is the knowledge gained through introspection [atma-anubhav] and which you have understood and realised on your own. For this reason, you will have to discern between good and evil, virtue and vice, auspicious and inauspicious, through your own introspection. This [introspection] is the path of self-realisation of the sants [bhakti saints and preachers]. Self-realisation is the only touchstone against which you can test truth and falsity, high and low.[65]

The Adi Hindu leaders preached that, through the exercise of introspection, it could be concluded that the distinction between 'high' and 'low' was neither pre-ordained and natural nor grounded in 'truth', but was socially determined, and that there was no inevitability about the 'low' functions that the untouchables were expected to perform in society as the servants of higher castes. They argued that the untouchables had been forced by the higher castes to perform certain jobs and services that involved the handling of 'impure', organic matter, and then, using the plea of ritual impurity, the high castes had accorded them a 'low', servile role or status. Ram Charan said in a speech in 1927:

They [untouchables] were made to do the most insulting and demeaning jobs, such as cleaning excreta and dirty clothes. They were repeatedly told that you are shudras and your only work is to serve *[gulami]*. Those who were thus made to serve *[gulam* or *dasa]* were then called untouchables.[66]

The Adi Hindu leaders, therefore, denied that untouchables should perform only 'low' and 'impure' occupations, on the argument that these functions had been imposed on them. Moreover, it was pointed out that the untouchables were forced by the higher castes to remain in 'low' positions on the grounds of their 'bad' or impure habits, such as

---

[64] *Acchutanand biography*, pp. 108–9.
[65] Ibid.   [66] Ibid., p. 83.

eating dead animals. However, such habits were argued to be the products of 'desperation bred by our poverty' and 'for survival'. The fact that the untouchables ate dead, rotten animals was attributed to their deprivation, which itself was seen to arise from the social oppression of the low castes by the higher castes.[67] With these arguments, the Adi Hindu leaders tried to reveal the underlying social and political dynamics of untouchability, as they diagnosed them. They then gave out a message to refuse to serve the higher castes passively and to remain ever subservient.

It is noteworthy, however, that the criticism of the caste system by the Adi Hindu leaders had the limitation that they focused on the lack of rights or opportunities for the untouchables and aimed mainly at challenging their social and political exclusion. Thus, even while they denied the validity of caste distinctions and exclusions, they concentrated primarily on bypassing the caste system, and did not launch a direct onslaught on some of the basic premises of the caste system, such as purity and pollution. The leaders did not jettison the notions of 'low' or 'impure', on which caste distinctions were based, but focused their attention on proving that such stigma and disabilities should not be attached to the untouchables. Instead, by arguing that 'low' work for the untouchables arose from upper-caste imposition and their own persistent poverty, they claimed that a 'low' position was not the true inheritance of the untouchables but the product of a historical 'wrong'. The fact that the Adi Hindu leaders did not directly engage with the underlying principles of purity and pollution in the caste system ultimately undermined the radical political potential of Adi Hinduism in challenging the caste system.

Despite this limitation, however, the Adi Hindu ideology mounted a powerful political critique of the caste system as an instrument of domination that evolved through historical struggles. In order to buttress this argument, the Adi Hindu leaders asserted their pre-Aryan ancestry as the original rulers of India. This, of course, enabled them to argue that they should re-inherit the ancient rights of which they had been deprived. The Adi Hindu ideologues sought to offer a historical explanation for the genesis of untouchability in order to show how 'low' functions came to be imposed on the untouchables. The Adi Hindu theory about the origin of untouchability began with an assertion of a glorious past of the so-called Adi Hindu ancestors of the untouchables in the pre-Aryan times and unfolded as an account of the process of Aryan subjugation of the original inhabitants and their decline to the

---

[67] Ibid., pp. 102–3.

rank of untouchables.[68] The claim of a separate racial origin of the untouchables was substantiated by arguing that bhakti was a pre-vedic religion. Even though bhakti had its roots in Hinduism, the Adi Hindu leaders denied such associations. Bhakti was claimed to be a distinct and egalitarian religious tradition that pre-dated vedic Hinduism. Simultaneously, the fact that untouchables practised bhakti was held to be the proof that they had descended from the ancient inhabitants of India.[69] The Aryans were accused of subsequently imposing the caste-based and ceremony-oriented vedic Hindu religion on the Adi Hindus.

The Adi Hindu leaders claimed that there had been ancient Adi Hindu kingdoms, capital cities, forts and a thriving civilisation. They alleged that, when the Aryans invaded the country, they conquered these Adi Hindus variously by brute force, repression and treachery. Being righteous, good and free from deceit, the Adi Hindus were no match for the cunning Aryans, even though they were heroic and brave. Having defeated and subjugated the Adi Hindus, the Aryans turned them into slaves in servitude and forced them to perform 'low' jobs. They then devised the caste system and oppressive social laws, embodied in the Vedas and codified in the *Manusmriti*, in order to relegate the Adi Hindus to untouchable status and to deprive them of their rights in society. Hinduism, with its caste system, was argued to be a political creation of the Aryans, who called themselves the higher castes. Ram Charan declared at a meeting in 1927: 'The rule of making shudras was not a religious one. It was naked politics.'[70] It was further held that the Aryans themselves assumed higher status as *brahmins*, *kshatriyas* and *vaishyas*, in order to make education, political or military power and wealth, respectively, their own exclusive preserves. The forcible and illegitimate imposition of low ritual status through ancient acts of conquest, expropriation and dispossession was, thus, diagnosed to be the source of the unequal division of labour in society and of political and social exclusion. The caste system was then projected as a political instrument of domination and denial of rights. It was deplored as the original and continuing cause of deprivation of the untouchables, on the argument that low status condemned them in perpetuity to menial

---

[68] The following account is based on extracts from speeches and writings of Achchutanand and Ram Charan, cited in their biographies. *Acchutanand biography*, pp. 54–71, 84–6; *Ram Charan biography*, pp. 5–10, 17–19, 80–4.

[69] Juergensmeyer has argued that, in the Punjab, Ad Dharm was projected as a *qaum* or independent religion, rather than simply as a religious *panth* or sect which worshipped god in a particular way. Juergensmeyer, *Religion as Social Vision*, pp. 45–55. The implications of Adi Hinduism in UP were similar, though the distinction between qaum and panth was not overtly articulated.

[70] *Ram Charan biography*, p. 84.

occupations and divested them of their rights to political power or social mobility.

The Adi Hindu leaders projected the past not only as a period when the forebears of the untouchables were the rulers, but also as a golden age of social equality. In the Vedas and other Hindu religious texts, there are accounts of warfare between Hindu gods and asuras or *rakshasas* (demons), in which the latter appear as evil and oppressive, and whom the gods vanquished. The Adi Hindu leaders interpreted these stories as references to the process of the conquest of the pre-Aryans by the Aryans. They claimed that the demons represented the Adi Hindu rulers, but denied the authenticity of the depiction of the demons as evil and malevolent. On the contrary, they argued, the Adi Hindu rulers were benevolent, peaceful and egalitarian, their subjects lived in perfect harmony and happiness, and there was no aggrandisement of one group over another. The Adi Hindu leaders held that the Aryans deliberately vilified the pre-Aryan rulers as demons, in order to justify their conquest of the original races, and in fact it was the Aryans who were belligerent and who unleashed violence and introduced inequality in Indian society.[71] The Adi Hindu leaders thus emphasised an essentially oppressive image of the Aryans. They then proceeded to condemn the higher castes of the twentieth century as upholders of the tradition of injustice of their Aryan progenitors, for not acknowledging the rights of the untouchables and for continuing to exclude and deprive them.

Through their newly constructed history of the original inhabitants of India, the Adi Hindu leaders outlined an idealised vision of social equality and of past power and glory of the untouchables, which had been lost and were to be reclaimed. By arguing that the caste system was a political instrument of the Aryans to deprive the untouchables, they declared that the untouchables should not remain condemned to menial occupations, illiteracy, poverty and powerlessness. They thus put forward an explanation for the experience of being deprived, menial servants in society and projected a remedy to overcome the situation by denying the legitimacy of the caste system as an alien imposition, rather than by claiming higher status within it. At the same time, their theory about the origin of the caste system as a form of social domination and their notion of a past golden age of social equality suggested a challenge to the hierarchical conception of society, whose potential implications went beyond their immediate practical concern of repudiating the connections between low caste status and menial work.

The Adi Hindu leaders also highlighted a self-image of the untouch-

---

[71] *Acchutanand biography*, pp. 54–71, 84–6; *Ram Charan biography*, pp. 5–10, 17–19, 80–4.

ables as the good, honest and truthful simple-folk, who had been
conquered and deprived. This self-image was, however, not simply a
passive or negative one of the good and helpless or meek and servile
victims. By asserting that the untouchables were the true masters of the
land, the Adi Hindu preachers cultivated a sense of entitlement to rights
and power at the same time as they heightened an awareness of historical
deprivation. The stress on atmagyan (self-knowledge) and introspection
as the source of independent knowledge without higher-caste imposi-
tions also enabled the exposition of a distinctive, autonomous, proud
and even defiant self-identity of the untouchables. Moreover, the Adi
Hindu leaders echoed and reinforced the notion of a separate collective
identity of the untouchables, which had already begun to be expressed
through bhakti. They portrayed bhakti as the distinctive religious
heritage of the untouchables, and posited the egalitarianism of bhakti
against the inequities of vedic Hinduism. It has been seen above that the
Adi Hindu movement spread beyond the ranks of the literate leadership
because it provided a political vocabulary for the untouchables to claim
rights and opportunities in urban society. The leaders drew upon the
familiar religious idiom of bhakti and animated it with visions of a new
order of equality and rights.

Self-assertion and social reforms

The spread of the ideology of Adi Hinduism was reflected in social
reforms among untouchable groups in the towns. The central focus was
on denying the religious rituals and ceremonies prescribed by the higher
castes for the untouchables, and, in particular, on defying the 'low'
social duties and labour imposed on them. Medieval bhakti devotionalism had rejected idolatry in vedic Hinduism and the trappings of
ceremonial worship that shrouded god behind a veil of rituals. The
denial of brahmanical rituals was also, of course, promoted by the Arya
Samaj with an aim to return to purified, uncorrupted and original vedic
Hinduism by undermining what they saw as subsequent incorporation
under brahmanical dominance. They did not, however, seek to deny
caste distinctions. The Adi Hindu leaders denounced brahmanical
Hindu ceremonies for a different reason. These ceremonies were argued
to have been designed by the higher castes as tools to deprive the
untouchables. In the opinion of the Adi Hindu leaders, the higher castes
stipulated elaborate and expensive modes of observance of religious
festivals for the lower castes in order to impoverish them, to ensure that
they would remain in a constant state of economic dependence or debt
bondage to the higher castes, and thereby forced them to continue to

perform menial labour. The Adi Hindu leaders preached the need for reform of social and religious practices as a means of achieving economic self-sufficiency and occupational diversification, as well as to redirect savings to gain education and better living conditions.[72]

These ideas found application in reforms spearheaded by various untouchable caste panchayats from the 1920s, which laid down the rules, customs and rites to be observed by caste members. Many panchayats denied that pilgrimages, the holding of expensive religious feasts, especially for brahmin priests, and elaborate observance of religious ceremonies were meritorious acts, and these were actively discouraged. Some panchayats also decided to streamline the ceremonies observed on the occasions of birth, marriage and death. These included *chhatai* and *barahi*, which were rites performed on the sixth and twelfth days after birth and death respectively. There were also attempts to dispense with lavish meals on these occasions, as such practices were seen to be mere emulation of the higher castes, leading to indebtedness and impoverishment.[73] Related to this were also attempts to avoid intoxicants, especially the consumption of alcohol, and, at times, to adopt vegetarianism. All these, however, were efforts not to raise ritual status by embracing brahmanical or purified Hindu practices, but rather to contend with the problems of unnecessary expenditure.[74] In all this, then, a key concern was to avoid indebtedness to the higher castes through reform of social practices. However, acute poverty also meant that they needed to borrow money in emergencies or for medical treatment and the schooling of children. To contend with this, attempts were also made to devise means to mobilise resources for the availability of credit within the community by cultivating savings habits. Informal savings groups were organised under the auspices of the local panchayats, whenever possible.[75]

While social reform attempts were partly aimed at achieving economic independence and gaining education, they were also envisaged as the means to undermine the control that the higher castes exercised over the untouchables. The emphasis on social resistance against the higher castes and especially against the imposition of 'low' functions on the untouchables was revealed in changing practices among urban sweepers

---

[72] Interview with Chedi Lal Sathi (untouchable politician) in Lucknow.
[73] Interviews with Chedi Lal Sathi in Lucknow, Nageshwar Valmiki (leader of the municipal sweepers' union in 1987) in Kanpur, and Sita Ram Visharad (untouchable politician) in Benares.
[74] For the economic importance of social reforms among low castes, see Lucy Carroll, 'The Temperance Movement in India: Politics and Social Reform', *MAS*, 10, 3, 1976, pp. 417–47.
[75] Interview with Chedi Lal Sathi in Lucknow.

and scavengers from the mid-1920s. The Ravidas chamar panchayats of Kanpur and Lucknow, in this period, resolved not to handle dead animals, as a mark of their refusal to perform a 'low' function that had been forced on them.[76] That actions such as these were not simply superficial attempts to gain social respectability in the eyes of higher castes is evident from similar instances elsewhere. The annual report of the Benares Municipal Board in 1924–5 stated that the number of chamars performing 'customary' sweeping and scavenging in households had declined dramatically, while there was a corresponding increase in the number of sweepers employed by the municipality.[77] This may partly have been due to differences in the rates of remuneration for private and municipal sweepers, even though the municipal report did not suggest this possibility. Instead, the Municipal Board report in the following year attributed the lack of customary sweepers to 'the infusion of a spirit of superiority in them'.[78] This suggests that the sweepers were unwilling to perform scavenging functions when these were expected from them as 'customary' services in private households, but were agreeable to being employed by the municipality, for in the latter case conservancy occupations could be seen as essential public utility services, rather than simply 'low' duties demanded from them. This clearly encompassed an effort to undermine the link between ritual status and 'low' role or duties in society, rather than being a simple act of 'sanskritisation' to emulate the higher castes in the quest for respectability.[79] Not surprisingly, it was also in the early 1920s that a police report noted 'a spirit of revolt' among untouchables and remarked that they were 'forsaking hereditary professions'.[80]

A similar attempt to defy 'traditional' 'low' activities found expression among the sweepers (mehtars) of Kanpur in a different way. The Kanpur mehtar panchayat decided to overcome an established custom whereby the untouchables, owing to their low status, were considered to be entitled only to left-over and rejected food and goods of higher castes, called *utran* (discarded, used or second-hand clothes), *jhutan* (left-over or half-eaten food) and *phatkan* (refused or extra bits, literally chaff separated from grain after winnowing). Under the initiative of their panchayat, sweepers in Kanpur refrained from eating jhutan,

---

[76] Interviews with D. C. Dinkar and Chedi Lal Sathi in Lucknow and Hanuman Prasad Kureel in Kanpur.
[77] Benares Municipal Board Annual Report, 1924–25, p. 13.
[78] Ibid., 1925–26, p. 17.
[79] For an argument about 'sanskritisation' in low-caste social movements, see M. N. Srinivas, 'A Note on Sanskritisation and Westernisation' in *Caste in Modern India and Other Essays*, Bombay, 1962, reprinted 1970, pp. 42–62.
[80] *PAI*, No. 13, 1 April 1922.

which the poverty-stricken sweepers used to collect and consume during cleaning and sweeping.[81] Acchutanand himself also preached that the untouchables did not deserve only jhutan, utran and phatkan.[82]

Defying the restrictions and functions imposed on the untouchables by the caste system was clearly a driving force behind their social reforms. This dimension was also revealed in a somewhat paradoxical way in the failure of a reform attempt by Adi Hindu leaders. In their efforts at levelling caste distinctions, Adi Hindu leaders in the towns sought to eradicate ritual barriers to social intercourse among various untouchable caste groups themselves, such as between chamars and mehtars, by urging commensality. They tried to organise inter-dining ceremonies called *kuccha* (raw) meals, where members of various un-touchable castes brought raw vegetables, which were cooked at the same place for shared meals. However, kuccha meals met with very little enthusiasm.[83] This suggests that the focus of social reforms among the mass of the urban untouchables was not on overcoming ritual barriers to social interaction, in spite of being urged by their leaders. They were not seeking to undermine caste divisions insofar as these defined a set of ritual practices to regulate social interaction based on purity and pollu-tion. Their attack on the caste system was directed specifically at its function as a vehicle for exclusion from rights or opportunities and for the imposition of 'low' roles on the untouchables, which in turn was seen to be the cause of their continuing deprivation and lack of power.

Institutional politics and party affiliations

As religious innovation and social reform gathered momentum among the urban untouchable poor, agitation in the public political realm for their rights was able gradually to develop. For, as Khare points out, the ideas of the untouchable ascetic leaders of the Adi Hindu movement such as Acchutanand provided not only 'an ideology of radical equality' and 'a strategy for doing better in everyday life', but also 'a political culture for civil rights and organised protest'.[84] However, by the early 1930s, rather than promoting mass organisation and action, the majority of the leaders of the Adi Hindu movement turned to political bargaining within representative institutions and concentrated on matters of public policy-making.[85] Agitational politics or social and religious activism

---

[81] Interview with Nageshwar Valmiki in Kanpur.
[82] *Acchutanand biography*, p. 51.
[83] Interview with Chedi Lal Sathi in Lucknow.
[84] Khare, *Untouchable as Himself*, p. 78.
[85] *Ram Charan biography*, pp. 22–47; C. P. Jijnasu, *Bharatiya Maulik Samajvad: Srishti Aur Manav Samaj ka Vikas Athba 'Bharat ke Adi Nivasi' Granth ka Pratham Khand,*

gradually came to assume a lower priority for them. Having established a base of support for the Adi Hindu movement and having demonstrated the strength of their constituency, the leaders now concentrated on consolidating their own position within political institutions. The rationale of the leaders in seeking places in political institutions was partly expressed in the following comment by a member of the deputation of the 'depressed classes' of UP, in an interview with the Indian Statutory Commission. When asked whether there had been any social or economic improvement among lower castes in the past 15 years, he stated : 'in social position there has been [improvement], but not beyond that. If I may say so, they [higher castes] are not going to give us any political status.'[86] It was this perception of their continued exclusion from political power that prompted untouchable leaders to concentrate their energies on registering their presence in institutional politics. This tendency was further encouraged by the sympathetic ear that the government lent to these leaders, often nominating them to local councils and the provincial legislature, or honouring them with titles.[87] Adi Hindu leaders such as Acchutanand stressed the benefits received by the untouchables under British rule, especially through missionary education and jobs in the British civil and military administration at the lower levels. He saw British rule, with the possibility of political representation of the untouchables that it presented, as a source of salvation for the untouchables as opposed to the ill-will of the upper castes.[88] More importantly, however, the refusal of the Congress to accept some of the demands of lower-caste politicians in constitutional deliberations in the 1920s and early 1930s, especially for separate electorates,[89] had gradually persuaded many untouchable leaders throughout India to rely on interest group politics. In their dealings with the government and various Indian political parties, the leaders realised that recourse to agitational politics alone did not automatically enable them to secure their demands without a foothold in the institutional arenas of

Lucknow, 1941, pp. 261–96; *PAI*, No. 11, 27 March 1937, reported that, at a meeting of the Working Committee of the Adi Hindu Depressed Classes Association in Allahabad, it was decided to hold an all-India conference to devise ways and means to secure government service and seats in legislatures.

[86] Interview with the Deputation from Depressed Classes, UP, Lucknow, 6 December 1928. *Indian Statutory Commission*, vol. XVI, Part I, Selections from Memoranda and Oral Evidence by Non-officials, London, 1930, p. 362.

[87] For instance, Adi Hindu leaders Shyam Lal Dhobi of Allahabad and Ram Charan of Lucknow had received titles from the British and had been nominated to the Councils.

[88] *Acchutanand biography*, p. 13; *PAI*, No. 26, 10 July 1926.

[89] Eleanor Zelliot, 'Congress and the Untouchables, 1917–1950', in R. Sisson and S. Wolpert (eds.), *Congress and Indian Nationalism: The Pre-Independence Phase*, Berkeley, 1988, pp. 182–91.

bargaining. Besides, by concentrating on caste-based agitational politics they ran the risk of being marginalised in nationalist politics as 'separatists' or being accused of 'British loyalism'. The efficacy of the strategy of activist political campaigns based on caste was, therefore, in doubt in the 1930s. Untouchable politicians found it more pragmatic to secure a foothold in representative institutions, from where they felt that they would be best able to change public policy in the interest of the lower castes. Ensuring political representation in this way could be seen to be a prerequisite for achieving social equality. By 1930, the national untouchable leader Ambedkar himself had come round to the view that political leverage was essential to achieve social justice.[90] Untouchable politicians elsewhere in India too tended to focus on institutional negotiations and reformist interest group politics, as was evident, for instance, in the Punjab among Ad Dharmis. Juergensmeyer argues that representative and electoral politics had become the norm of Indian politics by the 1930s and the Ad Dharmis had to operate within this framework if they were not to become marginal and banished to the political wilderness.[91] The Adi Hindu leaders of UP towns were no exception to this trend of reorientation towards institutional politics. The leaders gradually came to interpret the aim of wresting political power for the untouchables narrowly in terms of gaining access to local and provincial councils by a handful of untouchables. This was expected to provide benefits to the larger untouchable community, for the leaders would gain concessions or privileges and public policy benefits for the community through their negotiations within the corridors of power. Moreover, it was often the case with untouchable politics of this era that the poverty of a majority of the constituents constrained the mobilisation of resources to sustain organised mass political action. This too tended to tip the balance in favour of institutional rather than agitational politics.

The emerging institutional focus of the leadership inevitably had implications for the politics of the poorer untouchables. They could, of course, identify with the project of the leaders to enter representative institutions to bargain for greater rights for the untouchables. Securing the government's endorsement and institutionalisation of their rights in this manner, especially through the legislative process, could be seen by the untouchables as a significant precondition to undermining the perpetuation of their exclusion and powerlessness in the urban milieu. Moreover, the access of their leaders to the arenas of policy-making at

[90] Mrinal Gore, *The Social Context of an Ideology: Ambedkar's Political and Social Thought*, Delhi, 1993, pp. 123, 212–15.
[91] Juergensmeyer, *Religion as Social Vision*, pp. 142–55.

least opened up the possibility of securing patronage as well as more favourable policies for education, employment or housing, which had so far been largely outside their grasp. Education, in particular, as noted earlier, was a pivotal concern among them, both for better occupational opportunities and to deal with administrative institutions. In addition, as mentioned earlier, local policies increasingly affected their settlement patterns and sources of livelihood, as well as the working conditions of untouchable municipal employees. Gaining representation in urban administrative institutions to influence policy-making was thus becoming more urgent for them. The untouchable poor, therefore, often rallied behind their leaders in political campaigns. However, support for the leaders on this basis could only be of a limited nature, usually focused on specific issues. It was the radical religious ideas and the programme of social reform based on them that had captured the imagination of the untouchable poor, and contributed to the popularity and rapid expansion of the Adi Hindu movement in the 1920s. With an erosion of interest of the leadership in radical religious activism, and their increasing embroilment in institutional politics, the paths of the leaders and the led began to diverge. The Adi Hindu movement appeared to lose its momentum by the mid-1930s, at least in public political campaigns. Far fewer police or newspaper reports dealt with the subject compared with a few years earlier, except when concerned with developments in the councils or large national or provincial conferences of the leaders.

The Adi Hindu movement was, however, kept alive through localised initiatives, and primarily through continued bhakti religious expansion among the poorer untouchables. For this was the most potent and emancipatory aspect of the Adi Hindu movement, and formed the main element of the self-assertion of the untouchable poor. Bhakti resurgence and social reforms continued to gather momentum, albeit in an uneven and fragmented way, throughout the 1930s in local contexts. Ravidas or Kabirpanthi festivals grew more strident, and celebration of the anniversaries of these gurus became annual affairs in the towns. Indeed, these gradually came to assume a place in the calendar of urban public events. The growing prominence of these festivals in urban life clearly suggests that a redefined religious identity continued to be elaborated and nurtured by the untouchables. Religious expression helped the untouchables to mark their presence in urban life and symbolically to carve out a space and presence for themselves in the face of continued exclusion. Their newly constructed identity as Adi Hindus as well as a critique of caste exclusions had come to stay, even though Adi Hinduism as a political movement did not get off the ground. Significantly, Khare observed, based on his research a few decades later on an urban untouchable community in Lucknow, that 'there is no doubt any more that cultural radicalism is already integral to the self-definition of the contemporary Lucknow chamar'.[92] In this comment, Khare referred to the abiding influence of the social movement initiated by such radical ascetics as Acchutanand.

Although religious and social activism constituted the primary arena of the political action and assertion of the untouchable poor, yet overt political agitation, engaging the state and political institutions, of course occurred from time to time when they supported the leadership on specific issues. These political campaigns were, not surprisingly, largely sporadic or short-lived and confined to periods of political debates when the issue of the rights or entitlements of the untouchables assumed centre stage. The timing and immediate context of particular political campaigns were thus set by wider developments. Political agitation peaked during periods of deliberation about constitutional change and political representation, or during wider political debates which involved the question of the rights of backward communities or religious minorities. During these periods, Adi Hindu leaders not only became particularly active in the institutional political arena to demand special rights, but at the same time, at the local level in the towns, they organised political demonstrations and meetings in support of their political demands.

One such period of intense political activity occurred in 1928 during the visit of the Indian Statutory Commission. Contrary to the policy of non-cooperation of the Congress, Adi Hindu leaders refused to boycott the Commission. Instead, with a view to securing rights for their constituents, the leaders resolved to give evidence to the Commission and staged a campaign to attract the Commission's attention to the problems of the untouchables. The political campaign was led by the Adi Hindu Depressed Classes Association (also called the All-India Adi Hindu Mahasabha), which had been formed in 1925 as an apex organisation in the province. Widespread participation of urban untouchables in the political agitations is evident from police reports of frequent and well-attended meetings and demonstrations in this period, either organised by the Adi Hindu sabhas in the towns or by local caste groups.[93] These political events were organised to put forward demands for separate political rights as well as government jobs, scholarships and entry to schools and colleges. When the Simon Commission arrived in

[92] Khare, *Untouchable as Himself*, p. 88.
[93] References to meetings in the towns appear in *PAI*, No. 15, 21 April 1928; No. 21, 2 June 1928; No. 33, 25 August 1928.

Lucknow on 28 November 1928, the local Adi Hindu sabha, led by the prominent leaders Ram Charan and Shiv Dayal Singh Chaurasia, staged a street play and a crowded demonstration at the Charbagh Railway Station to present the demands of untouchables.[94] The Adi Hindu Depressed Classes Association demanded rights as well as preferential treatment, on the argument that, even though there had been beneficial change in the social position of untouchables and in their employment relations in the twentieth century, owing to their 'low' and 'depressed' status they continued to be confined to low-paid, menial jobs, and failed to acquire education, better employment or a voice in the representative institutions.[95]

In 1931–2, the Round Table Conferences and discussions over the issue of separate or joint electorates for untouchables provoked a renewed bout of political demonstrations. This was when Ambedkar and Gandhi had political disagreements, with Gandhi undertaking a fast until an agreement was reached in the form of the Poona Pact in 1932. Adi Hindu organisations in the towns campaigned to rally support among untouchables. In Lucknow, in October 1931, a meeting addressed by the Adi Hindu leaders Ram Charan and Chandrika Prasad Jijnasu was attended by 2,000–3,000 untouchables.[96] Large public meetings were also held in Kanpur and Allahabad where Adi Hindu leaders such as Swami Acchutanand and Shyam Lal delivered speeches.[97] At some of these meetings, Gandhi and the Congress were the targets of violent criticism for opposing separate electorates for untouchables and it was declared that the Adi Hindus must fight their own struggle, for they could not rely on the Congress.[98] At one meeting in Lucknow, attended by 600 sweepers and convened by the Congress at the time when Gandhi was fasting, a sweeper, Asrafi Lal, rose from the audience and held forth against Gandhi and the insincerity of the harijan uplift initiative of the Congress.[99]

From the time of this controversy over separate electorates, the Congress charged into the battle for the hearts and minds of the untouchables with much greater vigour than ever before. The harijan uplift initiatives were intensified. In contrast to the Adi Hindu movement, the Congress sought to present itself to the untouchables as

[94] Dinkar, *Swatantrata Sangram*, p. 80.
[95] Interview with the Deputation from Depressed Classes, UP, Lucknow, 6 December 1928, *Indian Statutory Commission*, vol. XVI, Part I, p. 362.
[96] *PAI*, No. 43, 31 August 1931.
[97] *PAI*, No. 39, 3 October 1931; No. 44, 7 November 1931; No. 46, 21 November 1931; No. 38, 24 September 1932.
[98] *PAI*, No. 40, 8 October 1932.
[99] *PAI*, No. 38, 24 September 1932.

the focus of an alternative identity as 'harijan' or the people of god. It also offered a competitive set of ideologies for their emancipation through acculturation and integration into the Hindu community. The very logic of Adi Hinduism, with a section of the Indian population claiming to be the true inheritors of the land, would threaten the Congress vision of the unity and indivisibility of the nation and its people, which underpinned the party's claim to sole nationalist leadership of the country. As Jijnasu, an Adi Hindu ideologue, pointed out: 'If we call ourselves Adi Hindus, then by the very implication of the term we assert a natural right over India.'[100] Achchutanand too repeatedly stressed what he saw as the prior, natural and superior claim of the untouchables to the nation.[101] The Gandhian movement could ill brook such potentially separatist and exclusivist claims of the untouchables to be Adi Hindus. While this militated against an alliance between Congress and untouchable politics, yet bridges could have been built through some other means. Gandhi's own idiom of devotional religion could potentially resonate with the bhakti religion of the untouchables and with the ascetic figures of the sants and gurus whom they increasingly consciously set up on a pedestal. However, the possibility of identification with Gandhian devotionalism was limited by the perception that the untouchables were the inheritors of a distinctive egalitarian, heterodox tradition of bhakti of pre-Aryan origin, which was not part of the mainstream Hindu devotionalism that Gandhi espoused. Gandhi's pietistic idiom of renunciant asceticism, while in tune with the devotionalism of many commercial and cultivating communities,[102] was, none the less rather far from the image of the radical social leveller sants whom the untouchables revered. Besides, as seen above, during Gandhi's fast to persuade Ambedkar to accept joint electorates, the Adi Hindu leaders had conducted extensive campaigns against the Gandhian position. They had above all widely aired the question of who would rule in independent India.[103] They had stressed that, unlike the rest of Indian society, the untouchables had to contend with 'double servitude' – first, to the higher castes and, second, to foreign rule.[104] They also frequently projected foreign rule as the less oppressive, and

---

[100] *Achchutanand biography*, p. 18.

[101] Ibid., pp. 18–20.

[102] D. Hardiman, 'The Crisis of the Lesser Patidars: Peasant Agitations in the Kheda District, Gujarat, 1917–34', in D. A. Low (ed.), *Congress and the Raj: Facets of the Indian Struggle, 1917–47*, New Delhi, 1977, pp. 59–61; Douglas Haynes, *Rhetoric and Ritual in Colonial India: The Shaping of a Public Culture in Surat City, 1852–1928*, Berkeley, 1991, Delhi, 1992, pp. 220–37.

[103] *Achchutanand biography*, p. 26; *PAI*, No. 26, 10 July 1926.

[104] A term used by Ambedkar in his evidence to the Simon Commission, cited in Dinkar, *Swatantrata Sangram*, p. 81.

even as a benign force,[105] which had opened up new opportunities for the untouchables through occupational mobility and education, and thus facilitated their political assertion. It was with this view that the Adi Hindu leaders of UP had refused to boycott the Simon Commission, defying the Congress, and presented their evidence to the Commission. Within this context, not surprisingly, the response of the untouchable poor to the Congress' harijan uplift overture was mixed.

The leadership of the Adi Hindu movement split over the issue of supporting the Congress in the early 1930s, and chose divergent political strategies to achieve their goal of advancing the interests of the untouchables. Some leaders of the original Adi Hindu Association preferred to avoid the help of the Congress in organising social reform work and in setting up schools for untouchables. Another section opted for a policy of pragmatic alliance and formed a break-away party called the Depressed Classes League. They were inclined to cooperate with the Congress in order to take advantage of the practical benefits of the party's 'constructive work' and the harijan uplift programme. It is, however, significant that, despite the disinclination of the Congress to acknowledge the claim of the untouchables to be the original inhabitants, the pro-Congress Depressed Classes League was cautious about advancing an alternative focus of identity of the untouchables as harijans. They continued to reiterate that the untouchables were the *pracheen nivasi* (ancient inhabitants) of India and that bhakti was their separate religion.[106] These ideas had clearly gained such favour among the urban untouchables by the 1930s that the Congress not only was unable to deny them actively, but also tacitly accepted them in its mobilisation initiatives for fear of alienating the mass of the untouchables. What is important here is that the Congress, even though it did find some response in its harijan uplift campaigns, did not succeed in providing an alternative emancipatory ideology or a different focus of identity for the untouchables as harijans within the Hindu fold. Not surprisingly, twenty-five small Hindu temples that had been opened for the use of untouchables in 1934 when Mahatma Gandhi visited Kanpur soon fell into disuse owing to the lack of interest of untouchables.[107] At the ideological level, then, it seems that, notwithstanding Congress initiatives to win over the untouchables, Adi Hinduism by the 1930s had

---

[105] *PAI*, No. 26, 10 July 1926.

[106] *UP Depressed Classes League ki Teis Saal ki Report, tatha Udyeshya, Karya Vivaran aur Appeal* (a pamphlet outlining the history, aims and programme of the Depressed Classes League), Lucknow, 1935, pp. 3–5, 10, N. P. Arora Collection, Printed material, Serial no. 7, NML.

[107] N. P. Arora and N. C. Chaturvedi, *Kanpur ke Gata Pachas Varsh ki Rajnitik aur Sahityik Jhanki*, Kanpur, 1951, p. 36

come to assume considerable preponderance among the untouchables, despite the difficulties of the movement in the arena of institutional and organisational politics.

As for the response of the untouchable poor, Gandhian organisations and institutions generated limited interest among them for the benefits that they offered by way of vocational training or schools for children.[108] There is, however, little evidence to suggest any major success of the harijan uplift initiative in these UP towns. The limitations of the Gandhian path of dalit emancipation have been extensively aired, not only by recent scholars but also by contemporary untouchable politicians themselves, such as Ambedkar.[109] For instance, the Gandhian approach based on 'constructive work' and social service was at best seen to be sufficient to improve individual untouchable lives, but not to achieve structural social transformation to reverse the 'low' position of untouchables.[110] Similarly Gandhian attempts to change the hearts of the higher castes about caste differences were viewed with considerable cynicism by contemporary untouchable leaders, not least because the political experience of the 1920s and 1930s had cast doubt on the willingness of the upper castes to concede rights and power to the untouchables. In addition to such general problems with the Gandhian harijan uplift initiative, what appears to have made the Gandhian way largely ineffective in the UP towns was the history of at least a decade of religious assertion and a movement against social exclusion through bhakti resurgence and Adi Hinduism. These provided a far more radical and assertive ideology of social liberation than that of the Congress. Moreover, the Congress side-stepped some of the central questions that concerned the urban untouchables. Gandhi and the Congress attempted to invest respectability in 'low' jobs, which was symbolised by high-caste Congress volunteers undertaking sweeping and cleaning. Gestures of this kind were, however, geared not to release the untouchables from their deprivation in menial jobs, but merely to dignify that work and erode the stigma attached to it with paternalistic, patronising, philan-

---

[108] For instance, near Allahabad, at Chandpur Salori, Ishwar Saran, a Congressman, set up a large *Harijan Ashram*, which drew untouchables from the city. Interview in Allahabad with C. S. Saran, son of Ishwar Saran.

[109] B. R. Ambedkar, *What the Congress and Gandhi Have Done to the Untouchables*, Bombay, 1945. More recent scholarly critiques include, Zelliot, 'Congress and the Untouchables', pp. 182–97; Vijay Prashad, 'Between Economism and Emancipation: Untouchables and Indian Nationalism, 1920–1950', *Left History*, 3, 1, Spring/ Summer, 1995, pp. 5–30; B. R. Joshi, *Democracy in Search of Equality: Untouchable Politics and Indian Social Change*, Delhi, 1982, pp. 42–48; Gore, *Social Context of an Ideology*, pp. 139–40; G. Omvedt, *Dalits and the Democratic Revolution: Dr. Ambedkar and the Dalit Movement in Colonial India*, Delhi, 1994, pp. 161–89.

[110] Gore, *Social Context of an Ideology*, pp. 139–40.

thropy. The approach here was a personalised moral and spiritual one, aiming at attitudinal transformation, rather than focusing on structural social and political change or challenging the social hierarchy. This Gandhian initiative scarcely provided either a powerful alternative vision or a convincing possibility of liberating untouchables from their 'traditional' occupations, which had been the key preoccupation of urban Adi Hinduism. It is, of course, well known that Gandhi did not question the principle of caste divisions, which further served to dilute the significance of the Gandhian movement for the untouchables.[111] Thus, there remained an ambiguity in the relationship between the Congress and the untouchables in UP towns where the Adi Hindu movement flourished. Had the Adi Hindu movement not developed in the UP towns, the Gandhian movement might have generated greater enthusiasm. Crucially, however, not only was there a public critique of the Gandhian position, but also, and more significantly, a radical and emancipatory alternative was available to the untouchable poor through their own engagement with the Adi Hindu movement.

The Gandhian harijan uplift programme was, however, not the only initiative to emanate from the Congress fold to integrate the untouchables in Indian nationalism and to offer a solution to the problem of their deprivation. From the mid-1930s, a left-wing group within the Congress, the Congress Socialist Party (CSP), attempted to organise untouchable occupational groups in trade unions on the basis of their workplace demands. This was possible owing to the enclaved nature of labour and employment of some sections of the urban untouchable poor, especially their concentration in municipal sanitation work. By the 1930s, these untouchable occupational groups, such as municipal sweepers, had begun to organise themselves to demand better wages and working conditions, as well as civic facilities in their residential neighbourhoods and schools for their children.[112] It was these trade union type organisations into which the Congress Socialists stepped and provided leadership, with considerable success in bringing about strikes.[113] However, in achieving this mobilisation, the Congress Socialist Party deployed a language of class about the relations between

[111] Zelliot, 'Congress and the Untouchables', pp. 184–5, 193; Joshi, *Democracy in Search of Equality*, pp. 42–8.

[112] *Report of the Benares Municipal Board Enquiry Committee, 1933*, Allahabad, 1933, pp. 178–80; Demands presented by Lallu Ram Sweeper of the Kanpur *Mehtar Sabha* (Scavengers' Union) to the Municipal Board, Serial No. 25, File No. 160/1938, Department XXIII, Municipal, Allahabad Commissioner's Office Records; *PAI*, No. 37, 17 September 1932.

[113] Interview with Nageshwar Valmiki in Allahabad. The organisational activities of the CSP will be discussed in detail in chapter 9 below.

employers and employees, and about the contradictions between capital and labour. They focused on securing largely 'economic' demands of wage or working conditions from the employers on behalf of the sweepers. Manifestly, this 'class' approach did not accommodate a broader range of political aspirations of the untouchables for rights, nor did it incorporate their social identity as an excluded section. The socialists tended to subsume caste under class-based politics. However, political action on the part of the untouchable workers, even in the form of the trade union movement, was related to their growing political awareness, which had developed through the bhakti and Adi Hindu movements. At times, the connections with Adi Hinduism were clearly stated in trade union action. In a charter of demands submitted to the Commissioner of Allahabad in 1939 by the association of municipal sweepers in the town, it was argued that as an 'untouchable Adi Hindu community' their own representatives should be given places on the committee set up by the provincial government to propose improvements in the working and living conditions of municipal employees.[114] Thus, workplace-based political action was also informed by the Adi Hindu and bhakti religious and social reform movements. The latter remained a prominent form of self-assertion for the untouchable poor. The experiences of the untouchables at their workplace and in wider social contexts were interconnected and the struggle against social exclusion was as significant as securing higher wages or better working conditions. The Congress Socialists were unable, however, to address these dual dimensions of untouchable politics, and their initiative was no more successful than the Gandhian one in this particular respect.[115]

There was yet another element in the uneasy relationship between Congress nationalism and the untouchable poor in the towns. The Congress attempt to incorporate untouchables into Indian nationalism was buttressed by religious reformist initiatives to 'purify' and assimilate lower castes into the Hindu fold. In this, the harijan uplift initiative of the Congress went hand in hand with the ongoing Arya Samaj campaigns of social reform and 'purification', both often undertaken by the same personnel, since the Congress and the Arya Samaj activist was frequently one and the same person. While the Congress invited the untouchables to join the national community, the Arya Samaj offered them membership in the Hindu community. In the 1920s, the Arya

[114] Serial No. 18, File No. 160/1938, Department XXIII, Municipal, Allahabad Commissioner's Office Records.
[115] For critical analyses of the economistic and class-based approaches of the Congress and Left parties to the problem of untouchable workers, see Prashad, 'Between Economism and Emancipation'; Omvedt, *Dalits and the Democratic Revolution*, pp. 177–85; G. Omvedt, *Dalit Visions*, Delhi, 1995, pp. 40–2.

Samaj and the Congress were joined by the Hindu Mahasabha in making overtures to the lower castes, especially under the leadership of Madan Mohan Malaviya, who was increasingly eager to consolidate the Hindu community, faced with the growing importance of communal representation in the electoral arena and the development of Muslim separatist politics.[116] The activists of these various organisations launched paternalist and philanthropic campaigns for the amelioration of the moral, material and educational conditions of the untouchables, in a bid to offer them an identity as Hindus and as worthy members of the national community. The reformers attempted to promote temperance, facilitate literacy, eradicate gambling and supposedly 'vulgar' forms of entertainment, and reform life-cycle ceremonies. They also tried to purge so-called 'superstitions' and various forms of religious beliefs which did not conform to 'respectable' Hinduism.[117] While some of these concerns for 'improvement', such as the avoidance of intoxicants or the cultivation of literacy and thrift, clearly overlapped with the untouchables' own social reform activities, yet the underlying rationale differed significantly. For the untouchables, as seen earlier, the adoption of temperance, the exercise of moderation in religious celebrations or even the attempt to embrace a more 'ascetic', devotional lifestyle, were all aimed, in no small measure, at achieving economic self-sufficiency and liberating themselves from the control of the higher castes and from the tyranny of social and occupational 'low' roles, not at the emulation of respectable social standards. However, for the nationalist, Arya Samajist and Hindu Mahasabha reformers, drinking, gambling and 'popular' religious practices constituted evil or bad habits, which had to be overcome, not simply to prevent indebtedness, but also to qualify for higher status and as fit and proper members of Indian society. Indeed, in the nationalist social reform approach, indebtedness was seen not as a product of poverty, but as a function of people living beyond their means by indulging in wasteful and disagreeable or immoral habits and activities.[118] Social training and behavioural reform for self-improvement, the inculcation of better 'habits' among lower castes and the censure of their existing practices, which were taken to be the mark of their 'lowness', thus formed central elements of nationalist and Hindu

[116] S. L. Gupta, *Pandit Madan Mohan Malaviya: A Socio-political Study*, Allahabad, 1978, pp. 297–300; R. A. Gordon, 'The Hindu Mahasabha and the Indian National Congress, 1915 to 1926', *MAS*, 9, 2, 1975, p. 170.
[117] Gupta, *Malaviya*, pp. 297–300; Jones, *Arya Dharm*, pp. 95–6; Ganesh Shankar Vidyarthi, 'Adi Hindu Andolan' (editorial article from the Kanpur newspaper *Pratap*, dated 27 April 1925), in R. K. Awasthi (ed.), *Kranti ka Udghosh: Ganesh Shankar Vidyarthi ki kalam se*, vol. II, Kanpur, 1978, pp. 798–801.
[118] Upadhyaya (ed.), *Dalitoddhar*, pp. 6–7.

reformism. These tendencies were especially prominent and therefore increasingly decisive in influencing the perceptions and responses of the untouchables from the 1920s, when campaigns for mass mobilisation were stepped up to consolidate both the national and the Hindu communities.[119]

In this respect, the attitude of Madan Mohan Malaviya, an important figure in initiating caste uplift programmes in UP from within a Hindu nationalist framework, is illuminating. Although he upheld the validity of caste distinctions and the varnashrama dharma, Malaviya opposed the exclusion of untouchables from *public* places and affairs, including temples, on the ground that the 'polluting' state of untouchability related to aberrant *personal* conduct and behaviour, which if eradicated would bring about the redemption and salvation of the untouchables and rectify their 'polluting' influence.[120] This emphasis on personal behavioural elements in the uplift of untouchables, rather than on public exclusion, led Malaviya to advocate that they should be given religious consecration, involving *diksha* (initiation) and *sanskar* (purification and reform). A person thus consecrated, he believed, would 'discard all evil habits and then become pure and religious'. Such a person would then 'cease to be called and treated as untouchable'.[121] Malaviya, moreover, exhorted the untouchables to give up evil habits, to educate themselves and to change their conduct and manner.[122] In particular, he advised the untouchables to acquire proper religious instruction in Hinduism, which would make them useful members of society.[123] In this context, it is also relevant that, according to one of his biographers, Malaviya attached supreme importance to primary education as 'a *sine qua non* of [national] efficiency and progress', which would 'solve the problems of ignorance, untouchability and communal bitterness, etc., and promote sanitary habits among the people'.[124] By making the people 'physically, morally and intellectually more efficient', as well as aware of hygiene and sanitation, Malaviya envisaged primary education for all, including and especially the lower castes and classes, to help in forging the future nation.[125] Underlying the reformist initiatives of such Hindu nationalists as Malaviya, then, were efforts to weld together the national or the Hindu community through the promotion of social and behavioural conformity and uniformity. In this respect, Carey Watt has argued that constructive nationalists in north India, with their prime concern to augment national efficiency and the numerical strength of

---

[119] Joshi, *Democracy in Search of Equality*, p. 44.
[120] Gupta, *Malaviya*, p. 333.   [121] Ibid., p. 334.
[122] Ibid., pp. 330–4.   [123] Ibid., p. 296.
[124] Ibid., p. 359.   [125] Ibid.

the Hindu community, focused their attention, in particular, on the education of the lower castes to make them more productive and efficient members of society.[126]

The elements of social control and discipline of the lower castes, as well as the imposition of a higher-caste value system that these approaches implicitly harboured or explicitly advanced, inevitably rendered the relation between the nationalist reformers and the untouchables increasingly tension-ridden from the 1920s. This contradiction was further accentuated against a background of Adi Hindu social reforms which sought precisely to reverse the tendencies of the upper castes to impose their own values and practices. As Barbara Joshi has pointed out, the obsession of the reformers with the 'ignorance' and 'poor manners' of the untouchables, as well as 'the penitential quality' of uplift initiatives, 'reemphasised the popular prejudiced attitude that social contact with all untouchables was disagreeable' and maintained 'many of the negative stereotypes of the untouchable'.[127] Small wonder then that the leaders of the twentieth century were at times seen by the untouchables as the successors of the ancient Aryan oppressors, but presenting themselves in a benevolent and philanthropic garb.[128]

The Arya Samaj and Congress activists were also obsessed with the promotion of cleanliness among untouchables as a significant step, not only in undoing the ill-effects of their contact with filth and dirt in the course of their 'impure' work, but also in bringing about their moral and material uplift. Of course, an accompanying idea was that it was not simply their work which made the untouchables physically dirty, but also their proneness to unhygienic habits. This overwhelming preoccupation with the supposed insalubrious disposition of the untouchable poor, while related to notions of ritual pollution, is most likely to have been further fuelled by the growing concern in the interwar period about the 'insanitary' living and working conditions of the urban poor and their unhygienic propensities. The untouchables, usually being the most 'low' and 'poor' of the urban population, could be perceived to be especially in need of being cleansed in the interest of sanitised, improved urban environments. The issues of ritual purity and physical cleanliness gradually seemed to become conflated, and fed off each other. Thus while the local authorities often zealously targeted untouchable neighbourhoods for 'improvement', the Congress volunteers enthusiastically descended into these residential areas armed with brooms to clean them

[126] C. A. Watt, 'Education for National Efficiency: Constructive Nationalism in North India, 1909–1916', MAS, 31, 2, 1997, pp. 362–5.

[127] Joshi, Democracy in Search of Equality, p. 44.

[128] Achhutanand biography, pp. 88–9.

out. Local Congress and Arya Samaj workers even arranged the distribution of soap and toothbrushes in the neighbourhoods of the untouchable poor to promote personal hygiene.[129] The untouchables were urged in a caste uplift manual of the Arya Samaj in Allahabad to shower and to brush their teeth everyday, to wash their bed-clothes and garments, and to clean their houses regularly. The untouchables were told:

Cultivate the habit of living purely [*shuddhata*]. Cleanliness is the root of contentment. . . . [If you stay clean] you will then see how much pleasure you feel. Your bodies will be less afflicted with disease. Your hearts will remain happy. Everyone will want to meet you. Your own thoughts and judgements will be wiser and more discerning. You will have less cares. People will automatically cease to look down upon you. They will sit together with you as equals and behave with you as brothers.[130]

Evidently, this promotion of cleanliness in the body and surroundings was a rather literal and misplaced approach to undermining the religious conceptions of ritual pollution and the social or political exclusions arising from them. As the above quotation shows, the task of reversing the deprivation of the untouchables was equated with making them physically clean, with which would automatically come health, happiness, superior thoughts and values as well as social equality, when all would want to sit next to them. The promotion of cleanliness here appears to have been envisaged as a measure to dragoon the untouchables into becoming tidy, orderly, happy, right-thinking, unthreatening and docile members of society. The radical edge of untouchable politics, which contested social exclusion and denied caste distinctions, was here considerably blunted and given a benign orientation. Indeed, untouchable politics were thus sought to be contained within manageable limits, and ultimately controlled and emasculated, as Vijay Prashad has argued in another context. Discussing some broadly similar developments in the Punjab to do with providing clean working conditions for urban untouchable sweepers, Prashad holds that 'the demands of the untouchables, therefore, were reinterpreted by the Congress in order to remove the antagonistic components'.[131] To the untouchables of the UP towns, the nationalist-reformist cleanliness initiative would have been at best irrelevant and at worst a form of censure by projecting them as behaviourally or characteristically unclean, which was more likely to accentuate, rather than undermine, their social and cultural exclusion. Indeed, the alienation and marginalisation that this implied were

---

[129] Interview with Gopi Dom in Benares; Joshi, 'Bonds of Community', pp. 257–8.
[130] Upadhyaya, *Dalitoddhar*, pp. 8, 11.
[131] Prashad, 'Between Economism and Emancipation', pp. 5–30.

precisely the conditions that untouchable social movements sought to reverse from the 1920s. It is not surprising, then, that the attempts at assimilation of the untouchables into the Hindu fold through reform and uplift did not succeed in cultivating an identity of the untouchables as Hindus, instead of as Adi Hindus. The relationship of the untouchable poor with the upper-caste nationalists and religious reformers remained uneasy in the UP towns, and neither provided an adequate focus for the politics of the untouchable poor. Instead, bhakti and Adi Hinduism formed the dominant and sustained form of their political expression and identity, despite the sporadic and uneven nature of agitational politics under the Adi Hindu banner.

6   Militant Hinduism

The major cities of UP in the interwar period emerged as the sites of unprecedentedly widespread and frequent communal violence between Hindus and Muslims.[1] This outbreak of violence was accompanied by an increasingly militant and martial public expression of both Hinduism and Islam. Religious processions and festivals proliferated and came to be observed with mounting zeal and fervour. Such religious expressions were characterised by aggressive chants and displays of arms and physical feats. Religious organisations multiplied in urban neighbourhoods, with intensifying rivalry and competition between contending groups of Hindus and Muslims. Most significantly, in this upsurge of religious militancy, some sections of the urban poor came to play a pivotal role. This chapter and the following one seek to shed light on this history of religious resurgence and strife among various groups of the urban poor.

The subject of religion and politics has engaged much scholarly attention. When urbanisation, religious conflict and the poor are discussed, some dominant themes run through most studies in different ways.[2] One theme is the segmentation of the labour market along the lines of caste or religious community, frequently reinforced by the divisive strategies of the employers and the state in recruiting, control-

[1] In Allahabad, minor skirmishes occurred between groups of Hindus and Muslims in 1917–18 at the time of religious festivals, but the city experienced its first series of extensive rioting from 1924 to 1926. Kanpur saw a localised religious affray in 1927, and an unusually violent riot engulfed the whole city in 1931. In 1931, Benares was torn by its first major communal riot. In Lucknow several communal clashes occurred between 1924 and 1926. Benares, Allahabad and Kanpur were rocked by further rioting between 1937 and 1939.
[2] Chitra Joshi, 'Bonds of Community, Ties of Religion: Kanpur Textile Workers in the Early Twentieth Century', *IESHR*, 22, 3, 1985, pp. 251–80; Dipesh Chakrabarty, 'Communal Riots and Labour: Bengal's Jute Mill-hands in the 1890s', in V. Das (ed.), *Mirrors of Violence: Communities, Riots and Survivors in South Asia*, Delhi, 1990, pp. 146–84 (previously published in *Past and Present*, 1981); Dipesh Chakrabarty, *Rethinking Working Class History: Bengal, 1890–1940*, Princeton, 1989, pp. 186–218; R. S. Chandavarkar, *The Origins of Industrial Capitalism in India: Business Strategies and the Working Classes in Bombay, 1900–1940*, Cambridge, 1994, pp. 421–3, 426–8.

ling, and reproducing labour. Competition among members of different communities for jobs is considered a significant factor in the formation and expression of religious identities. Various studies also point to the efficacy of past values, ideals and kinship ties for the poor in rapidly changing and hostile environments, especially in the burgeoning towns. Chitra Joshi, for instance, emphasises the 'continuity of "traditional" modes of thought and feeling among workers' and argues that the urban 'social milieu has to be located in a context where religious myths, legends and symbols retained their meaningfulness and motivational power for workers and also provided them with categories with which they created and apprehended their social world'.[3] It is also argued that, confronted with the bitterly divided and competitive conditions of work and urban living, the poor hark back to traditional ways of life and invoke the support of kin and community networks as ways of achieving both psychological succour and physical or material security. These approaches are illuminating in providing the background against which communal conflicts develop. They do, however, harbour two different kinds of analytical problem. On the one hand, they tend to reduce the question of religion and politics to material considerations. On the other hand, they ultimately beg the question why such conflicts should take religious forms or why religion should be invoked in the process of urban socialisation, unless it is implicitly assumed that religious community affiliations and values are both enduring and extremely powerful, and that the poor automatically draw upon them. The question 'why religion?' remains to be addressed.

Answers to this question have been offered, most notably, by some historians of the 'Subaltern' school. Their perspective on the subject hinges largely on the notion of community consciousness, and this, in turn, stems from some of their wider theoretical considerations. Three interrelated points are important here. First, in seeking to reveal the autonomy, subjectivity and agency of the subaltern classes, these historians have conceptualised the essence of subaltern mentality in terms of notions of community, which are frequently defined by religion. It has been argued that subaltern ideas of honour or shame and their codes of morality and justice are mediated through community or communitarian values, in which religion often plays a pivotal role.[4] Some Subaltern historians have buttressed this argument with the further, and second, point that, in contrast to ideas of individual citizenship or individualism, deriving primarily from the European 'Enlightenment',

---

[3] Joshi, 'Bonds of Community', pp. 251, 258.
[4] Chakrabarty, *Rethinking*, pp. 213–17; P. Chatterjee, *Bengal, 1920–1947: The Land Question*, Calcutta, 1984, pp. 136–7.

subaltern mentality is informed by pre-bourgeois or pre-capitalist notions of community.[5] This pre-existing community consciousness, focused largely on religion or caste, was then brought into play, expanded and magnified by the subalterns in their encounters with the large and decisive changes brought about by colonialism and capitalism, leading to the centrality of religious community identities in their political responses.[6] Thirdly, and related to the first two points, Subaltern historians have sought to liberate the analytical autonomy of culture from the tyranny of liberal rationalist interpretations. They have challenged the post-Enlightenment privileging of rationality, which permits the understanding of human action only in terms of 'economic interests', 'functional utility' or 'tangible need', thus delegitimising other forms of motivation to do with cultural ideals – the realm of faith and beliefs, religion and myth.[7] They have, therefore, in keeping with a range of critiques of master-narratives of modernity, tried to salvage the autonomous history of culture and religion, which is not a mere derivative or reflection of social or political histories.

In this particular respect, the approach of the Subaltern historians has found elaboration and support from others who are concerned to question post-Enlightenment epistemology and to emphasise the analytical importance of 'culture', without reducing all explanations to material issues. Peter van der Veer, in particular, has intervened in the debates on religion. In unravelling the origins of religious nationalism in India, he traces its roots to the long-term history of ritual transitions and transmissions, oriented around the practices of Hindu and Islamic institutions and organisations. Van der Veer ascribes singular centrality to religious rituals, discourse and practice as constitutive of social identity in Indian history, which, he argues, inevitably came to underpin imaginations of the nation in the colonial and post-colonial periods.[8] He seems to suggest that ritual practices and forms of communication based on religion provided the primary, if not the sole, basis for formation of social identities, and hence religion naturally provided the dominant idiom for the discursive forging of the nation. He appears to preclude any serious possibility of the existence of alternative foci of identity and modes of communication, other than religion. Although van der Veer is not specifically concerned with the subaltern classes, his

[5] Partha Chatterjee, *The Nation and Its Fragments: Colonial and Post-Colonial Histories*, Princeton, 1993, chs. 8, 11.

[6] Chakrabarty, *Rethinking*, pp. 213–17.

[7] Ibid., p. 212; G. Pandey, 'Liberalism and the Study of Indian History: A Review of Writing on "Communalism"', *EPW*, XVIII, 42, 15 October 1983, pp. 1789–91.

[8] P. van der Veer, *Religious Nationalism: Hindus and Muslims in India*, Berkeley, 1994, passim and especially pp. ix–xvi, 12–24.

affirmation of the primacy of religious constructions in shaping wider political identities and his attempt to undermine the narrative of secular modernity dovetail into the analytical perspective of the Subaltern historians.

The various concerns of the Subaltern historians, reinforced by such works as that of van der Veer, have converged to produce a view of religion and subaltern politics which harbours essentialised notions about the religious world-view of the subaltern classes, which seemingly over-determines their politics. Partha Chatterjee comments in his analysis of peasant politics in Bengal: 'The very nature of peasant consciousness . . . is religious. Religion to such a community provides an ontology, an epistemology, as well as a practical code of ethics, including political ethics. When this community acts politically, the symbolic meaning of particular acts – their signification – must be found in religious terms.'[9] Similarly, Dipesh Chakrabarty asserts that mill workers in Calcutta and its hinterland had 'a communal sense of identity and honour',[10] the strongest of which is religion, in addition to language and habitat. Further, he writes, 'distinctions based on birth – religion, language and kinship – were central to the jute mill workers' sense of identity', and hence 'religion, . . . ethnicity, or language or other similar loyalties, formed the stuff of his [worker's] politics'.[11] Chakrabarty goes on to elaborate that such community consciousness carries with it a hierarchical sense of social allegiances or political loyalties, which predisposes the subaltern classes to ally and identify with other members of their religious community, including social superiors and elites, irrespective of class or any other form of social contradiction.[12] He asserts: 'The power relations that made up their [the workers'] everyday life arose out of a culture that was hierarchical and inegalitarian, subordinating the individual to imagined communities of a distinctly pre-capitalist character.'[13] The implication here is that the consciousness of community precludes or prevents the articulation of class distinctions or egalitarian political discourses. Indeed, by imputing an essentially communitarian subjectivity to the workers, who allegedly espoused a hierarchical conception of society, Chakrabarty implies the culpability and complicity of the workers themselves in their own oppression. Most importantly, he is unwilling to countenance the

---

[9] Chatterjee, *Bengal, 1920–1947*, pp. 136–7.
[10] Chakrabarty, *Rethinking*, p. 213.
[11] Ibid., p. 217.
[12] Ibid., p. 229; Chakrabarty, 'Communal Riots and Labour', pp. 146–84.
[13] Chakrabarty, *Rethinking*, p. 229.

possibility that languages of class could develop by inflecting other languages of politics, including that of religious community.[14]

All these views, in various degrees, come surprisingly close to a primordialist interpretation of religion in political action, although with the difference that these historians do not argue for the static time-lessness of religious community consciousness. They would recognise that notions of community are historically constructed and dynamic, and that such notions found particular elaboration in the context of colonial and capitalist transformations. None the less, some questions remain: if and when the subaltern classes emphasised their religious identity in the colonial period, then did they do so because of the seemingly 'autonomous' meaning that religion and community carried for them? Were their actions always, inevitably or invariably conditioned by their supposedly pre-colonial, pre-bourgeois, pre-capitalist, religious community consciousness? It is, of course, axiomatic that the present carries more than just the vestiges of the past. Yet, were past traditions and notions not selectively chosen, given new content and significance, and then reconfigured and deployed in new forms? Indeed, rather than asserting pre-existing notions in changing contexts, albeit with embel-lishment and contextual reinterpretation, could new notions of religious tradition and of community have not been forged? Were the meaning and significance of particular forms of religious identity not constructed and reconstructed, even newly invented, rather than merely carried from the past and transplanted and cultivated on a larger and more intensive scale, in new and changing situations? These questions lead to another broader one: Is it necessary at all to deploy the arguably 'essentialised' concept of pre-capitalist or pre-bourgeois community consciousness and communitarianism in historical analysis to under-stand religious assertion or communal antagonism?

With regard to community consciousness, the nature of linkages between so-called elite and popular culture and politics also requires investigation. Sandria Freitag has shown that the early twentieth century was characterised by the growth of religious festivals and celebrations as collective activities, and by the shared participation of elites and popular classes in rites of community in the 'public arena'. This, she argues, contributed to the emergence of a cohesive sense of religious community and 'the elaboration in this period [1920s–1930s] of a sustained ideology of community that united "Hindus", and another that united "Muslims", residing in north Indian urban areas'.[15] However, in the

---

[14] Ibid., pp. 193–5.
[15] S. B. Freitag, *Collective Action and Community: Public Arenas and the Emergence of Communalism in North India*, Berkeley, 1989, p. 199.

context of growing class and social tensions in the interwar period, as seen in Part I of this book, and in view of the gradual separation of elite and popular cultural practices from the 1920s, noted by Nita Kumar[16] and Freitag herself,[17] it becomes relevant to take a closer look at the proposition about the power of shared rituals to forge unities. Many scholars now question an anthropological orthodoxy that rituals primarily play a role in reinforcing or reproducing social cohesion, and they are inclined to study rituals as sites of contest.[18] However, in studies of communal conflict in India, the unifying and integrative power of rituals continues to provide a powerful analytical perspective.[19] In contrast, the chapters here, by approaching the history of religious resurgence from the perspective of the poor, seek to ask whether it is, in fact, more appropriate to interpret religious assertion as a phenomenon encompassing different, often contradictory, initiatives of diverse groups, which did not necessarily amount to a cohesive, unifying community identity of the kind envisaged by Freitag.[20] Indeed, these chapters attempt to examine the assumption that a cohesive sense of community, either pre-existing or newly constructed, is necessary for the development of communal conflict. The intention is to explore the diverse reasons behind the outbreak of communal violence or the escalation of communal tension, without assuming that to explain and understand communalism it is necessary to identify and account for the development of a unified sense of community on the part of either Hindus or Muslims. Did such cohesive identities emerge after all, or do other social and political dynamics underpin communal conflict? Did a growing emphasis on religious identity, as expressed through expanding

---

[16] N. Kumar, *The Artisans of Banaras: Popular Culture and Identity, 1880–1986*, Princeton, 1988, pp. 176–8, 190–5.

[17] S. B. Freitag, 'State and Community: Symbolic popular Protest in Banaras's Public Arenas', in S. B. Freitag (ed.), *Culture and Power in Banaras: Community, Performance and Environment, 1800–1980*, Berkeley, 1989, pp. 223–4; S. B. Freitag, 'Enactments of Ram's Story and the Changing Nature of "the Public" in British India', *South Asia*, 14, 1, 1991, pp. 65–90. In this article, Freitag acknowledges the element of contestation present in collective activities in the public arena, but she still sees these as vehicles of 'assertion of values held in common' (p. 85) and of the expression of 'values and viewpoints held by the collectivity' (p. 67), and continues to confirm their ability 'to signify larger forms of community' (p. 83).

[18] Nicholas B. Dirks, 'Ritual and Resistance: Subversion as a Social Fact', in D. Haynes and G. Prakash (eds.), *Contesting Power: Resistance and Everyday Social Relations in South Asia*, Oxford, 1991, 1st edn of the University of California Press, Berkeley, 1992, pp. 213–38; Norbert Peabody, 'Inchoate in Kota?: Contesting Authority through a North Indian Pageant-play', *American Ethnologist*, 24, 3, 1997, pp. 559–84.

[19] See, for instance, Freitag, *Collective Action, passim* and especially pp. 5, 197–9.

[20] For arguments about internal fractures within religious community-based political movements, see G. Pandey, *The Construction of Communalism in Colonial North India*, Delhi, 1990, pp. 199–200, 205.

religious activities, necessarily contribute to a perceived sense of community unity or community consciousness? To address these questions, religious rituals and collective activities in these chapters are not studied simply to discern patterns of conflict between the two major religious communities. Collective religious actions are also dissected for their stratified and multi-layered nature, and analysed as sites of contest and political conflict *within* putative communities – conflicts which arose from the extensive and intensifying social tension of the interwar years. An analysis of religious activities and rituals within the social context of their production may well cast doubts on the proposition that rituals are constitutive of cohesive collective identity, irrespective of the conflictual social and material bases which underpin them.

To examine these various issues, this chapter and the next one explore the history of religious assertion among various groups of the Hindu and the Muslim poor in the early twentieth century, and, in particular, attempt to elucidate the links between poverty, deprivation and religious resurgence, and draw out the interplay of various overlapping identities of the poor based on caste, class, status, labour, occupation and religion.

Low-caste identity and Hindu militancy in the changing towns

The early twentieth century, and especially the 1920s and 1930s, saw a gradual, but radical, transformation in the nature of Hinduism. The public face of Hinduism from this period appeared less and less to be that of devotion and religious worship and more and more that of martial militancy. The dominant image of Hinduism emerged as one of very large crowds of people wielding staffs, flags, swords and other arms, marching in procession during religious festivals, imparting an aura of triumphant and aggressive expansionism to Hinduism.

Christopher Bayly has described the emergence of powerful Hindu mercantile classes, the development of Hindu corporate towns, and the consequent transformation of north Indian urban political culture and social ethos in the late eighteenth and nineteenth centuries.[21] These changes, as Bayly, Freitag and Vasudha Dalmia[22] have demonstrated, provided the context for Hindu revival and reform in the nineteenth century, which were manifested, first, in the proliferation of religious

---

[21] C. A. Bayly, *Rulers, Townsmen and Bazaars: North Indian Society in the Age of British Expansion, 1770–1870*, Cambridge, 1983.

[22] Freitag, *Collective Action, passim*; Vasudha Dalmia, *The Nationalization of Hindu Traditions: Bharatendu Harishchandra and Nineteenth-century Banaras*, Delhi, 1997, pp. 50–145.

rituals and celebrations in what Freitag calls the 'public arena' and, secondly, in the expansion of activities of religious organisations such as the Arya Samaj, the Sanatana Dharma Mahamandal and the Hindu Sabha. It is, thus, through the history of Bayly's rulers, townsmen and *bazars* that the patterns of Hindu assertion can be explained, to a large extent, until the turn of the century. By the 1920s, however, it is primarily in terms of the poor and the bazars that the acceleration in the scale and pace of Hindu resurgence has to be understood. In the years between the two world wars, when north Indian society and its economy underwent further crucial transformations, a section of the urban Hindu poor came to play a central role in the expression of Hinduism as a martial religion and helped to portray the Hindus as a community of aggressive combatants. Their increasingly strident and warlike involvement in Hindu festivals and celebrations fuelled the revivalist efforts of Hindu organisations, led by politicians and publicists and sponsored by affluent and influential merchants and local notables. These Hindu organisations had been trying to consolidate and regenerate the Hindu community from the late nineteenth century onwards by advocating a more militant form of Hinduism. Such attempts of the elites met with hitherto unseen success and gained in strength and intensity in the 1920s and 1930s, when some among the Hindu poor zealously presented themselves as the resurgent army of Hinduism. Hindu festivals, even when sponsored by the elites, now increasingly registered the prominent involvement of the poor.

Not all sections of the poor who were Hindus, however, involved themselves in religious resurgence in equal measure. It was among the growing numbers of the lower-caste or *shudra* labouring poor, who constituted the majority of the urban manual workforce, that a form of Hindu religious militancy developed most strikingly from the 1920s, and they emerged at the forefront of Hindu assertion. Police and newspaper reports repeatedly refer to various shudra caste groups as being involved in communal violence, and as prominent and militant participants in Hindu religious festivals and processions. A large number of those who came to the towns during the interwar years were agricultural labourers and poorer cultivators, who had increasing difficulty in finding sources of livelihood from the land and in the countryside because of the growing pressure of population, followed by the agrarian depression.[23] They belonged mainly to lower shudra agricultural and pastoral castes,[24] such as *ahirs* or *yadavs*, *kurmis*, *gujars*, *pasis* and *khatiks*. Being

---

[23] Discussed in chapter 2.
[24] D. N. Mazumdar, *Social Contours of an Industrial City: Social Survey of Kanpur, 1954–56*, Westport, Conn., 1960, p. vii; C. Joshi, 'Kanpur Textile Labour: Some

traditionally engaged in manual work as well as being illiterate, these shudra migrants to the towns sought unskilled jobs requiring physical labour. They found work as carters, porters and hauliers in the urban trading sector, in the wholesale and retail markets – the *mandis* and the bazars. They found unskilled manual work in the expanding small-scale manufacturing sector – the so-called 'bazar' industries. Many also worked in the construction industry as labourers, carpenters, bricklayers or masons. In fact, the shudras formed an overwhelming majority of manual workers and labourers in urban trade, industry and construction, and the term *kahar* (literally meaning carrier or bearer of load and originally referring to a particular caste of water-carriers), came to be used as a generic term to denote these low-caste manual workers in the bazars.[25] Some of them also diversified into petty trade, hawking and peddling to supplement their income, or engaged in service occupations such as laundering clothes (*dhobis* or washermen) and hair-dressing (*nais* or barbers). These urban occupational groups, as shown in Part I of this book, faced insecurity of employment and poverty, and their economic relations with the urban Hindu high-caste commercial classes began to intensify social tensions in the towns.

There was an important related development. As the urban labour market became overcrowded, the vastly expanded group of the shudra poor entered into direct competition with other contenders for jobs, such as the untouchable and the Muslim poor. The urban workforce at the turn of the century was, to a large extent, segmented along the lines of caste and religion. While the shudra poor worked in urban trade and manufacturing, the untouchable poor tended to be concentrated in sweeping and scavenging jobs, often employed by the municipal conservancy and sanitation departments, and they worked as domestic servants and retainers in the British cantonments and civil stations.[26] By the 1920s, the availability of such employment for the untouchables gradually began to dwindle. The cantonments and civil lines ceased to expand and recruit employees at the earlier rapid pace. The expansion of municipal sanitary and conservancy infrastructure slowed down after the great spurt of activity in the post-Mutiny decades. Moreover, the emergence of social movements for caste uplift and status mobility amongst these groups of untouchables[27] had prompted many of them to

Structural Features of Formative Years', *EPW*, XVI, 44–46, Special Number, November 1981, p. 1827; A. Niehoff, *Factory Workers in India*, Milwaukee, 1959, p. 34.

[25] Ram Shankar Shukla, 'Karmchari Sangathan aur Andolan Kyun?', *Kanpur Bazar Karmchari Federation: Rajat Jayanti Smarika*, Kanpur, 1977 editorial article (pages not numbered).

[26] See chapter 5.   [27] Ibid.

leave so-called 'menial' jobs and to seek work in urban trading and manufacturing. Jobs in these areas had so far been monopolised by lower-caste groups, other than the untouchables, since the orthodox high-caste merchants who dominated trade and manufacturing were often disinclined to employ untouchables. The untouchables now tried to compete with the shudras for these jobs in the bazars, although usually with little success. Similarly, competition developed between the Muslim poor and the shudra poor. The Muslim poor in the towns, most of whom had been engaged in artisanal work, had faced economic insecurity from the nineteenth century, owing to the decline of artisan industries.[28] In the interwar period, their condition worsened as artisan industries faced a further serious crisis with the depression.[29] The outcome was that the Muslim poor too sought employment as manual workers in trade, manufacturing and construction, as well as in petty trading and hawking. They, thus, increasingly attempted to make inroads into those areas of work in which the shudras had so far held sway, and the two sections came increasingly into direct competition with each other as the labour market became more and more crowded.[30] Thus, experience of the shudra poor in the towns encompassed growing occupational conflict with other groups of the poor, in addition to their increasing economic insecurity and marginalisation.

The marginalisation that shudra labourers encountered was, however, not only economic. Increasingly, they faced an erosion of status and respectability, for they were the objects of both the scorn and suspicion of their social superiors, who viewed them as virtual outcasts and as a lowly, volatile, floating, rootless, riff-raff population. This arose partly from the fact that the higher castes attached no worth to manual work and treated physical labour as demeaning. More importantly, all the measures of local administration and policing described in previous chapters were underpinned by the notion that the poor were prone to dirty or bad habits, immoral practices and lawlessness. Not only had municipal and policing policies adversely affected the work and housing of the poor, but, equally importantly, they had contributed to their

28 Kumar, *Artisans*, pp. 19–21; D. A. Thomas, 'Lucknow and Kanpur 1880–1920: Stagnation and Development under the Raj', *South Asia*, 5, 2 (New Series), 1982, pp. 68–72; Nevill, *Allahabad: A Gazetteer*, pp. 62–4; G. Pandey, 'Economic Dislocation in Nineteenth-century Eastern Uttar Pradesh: Some Implications of the Decline of Artisanal Industry in Colonial India', in P. Robb (ed.), *Rural South Asia: Linkages, Change and Development*, London, 1983, pp. 98–9.
29 *RDIUP*, 1929–30, 1930–31, 1931–32.
30 For instance, a pamphlet on the ahirs, published from Benares in 1927, mentioned that Muslim masons and bricklayers were increasing in number and posing a threat to those ahirs who worked in the construction industry. Baijnath Prasad Yadav, *Ahir Jati Ke Niyamavali*, Benares, 1927, p. 39.

social subordination and debasement, and reinforced their material deprivation and economic marginalisation. The increasingly overt expression of elite and official prejudices against the poor through interventionist policies, and the more and more clear characterisation of the poor by the upper classes and the authorities variously as low, violent, immoral or dirty, created an urgency for them to project their self-worth and self-esteem. The cultural and social subordination of the shudra poor was further reinforced by some upper-caste social reform attempts, like that of the Arya Samaj, which had been gaining momentum from the turn of the century. These reform initiatives were based, *inter alia*, on the notion of the inferiority of the religious and social practices of lower-caste groups, which needed to be purified.[31] Within a context of several interlocking processes which marginalised or censured the lower classes and castes, religious assertion emerged as an important mode of self-assertion for the shudra poor. It involved a redefinition of their caste status as the martial ruling classes or *kshatriyas* of the past, who had played a special role in the history of Hinduism. The underlying notion was that the warrior ancestors of the shudras had been the traditional defenders of Hinduism, and it was while defending Hinduism and the Hindu community against the supposedly oppressive Islamic conquerors and rulers of medieval India that the erstwhile warriors were defeated and displaced from power by the Muslims and forced to become subordinate shudras.

What were the reasons for and the nature of the espousal of a warrior identity by the shudra poor in the urban context? Why did the urban low-caste poor claim higher status and in particular stress their role as the warrior guardians of Hinduism? The shudra poor had found themselves in the social and economic milieu of the powerful Hindu commercial groups in the towns. The north Indian urban mercantile communities, composed overwhelmingly of Hindu higher castes, had gradually consolidated and enhanced their power and influence by the nineteenth century. Their ascendance had been marked by their promotion of Hinduism, the manifestations of which included the growing activities of the Arya Samaj, the Hindu Sabha and similar Hindu religious organisations as well as the establishment of Hindu educational and medical institutions and charitable trusts. A prominent and central mode of expression of power by these merchants was their patronage of religion, through temple construction or the sponsoring of festivals. Indeed, religious practice and display provided the major means for their projection of power and status. As Bayly has noted, 'it was

[31] K. W. Jones, *Arya Dharm: Hindu Consciousness in Nineteenth-century Punjab*, Delhi, 1976, pp. 95–6.

primarily in the field of religious patronage (and also ritual advancement) that the commercial notables expended the social energy derived from their wealth'. They were the key players in fostering the forces of Hindu cultural revivalism, puritanical social and moral reform and caste uplift, and 'it was through the active propagation of these religious and status concerns they came to contribute to the developing public politics of upper India'.[32] Thus, an increasingly confident and assertive Hindu cultural style had become central to the urban mercantile ethos, where piety, prosperity and political power all equally symbolised the growing dominance of commercial classes in the towns.[33]

It was within this environment of commercial communities that the shudra poor found themselves in a subordinate and debased position. In order to assert themselves, and faced with social and economic marginalisation as well as overt and growing upper-class disdain or prejudices, it became relevant for the shudra poor to claim their own pivotal role in the history of Hinduism. For, by projecting themselves as the defenders of Hindu faith and territory, the poor could try to match or confront the power of the merchants symbolically. If religion was integral to the constitution and expression of the power of the commercial classes, it was through this idiom that their power could be contested by appropriating the mantle of patron and protector of religion. Norbert Peabody has argued that 'a particular dominant structure defines *a centre from which* contestation evolves or develops. It defines a point of departure for resistance; not the extent of its universe'.[34] This analytical perspective helps to explain why religion should come to inform the political action of the shudra poor, within the 'dominant structure' of a Hindu commercial milieu. It was the element of self-assertion, and countering their social marginalisation vis-à-vis dominant groups with an overt Hindu religious culture, which brought martial religious militancy to the centre of shudra popular politics. A religious identity was asserted, not because of any powerful inherited commitment to one's religious community, but to contest the authority of dominant classes, whose primary mode of expression of power was religious. Central to the redefinition of the identity of the shudra poor as the descendants of brave and mighty defenders of Hinduism was their quest to carve out a more prominent position for themselves in urban society. Thus when, in 1923–4, some Muslims of Allahabad objected to the playing of music by Hindu *Ramlila* processions in front of mosques, with the local British administrators conceding this demand and the Hindu notables and merchants,

---

[32] C. A. Bayly, 'Patrons and Politics in Northern India', *MAS*, 7, 3, 1973, pp. 387–8.
[33] Bayly, *Rulers, Townsmen*.
[34] Peabody, 'Inchoate in Kota?', p. 562, emphasis in original.

in protest, threatening to suspend the celebrations, a section of the shudra participants of the Ramlila, notably the caste group of *mallahs*, or boatmen, sought to outdo the merchants in their zeal to defend Hinduism and formed a Khuni Dal (Suicide Corps). This dal pledged to sacrifice lives in order to continue the triumphal procession of Ram and to uphold the glory of Ram as the symbol of Hinduism, defying Muslim obstructions and official restrictions.[35] By stepping forward as the truer and more militant champions of Hinduism, these marginal people aspired to become central in urban society.

This assertion of Hindu militancy by the shudra poor is clearly in striking contrast to urban untouchable groups and their *bhakti* resurgence, described in the previous chapter. Being mainly located outside the bazars and mercantile milieu, the untouchables had sought to reject higher-caste versions of Hinduism and to deny the caste system, instead of seeking higher status and importance within it. For the shudra poor, in contrast, it was crucial to place themselves in positions of importance within the Hindu community, rather than outside it, because they were positioned squarely within the orthodox Hindu commercial environment. Some Adi Hindu leaders in the 1930s did, however, try to muster the support of the touchable shudras, and to offer them an alternative identity as Adi Hindus.[36] To this end, the Adi Hindu version of India's ancient history sought to accommodate the touchable shudras as part of the original inhabitants. It was suggested that the conquering Aryans, while trying to subjugate the 'original inhabitants' of India, were forced to strike a pact of peaceful coexistence with those pre-Aryan martial groups whom they could not defeat. Although the Aryans were inclined to consider these pre-Aryan groups to be shudras, yet owing to their military prowess the Aryans grudgingly accorded them kshatriya status and they were taken to belong to the lineage of the martial ruler Chandra *(Chandravamsis)*.[37] The Adi Hindu account of the history of the Chandravamsis further argued that these warrior groups did not, however, accept brahmanical ideology or vedic religion and indeed waged wars against inegalitarian Aryan practices. These Chandravamsis were also said to be much more 'truthful, moral, learned and pious' than the Aryans.[38] This aspect of the Adi Hindu history provided the possibility of including the shudras in the Adi Hindu fold as pre-Aryans.

[35] *Smarika: Sri Ramlila Committee, Daraganj, Prayag, 1979*, Allahabad, 1979, p. 41.

[36] This policy most probably derived inspiration from Ambedkar's attempts to build a broad oppositional alliance against the upper castes. G. Omvedt, *Dalit Visions*, Delhi, 1995, pp. 8–9.

[37] Chandrika Prasad Jijnasu, *Adi Hindu Andolan ka Prabartak Sri 108 Swami Acchutanand Harihar* (hereafter *Acchutanand biography*), Lucknow 1968, 2nd edn, p. 75.

[38] Ibid.

It also provided them the opportunity to claim a noble and martial identity as Chandravamsi kshatriyas, as indeed many of the shudra groups were already doing. Some of the Adi Hindu leaders such as Ram Charan Mallah of Lucknow, Shyam Lal Dhobi of Allahabad and Bhai Karori Mal Khatik of Kanpur were themselves touchable shudras and some of them formed the Adi Hindu Backward Classes Association for the touchable shudras.[39] However, this Adi Hindu initiative did not bear fruit and did not meet with any enthusiasm among their poorer brethren.[40] Adi Hinduism, with its integral link with heterodox devotional *nirguna* bhakti, remained popular only with the untouchable poor. Although the alternative Adi Hindu version of history and identity was available to the shudra poor, including a martial dimension, they preferred to see themselves as erstwhile kshatriyas belonging to the Hindu fold. The shudra poor were not inclined to ally with the heterodox dissenting traditions of devotionalism, for they needed a place for themselves in a predominantly Hindu higher-caste commercial milieu. The cultural radicalism and heterodoxy involved in bhakti Adi Hinduism were not viable options for the shudra poor, for these would inevitably have invited further marginalisation, even repression, from the upper castes. The social locations and life experiences of the untouchable and the shudra poor were manifestly and significantly different and their choice of politics differed accordingly. It is also significant that the untouchables and the touchable shudra poor had different past religious and cultural traditions, which played an important role in influencing the forms of identities to which they could relate. The untouchables drew upon a religious tradition of heterodox nirguna bhakti in their self-assertion, while the shudras elaborated upon a martial past and *saguna* tradition of devotionalism, which had been more prominent in their own history.

Claiming warrior ancestry and valorising physical prowess had some further crucial relevance for the shudra poor, in addition to their self-assertion in a dominant Hindu commercial culture. Their heightened self-perception of being strong and able-bodied erstwhile brave warriors was integrally linked with their occupational identity and self-image as manual workers. An article in the Silver Jubilee Souvenir of the *Palledar* (manual workers and coolies in the bazars) Union in the main Kanpur wholesale cloth market, describing the self-image of the manual

---

[39] C. P. Jijnasu, *Bharatiya Maulik Samajvad: Srishti aur Manav Samaj ka Vikas Athba 'Bharat ke Adi Nivasi' Granth ka Pratham Khand*, Lucknow, 1941, pp. 286–7.

[40] For instance, a police report noted that the Kushbaha Kshatriya Mahasabha (of low-caste groups of *koeris*, *kacchis* and *kachbandis*) of Allahabad refused to join the Adi Hindus and to separate themselves from Hinduism. *PAI*, No. 5, 4 February 1928.

labourers, extolled the virtues of the '*jujharu vyakti palledar*' or the 'fighting palledar', who was the pivot of bazar life as the carrier and transporter of goods, who never feared the hardest of physical labour and was fired with a militant, fighting spirit.[41] Relating physical strength to bravery and heroic deeds enabled them to cultivate a sense of pride and importance in their physical labour, to which little social worth was attached by the upper classes or castes.[42] Similar attempts by rural shudra groups in north India in the early twentieth century to dignify physical labour and to glorify its social and economic value through claims of kshatriya origin have been discussed by William Pinch. The 'amelioration of the stigma of physical labour' was central to the teachings of rural religious reformers of devotional sects who enjoyed a large following among shudra groups.[43] In the case of the urban shudra poor, in addition to the dignification of labour, claiming respectability through a high-caste martial tradition provided the possibility of replacing their lowly, violent, criminal and unruly image with the notion of being upright and orderly warriors. For the shudra poor, religious militancy developed as a means of demanding respect and expressing their self-esteem and dignity as the strong and mighty, in the face of social marginalisation and negative characterisation. The expression of masculinity and virility that this entailed may also be explained in terms of a need for a gendered assertion of selfhood that stressed the virtues of maleness and the physical prowess of the dominant sex in the face of the demeaning urban experience of exclusion and status diminution, which could be akin to emasculation and infantilisation. The religious resurgence of the shudra poor thus reflected an intermeshing of their newly emerging identities based on high-caste kshatriya status and Hinduism with those of physical labour and manual occupation. It would be a restrictive and partial interpretation to view this process simply in terms of attempts at integration into high-caste Hindu society.

Religious assertion also encapsulated the efforts of the shudra poor to fortify their own position in scarce urban occupations and on the land, as well as to maintain their occupational preponderance in the bazars in the face of mounting incursions from the Muslim and the untouchable poor. By emphasising physical strength and prowess as their specific tradition, the shudra poor tried to justify their own special suitability for manual work in the bazars.[44] The claim of being higher-caste martial

---

[41] Shiv Shankar Lal Trivedi, 'Jujharu Vyakti Palledar', *Kapra Bazar Palledar Union: Rajat Jayanti Smarika*, Kanpur, 1986, pp. 41–2.

[42] Shukla, 'Karmchari Sangathan aur Andolan Kyun?', also noted that *kulin* or upper castes were usually disinclined to undertake manual labour.

[43] W. R. Pinch, *Peasants and Monks in British India*, Berkeley, 1996, pp. 7, 107–12.

[44] Trivedi, 'Jujharu Vyakti Palledar', pp. 41–2.

kshatriyas helped in emphatically distinguishing them from the untouchables and Muslims. In addition, by portraying themselves as the long-standing defenders of Hinduism and thus, by implication, as the militant and committed protectors of Hindu local trading and commercial interests, they could project, to the merchants, their own indispensability and superior claim in the bazars. Protection of the bazars also meant that they were able to safeguard their own economic opportunities against rivals. The defence or expansion of Hindu commerce and industry, in which the shudra poor had a stake as labourers and petty traders, could easily overlap with their newly emphasised mission to uphold the Hindu faith and its territory. The shudra poor thus increasingly stood out as the strong and able guardians of the economy and culture of Hindu bazars. Evidence taken by the Kanpur Riots Inquiry Commission of 1931 included many references to the fact that local labourers acted as strongmen or toughs for a number of firms in the Kanpur markets.[45] Labourers were also reported to have been employed as 'lathbands', or 'specialists in lathi-wielding', by merchants, to act as guards of shops and to collect subscriptions for the Ramlila festival.[46] Moreover, in order to defend themselves against the urban improvement onslaught of the local authorities and to fend off claims to scarce land by members of other communities, such as the Muslims, the shudra poor frequently had recourse to religious symbols. They located a shrine or a temple in a disputed area and presented themselves as the defenders of such supposedly sacred sites in defence of their own rights to that land. They sought to stave off the municipal authorities or contending groups from other communities by accusing them of attacking Hindu interests. In all this, the shudra poor increasingly emphasised their religious identity and their centrality in militant Hinduism. This was their response not only to marginalisation in urban society vis-à-vis the upper classes and castes but also to competition from other groups of the poor. In an environment of growing conflict, rivalry and competition in the towns, religion was a means of self-preservation and self-defence as well as a form of self-assertion.

Ideological and cultural sources of martial religious assertion

What were the sources of the ideas that informed religious change among the shudra poor and the reconstruction of their identity as

---

[45] See, for instance, the 'Extract from the Note of SP, Cawnpore, dated 3 April 1930', cited in File No. 412/1931, Box No. 206, Police Department, GUP, UPSA.
[46] *PAI*, No. 18, 15 May 1926.

martial groups? The idea of a martial tradition of shudras was prevalent in rural popular culture, where song traditions and folklore extolled the courage and heroism of pastoral and agricultural groups and their bravery against unjust local tyrants in rural communities.[47] There were also numerous legends of shudra martial leaders and their exploits, and many of these shudra castes traced their lineage to mythical warriors.[48] Amongst pastoral groups such as the ahirs, warfare and victory had been a central motif of rural folk culture, because of a long history of cattle protection and raiding, which often developed into strife between rival groups under local chiefs. Many of these shudra peasants and pastoralists, from the medieval period and well into the nineteenth century, had also divided their time and work between agriculture and military service, and fought for regional armies as well as with armed ascetic orders which were engaged in trade and warfare.[49] Indeed, many of these peasants were armed until their demilitarisation under *Pax Britannica*, especially after the north Indian rural uprisings of 1857 and the assumption of the monopoly of legitimate violence by the modern state under colonialism.[50] Memories of battles fought by these pastoral groups and of kingdoms and territories lost and gained, as well as the values of strength, nobility, honour and loyalty, had been embodied in oral tales and sagas such as the *Loriki* of the ahirs or the well-known folk-epic *Alha*.[51] The Loriki, in particular, almosts deified the male warrior as the protector of women.[52] Such folk tales of martial valour depicted a world in which the shudras 'stand as equal to the "twice-born" warrior castes'.[53] The historical importance of military engagement in

---

[47] Shyam Manohar Pandey, *The Hindi Oral Epic Loriki (The Tale of Lorik and Canda)*, Allahabad, 1979, pp. 9–10, 15–21; Shyam Manohar Pandey, *The Hindi Oral Epic Canaini (The Tale of Lorik and Canda)*, Allahabad, 1982, pp. 19–24, 28.

[48] W. Crooke, *The Tribes and Castes of the North-Western Provinces and Oudh*, Calcutta, 1896, vol. I, pp. 50–6; vol. III, p. 261; vol. IV, pp. 139–41.

[49] Pinch, *Peasants and Monks*, pp. 24–30; Dirk H. A. Kolff, *Naukar, Rajput and Sepoy: The Ethnohistory of the Military Labour Market in Hindustan, 1450–1850*, Cambridge, 1990, passim and especially pp. 1–31.

[50] Ibid.

[51] D. M. Coccari, 'Protection and Identity: Banaras's Bir Babas as Neighbourhood Guardian Deities', in Freitag (ed.), *Culture and Power*, pp. 136–7; Pandey, *Loriki*; Pandey, *Canaini*; K. Schomer, 'Paradigms for the Kaliyuga: The Heroes of the Alha Epic and Their Fate', in S. H. Blackburn et al. (eds.), *Oral Epics in India*, Berkeley, 1989, pp. 140–54. This book also includes stories of alha and loriki, pp. 197–202, 212–15; Kolff, *Naukar, Rajput*, pp. 74–85.

[52] Interestingly, the UP version of Loriki, reports Flueckiger, is striking for its expression of a kshatriya ideal of warfare and chivalry, compared with the Chattisgarh version in Madhya Pradesh, where Lorik is presented more as a lover than a warrior. J. B. Flueckiger, 'Caste and Regional Variants in an Oral Epic Tradition', in Blackburn et al. (eds.), *Oral Epics in India*, pp. 33–54.

[53] Coccari, 'Protection and Identity', p. 136.

the life of peasants and pastoralists is also evident from the prominence of martial games and physical training centres (*akharas*) in village society from the medieval period.[54] It was against this background of a self-image and valued heritage of warfare, bravery and heroism that the shudra poor now began to assert themselves as the warrior defenders of Hinduism. The innovation here was the linking of the notion of a martial past with the history of Hinduism and the claim of a higher ritual status. New, too was the central metaphor of deprivation and the myth of dispossession from past power. In this, the shudra poor could turn to the new histories and theories of origin which were being produced by the various caste and religious movements emerging in north India from the late nineteenth century onwards.

Notions nurtured by the shudra poor with regard to Islamic oppression and the decline of various Hindu groups were derived from new myths about the supposedly detrimental impact of medieval Muslim rule on the Hindus. These myths drew inspiration from the writings of Orientalist scholars and colonial enthnographer-administrators of the nineteenth century, and were then embellished and propagated with vigour by Hindu revivalist and reformist organisations from the turn of the century, notably the Arya Samaj.[55] The concerted propaganda campaigns of the Arya Samaj and other such organisations about Muslim oppression had contributed to the wide publicity of these ideas, which the shudra poor could marshal for their own purposes. Another, more important and related, corpus of ideas was available to the shudra poor from the various lower-caste uplift movements that were emerging from the late nineteenth century. In contrast to the shudra poor, a section among the shudras in north India, both rural and urban, had gained affluence or education from the late nineteenth century, having been able to reap some benefits from the changes brought about by colonial rule, including agricultural expansion.[56] These upwardly mobile shudras, with aspirations to match the power and influence of the upper castes, had initiated caste uplift movements to claim higher status, and often asserted an ancient vedic religious and cultural heritage.[57]

---

[54] Kolff, *Naukar, Rajput*, pp. 28–9.

[55] Jones, *Arya Dharm*, pp. 145–53; C. Jaffrelot, 'The Ideas of the Hindu Race in the Writings of Hindu Nationalist Ideologies in the 1920s and 30s: A Concept between Two Cultures', in P. Robb (ed.), *The Concept of Race in South Asia*, Delhi, 1995, pp. 327–54; C. Jaffrelot, *The Hindu Nationalist Movement and Indian Politics, 1925 to the 1990s*, Delhi, 1996, pp. 11–25; R. Thapar, 'The Theory of Aryan Race and India: History and Politics', *Social Scientist*, 24, 1–3, 1996, pp. 3–29.

[56] Pandey, *Construction*, pp. 90–2.

[57] M. S. A. Rao, *Social Movements and Social Transformation: A Study of Two Backward Classes Movements in India*, Delhi, 1979, pp. 132–47; Pinch, *Peasants and Monks*, pp. 81–114; Pandey, *Construction*, pp. 90–2.

These movements tended to develop in collaboration with the Arya Samaj, which was trying to incorporate lower-caste groups within the fold of vedic Aryan Hinduism.[58] Pinch has traced the development of religious and social movements in north India from the nineteenth century among shudra peasants and artisanal and service communities, often those who were upwardly mobile and aspired to higher status. These communities came to associate their genealogical descent with royal kshatriya clans, including the divine lineages of Ram and Krishna. They emphasised a *Vaishnavite* saguna devotional bhakti ethic, with its assimilative view of the caste system, which accorded better status to lower castes and afforded them inclusion in the Hindu hierarchy.[59] The rural shudra social movements, in alliance with bhakti monks, concentrated on dignifying labour and on 'the inculcation of a just moral order'.[60] The peasants involved in these movements 'thought of themselves not as cosmically created servants (shudras) devoid of any history, but as the descendants of divine warrior clans (kshatriya) firmly rooted in the Indian past'.[61] Both these ideological dimensions could be of major significance to the urban shudra poor, many of whom would have had experience of the shudra social movements both in their recent rural past and through their continuing social contacts with the countryside.

In urban areas, the leadership of shudra caste movements at the beginning of the twentieth century came from a section of shudras who were both educated and relatively more affluent than the majority. Members of shudra groups such as *kalwars* (distillers), yadavs or ahirs, kurmis and khatiks were often successful urban traders, school teachers, clerks or lawyers. Some khatiks, traditionally pig rearers, cattle breeders and vegetable gardeners, had emerged as merchants of some standing in the towns. They owned wholesale vegetable businesses, dealt in poultry and pig products and by-products as contractors to the British or supplied pig bristles for the manufacture of brushware.[62] For the kalwars, government liquor contracts had brought prosperity, and many were urban landlords, bankers, contractors or government servants.[63] The dairy business had brought affluence to some ahirs, a caste of milkmen or cowherds. Moreover, an educated generation of ahirs and kurmis, both pastoral and agrarian castes, emerged by the 1920s, often

---

[58] Rao, *Social Movements and Social Transformation*, pp. 132–5.
[59] Pinch, *Peasants and Monks*, pp. 81–114.
[60] Ibid., p. 7.   [61] Ibid., p. 6.
[62] Rajnath Sonekar Shastri, *Bharatiya Varna Vyavastha mein Khatik Jati ki Utpatti Aur Uska Vikas*, Benares, 1975, pp. 107–8; interview with Shiv Mangal Ram Vaid, a leader of the khatik association in Benares; Lakshmi Kant Tripathi and Narayan Prasad Arora, *Kanpur ka Itihas*, Kanpur, 1950, vol. I, pp. 150–3.
[63] Bayly, 'Patrons and Politics in Northern India', pp. 380–1.

from upwardly mobile rural families, some of whom had moved to the towns and joined government services or entered the legal or teaching professions.[64] This shudra elite spearheaded caste movements in the UP towns. The context for their political action was partly set by the devolution of power in the councils and local bodies by the British government, and partly by the classification of population by castes and communities in the census operations.[65] Urban shudra elites found that they could gain influence in administrative institutions and representative bodies by portraying themselves to the British as historically 'backward castes' and, hence, deserving of special rights and privileges for their uplift.

Although some caste associations had begun to emerge in both rural and urban areas at the turn of the century among shudra groups,[66] it was from the 1920s that caste movements of shudra elites, to claim special political representation and to promote social reforms, gained momentum in the larger towns. The main impetus for their political action came from the changing political scene in the interwar period. With further devolution of power after the First World War by the government, the issue of the distribution of political representation among different communities gained greater urgency. This provided an incentive to the shudra elites to intensify their political activities. They were spurred on by the growing political importance of the issue of caste in the interwar period, owing to accelerating Arya Samajist *shuddhi* activities, followed by Gandhi's emphasis on caste uplift, as well as to the emergence of untouchable caste movements.[67] From the early 1920s, a number of shudra caste associations were organised in the towns.[68] The leaders and publicists sought to promote social and religious reform among the members of their caste. They were also

[64] *Bharatiya Yadav Sangh: Rajat Jayanti Smarak Granth* (Silver Jubilee Souvenir), Bombay, 1954, Part 3, pp. 55–66, Part I, pp. 56–7. For a history of the kurmi caste movement, its leadership and activities, see K. K. Verma, *Changing Role of Caste Associations*, New Delhi, 1979.

[65] For the background to the development of caste associations in Indian politics in the early twentieth century, see Lucy Carroll, 'Colonial Perceptions of Indian Society and the Emergence of Caste(s) Associations', *Journal of Asian Studies*, 37, 2, 1978, pp. 233–50; D. Washbrook, 'The Development of Caste Organisation in South India, 1880 to 1925', in C. J. Baker and D. Washbrook, *South India: Political Institutions and Political Change, 1880–1940*, Delhi, 1975, pp. 150–203; Bernard Cohn, *An Anthropologist among Historians and Other Essays*, Delhi, 1990, chs. 7, 10.

[66] The case of the urban kalwars in Allahabad, for instance, is discussed in Bayly, 'Patrons and Politics in Northern India', pp. 380–5.

[67] Shastri, *Bharatiya Varna Vyavastha mein Khatik Jati*, pp. 140–1.

[68] For instance, in Lucknow, the Awadh Shaundik-Kalwar Kshatriya Sabha was set up in 1921. *Kalwar Kesri* (monthly journal of the Awadh Shaundik-Kalwar Kshatriya Sabha), Lucknow, I, 1, Chaitra, *vikrami samvat* 1980, c. A.D. 1923, pp. 15, 51–66. In Kanpur, khatik associations were set up in the early 1920s. Interviews in Kanpur with Badlu

particularly active in setting up schools and advocating literacy, as well as in popularising new versions of the histories of their castes.

One of the most politically active and vocal among the shudra castes was the ahirs or yadavs. In 1922, an ahir conference was held in Lucknow, followed by another ahir *mahotsav* (festival) in Allahabad in 1923, where a provincial Mahasabha was inaugurated, with the new name of Yadav Mahasabha. The term yadav, to denote the ahirs, gained currency from this period. Rajit Singh, a yadav born in the Deoria district in 1897, and educated at Gorakhpur and Shikohabad, was instrumental in the formation of the Yadav Mahasabha. He had briefly worked in the Excise Department in Kanpur, but had resigned from his job to devote himself to organising yadav associations from 1921. In 1925, Rajit Singh settled in Benares and inaugurated the Benares Yadav Mahasabha, which soon emerged as the centre of the yadav caste movement in UP. From Benares, Rajit Singh edited the journal *Yadav*, and also published a history of the yadav castes, entitled *Yaduvamsa Prakash*.[69] Several other yadav histories were published in rapid succession in the 1920s, written by another younger yadav leader of Benares, Mannalal Abhimanyu, a lawyer who was the son of a school teacher.[70] He wrote *Ahir Vamsa Pradip* (1925) and *Yadukul Sarvasya* (1928), in which he attempted to demonstrate the kshatriya origin of the yadavs, with extensive references from both religious texts and British ethnographic tracts.

The propagandists or publicists of these caste movements, such as Mannalal Abhimanyu and Rajit Singh, had developed various theories about the genealogies and histories of their caste groups.[71] There were two dominant strands in the ideas that the shudra elite ideologues propounded. First, they portrayed their caste groups as socially 'backward' and materially deprived, for they found that such depiction enabled them to bargain effectively with the British government in

---

Ram Sonekar (khatik politician) and Chaudhuri Bandidin (khatik panchayat headman).

[69] Rajit Singh, 'Jivan Parichay Ki Ek Jhalak', in *Yaduvamsa Prakash*, revised edn, Benares, 1983, pp. 7–16, (this is an introductory autobiographical essay by Rajit Singh, published in his book, *Yaduvamsa Prakash*).

[70] *Bharatiya Yadav Sangh: Rajat Jayanti Smarak Granth*, Part I, pp. 56–7.

[71] These histories and genealogies were popularised through numerous caste journals and caste histories. For instance, Mannalal Abhimanyu, *Ahir Vamsa Pradip*, Benares, *vikrami samvat* 1982, c. A.D. 1925, *Yadukul Sarvasya*, Benares, *vikramabda* 1985, c. A.D. 1928, *Gop Jati Kshatriya Varna Mein Hai: Arthat 'Brahman Sammelan' ke Anargal Pralap ka Muhtor Jawab*, Benares, 4th edn, 1974; first published 1929; Rajit Singh, *Yaduvamsa Prakash*, Devi Prasad Singh, *Kurmi Kshatriya Darpan* (1910); *Chhatra Kuladarsh* (1912); Deep Narayan Singh, *Kurmi Kshatriya Nirnai* (1924); and Siva Prasad Singh, *Kurmi Kshatriya Itihas* (1936). Journals include *Kalwar Kshatriya Mitra, Kalwar Kesri, Yadavesh, Yadav, Kurmi Kshatriya Divakar* and *Kurmi Kshatriya Hitaishi*.

acquiring special privileges and preferential access to institutions of administration and representative politics. This depiction was also necessary in order to define and forge a wider constituency beyond their own ranks, whom they claimed to represent. Secondly, and at the same time as professing backwardness, they set out to prove that they had enjoyed higher caste position in the past, in an attempt to match their improving material conditions with higher ritual status. While a handful of shudra castes claimed *brahmin* or *vaishya* lineage, a large majority of them traced their origin to powerful kshatriya rulers and warriors and the traditional upholders of Hinduism. They further asserted that they had subsequently lost their power and had been degraded to lowly shudras in the course of external invasions, political usurpation or conquests, especially during the so-called medieval Islamic period in India. The shudra ideologues now advocated that the fallen kshatriyas should recover and cultivate their original martial customs and ceremonies, and return to the ancient Indian religious practices of higher castes, through the reform of their existing practices. This would enable them to reinstate themselves in their rightful, rediscovered and resurrected higher ritual position. The ideas and message put forward by the shudra elite ideologues thus had two important dimensions. On the one hand, they upheld the notion of past glory and political power, which could easily resonate with folk traditions of bravery and warfare. On the other hand, these ideologues attempted to foster an awareness of and provide an explanation for the present deprivation of a large section of the shudras, who were indeed poor. Thus, in the process of their own bid for power and respectability, as well as to fashion a constituency of support, the shudra elite came up with a new rhetoric of present deprivation and recovering past power and prosperity, which in turn produced a vocabulary and a set of ideas which could be relevant to the poorer shudras.

A poignant illustration of the dual dimension of the ideology of shudra caste movements comes from a pamphlet entitled *Ahir Jati Ke Niyamavali* or 'Rules of the Ahir Caste'. This was first published from Benares in 1927 by an ahir or yadav writer.[72] The *Niyamavali* laid down practical guidelines and directives for religious and social reforms, and for the return to purer and original Hindu practices *(Sanatana Dharma)* in order to achieve higher ritual status. However, the *Niyamavali* was in fact written as a manifesto or manual for social uplift of the poor and

---

[72] Yadav, *Ahir Jati Ke Niyamavali*, passim. Similar ideas were also expressed in Singh, *Yaduvamsa Prakash*, pp. 104–10; 'Smriti kal me Kalwar', *Kalwar Kshatriya Mitra* (Allahabad), 2, 17, August 1921, p. 151.

suggested practical ways to overcome material deprivation. It advocated a return to ancient religious rites and rituals, purged of expensive, wasteful and supposedly non-scriptural religious practices, mainly as a way of achieving economic self-sufficiency and freedom from indebtedness or exploitation. The *Niyamavali* ascribed yadav poverty to their *kuritiyan* or malpractices, which was a reference to local customs and popular religious practices as well as to the rituals and ceremonies observed at birth, initiation, marriage, and death. The emphasis was on *fizulkharch*, or unnecessary expenditure, arising from kuritiyan in religious festivals and social ceremonies, which contributed to impoverishment, and then to gambling, theft and indebtedness, as well as a general loss of respectability and status. Hence, it was recommended that rituals and practices should be reformed and cleansed of kuritiyan. A return to the streamlined, and less expensive, prescriptions of Sanatana Dharma was advocated, along with the advice to dispense with costly, non-religious accretions such as dowry exchange, feasts, drinking of alcohol, songs and dances. All this would help to curtail expenses, prevent poverty and increase savings, which should be directed to gaining literacy as well as to improving nutritional habits and to cultivating a better physique (*tandurusti*) and physical strength.[73] The overriding spirit of the *Niyamavali* and of similar propaganda by the educated shudras was certainly that of a revival of the supposed ancient practices of the shudras as erstwhile upper castes. Yet the justification for adopting reformed practices as a means of surmounting poverty and deprivation could enable the shudra poor to interpret and appropriate these ideas in terms of their own experience and concerns.

In many parts of rural UP, especially the eastern districts from where many migrated to the cities,[74] caste uplift movements had already gained ground amongst poorer shudra cultivators and cattle rearers by the turn of the century.[75] Some of the rural migrants who came to the towns in the 1920s and 1930s therefore must have had knowledge of, or possibly even involvement in, these caste movements in the countryside, and could draw upon their ideologies. Moreover, in the towns the ideologies of the caste movements were widely publicised by the leaders, not only through new caste histories, caste journals and a flurry of

---

[73] Yadav, *Ahir Jati Ke Niyamavali*, pp. 1–28. Similar themes echoed in Singh, *Yaduvamsa Prakash*, pp. 104–10.

[74] *RCLI*, III.I, pp. 140–2, Memorandum of the Government of U.P.; many urban labourers in Kanpur, for instance, came from the eastern districts (*purbi zillas*) of UP, according to *Kapra Bazar Palledar Union: Rajat Jayanti Smarika*, p. 49; *Kanpur Bazar Karmchari Federation: Rajat Jayanti Smarika*, Part II, p. 60.

[75] Pandey, *Construction*, pp. 90–4, 166; Rao, *Social Movements and Social Transformation*, p. 134; Pinch, *Peasants and Monks*, pp. 81–114.

pamphlet literature, but also at public meetings, especially from the 1920s. The theories propounded by the ideologues of the caste movements were, therefore, easily available to the poorer shudras. The shudra poor did not, however, simply adopt a martial Hindu identity at the behest of the leadership of the caste associations, but had reasons of their own to identify with the message of a martial past and present deprivation.

Shudra caste associations and the poor

Assertions of the kshatriya status of shudras by the political leaders of caste movements and their advocacy of the need to counter the deprivation and 'backwardness' of shudras groups could provide an ideological meeting ground for the leadership and the shudra poor in the towns. How far did this in fact contribute to political solidarity between the leaders and the mass of the shudra poor? Did the leaders enjoy the support of the poorer shudras in demanding special political representation or educational privileges and in their activities within local institutions?

In some cases, particular groups of poorer shudras allied with the leaders to further their own attempts to influence local policies. This dimension could become especially significant when municipal regulations impinged more and more extensively upon the activities of the poor, as they did in the 1920s and 1930s.[76] As seen in chapter 3, matters relating to municipal policies were far from being trivial considerations to the poor, and in fact exercised a powerful influence on their work, living conditions and social position in the towns. Various occupational groups among the shudra poor, thus, frequently needed to engage with or address the municipal councils for civic resources to improve the conditions of their trades and occupations or to demand educational facilities. In the 1930s, the dhobis (washermen) in Allahabad, for instance, had formed an association called the *chauhaddi*. Composed of representatives from various dhobi neighbourhoods in the town, the chauhaddi met once a month at an open meeting. This meeting was also attended by at least one member from each dhobi family in the town, and the day was observed as a monthly holiday by the dhobis. At these meetings, the dhobis discussed their needs and requirements, on the basis of which the urban authorities were approached to demand facilities such as tap-water connections, the paving of washing areas or *ghats* on river fronts and subsidised supply of

---

[76] Discussed in chapter 3.

washing soda.[77] A similar dhobi association in Kanpur, called the Rajak (Dhobi) Sudhar Sabha (Washermen's Reform Association), was also reported to have placed demands before the Municipal Board and the Improvement Trust for land to set up a dhobi ghat and a school for dhobi children.[78]

The yadavs of Benares, many of whom supplemented their incomes from manual labour by maintaining one or two milch cows or were, at times, full-time milkmen, also frequently approached the Municipal Board for the provision of adequate space for cattle sheds and grazing areas. The threat to the survival of the cow in the towns, owing to a lack of grazing space or cheap fodder and the impounding of grazing cows by municipal supervisors, was a problem specific to members of the yadav community.[79] Moreover, milkmen were subjected to municipal hygiene regulations and were fined for non-compliance, which was a source of friction between them and the municipal authorities. Their cowsheds were often the targets of municipal or Improvement Trust clearance drives for the insanitary conditions they bred in the central areas of the towns. Another caste group, the khatik greengrocers, needed to deal with the local authorities regularly because their shops were located in municipal markets and their trade was subject to a range of municipal regulations.[80] Issues like these, which affected particular shudra caste groups engaged in specific occupations, as well as more generalised demands for municipal educational facilities, often prompted the poorer shudras to support the caste-based political demands of their leaders for special representation in the local bodies, with the expectation that their demands might receive adequate attention in municipal councils if shudra leaders could enter these institutions. Political agitation by the shudra leaders was thus often buttressed by a wider social base of support from the poorer sections of their castes.

The relationship between the leaders and the led, however, does not appear to have been an entirely harmonious one, nor were the leaders always able to lead. Articles in the caste journals suggest that the poorer shudras did not extend unqualified or sustained political support to their leaders. Various factions of shudra politicians often vied with each

---

[77] Interview with Chaudhuri Chunnilal, whose father, Shyam Lal, was a prominent dhobi leader in the 1920s and a municipal commissioner.

[78] Land Required by the Dhobi Sabha, Kanpur Improvement Trust, File No. 436/I.T.

[79] *Yadavesh* (Benares), 6, 8, *vikrami samvat* 1998, c. A.D. 1941, pp. 123–8.

[80] In Lucknow, for instance, in 1933, the Improvement Trust and the khatik panchayat, under the leadership of several *chaudhuris*, or headmen, signed a formal 'Agreement', which laid down the rules, terms and conditions for the sole use of the vegetable market in Kaiserbagh by the khatik community. Printed copies of 'The Agreement' of 1933 are available at the office of the khatik panchayat in the Kaiserbagh market.

other to gain control of caste organisations. The usual strategy of the rival factions was to criticise each other by pointing out their short-comings as leaders and their inability to enlist the support of the masses. Competing factions sought to substantiate their superior claim to run and lead the caste organisation by arguing that they would reverse the general character of the leadership. Even though this was usually mere rhetoric on their part, nevertheless the criticisms they levelled at each other, which found their way to the pages of the caste journals, reflected the terms on which they were supported by the poorer shudras.

The leaders denigrated each other as mere canvassers of votes, attempting to enter political institutions, and for harbouring opportunistic motives of personal power and influence. One article in a yadav journal described the leadership as follows:

They will go to the doors of the *janata* [common people], spouting slogans and begging for votes. There will be dazzling performances and everyone will claim that he wants to go to the Municipal and District Boards to promote the welfare of the people. But by now, people have started to understand after several elections that our 'honourable' elected members will not put in appearances except on the days of the elections. After that it is impossible to say whether they are in this world or in another.[81]

The leadership was also condemned as a caste unto themselves, the *leadran qaum*, who were concerned only to gain power for themselves; it was declared that 'we do not need those leaders any more, who are only concerned about their seats of power [*kursi*, literally chairs]. We now need people who will rouse the yadavs and reach their hearts.'[82] Another constant and recurrent theme in caste journals was the reiteration that the activities of the leaders did not benefit the poorer shudras. In 1931, in an article about the failings of the leadership of the Yadav Mahasabha in Benares, it was stated that the leaders concentrated on 'the pomp and shine of the mahasabhas [i.e. conferences]', but the welfare of the mass of the yadavs and social reforms among them did not engage the leaders' attention.[83] Comments such as these suggest that claiming shared caste or martial identity was not sufficient to enlist the political support of the shudra poor; concrete action for their welfare was required. Thus, in an article in *Yadavesh*, the interests of the leadership of the educated *badelog* or big people, who were 'seeking political power only', were argued to be different from those of the poorer ahirs, and the need for *sacchi*, or 'true', public-spirited leaders was expressed.[84] Clearly, the

---

[81] *Yadavesh*, 2, 2, *vikrami samvat* 1993, c. A.D. 1936, pp. 22–3.
[82] Ibid., 2, 13, *vikrami samvat* 1994, c. A.D. 1937, pp. 16–17.
[83] *Yadav* (Benares), *Chaitra-Vaisakh* issue, *vikrami samvat* 1988, c. A.D. 1931, pp. 2–4.
[84] *Yadavesh*, 6, 1, *vikrami samvat* 1997, c. A.D. 1940, pp. 28–9.

language of deprivation that animated the caste movements drew attention to social stratification and a divergence of interests *within* the community, just as much as it pointed to the deprivation of the shudras compared with various higher castes.

It is difficult to gauge whether the nature of the criticism of the leadership in caste journals was an accurate reflection of the views of the poorer shudras. What it does indicate is that the political activities of the leaders were largely oriented towards gaining entry into representative and administrative institutions. In this, they enjoyed only occasional and qualified support of the poorer shudras, insofar as they were able or willing to voice the poorer shundras' specific demands in local bodies or provincial councils. The shudra leaders, with their limited political aims, could not provide an adequate or sustained political focus for the poor, as is evident from the discussion by the leadership about their own failings and deficiencies. Attempts by the leaders to forge caste-based political solidarities, cutting across social and economic differences, by emphasising a shared caste identity, clearly did not meet with resounding success. For the shudra poor, the assertion of a kshatriya identity was ultimately of greater political significance in the urban milieu than support for the political projects of leaders of the caste movements. It was for this reason that the political action of the shudra poor took the form mainly of religious or cultural assertion, rather than being expressed through overt political agitation in alliance with the leadership of caste associations.

Transformation of religious and cultural practices

The urban shudra poor came to express their Hindu martial identity and their self-perception as being strong and mighty through a wide range of changing cultural and religious practices in the 1920s and 1930s. These activities also reflected a heightened awareness of being deprived and powerless, as well as a perception of being the ordinary 'good' people.

There was a growing zeal among the shudra poor in celebrating certain religious festivals and ceremonies, which were usually observed mainly by the shudras but were also thought to be associated with a kshatriya past or to express a martial ethic. The most important example is the festival of *Holi*. Holi is especially favoured by shudra caste groups, for, unlike in the case of the other main Hindu festivals, the modes of celebration of Holi through revelry subvert the existing order of status, rank and power. As Mckim Marriott points out, Holi reflects 'an order precisely inverse to the social and ritual principles of routine life'.[85] Holi is unique in this respect and is distinguishable from all other Hindu festivals, which reinforce 'the separation of the lower from the higher castes and their strict order of ranking' and give expression to the 'order of economic dominance and subordination'.[86] Holi also features in some of the pivotal events and episodes of the heroic folk tales of shudra caste groups, such as the Loriki of the yadavs,[87] and thus carries martial connotations. The martial dimension of Holi also derives from its mythological association with Lord Krishna. Lord Krishna, the special protagonist of Holi, is a legendary warrior and a Hindu deity, whom some shudra castes, notably the ahirs or yadavs, claim to be their ancestor.[88] The festival of Holi, because of its connections with Lord Krishna, could be claimed to be originally a martial kshatriya practice. In Hindu mythology, Krishna is also notable as a lover, playing amorous melodies on his flute, and he personifies the ideal of romantic love and devotion.[89] From the early twentieth century, however, it was the martial essence of Krishna which found greater emphasis.[90] The tendency was to proclaim the need to revere the image of Krishna who killed the tyrant ruler Kansa and wielded his sword and *chakra* (discus). Krishna of the *sudarshan chakra* seemed more relevant for the age than Krishna of the flute.[91] Increasingly his most favoured and publicised images were those of the protector of cows and of the embodiment of the martial spirit in the *Bhagavad Gita*, who justified to Arjun the need to take up arms against his kinsfolk in the interest of righteousness, and indeed coaxed him to engage in slaughter as his essential 'duty' or *dharma*.[92] The celebration of Holi is also seen as a way of expressing reverence for a benevolent patron deity of the poor and the ordinary people. For, in Hindu mythology, Lord Krishna is reputed to have unfailingly defended and protected the oppressed or the underprivileged, whenever they faced hardship, injustice or exploitation.[93] The celebration of Holi marks the triumph of good over evil. It was thought to have been first celebrated to commemorate the annihilation of the evil demon ruler Hiranyakashipu by Lord Vishnu, in his incarnation as *Narasimha* (half man and half lion), to prevent Hiranyakashipu from

[85] Mckim Marriott, 'The Feast of Love', in Milton Singer (ed.), *Krishna: Myths, Rites and Attitudes*, Honolulu, 1966, p. 210.
[86] Ibid., pp. 206, 207.
[87] Pandey, *Loriki*, pp. 10–11.
[88] Crooke, *Tribes and Castes*, vol. I, pp. 50, 64. W. Crooke, *An Introduction to the Popular Religion and Folklore of Northern India*, Allahabad, 1894, p. 389.
[89] Marriott, 'Feast of Love', pp. 200–12.
[90] *Yadavesh*, 2, 1, Special Holi issue, *vikrami samvat* 1993, c. A.D. 1936, passim.
[91] *NNR*, No. 34/1930, pp. 2–3.
[92] *NNR*, No. 31/1925, p. 3; No. 32/1925, p. 2; No. 33/1925, p. 3.
[93] *Yadavesh*, 2, 1, Special Holi issue, pp. 2–3.

destroying his own son Prahlad, the symbol of the 'good', who was a devotee of Vishnu.[94] Taking this as the origin of Holi, the festival was projected as a metaphor for liberation from evil rule and domination.[95] One newspaper article poignantly expressed this perspective: 'This festival occurs every year to remind us of the power of our ancestors to humble the pride of oppressors.'[96]

Holi was being observed more extensively by the shudra poor in the 1920s and 1930s, and it emerged as the main festival of the bazars. There were growing and repeated demands by labourers in the bazars, especially in Kanpur, for extended holidays and closure of the bazars during Holi, in order to enable them to observe the festival properly and to attend fairs and public musical and dramatic festivals, more and more of which were being held during the festival season.[97] By the mid-1920s Holi had come to be celebrated over a period of seven days in the Kanpur bazars,[98] and police reports mentioned the new innovation of celebratory processions during Holi.[99] By the mid-1930s, the District Magistrate of Kanpur was issuing restraint orders during Holi to control what he saw as 'hooliganism' and excesses.[100] Moreover, the increasingly closer association of Holi celebrations with Hindu militancy appears to have eroded the participation of Muslim groups, who had played a prominent role in the festival before the 1920s.[101] Holi celebrations in the 1920s and 1930s were frequently the occasion for both minor skirmishes and serious clashes or riots between the shudra poor and various Muslim groups, who resented the growing stridency of the festival.[102] The extension of the scale of celebration of Holi reflected the concern of the shudra poor, first, to resurrect a supposedly lost kshatriya power and glory, secondly, to uphold Lord Krishna both as an icon of martial prowess and as a patron deity of the poor and the powerless, thirdly, to celebrate the triumph of the good, and, finally, to enact the symbolic inversion of the established order of power and hierarchy. The celebration of Holi and the related veneration of Lord Krishna thus encapsulated a range of emerging overlapping

[94] Ibid., pp. 3–5, 22; Crooke, *Popular Religion*, pp. 387–8.
[95] *NNR*, No. 10/1923, p. 3.
[96] *NNR*, No. 9/1926, p. 2.
[97] Interviews in the Kanpur wholesale markets of Generalganj, Naughara, Collectorganj and Kahu Kothi, with shop employees and bazar labourers, including Ram Kripal Yadav, Ramfer Khalifa and Datti Ram Yadav.
[98] *PAI*, No. 10, 13 March 1926.
[99] *PAI*, No. 13, 2 April 1927.
[100] *PAI*, No. 12, 28 March 1936.
[101] N. G. Barrier, *Roots of Communal Politics*, Columbia, n.d., pp. 236–8.
[102] *PAI*, No. 10, 13 March 1926; No. 11, 17 March 1928; *Aj* (Benares), Special Issue, 17 March 1938 (report on Holi riots).

identities and self-images of the shudra poor: those of Hindu religion, martial might and high status, as well as deprivation, powerlessness and goodness.

Another shudra religious practice, the worship of *beers*, although less important than Holi and confined to some regions of UP, was also gaining greater prominence amongst urban shudra groups and expressed attitudes similar to those of Holi. In Benares, worship had traditionally been offered by various shudra caste groups at the shrines of beers, literally the brave but here referring to the 'ascetic hero'. The beers represented the martial tradition of shudra pastoral castes and the beer shrines were dedicated to heroic martyrs who had met an untimely death or fallen in battle, often while defending family or community. The beers were revered by believers as courageous leaders and fighters, as individuals who championed the defenceless and as local neighbourhood guardians of the common-folk.[103] Although these shrines were of earlier origin, it was largely from the early twentieth century that prominent seasonal festivals and regular prayers or ceremonies became more widespread,[104] echoing a spirit similar to that of Holi. Diane Coccari, in her study of beer worship in Benares, argues that not only was the beer cult 'lower class and caste' in its following, but that it also displayed 'self-consciousness and rebelliousness *vis a vis* brahmanical modes of worship',[105] and even attempted 'to establish an alternate power base of resistance to traditional authority'.[106] Moreover, the worship at beer shrines encapsulated the efforts of shudra groups to stake their claims to and entrench themselves in urban neighbourhoods around the shrines, within a context of social marginalisation as well as urban overcrowding and growing conflict over land and space.

While heightened martial consciousness and awareness of deprivation were expressed by the shudra poor through their changing religious practices, their emerging emphasis on a Hindu identity was reflected in some innovations in folk song traditions. One such example was *Biraha*, which was prominent amongst shudra pastoral castes.[107] Biraha literally means 'separation from one's beloved' or 'songs of separation', but the songs are also sung in memory of traditional heroes and beers. Biraha is believed to have originated, possibly during the Mughal period, as a song tradition of peasant and pastoral groups who alternated between agriculture or animal husbandry and military service. Biraha songs

---

[103] Coccari, 'Protection and Identity', pp. 130–46.
[104] Ibid., pp. 143–4; *Bharatiya Yadav Sangh: Rajat Jayanti Smarak Granth*, Part I, p. 26.
[105] Coccari, 'Protection and Identity', p. 145.
[106] Ibid., pp. 143–4.
[107] Crooke, *Tribes and Castes*, vol. I, p. 61; Onkar Prasad, *Folk Music and Folk Dances of Banares*, Calcutta, 1987, pp. 94–5.

reflect the experience of fighting away from home and of martial achievements as well as the emotions of love in separation.[108] Rural Biraha, called *Khari Biraha*, was sung during cattle-grazing, at night to pass leisure hours, and at social ceremonies such as weddings or engagements as a competition between brides' and grooms' parties. Until the 1880s, Biraha was known almost exclusively as a form of folk music in the villages. From the early twentieth century, Biraha gradually developed into an important urban musical genre, especially in Benares, under the initiative of the well-known singer Bihari Guru (1857–1926). The urban version of Biraha, called *Shayri* or *Dangali Biraha*, came to be performed mainly at temple festivals or at *varshik sringars* (annual decorations of the deity).[109] This new religious orientation of Biraha in the town suggests that the shudra poor were gradually seeking to impart a religious significance to their cultural activities and associating them with Hindu festivals, departing from their rural tradition.

In Kanpur, a similar song tradition, *lavni* or *khayal*, began to incorporate religious concerns, such as cow protection, regeneration of the Hindu community and social reforms. One of the singers, Prabhu Dayal Maharaj (1865–1905), was especially prominent in this respect. His songs, imbued with Hindu religious sentiments, rivalled those of other contemporary performers and gained greatest popularity in Kanpur. His disciple, Chunni Guru (1870–1943), who was based at a temple of Hanuman (a lesser Hindu deity revered mainly by shudras), followed in his footsteps with Hindu devotional songs, and gained a large following amongst both the poor and the commercial classes.[110] Lavni was long known to have been practised by both Hindus and Muslims, and had been especially powerful for its syncretic spirit. However, the inclusion of overtly religious themes in some forms of lavni tended to erode its previous importance in a composite popular culture, in turn reflecting the changing preferences of the audience for a greater religious content. In addition to the expression of religious sentiments, martial themes were prominent in lavni. Such folk-singing frequently went together with *pahalwani*, or body-building and wrestling,[111] revealing the inter-linking of various forms of popular culture and expressing the martial self-image of many sections of the urban poor.

In the early twentieth century, a major locus of self-expression of the shudra poor gradually emerged to be the gymnasium or akhara for

[108] Kolff, *Naukar, Rajput*, pp. 74–6; van der Veer, *Religious Nationalism*, p. 110.
[109] Scott L. Marcus, 'The Rise of a Folk Music Genre: *Biraha*', in Freitag (ed.), *Culture and Power*, pp. 93, 113; Kumar, *Artisans*, pp. 152–3; Prasad, *Folk Music*, pp. 94–7.
[110] Swami Narayananand Saraswati, *Lavni ka Itihas*, Kanpur, 1953, pp. 171–2, 235–7.
[111] Pandit Gaurishankar Tripathi 'Piyush', 'Lakhnau mein khayalbazi aur Uski Parampara', *Chayanat*, 31–32, October 1984–May 1985, pp. 24–9.

physical culture and martial arts.[112] The term akhara refers to the spatial organisation or the site of activities and training of any specialised group. Of the many kinds of akhara, those for physical culture became pervasive in north India in the twentieth century. Although akharas of musicians, troupes of dramatic performers or practitioners of indigenous medicine also existed, they were fewer and less prominent. Akharas of a religious nature amongst Hindus had been in existence well before the twentieth century as the organisational location of religious sects or orders of ascetics, and these akharas related to a history of armed monasticism in north India. Historically, monks of the ascetic orders in north India were also influential merchants and soldiers, involved in commerce and in organising armies.[113] Many of these monastic types of akharas, often based at pilgrim centres such as Benares or Prayag in Allahabad, had evolved as centres of martial arts, weaponry and wrestling, practised by Hindu Vaishnavite and Shaivaite devotional religious orders who engaged in warfare for the control of pilgrim routes, which also doubled as key commercial arteries. It also appears that one of the functions of these religious akharas had been to defend shrines and monastic institutions against Muslim intervention or aggression. Hindu martial akharas were known to recruit shudra groups, who played a prominent role in warfare, military training and wrestling.[114] It is often believed that shudras were inducted into these akharas in large numbers during the reign of the Mughal ruler Aurangzeb for self-defence, when many of these monastic orders came under threat.[115] Akharas, pugilism and martial sports and games had also been a part of the rural culture of the mobile armed peasantry and pastoralists of north India from the medieval period.[116] Thus, amongst shudra agrarian and pastoral groups, a culture of participation in martial akharas had existed before the twentieth century. Moreover, shudra rulers and nobles of earlier centuries in various parts of India were the patrons and practitioners of physical culture and wrestling, and had actively promoted these activities amongst their subjects. The patronage of wrestling had been a

[112] The central importance of akharas in twentieth-century urban popular culture has been noted by a number of authors, notably Freitag, *Collective Action*, pp. 121–3; Kumar, *Artisans*, pp. 111–24.

[113] Pinch, *Peasants and Monks*, pp. 24–31; P. van der Veer, 'The Politics of Devotion to Rama', in D. N. Lorenzen (ed.), *Bhakti Religion in North India: Community, Identity and Political Action*, New York, 1995, p. 301; P. van der Veer, *Gods on Earth: The Management of Religious Experience and Identity in a North Indian Pilgrimage Centre*, London, 1988, ch. 3.

[114] Pinch, *Peasants and Monks*, pp. 24–31.

[115] J. Alter, *The Wrestler's Body: Identity and Ideology in North India*, Berkeley, 1992, pp. 223–4.

[116] Kolff, *Naukar, Rajput*, pp. 28–9.

part of the courtly culture of shudra, especially yadav, kings, and these rulers considered the physical prowess of their subjects, as manifested in wrestling, to be a key symbol of royal power and might.[117] The twentieth-century leaders of shudra caste movements sought to perpetuate and revive this tradition. They stressed the cultivation of physical culture as an integral aspect of the reassertion of the tradition of the shudras as martial, ruling kshatriyas.

It was the earlier north Indian shudra tradition of participation in martial–religious akharas that now began to be elaborated extensively in the early twentieth century in the towns by the shudra poor. The elements of the martial defence of religion and the expression of Hindu militancy embodied in the past akhara culture were, undoubtedly, significant factors in the popularity that akharas now gained amongst the shudra poor. The assertion of a kshatriya martial tradition of the shudras gave an impetus to the growth of akharas as centres of physical culture, wrestling, sword and club wielding or *lathi* fighting. In the 1920s and 1930s, such akharas proliferated rapidly in the towns.[118] Pahalwani, or the cultivation of physical prowess, especially wrestling, emerged as a coveted social and personal ideal in urban popular culture; being a *pahalwan* signalled a desirable strong and muscular masculine personality. In this respect, Shahid Amin's analysis, albeit in a different context, of the significance of pahalwani and akharas in the 1920s in the eastern UP countryside in Chauri Chaura helps to illuminate their relevance in popular politics. Amin comments: 'In a culture where docile postures and genuflexion were the palpable signs of subordination, *pahelwani* amounted to a literal and metaphorical flexing of peasant muscles' and constituted 'an exhibition of peasant prowess'.[119] The glorification of the physique through akhara activities also, of course, related to an attempt by the labouring poor to dignify physical work. The prominent feature of akhara activities was, however, not just the nurture of physical strength; such activities were also marked by an

---

[117] Alter, *Wrestler's Body*, pp. 72–5.

[118] N. P. Arora, *Pahalwani aur Pahalwan*, Kanpur, 1948, pp. 70–104; *PAI*, No. 40, 20 October 1923, mentions 150 Hindus in 9 akharas learning swordsmanship and wrestling in Allahabad in one particular week; *PAI*, No 41, 27 October 1923, reports 13 Hindu akharas staged displays of arms and drills, with 300 participants; *PAI*, No. 35, 6 September 1924, mentions 5,000 involved in a display of swordsmanship in Allahabad; *PAI*, No. 18, 15 May 1926, commented that 'an increased tendency to carry stout lathis is noticeable'.

[119] Shahid Amin, *Event, Metaphor, Memory: Chauri Chaura, 1922–1992*, Delhi, 1995, pp. 123–5. Amin, however, argues in a footnote that akharas and wrestling in the urban context were dominated by elite concerns of national regeneration, in contrast to the world of the peasants where akharas 'existed within a traditional and more stable domain of physical culture' (p. 229n). In this assessment, Amin underestimates the extent of a popular initiative behind akharas and wrestling in urban north India.

element of competition and combat. Various akharas assembled, often during religious festivals, to contend with each other at tournaments or *dangals*, where the aim was to outdo the opponent and attain victory in various martial arts. The ultimate achievement of akhara activities was considered to be victory in competitions, which echoed the spirit of triumph of the kshatriyas in martial encounters.

The aspiration for self-assertion through physical prowess as represented in akhara activities also found an interesting expression in the figure of the local hero as *dada*, literally meaning the elder brother or paternal grandfather. Dadas were neighbourhood bosses among the poor or in working-class localities, often based at akharas. They boasted muscular physique of exceptional quality and were reputed for having perfected their 'fighting' techniques, which enabled them to assert their power and superiority in the *mohallas*. They usually established their own informal mechanisms of enforcing local order and instituted protection rings for their clientele among the poor against the exertions of moneylenders, landlords or the subordinate police. They often exacted dues from workers in return for such protection, for which they inspired fear rather more than adulation. Of course, the police considered them to be thugs, or *goondas*. However, among the poor, despite the heavy-handedness of the dadas, they enjoyed a degree of legitimacy and popularity as protectors, suggested by the very use of the fictive kinship term of 'dada'. They were also looked upon as repositories of a certain heroism for being able to face up to powerful exploitative forces. Even if they did not always effectively or systematically surmount or subvert the power of various superior forces, or were tyrannical in their role as local patrons, still they symbolised the efficacy of flexing muscles and personified the possibility of forging alternative, contested bases of power, defying existing structures of exploitation. The figure of the dada, arguably a kind of non-deified, profane 'beer' of everyday life, could thus embody the aspiration of workers for self-assertion through martial masculinity and virility.

Apart from the cultivation of a physical and martial culture and masculinity, the formation of akharas among the shudra poor was also the result of the practical relevance of akharas in local conflict and competition in urban neighbourhoods. The akharas served as local organisational bases of the shudra poor in relation to other urban groups, such as the untouchables or Muslims, in rivalries over land or jobs. The khatik vegetable vendors in the Kanpur *sabzi mandi* (vegetable market), for instance, formed an akhara and an association called the Khatik Sevak Mandal (Khatik Service Association) in the 1930s, partly to contend with the Muslim *kunjra* greengrocers and partly to develop physical culture.[120] Akharas in the bazars frequently served as a base for the shudra labourers or vendors to resist the exertions of the police, the urban improvement authorities and municipal inspectors or superintendents. It cannot be over-emphasised that the growth of akharas, underpinned by the cultivation of Hindu martial culture, was also integrally related to the responses of the shudra poor to growing local-level competition and conflict in the towns.

It was from within an akhara milieu that a form of urban folk play developed in the early twentieth century, which came to enjoy phenomenal popularity among the poorer classes in the towns. This form of folk play was variously called *swang*, *sangit* or *nautanki*. Nautanki, which originated in the Punjab at the turn of the century and then spread to urban UP to the akharas of musicians,[121] was a musical form of theatre, rather like an opera, featuring male performers, miming, singing and dancing to the accompaniment of kettledrums. These nautankis dealt with religious devotees such as Prahlad or Gopichand and with well-known folk heroes and their tales of victory in love and war.[122] Kathryn Hansen, through her study of two typical and popular nautanki plays, has outlined some of the recurrent and key thematic features of nautanki.[123] First, the main virtues of the central characters were their devotion to duty and truthfulness and their commitment to protect and support ordinary, poor people. Frequently, the protagonist was a brave, righteous and heroic person, rising from humble origins to become a powerful protector of the common-folk. Secondly, nautankis persistently deployed the motifs of treachery and disguise as artistic devices to demonstrate that the true worth and identity of a person were not reflected in outward appearance, status or behaviour, but lay in his or her inner self; thus, the truly virtuous was the humble or the ordinary person, not those who enjoyed social standing. This idea was also often developed through comic interludes depicting the humiliation, harassment or punishment of such apparently respectable figures as wealthy merchants or *banias*. Thirdly, in the plays, the extant social order and quotidian world were inverted, albeit briefly, when 'the powerless

---

[120] Interviews in Kanpur with Chaudhuri Bandidin (head of khatik panchayat in 1987 and a vegetable merchant) and Badlu Ram Sonekar (khatik politician).

[121] For the history of nautanki, see Ramnarayan Agarwal, *Sangit*, Delhi, 1976; Indra Sharma 'Varij', *Swang Nautanki*, Publications Division, Ministry of Information and Broadcasting, Government of India, 1984; Kathryn Hansen, *Grounds for Play: The Nautanki Theatre of North India*, Berkeley, 1992.

[122] K. Hansen, 'The Birth of Hindi Drama in Banaras: 1868–1865', in Freitag (ed.), *Culture and Power*, p. 69.

[123] K. Hansen, 'Sultana the Dacoit and Harishchandra: Two Popular Dramas of the Nautanki Tradition of North India', *MAS*, 17, 2, 1983, pp. 313–31.

become powerful for a time and the powerful become powerless'.[124] Nautankis acknowledged that 'even the great must suffer and endure oppression at the hands of the lowest of the low'.[125] The plays projected a 'highly moral universe' where good triumphed over evil and 'good deeds and truthfulness were rewarded by the gods'.[126] The nautankis, however, did not suggest or advocate a radical restructuring of the social order, or challenge the status quo, for order was restored at the end of the play, after temporary inversion.[127] Nautankis, thus, did not represent a culture of protest of the poor, amongst whom the performances were popular; rather the plays served both as a vehicle for their self-expression as the heroic and the virtuous, even if destitute or powerless, and as a means of expressing their world-view and moral conceptions. As Hansen argues, nautankis 'reflected their tastes, dreams and beliefs'.[128]

Nautankis were based in akharas, where the performers were trained by the author-director. The performers were proficient not only in singing, miming or acting, but also in wrestling and other martial arts, which featured in the performances.[129] The organisation of nautanki performances and the form of exchange of dialogues were also in the akhara style of dangal or competition, involving musical or verbal contest and repartee, in which various characters were in a state of competition with one another.[130] This manner of performance imparted an atmosphere of combat and triumph to the plays and reinforced the thematic martial and heroic overtones. The centrality of this martial element is also evident from the cover of the chapbooks of nautanki plays written by one of the most popular dramatists, Sri Krishna Pahalwan of Kanpur. The chapbooks published in this period featured a portrait of him as a pahalwan, displaying the full splendour of his muscular body, clad only in a loincloth. The period of the rising popularity of nautankis in UP was from the 1910s and 1920s, when Sri Krishna introduced new characters and stories in nautanki plays and toured the towns of UP. The Hindu heroic and patriotic content of nautankis gained great prominence in Sri Krishna Pahalwan's plays, which focused on such figures as Haqiqat Rai, Veermati, Padmini and

---

[124] Ibid., p. 323.   [125] Ibid.
[126] Hansen, 'Birth of Hindi Drama', p. 71.
[127] Hansen, 'Sultana the Dacoit and Harishchandra', pp. 321–31.
[128] Hansen, 'Birth of Hindi Drama', p. 74.
[129] N. P. Arora's book on akharas and wrestling mentions that a number of akharas in Kanpur boasted nautanki performers amongst their participants. Arora, *Pahalwani aur Pahalwan*, pp. 70–104.
[130] Ibid., pp. 70–1.

Shivaji, who had defended Hinduism.[131] Nautanki was the object of elite disapproval, being regarded as 'low' or 'lewd' in character and essentially a form of entertainment for the lower classes.[132] In fact, in urban areas, the main clientele of nautanki came from the bazar poor, and it developed primarily in the bazar milieu.[133] Thus, for instance, Sri Krishna Pahalwan's nautanki plays and performers were products of the Kanpur bazars, where his troupe and akhara were based in the heart of the bazars at Hatia. The development of nautankis as the most important form of popular entertainment by the 1920s, similar to Hindi films of a later period, is emblematic of the nature of the transformation in urban popular culture in the early twentieth century, with a moral and martial spirit at its centre, along with a strong expression of the virtues and triumphs of the poor and the powerless, as well as a strain of Hindu heroism.

'Sachcha Hindu Sangathan': Complexities in the construction of Hindu community

The upsurge of militant Hinduism among the shudra poor would gradually come to reinforce and immeasurably accelerate the activities of various Hindu reformist and revivalist organisations in the 1920s and 1930s. In 1924, the Allahabad Ramlila procession included a 'great display of numbers and arms', and featured a *tableau-vivant* depicting a brahmin and a sweeper sitting together, with the slogan 'Sachcha Hindu Sangathan' – 'True United Organisation of Hindus'.[134] This tableau encapsulated the two key messages that were being propagated in UP from the early 1920s with ever greater stridency by Hindu publicists and by organisations such as the Arya Samaj and the Hindu Sabha. The salient themes of Hindu resurgence were, first, the integration of lower-caste groups into the Hindu fold in order to achieve greater cohesion and unity within the putative Hindu community, and, second, the militant expansion of religious festivals and other activities with heightened martial fervour in order to organise the Hindu community better.

---

[131] This is inferred from a number of plays by Sri Krishna Pahalwan, the texts of which were supplied to me by his son, Puran Chandra Mehrotra, in Kanpur.

[132] Hansen, 'Birth of Hindi Drama', pp. 71–4; Hansen, 'Sultana the Dacoit and Harishchandra', p. 314.

[133] Interestingly, the Kanpur school of nautanki is considered by some commentators to be 'vulgar' (*ashleel*) as well as less respectable and more lower class in character than the other main school of nautanki in UP, based at Hathras. This view is not surprising, since, in contrast to Hathras, the Kanpur nautanki enjoyed greater participation and input from bazar akharas and was more popular locally amongst the labouring classes. Indra Sharma 'Varij', *Swang Nautanki*, p. 148.

[134] *PAI*, No. 41, 18 October 1924.

The need to unify the Hindu community and to regenerate Hinduism had begun to be voiced from the late nineteenth century. In the forefront of this religious revivalism were the Arya Samaj, Hindu Samaj of Allahabad, Sanatana Dharma Mahamandal and the Sanatana Dharma Sabha. Prominent writers and political publicists such as Bharatendu Harishchandra, Madan Mohan Malaviya and Bishan Narayan Dar[135] had also declared the need to revitalise Hinduism.[136] From the early 1920s, however, the efforts of religious organisations to revive Hinduism and to unite the Hindu community gained new momentum and urgency as well as a far more activist focus than ever before. The wider context for this development was partly set by the recognition of communal representation in the political and constitutional reforms introduced by the British government after the First World War, which spurred on the political leadership of the various communities to attempt unification and numerical expansion. In part, the establishment of powerful Muslim organisations and Islamic religious ferment during the Khilafat movement also played a decisive role in galvanising Hindu communal organisations into action, with a projected need for defensive mobilisation.[137] Moreover, after the Non-Cooperation movement, a section of the Congress leadership in UP led by Madan Mohan Malaviya, in mounting its opposition against the Swarajist group, increasingly adopted a Hindu rhetoric in the 1920s and promoted the activities of religious organisations.[138] The interwar period in UP thus came to be characterised by a new zeal in the activities of the Arya Samaj, the Hindu Sabha and other Hindu organisations. They also launched an extensive and vigorous propaganda campaign in order to sculpt a pan-Hindu identity.[139]

In UP, the Arya Samaj launched the programme of shuddhi on a large scale in 1923 for reconversion from Islam to Hinduism and for the reclamation of lower castes into the Hindu caste hierarchy. In that year, in reaction to the conversion to Islam by the Mappillas in Malabar, Swami Shraddhanand made a determined bid to win over the Malkan Rajputs of Western UP, who had converted to Islam. In the wake of this reconversion drive, the shuddhi programme was vigorously extended by

[135] Dar rose to prominence as a Hindu leader during the cow protection movement of the 1890s and later became the Congress President in 1911.
[136] C. A. Bayly, *The Local Roots of Indian Politics: Allahabad, 1880–1920*, Oxford, 1975, pp. 104–17, 214–17; Freitag, *Collective Action*, pp. 208–9; Pandey, *Construction*, ch. 6.
[137] G. Pandey, *The Ascendancy of the Congress in Uttar Pradesh, 1926–34: A Study in Imperfect Mobilization*, Delhi, 1978, pp. 115–16.
[138] Ibid., pp. 115–27; D. Page, *Prelude to Partition: The Indian Muslims and the Imperial System of Control, 1920–1932*, Delhi, 1982, pp. 74–84.
[139] For instances of vigorous religious propaganda in the press, see *NNR*, Nos. 1, 9, 12, 13, 14, 15, 16, 20, 22/1923.

the Arya Samaj to other parts of UP, in order to draw in converts, and especially low-caste groups, to the Hindu fold.[140] To implement the national-level programme, a number of local-level organisations were formed. A reclamation or shuddhi society was inaugurated at the Arya Samaj office at Bulanala in Benares in 1923, followed by an Acchutod-dhar Sabha (Society for the Uplift of Untouchables) in Allahabad.[141] The concept of shuddhi was of earlier origin, but, as a police report commented, the militant activism of the Arya Samaj from 1923 and the application of shuddhi 'to mass rather than individual conversion gave it special prominence at this time'.[142] Another report at the time also mentioned that 'the outstanding feature of the period' was the promi-nence of the shuddhi issue, giving rise to 'a general awakening in religious sentiments'.[143] To spread its message, the Arya Samaj made use of forms of popular entertainment, alongside press campaigns, public meetings and processions. The well-known nautanki composer Sri Krishna Pahalwan, who had come under the influence of the Arya Samaj, wrote plays for the Arya Sangit (Nautanki) Samiti. Plays about Hindu martyrs such as *Dharmveer Haqiqat Rai or Maharani Padmini* advocated deep loyalty to Hinduism and the need to fight for one's faith. Quotations from these plays cited in Hansen's book on nautanki also show that they explicitly urged support for the Arya Samaj and expressed veneration for its founder, Swami Dayanand Saraswati.[144] The Arya Samaj, not surprisingly, had a very large number of copies of the play *Dharmveer Haqiqat Rai* printed, and sold them for the nominal sum of two *paisa* or distributed them free.[145]

   Alongside the Arya Samaj, the Hindu Sabha launched a major revival of its activities in 1922–3. The UP Hindu Sabha had been inaugurated in 1915 at Allahabad, with Madan Mohan Malaviya as its president. It was practically defunct during the Non-Cooperation years, but was revived with much fanfare at its Gaya conference in 1922 and at a subsequent session in Benares in 1923.[146] The importance of its revival

---

[140] P. Hardy, *The Muslims of British India*, Cambridge, 1972, pp. 208–9.

[141] *PAI*, No. 17, 5 May 1923; No. 21, 2 June 1923.

[142] Confidential note on 'Communal Friction in the United Provinces, 1924', by Assistant to Deputy Inspector General of Police, Criminal Investigation Department, UP, File No. 140/1925, Home Poll., GOI, NAI, (also included in File No. 206/1926, Home Poll, GOI, NAI).

[143] *PAI*, No. 16, 21 April 1923.

[144] Hansen, *Grounds for Play*, p. 110.

[145] Agarwal, *Sangit*, p. 131; *Jivan Parichay: Ek Jhanki: Sangeet Natak Academy 1967–68 ke Purashkar Se Vibhushit Nautanki Shiromani Pahalwan Sri Krishna Khattri*, Kanpur, *vikrami samvat* 2025, c. A.D. 1968, p. 3.

[146] Confidential note on 'Communal Friction in the United Provinces, 1924'; R. A. Gordon, 'The Hindu Mahasabha and the Indian National Congress, 1915 to 1926',

was not just that it resumed its activities, but that it now adopted a new focus and determined stance. The Hindu Sabha was an organisation of the orthodox higher castes, and until 1923 the Sabha had not been in favour of the reclamation of lower castes through shuddhi. However, a majority of the members of the Sabha resolved their differences with the Arya Samaj over shuddhi in the early 1920s. An alliance was forged with the Arya Samaj, under Malaviya's leadership, and the shuddhi programme was formally adopted by the Hindu Sabha at its 1923 Benares session.[147] In bringing about this reconciliation with the Arya Samaj, Malaviya stressed the need for Hindu unity, sinking all internal differences. Malaviya's biographer reports that he regarded the Arya Samaj and the Hindu Sabha not merely 'as members of the same family but as two brothers holding different and even opposing views on some aspects of [our] religion, but united in their faith in and devotion to [our] ancient religion and civilisation'.[148] This shift in the policy of the Hindu Sabha arose from the new preoccupation of stalwarts such as Malaviya to widen the Hindu fold and to promote the participation of various castes and sects in the activities of Hindu organisations. A set of plans was charted to strengthen the Hindu community in two important ways: first, the reclamation of lower castes (shuddhi), and, secondly, the promotion of a range of organisations (*sangathan*) and religious volunteer corps, extending down to the local neighbourhood. These programmes of shuddhi and sangathan were incorporated in resolutions adopted at the Benares session of the Hindu Sabha in 1923.[149] Malaviya's urgency to unify the Hindu community by drawing in all manner of castes and sects was amply demonstrated at the Allahabad Adh Kumbh Mela of 1924. Malaviya solicited the participation of the Sikh Akalis in the Hindu Sabha procession at the *mela* (fair) by promising to donate Rs 10,000 to the Akali Dal from Hindu Sabha funds.[150] The Akalis were, as a result, reported to have participated in a Hindu Sabha procession, chanting militant slogans which urged Hindus to rise and fight.[151] More importantly, members of low-caste groups were invited to attend a meeting at the Hindu Sabha *pandal* (pavilion) at the mela, where speeches were delivered on the unity of all Hindu castes. They were then escorted to the sacred *sangam*, the confluence of the holy

---

MAS, 9, 2, 1975, p. 170; PAI, No. 18, 12 May 1923; Mushirul Hasan, *Nationalism and Communal Politics in India, 1916–1928*, Delhi, 1979, pp. 254–5.

[147] Gordon, 'The Hindu Mahasabha', p. 170; S. L. Gupta, *Pandit Madan Mohan Malaviya: A Socio-political Study*, Allahabad, 1978, pp. 298–9.

[148] Gupta, *Malaviya*, p. 259.   [149] Ibid.

[150] PAI, No. 7, 16 February 1924.

[151] PAI, No. 3, 19 January 1924.

rivers in Allahabad, and allowed to bathe at the site to which low castes were traditionally prohibited access.[152]

The attempts of the Arya Samaj and the Hindu Sabha to strengthen and revitalise the putative Hindu community and to present a united image were given a militant organisational basis through the sangathan movement.[153] Sangathan was envisaged as the key initiative in 'eradicating the evil effects of years of emasculated existence of the Hindus and infusing manliness into them'.[154] Sangathan was also partly aimed at promoting the self-defence of the Hindu community by united action against what was perceived as Muslim onslaught and projected as historical oppression by Muslims. Although Hindu leaders were careful to emphasise that war and violence were not compatible with Hindu spirituality, yet, referring to Muslims, they stressed that 'not to give a fight when challenged was no less of a sin', which would lead to the violation of dharma, or religious virtue, and *nyaya*, or justice.[155] Sangathan was seen also as a form of national, not just Hindu, regeneration in the face of the demilitarisation and emasculation argued to have been perpetrated by the British on the Indian people. Sangathan thus equated the revitalisation of the nation with the resurrection of an imagined past virility and masculine prowess of Hindus. Moreover, the emphasis on physical strength was coupled with the notion of wielding arms, thus linking rejuvenated masculinity with weapons and violence – masculinity, muscularity, machismo and militarism, all went hand in hand.[156] Sangathan entailed the formation of self-defence and vigilante volunteer corps, youth organisations, wrestling dens, akharas and *vyamshalas* (gymnasiums) for training in discipline, physical prowess, martial arts and arms.[157]

As part of the sangathan strategy, Hindu organisations as well as the mercantile communities of north India tried to promote physical culture as a form of expression of Hindu power. Akharas and physical culture had gradually evolved as a central symbol of the resurgent power of the Hindus ever since the time of the Maratha ruler Shivaji in the eighteenth

---

[152] *PAI*, No. 8, 23 February 1924.
[153] Gupta, *Malaviya*, pp. 295–300.
[154] *NNR*, No. 31/1924. cites *Abhudaya* (Allahabad).
[155] Gupta, *Malaviya*, pp. 295–300, 326.
[156] These ideas about sangathan were elaborated, for instance, in a key text by Swami Shraddhanad, entitled *Hindu Sangathan: Saviour of the Dying Race* (1924). See also Swami Satyadev Paribrajak, *Sangathan ka Bigul*, Dehradun, 1926; Bandhusamaj, Kanpur, *Hinduon ki Tez Talwar*, Kanpur, 1927. I am grateful to Charu Gupta for these references.
[157] Gupta, *Malaviya*, pp. 294–7, 355–8; Confidential note on 'Communal Friction in the United Provinces, 1924'.

century, who had actively patronised wrestling and akhara formation.[158] This tradition spread and flourished in north Indian urban centres with Maratha pilgrims, especially in places such as Benares or Allahabad, where they often reinforced the akhara tradition associated with religious orders of armed monks. Based on these various traditions, the formation of akharas and the nurture of physical culture were stressed as a central plank of the revivification, reunification and empowerment of the Hindu community through sangathan. In support of these initiatives, north Indian urban merchants and notables also frequently made substantial financial donations or provided free land for the establishment of gymnasiums and wrestling dens. They were some of the greatest enthusiasts of akharas and dangals, and sponsored wrestling tournaments, often during religious festivals, and awarded trophies and prizes to the winners.[159] Moreover, in the 1920s and 1930s, activists of the Indian National Congress were advocating akharas, physical culture and good physique as means of character-building and patriotic education for the training of a citizen army and able freedom fighters against the Raj.[160] The Congress financed akharas with their own organisational resources or with funds from the municipalities over which the party had control.[161]

All of these groups – Hindu revivalists and reformists, and the Congress nationalists – found strong enthusiasts among the shudra poor in accelerating akhara activities. The diverse, but overlapping, efforts of various Hindu or nationalist organisations to promote physical and martial culture would not have met with any great success or gained rapid proliferation without very considerable expansion of akhara activities among the shudra poor or without the growing importance of wrestling and physical exercises in popular culture. Equally, elite patronage clearly played a role in sustaining the self-assertion of the poor through akhara activities. It is, however, important to note that, although the akhara initiatives of the poor and of their affluent patrons and religious or political leaders intersected, and shared or common practices thus emerged, yet the meaning and relevance of akharas for the shudra poor differed quite considerably from those of the leadership.

---

[158] Alter, *Wrestler's Body*, p. 73.

[159] Arora, *Pahalwani aur Pahalwan*, pp. 10–12.

[160] Gupta, *Malaviya*, pp. 355–8; Alter, *Wrestler's Body*, pp. 17–18. The enthusiasm of Congress nationalists for wrestling and body-building is also evident from Arora, *Pahalwani aur Pahalwan*. Arora, a well-known Congress leader of Kanpur, was himself an enthusiast and practitioner of wrestling, and his book on this subject reflects his keen interest.

[161] Evidence of Khaliluddin Ahmad Saheb, Honorary Assistant Collector, Kanpur, given to the Kanpur Riots Inquiry Commission of 1931. Reported in *The Pioneer* (Lucknow), 25 April 1931. Also mentioned in Freitag, *Collective Action*, pp. 225, 234.

The *form* of action may have overlapped, but the *content* diverged. The main aims of the leaders and patrons were variously to assert higher-caste status, to forge a strong and unified Hindu community or to promote nationalism, whereas for the poor the akhara culture, as noted earlier, expressed their own concerns about status and self-esteem, political assertion or resistance, as well as their more practical needs. It is, however, important that, in the process of linking the actions of the leaders and the shudra poor in the public sphere, a significant reorientation and transmutation gradually happened. What had originated as a celebration of manliness and physical strength among the shudra poor now tended to be expressed in violence and aggression through the sangathan movement, especially with the attendant elaboration of a notion of threat from the Muslims.

A projected need for protection from supposedly aggressive Muslims was at the heart of the sangathan movement. Apart from promoting akhara activities, the sangathan initiative also included the formation of volunteers corps, such as the Hindu Sevak Dals, not only for the expression of Hindu power and for martial display, but also for the protection of the Hindu community. In 1923, numerous branches of the Mahabir Dal (Group of the Brave) were formed in various urban neighbourhoods; they practised sword-fighting, wrestling and lathi-wielding.[162] Hindu volunteer corps named after famous warriors such as the Bhimsen Dal, Abhimanyu Dal and Mahabir Sena Sangh, mush-roomed in all the cities. A prominent element that emerged in their activities was an emphasis on defence against Muslims. Kenneth Jones points out that the Arya Samaj, drawing upon Dayanand's *Satyartha Prakash*, portrayed Islam as a 'religion of slaughter, both animals and men', impelled by 'brutality and sensuality'.[163] According to the Arya Samaj, Islam 'was born of violence and would always remain tied to religious warfare'.[164] Based on ideas of this nature, Hindu organisations in UP in the 1920s increasingly campaigned to forge a self-image of the Hindu community being at war, in which the Muslims supposedly acted with aggression and rapacity, while the Hindus reacted, in defence, with bravery, strength and a heroic martial spirit.

This notion of a need for Hindu 'self-defence' of necessity had to be fostered and justified, at the same time, through a stereotypical image of Muslims as fierce sources of danger from whom Hindus required pro-tection. A large body of Hindu propaganda in this period consistently

---

[162] *PAI*, No. 35, 8 September 1923; No. 36, 15 September 1923; No. 37, 22 September 1923; No. 40, 20 October 1923.

[163] Jones, *Arya Dharm*, p. 145.

[164] Ibid., p. 150.

portrayed Muslims as destructive, fanatical and sinister, intent on
desecrating Hindu shrines and temples, determined to construct
mosques on Hindu sacred sites, prone to kidnapping women and
children to convert them forcibly to Islam, and eager to violate Hindu
women.[165] A few instances from the press demonstrate the tone of this
campaign. The major Kanpur Hindu daily newspaper, *Vartman*, aired
the fanciful idea that 'there exists a secret but organised association
which instigates them [the Muslims] to perpetrate atrocities on the
Hindus, and in which the entire Islamic world is implicated'.[166] Another
well-known paper of Kanpur, *Pratap*, advised that 'Hindus should
abandon their cowardliness and impotency and make themselves so
strong that these [Muslim] *badmashes* [miscreants] may not dare to
oppress them'.[167] Both *Vartman* and *Pratap* also regularly accused
Muslims, whom they usually called 'goondas', 'ruffians' or 'badmash',
of 'thrashing', 'plundering', 'assaulting' and 'oppressing' the 'timid' and
'weak' Hindu 'sufferers'.[168] Another paper, *Abhaya*, in a single article
entitled 'Increase in hooliganism', succeeded in bringing together an
impressive array of negative attributes to describe the Muslims, ranging
from the usual mention of outrages perpetrated on Hindus to the moral
and social degeneracy of the Muslim community as a threat to the body-
civic of India:

Robbing people, molesting women and kidnapping children, as is done by
wolves, are specimens of their [Muslims'] civilisation. In throwing flesh inside
temples, setting fire to buildings and beating two or three men by ten or twenty
lies their heroism. Marrying the daughter of uncles is an example of their high
ideals. Can anybody sleep peacefully in the midst of such races and such a
religion? If not, then all should combine to crush the increasing hooliganism of
Muslims.[169]

The image of the violence and immorality of the Muslims thus fostered
was further strengthened with widespread propaganda about a history
of 'Muslim atrocities' on Hindus from medieval times, and bitter
invective was let loose about their historical treachery and oppression.[170]
These myths soon found their way into popular entertainment. Balb-
hadra Singh of Ranjitpurwa, Kanpur, wrote a nautanki play, *Birbala*, in
which the Mughal ruler Aurangzeb was shown to be craving for and

---

[165] Confidential note on 'Communal Friction in the United Provinces, 1924'.
[166] *NNR*, No. 30/1923, p. 3.
[167] *NNR*, No. 32/1923, p. 3.
[168] See, for instance, *NNR*, No. 36/1923, pp. 2–3; No. 37/1923, p. 2; No. 20/1924. p. 3;
     No. 24/1924, p. 2.
[169] *NNR*, No. 31/1925, p. 3.
[170] *PAI*, No. 31, 15 August 1925; No. 33, 29 August 1925; No. 45, 28 November 1925;
     No. 1, January 1926; No. 19, 21 May 1927; No. 20, 28 May 1927; No. 1, 5 January
     1929.

lusting after the central female character. Alleged historical crimes were thus linked with imagined contemporary behaviour through essentialised stereotypes of Muslims.[171] Not surprisingly, the *Lakshman* referred to the contemporary 'thrashing and spoliation' by Muslims as 'Aurangzebian tactics'.[172]

Between 1923 and 1925, when sangathan activities were rapidly accelerating, rumours and 'scare' stories about Muslims defiling or molesting Hindu women and abducting both women and children for conversion were rife in all the towns. At meetings of Hindu organisations, warnings were regularly issued about the propensity of Muslims to engage in such activities, and sangathan initiatives were strongly urged to prevent such abominations, thus also often precipitating assaults on Muslims.[173] In Benares, the local Hindu Sabha tried to raise subscriptions from the public to maintain a volunteer corps at railway stations to protect women and children from being kidnapped.[174] In Kanpur, the Sewa Samiti volunteers of the Congress were reported by the police to have made an 'intolerable nuisance of themselves' over women they suspected of being kidnapped and converted to Islam.[175] The Hindu Sabha in Allahabad even sent a formal letter to the paper *Bhavishya* to warn Hindus about the 'thousands' of Muslim goondas who were engaged in kidnapping on an organised basis.[176] Such vigorous and elaborate measures by the Hindu organisations to prevent kidnapping imparted an air of reality and immediacy to this imaginary threat.

The question, however, arises as to why these myths were believed by the shudra poor so widely and why they came to provide part of the justification for the formation of akharas and of martial mobilisation. Why and to what extent did these projects of Hindu self-protection overlap with the religious resurgence and martial assertion of the shudra poor? For the shudra poor, the portrayal of Muslims as violent helped them to fortify the myth of the loss of their past glory on account of Muslim oppression. Muslims being the villains responsible for the weakening of Hinduism and especially for the decline of shudras, the theory of 'Muslim atrocities' was necessary grist to the mill for the construction of their past. Besides, the imagination of a demonised

---

[171] Noted from the nautanki chapbook collection of Sri Puran Chandra Mehrotra, son of Sri Krishna Pahalwan.

[172] *NNR*, No. 36/1923, p. 3.

[173] Ibid., *PAI*, No. 37, 20 September 1924; No. 40, 11 October 1924; No. 25, 4 July 1925; No. 31, 15 August 1925; No. 32, 22 August 1925; *The Leader*, 3 August 1938, p. 10; *Pratap* (Kanpur), 27 March 1938, p. 8; *Pratap*, 11 September 1938, p. 8; *PAI*, No. 20, May 20 1939.

[174] *PAI*, No. 25, 4 July 1925.

[175] *PAI*, No. 40, 11 October 1924.

[176] *NNR*, No. 29/1925, p. 3.

figure of threat and fear provided the excuse for the shudra poor to put themselves forward as the defenders of Hinduism. The upholding of masculinity and physical strength in defence of community very closely corresponded to the concerns of the shudra poor, but these now assumed a more violent and aggressive orientation in the context of the wider religious propaganda. Moreover, as seen earlier, increasingly in the 1920s and 1930s the rationale behind the formation of akharas by the shudra poor was not only an expression of martial or religious spirit, but also a perceived need for defence against Muslim groups, in the face of growing competition and conflict. Shudra assertion in the form of akharas and self-defence corps thus gradually became more and more focused on antagonism against Muslims. All these developments served to heighten communal tensions, as various sections of Muslims began to feel threatened by what they saw as Hindu aggression and they reacted by expanding similar organisations of their own. It will be seen in the next chapter that martial activities amongst various sections of the Hindu and the Muslim poor mutually reinforced each other, and contending akharas then clashed, often developing into communal riots. Moreover, neighbourhood akhara-based conflicts increasingly over-lapped with local rivalries over jobs or land, as indicated earlier in the case of the khatik and kunjra vegetable sellers in Kanpur.

Simultaneously with shuddhi, sangathan and akhara expansion, Hindu revivalism from the 1920s found manifestation in the changing patterns of worship and observance of religious festivals. Regular prayers, often with an elaborate panoply of ceremonials, were intro-duced, even at previously abandoned temples, which led a police report of 1926 to comment that in Allahabad 'it is noticeable that in every temple, even those which have been practically disused, *"arti puja"* (special religious ceremony) and conch blowing have been restarted with great vigour'.[177] Festivals were celebrated with increasing grandeur and the display of arms, weaponry and physical force; new festivals and more elaborate modes of celebration were introduced. *Dadhkando*, *Shivaratri*, *Ramdol* and *Janmastami*, which had hitherto been minor public festivals, were celebrated on a grander scale, alongside Ramlila and Holi.[178] Processions began to be organised for occasions for which

[177] *PAI*, No. 8, 27 February 1926.
[178] *PAI*, No. 30, 5 August 1922; No. 36, 15 September 1923; *PAI*, No. 35, 6 September 1924; No. 36, 13 September 1924; No. 37, 26 September 1925; No. 8, 27 February 1926; *NNR*, No. 37/1924, p. 5; Chief Secretary, UP, to Secretary, Government of India, Home Department, Letter No. 1355–Z, dated 23 September 1924, File No. 249/X/1924, Home Poll., GOI, NAI; *FR*: second half of January 1926, first half of March 1926, second half of October 1926, File No. 112/IV/1926, Home Poll., GOI, NAI.

no such tradition existed.[179] In 1925, Hindu papers issued detailed instructions for the proper celebration of Janmastami, until then a minor festival. As the festival that commemorates the birth of Lord Krishna, the protection of cows was stressed, for Krishna, according to Hindu mythology, spent his childhood as a cowherd among communities of milkmen. Processions were organised with the *Bhagavad Gita* on display as a key religious text in which Lord Krishna expounded the duty to engage in warfare even against one's kinsmen.[180] In 1927, for the first time ever, a procession was taken out by the Arya Samaj in Kanpur on *Basant Panchami*, which met with much enthusiasm, being attended by about 2,000 people.[181] *Nagar kirtan* processions, which traversed various urban neighbourhoods singing devotional songs, were not only an innovation in the 1920s, but they were remarkably expanded with enlarged participation. They also often struck provocative postures by vigorously playing music in front of mosques.[182] In addition to these changes in religious observances, resolute attempts were made to prevent Hindus from joining Muslim festivals or visiting sufi shrines, and to exclude Muslims from taking part in Hindu sacred ceremonies and events, including the setting up of stalls or shops at religious fairs – all of which frequently reversed practices of the recent past.[183]

By the 1920s, then, Hindu festivals emerged as occasions for militant Hindu self-assertion. This process is best illustrated in the changing pattern of celebration of Ramlila in Allahabad. One of the most important annual Hindu festivals of north India, the Ramlila celebrates the victory of Lord Ram over his demon enemy Ravana. Warfare and victory are its central motifs, and the festival symbolises the affirmation and recreation of dharma or moral order.[184] From 1911–12, the Ramlila had been observed in Allahabad with greater pomp and show, under the auspices of the town's affluent Hindu merchants. Evening illuminations and tableaux or floats depicting events from the life of Ram, the martial hero, had been introduced in Ramlila processions,[185] and musical bands had begun to accompany the processions by 1916.[186] By the 1920s, the Ramlila in Allahabad developed into an even more explicit expression of

---

[179] *PAI*, No. 32, 22 August 1925.
[180] *NNR*, No. 31/1925, p. 3; No. 32/1925, p. 2; No. 33/1925, p. 3.
[181] *PAI*, No. 7, 19 February 1927.
[182] *PAI*, No. 9, 5 March 1927.
[183] *PAI*, No. 12, 18 March 1925; No. 20, 28 May 1927; *NNR*, No. 23/1912, p. 458; Barrier, *Roots of Communal Politics*, p. 237.
[184] C. J. Fuller, *The Camphor Flame: Popular Hinduism and Society in India*, Princeton, 1992, p. 125.
[185] Cited in *Smarika: Pajawa Ramlila Committee, 1982*, Allahabad, 1982, p. 31.
[186] Confidential Note on Music in Ramlila, by H. Crosthwaite, DM, Allahabad, dated 28 October 1926, File No. 613/1926, Box No. 473, GAD, GUP, UPSA.

a militant Hindu offensive. The Rani of Jhansi first appeared in the procession in 1911,[187] and a decade later, in 1922, an image of Shivaji as the defender of Hinduism and the epitome of victorious Hindu nationalism featured prominently alongside the usual images of Ram, Lakshman and Sita.[188] This marked a new intermeshing of nationalist images with Hindu symbolism. The Ramlila then gradually developed as a vehicle for the expression of Hindu power and Indian nationalism. The figures of *Bharat Mata* or Mother India, Mahatma Gandhi, Shivaji and the Rani of Jhansi graced the Ramlila processions, alongside images of *charkha* spinning and British police atrocities, such as at Jallianwala-bagh. The revered figures of Ram, Sita and Lakshman were dressed in hand-woven *khadi* clothes, with their denigrated adversary Ravana in foreign outfit.[189]

The ethos of the Ramlila was also increasingly that of a celebration of the newly developing physical prowess of the Hindus. Not only were public celebrations of festivals expanded in scale, they were also given an overtly martial content. Several armed Hindu akharas participated for the first time in the Allahabad Ramlila procession in 1923, which was considered to be 'a marked innovation' in a police report of the time.[190] Groups of processionists, called dals, dressed in martial costumes, carried spears, swords and lathis, and projected themselves as the army of Hindu nationalism. In their later reminiscences, veteran Ramlila participants of Allahabad highlighted the fact that the themes of Hindu martial valour and might had marked Ramlila celebrations. Describing the performance of Kalyan Chandra Mahile, popularly known as Chhunnan Guru, a prominent Ramlila participant and a well-known pahalwan of Allahabad, his brother later reminisced about his martial costume and 'the shining glory of his spear', which he held aloft as he rode on his horse.[191] One participant, recapitulating his childhood memories of rehearsals and exercises for Ramlila mock fights, wrote that they seemed like actual combat with war cries and that the festive season rang with the din of battle.[192] A further reflection of the expression of Hindu martial strength in the Ramlila was the formation of the Kesaria Dal and the Khuni Dal in 1924 as part of the Daraganj Ramlila celebrations. In that year, prior to the festival, some Muslim groups had

---

[187] Freitag, *Collective Action*, p. 202.
[188] *PAI*, No. 39, 7 October 1922.
[189] Ibid.; Harimohandas Tandon, *Prayagraj: Lala Manohardas ka Parivar*, Allahabad, 1993, p. 82; File on 'Innovations in Ramlila Processions at Allahabad', File No. 586/1921, Box No. 40, GAD, GUP, UPSA.
[190] *PAI*, No. 43, 10 November 1923.
[191] *Smarika: Pajawa Ramlila Committee*, 1982, p. 96.
[192] Dr Sureshwar Rai, 'Ramdal, Roshni aur Ramlila', *Dharmayug*, 12 October 1975, p. 6.

objected to the playing of music near mosques in the course of Ramlila processions. In protest, the organisers of the Daraganj Ramlila threatened to suspend the celebrations. A renowned local poet, Bacchan Lal 'Bibudhesh', composed a fiery poem calling upon kshatriyas to perform their traditional duty of defending Hinduism and accusing the Allahabad Hindus of being effeminate and giving in to Muslim threats. Spurred on by his stirring call to arms, the pahalwan *pandas* and *tirtha purohits*, who organise worship at the Prayag Kumbh mela, formed the Kesaria Dal (the Saffron-clad Group – saffron being the colour of Hinduism) and the mallahs, a shudra caste group, formed the Khuni Dal (Suicide Corps). Both dals pledged to lay down their lives to keep the glory of Ram, as the symbol of Hinduism, alive.[193]

Shudra groups, such as the Khuni Dal had by this time assumed a prominent position in the Ramlila celebrations. The patrons of the Ramlila wished to enlarge the scale of festival celebrations with a view to projecting an image of the organised cohesiveness of the Hindu community. The Ramlila processions, which had been confined to higher castes, gradually included low-caste dals from 1923–4.[194] By integrating lower-caste groups in Hindu festivals, especially those who claimed to be warlike kshatriyas, the Arya Samaj and the Hindu Sabha aimed to project an appearance of unity and militancy in the Hindu community. A police report on the 1923 Ramlila in Allahabad stated that the inclusion of low-caste groups by the Ramlila Committees 'had as its motive the raising of a force of men used to handle lathis, in order to impress the Mohammadans'.[195] Another report similarly noted that 'the prominent current running through the various [Hindu Sabha and Arya Samaj] proceedings was the political advance of the Hindu body politic'.[196]

While the involvement of shudra groups was actively encouraged by Hindu leaders and patrons of the Ramlila, their participation was also undoubtedly a product of the attempts of the shudra poor to express their centrality in martial Hinduism. The emphasis on a kshatriya identity by the shudra poor involved not only the cultivation of a martial tradition and the formation of akharas, but also their growing and militant participation in the major north Indian religious festivals, most notably the Ramlila. In the Ramlila processions before the 1920s, urban higher castes had been the chief organisers and participants, and the celebrations were financed and sponsored by merchants or local notables.

[193] *Smarika: Sri Ramlila Committee, Daraganj, Prayag, 1979*, p. 41.
[194] *PAI*, No. 41, 27 October 1923; No. 41, 18 October 1924.
[195] *PAI*, No. 41, 27 October 1923.
[196] Confidential note on 'Communal Friction in the United Provinces, 1924'.

The shudras had participated, but mainly as onlookers and crowds, and they had been employed by the merchants to transport floats or tableaux and carry lights and torches.[197] In the 1920s and 1930s, urban shudra workers and their akhara groups appeared in these processions in large numbers as active participants in the pageantry, equipped with swords or staffs, and chanting militant religious slogans. Moreover, various elements of the entertainment of the poor, such as street theatre or swang, mime, acrobatics, jesters or clowns, and folk songs began to feature more and more extensively in the Ramlila,[198] rivalling the floats and tableaux of the merchants and other urban notables. These were striking developments because, prior to the 1920s, shudra participation in Ramlila processions, although by no means unknown, was not as central, assertive, strident or warlike as in the 1920s and afterwards.

With the new accretions to the celebration of the Ramlila, between 1924 and 1926 the Ramlila emerged as the focal point of communal animosities in Allahabad. Until 1922, Muslim musicians used to play in the bands accompanying Ramlila processions. Increasing Muslim opposition to playing music had led to the formation of bands of purely Hindu musicians, who were reported to have deliberately created a din in front of mosques in 1924.[199] In that year, a riot occurred in the town after some Hindus blew conchs in front of the Kalwari Tola mosque, at the time of the call of *azan* to evening prayers, followed by the playing of music in front of the Jama Masjid on the first day of the *Dusserah*.[200] In 1926, some Muslim groups again demanded that music should not be played at any time in front of mosques in the course of Ramlila processions. A meeting was held in protest, where Madan Mohan Malaviya, the Hindu Sabha and Congress leader, addressed an audience of 10,000 people and vilified the obstructive attitude of the Muslims. The Ramlila was eventually abandoned because the district authorities failed to bring about a compromise over the music issue. In the place of the Ramlila, the comparatively unimportant Dadhkando festival was made the occasion for an impressive Hindu procession with armed dals, which was then attacked by some Muslims in front of the Shabrati Ki Mosque, and more extensive rioting ensued.[201]

Clearly, communal tensions were generated in the towns by the enlargement of festivals such as the Ramlila celebrations and by Hindu martial assertion, which were facilitated by the involvement of the

---

[197] Tandon, *Prayagraj*, pp. 176, 184.
[198] Similar developments, starting in the early decades of this century, have been reported for Benares in Kumar, *Artisans*, pp. 189–93.
[199] Confidential Note on Music in Ramlila, by Crosthwaite, DM, Allahabad, dated 28 October 1926.
[200] Ibid.   [201] Ibid.

shudra poor. None the less, it is necessary to ask whether we should therefore conclude that festivals such as the Ramlila in the 1920s and 1930s embodied the emergence of a cohesive sense of Hindu community amongst the diverse groups of participants, all of whom took to the same 'public space', as Freitag has argued. Is it, in fact, the case that shared participation in 'public arena' religious rituals constitutes and reflects a homogeneous community identity, which then comes to underpin communal conflicts?

Ramlila was perhaps the most important festival in north Indian Hinduism patronised by the merchants as a key marker of their power and status. In a recent history of one of the most influential houses of merchants and bankers in Allahabad, written by the present head of the family, it is stressed that the promotion of Ramlila was one of their main contributions to the religious and cultural life of the town. This account shows how the rising commercial fortunes of this banking house were mirrored in the growing pomp and show of the Ramlila procession that the family sponsored.[202] As one of the chief symbols of mercantile power, the Ramlila, above all, became the most important occasion for the shudra poor to establish their own prominence, and the site for them to contest the power of the commercial classes. Moreover, Ram personifies kshatriya power and kingship, and the shudras joined the triumphal march of Ram as the self-proclaimed valiant kshatriya army of Hinduism. Ram also, of course, personifies the ideal of just and benevolent rule. The reign of Ram, or *Ramrajya*, epitomises a utopian regime of welfare and egalitarianism, a theme which was highlighted and greatly popularised by Gandhi and some segments of the nationalist movement in this period.[203] The growing veneration of Ram by the shudra poor may partly have been related to this ideal. Pinch has demonstrated the importance of the veneration of Ram to rural shudras as a means of expressing social equality and the dignity of labour.[204] The roots of lower-caste urban migrant labourers in this rural context of Ram devotion may have further enhanced the importance of Ram in urban popular culture. In addition, by the 1920s and 1930s, among workers in Kanpur, Ram appears to have joined a pantheon of radical or revolutionary leaders as a great social leveller, along with Marx and Lenin.[205]

Not surprisingly, then, the Ramlila celebrations registered the

---

[202] Tandon, *Prayagraj*, passim.
[203] P. Lutgendorf, 'Interpreting Ramraj: Reflections on the 'Ramayan', Bhakti and Hindu Nationalism', in Lorenzen (ed.), *Bhakti Religion*, pp. 269–70.
[204] Pinch, *Peasants and Monks*, pp. 81–114.
[205] Joshi, 'Bonds of Community', pp. 259–60.

increasing participation of the urban shudra labouring poor. Some of the processions in each town had greater lower-caste participation and reflected their attitudes and concerns more clearly. One example, documented by Nita Kumar, is the Nakkataiya Ramlila of Chetganj in Benares, which was known for its lower-caste and lower-class character. It featured mimes and street theatre as well as the abusive demon brigades of Ravana.[206] Another example was the Daraganj Ramlila of Allahabad, which had a majority of shudra participants, such as the mallah or *nishad* caste group. They joined the Ramlila procession as the Hanuman Dal (the 'Band of Hanuman'), representing the valiant army of monkeys who fought on behalf of Ram in the epic battle of Ramayana, and who were, therefore, a central point of identification for the shudra poor in their newly envisaged role as the defenders of Ram and Hinduism. The invocation of Hanuman in this Ramlila is significant, for Hanuman is a lesser Hindu deity, revered especially by the practitioners of physical culture and wrestling, with his image being extensively worshipped at akharas all over north India in the early twentieth century.[207] Hanuman is also considered to be the first among the heroic godlings of popular Hinduism, especially of the lower castes.[208] The Daraganj festival also included swang and street theatre, in striking contrast to the other three major Ramlila processions of Allahabad, which were proud about the absence of such features. According to a prominent high-caste merchant and organiser of the grand Pajawa Ramlila of Allahabad, the Daraganj celebration, with its Hanuman Dal and swang, reflected the values of the 'common people' (*janjati*), in contrast to the other three, largely upper-caste-dominated, Ramlilas, with their Ram Dal, or army of Ram.[209]

These instances suggest that the modes of celebration as well as the meaning and relevance of the Ramlila, as in the case of the akharas, were different for various groups: for the merchant patrons, the grandeur of Ramlilas signified their dominance in urban society; for the Hindu organisations, which began to encourage lower-caste participation, the expanding celebration of the Ramlila was a means of demonstrating and bringing about the wider unity of all Hindus and cultivating the strength of the community; for the shudra poor, active and prominent participation in the Ramlila marked their efforts at self-assertion, claims to respectability and glorification of physical strength and labour. It also expressed their aspirations for an egalitarian social order, and their

---

[206] Kumar, *Artisans*, pp. 189–93.
[207] Alter, *Wrestler's Body*, pp. 198–213.
[208] Crooke, *Popular Religion*, p. 51.
[209] Tandon, *Prayagraj*, p. 77.

awareness of being the deprived and the powerless. This does not suggest that the Ramlila signified the emergence of either a cohesive sense of community or a shared notion about the significance of the festival. Instead, the festival was multi-vocal, registering varied levels of social construction of meaning. It incorporated contested and opposing visions and interpretations; it served as the site for struggle amongst various conflicting Hindu groups. This was possible because the figure of Ram and the concept of Ramrajya, especially as embodied in the popular syncretic bhakti text of Ramcharitamanas of Tulsidas, are open to divergent interpretations. As Lutgendorf has argued, 'Ramrajya has been viewed both as a harmonious but hierarchical order in which the privileged confidently enjoy their status and the dispossessed keep within their limits, or conversely, as a kingdom of righteousness in which the possibilities of freedom are made accessible to all'.[210]

Throughout the 1920s and 1930s, Ramlila emerged in various towns as the terrain of contests over rival forms of self-expression of the so-called leaders and the led. The leaders of Hindu organisations and nationalist reformers attempted to make the Ramlila a vehicle for the expression of Hindu power and Indian nationalism. Simultaneously, and more importantly, these leaders resolutely tried to purge the Ramlila of what they saw as the growing revelry brought in by lower-class participation. They launched concerted campaigns against the accretion of 'vulgar', 'obscene' and 'indecent' low-caste features, such as mimes, street theatre, popular songs, acrobatics and the use of abusive language in the processions by actors representing the demon army of Ravana.[211] Nita Kumar has argued about the Nakkataiya Ramlila in Benares that its revelry marked a 'statement of class identity'[212] by the lower castes and classes, and their rejection of dominant versions of acceptable public behaviour and morality in the face of growing and concerted attempts by reformers and revivalists to subordinate and control lower-class practices and to impose a version of Hinduism and Hindu practices which was thought to be pure, progressive, respectable and quintessentially Indian.[213] Kumar shows, that ritual reversal in the Ramlila of the lower castes and classes had been permitted in the past by the local elites. Then, from the early part of the twentieth century, especially in the 1920s and 1930s, even such ritual reversal was outlawed. The timing of this development is significant, for

[210] Lutgendorf, 'Interpreting Ramraj', p. 267.
[211] Kumar, *Artisans*, pp. 190–3; *Aj* (Benares), 6 October 1931, 14 October 1938; N. Kumar, 'Class and Gender in the Ramlila', *IESHR*, 29, 1, 1992, pp. 51–4.
[212] Kumar, *Artisans*, p. 5.
[213] Ibid., pp. 190–5.

it coincided with the growing participation of the poor and their self-assertion through religious celebrations. The festival was sought to be sanitised and 'disinfected', with popular practices stamped out. A struggle for control ensued, and eventually elite patronage was withdrawn, contributing to a separation of elite and popular practices. The controversy over 'reforming' or 'purifying' the Ramlila celebrations in this case indicates that both the leaders and the led were seeking to put their own imprint on these Hindu festivals, each trying to claim the festivals for the expression of their own concerns, identities and practices. It also appears that the reformist onslaught on religious festivals undermined the potential for unity within religious communities through shared rituals. For reformism helped to solidify class and social differences by privileging elite versions of cultural practices against popular initiatives. The withdrawal of elite patronage from popular practices and the simultaneous emergence of festival celebrations as sites of power struggle therefore meant that the integrative role of collective rituals was increasingly eroded. Instead of reaffirming community, the Ramlila here signalled the expansion of internal strife and social distinctions.

Attempts to cleanse and control popular culture in this period did not remain confined to the Ramlila. Holi, a key festival of the poorer shudras, and nautanki, the major genre of their entertainment, were also particularly important targets of reformism. Drinking and gambling, in which the poor frequently indulged publicly during the Holi season, were outlawed by Hindu reformers and nationalist leaders.[214] Kumar documents how in Benares, especially in the 1920s, the shouting or singing of obscenities, 'indiscriminate colour throwing and the general debauchery and tomfoolery' in Holi were intended to be eliminated by 'self-consciously "cultured" people to keep even ritual reversal in control'.[215] She shows that popular celebrations of Holi were condemned as degenerate or even bestial and, to improve this situation, nationalist slogans and processions were introduced, much like in the Ramlila.[216] The lower castes and classes were exhorted to observe the festival with proper piety and decorum, instead of revelry and entertainment. The Arya Samaj, in particular, emphatically condemned 'licentious merriment' and prescribed the celebration of Holi with 'purity and sobriety' and according to 'ancient customs', which were argued to be both 'beneficial and scientific'.[217] The leaders of the shudra caste associations, themselves increasingly part of the rank of the urban elites,

[214] NNR, No. 10/1922, pp. 263–4; Aj (Benares), 20 October 1938.
[215] Kumar, Artisans, pp. 176–7.   [216] Ibid.
[217] Jones, Arya Dharm, pp. 95–6.

also shared the concern of the leaders of Hindu organisations such as the Arya Samaj to impose their own vision of reformed and pure Hinduism on Holi, in an effort to express purer high-caste status.[218] While these reform initiatives undoubtedly related to imperatives to invent an authentic and uniform Hindu national culture, identity and lifestyle, at the same time the importance of reformism in urban social control and in the self-definition of the middle classes in contradistinction to the poor is also undeniable.

Nautanki, too, was the object of control and reform in the 1920s and 1930s. The attack on nautanki, as Hansen points out, emanated from various sources. The colonial government, by invoking the Dramatic Performances Act of 1876, sought to prohibit performances that were considered seditious, defamatory or 'likely to deprave and corrupt persons present'.[219] The Arya Samaj and the like were not far behind. They stepped in with their reformist social agenda in ensuring proper standards in nautanki plays, which found reflection in the directives given to the nautanki authors by their publishers. The authors were urged to write plays imbued with 'sentiments of devotion and valour', and were warned not to 'damage the country by writing lewd and impure' compositions.[220] The main targets of the reformers appear to have been vulgar language and erotic topics. However, the presence of subversive or emancipatory themes in these nautankis, which found elaboration away from the ambit of elite control and direction, was also most likely to have reinforced reformist zeal to regulate nautankis. Hansen argues that 'the opprobrium of the elite' had to do with the 'symbolic inversions of the power structure of the society at large' and with 'the debunking of authority'.[221] Even more significant and telling is the fact that 'just as mass appeal of the svang stage became recognised, some quarters attempted to convert svang and nautanki to more edifying form, one beneficial to the building of moral character. The impact of the new political ideology [of reformism] seemed to intensify just as nautanki took root in Kanpur.'[222] This suggests a direct, even causal, link between reformist drives and the urge to impose social control in a period of expansion in the ranks of the urban poor and their growing self-assertion through cultural forms. These developments also coincided with growing elite efforts to guide and direct entertainment habits among the poor, especially by making provision for appropriate and wholesome leisure activities and recreational facilities, such as would be

---

[218] *Yadavesh*, 2, 1, Holi Special Issue, *vikrami samvat* 1993, c. A.D. 1936, p. 22.
[219] Hansen, *Grounds for Play*, p. 105.   [220] Ibid.
[221] Hansen, 'Birth of Hindi Drama', p. 73.
[222] Ibid., p. 106.

strongly recommended by a Committee of Inquiry investigating the conditions of labour in Kanpur in the late 1930s.[223] The report of this Committee clearly shows the concern to 'improve' the moral and social life of the labouring poor through the regulation of their leisure activities, in order to ensure that the entertainment habits of the working classes did not find 'unhealthy and anti-social outlets'[224] and to prevent the degradation of the moral quality of the urban workforce.

The controversy concerning public behaviour and morality in the 1920s and 1930s was not focused simply on the proper celebration of religious festivals or on nationalist conduct. These were also part and parcel of a range of interconnected developments in public life which related to the control and reform of the poor.[225] Contests in the ritual arena of festivals; struggle over issues of sanitising and 'improving' the towns; control of the 'dangerous classes' through policing; or uplifting the lower castes to acceptable standards of respectability and moral conduct – all these were interlinked developments set in the context of rising urban class tensions. Undoubtedly, an important source of reformist drives lay in the history of religious revival and nationalist reform. Such reformism was also associated with the gradual development of a puritanical social ethic from the nineteenth century onwards among the emerging new professional and commercial middle classes, who were eager to distance themselves from what they saw as the immorality and vulgarity of plebeian and street culture. They were concerned to forge a definitive new respectable identity for themselves and to define an ideal national culture, partly in response to social and cultural contact with the West and partly to register their own newly gained social prominence in the towns.[226] However, this puritanical reformism and its related denunciations of popular culture do not seem to have arisen only from middle-class imperatives of internal self-definition, their need 'to formulate an ideological basis for their identity as a social class'[227] and to set themselves apart from popular practices or to sculpt a respectable public sphere and civic culture. Reformism has also to be understood in terms of a parallel history of escalating urban class tensions in the 1920s and 1930s. Reformism seems to have been crucially driven by the

[223] *KLIC Report*, pp. 422–3.
[224] Ibid., p. 422.
[225] For instance, in her analysis of the Benares Nakkataiya Ramlila, Nita Kumar argues that the festival has to be seen as 'the field for control and domination, expressing social relations'. Kumar, 'Class and Gender in the Ramlila', p. 39.
[226] Sumanta Banerjee, *The Parlour and the Streets: Elite and Popular Culture in Nineteenth Century Calcutta*, Calcutta, 1989, pp. 15, 71–3, 205–6; Bayly, 'Patrons and Politics in Northern India', pp. 349–88; Hansen, 'Birth of Hindi Drama', pp. 62–92; Dalmia, *Nationalization of Hindu Traditions*, pp. 50–145.
[227] Banerjee, *Parlour and the Streets*, p. 72.

accelerating urgency of the upper classes and the elites to achieve social control, and not merely to assert cultural superiority. It is scarcely a coincidence that nationalist and religious reformism in UP, spearheaded largely by urban-based leaderships, was most concerted in the 1920s and 1930s, when the urban poor emerged as a major social force to be reckoned with. It is also significant that strikingly similar processes were at work in the field of Islamic reform and revival.

The evidence of the Ramlila, Holi or nautanki, and the trends that they signal in Hindu resurgence, would therefore indicate that shared participation in festivals did not override social distances or class prejudices, which were becoming central features of urban life in this period. On the contrary, the festivals and the related process of Hindu resurgence incorporated and articulated precisely these growing social cleavages and conflicts, rather than diffusing them. Indeed, even the very fact that these festivals and religious celebrations proliferated in this period with wider participation was a product of the emergent social conflicts. For the festivals emerged as the sites where class differences were fought out and contending or opposing groups fiercely sought to inscribe their presence and their values in the ritual arena. The process of Hindu resurgence constituted the very terrain of struggle amongst various opposing sections of Hindus, not simply over doctrine, but more crucially over questions of class, status and power. Contrary to Dipesh Chakrabarty's suggestions, religious identity is clearly able to reflect and articulate class, and scarcely suggests hierarchical forms of loyalty and allegiance. Furthermore, the pattern of Hindu upsurge in the 1920s and 1930s seen in this chapter hardly confirms the elaboration of 'a sustained ideology of community that united the Hindus', as Freitag claims. The cohesiveness of the Hindu community that these festivals are thought to represent was only superficial. The elaboration of a seemingly uniform set of religious practices in fact encompassed very different and contested appropriations. It is, therefore, untenable to interpret the history of early twentieth-century communalism in terms of the development of unified and cohesive community consciousness, not least because this line of interpretation underplays deeper conflicts of class, caste or status, and thus infers the creation of communities where such communities did not come into being. Arguably, what has so far been interpreted primarily as the history of construction of community could be understood more appropriately as the history of class conflict. Evidently, class is imbricated in the history of community. On a different, but related, note, it is also important to recognise that communal strife does not have to be accompanied by the growth of unified community identities. Communal tension and violence can be precipitated by revivalist and assertive religious activities of a diverse, even conflicting, range of social groups within a putative community, who compete and clash with similar diverse groups from another community, without these necessarily giving rise to homogeneous and sustained conceptions of community on either side. Interpretations of communal conflict based on the emergence of unified communities have the further grave implication of viewing communalism in twentieth-century India in terms of a unilinear, cumulative and even irreversible progression towards partition and continued sectarian strife and polar-isation afterwards.

It would be of comparative interest to cite here the concept of 'moral ethnicity', which John Lonsdale has advanced in his work on the Kikuyu tribe of Kenya and their Mau Mau movement of the late 1940s and 1950s. In discussing the nature of ethnic identity formation among the Kikuyu, Lonsdale argues that the process was not simply about sketching external boundaries of community and the exclusion of out-siders, but also, and more crucially, about redefining the terms of internal relationships within the community. Kikuyu ethnicity, Lonsdale argues, served as an arena for moral debate – hence the coinage 'moral ethnicity' – about how unequal relations within the community were to be restructured and negotiated. A shared ethnic discourse was con-structed in order to conduct what Lonsdale describes as a moral argument *within* the community 'over domestic civic virtue', codes of political conduct, leadership and moral authority, as well as the distribu-tion of power and resources. Thus, Lonsdale holds: 'A common ethnicity was the arena for the sharpest social and political division.'[228]

It should, however, be recognised that common participation in religious festivals and organisational activities in UP in the 1920s and 1930s did bring the diverse groups into the same 'public arena', and tended to present a united image of the Hindu community to the Muslims, ultimately intensifying communal tensions and opening up a rift in the nationalist movement led by the Congress. From the early 1920s, efforts by Hindu organisations to promote Hindu unity and to rejuvenate Hinduism contributed to the growth of self-defence corps and akharas, as well as to increasing stridency in religious celebrations. The most significant feature of religious developments in this period was, however, the growth of local religious organisations and activities among the Hindu low-caste poor. The shudra poor, who were seeking to define an important role for themselves in Hinduism as erstwhile martial kshatriyas, found a means of self-expression by playing a

[228] B. Berman and J. Lonsdale, *Unhappy Valley: Conflict in Kenya and Africa: Book 2: Violence and Ethnicity*, London, 1992, p. 268.

prominent part in Hindu festivals and volunteer corps. The militant religious assertion of the shudra poor was their response to growing social conflict and marginalisation in the towns. The interplay and interweaving between their identities, based simultaneously on labour, deprivation and martial Hinduism, helped to give a newly emergent militant version of Hindu religion centrality and potency in the politics of the urban shudra poor, as well as in the evolving urban political culture. This gave an immediacy to religious issues in urban neighbourhoods. It engendered religious tensions in the locality and intensified contests over priority and precedence in religious celebrations. Local-level akharas in urban neighbourhoods now multiplied rapidly, with an overtly religious orientation. Moreover, in their attempts to portray themselves as the defenders of Hinduism, the shudra poor often placed themselves in opposition to Muslims. The growth of local Hindu organisations affected various groups among the Muslim poor directly, for they had to contend with the numerous akharas and volunteer corps in urban neighbourhoods. On a broader level, the participation of diverse caste and social groups among Hindus in religious organisations and festivals, coupled with deliberate attempts by revivalist organisations to project Hindu militancy and unity during religious celebrations, could also convey to the Muslims in the towns an image of the Hindu community as a resurgent and unified group. This could reinforce the sense of religious threat and challenge that the Muslim poor faced in their neighbourhoods. The following chapter turns to the history of religious resurgence among various groups of the Muslim poor.

7   Resurgent Islam

One of the focal points of scholarly discussion on the subject of Islamic assertion in India in the nineteenth and twentieth centuries has been the extent and reach of revivalist and reformist ideas and practices beyond the ranks of the religious leadership. Some historians have emphasised the shift towards more uniform scriptural or textual norms in Indian Islamic religious and social practices as the key development in this period.[1] Others have drawn attention to the uneven spread, penetration and stratified nature of such trends, as well as the persistence of syncretic traditions and pluralism in belief and ritual, with many local variants and differentiation along the lines of class and status.[2] Gail Minault, for instance, points to potentials of class tension in Islamic assertion, when she comments: 'Religion offers a sheet anchor in a time of economic, political and moral uncertainty, threat and instability. Islam also offers an ideology supportive of private property, for those who have it or fear losing it, and supportive of egalitarianism for those who have not.'[3] Such questions of internal cohesion and contradiction within resurgent Islam form the focus of investigation here, with the aim of unravelling the specific nature of religious change among the poorer Muslims of UP towns – artisans and labourers, pedlars and petty traders.

Expansion of Islamic practices in the public arena

The extensive movements of religious revival and reform that charac-terised north Indian Islam in the nineteenth and early twentieth cen-

---

[1] Francis Robinson, 'Islam and Muslim Society in South Asia', *Contributions to Indian Sociology* (n.s.), 17, 2, 1983, pp. 185–203.

[2] Imtiaz Ahmad, *Ritual and Religion among Muslims in India*, Delhi, 1981, pp. 1–19; Gail Minault, 'Some Reflections on Islamic Revivalism vs. Assimilation among Muslims in India', *Contributions to Indian Sociology* (n.s.), 18, 2, 1984, pp. 301–5; N. Kumar, *The Artisans of Banaras: Popular Culture and Identity, 1880–1986*, Princeton, 1988, pp. 138–47, 211–17.

[3] Minault, 'Some Reflections on Islamic Revivalism', pp. 304–5.

244

turies[4] did not leave the poorer Muslims untouched. Their involvement was also to influence the course of Islamic revivification movements, just as the participation of the Hindu poor had been central to resurgent Hinduism. Poorer Muslims both drew upon and contributed to the changing rituals and practices of the Muslim service gentry, middle classes and Islamic learned men, who had been at the forefront of religious assertion.[5]

Of the emerging trends of religious change from the nineteenth century onwards, some developments were to be of particular significance in the gradual transformation of ritual practices and religious expression amongst the Muslim poor. One important and well-documented dimension of Islamic revitalisation movements, shared by a number of different schools of thought, albeit with divergent emphases, was the central importance attached to a restoration of the puritanical spirit of early Islam, a return to the textual norms of the faith (*shariat*) and a greater personal adherence to the basic tenets of Islam. In order to return to original scriptural Islam, a large section of the learned religious leadership (*ulema*) ascribed overwhelming importance not only to the *Quran* but also to the veneration of the Prophet, and to his life and traditions (*Hadith*) as the model of right conduct for all Muslims to follow.[6] Those among the religious leaders who were ardent sufis, such as the ulema of the Firanghi Mahal seminary in Lucknow, were also particularly concerned to immerse themselves in the adoration of the Prophet and to emulate him, for this played an important role in Islamic mysticism.[7]

Such attempts to highlight and re-emphasise the authentic traditions of the Prophet contributed to the elaboration, often innovation, of public rituals relating to his life in the latter half of the nineteenth

---

[4] A vast body of literature discusses Islamic reform and revival movements. See, for example, B. Metcalf, *Islamic Revival in British India: Deoband, 1860–1900*, Princeton, 1982; Aziz Ahmad, *Islamic Modernism in India and Pakistan, 1857–1964*, London, 1967; Peter Hardy, *The Muslims of British India*, Cambridge, 1972; F. Robinson, *Separatism among Indian Muslims: The Politics of United Provinces' Muslims, 1860–1923*, Cambridge, 1974; F. Robinson, 'Ulema, Sufis and Colonial Rule in North India and Indonesia', in D. Kolff and C. A. Bayly (eds.), *Two Colonial Empires*, Dordrecht, 1986, pp. 9–34; Ziya-ul-Hasan Faruqi, *The Deoband School and the Demand for Pakistan*, London, 1963; M. Mujeeb, *The Indian Muslims*, London, 1967.

[5] C. A. Bayly, 'The Small Town and Islamic Gentry in North India: The case of Kara', in K. Ballhatchet and J. Harrison (eds.), *The City in South Asia: Pre-modern and Modern*, London, 1980, pp. 20–48; Robinson, 'Ulema, Sufis', pp. 9–34.

[6] Robinson, 'Ulema, Sufis', pp. 9–34; Robinson, 'Islam and Muslim Society', pp. 198–9; Metcalf, *Deoband*, pp. 56–7.

[7] F. Robinson, 'The "Ulama" of Farangi Mahall and their *Adab*', in B. Metcalf (ed.), *The Place of Adab in South Asian Islam*, Berkeley, 1984, pp. 164–5; Metcalf, *Deoband*, pp. 165–6; Robinson, 'Islam and Muslim Society', pp. 198–9.

century and the early twentieth century.[8] Although the example of the Prophet had to be followed in personal behaviour, a corpus of public rituals was introduced by some ulema to underscore the importance of the Prophet's life and for the exposition of his virtues.[9] The arena of reform and revival, thus, broadened beyond the realm of private piety to incorporate public observance of religious events and sacred occasions. Religious assertion tended to take the form, not just of conforming to proper Islamic norms in personal or private worship, but increasingly also of expression *in public* of inner religious emotions and personal devotion focused on Islamic symbols and the figure of the Prophet. These tendencies were also prominent among a section of sufi leadership, who sought to reform and strengthen Islamic mysticism.[10] They encouraged the public display of spiritual ecstasy and mystical experience, although not without some controversy, as some sections of the orthodox ulema sought to contain mysticism and to confine religious practices to strictly scriptural forms.[11] The religious promoters of the outward, public demonstration of emotional loyalty to Islamic symbols often found allies in some parts of the provincial Urdu press.[12] This was particularly apparent during the controversy over the demolition of a part of a mosque in Kanpur in 1913, in the course of which the particular mosque was presented, not only in political speeches by the militant ulema but also extensively in the Urdu press, as the focus of intense and passionate attachment and identification for all Muslims. Enactment of ritual lamentation and collective expression of mourning in public at the damage done to the mosque, and thus to a vital Islamic sacred site, formed the key features of the political agitation against the demolition of the mosque, as will be seen below.

All these forces of change contributed to a substantial transformation of Islamic practices in the public sphere by the early part of the twentieth century. Public religious meetings for prayers and for lectures on the virtues of the Prophet, coupled with processions and illuminations, were

[8] Robinson, 'Islam and Muslim Society', pp. 198–9.
[9] Not all schools of ulema were unanimous on these innovations. The Deobandis, for instance, did not support some of these initiatives. Metcalf, *Deoband*, pp. 150–1.
[10] Robinson, '*Adab*', pp. 156, 164–5; F. Robinson, 'Problems in the History of the Firangi Mahall Family of Learned and Holy Men', in N. J. Allen et al. (eds.), *Oxford University Papers on India: Volume 1, Part 2*, Delhi, 1987, pp. 6–7.
[11] Metcalf, *Deoband*, pp. 148–51; S. Muzaffar Hasan, *Aaqab Shah Badiuzzaman*, Lucknow, 1984, pp. 297–301. This book mentions how Mohammad Hussain of Allahabad, a leading sufi, invited the censure of a section of the local orthodox ulema for his ecstatic mysticism.
[12] Gilmartin emphasises the role of the Urdu commercial press in this respect in the case of the Punjab. D. Gilmartin, 'Democracy, Nationalism and the Public: A Speculation on Colonial Muslim Politics', *South Asia*, 14, 1, 1991, pp. 132–3.

gradually introduced in UP from 1892 by Maulana Mohammad Hussain, a leading *alim* (singular of ulema) of Allahabad, on the occasion of *Meraj Sharif*, also referred to as *Rajbi Sharif*, after the month of *Rajjab* in which it is celebrated.[13] Meraj, the festival which marks the Prophet's ascension to heaven, although a significant moment in the life of the Prophet and in the history of Islam, had been a matter of private celebration confined mainly to the 'pious and the educated', and was a relatively unimportant public event until the nineteenth century.[14] It gradually became a prominent festival by the first few decades of the twentieth century in many UP towns, attracting large numbers of people to prayer meetings and lectures on the Prophet's life, often along with the recitation of religious poetry and festive processions.[15] An even more important celebration blossomed on the occasion of the Prophet's birth and death, which fall on the same day – the 12th of the month of *Rabi-ul-awwal*. Celebration of this festival, termed the *Id-milad-ul-nabi*[16] or *Barawafat*, came to be undertaken on a far more extensive scale from this period by some sections of the ulema.[17] In Lucknow, expanded celebrations were instituted in the mid-nineteenth century by the Firanghi Mahal ulema, with the extensive public recitation of verses in praise of the Prophet (*Maulud Sharif*).[18] In Allahabad, around the turn of the twentieth century, large public Maulud gatherings began to be held over a period of twelve days, culminating in the grandest meeting on 12th Rabi-ul-awwal.[19] Public processions and street illuminations were gradually introduced to mark Barawafat in all towns by the early decades of the twentieth century.[20] Religious meetings as well as newly

---

[13] Interview with Suhaib Faruqi of Daira Shah Hujjatulla, Bahadurganj, Allahabad, and Haji Mohd. Osmani in Allahabad; C. A. Bayly, *The Local Roots of Indian Politics: Allahabad, 1880–1920*, Oxford, 1975, p. 81; Hasan, *Aaqab*, pp. 297–300.

[14] G. de Tassy (translated and edited by M. Waseem), *Muslim Festivals in India and Other Essays*, Delhi, 1995, p. 159; A. Schimmel, *Islam in the Indian Subcontinent*, Leiden, 1980, p. 122.

[15] *PAI*, No. 11, 15 March 1924; No. 9, 7 March 1925; Bayly, *Local Roots*, p. 81; Hasan, *Aaqab*, p. 297; Parliamentary Papers, East India. (Cawnpore Riots), *Report of the Commission of Inquiry into the Communal Outbreak at Cawnpore and the Resolution of the Government of U.P.* Session: 1930–31, vol. XII, Cmd. 3891 (hereafter *KRIC Report*), pp. 7, 10.

[16] Milad refers to the birthday or nativity of the Prophet.

[17] The Deobandis did not support this and there was no universal consensus over this particular practice. Metcalf, *Deoband*, pp. 150–1.

[18] Robinson, *'Adab'*, pp. 166–7; interview with Maulana Matin Mian of Firanghi Mahal, Lucknow.

[19] Interview with Zahid Fakhri of Daira Shah Ajmal, Allahabad; similar developments in Kanpur have been reported in N. G. Barrier, *Roots of Communal Politics*, Delhi, n.d., p. 239.

[20] Interview with Zahid Fakhri and Haji Mohd. Osmani of Daira Shah Ajmal, Allahabad; *KRIC Report*, pp. 7, 10; Hasan, *Aaqab*, pp. 297–300.

launched processions on these occasions also incorporated armed displays, with *lathis* and swords, of the kind that had hitherto been confined to *Mohurram* celebrations.[21] *Shab-i-Barat*,[22] a festival to remember the ancestors or to commemorate the dead, had been primarily oriented around private prayers, family feasts and the exchange of gifts among kin, but it gained greater public prominence. Special significance was attached to the fireworks display on this occasion as an expression of the martial spirit in Islam.[23]

Mohurram, already a prominent festival, although not directly related to the life of the Prophet, saw further expansion from the nineteenth century.[24] Mainly a Shia festival to mark the martyrdom and suffering of Hassan and Hussain,[25] Mohurram was also observed as a major event by Sunnis all over north India, with some modifications. The occasion became especially striking in the early twentieth century for its increasingly elaborate public pageantry with processions and ornate *tazias*, as well as for the accentuation of its martial metaphor, as expressed through the expanding participation of *akharas* and the public exhibition of arms. *Majlis* religious gatherings to lament the fate of the martyrs also proliferated. As the occasion of mourning *(matam)* for martyrdom and suffering, Mohurram served as a powerful metaphor for the loss of Muslim power in India with the advent of British rule.[26] The festival thus assumed a particular political importance and emotional poignancy. With its grand processions and the 'emotionally charged renderings of *marsiyas*, passion plays and *zikrs*',[27] Mohurram evolved as the key public platform for symbolically enacting the tragedy of Islamic

---

[21] At the Daira Shah Ajmal, one of the great medieval sufi shrines of Allahabad, akharas staged armed drills and combats on the Barawafat day: interview with Zahid Fakhri, Allahabad; *PAI*, No. 42, 3 November 1923; No. 27, 12 July 1924; No. 39, 10 October 1925; No. 30, 30 July 1932.

[22] Celebrated as the day when the fate of all humans is recorded in the heavenly register of God and as a day of remembrance of the dead. Shia Muslims, additionally, consider this day to be the birth anniversary of Imam Mahdi, and also treat it as a day of remembrance of the martyrdom and suffering of Hassan and Hussain. G. A. Herklots (ed.), *Qanoon-e-Islam or the Customs of the Mussulmans of India by Jaffur Shurreef*, Madras, 1895, pp. 166–8; W. Crooke (ed.), *Observations on the Mussulmauns of India by Mrs Meer Hassan Ali*, Oxford, 1917, pp. 161–2.

[23] *NNR*, No. 29/1912, p. 701, extract from *Al Bashir* (Etawah), 9 July 1912; de Tassy, *Muslim Festivals*, p. 159.

[24] Kumar, *Artisans*, pp. 211–17.

[25] Schimmel, *Islam in the Indian Subcontinent*, p. 125.

[26] K. H. Ansari, *The Emergence of Socialist Thought among North Indian Muslims (1917–1947)*, Lahore, 1990, pp. 126, 489n.

[27] Ibid. Marsiyas are elegiac hymns or laments. Zikr literally means remembering and refers to a sufi religious ceremony or act of devotion.

decline in India and as the rallying focus for 'national war' against colonial rule.[28]

Through these religious innovations, a set of increasingly assertive, elaborate, vigorous as well as more overtly martial public rituals gradually emerged in north Indian Islam. The prominence of the martial element partly related to the early history of Islam in the Middle East and resonated with the tradition of *jihad* or holy war in defence of Islam, which came to be seen as especially relevant within the context of the erosion of Muslim power in the subcontinent. In some cases, the martial overtone in religious rituals related to the warrior tradition of north Indian sufism.[29] There was also clearly an emulation of or a competition with the proliferating Hindu processions and armed displays. The ulema and their patrons, the local Muslim elite, intended to face up to Hindu assertion in the public arena, as well as to match the growing power and influence of the urban Hindu commercial and landowning classes, who expressed their dominance through the expansion of Hindu celebrations.

A good deal of the expansion of public rituals from the later nineteenth century was promoted not only by the revivalist or reformist ulema, but also very prominently by the *shaikhs, pirs* and *sajjada nashins*[30] of some urban sufi shrines, such as the famous medieval *dairas* of Allahabad.[31] This was the period when some dominant sections within the north Indian Islamic leadership, notably the scholars and theologians of the Deoband seminary, were seeking to restrain certain practices of mystical Islam as they tried to orient their religion more in the direction of scriptural orthodoxy.[32] They did not, of course, intend to undermine Islamic mysticism altogether, for they were often themselves sufis, as most ulema were, and mysticism was an important dimension of their faith. They were concerned to discard those aspects of popular sufism which they considered to be infiltrations from Hinduism or accretions from local customs and practices not sanctioned by Islamic texts. They also denied the legitimacy of those elements of sufism which elevated the status of saints, undermined the doctrine of *tauhid* (unity of God), and acknowledged the principle of intercession

---

[28] *NNR*, No. 5/1910, pp. 119–20, extracts from *Swarajya* (Urdu) (Allahabad), 29 January 1910.

[29] P. van der Veer, *Religious Nationalism: Hindus and Muslims in India*, Berkeley, 1994, pp. 34–5; N. Kumar, 'The "Truth" about Muslims in Banaras: An Exploration in School Curricula and Popular Lore', *Social Analysis*, Special Issue on 'Person, Myth and Society in South Asian Islam' (P. Werbner, ed.), 28, July 1990, 84–5.

[30] All these terms refer to a sufi spiritual guide, the head of a sufi shrine and the successor to the saint of a shrine.

[31] For an introduction to the dairas of Allahabad, see Bayly, *Local Roots*, pp. 79–81.

[32] Metcalf, *Deoband*, pp. 148–51.

or mediation by saints between God and humans. In response to these endeavours to purify sufism, sufi elders as well as some schools of ulema, such as the Firanghi Mahalis of Lucknow, who were less rigid in their approach to sufism, attempted to popularise a reformed version of sufism, more in tune with scriptural Islam, but one that would not modify prevalent sufi practices beyond recognition.[33] Sufi reformism was also promoted by the Barelvi ulema, followers of Maulana Ahmad Raza Khan of Bareilly. These ulema set themselves apart from the Deobandis and promoted a religious outlook which sought to preserve intercession and customary practice.[34] Various groups of sufis were, however, not only concerned to preserve their mystic heritage in the face of the rising tide of textual orthodoxy. They had also to be mindful of the possibility that an over-emphasis on the scriptures and the attendant puritanical and fundamentalist propensities to outlaw popular non-scriptural practices might lead to a depletion in the ranks of their followers in local communities, especially the poor and lower classes, most of whom in north India based their religious life around the shrines and tombs of saints and practised the mystical version of Islam.

The solution envisaged by many sufis was to emphasise the public expression of mystic religious sentiments and practices in order to nurture popular enthusiasm and, at the same time, to bring popular sufism closer to the traditions of the Prophet as a reformist endeavour. These measures were attempted with much success in Allahabad, for instance. Here, Maulana Mohammad Hussain (c. 1853–1933), an eminent alim associated with the medieval sufi shrine of Daira Shah Hujjatulla, in his early career in the 1880s and 1890s tried to promote a purified, fundamentalist version of Islam, which soon earned him the reputation of being an orthodox, puritanical 'Wahabi' and made him rather unpopular in the town. Gradually, however, he also embraced sufi beliefs, came to acknowledge the importance of intercession, wrote and recited passionate mystical poetry, and eventually emerged to be one of the most popular religious figures in Allahabad, especially revered by the lower classes for his ecstatic devotion, but criticised by some of the orthodox ulema of the town.[35] At another sufi shrine of Allahabad, the influential Daira Shah Ajmal, important initiatives were undertaken

---

[33] Robinson, 'Adab', pp. 156, 164–5; Robinson, 'Problems in the History of the Firangi Mahall Family', pp. 6–7.

[34] The sufi leaders of the dairas of Allahabad, for instance, had strong Barelvi leanings. For a discussion on the Barelvis, see Metcalf, Deoband, pp. 296–314.

[35] Mohammad Mian Faruqi (compiler), Sawane Hyat: Maulana Al-Haj Shahid-e-Ishq Shah Mohammad Hussain Rahamatullah Alay Allahabadi ma Adbiyat, Malfuzat, Maqtubat, Karamat (hereafter Mohammad Hussain biography), Allahabad, c. 1933, pp. 23–6, 59–64, 84; Hasan, Aaqab, pp. 297–301.

by the sajjada nashin, Maulana Mohammad Fakhir (Rashid Mian), to link sufi events or celebrations with rituals based on the Prophet's life. Here, the commemoration ceremonies to mark the death anniversary of the saints of the shrine (*urs*)[36] were shifted to the Maulud day (the Prophet's nativity), and the two celebrations dovetailed into each other. On that day, the relics of the Prophet and his followers, preserved at the daira, were displayed alongside those of the local saints, and all were taken out in a ceremonial procession for viewing by the devotees. Both Maulud Sharif in memory of the Prophet and sessions of sufi poetry and *qawwali* songs (*mehfil sama*), performed during urs, featured prominently in the celebrations.[37] The festivities also included the gathering of akharas and the display of physical culture and wrestling, as well as elaborate martial pageantry, with the sajjada nashin and his chief disciples and members of the family leading religious processions dressed in ritual martial regalia and armed with swords, including a sacred sword which was believed to have been bequeathed to one of the medieval saints of the shrine by Baba Khizir, an important saintly figure in Indian sufism.[38] Similarly, the month of Rajjab was treated as a period of general festivities and holiness in Allahabad, both as the time of Meraj Sharif – the Prophet's ascension – and as the month of the urs of Shah Mohibullah Allahabadi, founder of the important shrine of Daira Shah Hujjatulla, as well as of other saints of the *Chisti silsila* (religious order), to which this shrine linked its spiritual lineage.[39] Elsewhere, such celebrations may not have been merged on the same day or month, but increasingly Prophetic celebrations were given equal emphasis with sufi rituals.

These efforts to maintain sufi practices and to temper puritanical tendencies ensured that, despite attacks on some aspects of mysticism in this period and a scriptural revival, sufi shrines did not inevitably lose their importance. Many shrines which adapted themselves in the above ways, such as the ones in Allahabad, sustained their popularity amongst the Muslim masses as spiritual centres and even expanded their activities and their following, and experienced something of a revival, after some setbacks during the political turmoil of the eighteenth and nineteenth centuries. However, they did increasingly tend to be more overtly 'Islamic' and 'revivalist' in their public image, especially because the

---

[36] Urs literally means 'wedding', and refers to the celebration of a sufi saint's final union with God, i.e. the saint's death anniversary, which is the major annual festival at most sufi shrines.

[37] Interview with Zahid Fakhri of the Daira Shah Ajmal, Allahabad; Khalid Mian Fakhri, *Taskira Aulia*, Karachi, n.d., c. 1976, p. 60.

[38] Interview with Zahid Fakhri in Allahabad.

[39] Interview with Suhaib Faruqi in Allahabad.

closer linkage of sufism with the traditions of the Prophet enhanced the distinctly Islamic character of sufi mysticism. This tended to dilute the syncretic features of sufism, set it apart from Hindu devotionalism and, to some extent, eroded popular local customs and practices.

One impact of these developments was, inevitably, the slow but steady waning of Hindu participation in Muslim festivals and of syncretic cultural interactions through sufism. Of course, these trends were reinforced by the currents of religious and cultural separation unleashed by Hindu revivalism.[40] The distance between Islamic mysticism and Hindu devotionalism also widened owing to an emphasis on the martial spirit of the former. The growing display of arms in the various sufi ceremonies and festivals not only highlighted the history of warfare in classical Islam or the tradition of jihad, but also, at the same time, harked back to the martial dimension of Indian sufism, as embodied in the figures of *ghazis* (victorious soldiers) and *shahids* (martyred fighters), to whom numerous shrines had been dedicated all over north India.[41] The emphasis on this particular martial aspect of Islamic mysticism helped to distinguish it from north Indian Hindu bhakti. Martial militancy was also, of course, developing as a central feature of Hinduism in this period. However, its inspirations were drawn from different sources and traditions, as seen in the previous chapter. Islamic and Hindu martial assertion, therefore, came to develop largely in competition and conflict with each other. Moreover, the differences in the lineages of martial Islam and Hinduism were especially emphasised in this period by the publicists of revivalist or reformist movements, thus opening up the possibility of creating a religious and cultural rift.

Religious assertion and the Muslim poor

By the early part of the twentieth century, then, Islamic practices in the public arena had undergone significant changes. More assertive, elaborate and self-conscious versions of Islam in public religious observances had emerged, linking scriptural elements with mysticism and giving prominence to the public display of personal emotional piety, and at the same time infusing many of these practices with a greater martial spirit. It was through these kinds of gradual but significant changes in rituals and practices in the public sphere that the ripples of the impact of the Islamic reform and revival movements of the learned ulema of the seminaries and the sufi elders were to be felt beyond their own ranks,

---

[40] Barrier, *Roots of Communal Politics*, p. 237; *PAI*, No. 21, 6 June 1925; No. 22, 12 June 1926; No. 23, 19 June 1926; No. 29, 31 July 1926; No. 20, 28 May 1927.
[41] van der Veer, *Religious Nationalism*, pp. 34–5.

and beyond the social groups from which they were themselves drawn – the erstwhile Islamic gentry and the Muslim administrative and political elites of north India.

By the 1920s and 1930s, poorer Muslims had become widely involved in public religious activities. Very large gatherings and processions during the religious festivals of Mohurram, Maulud or Rajbi Sharif became commonplace, at times celebrated over a number of days, staged on public roads, involving up to 40,000 participants, and frequently reported to have been fuelled by the initiative of the 'lower classes'.[42] The participation of the poor ensured the continued and sustained expansion of these festivals, at times in the face of growing opposition from a section of the Muslim elite and the puritanical ulema, notably the Deobandis and the Ahl-i-Hadiths.[43] Some forms of religious celebration of the poor, especially of the sufi ecstatic and emotional kind, including music sessions at shrines, or enthusiastic public demonstration of piety through processions or meetings, tended, in particular, to face censure. These were frequently seen by those inclined towards religious orthodoxy as largely popular entertainment devoid of spirituality, which needed to be purified or reformed to conform to the fundamental doctrines of Islam.[44] In Lucknow, for instance, towards the end of the nineteenth century one observer noted that, in cases where Mohurram had become carnivalesque, Islamic religious leaders did not favour excessive 'outward show of sadness' and increasingly railed against the 'mixture of pageantry with the deeply expressed and public exposure of grief'.[45] Similarly, a Lucknow newspaper in 1913 published the views of a correspondent who launched into a fierce condemnation of the musical performances at the Shahmina sufi shrine in Lucknow for being immoral and impious, and he urged the ulema of Firanghi Mahal and the Nadwat-ul-Ulema to curb these activities.[46] In seeking to reform the nature of celebration of festivals, the religious leadership, or those favouring scriptural orthodoxy, appeared to have become concerned not only about the violation of doctrinal norms but also about their own limited influence to restrain or control what they saw as

---

[42] For instance, *PAI*, No. 11, 15 March 1924; No. 8, 27 February 1926; No. 49, 12 December 1931; No. 50, 19 December 1931; No. 32, 16 August 1930; No. 27, 15 July 1933; *KRIC Report*, pp. 7, 10; Barrier, *Roots of Communal Politics*, pp. 239, 256–7.

[43] The puritanical ulema opposed the expanded celebration of Barawafat or Meraj, as well as the urs ceremonies. Metcalf, *Deoband*, pp. 150–1.

[44] Kumar, *Artisans*, pp. 138–9; Schimmel in her study of Islam in various parts of India also mentions reformist drives against Mohurram and against the use of fireworks in Shab-i-Barat. Schimmel, *Islam in the Indian Subcontinent*, pp. 121–3.

[45] Crooke (ed.), *Observations on the Mussulmauns of India by Mrs Meer Hassan Ali*, pp. 29–30.

[46] *NNR*, No. 24/1913, p. 583, cites *Tahrif* (Lucknow), 7 June 1913.

manifestations of popular excesses.[47] Such concern to direct or regulate popular religious observances seemed not simply to have arisen from the need to enforce right conduct among the poor in the interest of religious revival or reform, but could also, and equally crucially, have been related to the possibility of the assertion of individual autonomy against community cohesion. The potential for individual self-assertion, as well as the consequent danger of subversion of religious authority, was implicit in the practice of intense personal devotion. This is because the individual alone was responsible for personal acts of piety, thus attaching paramount importance to the autonomy and agency of the individual self.[48] The emphasis on the public display of personal religious emotions from the inner realm of the mind or the heart thus accentuated an element of autonomous self-expression,[49] which could, in turn, easily precipitate tensions between the leaders and the led, and between elite and popular practices within resurgent Islam. Indeed, such tensions may well have fuelled elite efforts to regulate religious observances, as in the case of Mohurram, cited above. Trends of this nature were to become obvious during the period of the *tanzeem* movement from the mid-1920s, which will be discussed later in this chapter. The existence of such internal friction within resurgent Islam suggests that a significant impetus for the expansion of Islamic practices in the public arena in the early twentieth century would have come from the poorer Muslims. The growing significance of religious innovation in the public sphere, thus, cannot be understood simply in terms of the efforts of a section of the ulema and sufis. Why and how were the various innovations and modifications in Islam relevant to the Muslim poor? For what reasons and in what ways did changing religious practices come to provide a focus of action and identity for them?

A large section of poorer Muslims in north India had been engaged in artisan crafts,[50] and many of them, faced a disruption of their erstwhile occupations and lifestyles in the nineteenth and twentieth centuries.[51] It

[47] This will be discussed further later in this chapter.

[48] Francis Robinson, 'Religious Change and the Self in Muslim South Asia since 1800', *South Asia*, 20, 1, 1997, pp. 6–7, 9–10.

[49] Gilmartin, 'Democracy, Nationalism and the Public', p. 132.

[50] For Muslim occupational groups in north India, see Ghaus Ansari, *Muslim Castes in Uttar Pradesh*, Lucknow, 1960; Muslim caste and occupational groups are also tabulated in *Census of India, 1951: Estimated Population by Caste: 1: Uttar Pradesh*, Office of the Ministry of Home Affairs, Government of India, 1951, Tables II and III (i).

[51] G. Pandey, *The Construction of Communalism in Colonial North India*, Delhi, 1990, pp. 66–108; G. Pandey, 'The Bigoted Julaha', *EPW*, XVIII, 5, 29 January 1983, pp. PE19–28; G. Pandey, 'Economic Dislocation in Nineteenth-century Eastern Uttar Pradesh: Some Implications of the Decline of Artisanal Industry in Colonial India', in P. Robb (ed.), *Rural South Asia: Linkages, Change and Development*, London, 1983, pp. 89–129; *BEC*, II, pp. 371–91, 392–411, 418–23, Surveys of small-scale and

was primarily these communities of artisans or erstwhile artisans, at times joined by some others involved in service occupations, who emerged to be at the forefront of urban Islamic resurgence. A large number of these Muslim artisans, whose history is well known, were engaged in handloom weaving, especially coarse cotton cloth, and had been based in small towns or *qasbahs* and in the countryside until the early nineteenth-century.[52] Other artisans were engaged in hand-embroidery, metal- and woodwork, dyeing and calico printing. Demand for the products of these Muslim artisans of both the countryside and towns began to drop because of the import of cheap manufactured goods of various kinds, including machine-made cloth, from the mid-nineteenth century[53] and then at an even more accelerated pace from the latter half of the nineteenth century as the railways rapidly penetrated the north Indian market with a wide range of products.[54] This rendered the economic position of many artisans, such as rural weavers, much more vulnerable than ever before, especially when many of them had already been in a position of subsistence or near-subsistence.[55] Those who were based in the qasbahs and villages often left in search of employment in the emerging manufacturing towns such as Kanpur.[56] Some also shifted to nearby larger urban centres,[57] often in quest of new markets for their products. Handloom weavers, in particular, appear to have become increasingly urbanised.[58] Some of these migrants, as well as a section of those artisans who were already located in the towns, tried to persist in eking out a meagre living from the remnants of their crafts. Others lacked this option, such as the calico printers of Lucknow, whose

artisan industries in Allahabad, Lucknow and Benares; C. A. Silberrad, *A Monograph on Cotton Fabrics Produced in the Northwestern Provinces and Oudh*, Allahabad, 1898, pp. 45–8; C. A. Bayly, *Rulers, Townsmen and Bazaars: North Indian Society in the Age of British Expansion, 1770–1870*, Cambridge, 1983, pp. 357–8; Bayly, *Local Roots*, p. 255.

[52] In 1931, julaha or ansari weavers formed the largest non-elite Muslim caste group in UP and were reported to number over 1 million, of whom 44.9% were engaged in weaving, with the rest in transport, trade, general labour and agriculture-related industries. *Census 1931*, pp. 439, 619.

[53] Bayly notes that, by the 1870s, 40% of the population of several districts in north India were being supplied with imported cloth. Bayly, *Rulers, Townsmen*, p. 446.

[54] *Report of the Fact Finding Committee (Handloom and Mills), 1942* (Chairman P. J. Thomas), Delhi, 1942 (hereafter *Handloom and Mills Committee, 1942*), pp. 5–6, 37; Pandey, 'Economic Dislocation', pp. 89–129.

[55] Pandey, 'Economic Dislocation', pp. 89–129; *Handloom and Mills Committee, 1942*, p. 64; Nevill, *Allahabad: A Gazetteer*, p. 95; Nevill, *Lucknow: A Gazetteer*, pp. 38–9.

[56] Bayly, *Rulers, Townsmen*, pp. 356–7.

[57] Bayly, 'The Small Town and Islamic Gentry', pp. 29–30; Bayly, *Local Roots*, p. 255; Bayly, *Rulers, Townsmen*, pp. 357–8.

[58] *Handloom and Mills Committee, 1942*, pp. 65–70. This development is possibly reflected in the fact that between 1881 and 1931 Muslims in UP became far more urbanised than Hindus, *Census 1931*, p. 138.

industry was nearly eradicated by the twentieth century.[59] The displaced artisans had to turn to wage-work in new small-scale industries, general manual labour, menial tasks, construction work and driving horse-drawn hackney carriages as well as peddling and petty trade, including vegetable vending.[60]

Along with the artisans, some Muslim service castes also faced the loss of their erstwhile occupations, with the decline of the courtly classes whom they served in the past and because of the alteration of earlier patterns of consumption, trade and transport. Caste groups such as *bhatiyaras* or innkeepers and *banjaras* or itinerant traders gradually declined as social units by the twentieth century.[61] In contrast to these declining caste groups, in his study of Muslim castes in UP Ghaus Ansari reports that by the twentieth century some occupational groups, often categorised as caste units in the census, had registered a numerical increase, such as bakers (*nanbai*), cooks (*bawarchi*), confectioners (*halwai*) and butchers (*qassabs*) as well as beggars or *faqirs*.[62] Ansari concludes that the expansion of these occupations suggests that displaced Muslim artisans or service groups shifted to these alternative forms of work or took to begging.[63] Indeed, in Ansari's view, the state of flux in the occupation of many Muslim groups can be surmised from the disappearance or rapidly dwindling number of some caste occupational groups, the appearance of new ones and the increase in number of some others.[64]

Poorer Muslims in the towns often found that employment opportunities for them were limited because the bazars and mandis, as well as many of the small-scale industries, were dominated by Hindu merchants and traders, who were usually disinclined to employ Muslims. There was only a handful of Muslim merchants or entrepreneurs in the towns, most of whom usually specialised in a few specific trades and industries,[65] to which Muslim workers were also confined for employment. Not surprisingly, the demographic profile of the markets, including 'bazar' industries, and the composition of their labour force tended to be predominantly Hindu. In Kanpur, for example, the tenement census of 1931 showed that in the central bazar areas of Nayaganj and Dalmandi, where the wholesale spice and pulses markets were located,

---

[59] *BEC*, II, p. 401; the decline of cloth printers (*rangrez*) as an occupational caste group by the early twentieth century has been noted in Ansari, *Muslim Castes*, p. 47.
[60] *Handloom and Mills Committee, 1942*, pp. 64–5; Pandey, 'Economic Dislocation', pp. 89–129.
[61] Ansari, *Muslim Castes*, p. 49.
[62] Ibid.   [63] Ibid.   [64] Ibid., pp. 48–9.
[65] See lists of trading and manufacturing firms in *The Trade and Industries Directory of the United Provinces, 1935*, pp. 67–87, 134–54, 176–216, 298–323.

100 per cent of the population was Hindu. In the Collectorganj grain market area and in the Generalganj wholesale cloth market, Hindus formed 90.2% and 94.7%, respectively, of the local population.[66] The limited access of Muslim groups to the bazars meant that they had to seek jobs elsewhere. Many derived their livelihood as butchers (*qasais*), carpenters, masons and bricklayers, or they were forced to continue as artisans. Most of these were trades and services in which Muslims had been historically engaged and poorer Muslims now crowded into these occupations in the absence of other newer avenues of employment. Often they had no choice but to cling tenaciously to their traditional occupations. Poorer Muslims also worked in urban factories and work-shops, though they often found themselves confined to particular enclaves. In Kanpur, for instance, Muslim groups concentrated in the leather factories and workshops, where caste Hindus seldom sought employment for fear of ritual pollution from contact with leather.[67] Muslims belonging to the *ansari-julaha* caste of weavers predominated in the weaving departments of the Kanpur textile mills, building upon a historical tradition of weaving skills.[68] In Allahabad, Muslim workers flocked to the steel trunk, metal bucket and *bidi* (Indian cigarettes) industries, for the owners of these workshops were Muslims[69] and did not discriminate against members of their own community.[70] Evidently many Muslim occupational groups were forced to adapt to new condi-tions and experienced economic instability and displacement. Although, arguably, not all were necessarily far worse off than in the past, their experience of occupational disruption could breed a sense of disposses-sion and of blocked or lost opportunities.

Those who remained in their past occupations, such as artisans, usually found themselves much worse off than before. The key change in their situation entailed not so much rapid impoverishment as a result of the destruction of markets for their products as a loss of economic autonomy and far greater dependence than ever before on merchants and moneylenders. As the UP Provincial Banking Enquiry Committee of 1931 reported, and from evidence given to the Committee, it appears that, in most artisan industries, the extent of indebtedness of workers as

---

[66] Calculated from *Census 1931*, pp. 172–83, Subsidiary Table No. V: Housing Statistics (Tenement Census) (ii).

[67] *RCLI*, III:I, p. 241, Evidence of the Superintendent, Harness and Leather Factory, Cawnpore.

[68] C. Joshi, 'Kanpur Textile Labour: Some Structural Features of Formative Years', *EPW*, XVI, 44–46, Special Number, November 1981, p. 1825.

[69] A. C. Chatterjee, *Notes on the Industries of the United Provinces*, Allahabad, 1908, p. 131.

[70] Interview with Dr Z. A. Ahmad, a leader in the Communist Party of India (CPI), who organised trade unions of steel trunk and bidi workers in Allahabad in the 1930s.

well as their dependence on financiers, merchants and dealers had increased considerably by the early twentieth century.[71] One survey report submitted to the Enquiry Committee stated somewhat dramatically: 'Poverty and helplessness are writ large on the workers of trade after trade. Perhaps the best material for a study in poverty will be found among these handicraftsmen.' The survey also referred to the workers' 'submission to a more or less constant want for a period of about half a century'. The workers, the survey further commented, 'have been brought completely under the thumb of the middlemen and the large dealers and it seems that courage and hope for concerted action has been crushed out of them . . . the workers are living either steeped in debt or on the verge of starvation'.[72] In many cases, the shrinking of local markets for artisanal products meant that their goods had to be exported from their immediate vicinity, and their markets extended to wider geographical arenas of commercial activity. This forced the artisans to rely almost entirely on merchants and dealers for their products to reach distant markets, and the latter inevitably skimmed off a large share of the profits, contributing, in turn, to a decline in the earnings of the artisans.[73] Similarly, some workers needed to procure raw materials such as mill-spun cotton yarn from further afield through rail-borne trade, and, in some cases, they found the price of raw materials rising. This left the artisans at the mercy of the merchants for access to raw materials and for credit.[74] An official enquiry report on the condition of handloom weavers in India commented: 'the working weaver is so inexorably tied to the financier that he is not able to sell his labour in a free market, nor sell his product at the highest available price'.[75] This statement, although not specifically referring to weavers in UP towns, might well describe their situation. Some of the handloom weavers had tried to adapt to their difficult economic circumstances by using cheaper mill-spun yarn instead of the more expensive, locally produced, hand-spun variety, which they had used in the past.[76] This was, however, at a cost to themselves, for it radically altered the organisation of the handloom weaving industry and the status of the weavers by forcing them to rely on dealers and merchants in machine-manufactured yarn. Most artisans thus lost their independent status and

---

[71] *Handloom and Mills Committee, 1942*, pp. 69–70; *BEC*, I, pp. 246–55; *BEC*, II, pp. 392–411.
[72] *BEC*, II, p. 407, extracts from a survey by Ardhendu Bhattacharya.
[73] *BEC*, II, p. 404; *Handloom and Mills Committee, 1942*, pp. 65–70.
[74] *Handloom and Mills Committee, 1942*, pp. 69–70; Pandey, 'Economic Dislocation', p. 108.
[75] *Handloom and Mills Committee, 1942*, p. 70.
[76] Ibid., p. 6.

came to work for merchants and moneylenders on a contract or wage basis, with piece- or time-rate payment.[77] This reinforced their indebtedness and dependence on the merchants, especially because most of them operated under the *baqidari* system. To add to their vulnerabilities, the patronage that many artisans had received from the courtly classes of the Mughal period and of the successor states had also eroded by this time, forcing them to rely solely and overwhelmingly on the merchant-financiers, who were more often than not Hindu. Some sections of the artisans, however, gradually began to adjust to the changing economy by the turn of the century. Yet, no sooner had they done so than some of them were exposed to further economic problems in the interwar years, especially to the ravages of the economic depression. The handloom weavers, in particular, were severely affected. In the nineteenth century they faced competition largely from foreign mill cloth, as the Indian mills produced mainly yarn and little cloth. However, by the time of the First World War, Indian mills too came to produce cloth extensively, accentuating the competition for handloom weavers.[78] Their hardship became even more acute as a result of the disruption of the supply of yarn during the war as well as of price rises. By the time of the depression, the situation was worse, with the influx of cheap foreign cloth, especially Japanese products, threatening a glut in the market. The Indian mills tried to undercut foreign products as well as each other, thus contributing to a general decline in cloth prices. The handloom weavers found their income further reduced and were forced to work far harder or risked unemployment.[79]

The experience of the various groups of Muslim artisans or erstwhile artisans and some service groups was, of course, scarcely uniform. Some suffered more than others, some persevered in their traditional crafts under worsening conditions, and some diversified into other trades and occupations. A small minority even managed to surmount the economic difficulties and turned the economic changes under colonialism to their advantage. A section of erstwhile weavers, for instance, managed to enter the growing cloth trade as merchants, rather than continuing in artisanal production.[80] However, lacking the capital to invest in a commercial world dominated by Hindu merchants, branching out into trade was not an option open to most artisans, and the handful of new businessmen remained exceptional for much of the early twentieth century. Not all artisan industries, however, went into absolute or terminal decline. The specialised silk-weaving industry of Benares, for

---

[77] Ibid., pp. 6, 69–70; *BEC*, I, pp. 246–55.
[78] *Handloom and Mills Committee, 1942*, pp. 9–10.
[79] Ibid., pp. 20–2.   [80] Ibid., pp. 64, 71–2.

instance, continued to hold its own until the First World War,[81] although here too the role of the merchant-financiers was undoubtedly enhanced owing to the artisans' need to have access to distant markets and to secure credit. Despite the diversity of situations of the poorer artisans and service groups, a substantial section of them experienced, to a greater or lesser extent, either displacement and dispossession, often with little hope of occupational diversification, or growing economic dependence on merchant-financiers and the consequent loss of what they saw as their '*azadi*' or independent status, usually coupled with a slide into the dreaded condition of mere wage labour or work as a servant: '*naukri*' and '*ghulami*'.[82] Although their position in the towns was frequently much worse, these changes did not necessarily mean that their economic conditions plummeted and that they were invariably driven to abject penury or pauperism, or that they had been significantly prosperous in the past.

More importantly, the transition in their condition, especially the loss of economic independence or 'azadi', the lapse into the perceived state of 'ghulami', and the experience of lack of opportunities, came to be *seen* by the artisans and service communities as a humiliating or subordinating process of decline, and this was increasingly juxtaposed against an imagined past golden age. This perception did not, however, arise spontaneously from their objective material condition, but also related to a wider discourse of decline of the Indian Muslim community, which was orchestrated steadily from the early nineteenth century by Islamic publicists and religious leaders. This rhetoric of Muslim decline and victimhood was of central significance in prompting the Muslim artisanal and service classes to interpret and explain their condition in terms of a history of decline. Having to face up to a growing sense of insecurity and dislocation, and often an actual or dreaded loss of their status as independent artisans, they increasingly drew upon the idea of Muslim decline and came to construct and imagine their past in terms of a proud and idealised heritage, which was rapidly eluding them.[83] Their sense of loss of respectability and social diminution was further aggravated by the fact that some of these artisans, for instance the julaha weavers, were labelled as violent and fanatical by the British,[84] and seen as a particularly undesirable segment of the labouring classes. Moreover, as a section of the urban labouring poor, they increasingly found

[81] Ibid., pp. 18–20.
[82] Pandey, *Construction*, pp. 101–2; Pandey, 'Economic Dislocation', p. 113; Kumar, *Artisans*, p. 55; interviews in Benares with Nuruddin Ahmed and other weavers.
[83] Pandey, *Construction*, pp. 66–108.
[84] Ibid.; Nevill, *Benares: A Gazetteer*, pp. 103–4.

themselves identified as undesirable riff-raff, the flotsam and jetsam of the urban population, and as a source of 'social and moral evils' and 'a menace to the peace, health and prosperity of the city'.[85] For a people who already perceived themselves to be facing social decline, such characterisations were especially abhorrent as additional forms of subordination and marginalisation. All these factors together contributed to a sense of loss of self-worth and social status. The artisans came to fear the disappearance of their valued skills as handicraft workers, the destruction of the sources of their ancestral livelihood, the violation of their established ways of life, and the erosion of their past cultures.[86] The dread of the obliteration of their independent identity and standing became especially acute because of their subordination to the increasingly powerful commercial classes, who did not just happen to be Hindus, but were also aggressive in their religious and cultural expression, often marginalising the practices of other communities. The commercial people were assertive in claiming Hindu priority and precedence in urban rituals and festivals, and enthusiastic in their patronage of revivalist movements. They were also frequently overzealous and overbearing in sponsoring moralistic social reform activities which exhorted the lower castes and classes to adopt 'respectable' modes of behaviour.[87] Above all, by the 1920s, they lent their support to *shuddhi* campaigns to coax lower-class Muslims to reconvert to Hinduism.

Against this background, the poorer Muslims of artisan communities and some service occupational groups seized upon the changing religious practices described earlier, which gradually came to provide a focus of organisation and identity for them from the later nineteenth century. The confident public elaboration of rituals, as well as their martial overtones, was relevant to the poorer Muslims in dealing with, at least symbolically, their sense of marginalisation and in contesting the dominance of the Hindu commercial groups. As in the case of the *shudra* poor, the religious idiom was appropriate and relevant for the Muslim poor and artisanal communities as a form of political assertion. This is because religious patronage had been a central form of expression of the power of the Hindu commercial classes and it was through this idiom that their power could be best contested. Subordinated as they were within a Hindu mercantile milieu and in the face of a real or

---

[85] *BEC*, II, p. 407, extracts from a survey by Ardhendu Bhattacharya.
[86] Pandey, *Construction*, pp. 66–108; Pandey, 'Bigoted Julaha'.
[87] C. A. Bayly, 'Patrons and Politics in Northern India', *MAS*, 7, 3, 1973, pp. 387–8; Pandey, *Construction*, pp. 79–82; S. B. Freitag (ed.), *Culture and Power in Banaras: Community, Performance, and Environment, 1800–1980*, Berkeley, 1989, p. 22; Vasudha Dalmia, *The Nationalization of Hindu Traditions: Bharatendu Harishchandra and Nineteenth-century Banaras*, Delhi, 1997, pp. 50–145.

perceived loss of past cultures and lifestyles, Muslim artisans or erstwhile artisans now tended to project their religion as a major mark of
their heritage, autonomy and respectability. This was in part because
religion was one of the very few symbols of their identity that they could
still conceivably cultivate in their depleted material circumstances, and
for which, crucially, they frequently enjoyed the support and patronage
of urban Muslim elites and the religious leadership. Moreover, as
Pandey argues in the case of Muslim julaha weavers in north Indian
qasbahs, work and worship were integrally linked in artisanal culture
and, with an accentuated sense of loss of work, they embraced worship
more ardently and came to reify their religious identity.[88] Through a
process of participation in renovated ritual practices, the Muslim poor
were able to express their own distinctiveness. They could envisage
religion as a means to prevent themselves from being effaced and
engulfed amidst the burgeoning ranks of the urban poor and in a
powerful commercial milieu. Within a changed social context, religion
could now assume and be given a new and greater significance, and
Islam could be constructed as a central marker of identity and as a
vehicle for the expression of respectability.[89]

Francis Robinson has argued that notions of the primacy of the
individual and of personal autonomy and 'empowerment' in religious
practice were key elements in nineteenth- and twentieth-century Islamic
religious change.[90] This element of 'empowerment' through religion
was also undoubtedly of significance in the self-assertion of the Muslim
poor in a religious idiom. The Muslim poor thus increasingly turned to
greater and more public observance of Islamic practices, such as those
relating to the life of the Prophet, and engaged in overt demonstrations
of personal religious emotion and piety in the public arena. They also
took part in some of the changing sufi practices with great eagerness, the
devotional content of which could help them to cultivate a sense of inner
self-worth and personal autonomy in the face of external and material
forms of subservience. Moreover, the sufi shrines, with their rootedness
in the locality and their mapping of the sacral landscape, enabled the
cultivation of a sense of belonging and entrenchment in urban and
sacred space and territory, which was particularly valuable in a time of
displacement and marginalisation. Alongside history and a glorified

---

[88] Pandey, *Construction*, pp. 97–9.
[89] Processes of 'Islamisation', which have also been termed 'ashrafisation' in some
contexts (adoption of the religious practices and ways of the ashraf or upper classes,
especially by upwardly mobile sections of Muslims), have been well documented by
historians in recent years. See, especially, Pandey, *Construction*, pp. 66–108; Rafiuddin
Ahmed, *The Bengal Muslims, 1871–1906: A Quest for Identity*, Delhi, 1981.
[90] Robinson, 'Religious Change and the Self', pp. 6–7, 9–10.

past, geography and sacred space assumed centrality in the emerging identity of the Muslim poor. Although these poorer Muslims became involved in the Islamic revivification endeavours of religious leaders, the context of their changing religion and their imperatives were clearly different. The preoccupation of the leaders was to contend with the decline in Muslim political dominance, the erosion of the power and influence of Muslim elites and a perceived sense of crisis in Indian Islam. In contrast, the religious resurgence of the artisans and service classes was grounded in their experience of economic and social dislocation and diminution. Moreover, rather than simply placing a stress on community identity or communitarianism, the articulation of personal autonomy and self-worth was also arguably significant in their religious resurgence.

Religion and artisanal identity

Although the new emphasis of the Muslim poor on religion was closely related to a growing awareness of deprivation and dispossession, at the same time it encapsulated an assertion of past superiority and respectability, mainly through the projection of an idealised past culture as artisans. This trend, coupled with a respectable, high-status religious identity, was particularly noticeable among the most numerous of Muslim artisan communities in UP – the julaha handloom weavers, whose case is well documented.[91] Religious assertion among them developed in dialogue with the construction of other forms of self-image based on artisanal work and occupation. Religion was one of a number of interweaving identities, all of which were being reconstructed and reimagined in the context of extensive social change. Such interlinking of multiple identities has been noted by Nita Kumar for a more recent period in the case of the silk weavers of Benares, for whom changes in religious practices, Kumar argues, were 'as much part of occupational consciousness as of religion'.[92] Similarly, Gyan Pandey has shown for the handloom weaving julaha communities of eastern UP and western Bihar qasbahs that the decline in their position stimulated the construction of an identity as respectable artisans, which found expression in heightened piety and religious activity, as well as in the assertion of a glorified artisan identity as ansaris, tracing their lineage back to the days of the Prophet.[93] These tendencies did not remain confined to the erstwhile artisan centres and qasbahs that Pandey has studied, but

---

[91] Pandey, *Construction*, pp. 66–108; Pandey, 'Bigoted Julaha'.
[92] Kumar, *Artisans*, p. 215.
[93] Pandey, *Construction*, pp. 66–108; see also, Kumar, *Artisans*, pp. 49–52.

developed all over UP, including towns such as Benares and Lucknow with significant established artisanal populations as well as in places such as Kanpur or Allahabad, to which artisans from many declining qasbahs and the countryside increasingly migrated. Artisans in these towns, particularly the julaha weavers, projected their identity as *mominansaris* or the pure, honest, honourable, faithful, good people,[94] in sharp contrast both to British official perceptions and to the stereotypes peddled by some Hindu religious organisations, which portrayed them as violent fanatics. Even former Muslim artisans, who no longer remained in artisanal occupations and took to manual labour or petty trading, came to revel in an idealised imagined past of artisanal culture and harboured a self-image as dispossessed, independent craftsmen. As we shall see below, textile mill workers in Kanpur or labourers in Allahabad who were no longer practising handloom weavers none the less identified themselves as momin-ansaris and undertook political initiatives based on an artisanal identity. This assertion of the past glory of their work and their high status enabled all these groups to face up to the erosion of their occupational dignity and the loss of their economic independence as they became wage-labouring 'servants'. Not surprisingly, the tendency of imagining a glorious history and past superior status was soon to develop among other declining Muslim caste or occupational groups, although the momin-ansari initiatives remained the most powerful and politically assertive, partly because of the numerical preponderance of weaving castes in urban UP and partly because the ansari movement became effectively institutionalised through an organised political party. In all cases of imagination or invention of new identities, an overt display of religious piety formed an integral aspect of the assertion of a respectable and devout past.

It was by drawing upon weaver artisanal identities that, in the 1920s and early 1930s, Maulana Azad Subhani, an alim of Kanpur, adopted the symbol of the *garha* or handwoven coarse cloth produced mainly by Muslim artisans, in an attempt to form political organisations of Muslim working-class groups throughout UP and to mobilise them for pan-Islamic and nationalist movements. Maulana Subhani spearheaded a campaign to boost the market for garha and to revive its production. He saw the garha movement as a means of regenerating the depressed economic conditions of Muslim weavers and to contend with what he argued to be the extreme poverty and destruction of independent artisanal status particular to them. Subhani also made British rule squarely responsible for the decline of Muslim weavers, and urged all

94 Kumar, *Artisans*, p. 52; Pandey, 'Bigoted Julaha', p. PE21.

weavers to fight against imperialism.[95] Although the campaign for garha was not directly relevant to the large number of erstwhile artisans who did not produce cloth, or to other artisanal or service groups, the movement captured their imagination and proved to be a successful political rallying point. The symbolism and ideology of the garha movement not only underlined the newly emphasised artisanal identity of the momins or ansaris, but also, at the same time, articulated an explanation for the decline of all Muslim artisanal and service communities, and identified a political strategy directed against British colonialism, which was projected as the cause of their deplorable plight.

These political tendencies contributed, by the late 1920s, to the formation of ansari-momin political organisations in many UP towns. The Momin Conference, also called the Jamiat-ul-Ansar, was first inaugurated in Bengal in 1911, but gained momentum from the mid-1920s in north India.[96] The annual national meeting of the All India Momin Conference was held in Allahabad in 1929, and the 1937 annual meeting, held in Kanpur, drew a large gathering, mainly consisting of local mill workers.[97] The leaders of the Momin Conference argued that they had a proud past as independent and upright artisans producing a basic necessity of life – cloth – but that new technology and capitalism brought in by British imperialism had caused the ruin of the ansaris. As a result of this, they had lost their cultural distinctiveness and social status; the community had disintegrated because of poverty and occupational dislocation, and they had come to be degraded and looked down upon.[98] The Momin Conference aimed to revive the traditional crafts of the weavers as well as to promote self-respect, devout religious conduct and economic independence, especially of the poorer weavers.[99] The object of the organisation was to unite all ansaris whatever their current work or condition and to uplift the reconsolidated community through a revival of the weaving industry and the restoration of traditional occupations. Through its resolute anti-colonialism and emphasis on the use of indigenously produced garha, the Momin Conference tended to be close to the Congress in its party political affiliation and shared the

[95] *PAI*, No. 40, 10 October 1931; No. 25, 25 June 1932; No. 27, 9 July 1932; No. 28, 16 July 1932; No. 33, 20 August 1932; No. 45, 12 November 1932; *NNR*, Nos. 6, 11, 24, 25/1932.
[96] Interview with Habibur Rahman 'Betab' (office bearer and volunteer-activist of the Momin Conference in the 1930s) and Jameel Akhtar Nomani (former editor of *Siyasat*) in Kanpur; *Souvenir: Congress Centenary Celebration: Organised by All India Momin Conference (New Delhi, December 3–4, 1984)*, pp. 14–15, 43.
[97] Ibid.; *PAI*, No. 41, 23 October 1937.
[98] Presidential Address delivered by Molvi Sheikh Abdul Aziz at the 1937 annual national meeting of the Momin Conference. *Souvenir: Congress Centenary Celebration*, pp. 1–9.
[99] Ibid.

nationalist *swadeshi* ideology of the importance of hand-woven cloth.[100] It distanced itself from the Muslim League, which was argued to be a party of the English-educated, upper classes, who were seen to be forcibly trying to absorb the momins into the fold of the League and seeking to exploit the poorer Muslims for their own political ends.[101] The leaders of the Momin Conference held that the Muslim League was 'controlled and manned chiefly by such Muslims as belong to the rich section or the Superior-Group, whose interests are obviously antagonistic to those of the poorer section or the Inferior-group Muslims'.[102] The term 'momin' itself emphasised this distinction, for it means honest and true to tradition, faithful and honourable, referring to ordinary, good, pious, god-fearing people.[103] The Momin Conference, thus, not only expressed deep political distrust of the 'upper classes' and the Muslim League, but also set itself up as an organisation of the common Muslims, with the aim to 'overcome the suppression of the [momin] community'.[104] By the late 1930s, this conflict between the Momin Conference and the Muslim League took a violent form in some places. In Kanpur, the Captain of the Momin Volunteer Corps, Abdullah, a mill worker, was allegedly killed by 'Muslim League miscreants'.[105]

The leadership and wider initiative behind the Momin Conference at the provincial level and in the towns often lay with the more affluent, commercially successful and educated ansaris who had turned to the cloth trade and were merchants or cloth shopowners.[106] However, a large number of urban poorer Muslims who belonged to the julaha-ansari community, but many of whom were now in other occupations,[107]

---

[100] *NNR*, No. 42/1937, p. 2; No. 44/1937, p. 2; Hasan Nishat Ansari, *The Momin–Congress Relation. A Socio-historical Analysis*, Patna, 1989.

[101] *PAI*, No. 16, 28 April 1928; No. 37, 13 September 1938; No. 44, 5 November 1938; *NNR*, No. 44/1937, p. 2, cites report from the *Momin Gazette*.

[102] Letter from Abdul Qaiyum Ansari, Vice-President, All India Momin Conference, to the President of the Indian National Congress, dated 8 October 1939, Correspondence relating to the Jamiat-ul-Momineen, October–December 1939, Jawaharlal Nehru Papers, Part II, Subject File No. 136, NML.

[103] Kumar, *Artisans*, p. 52.

[104] 'A statement regarding the aims, objects, policy and programme of the All India Momin Conference', Correspondence relating to the Jamiat-ul-Momineen, October–December, 1939, Jawaharlal Nehru Papers, Part II, Subject File No. 136, NML.

[105] *National Herald*, 8 September 1938; interview with Habibur Rahman 'Betab' in Kanpur.

[106] Interview with Zamiruddin Ansari (office bearer of the Momin Conference in 1993) in Allahabad; *Handloom and Mills Committee, 1942*, pp. 64, 70–72. This report mentions that some erstwhile weavers had turned to business in cloth.

[107] Only half of the entire momin population in India in the 1930s was said to have been engaged in textile weaving; the rest were in other occupations. Letter from Abdul Qaiyum Ansari, Vice-President, All India Momin Conference, to the President of the Indian National Congress, dated 8 October 1939.

identified with the political ideology of the Momin Conference. The Momin Conference's emphasis on reversing deprivation and securing the economic independence of past and present artisans inspired the mass of the poorer momins. In the Kanpur mill districts, and in the neighbourhoods of poorer ansaris in Allahabad who worked in the bidi and steel trunk workshops or as manual labourers and construction workers, poorer momins formed volunteer corps or musical bands and organised drills and marches, in an attempt to animate and express their artisanal and religious identity. These local neighbourhood units of the Momin Conference also concerned themselves with the promotion of education and the cultivation of thrift and saving habits to deal with their poverty and indebtedness. Of course, they emphasised greater and better observance of religious rituals and public piety in order to present themselves as devout Muslims, which would match their rediscovered respectable artisan identity.[108]

It is interesting that in Allahabad the poorer momins, such as those employed in the bidi or steel trunk workshops, appeared to have had a somewhat uneasy relationship with the leadership of the town unit of the Momin Conference, which was largely dominated by the relatively better-off Muslim cloth merchants with shops in the central business districts, and with whom the poorer momins did not have much in common.[109] Moreover, at the first All India meeting of the Momin Conference in Calcutta in 1928, Allahabad was selected as the place in UP where the programme of the momin reform movement would be set in motion and momin organisations would be developed.[110] The first annual All India meeting of the Momin Conference in UP was also held in Allahabad in 1929. The Momin Conference here saw the regular involvement of the political leadership, thus probably imparting an elite image to it. The actual organisation of the Allahabad Momin Conference therefore tended to be somewhat sectional and narrow in its social base, although a large number of momins clearly identified with the message of the party and formed their own volunteer corps in the poorer neighbourhoods. The Kanpur organisation, in contrast, was dominated by mill hands, possibly because of their numerical preponderance, greater political militancy and better organisational strength in the town, partly derived from their workplace politics.[111]

These cases of the development of ansari political organisations in the

[108] Interview with Habibur Rahman 'Betab' and Jameel Akhtar Nomani in Kanpur, interview with Zamiruddin Ansari in Allahabad.
[109] Interview with Zamiruddin Ansari in Allahabad.
[110] Extract from Para 1166, 'Bengal Secret Abstract', No. 15, 11 April 1928, cited in *PAI*, No. 16, 28 April 1928.
[111] Interview with Habibur Rahman 'Betab' in Kanpur.

1920s and 1930s demonstrate the importance of an artisanal tradition in the religious assertion of a section of the Muslim poor. At the same time, the differences in the Allahabad and Kanpur cases illuminate the simultaneous importance of class, occupational and neighbourhood affiliations in shaping the contours of political solidarities and identities. A collective sense of community based on religion and shared interests or the plight of all Muslims did not develop among the poorer Muslims, notwithstanding an emphasis on Islam as an integral part of their artisanal identity. The heightened awareness of religious identity here was not poised to override other distinctions of occupation, work, neighbourhood, status or class to bring about the unity and cohesiveness of all Muslims.[112] This conclusion is consistent with the argument in the previous chapter that it is necessary analytically to separate the two issues of religious identity and sense of community; that is, the awareness of religious identity, even when articulated through shared collective action with elites in the public arena, does not unambiguously amount to the imagination or conception of a wider, cohesive community based on religion.

Religious identity and the metaphor of Muslim decline

Alongside artisanal and occupational identity, an awareness of deprivation and dispossession was central to the emerging religious assertion of the Muslim poor and their perception of themselves. One crucial factor in this was the discourse of Muslim decay and decline, which was part of a strident and increasingly orchestrated campaign conducted by the ulema and the north Indian Muslim political leadership. The sense of deprivation of the Muslim poor, while undoubtedly grounded in their changing social experience, was also discursively constructed. Wider political ideologies and rhetoric configured their understanding of the nature of their deprivation in specific ways. They conceptualised and made sense of their plight in dialogue with a projected history of the decline of the Indian Muslims and of Islam worldwide. This perspective gave centrality to religion in their political action and identity. It also made them prone to viewing themselves as relatively more deprived than the poor of other Indian communities.

The agitation against the proposed demolition of a portion of a mosque in Kanpur in 1913 by the municipal council provides an interesting example of how the threatened mosque was projected as a

---

[112] Nita Kumar recently detected that the julaha weavers of Benares never spoke in terms of 'all we Muslims', despite a keen consciousness of their religious identity. Kumar, *Artisans*, p. 215.

symbol of what Freitag describes as 'mourning and martyrdom' and how it served as a metaphor for the deprivation of Muslims.[113] When a part of the Machhlibazar mosque in Kanpur was earmarked for demolition for the construction of a major thoroughfare by the largely British-dominated Municipal Board in 1913, a campaign was organised by the local ulema and political leadership, directed primarily against the colonial government.[114] The campaign dwelt on the theme of defeat and victimisation of Muslims at the hands of British and imperial powers worldwide. Many meetings were convened not only to lament the fate of the mosque in question but also to mourn the decline of Islam and Muslim communities more generally. The campaign to save the mosque generated unprecedented excitement amongst the local Muslim poor, including julaha mill workers and lower-caste pedlars (*bisatis*), who made up the majority of worshippers at the mosque. They swelled the crowds at meetings to protest against demolition, and staged processions, often in the mode of the mourning rituals of Mohurram.[115] A newspaper described large groups of people heading towards the Kanpur Idgah to attend a major protest meeting. Barefoot and carrying black flags, they halted at regular intervals to recite an elegy and to repeat the following refrain: 'O God, help us *oppressed Muhammadans*; (regard the) demolition of the mosque of the *helpless*' (emphases added). These proceedings closely replicated the ritual mourning enactments of Mohurram. The newspaper further noted that the words of mourning brought 'tears to the eyes of hundreds of Muhammadans, many of whom wept so bitterly that they remained speechless for a long time'.[116] Maulana Azad Subhani, a popular local leader and mastermind of the garha movement, who was considered in government circles to be a 'key agitator' and said to possess 'a gift of fiery theological exhortation',[117] linked the mosque issue with the tribulations and martyrdom of Hussain and Hassan. In his 'passionate oration' Subhani declared: 'Today we have our Karbala [the site of martyrdom]; this is the time to interpret it: Hasan and Husain have had their throats cut.'[118]

The mosque issue precipitated a violent confrontation in August 1913, when, following a protest meeting, 10,000–15,000 people proceeded

[113] S. B. Freitag, *Collective Action and Community: Public Arenas and the Emergence of Communalism in North India*, Berkeley, 1989, pp. 210–16.
[114] Minutes by the Lieutenant Governor of UP, James Meston, on the Cawnpore mosque and riot, File No. Proceedings 100–118/October 1913, Home Poll. (A), GOI, NAI.
[115] Ibid.
[116] *NNR*, No. 33/1913, pp. 815–16, cites a report from *Muslim Gazette* (Lucknow), 6 August 1913.
[117] Minutes by the Lieutenant Governor of UP, James Meston, on the Cawnpore mosque and riot, Part II, pp. 20–1, 23, 35–6.
[118] Ibid., Part II, p. 23.

to reconstruct the demolished part of the mosque. The police intervened to stop them and, when the crowd turned against them, they fired on the crowd.[119] This shooting incident caused widespread outrage amongst many different Muslim groups, not only in Kanpur but throughout the province. The orchestrated imagery of victimhood of Muslims was now further magnified, especially in the local Urdu press. Shibli Nomani, the renowned scholar-historian from the Nadwat-ul-Ulema seminary of Lucknow, composed a poem entitled 'We are the victims of the fight at Kanpur', which was widely publicised. Numerous such poems were composed in which the victims of the police shooting were hailed as *shahids* or martyrs.[120] Much of the Kanpur mosque campaign was, in fact, carried out through a particular genre of political verse emerging from this period, which was reminiscent of and reso-nated with the matam (mourning) and marsiya (a lament)[121] traditions of Islamic verse, and related to the elegiac hymn and ritual mourning of Mohurram.[122] This served to accentuate and nurture a sense of depriva-tion and victimhood. It also provided a popular idiom for the transmis-sion and dissemination of the ideas underpinning the mosque agitation. It enabled the poor to cultivate the public expression of emotional attachment and devotion to religious symbols.

Arguably, however, the propaganda around the mosque elicited a passionate response among the poorer Muslims not simply because of the extensive deployment of familiar religious motifs, mourning rituals or an emotive appeal, but equally because this propaganda was set against a backdrop of their perceived occupational, social and cultural degradation. The imagery of destruction and loss and of decline or decay in the mosque campaign animated the poor and facilitated their identification with the agitation. The nature and extent of victimhood or martyrdom of Muslims under colonialism may have been magnified in the political propaganda of the leaders, but the emotions they unleashed were not simply conjured up through fiery speeches. If martyrdom was a rhetorical device deployed by the leaders for political mobilisation or to highlight the decline of Muslim power in India, for the poorer Muslims deprivation was an immediate and real experience. However, as argued

[119] Ibid., Part II, passim.
[120] *NNR*, No. 37/1913, pp. 950, 1020–3; No. 38/1913, pp. 1054–6, 1060–1.
[121] A marsiya is a lament or threnody at the death of a friend, relative or patron. In the context of Mohurram, marsiyas are chants and poems bearing on the heroic struggle and sufferings of Hussain. The Mohurram festival is celebrated to lament the tribulations of Hussain and his family and followers, which culminated in the tragedy of the Karbala. Muhammad Sadiq, *A History of Urdu Literature*, Delhi, 1984, ch. 10, discusses the marsiya.
[122] Ansari, *Emergence of Socialist Thought*, p. 489n, notes that some Shia writers in the 1920s and 1930s developed a new kind of marsiya with a radical political content.

earlier, the acute sense of deprivation of the Muslim poor did not simply spring out of their objective experiences, but was discursively constructed in synergy with the wider rhetoric of decline and backwardness – this was a two-way interactive process. The moment was right for such a rhetoric to be eagerly embraced by the Muslim poor. This rhetoric also accentuated the development of the theme of deprivation as a central motif in the religious assertion and political action and ideology of the Muslim poor throughout the 1920s and 1930s. This could, moreover, heighten awareness specifically of the deprivation of the poorer sections of Muslims and, in turn, draw attention to internal differences within the community, thus fragmenting the construction of an overarching religious community identity, even within a broader rhetoric of the collective decline of the Muslim community and Islam worldwide.[123]

The Kanpur mosque agitation was significant in marking a step towards the elaboration of anti-colonial nationalism among the Muslim poor. The prominence of the theme of deprivation in the mosque agitation meant that the campaign could be seen by the poor not only as heroic action in defence of Islam against colonial rule, but also as a struggle that would rescue the poorer Muslims from their misery. Religious publicists and leaders, while condemning the attack on Islamic sites, at the same time identified the government and British imperialism as the cause of the deprivation of many Muslim groups. This enabled the poor to envisage the possibility of improving their position through a struggle against oppressive British rule, accompanied by a spirited defence of their religious rights. Thus, it is possible to trace the roots of religious nationalism, pan-Islamism and anti-colonialism amongst the Muslim poor – which would later develop into the Khilafat movement – to the Kanpur mosque issue and to the campaigns to save Islamic holy sites in the Middle East that took place during this time. Just as the mosque issue was situated by the political publicists within the context of what they argued to be a broader history of victimisation of Islam and Muslims, the Muslim poor could also locate their own plight within these wider processes. The defence of Islam and its sacred sites, as well as opposition to the government, could all become so important to the poorer Muslims precisely because the notion of victimisation and deprivation of Muslims under colonial rule, as it was fleshed out in the mosque agitation and similar campaigns, came to assume such centrality in the understanding of their own experience.

---

[123] However, Freitag argues that with this mosque agitation and similar political developments around that time 'a vision of a declining community had been articulated that connected Muslims throughout India and outside'. Freitag, *Collective Action*, p. 216.

Religious resurgence, patronage and leadership in the locality

Islamic resurgence among the Muslim poor related to their newly constructed respectable artisanal identity and to their growing awareness of deprivation. The patterns of their religious expression were also influenced by the nature of leadership and patronage in the locality. The Muslim poor not only drew upon the rhetoric of decline and deprivation of the political leadership, but also tapped into some of the activities and organisations of the religious leadership and Muslim elites that were emerging from the late nineteenth century in the towns. The ulema and sufis from the later half of the nineteenth century began to initiate and develop a range of welfare, social service and organisational activities, which at times doubled as vehicles for political mobilisation. They were concerned both to regenerate or energise Islam and to promote or protect the interests of various Muslim groups. Their aim was to grapple with what they perceived to be the destruction of Muslim political power, the marginalisation of Islam in public life, the crisis of religious education, and the social and cultural ascendance of Hindu commercial and land-owning classes, often at the expense of Muslim elites and gentry. In their organisational and social service activities, the ulema and sufis received the patronage of local Muslim notables and propertied groups whose interests they usually represented and with whom they frequently shared the same social background. Having lost their erstwhile sources of power in pre-colonial Islamic state politics, the religious leaders gradually focused on anchoring their authority and legitimacy within the community, in order to recast their social and political role in changed contexts. They based their activities at local mosques and shrines, at the numerous new religious schools (*madrassa*) and at a wide range of newly formed, often short-lived, organisations or *anjumans*.

In Kanpur, the ulema established educational institutions such as the Faiz-e-Am Madrassa, Madrassa Jam-e-Uloom, Halim Muslim School, Madrassa Illahiyat, as well as a range of anjumans, including the Anjuman Islamia, Anjuman Mohammadia and Anjuman Hifazat-ul-Islam, to name but a few.[124] In this, they had the support of the wealthy hide and skin merchants and manufacturers of leather goods, including the well-known Hafiz Mohammad Halim, and of the handful of Muslim traders involved mainly in the timber industry, in haberdasheries and

---

[124] Interview with Jameel Akhtar Nomani and Mohd. Ilyas Khan Adeeb in Kanpur; N. P. Arora, *Kanpur ke Prasidh Purush*, Kanpur, 1947, pp. 97–103; Syed Ishtiaq Hussain Azhar, *Sheikh ul Isatazza: Maulana Gulam Yahiya Hazarwi*, Karachi, 1976–7, pp. 42–4, 53.

general merchandise shops (*bisatkhanas*) and in the wholesale vegetable business, as well as of professional people and politicians such as the renowned barrister and member of the Legislative Council Hafiz Hidayat Hussain. In Benares, some of the more prosperous Muslim merchants and elites patronised similar organisations and ulema,[125] as did the *taluqdar* landowners in Lucknow.[126] In Allahabad, Maulana Mohammad Hussain, one of the most influential ulema of the town, who was also connected with the famous sufi shrine of Daira Shah Hujjatulla in Bahadurganj, formed the Anjuman Rifa-i-Islam in the 1880s and 1890s with locally raised subscriptions. His son Maulana Vilayat Hussain and grandson Maulana Mohammad Mian Faruqi followed in his footsteps to establish the Madrassa Mohammadia Imdadia in 1924.[127] Shah Mohammad Fakhir (also known as Rashid Mian) and his son Maulana Shahid Fakhri, who belonged to another influential family of sufi shaikhs based at the Daira Shah Ajmal shrine, were equally prominent local leaders. These Allahabad families often represented the interests of landed and service Muslim groups of the town and its hinterland.[128] However, the nuclei of activities that these leaders generated, in their local organisations as well as at mosques and shrines, were also to provide the organisational bases and agitational platforms for various groups of the poor.

Beginning in the last half of the nineteenth century, a wide and diverse range of activities were undertaken by these religious leaders – ulema and sufis – in the various towns with the support of their patrons. They established orphanages (*Islami yetimkhana*) for Muslim children, apparently with the aim of preventing Christian missionaries from taking on Muslim orphans and raising them in an alien faith. They facilitated the renovation, repair and upkeep of urban mosques, Idgahs (compounds for Id prayers) and graveyards. Many of the organisations (anjumans) they established were intended for the protection of the rights and the furtherance of the needs of many different urban Muslim groups. The work of the anjumans covered, depending on the need of the moment, the organisation of religious meetings or ceremonies, the provision of religious teaching, the formation of akharas, the protection

[125] Kumar, 'The "Truth" about Muslims in Banaras', p. 89.
[126] S. Ganju, 'The Muslims of Lucknow, 1919–1939', in K. Ballahatchet and J. Harrison (eds.), *The City in South Asia: Pre-modern and Modern*, London, 1980, p. 285.
[127] *Mohammad Hussain biography*, pp. 28–30, 51–3; Mohammad Mian Faruqi, 'Biography of Maulana Vilayat Hussain', Urdu Manuscript, n.d. (hereafter 'Vilayat Hussain biography'), pages not numbered; Mohammad Mian Faruqi, 'Mukhtasar Halat-e-Zindagi' (a brief autobiography), Urdu manuscript, n.d. (hereafter 'Mohd. Mian Faruqi autobiography'), p. 1 (these manuscripts were made available to me by Suhaib Faruqi of Daira Shah Hujjatulla, Bahadurganj, Allahabad).
[128] Bayly, *Local Roots*, pp. 79–81.

of *waqf* (religious endowments) properties, the provision of relief in Muslim areas during riots, mounting legal defence on behalf of those arrested during communal riots or prosecuted for violence, championing the cause of Muslims in local politics and in municipal institutions, as well as campaigning for the protection of housing of poorer Muslims and seeking to improve their economic condition and employment opportunities.[129]

While activities of this kind were initiated by various anjumans around the turn of the century, by the 1920s many of these functions were to assume greater urgency, especially for the poorer Muslims, with the intensification of urban tensions over land and work as well as the escalation of religious competition with various Hindu organisations. In Allahabad, the Anjuman Rifa-i-Islam,[130] originally founded at the Daira Shah Hujjatulla around the turn of the century, played a more and more vigorous role in the 1920s and 1930s under the leadership of the sufi pirs of the shrine, Maulanas Vilayat Hussain and Mohammad Mian Faruqi. The anjuman ran *maktabs* and *madrassas* (religious schools), raised funds to support local Muslim associations in various mohallas to defend mosques, shrines or graveyards, and promoted physical training as part of a Muslim defence effort.[131] These leaders also took initiatives to promote the economic interests of Muslim petty traders and other occupational groups, and were even involved in organising trade unions of Muslim labourers, often ideologically buttressed by a militant egalitarian version of Islam or Islamic socialism.[132] They also launched vigorous campaigns to protect land belonging to Muslims, including the settlements of poorer Muslims from Improvement Trust acquisitions. For this purpose, in 1926 they formed, along with other local notables, a new organisation – Ajuman Mohafiz Imlak Mussalmanan (Society for the Protection of Property Belonging to Muslims), which staged several meetings at mosques and shrines to address the problems arising from municipal and Trust policies.[133]

---

[129] Some of these points will be discussed further later in this chapter. Interview with Jameel Akhtar Nomani and Mohd. Ilyas Khan Adeeb in Kanpur; Arora, *Kanpur ke Prasidh Purush*, pp. 97–103; Azhar, *Sheikh ul Isatazza*, pp. 49, 52–3; *Mohammad Hussain biography*, pp. 28–30, 51–3; 'Vilayat Hussain biography'; 'Mohd. Mian Faruqi autobiography', p. 1.

[130] *Mohammad Hussain biography*, pp. 28–9.

[131] *PAI*, No. 14, 9 April 1938; No. 15, 16 April 1938; interview with Maulana Mohammad Mian Faruqi of Daira Shah Hujjatulla.

[132] Interview with Maulana Mohammad Mian Faruqi, who organised trade unions among the Muslim workforce in the bidi, metal bucket and steel trunk workshops in Allahabad. These points will be discussed later in this chapter and in chapter 9.

[133] AIT File No. 1/3, Mirganj Open Area Scheme.

In addition to these new functions that the religious leaders gradually developed from the late nineteenth century onwards, they further expanded some of their traditional functions within the community. The Graeco-Arabic humoral system of medicine – *yunani tibb*, which the ulema and sufi practised historically – was reinvigorated in the nineteenth century as a part of the wider Islamic regeneration movements of north India[134] and assumed a more prominent place in the everyday work of the sufi pirs and ulema.[135] Shah Mohammad Fakhir of the Daira Shah Ajmal, for instance, actively developed *hakimi* (yunani medicine) practice as an important aspect of his sufi leadership around the turn of the century.[136] Those religious leaders who were sufi pirs also practised *amaliyat* or prescriptions of certain prayers, sacred readings and phrases, which were often dispensed in the form of *tawiz* (amulets), and which were expected to secure practical benefits such as employment, desirable marriage or recovery from illness. This was associated with the miraculous ability (*karamat*) that sufi pirs were believed to have in healing and in changing people's fortunes.[137] As practitioners of tibb and amaliyat, the sufi pirs were in close contact with the care and cure of the poor in the towns and in their daily lives.[138] Some of them were also thought to have miraculous power, such as Maulana Mohammad Fakhir of Daira Shah Ajmal in Allahabad. He was believed to have thrown a pitcher used for ritual ablution from a mosque at a particularly noisy Hindu procession during prayers, which exploded with an uncharacteristic bang like a bomb and caused the processionists to run for cover.[139] This act earned him legendary fame in the town for deploying his special powers to humiliate the Hindus during a period of heated controversy over the playing of music in front of mosques, and fortified his leadership authority. The sufi pirs and ulema were also great patrons of akharas for physical training, lathi and sword play, and wrestling.[140] Their shrines and mosques were frequently the site of these

---

[134] B. Metcalf, *Perfecting Women: Maulana Ashraf Ali Thanawi's 'Bihishti Zewar': A Partial Translation with Commentary*, Berkeley, 1990, p. 10; B. Metcalf, 'Hakim Ajmal Khan: Rais of Delhi and Muslim Leader', in R. Frykenberg (ed.), *Delhi through the Ages*, Delhi, 1986, pp. 299–315.
[135] 'Mohd. Mian Faruqi autobiography', p. 1; 'Vilayat Hussain biography'; *Mohammad Hussain biography*, p. 9; Bayly, *Local Roots*, p. 81; Fakhri, *Taskira Aulia*, p. 52.
[136] Interview with Zahid Fakhri in Allahabad.
[137] Metcalf, *Deoband*, pp. 190–4, 176–7.
[138] Interview with Mohammad Mian Faruqi.
[139] Interview with Zahid Fakhri in Allahabad; Fakhri, *Taskira Aulia*, p. 60.
[140] For instance, both Daira Shah Ajmal and Daira Shah Hujjatulla had akharas on their grounds, and Mohammad Hussain, Mohammad Fakhir, Shahid Fakhri and many of the members of their families were well known for their own prowess in the martial arts. Interview with Zahid Fakhri and Suhaib Faruqi in Allahabad; Fakhri, *Taskira Aulia*, p. 52; also see, Kumar, 'The "Truth" about Muslims in Banaras', p. 85.

activities, often with financial input from the towns' affluent Muslims. This particular activity developed increasingly vigorously in the interwar years, within a context of growing Hindu martial assertion and the perceived need to match that and to protect Muslims.

As the focus of such a wide, and widening, range of activities, including, of course, the expansion of public religious display, many of the urban mosques and sufi shrines, as well as the anjumans and madrassas, developed as centres of community organisation and support, where people came for advice, consolation and material help. These institutions and organisations were also increasingly centres for political discussion and debate, and channels for the dissemination of ideas and information. The lectures and public addresses at the mosques and shrines during Friday prayers, Milad Sharif gatherings, Id celebrations and Rajbi or Barawafat meetings came to play a more and more important public political function.[141] In all this, not only did the ulema and sufi provide spiritual leadership but, in order to maintain and extend their sway in the locality, they also sought to reorient the nature of their leadership by redefining, recasting and even re-inventing their role in terms of the changing needs of their flock. They infused their leadership with new purpose and presented new concerns of local import and relevance. They also tried to address themselves not just to long-term urban inhabitants but also to newer social groups, including migrants to the towns. Moreover, some of these leaders expressed themselves in an idiom of poverty. *Faqr (Fakhr)* or poverty was the ideal of the Prophet,[142] and some sufi pirs stressed this element in their practice, as did Mohammad Fakhir of Daira Shah Ajmal by incorporating the term 'Fakhir' (poor or beggar) in his own name. Some sufi leaders were also prominent in publicising an egalitarian version of Islam, and at times professed their adherence to Islamic socialism.

These sufis and ulema did not, however, entirely gear their lives and activities to the welfare of the poor. Indeed, their organisations and institutions were able, or willing, to deliver the needs of the poor only in limited ways. Their social origin, after all, lay with the Muslim propertied classes, landowners or service elites, and some of them were politically far from radical. They were also often well entrenched in the local factional politics of the towns.[143] Frequently, there were rivalries amongst various families of sufis and various groups of ulema, as they

---

[141] See, for instance, *PAI*, No. 32, 19 August 1922; No. 36, 16 September 1922; No. 37, 23 September 1922; No. 38, 30 September 1922. Similar meetings are mentioned in police reports throughout the 1920s and 30s.

[142] Schimmel, *Islam in the Indian Subcontinent*, p. 138.

[143] Bayly, *Local Roots*, pp. 79–81, 252, 255; Robinson, 'Ulema, Sufis', pp. 9–34.

vied for leadership positions. Equally, the relationship of this religious leadership with the emerging new rank of professional Muslim politicians was not entirely harmonious. However, they did frequently have to depend on each other. Sufi families and ulema relied on local notables, landowners and emerging professional politicians for patronage, while the latter looked to the religious heads to marshal the support of poorer Muslims behind their own political campaigns.[144] It should also be borne in mind that these foci of patronage did not operate equally effectively everywhere. In Allahabad and Lucknow, with long-established sufi shrines and influential local schools of ulema, religious leadership and patronage could work more smoothly than in Kanpur, where not only did such traditions develop more recently, but the large population of migrant workers could not always be adequately integrated into such patronage structures.

Notwithstanding these various obvious ambiguities and limitations, the ulema and sufis actively reoriented older structures of patronage to mobilise a wide constituency of support for Islamic revivification and the regeneration of the Muslim community. The range of activities that the religious leaders initiated had implications for the political identity and organisation of the Muslim poor. First, a recurrent motif in all activities of the local religious leadership was their rhetorical emphasis on Muslim decline and the need for special organisational and political initiatives for the defence and reorganisation of the community. The ubiquitous theme of the deprivation of Muslims easily attracted the poor and helped to nurture a political vocabulary in which religion played an important role. Secondly, the fact that the local religious leadership sought to extend patronage and support to the poor, even if limited in nature, meant that religious community affiliations came to play a part in the politics of the poor. Both the wider discursive context and the patterns of leadership and patronage, therefore, tended to accentuate the role of religious linkages in the politics of the Muslim poor, and reinforced the trends of ritual elaboration and religious resurgence. However, the linkages forged between the leaders and the led through these structures were fragile and prone to tensions, which would become more and more evident in the 1920s and 1930s when the leadership found it increasingly difficult to exercise control over their followers in the face of growing religious militancy and political ferment.

---

[144] F. Robinson, 'Professional Politicians in Muslim Politics, 1911–1923', in B. N. Pandey (ed.), *Leadership in South Asia*, New Delhi, 1977, p. 386.

Radical Islamic egalitarianism, nationalism and socialism

The religious identity of the Muslim poor in the interwar years came to encompass ideas of radical egalitarianism, socialism and anti-colonial nationalism. Many of the ulema and sufis, who extended patronage or support to the poor and stood as their champions, also involved themselves in the politics of nationalism, pan-Islamism or Muslim 'separatism'. This dual role of the leadership helped to link local concerns with wider politics and to draw the poor into wider political movements. The ulema and sufis provided the local leadership for the first major initiative in Muslim mass politics during the Khilafat movement. While a new breed of professional Muslim politicians had emerged by this time in the province,[145] the substantial responsibility for local-level political mobilisation amongst the poor lay largely with the ulema and sufis. Urban mosques and shrines served as the nuclei for political mobilisation, where volunteer corps were organised, speeches delivered, and rallies or meetings held. The dairas of Allahabad provide the most apt instances. The pirs and ulema of both the main shrines of Daira Shah Ajmal and Daira Shah Hujjatulla espoused the Khilafat cause, and it was at these dairas that the most impressive and spectacular gatherings were staged in support of Khilafat,[146] involving vast numbers of the town's Muslim population, including the poor. With the Khilafat movement, the earlier trend of defence of Islam and efforts to stem the material and social decline of Indian Muslims, as epitomised by the Kanpur mosque episode, expanded into pan-Islamic, anti-colonial nationalism among the poor.

While the defence of Islam and anti-colonialism clearly animated the Khilafat movement, the participation of the poor also related to a great extent to a militant egalitarian rhetoric of the leadership, specifically concerned with the plight of the Muslim poor.[147] The fate of the Caliphate was of little direct relevance to most ordinary Muslims. The Caliph could, however, be seen as a potent symbol of dispossession with whom the poor could identify and around whom they could rally in an attempt to struggle against colonial rule, which was portrayed by many

---

[145] Ibid., pp. 372–94.
[146] Maulana Vilayat Hussain of Daira Shah Hujjatulla was the Secretary of the Khilafat Committee in 1919, and Maulana Mohammad Fakhir of Daira Shah Ajmal was arrested for his political activities during the Khilafat movement. 'Vilayat Hussain biography'; Bayly, *Local Roots*, p. 254; Fakhri, *Taskira Aulia*, p. 53; photographs of meetings at the Daira Shah Ajmal during the Khilafat movement, published in *Taskira Aulia*, show large mass gatherings.
[147] Ansari, *Emergence of Socialist Thought*, pp. 48–50.

leaders as the real source of the troubles of the poor. Colonialism was held responsible for India's economic decline, including the destruction of artisanal crafts, and for the economic hardships brought on by the First World War.[148] The central mobilising symbol of swadeshi home-spun cloth in the Non-Cooperation–Khilafat movement was also especially meaningful to many Muslim artisanal groups, notably weavers, to whom it represented the social and economic crisis that they faced. The Khilafat leaders were able to stimulate popular participation, in part, through radical populist slogans about the evils of colonialism and by addressing local issues and specific economic grievances relevant to the poor. More importantly, however, the Khilafat movement was ideologically projected as a broader egalitarian campaign to overcome deprivation, especially by a militant section of the ulema with a socialist political orientation. They painted the Khilafat movement as the struggle of the poor against the British, and Islam as primarily an egalitarian religion of the poor.[149] This provided the rallying point of political action for poorer Muslims in the Khilafat movement, similar to the theme of deprivation during the Kanpur mosque campaign earlier. Significantly, if the general decline of the Muslim community had been stressed during the Kanpur mosque protest and the issue of the specific deprivation of the poorer Muslims had been more implicit than explicit, the latter became a focus of the political campaigns of the ulema of socialist persuasion during the Khilafat movement. The interaction between the difficult material circumstances of the Muslim poor and socialist political rhetoric provided the potent brew which spurred on popular political action in the Khilafat movement. Furthermore, from around the time of the Kanpur mosque agitation, a genre of Urdu agitational poetry had begun to emerge, drawing upon traditions of religious and Persian verse, which developed in the years leading up to the First World War and came to play an important role by the time of the Khilafat movement.[150] This provided a familiar mode of communication and enabled the effective transmission of messages between the poor and their leaders. The Khilafat movement aroused such enthusiasm among the poorer Muslims that, long after the Congress declared the end of the Non-Cooperation movement, processions and drills by Khilafat volunteers as well as political meetings, frequently at religious gatherings, continued unabated well into 1922. One police report at the time

[148] Ibid.   [149] Ibid.
[150] Freitag, *Collective Action*, p. 227; Gail Minault, *The Khilafat Movement: Religious Symbolism and Political Mobilization in India*, Delhi, 1982, pp. 154–63; Ansari, *Emergence of Socialist Thought*, p. 94; Gail Minault, 'Urdu Political Poetry during the Khilafat Movement', *MAS*, 8, 4, 1974, pp. 459–71.

mentioned the '*josh*' or zeal of Khilafat volunteers[151] and another pointed out the predominance of the 'poorer classes' at religious meetings where political speeches were delivered.[152] Indeed, by this time, the leadership appeared to be losing their initiative or control of the movement to the poor,[153] thus confirming the serious concern that some Khilafat leaders had expressed from the outset about the potential dangers of unbridled popular militancy.[154]

One of the most significant developments related to the Khilafat movement was the emergence of Islamic socialism as an important element in the politics of the poor. It brought together the multiple levels of identity of the poor based on religion, deprivation and artisanal occupation as well as opposition to British rule. The prominent role played by Muslim socialist leaders contributed overwhelmingly to mass participation in the Khilafat movement. The Islamic socialists became a decisive political force by the 1920s, especially in places such as Kanpur which had a large concentration of Muslims in the industrial workforce.[155] The Islamic socialist leaders of this generation[156] came from the erstwhile qasbah service gentry with a tradition of religious leadership, and many had been active in the early twentieth-century pan-Islamic campaigns in defence of sacred sites in the Middle East and were associated with such organisations as the Anjuman Khuddam-e-Kaaba. Many were ardent sufis and ulema, and some were trained at or had connections with the well-known seminaries of Deoband or Firanghi Mahal, as well as the Aligarh College and School. Their leanings towards socialism developed from their identification with the anti-imperialism and anti-capitalism of Bolshevism, both of which had also been central to much of early twentieth-century Islamic thought in north India. For a section of these Islamic socialist activists, their interest in Bolshevism was not confined to anti-colonialism and anti-capitalism. They went on to emphasise the egalitarian or redistributive content of socialism, which they saw as central also to Islamic philosophy. Islam and socialism were both pivotal in their political perspective as the source of social emancipation of the poor. For them, a true Muslim was a socialist, as both Islam and socialism, they believed, stood

[151] *PAI*, No. 3, 21 January 1922.
[152] *PAI*, No. 36, 16 September 1922.
[153] *PAI*, No. 16, 21 April 1923.
[154] Mushirul Hasan, *Nationalism and Communal Politics in India, 1916–1928*, Delhi, 1979, p. 169.
[155] Two of the most prominent leaders, Azad Subhani and Hasrat Mohani, were based mainly in Kanpur in this period. Ansari, *Emergence of Socialist Thought*, p. 48.
[156] The account here is based on the history of Islamic socialism in this period in ibid., chs. 1, 2; also see Bayly, *Local Roots*, p. 254.

for equality above all. The growing emphasis on the religious commitment of the individual and personal piety in Islamic reformism from the
nineteenth century also helped to fortify the Islamic socialist message of
egalitarianism and of the subversion of the social order or established
hierarchy by upholding the primacy of the individual. Some of the
socialist leaders preached their ideas of egalitarianism through the idiom
of sufi Islam, which could, in essence, be seen to level social distinctions
through personal devotion. Thus, Maulana Hasrat Mohani, one of the
most popular Muslim socialist leaders, with a large following among the
Muslim poor, described himself as a 'momin sufi'. The term 'momin'
probably served here as a metaphor of identification with the honest and
pious common-folk, while the reference to sufism pointed to egalitarianism. He also maintained, 'my creed is *derveshi* [mystic asceticism]
and revolution'.[157]

Hasrat Mohani, along with his equally well-known contemporary
Maulana Azad Subhani, preached that socialism and Islam were one;
that the cardinal principles of socialism were anti-landlordism, anti-
capitalism and equality, which were also central to Islam.[158] Azad
Subhani, when outlining his vision of a nationalist organisation and the
future independent nation, specified the key groups in society and polity
as 'kisans [peasants], labourers, students and ulema'.[159] His stated
political objective was the religious and social improvement of the lower
classes. Subhani's radical views were reported to have alienated the
'better class Muslims', who were suspicious of his leanings toward
communism and of his messages of social levelling and the redistribution of property.[160] Subhani's vision of emancipation of the poor also
informed the garha movement of the 1920s and 1930s, which he
initiated in order to promote the production of and demand for
handwoven cloth. The movement was geared to solving the problems of
unemployment and poverty of large sections of Muslim artisans, and
this issue gained even greater importance during the economic depression of the early 1930s.[161] Hasrat Mohani, who regarded himself a
'Communist Muslim', believed that the true value of Islam lay in its
belief that no one must go hungry. He pointed to the fundamental
importance of charity or the giving of alms in Islam in the form of *zakat*

---

[157] Cited in Ansari, *Emergence of Socialist Thought*, p. 490n.
[158] Ibid., p. 48.
[159] *PAI*, No. 5, 3 February 1923.
[160] *PAI*, No. 18, 15 May 1926.
[161] *NNR*, Nos. 6 (p. 5), 24 (p. 4) and 25 (p. 3)/1932; Nos. 6, 11, 24, 25/1932 report press
propaganda about garha promotion; also see, *PAI*, No. 40, 10 October 1931; No. 25,
25 June 1932; No. 27, 9 July 1932; No. 28, 16 July 1932; No. 33, 20 August 1932;
No. 45, 12 November 1932.

or *ushr*, which were taxes aimed at the redistribution of wealth from the rich to the poor, and which recognised society's responsibility for the welfare of the poor. This, he argued, was identical to the norms of equitable redistribution in socialism. Both socialism and Islam, in his view, prevented the wealthy from having too much wealth and both were grounded in the ideal of even allocation.[162] The egalitarianism of Mohani and many of his contemporaries also prompted them to forge new modes of political communication and mobilisation, especially through literary forms, in order to translate their ideas into action. Hasrat Mohani, for instance, was an effective and popular exponent of the new genre of agitational poetry that developed in the 1910s and 1920s.[163]

The message of the Islamic socialist leaders such as Subhani and Mohani contained several interrelated themes: a condemnation of colonial rule; a mission to eradicate the misery of the poor and to ensure equality and justice; an advocacy of the social responsibility of the elites; as well as an emphasis on the cultivation of personal and political autonomy and social subversion through sufi mysticism. Moreover, pan-Islamic, anti-colonial nationalism was urged as the vehicle for the emancipation of the poor. The political prominence of emancipatory and redistributive themes in Islam fortified the forces of religious resurgence among the poor. The resurrection and cultivation of 'true' egalitarian Islam assumed an urgency. Islamic socialism remained an abiding inspiration for political action by the Muslim poor well into the 1930s, encouraging the activists of the Congress Socialist Party to draw upon it for the purpose of nationalist and trade union mobilisation. These developments are addressed in chapter 9.

The growing currency of socialist ideas among the Muslim poor often stimulated their political organisation and protest at the workplace. Islamic socialist leaders such as Mohani and Subhani were not only key leaders in the Khilafat movement, but also instrumental in the organisation of some of the early workers' unions in places such as Kanpur in the 1910s and 1920s. Both leaders were particularly active in the early Communist movement in India and at the first All India conference of the Communist Party in Kanpur in 1925.[164] Mohani and Subhani were evidently held in great esteem by mill workers in Kanpur. One worker, Sudarshan Chakr – who was, in fact, Hindu – in his history of the

---

[162] Asar bin Yahiya Ansari, *Hasrat Mohani: Ek Siyasi Diary*, Bombay, 1977, p. 126; Maulana Jamaluddin Abdul Wahab et al., *Qulliat-e-Hasrat*, Karachi, 1976, p. 37.
[163] Ansari, *Emergence of Socialist Thought*, pp. 94, 98–9, 264.
[164] Wahab et al., *Qulliat-e-Hasrat*, p. 36; Ansari, *Emergence of Socialist Thought*, pp. 69–70; Sudarshan Chakr, *Kanpur Mazdur Andolan ka Itihas*, Kanpur, 1986, pp. 17–19.

Kanpur labour movement described Mohani as the personification of the ideals of equity and independence (*samanta* and *swatantrata*) and of humility and simplicity.[165] Mohani and Subhani are, indeed, considered legendary pioneering figures in the history of labour struggles in UP. The messages of equality and redistribution popularised by these leaders were enthusiastically embraced by Muslim workers in the Kanpur textile mills, especially those belonging to the julaha caste. These workers were believed to be the most militant in the early years of labour politics in Kanpur from the 1910s,[166] and Islamic socialism undoubtedly contributed to their political radicalism. Ramzan Ali, mill worker, prominent early labour activist and founder member of the Kanpur Mazdur Sabha (Labour Union), for instance, had come under the influence of Hasrat Mohani and his socialist ideas. Islamic socialist ideas, with their syncretic sufi overtones, were also a motivating force behind Ramzan Ali's well-known efforts to promote unity among workers of various castes and religions, in particular by organising '*chana bhoj*' – a form of collective meal eaten during festivals by workers of all communities.[167]

It is worth briefly considering, at this stage, the implications of the association of labour politics with an egalitarian ideology which drew inspiration from religion. Although Islamic socialism was an important force in Kanpur in the first few decades of the twentieth century, it does not appear to have played a divisive role in fuelling communal tensions during this period at the workplace. Indeed, the political message of the Muslim socialist leaders seems to have been espoused even by non-Muslim mill hands, as evident from Sudarshan Chakr's admiration for Hasrat Mohani, noted above. Politics at the workplace did, of course, face fragmentation along 'communal' lines and religious demands were put forward within the mills, especially in interwar Kanpur. However, in origin this had little to do with Islamic socialism, but rather with wider political developments. The segmentation of the labour market and of the workforce along the lines of religious community, and the deliberate strategies of employers or the state to exploit such divisions for the control and discipline of workers, often provided the basis for communal rifts in workplace politics.[168] Moreover, the regime of work discipline in factories enforced by the management frequently targeted religious

---

[165] Chakr, *Kanpur Mazdur Andolan*, pp. 17–19.
[166] Joshi, 'Kanpur Textile Labour', pp. 182–5.
[167] N. P. Arora, 'Swargya Shri Ramzan Ali: Kanpur Mazdur Sabha ke Janamdata', *Veer Bharat*, 15 July 1947, p. 6 (editorial article), Narayan Prasad Arora Collection, Writings by Arora, Serial No. 12, NML.
[168] C. Joshi, 'Bonds of Community, Ties of Religion: Kanpur Textile Workers in the Early Twentieth Century', *IESHR*, 22, 3, 1985, pp. 251–80; R. Chandavarkar, *The Origins*

activities and prayers during working hours, and the consequent demands to do with the preservation of religious rights thus related to conflict over discipline and control.[169]

Far more important than these, however, were escalating movements of religious revival among the urban labouring poor from the 1920s, which penetrated labour politics and extended into workplace relations. Thus, for instance, during the shuddhi–sangathan campaigns of the mid-1920s, Muslim mill workers were reported to have become more zealous about their prayers in response to Hindu revival, and many Muslim labourers of the Swadeshi Cotton Mills left work for not being allowed to offer prayers during working hours.[170] A few years later, as religious activities accelerated among the workers in their residential neighbourhoods, and following a major riot in Kanpur in March 1931, Muslim mill workers declared the intention of forming their own separate labour association at the offices of the Urdu newspaper *Gharib*, and not to have their grievances redressed through the existing Mazdur Sabha.[171] They seemed to fear that they would not be adequately represented by the largely Hindu leadership of the Mazdur Sabha, many of whom were activists of the local Congress Party and had shown themselves to be inclined towards resurgent Hinduism through the sangathan movement and the Civil Disobedience campaigns. In such a situation, Hasrat Mohani had to be elected to the executive committee of the Kanpur Mazdur Sabha in order to allay the suspicions and misgivings of the Muslim workers.[172] In both these cases, communal tensions arising outside the context of work impinged upon workplace relations and political organisation. Again, during provincial autonomy and the Congress Ministry period in the late-1930s, fear of Hindu political dominance through the ruling Congress Party, coupled with the efforts of the Ministry to curb labour unrest, prompted some sections of Muslim workers in Kanpur either to lend only qualified support to the Mazdur Sabha or to rally behind the Muslim leaders of the Communist Party, and eventually by the early 1940s to turn to Muslim political organisations.[173] Similarly, in Kanpur and elsewhere, in the mid- and late-1930s, when Congress Socialists and Communists

---

of *Industrial Capitalism in India: Business Strategies and the Working Classes in Bombay, 1900–1940*, Cambridge, 1994, pp. 421–3, 426–8.

[169] Subho Basu, 'Strikes and "Communal" Riots in Calcutta in the 1890s: Industrial Workers, *Bhadralok* Nationalist Leadership and the Colonial State', manuscript article.

[170] *PAI*, No. 42, 25 October–1 November 1924.

[171] *PAI*, No. 43, 31 October 1931.

[172] Joshi, 'Bonds of Community', pp. 271–2.

[173] Ibid., pp. 271–2, 279–80.

sought to organise trade unions in a number of industries, the Muslim
political activists amongst them, including some who were ulema such
as Maulana Mohammad Mian Faruqi of Allahabad, often worked in
enclaves of Muslim occupational groups[174] as the only effective strategy
of mobilisation. In the wake of the extensive competitive religious
mobilisation in the public sphere through Hindu sangathan and Islamic
tanzeem, it was particularly difficult to forge combined labour organisations of Hindu and Muslim workers. It seems more likely, then, that it
was not the religious content of the Islamic socialist message per se but
wider political developments that exercised a more powerful fragmenting influence in workplace politics.

Interestingly, such vertical mobilisation in labour politics in the 1930s
along religious community-based leadership structures and the invocation of socialism with an Islamic orientation did not inevitably
strengthen ties within the putative Muslim community, overriding all
social or class differences. For instance, the almost exclusively Muslim
workforce of the bidi and steel trunk industries in Allahabad in the
1930s formed unions led by Islamic socialist leaders, most notably by
the eminent alim Maulana Mohammad Mian Faruqi of the Daira Shah
Hujjatulla. However, this did not prevent the workers from vocally
condemning the rich and the elite of their own community in the locality
for exploiting the Muslim poor, especially as their employers were
Muslims. At a meeting in 1937 these workers were reported to have
denounced the wealthy and the upper classes of their community for not
being devout Muslims, for squandering money on debauchery and for
the un-Islamic practices of consuming alcohol and pork.[175] Significantly, the workers emphatically disqualified some sections of the elite
from their own definition of community, not primarily as economic
exploiters, but for supposed irreligious behaviour. The poor here specifically invoked revivalist prescriptions for the right conduct of devout
Muslims, but not to cement together various sections of the community.
They deployed such ideas for exactly the opposite purpose – to underscore contradictions and articulate social tensions within the community. It has been asserted by some historians that protest at the workplace
among labourers occurs through a religious idiom owing to their 'pre-
bourgeois' forms of social consciousness and political culture, in which
'a communal sense of identity', informed primarily by religion and often
derived from their past rural traditions, plays a central role.[176] Such

---

174 This point will be discussed further in chapter 9.
175 *PAI*, No. 20, 29 May 1937.
176 Dipesh Chakrabarty, *Rethinking Working Class History: Bengal, 1890–1940*, Princeton,
    1989, pp. 212–13.

'pre-bourgeois' consciousness is also argued to instil a hierarchical sense of allegiance to leaders of the community or elites, which predisposes workers to forge vertical alliances with their social superiors, irrespective of internal tensions or social differences within the community. The evidence from Allahabad here does not bear this out. Moreover, the instances cited earlier of Muslim workers in Kanpur or Allahabad putting forward religious demands or forming separate organisations, precisely at moments when religious conflict became more pronounced in urban politics, suggests that religious issues assumed importance in workplace disputes not because of the elaboration of prior community consciousness, but as a result of new political developments and the escalation of religious activities in the locality.

The history of religious resurgence among the Muslim poor illuminates the interpenetration of a range of different identities and highlights the complexities and ambiguities involved in their definition of community affiliations. Clearly, there was internal contestation and class tension within resurgent Islam, which were to become more pronounced during the period of the tanzeem movement from the mid-1920s to the 1930s, even at a time when Islam emerged as a significant focus for political action and identity of the poor, and when communal conflict became pervasive for a few decades.

Tanzeem and communal conflict

As seen in the previous chapter, in the wake of the Khilafat movement came shuddhi and sangathan, and the strident expansion of activities by the Arya Samaj, the Hindu Sabha and related organisations. The unprecedented ascendance of militant Hinduism, especially the expansion of festival celebrations, martial displays and akhara-based activities, considerably heightened the atmosphere of Hindu religious ferment in urban neighbourhoods. In response, the poorer Muslims now elaborated their religious activities and focused them more directly against resurgent Hinduism. Religious identity was further fleshed out, alongside the emphasis on an experience of deprivation, the self-conscious articulation of an artisanal tradition and the aspirations for egalitarianism.

The reaction of the Muslim poor to shuddhi and sangathan emerged in the form of tanzeem or 'organisation' and *tabligh* or 'propagation of religion' by the mid-1920s. These aimed to rejuvenate Islam and to promote greater adherence to Islamic rituals and duties. The concepts of tanzeem and tabligh initially came from some of the influential schools of ulema in the province,[177] which sketched out a plan of action

---

[177] Minault, *Khilafat*, pp. 193–4; *PAI*, No. 46, 5 December 1925.

to meet the challenge of shuddhi and sangathan.[178] However, various schools of the ulema were in disagreement over doctrinal matters[179] and, at the provincial level, the ulema as well as the Khilafat and Muslim League leaders were in a state of political confusion and disarray after the gradual petering out of the Khilafat movement, especially when the Khilafat issue itself became irrelevant as a rallying focus with the dissolution of the Caliphate in Turkey.[180] Thus, although the ulema and a section of the Muslim leadership put forward the ideas of tanzeem and tabligh, they did not, or could not, come up with any organised or coordinated attempts to promote these across the province, especially at the local urban level.[181] The tanzeem movement developed largely through neighbourhood-based localised activities, without any significant involvement or direction of the provincial Muslim political leadership. Not surprisingly, Mushirul Hasan, who concentrated his analysis largely on provincial elite Muslim politics, when describing political trends after the Khilafat movement commented that 'among Muslims, there is no evidence of any organised or effective revivalist activity after the Khilafat movement' and that tanzeem and tabligh 'were merely in the form of local organisations'.[182] Similarly Sandria Freitag shows that the branches of national-level political organisations formed in urban areas during the Khilafat movement had, by the mid-1920s, come to be dominated by 'very localised interests' and 'any overt coordination among them had atrophied'.[183] 'This', she states, 'resulted from efforts in the neighbourhoods to express sentiments in locally meaningful terms'.[184] Tanzeem organisations in the towns emerged largely as local initiatives, with a significant role played by the poorer Muslims, who had to contend daily with Hindu assertion in urban localities.

Leadership was based almost entirely at the local level and was given by ulema or sufi pirs in the towns, such as Maulana Vilayat Hussain in Allahabad, the influential alim connected with the Daira Shah Hujjatulla shrine. He set up the Anjuman Tahafuz-i-Islam in 1924 and a range of

---

[178] *PAI*, No. 46, 15 December 1925, lists the tanzeem objectives as outlined by Dr Kitchelew.

[179] Hasan, *Nationalism and Communal Politics*, p. 251.

[180] D. Page, *Prelude to Partition: The Indian Muslims and the Imperial System of Control, 1920–1932*, Delhi, 1982, pp. 27, 40–1; Robinson, *Separatism*, pp. 342–4; Hasan, *Nationalism and Communal Politics*, pp. 196–203; A. Jalal and A. Seal, 'Alternative to Partition: Muslim Politics between the Wars', *MAS*, 15, 3, 1981, p. 417.

[181] Confidential note on 'Communal Friction in the United Provinces, 1924', by Assistant to Deputy Inspector General of Police, Criminal Investigation Department, UP File No. 140/1925, Home Poll., GOI, NAI; Hasan, *Nationalism and Communal Politics*, p. 197.

[182] Hasan, *Nationalism and Communal Politics*, pp. 250–1.

[183] Freitag, *Collective Action*, p. 231.

[184] Ibid., pp. 231–2.

similar other organisations,[185] all of which aimed to propagate Islam, to prevent the conversion of Muslims to Hinduism through shuddhi, and to organise local Muslims to defend themselves against what they perceived to be a Hindu religious offensive. In Kanpur, some local ulema and politicians cooperated under the patronage of Hafiz Hidayat Hussain, a barrister and member of the Legislative Council, and undertook a range of activities through the institutional framework of the Anjuman Hifazat-ul-Islam and the Anjuman Islamia.[186] Similarly, the ulema of the Madrassa Illahiyat, established in 1912 under the patronage of local leather merchants in Kanpur, now geared themselves specifically to the tabligh initiative.[187] Organisations for the advancement and defence of Islam inaugurated or reactivated in the mid-1920s included the Anjuman Tabligh-ul-Islam in all the towns, the Anjuman Taid-ul-Islam in Benares, and the Anjuman Moid-ul-Islam in Lucknow.[188] These anjumans tried to organise more vigorous preaching of Islam, promote better religious education and observance of religious duties, raise awareness about fundamental religious doctrines, construct and renovate mosques and religious institutions, and, through all this, prevent the conversion of Muslims to Hinduism.[189] The activities of these anjumans also included efforts to improve the economic plight of various Muslim groups and to reduce the economic power and influence that Hindu commercial communities exercised over them. In all these activities, the leadership of the various anjumans were chiefly concerned to constitute and invigorate a large and unified community of devout practitioners of reformed and purified Islam, who would be more conscious of their distinctive religious identity and interests and thus able to combat and resist the militant Hindu onslaught. The activities initiated by the local leadership were, however, gradually taken over by the poorer Muslims, who soon came to set the pace of religious and political developments. Faced as they were with sustained Hindu militancy in their neighbourhoods, asserting their religious identity was of utmost urgency to them. Moreover, with the growing scarcity of and competition over urban resources and economic opportunities in the interwar period, the desire to combat the economic power of Hindu merchants and entrepreneurs was no less important to them than to the local leadership. Thus, while the organisations and activities of the local ulema and sufis in the towns, supported by local Muslim notables,

185 *PAI*, No. 42, 25 October–1 November 1924; interview with Maulana Mohd. Mian Faruqi in Allahabad.
186 *PAI*, No. 38, 27 September 1924; No. 47, 6 December 1924.
187 Azhar, *Sheikh ul Isatazza*, pp. 52–4.
188 *PAI*, No. 21, 2 June 1923; No. 26, 7 July 1923; No. 13, 13 March 1923.
189 *PAI*, No. 21, 2 June 1923; No. 26, 7 July 1923.

provided the initial stimulus for tabligh and tanzeem, local neighbourhood-based tanzeem akharas, volunteer groups and religious activities
began to develop rapidly and extensively among the Muslim poor from
1923–4.[190] In these endeavours, they built upon the trend of religious
resurgence from the later nineteenth century and, in particular, elaborated on the political experience, organisations and activities of the
Khilafat years.

In tanzeem among the poor, many of the various trends of religious
revival and expansion from the late nineteenth century were to come
together and religious identity was more clearly defined. Cultivation of
martial practices, expansion of akhara activities and festival celebrations,
renovation of mosques and shrines, greater personal adherence to
Islamic practices – all played a role in tanzeem initiatives. While there
was significant continuity with the past, there were also decisive points
of departure. Islamic revivalist tendencies amongst the poor, which had
developed largely in response to the social changes of the nineteenth and
early twentieth-centuries, were now directed against Hindu assertion. If
decline, defeat and martyrdom had earlier been attributed to the British
and western domination during the Kanpur mosque campaigns and the
Khilafat movement, the responsibility for the deprivation and subordination of Muslims was now specifically and overwhelmingly ascribed to
Hindu power – both in the economy and in politics. In the process, the
Islamic religious expression of the poor assumed a more aggressive and
combative orientation against Hindus, at times at the cost of the
vigorous development of radical egalitarian ideas.

Key features of tanzeem initiatives were their rootedness in the
locality, their martial overtones, and their anti-Hindu mobilisation, with
an emphasis on greater public religious display with the larger and more
extensive participation of the poor. In Kanpur, the tanzeem initiative of
the Muslim poor in urban neighbourhoods started in the mid-1920s. A
series of Rajbi Sharif meetings in 1924 and 1926, for instance, were
reported to have attracted the participation of 4,000 and 2,000–5,000
people, respectively,[191] and the display of physical feats became more
prominent during the 1925 Milad gatherings.[192] In many of these
religious meetings, the Arya Samajists and their religious initiatives of
shuddhi and sangathan were severely vilified.[193] Milad sessions also
competed with the growing numbers of Hindu katha ceremonies for

[190] Freitag, Collective Action, pp. 230–7.
[191] PAI, No. 11, 15 March 1924; No. 8, 27 February 1926.
[192] PAI, No. 39, 10 October 1925.
[193] PAI, No. 38, 3 October 1925.

exposition on religious themes, especially in the mill districts.[194] In Allahabad, organisational reaction to shuddhi and sangathan of the Muslim poor, similar to the Kanpur ones, took the form of *Ali Ghol* akharas (Ali's bands), with apparent support from some prominent Muslims of the town.[195] These akharas undertook vigorous and elaborate martial displays during religious festivals. Based in various *mohallas* (neighbourhoods) of the town, akharas gave a major boost to swordsmanship and lathi wielding, and organised parades and marches.[196] The akhara participants came from Muslim lower-caste occupational groups, including artisans and petty traders. The akharas were concentrated in areas such as Atala, which had a high concentration of Muslim poor in the town, including labourers working in small workshops located within the neighbourhood.[197] Small wonder then that, by 1926, such groups as the *kunjras* (vegetable sellers) and *kasais* (butchers) in the town were branded as 'fanatical and reckless' by British district officials,[198] in addition to the julaha-momin-ansaris, already for long labelled as religious zealots. In response to the introduction of armed Hindu akharas in the *Ramlila* in 1923, these Ali Ghol akharas staged impressive demonstrations of arms in tazia processions during Mohurram in that year.[199] In addition, the akharas began to be involved with festivals in which martial activities had played a relatively minor role in the past. Lathi play was unusually combined with Milad Sharif in 1923[200] and martial displays were organised on the occasion of Id in 1924.[201] An indication of the rapid growth of these akharas in this period and the extent of participation in them comes from a congregation of some akhara participants after the Mohurram in 1923. A section of the participants, numbering 2,500, gathered after the festival. Awards for excellence in performance were distributed by Zahur Ahmed, a prominent Muslim lawyer of Allahabad, to twenty-five of the akharas

---

[194] *PAI*, No. 42, 2 November 1929.
[195] *NNR*, No. 35/1923, pp. 2–3.
[196] *PAI*, No. 34, 1 September 1923; *PAI*, No. 40, 20 October 1923, estimated that 600 people in 31 Muslim akharas were learning sword wielding, and 250 Muslims in 8 akharas were practising wrestling; *PAI*, No 41, 27 October 1923, reported armed displays by 12 Muslim akharas, with 250 people participating; *PAI*, No. 34, 30 August 1924, reported the involvement of 400 people at a display of swordsmanship by Muslim akharas; *PAI*, No. 38, 27 September 1924; Confidential note on 'Communal Friction in the United Provinces, 1924'.
[197] *PAI*, No. 40, 20 October 1923.
[198] Note by DM, Allahabad, dated 23 May 1926, File No. 246/1926, Box No. 467, GAD, GUP, UPSA.
[199] *PAI*, No. 41, 27 October 1923.
[200] *PAI*, No. 42, 3 November 1923.
[201] *PAI*, No. 27, 12 July 1924.

which had participated in Mohurram processions.[202] It is significant in this respect that some of the mixed Hindu–Muslim akharas which originated before the 1920s now became based exclusively on one community or another,[203] just as bands playing music at the Ramlila processions excluded Muslims and became entirely composed of Hindus from this time.[204]

Armed religious parades and the craze for physical exercise among rival and competing Muslim and Hindu akharas generated extensive panic and a spate of communal clashes in the towns during the 1923–6 period. In Allahabad in 1923, there was widespread apprehension that riots would occur during the Hindu *Dadhkando* festival. All shops were closed on the day of Dadhkando and goods were removed from shops by some merchants for fear of looting. Many people attempted to flee from the city.[205] Though riots did not actually happen during the Mohurram–Dadhkando–Dusserah festival season in 1923, the scare in the city clearly indicates the extent of communal tensions arising from the aggressive competition between Hindu and Muslim akharas. In the following year again, in response to the armed displays during Dadhkando, large Ali Ghol akharas escorted processions at the time of the Islamic festival of *chehlum*, which had hitherto been a relatively insignificant public event. Communal tensions mounted, and police reports noted that bricks were being amassed in households for use in the event of a riot. A riot did eventually break out during the Dusserah that year.[206] During the next festival season in 1925, several communal skirmishes occurred at the time of Dadhkando, along with the violent exchange of bricks between some Hindu and Muslim mohallas at night.[207] Throughout this period and in 1926, the questions of playing music in front of mosques and of priority and precedence in processions and festivals remained central features of politics in Allahabad, and the flashpoint of many tense situations.[208] Moreover, while various Muslim groups stepped up their religious organisation in response to aggressive Hindu expansion, Islamic counter initiatives, even if defensive in nature, were no less martial and violent. Clearly, the institutionalisation of religious mobilisation among the poor through Hindu and Muslim akharas and volunteer corps, their entrenchment in the locality, and

[202] *PAI*, No. 36, 15 September 1923.
[203] Ibid.
[204] *PAI*, No. 39, 4 October 1924.
[205] *PAI*, No. 37, 22 September 1923.
[206] *PAI*, No. 36, 13 September 1924; No. 37, 20 September 1924; No. 38, 27 September 1924; No. 39, 4 October 1924; No. 40, 11 October 1924.
[207] *PAI*, No. 34, 5 September 1925; No. 37, 26 September 1925.
[208] *PAI*, No. 16, 1 May 1926.

their rivalry to outdo each other during festivals were important pre-
cipitants of communal clashes and neighbourhood religious tensions.

A further dimension to neighbourhood religious conflicts was the
gradual rise to prominence and penetration of a Hindu religious idiom
from the 1920s in the activities of the Congress or nationalist volunteer
corps. After the breakdown of the Khilafat–Non-Cooperation movement, a section of the Congress leadership openly adopted a Hindu
rhetoric. Leaders such as Madan Mohan Malaviya linked the resurgence
of the Hindu community with the achievement of national independence. The struggle within the Congress between the Swarajists and
Hindu nationalists such as Malaviya and the consequent prominence of
religious propaganda by some Congressmen have been documented by
historians.[209] However, it was not simply the Hindu rhetoric of provincial Congress leaders, but more importantly the actual involvement of
local Congress activists and volunteers in religious activities in the
towns, that reinforced communal tensions in urban neighbourhoods.[210]
Nationalist or social service oriented volunteer groups attached to the
Congress, for instance, often doubled and functioned as volunteer wings
of Hindu organisations.

The *Sewa Samiti* is an interesting example of this trend. The Sewa
Samiti was initially established at Allahabad between 1910 and 1912,
under the stewardship of provincial Hindu leaders such as Malaviya.[211]
Its declared task was to extend social service, to provide elementary
education and to train 'men as national missionaries', who would
promote 'by constitutional means the national interests of the Indian
people'.[212] Modelled on the Boy Scouts, but re-imagined in an indigenist
Hindu idiom, the Sewa Samiti movement aimed to train youth in
'patriotism, obedience, discipline, resourcefulness, self-reliance, physical culture, sense of honour and above all social service'.[213] Leaders
such as Malaviya saw the Sewa Samiti as the nucleus of a 'future citizen
army'.[214] The Sewa Samiti was thus conceived primarily as a nationalist
political organisation, but from an early stage the Sewa Samiti volunteers also played an active role at Hindu fairs and festivals. In March

[209] Page, *Prelude*, pp. 74–84; G. Pandey, *The Ascendancy of the Congress in Uttar Pradesh,
1926–34: A Study in Imperfect Mobilisation*, Delhi, 1978, pp. 115–27.
[210] Joshi, for instance, documents the religious affiliations of some Kanpur Congress
leaders. Joshi, 'Bonds of Community', pp. 273–5.
[211] S. L. Gupta, *Pandit Madan Mohan Malaviya: A Socio-political Study*, Allahabad, 1978,
pp. 355–8.
[212] 'The Sewa Samiti Movement in the United Provinces', A Note by the Assistant to the
Deputy Inspector General of Police, Criminal Investigation Department, UP, dated
18 December 1919, File No. 604/1920, Box No. 132, GAD, GUP, UPSA.
[213] Gupta, *Madan Mohan Malaviya*, pp. 355–7.
[214] Ibid., p. 357.

1917, the members of the Allahabad Sewa Samiti joined in Hindu processions during *Holi*, wearing nationalist 'Vandemataram' badges. In December of the same year, the Allahabad Sewa Samiti appealed for Rs 25,000 in order to raise 700 volunteers for service at the Kumbh Mela, a major Hindu fair. The appeal met with success and about 800 Sewa Samiti volunteers assembled at the Kumbh Mela in February 1918.[215] By the 1920s, the Sewa Samiti was openly promoted as both a Hindu and a nationalist volunteer corps. At a Sewa Samiti meeting at Lucknow in 1926, for instance, Jai Dayal Awasthi, a Congress activist, said that Sewa Samiti volunteers were training themselves alongside the Hindu Sabha volunteers to oppose the Muslims.[216]

In addition to Sewa Samiti activities, meetings and demonstrations of Congress volunteer groups were often the occasion of campaigns for Hindu advancement. Congress volunteers participated in religious festivals and processions and, indeed, they appeared to be involved almost exclusively in Hindu ones. Instances are legion. At a meeting during the Congress National Week celebrations in Lucknow in 1924, Gauri Shankar Misra, a Congress activist, urged sangathan and the raising of funds to promote Hindu volunteer organisations. Another activist, Gopi Nath, claimed that the Hindu Sabha, Sikh Dals and other Hindu organisations had been formed in alliance with the Congress to resist the British government.[217] In 1927, the local Congress organisation in Kanpur staged a Holi procession, which was itself an innovation.[218] In Benares, at a Hindu *Harinam Jas Sammelan* procession organised by the Sanatana Dharma Sabha in 1932, Congress volunteers participated with nationalist flags.[219] The town Congress committees also often funded Hindu akharas and volunteer corps.[220]

For Muslim groups, even more menacing than these Hindu religious activities were the actual anti-Islamic demonstrations by Congress activists and volunteers in the towns. In Kanpur in 1927, some Muslims had attacked a musical band accompanying a Hindu marriage procession. In retaliation, Congress volunteers, headed by the city's prominent Congress leaders, G. S. Vidyarthi, Narayan Prasad Arora, G. G. Jog and Bir Bahadur Tiwari, played music before the Moolganj mosque for forty

---

[215] 'The Sewa Samiti Movement in the United Provinces'.
[216] *PAI*, No. 16, 1 May 1926.
[217] *PAI*, No. 14, 5 April 1924.
[218] *PAI*, No. 13, 2 April 1927.
[219] *PAI*, No. 1, 9 January 1932.
[220] Evidence of Khaliluddin Ahmad Saheb, Honorary Assistant Collector, Kanpur, given to the Kanpur Riots Inquiry Commission. Reported in *The Pioneer* (Lucknow), 25 April 1931; also mentioned in Freitag, *Collective Action*, pp. 234, 241, 245.

minutes.[221] A few days later, 300 Congress Sewa Samiti volunteers with lathis and *kantas* (axes) went in procession with a musical band to a mosque and played.[222] In connection with the same dispute, a *Nagar Kirtan* (singing of devotional songs) procession organised by the Arya Samaj, which was attended by 4,000 people, including Congress volunteers and prominent Congress leaders such as Dr Jawaharlal Rohatgi, deliberately halted before a mosque to play music.[223] The signal that these events and activities sent to the Muslims about the Congress could scarcely have been mitigated by the fact that some of the Congress leaders and activists involved in these were known for their 'secular' attitude and sympathy for the Muslims, such as Ganesh Shankar Vidyarthi, who was to be killed during the 1931 Kanpur riots while trying to save some Muslim people.[224] Not surprisingly, Urdu newspapers of the 1920s and 1930s reported the alarm caused to Muslims by such activities. One newspaper was surely not an exception in stating in 1924 that Muslims were fearful of organised attacks by Hindus, who not only professed to be Congressmen but also openly promoted shuddhi and sangathan.[225] The same newspaper was reported to have argued on another occasion that, in view of the shuddhi and sangathan activities of the Congress, it would appear that 'Muslims can get liberty in India on condition that they accept the Aryan civilisation'. The paper concluded, 'if this is so, they [the Muslims] should discard the Congress as useless and should themselves find out the way of their salvation'.[226]

Tanzeem naturally came to encapsulate a reaction against such growing and obvious links between Hinduism and Congress nationalism at the local level. This aspect of tanzeem gained further importance in the early 1930s, within a context of the aggressive expansion and frenetic activities of Congress volunteer corps in urban neighbourhoods during the Civil Disobedience movement. These Congress volunteers often tried to force Muslim groups to fall into line. They also expressed overt opposition to the tanzeem movement, often through aggressive or offensive language and gestures.[227] For instance, a number of those giving evidence to the Kanpur Riots Inquiry Commission in 1931 reported that the *Vanar Sena* volunteers of the Congress took out *prabhat pheries* (morning processions) in the course of which they regularly shouted strong anti-Muslim and anti-tanzeem

[221] *PAI*, No. 7, 19 February 1927.
[222] *PAI*, No. 8, 26 February 1927.
[223] *PAI*, No. 10, 12 March 1927.
[224] A similar case is cited in Pandey, *Construction*, pp. 256–7.
[225] *NNR*, No. 36/1924, p. 2, cites the *Al Khalil*.
[226] *NNR*, No. 30/1923, p. 4, cites the *Al Khalil*.
[227] Joshi, 'Bonds of Community', pp. 275–6.

slogans.[228] These developments affected the character and orientation of the tanzeem movement in the 1930s. The target of tanzeem now became not only Hindu resurgence but also increasingly and more clearly the Congress, as the party became more and more obviously implicated in Hindu revival at the local level, which was evident from the conduct of its volunteers and activists in the urban neighbourhood. A pamphlet entitled 'Congress aur Mussalman', printed and widely circulated in Kanpur in 1930, expressed the opinion that the shariat does not allow Muslims to cooperate with the Congress or to take part in a movement which aims merely at establishing Ramraj,[229] presumably because this projected future nation and the reign of Ram would be akin to *dar-ul-harb* (infidel territory), and would have no place for Muslims. The direct experience of the Muslim poor of interlinked Congress and Hindu religious mobilisation in the locality and a sense of onslaught on their rituals and practices, as well as on their political autonomy, now opened up the issue of their own space in the future nation. The idea could take root among the Muslim poor that they were an abused or embattled minority, at the hands not just of the British but also of the Congress and Hindu groups. This was clearly a shift from the Khilafat period, and manifested itself in more concerted religious activities by the Muslim poor. Such activities were now driven by the need to express their distinctive identity and to inscribe their presence and space in the political landscape and ritual culture of the towns, and by implication to stake their claim in the future nation.

Thus, in Kanpur, by the summer of 1930, tanzeem volunteer corps and akharas had been formed in almost every mohalla where Muslims lived.[230] The committee constituted by the Congress to inquire into the Kanpur riot of 1931 reported that, in the period before the riot, 160 new anjumans had sprung up in the city, usually connected with a mosque, with the number of volunteers running into thousands.[231] These volunteer corps patrolled various neighbourhoods every day,[232] often armed with lathis, spears, swords and kantas.[233] While the assorted tanzeem organisations were rooted in their various mohallas, on Sundays they amalgamated in collective processions and the number

---

[228] Evidence of Riaz Ali, given to the Kanpur Riots Inquiry Commission, 1931, reported in *The Leader* (Allahabad), 29 April 1931; *Tanzeem* in Kanpur has been described in Freitag, *Collective Action*, pp. 230–9; Joshi, 'Bonds of Community', pp. 273–5; *KRIC Report*, pp. 8–13.

[229] *PAI*, No. 25, 28 June 1930.

[230] Reported in *The Pioneer*, 26 April 1931; Barrier, *Roots of Communal Politics*, p. 256.

[231] Barrier, *Roots of Communal Politics*, p. 256.

[232] *PAI*, No. 31, 9 August 1930; Barrier, *Roots of Communal Politics*, pp. 256–7.

[233] *PAI*, No. 43, 1 October 1930.

of processionists swelled on the way.[234] Local tanzeem akharas also often gathered at one place for drills and armed parades. On one occasion in August 1930, 4,000–5,000 Muslims were reported to have participated in akhara performances.[235] In addition to staging armed displays, tanzeem organisations and activities highlighted the distinctive marks of Islam. Tanzeem processionists carried flags and banners in green – the colour signifying Islam. During their drills and physical exercises the volunteers issued words of command in Persian, a language associated with Islam.[236] Some also wore khaki uniforms and in their processions sang tanzeem songs, which abused Hindu shuddhi initiatives and urged Muslims to rise to the defence of their religion.[237] Tanzeem volunteers patrolling the streets everyday concentrated on preaching strict religious conduct.[238] They shouted slogans such as 'Say your prayers regularly', 'Allah-o-Akbar' or 'Islam Zindabad', and neighbourhood tanzeem committees urged residents of their mohallas carefully to observe Islamic religious practices.[239]

A major thrust of the Kanpur tanzeem movement in the 1930s, as in the previous decade, was the elaboration of religious festivals. Unprecedentedly large processions were organised for Barawafat and Rajbi Sharif in 1930, 1931 and 1932, with, for instance, 30,000–35,000 people participating in the Barawafat procession in August 1930,[240] and 40,000 joining the 1931 Rajbi procession.[241] Daily meetings with large gatherings were held during the 1932 Rajbi festival, which unusually spread over several days.[242] Some of these festivals registered striking expansion in direct retaliation against the proliferation of Hindu festivals. In 1932, the relatively new innovation of the Rathyatra procession by the Arya Samaj amassed 40,000 people, and in riposte Barawafat was celebrated with great éclat, and Milad meetings were planned on public roads, but were prohibited by police orders.[243] After the largest ever Dusserah in the history of Kanpur was organised in 1930,[244] in the following year in retaliation, and in the wake of a serious riot, the

234 Freitag, *Collective Action*, p. 237.
235 *PAI*, No. 32, 16 August 1930; Barrier, *Roots of Communal Politics*, p. 256.
236 *PAI*, No. 39, 3 October 1931.
237 Barrier, *Roots of Communal Politics*, pp. 256–7; translations of tanzeem songs were submitted to the Kanpur Riots Inquiry Commission, some of which have been cited in Freitag, *Collective Action*, p. 235.
238 *PAI*, No. 31, 9 August 1930.
239 *PAI*, No. 31, 9 August 1930; No. 32, 16 August 1930; also cited in Freitag, *Collective Action*, pp. 235–7; *PAI*, No. 43, 1 October 1930; No. 15, 18 April 1931.
240 *PAI*, No. 32, 16 August 1930; Barrier, *Roots of Communal Politics*, p. 256.
241 *PAI*, No. 49, 12 December 1931; No. 50, 19 December 1931.
242 *PAI*, No. 50, 17 December 1932.
243 *PAI*, No. 28, 16 July 1932; No. 30, 30 July 1932.
244 *PAI*, No. 40, 11 October 1930.

Mohurram celebration was on a much larger scale than in previous years.[245] Religious meetings, especially Maulud gatherings, became the forum for mounting rhetorical attacks against Hindu revivalism and the Congress.[246]

The importance of all these developments in religious organisation and celebration lay in their depth, spread and rootedness in the neighbourhoods, involving large numbers over vast areas. Police reports throughout 1930 and 1931 remarked on the increasing pace and strength of tanzeem in Kanpur, with more and more meetings, larger numbers attending meetings and festivals, mounting political propaganda, anti-Congress political demonstrations, and the consequent spate of clashes with Hindu or Congress volunteers.[247] This, not unexpectedly, bred very intense communal tensions between rival Hindu and Muslim groups in the urban localities. Such tensions often escalated into riots, and contributed to an increase in the scale of clashes and violence when riots did occur. Thus, for instance, the March 1931 riots in Kanpur were remarkable for the sheer number of violent incidents, spread all over the town and involving many different local groups.[248] These riots were indeed unprecedented in this respect and should rightly be considered a landmark. The riots indicated the extensive spread as well as the local rootedness and penetration of competitive religious mobilisation in the urban neighbourhoods. Not surprisingly, the competition in the locality between the Hindu akharas and the prabhat pheries of Congress volunteers on the one hand, and the Muslim tanzeem organisations, on the other, was identified by the Kanpur Riots Inquiry Commission as a 'major predisposing' cause of the riot in 1931.[249] The Kanpur riot has been seen to signify a clash between two communities, whose members participated in a wider and more generalised, supra-local religious identity and a sense of shared interests.[250] The localised nature of clashes in the riots, however, calls for a qualification of this proposition. The dispersed nature of the religious activities that underpinned the riots warrants a re-examination of the notion that these riots signalled the collective imagination of shared interests of the community by diverse sections of Muslims.

[245] *PAI*, No. 22, 6 June 1931.
[246] Barrier, *Roots of Communal Politics*, pp. 239–40.
[247] See, for instance, *PAI*, No. 34, 30 August 1930; No. 35, 6 September 1930; No. 36, 13 September 1930; No. 39, 4 October 1930, as well as almost every weekly report in 1931.
[248] Pandey, *Ascendancy*, pp. 129–42; Freitag, *Collective Action*, pp. 244–5; Joshi, 'Bonds of Community', pp. 269–71, The Kanpur riots of 1931 have been very well documented in the *KRIC Report* and Barrier, *Roots of Communal Politics*.
[249] *KRIC Report*, pp. 7–12.
[250] Freitag, *Collective Action*, pp. 239–48.

The most significant fact about tanzeem was not only that it was rooted in the locality, but also that it came to represent the independent political initiative of the poor and the growing distance between them and the local leadership. 'One remarkable thing' about the Kanpur tanzeem movement, reported by the Kanpur Riots Inquiry Commission, was that 'no leading Muslim belonged at any given time to the tanzeem',[251] and that no central tanzeem committee coordinated the diverse neighbourhood-based initiatives.[252] A police report also noted that at a tanzeem procession of 30,000–35,000 people on 8 August 1930, the day of the Maulud festival, 'better classes of Muslims held aloof'.[253] Maulana Abdul Qafi of the Anjuman Islamia, an organisation of prominent Muslims in the city, mentioned to the Riots Inquiry Commission that a similarly large tanzeem procession was taken out on 21 December 1930, but asserted that this procession 'had nothing to do with our organisation', referring to the tanzeem committee that had been formed by the town's leading Muslims.[254] Narayan Prasad Nigam, Vice President of the Kanpur Municipal Board, in his evidence confirmed that he had never noticed any prominent Muslim person of the town taking part in tanzeem activities.[255] Clearly, in Kanpur and elsewhere too, one stream of the tanzeem movement was undoubtedly not related to the efforts of the local leadership, but was a product of initiatives by disparate groups of the Muslim poor in their neighbourhoods, 'without reliance on, or much public support from, the prominent Muslims of the city',[256] and, at times, in the face of elite opposition and censure. Two parallel and even divergent or conflicting strands of tanzeem initiative were, thus, elaborated, and indeed tanzeem seemed to deepen political tensions within the putative Muslim community, in at least two ways.

First, the religious ferment amongst the poor began to pose a fundamental problem of political control for the leaders, which was already becoming manifest towards the later part of the Khilafat movement.[257] The ulema and local political leaders were, of course, eager to mobilise mass support, but on their own terms and under their own control and direction. Yet they now increasingly found themselves being overtaken by their followers, and at times even caught unawares in the consequent conflagration of riots and violence, as suggested by the evidence given to

---

251 *KRIC Report*, p. 11.
252 Ibid.
253 *PAI*, No. 32, 16 August 1930.
254 Reported in *The Pioneer*, 26 April 1931.
255 Ibid., 24 April 1931.
256 Freitag, *Collective Action*, p. 239.
257 *PAI*, No. 16, 21 April 1923.

the Kanpur Riots Inquiry Commission by prominent Muslims, who either claimed ignorance of popular initiatives or disowned them. As Freitag has pointed out, the tanzeem movement 'most dramatically' posed the problems 'of weakening of control over those involved in collective action'.[258] Moreover, ardent public expressions of attachment to religious symbols as an extension of personal devotion had subversive political implications in that they could help to articulate individual autonomy and initiative and thus potentially undermine the authority of leaders.[259]

Secondly, the tanzeem initiatives of the poor would also have attracted the censure of a section of the religious leadership for their excess of emotional zeal and public religious demonstrations, detracting from true piety. The ulema of the Deoband school, in particular, had already been averse to the elaboration of such festivals as the Maulud or Rajbi Sharif, for not conforming to textual prescriptions. The growing stridency of these festivals among the poor would now have irked such ulema even more. The unbridled emphasis on armed displays and processions could be considered to be increasingly undermining the true spirit of the festivals, with non-scriptural accretions being enhanced at the cost of reverence for the Prophet. Innovations in religious observance could not sit comfortably with the eagerness of a section of the religious leadership to promote a pure and reformed community of believers. Not surprisingly, a section of the local ulema vehemently disowned the more vigorous tanzeem initiatives in Kanpur. Indeed, this appears to have caused a rift among the ulema themselves in Kanpur, with those who supported the popular brand of tanzeem forming a separate Jamiat-i-ulema-i-Hind, Kanpur.[260]

More importantly, concerns for the purity of religious practices increasingly seemed to go hand in hand with a growing suspicion of or aversion toward lower-class culture and practices,[261] most likely born of a fear of the autonomous initiative and political assertion of the Muslim poor, which characterised the tanzeem movement. There were efforts on the part of the leadership and the ulema to elicit, or if necessary enforce and impose, conformity with scriptural norms. This was attempted by the Anjuman Hifazat-ul-Islam, Anjuman Tabligh-ul-Islam and Anjuman Islamia in Kanpur, formed on the initiative of some of the

[258] Freitag, *Collective Action*, p. 238.

[259] Robinson, 'Religious Change and the Self', pp. 6–7, 9–10.

[260] I. H. Qureshi, *Ulema in Politics: A Study Relating to the Political Activities of the Ulema in the South Asian Subcontinent from 1536 to 1947*, Delhi, 1980, p. 302.

[261] Nita Kumar discusses the aversion of Muslim elites to the lower-class culture of the artisans in Benares today, and traces the development of this trend gradually from the early part of the twentieth century. Kumar, *Artisans*, pp. 138–9, 145–6, 211.

prominent notables and ulema of the city. They organised groups of preachers to hold regular religious sessions in urban neighbourhoods, in order to ensure better observance of religious practices and to promote adherence to the scriptures, rather than to local, popular practices.[262] The Anjuman Hifazat-ul-Islam, in particular, tended to be somewhat forceful and overzealous, even coercive, in seeking to create better Muslims, for the Anjuman went so far as to threaten those who did not conform with boycott or eviction from their houses. This Anjuman was also eager to prevent the involvement of Muslims in Hindu festivals such as Diwali, and was especially concerned to curb certain forms of lower-class activities during festivals, such as gambling.[263] Clearly, 'Islamisation' was a stratified process, with the leaders chiefly concerned with purified religious conduct and controlled religious mobilisation of a wider constituency of the Muslim poor in the public arena, while the Muslim poor were more inclined towards overt public enactment of rituals or martial display, which could enable them to inscribe their own space in urban politics. The tensions within tanzeem were not simply about two different – elite and popular – versions of religious practices jostling against each other or a simple separation of and distancing between elite and popular culture,[264] but also about two sets of social forces locked in a struggle for control and self-expression. With tanzeem, then, as with some of the Hindu religious festivals, the questions of the purification of religious tradition and reform of or control over lower-class practices – and consequently the issue of the expression of lower-class identity and independent political initiative – all increasingly emerged as central points of contestation in Islamic religious resurgence. These contradictions were, moreover, under-pinned by the developing forces of urban class tensions in the interwar period.

It should be mentioned here that the concern to control and curb lower-class religious activities was not uniform in all towns. In Alla-habad, some leading Muslims encouraged or patronised tanzeem activ-ities and supported the akharas,[265] and they appeared to be somewhat less anxious about lower-class religious zeal than in Kanpur or Benares. This was possibly because the shrine-based patronage structures, dis-cussed earlier, under the leadership of sufi pirs and ulema had ensured

[262] *PAI*, No. 21, 2 June 1923; No. 26, 7 July 1923.
[263] *PAI*, No. 42, 25 October–1 November 1924.
[264] The remarkable separation of elite and popular culture in north India from the 1920s as part of a history of nationalist, Hindu and Islamic social reformism, especially in Benares, has been discussed, for instance, in Kumar, *Artisans*, and Freitag (ed.), *Culture and Power*.
[265] *PAI*, No. 36, 15 September 1923.

that these religious leaders of Allahabad were better able to exercise influence over their followers, and the problem of local control was less acute than, say, in Kanpur. In some ways the Allahabad leadership was also distinctive in that it sought to provide a focus of politics for poorer Muslims on a range of material issues, which could further ensure that the poor did not step entirely out of line. In Kanpur, the local leadership had limited control over the tanzeem initiatives of the poor. These differences, in fact, serve to highlight the point that the question of political control came to the fore with the tanzeem movement, and indeed deepened internal tensions within what appeared to be shared initiatives for religious assertion and defence of 'community'.

A brief digression to a different context and a later period of religious assertion among poorer Muslims would further illuminate how the attempts of the poor to express their own religious initiative and thus to make an impact on the urban public arena encountered elite rejection. A problem similar to that of tanzeem over discipline and control was to become evident a few years later in Lucknow in the course of the conflict between the Shia and Sunni Muslim sects between 1935 and 1939. The sectarian dispute originated between 1905 and 1907, when an upwardly mobile section of Sunnis as well as some politically assertive lower-class groups such as labourers, butchers and ekka drivers defied attempts by some among the Shia leadership, who came mainly from the erstwhile ruling classes and elites of Lucknow, to impose certain changes and reformed practices in the celebration of the Mohurram festival.[266] Sunni groups, concerned to contest the authority of the Shia leadership, instituted some new practices of their own, especially the recitation of verses called the *Madeh Sahaba*, which were offensive to Shia religious sensibilities and around which considerable local tensions were generated, contributing to the outbreak of violence between the two sects. The first phase of Shia–Sunni disputes in Lucknow abated by 1908, but resurfaced again in a second protracted episode from 1935 until 1939. This second stage of the controversy had several new political dimensions,[267] but the most relevant development for the discussion here related to the significant initiatives displayed by poorer Sunni Muslims and the consequent fissures within the Sunni community. A substantial section of the educated Sunni leadership as well as several of the influential ulema, including those of the two prominent seminaries of Firanghi Mahal and the Nadwat-ul-Ulema, held aloof from the more overtly agitational and confrontational aspects of the Sunni campaign for rights to recite the Madeh Sahaba and to practise their own preferred

[266] Freitag, *Collective Action*, pp. 249–79.
[267] Ibid.

version of festival celebrations. This moderate leadership favoured a negotiated settlement with the Shia community, in cooperation with the provincial government. The District Magistrate of Lucknow reported that this 'Constitutional Party', supported by 'more respectable' and 'responsible' Sunnis of the town, was 'definitely against any breach of orders' given by the government. They were eager for a peaceful solution, which would avoid outbreak of disorder or violence. In contrast, the local Ahrar Party, with a more militant, activist political orientation, according to the District Magistrate contained 'no man of a moderate social position in its ranks', and was taking out 'new and unheard of processions with public recital of the Madeh Sahaba'. However, the 'men of high position' of the Constitutional Party, although desiring moderation in political action on the part of the Ahrar Party, were, none the less, disinclined to engage in negotiations with those 'whom they regard[ed] as riff-raff'.[268] In addition to the Ahrar Party, a local alim, Maulana Abdul Shakoor, head of a Sunni religious institution – Dar-ul-Muballagin – established in 1931, was noted for his anti-Shia militancy and had a substantial following among the town's poorer Sunnis.[269] The neighbourhood of Patanala, where the Dar-ul-Muballagin was based, was frequently the flashpoint of agitation and violence. Reports on the Shia–Sunni disputes clearly indicate the popular support enjoyed by these two militant strands of the Sunni political campaigns. The Deputy Commissioner, for instance, observed that the civil disobedience agitation, declared by the more radical Sunni leaders and largely opposed by the moderates, attracted *razakars* or volunteers from the 'lowest strata of Lucknow Muslims'.[270] These developments in Lucknow in the late-1930s, which were remarkably similar to those during the tanzeem movement of the early 1930s, not only demonstrate the ongoing efforts at political assertion by the poorer Muslims through public religious expression, but also reveal the persistent attempts by the poor to seize political control and initiative, even in

[268] Deputy Commissioner, Lucknow, to Commissioner, Lucknow, Letter No. D.O. 215–C.R., dated 29 August 1936, File No. 5/15/1936, Home Poll., NAI, GOI. Social tensions among Sunnis are also mentioned in Kotwali, Chauk, Lucknow, to Commissioner, Lucknow, Letter No. D.O. 185, undated; Deputy Commissioner, Lucknow, to Commissioner, Lucknow, Letter No. D.O. 253–C.R., dated 25 April 1939, File No. 65/1939, Box No. 602, GAD, GUP, UPSA.

[269] Ganju, 'Muslims of Lucknow', p. 287; Deputy Commissioner, Lucknow, to Commissioner, Lucknow, Letter No. D.O. 112–C.R., dated 2 March 1939, File No. 65/1939, Box No. 602, GAD, GUP, UPSA; Note by Khan Bahadur Rahman Baksh Kadri, P.A., to D.C., dated 7 November 1938, File No. 5–20(25)/(1938–9, 1940–41), Lucknow Deputy Commissioner's Office Records.

[270] Deputy Commissioner, Lucknow, to Premier, UP, letter dated 26 October 1938, File No. 5–20(25)/(1938–9, 1940–41), Lucknow Deputy Commissioner's Office Records.

a place such as Lucknow with a history of established religious leadership. Indeed, the leadership appeared to have lost control and abdicated its role in the wider political arena by holding aloof from the activist agitations, and sought instead to rely on the government to bring about a constitutional solution and thus to curb the tide of popular militancy. As Freitag notes, in this case 'the pattern experienced in other north Indian cities, in which elites first tried to purge public arena activity through reformism and then increasingly withdrew from collective exercises, held true'.[271]

To return to the history of tanzeem in the early 1930s, the discussion on the tanzeem movement has so far concentrated on its relation to resurgent Hinduism and Congress nationalism from the mid-1920s onwards, and the consequent competitive religious mobilisation in urban neighbourhoods. However, the longer-term trends of Islamic assertion, which related to artisanal identity, egalitarian aspirations and an awareness of deprivation, also persisted, although these elements seemed to enjoy less overt emphasis than anti-Hindu and anti-Congress ideas. In some cases though, egalitarian ideas and artisanal identity found further elaboration in the interwar period and became a significant factor in tanzeem initiatives, especially in Benares. Here, a strident tanzeem movement emerged by the mid-1920s and accelerated in the early 1930s among Muslim artisans – the ansari or momin weavers, who were engaged in the silk-weaving industry. These weavers formed not only the substantial majority of the population of the Muslim poor in the town in the 1930s, but also 25–30 per cent of the overall urban population.[272] Their residential settlements and their places of work, usually one and the same, were concentrated mainly in the Madanpura, Alaipura, Adampura and Jaitpura areas in the town. Their common occupation as silk weavers and their artisanal identity as momin-ansaris, as well as their shared settlements, could form the basis of political solidarity.

In Benares, resurgent Hinduism had been in steady ascendance from the nineteenth century. Not only was the town believed to be one of the most important Hindu sacred places in north India, but also, as Vasudha Dalmia has shown, from the eighteenth century onwards and

---

[271] Freitag, *Collective Action*, p. 277.
[272] *BEC*, II, pp. 390, 372: 35,000 people were engaged in the silk industry in the early 1930s in Benares according to evidence given to the Provincial Banking Enquiry Committee of 1931. The size of the weaving community would have been larger with the dependants and families of the actual weavers. The total population of Benares in 1931 was 201,137. *Census 1931*, p. 127; *Handloom and Mills Committee, 1942*, pp. 44, 66. According to this report, in 1942 the size of the weaving community was 50,000, with about 25,000 looms.

more particularly in the nineteenth century, the city emerged as a key site for the definition of Hindu traditions in north India. This occurred initially under the patronage of local ruling houses and Brahmanical groups, and then under the auspices of an ascendant merchant community.[273] Benares was the nucleus of activity of the Hindu Sabha stalwart Madan Mohan Malaviya, the site of the Benares Hindu University, as well as a major focus of activity of the Arya Samaj and the Bharat Dharma Mahamandal.[274] It was also the centre of the Hindi-Nagri movement, led by a conservative alliance of upper-caste Hindus and commercial communities.[275] The Nagri Pracharani Sabha was based here and printing presses in the town produced the largest number of published works in Hindi in the province. Benares was also a key base of the *yadav* movement and militant shudra religious assertion. In the early 1920s, provincial-level shuddhi and sangathan campaigns were formally launched from Benares with great fanfare. It was here at a conference in 1923 that the Hindu Sabha joined the Arya Samaj formally in the shuddhi–sangathan onslaught.[276] The outcome was an extensive public focus not only on the 'purification' and inclusion of lower-caste groups in the Hindu fold, but also on the reconversion of lower-caste Muslims to Hinduism, with the Arya Samaj making most exaggerated claims about its proselytising achievements, thus fuelling a sense of threat among Muslim groups.[277] The ranks of the religious activists of the Samaj and the Hindu Sabha were swelled by Congress workers by the early 1930s, especially during the Civil Disobedience movement. Although the Congress organisations did not directly sponsor shuddhi and sangathan work, the Arya Samaj activists who undertook these activities in Benares were also mostly Congress members.[278] The overall tenor of much of the combined activities of the religious organisations and the Congress from the 1920s was one of reformism in public life, some of which was specifically geared to uplift and 'improve' the conditions of the lower classes. Such reformist zeal was invariably combined with a negative view of lower-class practices, a moral discourse and an interventionist social reform activism, which took such concrete forms as preaching the virtues of thrift and temperance

---

[273] Dalmia, *Nationalization of Hindu Traditions*, pp. 50–145.

[274] Nevill, *Benares: A Gazetteer*, p. 94.

[275] C. King, *One Language, Two Scripts: The Hindi Movement in Nineteenth-century North India*, Bombay, 1994, pp. 141–8.

[276] R. A. Gordon, 'The Hindu Mahasabha and the Indian National Congress', *MAS*, 9, 2, 1975, p. 170.

[277] *PAI*, No. 16, 21 April 1923. An Arya Samaj activist in Benares orchestrated the claim that 12,000 Rajputs who had converted to Islam had been won back to Hinduism.

[278] *PAI*, No. 15, 14 April 1923.

and attempts to promote these by coercion, if necessary, as well as efforts to reform the nature of public arena activities and religious celebrations.[279] For the Muslim weavers, all these activities, and above all the reconversion propaganda, constituted ever-increasing attempts to interfere in, overwhelm and erode their religious and cultural identities.

Their response was to rally around Baba Khalil Das, a new leader who shot to unprecedented prominence in Benares among the Muslim weavers in the late 1920s, mainly for his ability to stand up to the Hindu religious reformers and revivalists.[280] Baba Khalil Das came to Benares from Bihar at the time when the Arya Samaj stepped up its shuddhi and sangathan programmes.[281] His main qualification was that he was well versed in Hindu religious scriptures and was thus able to hold his own against Hindu religious leaders in debates about caste, conversion and religion. He was called Baba Khalil Das *Chaturvedi*, supposedly for his knowledge of the four Vedas.[282] The tanzeem movement gained ground under Khalil Das by the early 1930s, and large meetings, at times attended by up to 25,000–30,000 people, were frequently reported to have been addressed by Khalil Das.[283] This movement demonstrated a number of interlinked dimensions, many of which have been seen earlier in the cases of Kanpur and Allahabad.

Drawing upon trends of religious change which were gradually developing from the later nineteenth century, the weavers gave more and more prominence to Islamic religious symbols in public life, specifically as a counter to Hindu or Congress onslaught. Tanzeem volunteers wore green badges and carried red flags with white crescents, all of which were symbolic markers of Islam. They also wore and urged the use of Turkish caps as the chief emblem of Islamic dignity, and accused Gandhi of duping Muslims into wearing the Gandhi cap and thus erasing their identity.[284] They urged greater adherence to Islamic practices, including the abandonment of intoxicants.[285] In addition, Khalil Das emphasised self-protection, unity and organisation for the weavers as well as the need for literacy and a

[279] Kumar, *Artisans*, pp. 174–97. S. B. Freitag, 'State and Community: Symbolic Popular Protest in Banaras's Public Arenas', in Freitag (ed.), *Culture and Power*, pp. 223, 225–6.

[280] *PAI*, No. 27, 11 July 1931, noted that Khalil Das' followers were chiefly Muslim weavers.

[281] *The Leader*, 29 April 1931, p. 5.

[282] Interview with Nuruddin Ahmad, weaver, Pilikothi, Benares; *Ranbheri* (published by the Benares City Congress Committee), 29 August 1930, p. 7.

[283] Reported in *Aj* (Benares), 18 April 1931; *The Leader*, 29 April 1931, p. 5; *PAI*, No. 29, 26 July 1930; No. 30, 2 August 1930.

[284] *PAI*, No. 21, 2 June 1923.

[285] *PAI*, No. 28, 19 July 1930.

printing press.[286] Numerous tanzeem akharas and volunteer corps were formed in the neighbourhoods of the Muslim artisans. They not only staged drills and parades with arms, but also organised religious instruction and training for basic literacy.[287] A resolute anti-Congress position was also expressed through the tanzeem initiatives and meetings.[288] Khalil Das was reported to have led large processions, whose object was thought to be to demonstrate the strength of the Muslims to the local Hindus, who had been pressing them against their will to join the Congress and to undertake the picketing of cloth shops selling 'foreign' material during the Civil Disobedience campaigns.[289]

As in the case of the Kanpur tanzeem, in Benares too Khalil Das' movement represented lower-class self-assertion, as much as defence against Hindu onslaught. Local Muslim leaders remained distant from and critical of Khalil Das and his followers. One newspaper report at the time claimed that 'leading Muslims' of the town had never participated in Khalil Das' movement.[290] Indeed, Khalil Das seems to have been the target of attack from all quarters for what was seen as his rabble-rousing and fomenting of religious hatred. The tanzeem movement he led among the poorer Muslims was held responsible for the communal riot in Benares in 1931.[291] Moreover, a section of better-off Muslims in the town, who belonged to the same artisanal community of ansaris as the mass of the poor weavers, but who were often independent owners of loom or weaving workshops, employers of labour or cloth merchants and who lived in the more affluent neighbourhoods such as Madanpura, appear to have held aloof from Khalil Das' movement. More importantly, from this time onwards, they gradually became more scriptural and puritanical in their own religious approach. Mary Searle-Chatterjee shows that, from the 1930s, a movement towards purist 'Wahabi' Islam began to gain ground among a prominent cluster of better-off merchant families of artisan origin, who appeared to set themselves apart deliberately from the poorer sections and looked towards the orthodoxy of Deoband for religious inspiration.[292] Nita Kumar too has pointed out that, among weavers today, 'wahabiyat' is considered to be an affair of the rich and influential Muslims who, in alliance with the Hindu

[286] *PAI*, No. 27, 11 July 1931; No. 29, 26 July 1930.
[287] *PAI*, No. 4, 3 February 1934.
[288] *PAI*, No. 22, 7 June 1930; No. 29, 26 July 1930.
[289] *PAI*, No. 27, 12 July 1930.
[290] *The Leader*, 29 April 1931, p. 5.
[291] *The Leader*, 19 February 1931, p. 10; *Aj*, 14 February 1931, p. 4.
[292] Mary Searle-Chatterjee, '"Wahabi" Sectarianism among Muslims of Banaras', *Contemporary South Asia*, 3, 2, 1994, pp. 83–95.

merchant-moneylenders, were concerned to preserve a 'hierarchy where weavers were at the bottom of the ladder'.[293]

The spread of the tanzeem movement in Benares further fuelled the religious expansion of Hindu organisations, and contributed to an escalation in local competition and communal conflict. Khalil Das' movement elicited a counter-reaction from the Arya Samaj and from such Hindu shudra caste groups as the ahirs, who were active participants in volunteer corps and akharas, and who, in Benares, were involved in an especially active yadav caste movement. On the initiative of local Arya Samaj activists such as Ganga Singh and Ram Anurag Sharma, the Mahabir Dal volunteers regularly patrolled urban mohallas in 1930–1 to prevent what they saw as the tanzeem menace. Efforts were stepped up to form Mahabir Dals, Hanuman Dals and wrestling akharas.[294] On one occasion, a large procession of 10,000 Hindus, which included Congress volunteers carrying the national flag, was organised by the Mahabir Dal as a direct retort to Baba Khalil Das' tanzeem processions.[295] The police also reported that purchases of daggers, swords and spears had increased considerably among Hindu volunteer groups in 1930 in response to the tanzeem movement.[296] The ahirs in particular, who played an important role in militant Hinduism, retaliated strongly against the tanzeem movement. In July 1930, about 200 ahirs marched in procession to Trilochan, a sacred Hindu site, and performed a religious ceremony in response to tanzeem processions.[297] Thus, in riposte to the organisational endeavours of the Muslim artisans, various groups of Hindus in Benares redoubled their own religious initiatives. Animosities and tensions in urban neighbourhoods increased and took the form of defence of space and territory through neighbourhood patrols and vigilante organisations. This created a relentless cycle and an escalating spiral of mutual competition and hostility among local Hindu and Muslim religious organisations. This led several newspapers to attribute the Benares riots of February 1931 to the tanzeem movement and the growing rivalries between Hindu and Muslim organisations.[298]

Tanzeem in Benares encapsulated an expression of resistance by the Muslim artisans against the Hindu merchants. The Hindu merchants controlled the financing, production and marketing of silk cloth and

[293] Kumar, *Artisans*, p. 138.
[294] *PAI*, No. 30, 1 August 1931.
[295] *PAI*, No. 30, 2 August 1930; No. 28, 18 July 1931; No. 29, 25 July 1931; No. 30, 1 August 1931.
[296] *PAI*, No. 31, 9 August 1930.
[297] *PAI*, No. 30, 2 August 1930.
[298] *The Leader*, 19 February, 1931, p. 10; *Aj*, 14 February 1931, p. 4.

were the creditors and employers of the weavers. Sandria Freitag has argued that, until the economic depression, the weavers and the Hindu merchants had an economic relationship of interdependence in Benares, with the merchants supplying yarn to 'independent' self-employed artisans and marketing their products. This, Freitag claims, *inter alia* contributed to social and cultural integration between Hindus and Muslims in Benares. Communal relations were, thus, relatively harmonious until the ravages of the depression destabilised the relationship between weavers and merchants and caused a sharp break in 1930–1.[299] However, Freitag does not attach sufficient importance to the fact that the escalation of shuddhi and sangathan in the 1920s had already created religious tensions. More importantly, the relationship of interdependence had never been an equal one and the balance of economic power had been weighted in favour of the merchants, at least from the nineteenth century. The artisans may have been 'independent' in the sense of being self-employed, often working at home with their own looms, but they were dependent on the merchants for marketing their products, raw materials and credit. Indebtedness, importantly, was the most compelling form of dependence and brought about the dreaded lack of 'azadi' for the artisans, while it also caused abject poverty in many cases. According to evidence given to the Banking Enquiry Committee in 1929, 60 per cent of artisans worked for middlemen and workshop owners, of whom only 25–30 per cent worked at home. Out of 35,000 persons engaged in the silk industry, more than half were reported to have been merely wage-earners.[300] The picture is, thus, more complex than Freitag envisaged. Social integration based on economic mutuality between Hindus and Muslims prior to the 1930s was hardly as significant as she suggests, and cannot adequately explain why religious conflicts were not acute in Benares until the 1920s. The intensification of religious competition between Hindus and Muslims from the 1920s provides a more plausible explanation for increasing sectarian tensions, leading to violence and riots by the early 1930s. Freitag is, however, right in identifying the depression as one of the contributing factors in sharpening contradictions between Hindu merchants and Muslim artisans. Although the material concerns of the weavers were articulated from the 1920s at tanzeem meetings,[301] it was in the early 1930s that these became especially prominent.

The tanzeem movement, in fact, became most strident in the early

[299] Freitag (ed.), *Culture and Power*, pp. 13–14; Freitag, 'State and Community', pp. 224–7.
[300] *BEC*, II, pp. 371–2, 390.
[301] *PAI*, No. 3, 24 January 1925.

1930s, at a time when demand for and the price of artisanal products slumped and exposed the artisans to greater economic hardships and increased their dependence on the merchant-financiers.[302] The merchants in Benares provided credit and yarn on loan either direct to weavers who worked at home, or to master-artisans *(karkhanadars)* who, in turn, employed weavers on a wage basis to work in workshops *(karkhanas)*. Both independent weavers and the karkhanadars supplied their finished products to the merchants for marketing, as neither had direct access to the markets.[303] These merchants-financiers were, as a result, able to skim off a good deal of the profits of the weavers.[304] Giving evidence to the Banking Enquiry Committee on the economic conditions in the silk industry, based on surveys conducted in 1929 at the time of the gradual onset of the depression, one witness wrote: 'More than half of them [weavers] are merely wage earners, and the rest, though working in slightly more favourable circumstances, are not better off and are fast being reduced to the position of wage earners . . . 90% of the weavers live on the bare subsistence level; . . . Most of the weavers are sunk deep in debt.'[305] In the middle of such already difficult circumstances, the depression struck the industry with full force. The slump in demand and prices, coupled with the dumping of cheap artificial silk products on the Indian markets, especially from Japan, adversely affected the silk-weaving industry, and had a particularly negative impact on wages.[306] The relatively high price of yarn owing to protective tariff duties further worsened the situation.[307] To add to the troubles of the weavers, the policy of the Congress to promote swadeshi meant that they encountered opposition for using mill-spun yarn.[308] A shift to more expensive handspun varieties would have further aggravated their economic hardship. Moreover, some of the merchant dealers were reported to have refused to buy cloth from the weavers if they did not use *khadi* and used this 'nationalist' argument to tighten their hold over the weavers.[309] As a consequence of all this, and especially because of falling demand, the weavers would inevitably have faced not only a reduction in their income or unemployment, but also greater indebtedness, especially to merchant-creditors, almost all of whom were Hindus.

[302] *Handloom and Mills Committee, 1942*, pp. 18–20.
[303] *BEC*, II, p. 372.
[304] Ibid., p. 390.
[305] Ibid., extracts from a survey of the small urban industries of Benares by S. N. Majumdar Choudhury.
[306] Annual Administration Report, UP, 1929–30; *Handloom and Mills Committee, 1942*, pp. 18–20.
[307] *Handloom and Mills Committee, 1942*, pp. 18–20.
[308] Ibid., p. 15.
[309] *PAI*, No. 24, 21 June 1930.

As discussed in chapter 2, the artisans worked within a system of baqidari payment, which meant that they took advance loans against future wages. With a collapse in demand for their goods and the consequent shortage of work, they were likely to have had mounting loans, and possibly forcible recovery by the creditors. This would have been the case for both the weavers who worked directly for the merchants and those based at workshops of karkhanadars. The karkhanadars would also have encountered mounting deficits and a credit squeeze with falling demand, and may well have been unable to maintain production, so failing to provide employment to the weavers and thus exposing them further to the exertions of the merchant-creditors. The karkhanadars themselves would have either faced economic ruin and joined the ranks of wage-earners, or tried to pass on their own losses to the workers. The depression, therefore, was likely to have generated some friction within the weaving community between the karkhanadars and their employees.[310] At the same time, it sharpened antagonisms against the Hindu merchant-financiers and, on occasion, tended to unite various segments of the weaving community – wage workers and workshop owners – in opposition to them.

Within such a context, the tanzeem movement could serve to articulate the intensifying material concerns of the weavers. Khalil Das started an Urdu weekly paper, *Khadim*, to instruct his followers, in which he advised them to practise thrift both to avoid indebtedness to Hindu merchants and to gain literacy, and urged them to unite against the merchants.[311] He also advocated the need for a bank for the Muslim artisans, presumably as the key means to erode their dependence on the Hindu financiers.[312] In 1933, at tanzeem religious congregations at the Fatman Idgah and the Latbhairo mosque, addressed by Baba Khalil Das and attended by 2,000 and 10,000 people, respectively, prayers were offered for the economic improvement of the artisan community and the revival of their trade.[313] Why should such economic concerns have been expressed in a religious idiom? The egalitarian content of Islam, with its message of redistribution and welfare of the poor popularised by the Islamic socialists, may well have prepared the ground for the Benares artisans to make religion their rallying ideology against economic exploitation. This resistance against merchants in a religious

---

[310] Even during better times, it seems that the relation between the karkhanadars and weavers was not too harmonious. An attempt to form a joint organisation of karkhanadars and weavers had failed in the early 1920s, although a panchayat of the karkhanadars existed to ensure control over the wage-earners. *BEC*, II, p. 371.

[311] *PAI*, No. 41, 17 October 1931; interview in Benares with Nuruddin Ahmed, weaver.

[312] *PAI*, No. 28, 18 July 1931.

[313] *PAI*, No. 26, 8 July 1933; No. 35, 9 September 1933.

idiom was also conditioned by the fact that the crucial economic divide between the weaving community, including the master-artisans, on the one hand, and their creditors and financiers, on the other, overlapped with a religious divide. It was also due in part, and more importantly, to the fact that Hindu revivalism and Congress ascendance in Benares marked the superior economic power of Hindu merchants, who did indeed finance and patronise many of these activities. The particular stridency of these activities in the 1920s and 1930s coincided precisely with the hardships of the depression, and economic subordination could thus be seen to be reinforced by political coercion, at times in quite obvious and overt ways – for instance, when some of these Hindu merchants tried to deploy their economic hold over the weavers to coerce them to use khadi, and refused to have transactions with them if they did not comply.[314] From the weavers' point of view, the figure of the Hindu merchant epitomised a continuum of oppression, directly or indirectly, stretching from economic exploitation, to religious aggression, to reformist and Congress onslaught. The antagonism of the artisans against the Hindu merchants was manifested during the major riots in Benares in February 1931. During the Civil Disobedience movement, a Muslim merchant, Agha Mohammad Jan, who had refused to fall in line with the economic boycott policy, died after being attacked by a Congress activist. His funeral procession was accompanied by 5,000 Muslims, many of whom donned tanzeem badges. Some processionists proceeded to destroy shops of Hindu merchants and rioting ensued in the bazars.[315] It should be borne in mind, however, that while the developments described here suggest that there were obvious signs of unity among weavers against the Hindu commercial classes, yet all could not have been well *within* the weaving community. For, squeezed as the karkhanadars were between the merchants and the weavers who worked for them, some would invariably have attempted to avoid their own ruin by seeking to pass on their losses to the workers. The consequent tensions within the community may thus have undermined internal cohesion. This quite possibly explains the lack of unanimity about Khalil Das' movement, as well as the emergence of more purist 'wahabi' religious tendencies among a section of somewhat better off Muslim merchants of weaver caste from this time,[316] who were aware of a threat from the religious assertion of the poorer weavers,

---

[314] *PAI*, No. 24, 21 June 1930.
[315] Extracts from a report on the Benares riots of 12–16 February 1931 taken from File No. 1089/1931, cited in File No. 10/19/31, Home Poll., GOI, NAI; File No. 1263/1931, Box No. 211, Police Department, GUP, UPSA; *Aj*, 13 February 1931, p. 4.
[316] Searle-Chatterjee, '"Wahabi" sectarianism', pp. 83–95.

under a new leader – Khalil Das – who provided an alternative locus of political authority and legitimacy. While puritanical practices amongst the better-off clearly encapsulated their attempts to define their own respectability and distance from the poorer members of the community, it is also possible that a stricter and more orthodox version of Islam could have been seen by them as a potential tool for social and moral intervention to discipline and subordinate the poor.

The economic dimension of the tanzeem movement was not confined to Benares, but was also significant in other towns, albeit with a somewhat different emphasis. The aim of tanzeem was not just to defend the faith or to organise against Hindu resurgence, but also to improve or safeguard the economic condition of Muslim groups, especially against mounting material pressures from the 1920s.[317] The economic boycott of Hindu establishments thus emerged as an important plank for tanzeem in all the towns. For instance, in Kanpur, the Anjuman Hifazat ul-Islam spearheaded an economic offensive by proposing to open all kinds of new Muslim-owned shops. The leaders of the Anjuman argued that Hindu shopkeepers charged higher rates to Muslim customers. The Anjuman therefore undertook plans to open larger numbers of Muslim-owned vegetable and grain shops and sweetmeat and betelnut *(pan)* stalls, in order to make Muslims independent of the Hindus.[318] In Allahabad, Maulana Vilayat Hussain had urged Muslims not to buy clothes or confectionery from Hindu shops during Id and other festivals, and to avoid Hindu provisions shops.[319] Under the auspices of the various anjumans that he had formed for the improvement of the economic conditions of Muslims, new shops were set up for cloth, provisions, sweets and tobacco.[320] These were undoubtedly related to the initiatives of Muslim entrepreneurs to strengthen their own position, but popular enthusiasm for them was also remarkable. During the Barawafat festival in 1925 in Allahabad, Hindu halwais (confectioners) were reported to have sustained a loss of about Rs 10,000.[321] Hindu cloth merchants suffered similar large losses during Id, even though they were reported to have reduced the prices of their goods.[322] The poorer Muslims may not have had anything to gain directly from such a successful commercial boycott of Hindus, but they could see this as a part of a wider campaign to undermine the economic preponderance of

[317] Discussed in chapter 2 above.
[318] *PAI*, No. 42, 25 October–1 November 1924; No. 20, 29 May 1926; Barrier, *Roots of Communal Politics*, pp. 242–3.
[319] *PAI*, No. 44, 15 November 1924; No. 45, 22 November 1924; No. 17, 9 May 1925.
[320] *PAI*, No. 45, 22 November 1925.
[321] Ibid.
[322] *PAI*, No. 14, 18 April 1925; No. 17, 9 May 1925.

the Hindu commercial classes in the towns and thus to reduce the economic subordination of the Muslim poor to them. Of course, there was retaliation from the affected Hindu groups. The shops of Muslim kunjra greengrocers in Allahabad were boycotted by many Hindus.[323] Muslim pedlars and hawkers were also forcibly prevented from setting up stalls at some of the major Hindu melas such as the Kalyani Devi mela.[324] These rivalries were clearly escalating within a context of growing religious tensions and were one of many attempts by members of each community to undermine the other.

The tanzeem movement and Islamic assertion among the poor, then, had several different facets. They marked the defence of various Muslim groups in urban neighbourhoods in reaction to the growth of Hindu organisations and religious revivalism from the early 1920s. Tanzeem also had an economic dimension, including attempts to improve the material conditions of Muslim petty traders or shopkeepers, and to resist Hindu merchant-creditors. Finally, tanzeem was a response of Muslim groups to the growing self-confidence of Congress nationalism and its overt association with Hinduism. The impact of these developments was of immense importance in wider political developments, in at least two crucial respects. First, religious confrontations multiplied in the localities, with the poor as major players, and their role became increasingly central to the escalation of communal violence in UP. Secondly, the growing alienation of many groups of poorer Muslims from the Congress in this period ultimately stengthened trends of 'separatism' in elite Muslim politics. In the long term, these developments also threw up contradictions in the very definition of being 'a nationalist'. Muslim masses, alongside the so-called 'separatist' elites, were increasingly identified as being against nationalism because of their growing opposition to and alienation from the Congress, despite the long history of anti-colonial resistance by poorer artisans or erstwhile artisans. In addition, the most significant features of the tanzeem movement in the towns were, first, its localised nature, and, secondly, the fact that the pace of the movement was set, to a great extent, by the initiatives of the Muslim poor. They expressed their own version of Islam, even in the face of elite opprobrium, and much of the tanzeem movement related to specific concerns and imperatives of the poor. With tanzeem, the politics of the Muslim poor came into its own, and through it they sought to inscribe their presence and identity in urban public life. Tanzeem, of course, helped to nurture other aspects of the religious resurgence among the poor which had been developing from

[323] *PAI*, No. 45, 22 November 1925.
[324] *PAI*, No. 12, 28 March 1925.

the later nineteenth century. These included an identity defined by deprivation, decline, simplicity and goodness; an assertion of an imagined past golden age of artisanal communities; and aspirations for egalitarianism, often associated with a socialist rhetoric in resurgent Islam.[325]

Local conflict and communal violence

With competitive religious activities of the Hindu and the Muslim poor becoming rooted in urban localities, communal tensions came to overlap with, and fortify, various other forms of conflict in urban neighbourhoods. Communal riots gained in depth, breadth and ferocity owing to the unprecedented conflicts unleashed by municipal and Improvement Trust policies as well as by the paucity of jobs and infrastructure under demographic pressure. The fact that the labour market was segmented along community lines, as were residential settlements, ensured that attempts by the poor to retain or secure control over employment, land or housing often took on a communal colour. Moreover, with the mounting scarcity of housing and land for settlement or for petty trading, the politics of space and territory assumed central importance in the lives of the poor, in which the sacred and the profane intermingled. To prevent displacement, dispossession and eviction, various groups of the poor often tried to retain or stake their claims to land by using religious symbols. A mosque, a shrine or a temple would be set up to demonstrate that land connected with such religious activities or institutions was sacrosanct and could not be interfered with. The deployment of religious idioms by the poor in this way to maintain their own foothold on land would thus frequently take the form of religious agitation and reinforce religious mobilisation in the locality. Communal tensions and riots would then manifest themselves in local-level clashes over material issues, as an existing body of literature has emphasised.[326] However, without religious resurgence of the kind seen so far, material rivalries in the locality would have been unlikely to take an overt and violent communal orientation. It should be emphasised that economic tensions alone would not inevitably precipitate extensive communal riots. Struggles over space and territory, while arising partly from scarcity, could assume exaggerated and magnified symbolic significance only as an integral part of the escalating process of religious confrontation in the locality. Material rivalries thus have to be seen symbiotically in relation to religious change in understanding

---

[325] Islamic socialism and nationalism will be discussed further in chapter 9.
[326] For accounts of communal riots based on this analytical perspective, see, for instance, A. A. Engineer (ed.), *Communal Riots in Post-independence India*, Delhi, 1984.

communal conflicts. It is the interplay of the two simultaneous developments that ultimately determined the occurrence, patterns and nature of
communal violence. The growing religious rivalries of the poor over
festival celebrations, akhara-based activities and martial display, on the
one hand, and tensions arising from urban local policies and municipal
issues, on the other, were all grounded in the urban locality, and one set
of conflicts could extend into, exacerbate and reinforce the other.
Examples from Benares and Allahabad illustrate these interconnections.[327]

In Allahabad, the Mirganj Scheme was proposed soon after the
Improvement Trust first started its activities in the early 1920s.
Although located amidst the Hindu-dominated trading area in the town,
a number of Muslim petty traders and hawkers, especially greengrocers,
had shops or stalls in the area and it covered one of the important
settlement zones of Muslims in the city, with a significant concentration
of the Muslim poor. The Mirganj Scheme entailed the displacement of a
large number of poorer Muslim inhabitants and the eviction of Muslim
petty traders, as well as the demolition of a mosque and an *auqaf*
(Islamic religious endowment) property.[328] The issue of control over
land affected by the Mirganj Scheme overlapped with the question of
trading rights and access to market areas for Muslim kunjra vegetable
vendors. They were threatened with eviction from the Allabande ka
Phatak area and the vegetable market in Chowk, at a time when the
Municipal Board was also opening up another one.[329] The kunjras
regarded their removal by the Improvement Trust as a deliberate
conspiracy to redirect trade to the new municipal vegetable market in
Mirganj, in order to give a boost to the Hindu khatik greengrocers, who
predominated there.[330] In some sections of the Muslim press, the case
of the kunjras was projected as the first step 'towards the general
expulsion of the Muslim community as well'.[331] Kunjras were prominent participants in akhara activities at this time for religious defence
and self-expression, which provided them with a base of local resistance
against the khatiks. They also campaigned in the town to persuade
Muslims to boycott Hindu traders, and this overlapped with tanzeem

---

[327] Other examples have been explored in Nandini Gooptu, 'The Political Culture of the
Urban Poor: The United Provinces between the Two World Wars', Ph.D. thesis,
University of Cambridge, 1991, ch. 5.
[328] Allahabad Improvement Trust (hereafter AIT) File No. 1/3, Mirganj Open Area
Scheme.
[329] *PAI*, No. 15, 23 April 1927; *NNR*, No. 41/1926, pp. 4–5; No. 43/1926, p. 6.
[330] *NNR*, No. 43/1926, p. 6.
[331] *NNR*, No. 41/1926, pp. 4–5.

initiatives to strengthen or safeguard the economic position of Muslim traders, discussed earlier in this chapter.[332]

Political agitation by the various Muslim groups against the Mirganj Scheme reached a peak around 1926–7. This was also, of course, the time of intense religious competition in Allahabad through rival shuddhi–sangathan and tanzeem initiatives. In that context of religious rivalry, the Mirganj Scheme assumed an overt 'communal' colour. It was alleged by some Muslim leaders that, although the Mirganj Scheme had stalled earlier after initial proposals, it was deliberately revived in 1924 by the Improvement Trust under the influence of Hindu pressure groups in the wake of communal friction during the Dusserah festival of 1924.[333] Several organisations were set up from 1924 onwards to organise opposition to this and other improvement schemes. The most prominent one was the Anjuman Mohafiz Imlak Mussalmanan (Society for the Protection of Property Belonging to Muslims), set up in April 1926 under the initiative of the town's Muslim leaders and notables, with Maulana Vilayat Hussain, leading alim and sufi shaikh of the Daira Shah Hujjatulla, as President.[334] At a series of well-attended meetings at mosques and shrines,[335] organised by this anjuman, allegations were voiced against 'Hindu' attempts to deprive and dispossess Muslims, especially poorer Muslim residents and traders.[336] In an effort to stop the implementation of the Mirganj Scheme, local Muslim groups claimed that the area had been a Muslim graveyard, since some bones had been unearthed during excavations by the Trust. The Trust was thus accused of defiling a sacrosanct Islamic site, in addition to demolishing a mosque and an auqaf property in the area.[337]

During Ramlila, Dadhkando and Mohurram festivals between 1924 and 1926, several communal clashes occurred in Allahabad. While the immediate occasions for the riots were disputes over the playing of music near mosques and the competitive activities of sangathan and tanzeem akharas, at the same time the Mirganj issue and the controversy over the kunjras were far from being marginal to the riots. In October

[332] *PAI*, No. 42, 25 October–1 November 1924; No. 47, 6 December 1924.
[333] Memorial submitted to the Governor of UP by the Executive Committee of the Anjuman Mohafiz Imlak Mussalmanan, AIT File No. 1/3, Mirganj Open Area Scheme.
[334] Ibid.; another such organisation was the Anjuman Tahaffuz-i-Islam, *PAI*, No. 42, 25 October 1924.
[335] Meetings were held at the Jama Masjid, the Imambara and the Daira Shah Mohibullah, and in various Muslim-majority neighbourhoods. AIT File no. 1/3, Mirganj Open Area Scheme.
[336] Reports of 11 of these meetings held between April and August 1926 are included in this file, ibid.
[337] *PAI*, No. 42, 25 October–1 November 1924.

1924, a riot started with skirmishes during the Ramlila procession, but escalated afterwards when Hindu *'lathiwalas'* (men armed with lathis) attacked the vegetable market of the kunjras 'with the evident intention of looting it'.[338] During the September 1926 communal disturbances, a similar pattern was noticed. Rioting began when a Dadhkando procession was assailed by a number of kunjras.[339] The scene of communal affrays soon shifted to areas affected by the Mirganj Scheme and to Allabande ka Phatak, a neighbourhood inhabited by kunjras.[340] In these cases, local neighbourhood tensions relating to trading opportunities and access to land clearly ran alongside and reinforced hostilities among rival religious organisations and over celebration of festivals, and contributed to the intensity and spread of rioting to wider areas.

In a similar instance in Benares in the 1920s and 1930s, struggle for control over land ran parallel to communal animosities arising from religious resurgence, and together created the conditions for communal violence. Land connected with the Dayanand Anglo Vedic (D.A.V.) College and School of the Arya Samaj was at the centre of conflict. The disputed land was located in the north-western corner of the D.A.V. College in Ausanganj, adjacent to which lay a graveyard used by the poorer Muslim artisans of nearby Narharpur. The controversy began in 1925, when land near the graveyard was acquired for the D.A.V. College by the Municipal Board. During land acquisition proceedings, a municipal latrine in the area, used by the Narharpur Muslim artisans, was demolished by the D.A.V. College. This met with opposition from the Muslim artisans, and the College eventually had to rebuild the latrine.[341] The dispute in the area partly related to the restrictions placed on the Narharpur artisans over the use of land as a result of the land acquisitions for the D.A.V. College. The significance of the issue was, however, greatly magnified by the fact that the D.A.V. College of the Arya Samaj was a symbol of Hindu resurgence in the city and was thus in itself a target of the Muslim artisans' discontent. It is not surprising that the trouble in the area started in 1925 when shuddhi and sangathan were emerging with far greater force than ever before in Benares, mainly on the initiative of the Arya Samaj.

The second stage of this dispute coincided with the next phase of heightened communal tensions in 1931, when the tanzeem movement

---

[338] DM, Allahabad, to Commissioner, Allahabad Division, Urgent D.O. Letter No. 207/ S.T., dated 8 October 1924; Report of the Commissioner, Allahabad division, on 'The Allahabad Disturbances, 1924', File No. 249/xii/1924, Home Poll., NAI, GOI.

[339] *PAI*, No. 36, 18 September 1996.

[340] *Abhyudaya* (Allahabad), 18 September 1926.

[341] Cited in DM, Benares, to SP, Benares, Letter dated 2 November 1931, File No. 71/ 1923–27, Department VIII, Appropriation of land, Benares Collectorate, ERR.

against Hindu resurgence and the Congress gained ground among local artisans, led by Baba Khalil Das. In 1931, when the D.A.V. College constructed a wall between its compound and the graveyard, the artisans of Narharpur piled loose earth near the wall to elevate the land on the side of the graveyard, enabling them to cross over the wall into the D.A.V. College compound in defiance and violation of the very purpose of the wall, which was to prevent Muslim incursions. The artisans also started to convert a tomb in the graveyard into a mosque.[342] This attempt by the artisans to enhance the symbolic content and sacred meaning of the land was clearly aimed at preventing any further spatial expansion of the D.A.V. College. It also marked the religious resistance of the artisans, for they simultaneously blocked access through the graveyard to a Hindu temple near the D.A.V. College. On the intervention of the District Magistrate, the artisans ultimately removed the pile of earth in the graveyard next to the College, and agreed to grant restricted access to the temple.[343] In 1933, however, the dispute was revived when the D.A.V. College constructed a boundary wall near the latrine that had been the object of the 1925 controversy. This wall stretched across a passageway through the College compound, which the Narharpur artisans had customarily used to travel between two mosques with their funeral processions.[344] When the Narharpur Muslims pulled down the wall, the district authorities, apprehensive about communal clashes in the area, persuaded the D.A.V. College to concede right of way to the Muslims.[345]

Conflicts resumed in October–November 1938 and coincided with a third phase in provincial-level communal tensions during the period of the Congress Ministry. The object of controversy, this time, was the stone statue of a lion in the Muslim graveyard.[346] The lion was situated near the Hindu temple, but was located on graveyard land. During the *Diwali* festival in October 1938, some 'Hindus'[347] were reported to have offered *puja* (prayers) at the statue and put up some illuminations. The Narharpur Muslims naturally construed this as a renewed Hindu attempt to encroach on graveyard property and as a religious affront. They were perhaps especially sensitive owing to a wider Muslim League political campaign concerning the Congress Ministry at this time,

---

[342] Gauri Shankar Prasad, Secretary, D.A.V. School, to District Magistrate, Benares, Letter dated 11 November 1931, ibid.

[343] Note from Deputy SP, Benares to SP, Benares, dated 23 November 1931, ibid.

[344] Note, dated 11 November 1933, addressed to the D.M, Benares (signature of sender illegible); Note from SP, Benares, to DM, Benares, dated 8 November 1933, ibid.

[345] Ibid.

[346] *Aj*, 23 November 1938, p. 6.

[347] It is not clear from official and newspaper reports who the Hindus were.

alleging that the Ministry, armed with governmental power, was allowing party activists and local administrations to trample upon the rights of the Muslims.[348] The local Muslim inhabitants vigorously objected to the innovation of worship by the Hindus. The District Magistrate commented that the Muslims resented the offer of worship at the statue, for it 'interfered with their possession of the land'.[349] A month later, 250 Hindus again performed *arti puja* at the statue, along with loud music. Shortly afterwards, 200 Muslims from nearby Narharpur artisans' settlements arrived with lathis, and were pelted with stones by the Hindu worshippers. The Superintendent of Police soon arrived at the scene, dispersed both groups and imposed orders under Section 144 to prevent public gatherings. Some Muslims, driven from the graveyard, attacked Hindu shops in the vicinity, and were, in turn, showered with brickbats from Hindu houses.[350] Local Arya Samaj activists regarded this incident as an instance of Muslim recalcitrance on the doorstep of their D.A.V. College. They claimed that the entire plot of land on which the lion stood, including the graveyard, was in fact sacred Hindu land, according to *Kashi Khand*, a religious text.[351] This dispute over the Sher Ki Takia (Tomb of the Lion) generated much local tension, and apparently in retaliation, on 4 February 1939, an Arya Samaj procession stopped in front of the mosque of Langra Hafiz in Phatak Sheikh Salim 'for some unaccountable reason' and played music.[352] The throwing of brickbats and fisticuffs ensued in front of the mosque, as the Muslims inside the mosque hit back. The Superintendent of Police eventually arrived with his forces and put a stop to the encounter. The following day, an Arya Samaj meeting was held in defiance of prohibitory orders by the police, as a show of force to both the authorities and Muslim groups. The youth wings of the Arya Samaj – Arya Kumar Sabha and the Arya Naujuvak Sabha – as well as some students of the D.A.V. School and the Benares Hindu University participated in this meeting.[353] This prominence of students in the

---

[348] This point will be discussed further in chapter 9.
[349] DM, Benares, to SP, Benares, Letter dated 1 December 1938; SP, Benares, to Deputy IGP, UP, III Range, D.O. Letter No. G/24–5, dated 22 November 1938; Note from SP, Benares, to DM, Benares, dated 21 November 1938, File No. 7/1938–43, Department XXIV, Public Works Department, Building and Roads Branch, Benares Collectorate, ERR.
[350] Ibid.
[351] From Ram Narayan Misra, President, Nagri Pracharani Sabha to DM, Benares, dated 15 March 1939, ibid.
[352] Press Communiqué, issued by the District Magistrate, Benares, dated 5 February 1939, File No. 67(3)/1939 & K.W., Box Nos. 603–604, GAD, GUP, UPSA; *PAI*, No. 7, 18 February 1939.
[353] File No. 67(3)/1939 & K.W., Box Nos. 603–604, GAD, GUP, UPSA; *PAI*, No. 7, 18 February 1939.

agitation was quite possibly related to the dispute in the graveyard near the D.A.V. College grounds. In an atmosphere of heightening tension, further controversies surfaced in the town a month later in early March during Mohurram, over processions and the right of way. Eventually, a major riot broke out. The city was engulfed by fire and torn by pitched battles over several days. The Hindu Kapra Bazar and the Bara Bazar as well as the few Muslim shops in the predominantly Hindu-dominated grain market in Bisheshwarganj were looted. Significantly, Narharpur and Ausanganj were the scenes of extensive violence, and the mosque in the Muslim graveyard near the Sher Ki Takia was wrecked by Hindu crowds.[354] This series of developments from 1925 until 1939 in Benares, as well as the Allahabad case discussed earlier, provide interesting instances of the several interconnected issues that accentuated communal tensions and conflicts at this conjuncture in north Indian history. Communal violence was ignited by a number of overlapping factors which assumed new and far more magnified relevance, including concerted religious competition and antagonism in the locality; intense conflict over the control of land, space and territory; and contests over priority and precedence in rituals. These diverse constitutive elements of communal conflict reflected the complexities of the political preoccupations of the poor in the interwar years, which were also to find expression through nationalist politics, albeit in different ways.

[354] Confidential D.O. No. 335, dated 6 March 1939, addressed to Mr Horton, IGP, UP, File No. 67(3)/1939 & K.W., Box Nos. 603–604, GAD, GUP, UPSA.

8   Nationalist action

Recent analyses of popular participation in the nationalist movement have been dominated by two interconnected themes. The first relates to the issue of the 'imperfect mobilisation'[1] of the masses by the Indian National Congress and the attempts of the party to appropriate various forms of autonomous popular political initiatives under the nationalist umbrella, while at the same time restraining and containing their militancy and radicalism.[2] The second theme deals with the understanding of nationalism by the subaltern classes in terms of their own world-view, traditions and notions of moral community. Subaltern culture and traditions, including religious belief and codes of conduct, have been argued to have determined and informed the nature of their perception of nationalism and the figure of Gandhi.[3] Central to both these themes, and connecting them, is the notion of the autonomy of subaltern political action and consciousness. This emphasis on the social, cultural and ideological autonomy of the subaltern classes has, however, often encouraged a shift away from unravelling the processes of reconstruction of culture and tradition that were facilitated precisely

[1] Gyanendra Pandey, *The Ascendancy of the Congress in Uttar Pradesh 1926–1934: A Study in Imperfect Mobilization*, Delhi, 1978.
[2] Ibid.; G. Pandey, 'Peasant Revolt and Indian Nationalism: The Peasant Movement in Awadh, 1919–22', in R. Guha (ed.), *Subaltern Studies I: Writings on South Asian History and Society*, Delhi, 1982, pp. 143–97; G. Pandey, 'A Rural Base for Congress: The United Provinces, 1920–40', in D. A. Low (ed.), *Congress and the Raj: Facets of the Indian Struggle 1917–47*, Delhi, 1977, pp. 199–223; D. Hardiman, 'The Crisis of the Lesser Patidars: Peasant Agitations in Kheda District, Gujarat, 1917–34', in Low (ed.), *Congress and the Raj*, pp. 47–75; D. Hardiman, *Peasant Nationalists of Gujarat: Kheda District, 1917–34*, Delhi, 1981; S. Amin, 'Gandhi as Mahatma: Gorakhpur District, Eastern U.P., 1921–2', in R. Guha (ed.), *Subaltern Studies III: Writings on South Asian History and Society*, Delhi, 1984, pp. 1–61; S. Sarkar, *'Popular' Movements and 'Middle Class' Leadership in Late Colonial India: Perspectives and Problems of a 'History from Below'*, Calcutta, 1983.
[3] D. Hardiman, *The Coming of the Devi: Adivasi Assertion in Western India*, Delhi, 1987, pp. 166–77; Pandey, 'Peasant Revolt and Indian Nationalism', pp. 169–75; Amin, 'Gandhi as Mahatma', pp. 2, 19, 29, 37–8, 44, 54; S. Sarkar, 'The Conditions and Nature of Subaltern Militancy: Bengal from Swadeshi to Non-Cooperation, c. 1905–1922', in R. Guha (ed.), *Subaltern Studies III*, pp. 271–320.

by the infusion of Congress nationalist rhetoric and ritual in the political arena.[4] The actual content of the nationalist message for political mobilisation has tended to be underplayed in such interpretations, for it is seen as no more than a catalyst in subaltern politics. Subaltern nationalism is seen to be primarily autonomously generated, shaped largely by the values, practices and material concerns of the subaltern classes themselves and only marginally in interaction with wider political events and ideologies. This approach, often verging on a quest for the 'originary' or pure subjectivity of the subalterns, discounts the significance of the dynamic transformation of popular culture through the very experience of engaging with nationalist discourse, action and symbolism, including a political vocabulary of citizenship rights or democratic participation. This chapter and the following one adopt the perspective that popular nationalism cannot be understood simply with reference to pre-existing traditions and cultural conceptions. While the importance of traditions is undeniable, any analysis also needs to take into account the remoulding of subaltern political ideas by nationalist propaganda and action. It is not simply that traditional norms of justice or legitimate authority were brought to bear on nationalism; equally importantly, the traffic flowed in the reverse direction, with new notions of equality or rights being forged through involvement in nationalist action. This is not to revert to a framework of percolation of ideas and political mobilisation from above, or analytically to undermine subaltern agency and autonomy, but to reinforce the latter by focusing on the appropriation and differential reinterpretation of new ideas and ideologies by the subaltern classes, eschewing an 'essentialised' or static view of their culture and mindset. This analytical approach is particularly relevant in the urban context, where both the words and the deeds of nationalist activists became ubiquitous in public life by the 1920s and impinged upon the poor more directly and pervasively than ever before.

Shahid Amin, in his recent work on Chauri Chaura, appears to have adopted a perspective similar to the one advocated here, and has shifted from his earlier position, as epitomised in his analysis of the popular understanding of Gandhi as the Mahatma. In this work, he argued that Gandhi's figure was viewed through the past cultural conceptions of 'worship of the worthies' and beliefs in the 'thaumaturgic' or magical power of individuals.[5] In the monograph on Chauri Chaura, however,

[4] Historians vary in their emphases. While Hardiman seems to discount the importance of wider political ideas, Pandey and Sarkar are more inclined to acknowledge the significance of the interface between subaltern and elite nationalisms. Hardiman, *Devi*; Pandey, 'Peasant Revolt and Indian Nationalism'; Sarkar, 'The Conditions and Nature of Subaltern Militancy'.
[5] Amin, 'Gandhi as Mahatma', pp. 2, 19, 29, 37–8, 44, 54.

Amin also stresses the uniqueness of the time and the singularity of the nationalist discourse that made new constructions and hitherto unimaginable imaginings possible for the villagers. A striking illustration of this point is the subalterns' interpretation of the figure of the volunteer *satyagrahi*, (nationalist activist offering passive resistance), locally called the *otiyar*. Amin does not identify the significance of the otiyar to local people in terms of the familiar figures of the renunciant ascetic or religious mendicant. He argues instead that a new conception, specifically rooted to the time and space of the nationalist movement, emerged. Thus, 'volunteer – a new idea – comes into the village'.[6] Amin concludes, based on his interview with Naujadi Pasin:

the old woman has no urge to hurl her otiyars back into the enveloping fold of a context-free meaningful past. Naujadi remembers them in relation to a specific present: 'the time of Gandhi-raj and of the turmoil *[utpat]* we *[hamman]* all created.'[7]

Amin's work brings out the transformative potentials and the unique nature of the nationalist period and its politics, which generated its own myths, metaphors and folklores of power and emancipation, rather than simply stimulating the recasting of traditions.

This chapter and the following one on nationalist politics focus on the change in ideas and the new forms of contest and resistance of the subaltern classes that developed within the context of the emerging nationalist propaganda and public oppositional acts of the Congress. The discussion, in particular, seeks to unravel the changing notions of power and authority, of ideal polity, of social and political emancipation, and ultimately of visions for the future independent nation and its people. This analysis is undertaken through an exploration of both political action and changing forms of cultural expression among various sections of the urban poor. As in previous chapters, the analysis here deals with the interplay of various overlapping identities of the poor, and examines how the languages of nation, class and religion inflected each other.

The previous three chapters have suggested the importance of urban local conflicts in influencing the participation of various groups of the urban poor in caste and communal politics. These two chapters on nationalism attempt a similar investigation of the symbiosis of wider developments in the nationalist movement with the political action of the poor in the urban locality. It is considered how the changing ideology

---

[6] Shahid Amin, *Event, Metaphor, Memory: Chauri Chaura, 1922–92*, Delhi, 1995, pp. 175–89.
[7] Ibid., p. 189.

and practice of Congress nationalism lent themselves to contextual interpretation by the poor in terms of their own local and specific concerns. How far did nationalism enable the poor to explain, understand and negotiate their social tensions and competition in the locality? Why did the poor often articulate their political action at workplaces and neighbourhoods in the language of nationalism and to what extent did this constitute support for the nationalist movement?

Civil Disobedience movement, the poor and crowds

During the Civil Disobedience movement of the early 1930s, the participation of urban masses in nationalist agitation became especially evident and more extensive than in the 1920s. One of the most striking features of the Civil Disobedience movement was the gathering of large crowds along routes of, and often accompanying, Congress processions, as well as at meetings and at sites of pickets outside foreign goods' shops. While nationalist demonstrations were organised and initiated by a handful of Congress activists and volunteers, these occasions were frequently characterised by the presence of large crowds. It was usually through these crowd gatherings that various groups of the urban poor participated in the Civil Disobedience movement. In the earlier nationalist campaign of the Non-Cooperation movement, the involvement of the urban poor through crowd demonstrations, although noticeable,[8] was less extensive than in the Civil Disobedience movement. While meetings, pickets and processions did feature in the Non-Cooperation movement, their scale and extent were to expand significantly by the time of the Civil Disobedience movement. The plan of action adopted by the Congress in the towns during Non-Cooperation had been aimed primarily at rousing students, professional groups and government employees to boycott educational and government institutions. Resignations from schools, colleges, courts and government offices, the formation of Congress volunteer corps and public demonstrations by students and youth from middle- and lower-middle-class backgrounds had been the central features of the Non-Cooperation movement in the towns.[9] After the termination of the Non-Cooperation movement, there was a period of depleted enthusiasm among these groups for Congress politics, which was reflected in a substantial drop in Congress membership.[10] The

---

[8] Pandey, *Ascendancy*, p. 1.
[9] Ibid., pp. 1, 10–11; S. Sarkar, *Modern India, 1885–1947*, Delhi, 1983, pp. 222–4; Gail Minault, *The Khilafat Movement: Religious Symbolism and Political Mobilization in India*, New York, 1982, pp. 116–21.
[10] Pandey, *Ascendancy*, pp. 37, 154.

leadership of the Congress in UP, therefore, realised by the late 1920s that the success of any future nationalist agitation would depend on enlisting the support of the urban and rural masses.

This new preoccupation of the leadership was given practical shape by the launching of what Gyanendra Pandey has described as 'a gigantic propaganda campaign' by the Congress from 1929, first initiated in the context of opposition to the Simon Commission.[11] This campaign involved the extensive organisation of meetings, pickets, *hartals* (strikes) and processions, as well as the celebration of 'national days' and 'weeks'. Through these political demonstrations in the public arena, the Congress was attempting to develop a repertoire of powerful oppositional political rituals which gave concrete embodiment to the message of nationalism through acts of symbolic protest or defiance – 'propaganda by deed' in Pandey's words.[12] The aim of these public political enactments was to spread the nationalist message and, more importantly, to enlarge the space for the involvement in political demonstrations of diverse urban groups who were not directly connected with the Congress party and its volunteer organisations. This strategy of raising mass support through propaganda campaigns and public political rituals was vigorously adopted by the Congress during the Civil Disobedience movement.

The Civil Disobedience movement began in March–April 1930 and, after the suspension of agitations in March 1931 following the Gandhi–Irwin Pact, was resumed in January 1932. The strategy of the Congress to attract popular participation during these campaigns was evidently fruitful. Crowds of people joined Congress processions, attended nationalist meetings and were present at pickets of foreign goods' shops and at bonfires of foreign cloth, or at the drills, parades and flag-hoisting ceremonies of the Congress volunteers. From mid-April 1930, soon after the beginning of public campaigns for the Civil Disobedience movement in the previous month, Police Abstracts of Intelligence began to report the presence of thousands at meetings, processions and pickets. The numbers present at meetings and processions on various 'national days', 'boycott weeks' and 'flag days' and to protest against the arrest of Congress leaders were estimated by the police to range from 2,000 to 20,000, with one of the largest meetings reported to have been held at Kanpur in August 1930, on the final day of the 'boycott week', attended by 70,000 people.[13] Similarly large crowds were reported to

[11] Ibid., p. 81.   [12] Ibid., p. 84.
[13] *PAI*, No. 14, 12 April 1930; No. 15, 19 April 1930; No. 17, 3 May 1930; No. 18, 10 May 1930; No. 19, 17 May 1930; No. 26, 5 July 1930; No. 27, 12 July 1930; No. 31, 9 August 1930; No. 32, 16 August 1930; No. 33, 23 August 1930.

have assembled during the second phase of the Civil Disobedience movement from January 1932.[14] The Congress was also able to organise successful hartals in the bazars, enforcing the closure of shops and the immobilisation of various forms of transport. Processions, pickets and hartals served not only as instruments for Congress propaganda, but also as theatres of nationalist action – arenas where the urban masses could get involved. The Congress confined the actual organisation of demonstrations to its members and volunteers, but at the same time created a platform for wider participation by staging public agitational events.

Who among the urban poor formed the crowds and joined the processions, pickets, demonstrations or hartals? The Congress had largely concentrated its propaganda campaigns in the bazar areas of the towns and it was here that the largest crowds were formed by local people. While the processions of local Congress volunteer groups in various urban neighbourhoods were dispersed across the town, the major Congress processions targeted the central business districts and markets. The newspaper *Vartman* published notices of the routes of the main Congress processions every day in Kanpur during March and April 1930. The processions covered the trading zones of the town, which included Chowk Saraffa, Naughara, Generalganj, Kahukothi, Nachghar-Birhana, Parade, Nayaganj, Moolganj, Thathrai, Chatai Mohal, Shatranji Mohal, Lathi Mohal, Sikri Bazar, Juta Bazar, Naryel Bazar and Prayagnarayan.[15] Similarly in Benares, Congress processions toured the bazar areas in Chowk, Kapra Chowk, Dalmandi, Bulanala, Nai Sarak, Chetganj and Bansphatak.[16] In Lucknow, Congress processions were confined to the Hindu markets in and around Aminabad. As the sites of shops and commercial establishments, the bazars were also inevitably the centres of pickets to prevent trade in foreign goods. Congress hartals similarly affected the bazars of necessity, for the closure of shops had to be enforced here. The local people who thus became involved in Congress demonstrations and 'events' prominently included the bazar poor – the daily congregation of labourers, workmen, vendors and hawkers, many of whom were lower-caste Hindus.

Police and government reports referring to the crowds during the Civil Disobedience movement mentioned the 'bazar scum', 'vaga-bonds', 'irresponsible classes', people of a 'very poor quality', 'forces of discontent' in the bazars and 'low class elements', 'unemployed or loafer

[14] *PAI*, No. 2, 16 January 1932; No. 3, 23 January 1932; *FR*: first half of January 1932 and first half of April 1932, File No. L/P&J/12/45, IOR.
[15] *Vartman* (Kanpur), 30 March 1930, p. 2; 12 April 1930, p. 1; 14 April 1930, p. 1.
[16] *Aj* (Benares), 30 April 1930, p. 6.

classes' or 'disorderly elements in the city'.[17] In official parlance, these epithets were usually reserved for the labouring poor and those who were labelled as the 'floating population'. This unmistakably points to the manual labourers, job hunters, hawkers and street-vendors who thronged the bazars.[18] In addition to these generic references, government officials in their reports on Congress agitations were at times somewhat more specific in their identification of the groups of people who joined pickets and hartals. The District Magistrate of Kanpur and the Commissioner of the Allahabad Division in 1932 noted that the crowds at Congress pickets of foreign cloth shops in Kanpur were composed of employees and workers in the cloth market and people coming in from adjacent bazar areas.[19] A government report drew attention to 'shopkeepers', 'a sprinkling of beggars' and people in 'miscellaneous occupations'.[20] The Collector of Kanpur, describing the pickets in the cloth market in 1930, commented: 'crowds of mohalla people gather and they all show strong sympathy with the volunteers and help them in every way'.[21] Police reports also noted that workers in the cloth market were refusing to handle foreign cloth.[22] A corroboration of these official observations can be found in an article on political agitation in the bazars, published in the Silver Jubilee Souvenir of the Bazar *Karmchari* (Employees) Federation of Kanpur in 1977. In this article, Rewa Shankar Trivedi, a shop employee and former office bearer of the union of bazar karmcharis, mentioned that bazar workers had lent support to Congress picketers during the nationalist movement in the 1930s. He wrote:

Congress volunteers were picketing shops; arrests and lathi charges were happening . . . In the course of their daily work, when pickets were in progress, workers always gave their support and participated by joining in the slogans and protecting volunteers from the police. In carrying goods or in walking in and out of shops, the workers would have to trample over the prostrate bodies of the

[17] *PAI*, No. 28, 19 July 1930; No. 6, 13 February 1932; No. 15, 16 April 1932; *FR*: first half of January and first half of April 1932, File No. L/P&J/12/45, IOR; File No. 14/28, Poll. of 1932, Serial Nos. 1–22, P/CONF/81 (1932), India Conf. Proceedings, 3B, Home Department, IOR.

[18] Pandey noted the participation of 'small peddlers and hawkers, personal servants and other odd-job men' in the Civil Disobedience movement. Pandey, *Ascendancy*, p. 108.

[19] Draft of a letter (undated) from the DM, Kanpur, to Mr Carnegie, President of the Upper India Chamber of Commerce; Commissioner, Allahabad Division, to Chief Secretary, UP, Letter No. 2353, dated 25 April 1932, File No. 12/1931, Department XX, Police, Allahabad Commissioner's Office Records.

[20] *FR*: second half of March 1932, File No. L/P&J/12/45, IOR.

[21] Collector, Kanpur, to Commissioner, Allahabad Division, Confidential Letter No. 387–B/30, dated 8 July 1930, File No. 151/1930, Box No. 89, Police Department, GUP, UPSA.

[22] *PAI*, No. 18, 10 May 1930.

volunteers [who lay down in front of the shops to stop business]. But the workers were not willing to do this and disobeyed the orders of their employers. Many workers were dismissed for this offence.[23]

Ekka-tonga walas and carters were other groups mentioned in police reports. They showed solidarity with Congress hartals by refraining from plying their vehicles.[24] The Governor of UP, after a tour of the Province during the Civil Disobedience movement, also reported that in Kanpur and other towns 'practically all ekkas and tongas carried national flags'.[25] On one occasion, such transport workers in Kanpur were reported in a newspaper to have refused to allow a speaker to address a meeting because he was urging them not to observe hartals.[26] Bazar labourers, including those employed in small workshops, transport drivers and street-vendors were, clearly, some of the key participants in the Congress agitations.[27]

How did the crowds of the bazar poor, organisationally separate from the Congress activists, become part of the nationalist action? Some evidence comes from comments by government officials. Referring to a crowd gathering in Lucknow on 25 May 1930 that 'ran into thousands' at a site near Hazratganj where a Congress procession had been intercepted by the police, Mr L. S. White, a British official, noted:

a very great proportion of the crowd that accompanied the procession were sympathetic towards it and were in a sense giving it their *moral support* against the authorities . . . as on other occasions many of them were joining the members of the procession in uttering well known slogans.[28]

Similarly, describing crowd gatherings at pickets of foreign cloth shops in the Generalganj market in Kanpur, the Commissioner of the Allahabad Division commented:

It must be remembered that the responsibility for the situation by no means only rests with those actually picketing . . . *by far the most dangerous element is provided by the large crowds* collected, which call out revolutionary cries and jaunt and jeer at the police and *provide at the same time the most obvious and adequate symbol of a contempt of Government authority.*[29]

---

[23] *Kanpur Bazar Karmchari Federation: Rajat Jayanti Smarika* (Silver Jubilee Anniversary Souvenir) (hereafter *Karmchari Smarika*), Kanpur, 1977, Part II, pp. 22–3, article by Rewa Shankar Trivedi.
[24] *PAI*, No. 19, 17 May 1930.
[25] Report of the Governor of UP on his tour of the Province, File No. 249/1930 & K.W., Home Poll., GOI, NAI.
[26] *The Leader*, 6 September 1933, p. 7.
[27] Pandey, *Ascendancy*, p. 108, mentions similar groups.
[28] *Mr. L. S. White's Report on the Incidents Which Occurred in Lucknow on 25–26 May 1930*, Nainital, 1930, pp. 2, 4, emphasis added.
[29] Commissioner, Allahabad Division, to the Chief Secretary, UP (undated letter), File No. 12/1931, Department XX, Police, Allahabad Commissioner's Office Records, emphasis added.

It is interesting that in both cases the British officials concerned did not simply portray the crowds as posing a problem of law and order, even though it could be expected that they would seek to discredit the Congress by accusing the party of rabble-rousing and unleashing crowd violence and disorder. Instead, they argued that the crowds also constituted a defiance of the authority of the government. Mr L. S. White, in his report on the crowd gathering in Lucknow, in fact asserted that 'there was no display of violence' on the part of the crowd, but argued that the police felt obliged to disperse it owing to the fact that the crowd was 'giving it [the Congress procession] their moral support'.[30] The British officials therefore appear to have been as much, if not more, concerned about 'the contempt of Government authority' and 'moral support' for the Congress constituted by the crowds, as they were anxious about actual or potential violent action. In particular, the authorities betrayed their fear about crowds who 'jaunt and jeer at the police' as marks of resistance or acts of defiance against the government and support for the nationalist movement. It is possible that this interpretation was coloured by the official mind reading a challenge to the power and authority of the state in every form of collective activity. However, descriptions or reports of crowd demonstrations, even when isolated from the official understanding of them, as well as coming from other sources, confirm that crowds were composed not of mere idle and amused onlookers, or people looking for trouble, but of those who expressed considerable active support for Congress processionists or picketers.

In the Lucknow incident of 25 May 1930, cited above, a large crowd had collected at a site where the police declared the Congress procession unlawful, prohibited it from proceeding and tried to disperse both the processionists and the crowd. In spite of repeated warnings by the police and threats of baton charges and firing, the crowd stood its ground alongside the procession, and eventually faced police shooting.[31] In Allahabad, on 8 and 9 April 1932, large crowds had swelled Congress processions which were trying to enter the civil lines in defiance of government orders. When the police stopped the procession on both occasions and attempted to arrest Congress volunteers, the crowds intervened by pelting them with stones and brickbats.[32] On 5 January 1932 in Benares, the police prevented a Congress procession from entering the Town Hall grounds to hold a meeting. In protest, a crowd of 20,000 people accompanying the procession, and described in a government report as composed predominantly of 'low class elements',

[30] *Mr. L. S. White's Report*, p. 4.
[31] Ibid.
[32] *FR*: first half of April 1932, File No. L/P&J/12/45, IOR.

attacked the police with brickbats. The police opened fire to disperse the crowd, leaving three dead and fifty wounded.[33] At pickets of foreign cloth shops, crowds lent similar support to Congress volunteers and faced police action. When pickets were set up in the Generalganj cloth market in Kanpur, the crowds hurled verbal abuse and often shoes or brickbats at the merchants' shops. Members of the crowds surrounding the sites of pickets, who could espy approaching policemen, often alerted the Congress volunteers, helping them to disappear quickly and evade arrest.[34] These instances indicate that, even though the Congress engaged only its volunteers and activists to stage processions or pickets, the crowds became part of the action, often giving active assistance such as in compelling merchants to stop the sale of foreign goods and attempting to prevent the police from arresting Congress volunteers or leaders. Analysing similar crowd events in Bombay during the Civil Disobedience movement, Masselos remarked that the crowds of on-lookers came to form a 'massive chorus of observer-participants'.[35] The evidence cited here confirms Masselos' interpretation that the crowds of the poor did not remain a passive audience. They were crucial actors and had a decisive political impact on the British authorities.

The enthusiasm of the poor for nationalist action expressed in crowd gatherings was reflected in popular cultural forms, especially urban folk music. It is, of course, not possible to pin down oral traditions precisely to the years of the Civil Disobedience movement. More broadly, how-ever, folk songs and cultural performances during the 1920s and 1930s undoubtedly registered a growing interest in nationalism. Urban folk song genres of the period – *alha, doha, kajri, chaubola* and *khayal-lavni* – all began to incorporate nationalist themes.[36] Many of these musical traditions even received a boost during this period as vehicles for expressing nationalist sentiments and visions. Khayal-lavni was one such especially popular form of urban folk-singing. Lavni had its enthusiasts and patrons amongst the towns' elites, including some nationalist poets and activists, such as Balkrishna Sharma Naveen and Acharya Sanehi of

---

[33] *FR*: first half of January 1932, File No. L/P&J/12/45, IOR.

[34] A Note on Congress rowdyism in the Generalganj area since 1 April 1932, by the SP, Kanpur, dated 5 April 1932, File No. 12/1931, Department XX, Police, Allahabad Commissioner's Office Records.

[35] J. Masselos, 'Audiences, Actors and Congress Dramas: Crowd Events in Bombay City in 1930', in J. Masselos (ed.), *Struggling and Ruling: The Indian National Congress, 1885–1985*, London, 1987, p. 82.

[36] Dr P. Chand 'Manav', 'Uttari Bharat ke Khayal-Lavni ka Sahityik Swarup', paper submitted to the UP Sangeet Natak Academy, Lucknow, for the Khayal-Lavni Festival, Firozabad, 30 September–2 October 1984 (manuscript), pp. 3–4; N. Kumar, *The Artisans of Banaras: Popular Culture and Identity, 1880–1986*, Princeton, 1988, p. 151; Pandey, *Ascendancy*, p. 82.

Kanpur. However, lavni was primarily a song tradition of the poor, or of 'ordinary' people and 'mehnat-mazdur' (labourers and manual workers), in the words of one commentator.[37] In Kanpur, for instance, khayal-lavni performances and musical sessions were regularly held in places such as Hatia, Generalganj, Kahu Kothi, Shivala, Parade and Chowk[38] – all of which were in the bazars where the poor worked and often lived. In Lucknow, one of the nuclei of performances and *dangals* (competition among rival performers) was based at the betel-nut (*pan*) stall in Chowk of one of the most popular singers of the 1930s, Maikulal, who was a *shudra kahar*. The khayal-lavni songs popular in Maikulal's circles dealt with political and nationalist themes, in particular the heroic exploits of revolutionary leaders.[39] In the 1920s and 1930s, this genre of vocal music in the various towns came to include not only the traditional religious and philosophical themes, but also the achievements of histor-ical and contemporary heroes, leaders and '*beers*' (brave martyrs), and stories of their sacrifice and daring for the nation. Scores of lavni were also composed on the Civil Disobedience movement and its key motif of *satyagraha* or non-violent resistance, as well as on the various nationalist leaders, describing their ideals and extolling their greatness.[40] Khayal-lavni songs also often served as a vehicle of social critique.[41] The frequent inclusion of both nationalist themes and social commentary in these song traditions suggests not only the growing popularity of the nationalist movement, but also the significance of nationalism for the poor as a means of bringing about social change. How and why was the nationalist message of the Congress interpreted and understood in this way?

Civil Disobedience propaganda, the nationalist message and the poor

During the Civil Disobedience movement, the Congress committees in the towns stepped up the enlistment of volunteers. The volunteers

---

[37] Shivprabhu Sharma, 'Pandit Banarsidas Chaturvedi se Baatchit: Khayal Khojak Mandal', *Smarika: Khayal-Lavni Samaroh* (Souvenir of the Khayal-Lavni Festival), Firozabad, 30 September–2 October 1984, Sangeet Natak Academy, Kaiserbagh, Lucknow, 1984, 20.

[38] Swami Narayananand Saraswati, *Lavni ka Itihas*, Kanpur, 1953, p. 16.

[39] Krishnamohan Saxena, 'Baatchit Pandit Amritlal Nagar se: Khayal-lavni parampara aur Lucknow ke khayalgo ustad Maikulal', *Smarika: Khayal-Lavni Samaroh*, pp. 29–32.

[40] Swami Narayananand Saraswati, 'Khayal-lavni parampara', *Smarika: Khayal-Lavni Samaroh*, pp. 3–18; Sharma, 'Pandit Banarsidas Chaturvedi se Baatchit', pp. 19–22; Saraswati, *Lavni ka Itihas*, pp. 94–5.

[41] Saxena, 'Baatchit Pandit Amritlal Nagar se', pp. 29–32.

trained in physical exercises, organised drills, and regularly staged ceremonial hoistings of the national flag. They marched in processions through various urban neighbourhoods, chanting nationalist slogans, singing patriotic songs and often carrying posters and tableaux or floats. Descriptions of these processions in the newspapers and police reports as well as nationalist press campaigns indicate the key elements of the Congress message. Not surprisingly, political repression and economic exploitation, as the two props of illegitimate foreign rule, were ubiquitous and prominent in the political propaganda of the Congress, as typified, for instance, in the *Satyagraha Samachar*, which was a broadsheet published by the Allahabad District Congress Committee to report on the progress of the Civil Disobedience movement and to expound its guiding rationale. In the light of police shooting and baton or spear charges on unarmed nationalist gatherings, the *Satyagraha Samachar*[42] of 31 May 1930 proclaimed that *goondashahi*, or the Rule of Thugs, prevailed in the country. The editorial article on 29 May 1930, entitled '*Sarkar ki lathi*' (The disciplining baton of the government), condemned the rule of the government rod in the following manner: 'The Government has now adopted the policy of beating with lathis and at every place it causes lathi charges to be made [sic]. We wonder very much how this government which makes boast [sic] of being civilised can practise such barbarity . . . At one place it proclaims martial law, at another it orders firing or punishes little children and women with lathis.' Here the government's own discourse about violation of the law and disorderly political behaviour levelled against the nationalist movement or against 'unruly' mobs was inverted and turned against the government itself to expose it to be the real *goonda* (thug), responsible for barbarism and violence. The motif of brutal police action (*zulm*) was also a predominant and recurrent one, which was given visual representation in Congress processions. In Benares, for instance, a Congress procession in April 1930 halted at frequent intervals to enact the following scene: a person wearing the uniform of a *kotwal* or law and order official ordered others, dressed as *sipahis* or constables, to beat up some men in the *khadi* (handspun cotton) outfit of Congress satyagrahis.[43] In another procession in the following month, three men, impersonating the Divisional Commissioner, the District Magistrate and the Superintendent of Police, carried toy guns, and another,

---

[42] Extracts from *Satyagraha Samachar* (published by Allahabad District Congress Committee, printed at Abhyudaya Press), File No. 106/1930, Box No. 87, Home Police Department, UPSA, GUP.
[43] *Aj*, 30 April 1930. p. 6.

dressed as a constable, occasionally fired an airgun.[44] On 'Jallianwalabagh Day' in 1930 in Kanpur, partial hartal was enforced and a procession of 2,000, watched by another 10,000–15,000 people, featured tableaux on police oppression, especially on the themes of peasants in Bardoli, ill-treatment of political prisoners and the Jallianwalabagh incident.[45]

This message of rule by force and coercion by the colonial state ran parallel to colonial economic domination as the other obvious key theme. On 23 April 1930, the *Satyagraha Samachar* held the British government responsible for the poverty of 90 per cent of Indians and for destroying the trade, commerce and industry of the country, thus causing widespread unemployment and hardship. This message was powerfully enacted in the public arena. One procession, for instance, carried an effigy of a Member of Parliament, upon which was written that the British had bled India white, but now the people of India have been awakened and the British must leave.[46] Far more dramatic were the bonfires of foreign goods. The campaign against foreign cloth was, of course, projected by Gandhi as the struggle against colonial exploitation and against the consequent deprivation and dispossession of the large majority of Indians. The commoditisation of cloth was held up as the most poignant symbol of the adverse consequences of colonialism. In Gandhian thought, cloth was central to the harmonious, self-sufficient local economy of India, but the colonial economic system reduced cloth to a mere commodity for exchange. By challenging transactions in foreign cloth, Gandhian nationalism held out the promise of the restoration of a putative past golden age of economic interdependence, mutuality and neighbourliness as well as purity and godliness, which homespun cloth was projected to signify.[47]

Besides focusing on the two key messages about economic and political domination, in certain cases Congress propaganda also drew upon prevalent discontent in the town against urban maladministration and unpopular municipal policies, and incorporated the local authorities in nationalist demonology. A Congress procession in Benares in November 1930 included the effigies of the chairman and the executive officer of the Municipal Board, with messages stuck on them to show

[44] *PAI*, No. 20, 24 May 1930. Similar were processions reported in *PAI*, No 22, 7 June 1930.
[45] *PAI*, No. 47, 29 November 1930.
[46] *PAI*, No 22, 7 June 1930.
[47] For the importance of homespun cloth in nationalist politics, see C. A. Bayly, 'The Origins of Swadeshi (Home Industry): Cloth and Indian Society, 1700–1930', in Arjun Appadurai (ed.), *The Social Life of Things: Commodities in Cultural Perspective* (Cambridge, 1986), pp. 285–321.

that they were urging people to buy foreign goods. The slogans chanted included 'Down with the traitor (*deshdrohi*) Chairman' and 'Down with the puppet Chairman and Executive Officer who dance to the tune of the British Government'.[48] By ingeniously portraying municipal functionaries as champions of foreign goods, the Congress processionists attempted to attribute the ill-effects of local administration to what they projected as the treacherous and unpatriotic alliance of some municipal functionaries with the British government. In Benares, a Congress procession in April 1930 featured two donkeys wearing hats and coats and labelled as 'foreign cloth-wearing strange animals', which amplified this theme of the menace of the Indian collaborators of the Raj.[49]

In addition to the dissemination of the Congress message through the press or tableaux and play-acting in processions, other forms of visual representation reinforced and magnified the key nationalist themes. A number of brands of cigarettes and matches, for instance, which were often called '*swadhinta*' (freedom), '*swatantrata*' (independence), '*swadeshi*' (national or home industry) or '*swatantra bharat*' (independent India), featured on their cartons or wrappers the national flag in various forms, images of Congress volunteers, the spinning-wheel or the map of India, supplemented in some cases with nationalistic catch-phrases.[50] Calendar images, photographic prints[51] and chromolithographs[52] with nationalist iconography, depicting national heroes, nationalist leaders, the map of the nation, as well as the evils of British rule, flooded the market. Mock currency notes of a future independent India were also circulated, with Gandhi, Nehru or Bhagat Singh appearing on them.[53] Of course, the newspaper and pamphlet presses were central to the dissemination of nationalist messages. Despite the general low level of literacy, the messages in print found an extensive airing, being spread by word of mouth.[54]

The message broadcast by the Congress through all these media was simple and direct: the British government was responsible for India's poverty and for the misery and deprivation of its masses. Two main

---

[48] *Aj*, 24 November 1930, p.5.
[49] *Aj*, 30 April 1930, p. 6.
[50] *PAI*, No. 45, 15 November 1930.
[51] *PAI*, No. 41, 18 October 1930, for instance, reported that Bhagat Singh's photograph was a bestseller.
[52] For nationalist images in chromolithographs, see Christopher Pinney, 'The Nation (Un)Pictured: Chromolithography and 'Popular' Politics in India, 1878–1995', *Critical Inquiry*, 23, 4, 1997, pp. 834–67.
[53] Interview with Shri Amritlal Nagar in Lucknow, with his collection of some of these currency notes. Circulation of such notes in eastern UP is also mentioned in Amin, *Event, Metaphor*, p. 171.
[54] Pandey, *Ascendancy*, pp. 76–9.

aspects of British rule were highlighted: first, state oppression, police atrocities, brute force and coercion as the bases of colonial power and rule; second, the economic foundations of power, and colonial economic domination as the reason for the poverty of the Indian people and the underdevelopment of the economy. The ultimate and rather uncomplicated message of the Congress appeared to be that British rule was the root of all evil. All Indians must, therefore, join the Congress to fight British rule by attacking the twin pillars of government strength – trade in foreign goods and the police, as well as the government's indigenous allies, such as those in the institutions of local administration. The general nature of this message meant that it could be understood in a variety of ways by diverse social groups or political constituencies.[55] For the urban poor, in particular, the themes of political control, police repression, the tyranny of the local authorities and above all economic hardship could be understood in terms of their own experience. Colonialism could be seen not simply as the source of the deprivation and powerlessness of the nation, but also as the cause of their own specific plight.

Civil Disobedience and local conflicts of the poor

While the relevance of nationalist action for the poor and their involvement in the Civil Disobedience movement related, in part, to the nature of the Congress message, their participation was also stimulated by the possibility of articulating a range of discontent and grievances, which became important in the interwar years and were especially sharpened in the early 1930s' economic depression with which the Civil Disobedience movement overlapped. Nationalist agitation assumed such potency for the poor because it provided the political platform and a legitimising ideology to address the issues of exploitation, discipline or control. It should, however, be emphasised that the unrest of the poor arising from economic or political conditions did not automatically and spontaneously feed into the Civil Disobedience movement, but was also fuelled by nationalist propaganda – the two reinforced and magnified each other. Explanation and analysis of the economic and political situation put forward by the Congress helped to accelerate political action and shaped its forms and nature. At the same time, the generalised metaphors of British repression and exploitation in nationalist rhetoric proved to be strongly emotive for the poor in the light of their own experience of injustice, deprivation and the violence of everyday life.

[55] Ibid., pp. 95, 101–6.

Mounting conflicts among the poor over jobs, housing, shop space and trading opportunities, as well as over municipal policies and policing, all fed into the nationalist movement. Urban social tensions and conflicts of the 1920s, in addition to fuelling caste and religious politics, were, by the 1930s, also contributing to overt acts of protest. The years of the economic depression, with which the Civil Disobedience movement coincided, were characterised by a decline in wages[56] and keener competition for jobs because of further migration from the countryside and demographic pressures as well as the slowing down of industrial production and trade.[57] Around the time of the Civil Disobedience movement, unrest gradually gathered momentum among various occupational groups in the bazars against employers, merchants, urban authorities and the police. The newspaper *Vartman*, for instance, reported in March 1930 that Kanpur cloth market workers were protesting against arbitrary dismissal and wage reductions, both of which affected them acutely during the depression.[58] In 1931, a *Bekar Sabha* (Association of the Unemployed) had been formed in Kanpur by some dismissed industrial workers and bazar labourers.[59] Discontent was being voiced in the towns against municipal policies and the police. The ekka-tonga walas in Kanpur had formed a union in 1929, and went on strike against police harassment, municipal licensing policy and harsh penalties or fines.[60] A similar strike occurred in Lucknow in 1932.[61] An editorial in *Vartman* in 1930 reported unrest among *khonchawalas* (street-vendors) in Kanpur, who, as objects of municipal anti-encroachment measures, had lost their shop space and had to pay fines, when their incomes were already low owing to the trade depression.[62] Elsewhere in *Vartman*, it was reported that hawkers in the Chowk area in Kanpur had refused to allow the municipality to demolish their stalls and had protested that encroachments by *rais* (affluent, upper-class) householders and shopkeepers in the area were spared demolition.[63] High rents for shop space and residential accommodation, at a time of economic hardships, were yet another focus of discontent, often shared by the middle classes and the poorer labourers and traders. In Benares, under the auspices of the *Kiraya Klesh Nibarani Sabha* (Association for

---

[56] S. G. Tiwari, *Economic Prosperity of the United Provinces: A Study in the Provincial Income, Its Distribution and Working Conditions, 1921–39*, Bombay, 1951, pp. 197, 201.
[57] Discussed in chapter 2 above.
[58] *Vartman*, 3 March 1930, p. 1.
[59] *PAI*, No. 20, 23 May 1931; for similar developments in Benares, see *Aj*, 4 November 1931, p. 6.
[60] *PAI*, No. 20, 25 May 1929.
[61] *PAI*, No. 17, 30 April 1932.
[62] *Vartman*, 13 April 1930, p. 2.
[63] Ibid., 10 March 1930, p. 2.

the alleviation of rent-distress), meetings, hartals and processions were organised in 1931, demanding decreases in house and shop rents and rent ceiling regulations,[64] and on one occasion retail shopkeepers in the Dussaswamedh municipal market threatened not to pay rents.[65] In Kanpur, the Town Congress Committee was reported to have urged the Municipal Board in 1930 to review rents in the city and to impose rent ceilings.[66]

By the early 1930s, then, labourers, hawkers, transport pliers and unemployed job seekers in the bazars were growing increasingly restive. It was precisely at this time that the Congress presented, through its vigorous propaganda campaign, a wider systemic and structural explanation for economic and political problems in terms of colonial rule. Further, the Congress Civil Disobedience campaign happened to focus on precisely some of the most potent targets of popular hostility as they had emerged by the 1930s – the merchants, the police and the local authorities. Nationalist action thus provided a platform to confront specific figures of discontent, while at the same time helping to express a generalised aspiration for political and social change. The case of the workers in the Kanpur cloth market provides an interesting example. Here the shops of the cloth merchants in the bazars were prime targets of the Congress picketers. The District Magistrate reported that crowds at these pickets 'take to violence, throwing stones into shops and beating. They are greatly excited and there is always a danger of the shops being looted or burnt.'[67] Rewa Shankar Trivedi, a worker in a cloth shop in Kanpur, in his article on nationalist campaigns in the bazars cited earlier, explained the reasons for the participation of bazar workers in such Congress agitations, particularly at pickets against merchants of foreign goods:

We were fighting for our rights against *dasata* [servitude] . . . The workers had ranged themselves against their employers . . . On the one hand, it was the workers' struggle for their rights in the bazar . . . on the other hand, it was a struggle to stop business in foreign cloth.[68]

It is not surprising that a bazar worker would highlight in his later reminiscences that they had supported the nationalist movement as evidence of their past political achievements. Yet it is significant that he

---

[64] *Aj*, 3 October 1931, p. 6; 29 October 1931, p. 6; *PAI*, No. 3, 24 January 1931; No. 29, 25 July 1931; No. 39, 3 October 1931.
[65] *Aj*, 7 October 1932, p. 6.
[66] *Vartman*, 10 February 1930, p. 2.
[67] Draft (undated) letter of the District Magistrate, Kanpur, to the President of the Upper India Chamber of Commerce, File No. 12/1931, Department XX, Police, Allahabad Commissioner's Office Records.
[68] *Karmchari Smarika*, Part II, pp. 22–3.

did not assert that their participation was entirely or chiefly for patriotic reasons, but he emphasised the relevance of the nationalist movement to 'the workers' struggle for their rights in the bazar'. Trivedi's article thus suggests that the Civil Disobedience movement had been understood by the bazar workers partly in terms of defiance or challenge to merchants and employers. Although not all merchants were targets of Congress pickets, but only merchants of foreign cloth, this form of political action could be taken as emblematic of a wider struggle against the commercial classes and for 'our rights against dasata', where the term 'dasata' refers less to national political dependence than to the social and economic servitude of workers. Nationalism lent ammunition to political action by enabling the poor to devise a legitimising ideology and marshal the moral courage to confront merchants. Moreover, the trade in foreign cloth elicited such great passion because Congress rhetoric had constructed foreign cloth as the symbol of the decimation of the Indian economy and, hence, of the deprivation of the people. In addition, the significance of pickets of foreign cloth lay in resistance not just against cloth of alien origin, but also crucially against the economic transactions underlying the sale of cloth. These transactions exemplified the commercial culture of the bazars and the nexus of exchange, credit and profits, which were at the heart of the economic exploitation faced by the urban poor. From this perspective, too, the campaign against foreign cloth could signify a fight against dasata. Furthermore, the very nature of the labour market, with shifting jobs and changing employers, as well as the fear of dismissal and loss of employment or debt dependence on employers, frequently made it ineffective or difficult to organise protest at the workplace directly against specific employers. Instead, the tensions arising from the context of employment relations found generalised expression through nationalism.

In Civil Disobedience propaganda, the Congress often attacked the municipal authorities, as in the case of the Benares procession mentioned earlier. On another occasion in 1932, a Civil Disobedience hartal was announced in Kanpur to protest both against the arrest of the Congress leader Dr Kitchlew and against municipal policies, especially the levying of heavy fines for encroachment.[69] The Congress leaders in all the towns in this period were campaigning for rent reductions and against municipal fines, taxes and anti-encroachment drives.[70] In these cases, too, participation in Congress demonstrations could be seen by hawkers, ekka-tonga drivers and cartmen as a means of confronting and

[69] *PAI*, No. 36, 10 September 1932.
[70] Cited above and *Vartman*, 13 April 1930, p. 2.

contesting the power of the urban authorities and their policies, and possibly of replacing them with a new political order.

Alongside targeting merchants and the urban authorities, defiance of the police, as a part of the Civil Disobedience movement, provided yet another agitational focus of political action for the bazar poor – labourers, transport workers, petty traders, carters and hauliers – all of whom harboured resentment against police harassment, arbitrary arrests and the exaction of bribes. The harsh treatment meted out to crowds at pickets or processions during the Civil Disobedience movement in itself heightened hostility against the police[71] and served to augment popular support for the Congress. As the Civil Disobedience movement progressed, the government expanded its regime of repression and control, bringing about what D. A. Low has termed a state of 'civil martial law'.[72] As the towns became scenes of crowded nationalist processions and pickets, the demonstrators were handled with overt violence by the police, using batons, polo sticks and guns.[73] In the cloth market in Kanpur, even a merchant commented adversely on 'the somewhat indiscriminate action of the police in dealing with processions and crowds'.[74] He recounted an incident when a Congress volunteer had been arrested and a crowd, chanting nationalist slogans, followed him and the policemen accompanying him. This crowd and other onlookers were pursued and beaten up by another group of policemen, without any provocation.[75] Such action stirred up the brewing antagonism of the bazar poor against the police and lent greater purchase to the Congress' condemnation of the police for the exercise of absolute power, oppression and zulm. Moreover, police intervention at pickets and their attempts to curb political agitations in the bazar had been partly geared to protect the merchants, who were openly demanding stricter policing against the disruption of trade and commerce.[76] To the poor there was a nexus between the colonial state and economic exploiters. Bazar workers' resistance to merchants thus extended to and reinforced

[71] *PAI*, No. 22, 7 June 1930.
[72] D. A. Low, '"Civil Martial Law": The Government of India and the Civil Disobedience Movements, 1930–34', in Low (ed.), *Congress and the Raj*, pp. 165–98.
[73] DM, Kanpur, to Chief Secretary, UP, Letter No. 4038/XVIII-15, dated 19/20 March 1933; DM, Allahabad, to Chief Secretary, UP, Copy of D.O. Letter No. 3351/S.T., dated 16 May 1933, File No. 37/1930, Department XV, GAD, Allahabad Commissioner's Office Records.
[74] Copy of a letter from a merchant (not signed) addressed to the President of the Upper India Chamber of Commerce, dated 8 April 1932, File No. 12/1931, Department XX, Police, Allahabad Commissioner's Office Records.
[75] Ibid.
[76] Letter No. 48–B/1932, dated 26 February 1932, DM, Kanpur to Chief Secretary, UP, ibid.

hostility against the police. At the same time, the police in this period were most evidently acting on behalf of the government in repressing political agitation. Anger and protests against police action could, thus, become generalised into anti-British sentiments among the poor and account for their support for nationalist campaigns. Not surprisingly, Congress processions organised in violation of prohibition orders by the police attracted especially large crowds, including those supposed to be 'mainly composed of disorderly elements in the city'.[77] These crowds, according to British officials, lent 'moral support' to the processionists.[78] Such 'moral support' frequently developed into attacks on individual policemen or on police stations and into direct clashes with the police forces who attempted to disperse Congress processions and accompanying crowds.[79] While Congress processionists defied police orders as a form of 'civil disobedience', the crowds of the urban poor vented their anger or protests against the police.

At one level, then, the participation of the poor in nationalist agitations, in the form of crowd assemblies, related to local conflicts in the towns between the poor and the police, merchants or municipal authorities. Since their objects of discontent often coincided with the targets of the Civil Disobedience campaign, they found a means to articulate local protests or resistance through the nationalist movement. However, various groups of the poor took part in the Congress agitations for other, less instrumental, reasons too. The Civil Disobedience movement provided a general arena for them to confront or challenge the symbols of power and authority. They could question their own exclusion from power and assert their rights, even if this could be achieved only symbolically through ritualised political action.

The theatre of nationalism: political ritual and symbolic protest

By far the most important feature of the Civil Disobedience movement was the 'propaganda by deed' of the Congress. This encompassed acts of political opposition and protest that the Congress elaborated through pickets, processions, meetings, drills and hartals. The commitment of the Congress to non-violence and passive resistance meant that public nationalist events were largely in the form of ritualised and symbolic

---

[77] *PAI*, No. 15, 16 April 1932.
[78] *Mr. L. S. White's Report*, p. 4.
[79] *PAI*, No. 27, 12 July 1930; DM, Allahabad, to Chief Secretary, UP, D.O. Letter No. 3351/S.T., dated 16 May 1933 (copy), Serial No. 240, File No. 37/1930, Department XV, GAD, Allahabad Commissioner's Office Records; *FR*: first half of April 1932, File No. L/P&J/12/45, IOR; *Mr. L. S. White's Report*.

action, rather than being direct attacks on institutions of the colonial government. The nationalist repertoire of oppositional acts was forged to signify variously defiance of authority, protest against exclusion from power in the apparatus of government, violation of laws, challenge to the legitimacy of the established political order, as well as assertion of political rights. It was, to a great extent, in the corpus of meanings which could be extracted from these ritualised political actions of the Congress that the possibility of creative appropriation, reinterpretation and recon-struction of nationalism lay for the poor.

One of the most significant forms of political action that the Congress developed gradually from the 1920s, and more vigorously in the 1930s, was the formation of volunteer corps,[80] which engaged in various forms of physical culture and drills, and formed the backbone and nuclei of meetings, processions and pickets. These volunteer organisations were formed with the specific aim 'to raise a trained and disciplined army for the cause of India's freedom'.[81] Many of them, like the Hindusthani Sewa Dal, were fired by an 'avowedly militaristic vision' and received training in drills and handling weaponry.[82] The volunteer corps were also organised on the principles of a military or police hierarchy led by captains or *naiks*.[83] According to various police reports of the 1920s and 1930s, these corps 'model[led] themselves on the pattern of the military and police forces', sought to 'override law and authority' or to 'usurp the functions of the police'[84] and were a cause for serious concern on account of their 'subversive militarism' and 'utter disregard for law and order'.[85] Volunteers also organised pickets and processions, which frequently breached the law and prohibitory orders, and sought to enter areas where such activities had been banned, thus transgressing the spatial restrictions and exclusions stipulated by the government.[86] Through their orderly marches of a semi-military nature, with uniforms and real or mock arms, as well as their flag-hoisting ceremonies, drills and parades, the Congress volunteers regularly emulated precisely the rituals and symbols which epitomised formally constituted state power.

[80] *PAI*, No. 10, 9 March 1929, Appendix No. 4: Supplement to the 'United Provinces Secret Abstract'; for the development of the nationalist volunteer movement, see *PAI*, No. 29, 27 July 1935, Appendix No. 1; File No. G-5 (Part 4)/1940, AICC Papers, NML; Pandey, *Ascendancy*, pp. 39, 44–5.

[81] *PAI*, No. 29, 27 July 1935.

[82] Ibid.

[83] *PAI*, No. 14, 12 April 1930.

[84] Note on the Volunteer Movement in the United Provinces, by T. A. L. Scott O'Connor, Criminal Investigation Department, UP, dated 27 May 1922, File No. 604/1920, Box No. 132, GAD, GUP, UPSA.

[85] *PAI*, No. 29, 27 July 1935, Appendix No. 1.

[86] See, for instance, *Mr. L. S. White's Report*.

They also, at times, attempted to organise parallel administrative and judicial processes in urban neighbourhoods, in order to deny the legitimacy of the ruling apparatus of colonialism. These actions of the volunteers metaphorically marked, first, a contestation of the authority of what was seen as an illegitimate state, including its monopoly over the armed forces and a repressive apparatus of law and order, and, second, an assertion of entitlement to political power from which the colonial state excluded the Indian people. Moreover, by laying claim to the exclusive rituals of state power and prohibited space, the volunteers challenged exclusion itself as a form of exercise of power and a key instrument of domination. At the same time, the volunteers' replication of state rituals projected the possibility of fashioning a contested political order and alternative centres of power for themselves. This, in turn, could implicitly offer the hope of displacing the extant political system. In all its actions then, the nationalist volunteer corps symbolically represented defiance against the imposition of control and authority. Such acts of defiance appealed strongly to the poor in the interwar UP towns, for they faced the increasingly coercive and intrusive quotidian presence of the state and political authorities as well as the 'improvement' and reform onslaught of urban elites. In an environment where the experience of exclusion, marginalisation and social censure was central, the poor could involve themselves in the volunteer movement for political assertion and to register their presence in the urban public sphere. With its powerful political symbolism and contestatory vision, the volunteer movement offered a potent political weapon to the poor and, thus in turn, could draw them towards Congress nationalism. Not surprisingly, the bazar poor lent direct and active support to the volunteers and, with time, the volunteer movement came to assume central importance in popular politics. The participation of the poor themselves in the volunteer movement steadily increased from the period of the Civil Disobedience movement, as compared with the prominence of the middle classes as volunteers during the Non-Cooperation period.[87] By the late 1930s, volunteer corps were to emerge as a key site of political expression of the poor.

The martial culture of *akharas* also played a central role in the conception of the volunteer movement. Local Congress leaders actively promoted physical exercise, wrestling, gymnastics and the formation of akharas, such as the Tilak Vyamasala in Kanpur, established in 1926.[88] Congress volunteers often trained at these akharas. Notwithstanding Gandhi's emphasis on passive and non-violent resistance, body-

[87] Pandey, *Ascendancy*, p. 95.
[88] File No. G-5 (Part 4)/1940, AICC Papers, NML; *PAI*, No. 24, 22 June 1929.

building, wrestling, the martial arts and the worship of a strong physique and masculinity were important aspects of the construction of a nationalist person and expressions of the strength of the nation.[89] In this nurture of an ideal of physical and martial prowess there was a direct overlap between the initiatives of the Congress and the emerging political culture of a significant section of the manual labouring poor in the towns. As chapter 6 has shown, martial activities in the public space had gradually emerged as a central feature of the political action of the poor, especially low-caste Hindu labourers. The volunteer movement epitomised precisely this spirit. The self-assertion of the poor as upright, orderly warriors in order to counter their lowly unruly image, which was expressed through the growing popularity of the akharas, gradually dovetailed into the nationalist volunteer movement. The poor could now amplify their self-image as warriors of Hinduism to that of brave, strong nationalists, confronting a powerful colonial state and seeking to bring about a new social and political order.

In addition to involvement in the volunteer movement, participation in Congress demonstrations, processions and hartals could similarly reinforce the efforts of the urban poor at political assertion and provide them with a powerful repertoire of action to etch a presence for themselves in the politics of the towns. The Congress had introduced a calendar of regular nationalist occasions to mark 'national' and 'independence' 'days' or 'weeks' as well as the birth anniversaries of major Congress leaders or national heroes. On each of these days or weeks, special meetings, processions, pickets and hartals were organised. As seen above, the bazar poor were frequently involved in all of these events, often lending the main or crucial weight and substance to the event through their presence, and so magnifying the significance of the occasion in the eyes of the colonial authorities. As the Commissioner of the Allahabad Division commented on Congress pickets: 'by far the most dangerous element is provided by the large crowds collected, [who] . . . provide . . . the most obvious and adequate symbol of contempt of Government authority.'[90] The 'crowds' of the poor here had clearly seized the initiative and even rendered the Congress activists less relevant. Thus, by the very act of their participation or *yogdan*, the bazar poor immediately registered their powerful presence in urban nationalist politics. The distinction between the leaders and the led became blurred. As in the case of religious rituals and festivals such as the Ramlila seen in chapter 6, the poor could contest or match the

[89] See discussion in chapter 6 above.
[90] Commissioner, Allahabad Division, to the Chief Secretary, UP (undated letter), File No. 12/1931, Department XX, Police. Allahabad Commissioner's Office Records.

power and authority of the elites through their own action in the public space and by carving out their own indispensable role in the nationalist movement. This was their statement in the public arena for inclusion in the national community, instead of being marginal outcasts in the urban setting. In similar vein but for a different context, Shahid Amin has argued that, through their nationalist acts as volunteers or processionists, the villagers of Chauri Chaura experienced a sense of empowerment and envisaged the realisation of a different balance of power, however briefly.[91] Similarly, Pandey holds that '[t]he special merit of propaganda by deed lay . . . in ridding men of the mentality of dependence, of the inferiority complex that long subjection brings and of fear'.[92]

Participation in the nationalist movement, including volunteer activities, was a politically transformative experience for the poor. In the course of their engagement in nationalist action, they began to forge new social and political visions from this period. The most powerful reflection of these changes in the political perception of the poor may be discerned in some striking shifts in cultural practices and performances of the period. The following section provides an analysis of these cultural expressions to identify new concepts of a just society and polity, of emancipatory political change and of social liberation.

New political visions and cultural expression

As mentioned in chapter 5, *nautanki* or *swang* folk theatre was by far the most popular urban entertainment and performance genre in the early twentieth century,[93] incorporating folk songs such as khayal, alha, kajri and chaubola, as well as dance, mime and the martial arts. From its late-nineteenth-century origin in the Punjab, nautanki developed in UP at akharas for musical and dramatic performances. The earliest productions and compositions of nautanki in UP emerged from the Mathura and Hathras region at the turn of the century. Subsequently, Kanpur developed as a key centre from the 1910s, and gradually ushered in the period of the greatest popularity of nautanki in the 1920s and 1930s. At Hathras, a handful of akharas had monopoly over composition and performance. In Kanpur, in contrast, the main proponent of the genre, Sri Krishna Pahalwan, made it more broad based by involving singers

---

[91] Amin, *Event, Metaphor*, pp. 175–89.
[92] Pandey, *Ascendancy*, p. 92.
[93] The following account is substantially based on Kathryn Hansen, *Grounds for Play: The Nautanki Theatre of North India*, Berkeley, 1992; Ramnarayan Agarwal, *Sangit*, Delhi, 1976; Ramnarayan Agarwal, 'Nautanki ka Uday, Vikas aur Vartman Sthiti', *Chayanat*, 14, July–September 1990, pp. 23–8.

and performers from a large number of local akharas of music and body-building, in addition to his own and a few other related nautanki akharas.[94] This opened up the possibility of wider participation and improvisation in the plays, although the main outlines of the stories were sketched out by the author-directors of the akharas, such as Sri Krishna himself, drawing upon mythological legends, historical tales and contemporary events. The index of popularity of nautanki plays and their centrality in the cultural practices of the poor, however, did not lie in direct participation, but in audience response and the large attendance that nautanki performances enjoyed. Nautankis were staged at fairs and festivals[95] such as *Ram Navami, Holi, Burhwa Mangal* or *Chaupahi,* most of which were particularly important amongst the bazar poor. The bazars, in fact, formed the main venue for performances,[96] largely funded by raising subscriptions from the local people – workers, labourers and traders – to meet the fees of the actors and the expenses of the troupes.[97] Apart from the actual nautanki performances, the songs from the plays were also extremely popular and were sung at improvised sessions of music in the evenings, when bazar workers congregated after their work. Chapbooks of nautanki plays were extensively published from the early twentieth century, and provide excellent glimpses of the changing political attitudes of the poor.

As noted in chapter 6, nautanki was considered by the urban elites to be a 'vulgar' form of entertainment, 'low' or 'lewd' in character. The plays were increasingly condemned as a practice of the lower classes in need of reform, especially during the period of prominence of the Kanpur plays, when nautanki became popular among the bazar poor.[98] It is the 'low-class' character of nautankis that renders them an extremely important source for an analysis of the attitudes and perceptions of the poor in the early twentieth century, when nautanki enjoyed its greatest popularity. During this period, nautanki underwent several thematic mutations and transitions. These provide an insight into changes in the political perceptions of the poor as they became involved in diverse forms of political action, based not only on nationalism but also, simultaneously, on religious or caste identities. It will be recalled

---

[94] D. L. Swann, 'Nautanki', in F. P. Richmond, D. L. Swann and P. B. Zarrilli (eds.), *Indian Theatre: Traditions of Performance,* Honolulu, 1990, p. 267.

[95] Ibid., p. 269.

[96] Interview in Kanpur with Puran Chandra Mehrotra, son of Sri Krishna Pahalwan.

[97] Swann, 'Nautanki', p. 269; Sri Krishna introduced the sale of tickets in some cases from the 1910s, when he staged plays in cinema or theatre halls, such as the Baikunth Talkies at the heart of the market area in Moolganj, Kanpur. *Jivan Parichay: Ek Jhanki: Sangeet Natak Academy 1967–68 ke purashkar se vibhushit nautanki shiromani Pahalwan Sri Krishna Khattri,* Kanpur, *vikrami samvat* 2025, c. A.D. 1968, p. 5.

[98] Hansen, *Grounds for Play,* pp. 105–6.

that nautankis expressed a martial ethic, which was a focal point of popular culture in the early twentieth century and was also central to the social and cultural assertion of the poor. Nautankis also harboured a strong strain of Hindu heroism, particularly notable in the plays of Sri Krishna of Kanpur. As discussed in chapter 6, nautankis expressed a self-image of the common people as upright, virtuous and righteous. In addition, nautanki was an important vehicle for the expression of changing ideas about the nature of the polity, political authority, ideal society, community and forms of leadership. These folk plays frequently articulated political and social visions that contested established hierarchies and values.[99]

Nautanki in its early phase at the turn of the century in UP, before it became so widespread in the 1920s, was largely controlled by some akharas based in Hathras, Mathura and Amroha, where the guiding spirit came from Hindu religious devotionalism.[100] Nautanki stories focused mainly on ascetic kings, such as Gopichand Bharthari and Raja Harishchandra, who abdicated or forfeited their royal positions and espoused spiritual pursuits instead.[101] In the case of the rulers in these plays, the real authority to rule was divorced from actual power. These 'dramas of dispossession',[102] reflecting the displacement of Indian rulers from power with the entrenchment of British power, groped for a model of ideal leadership appropriate for the changing times. The figure of the leader envisaged here was one of a royal renouncer, whose legitimacy and authority derived from his penance, sacrifice and spiritualism, and not from his actual grasp over state power or political machinery. This model of leadership, based on the ascetic renouncer of Hindu devotionalism, came to coincide well with the figure of Gandhi. These early nautanki plays anchored political authority to foundations of moral righteousness, asceticism and self-sacrifice, as Gandhi would soon come to do.[103] However, renunciation, as a coveted political ideal and a model of ethical conduct, was to become increasingly the preserve of the Hindu upper-caste commercial communities and middle classes in the 1920s and 1930s, and came to underpin their vision of nationalism.[104] It is no coincidence that the renouncer King Harishchandra

[99] Ibid., passim.
[100] Agarwal, 'Nautanki ka Uday, Vikas aur Vartman Sthiti', p. 24; Hansen, *Grounds for Play*, pp. 70–3.
[101] Hansen, *Grounds for Play*, pp. 119–27.
[102] Ibid., p. 92.
[103] Gandhi himself saw Harishchandra as a model of personal conduct devoted to the quest for 'truth'. Raghavan Iyer (ed.), *The Essential Writings of Mahatma Gandhi*, Delhi, 1990, pp. 223–7.
[104] Douglas Haynes, *Rhetoric and Ritual in Colonial India: The Shaping of a Public Culture in Surat City, 1852–1928*, Berkeley, 1991; Indian edn, Delhi, 1992, pp. 227–9.

became a staple of the middle-class Parsee theatre of the 1920s and 1930s, and subsequently of early Indian cinema.[105]

By the 1920s, the nautankis gradually registered some shifts away from a focus on royal renouncers or moral asceticism and towards new social visions and political preoccupations. This was the period of the greatest popularity of nautanki. The more formal literary style of the Hathras school of earlier origin was gradually superseded by colloquial intrusions in the newly emerging Kanpur school from around 1911, which was soon to outstrip the former in audience.[106] 'Vulgar' language and 'erotic topics' now became integral features of nautanki, which Hansen has argued to be suggestive of the increasingly popular character of nautanki.[107] The more 'popular' character of the Kanpur school from this time is likely to be related to the erosion of the monopoly of a handful of akharas of the Hathras–Mathura school and the greater democratisation of the Kanpur school, which permitted improvisation and the inclusion of new themes and preoccupations. In this period, contradictions in urban society sharpened and the poor appeared at the forefront of a range of political and social movements. To the majority of the audience of nautanki – the lower castes and classes, especially the bazar poor – social and cultural assertion as well as the valorisation of a culture of martial prowess had become central. Nautankis of the 1910s and 1920s began to reflect these changes. They also increasingly dealt with issues of justice, equality and entitlement, suggesting the changing preoccupations of popular politics. The older plots and themes did not entirely disappear, nor were the plays dealing with the issue of renunciation in public life jettisoned. However, saintliness and renunciation had to compete with other values. The source of moral authority of the ruler and of a legitimate polity gradually seemed to have been relocated elsewhere, in tune with the enlargement of the arena of political action and the involvement of the poor.

As Hansen shows, one set of nautankis that emerged during this more popular phase drew inspiration from Rajput chivalric, martial and romantic tales, such as those of the chieftains Alha and Udal or the

---

[105] K. Hansen, 'The Birth of Hindi Drama in Banaras, 1868–1885', in S. B. Freitag (ed.), *Culture and Power in Banaras: Community, Performance and Environment, 1800–1980*, Berkeley, 1989, p. 75; A. Rajadhyaksha and P. Willemen (eds.), *Encyclopaedia of Indian Cinema*, Delhi, 1994, pp. 225, 503, 542–3, 550. The first Indian feature film of the 'silent' era by D. G. Phalke in 1913 was *Raja Harishchandra*, followed by several other versions, both 'silent' and 'talkies', including in Hindi and regional languages.

[106] Indra Sharma 'Varij', *Swang Nautanki*, Publications Division, Ministry of Information and Broadcasting, Government of India, 1984, p. 148.

[107] Hansen, *Grounds for Play*, pp. 105–6.

nobleman Amar Singh Rathore.[108] These plays were based not on mythology, as in the earlier stories of ascetic kings, but on historical events or heroic legends, drawn especially from a period when Islamic rule was being established in the Indian subcontinent and was encountering the resistance of Hindu royal houses. These plays celebrated India's folk heroes, selected largely from a Hindu heroic tradition. They revolved around the themes of displacement and usurpation. This metaphor of dispossession as well as the Hindu martial essence of the heroes overlapped with the central motifs of low-caste movements and the religious resurgence of the Hindu poor. They also played upon the theme of loss of independence and alien domination, and thus began to articulate nationalist aspirations. These nautankis thus established important cognitive bridges between nationalism and caste or religious movements. These nautankis of Rajput heroes also incorporated new ideas about the polity and leadership. The celebrated qualities of the heroes of the new plays and the source of their moral authority were different from those of the ascetic king. Amar Singh Rathore's status as hero, for instance, hinged on 'his willingness to lay down his life in defense of a code of honor rooted in loyalty, mutual trust, fearlessness, and benevolence'.[109] Renunciation and spiritualism appear no longer to be central to the image of the ideal leader and to the source of political authority. The heroes are now distinguished for their martial might, loyalty, forbearance and steadfast resolve.[110] More significantly, the hero is not the actual ruler or a royal figure. He is usually an outsider, often not of high birth, but is superior to the ruler in stature and moral fibre. These legends of asymmetry in birth and merit[111] challenged the hierarchies of clan and caste, and staked out the entitlement of outsiders to power. The heroes are like 'the ordinary person who strives for a sense of belonging in an indifferent world'.[112] The hero here expressed the conception of a new kind of ideal leader, and also represented a self-image of the poor. The plays celebrated the inner worth of a person – not their status or position. They also questioned exclusion and imbalances in the political system or in the extant social order, and thus dovetailed into some of the key motifs of both caste or religious movements and the nationalist movement.

The 1920s and 1930s saw another important shift in the content of nautankis. Nautankis, along with a related corpus of alha and lavni songs, increasingly incorporated nationalist themes. Their central motifs were the zulm or tyranny, atrocity and brutality of colonial rule, as well as the celebration of the heroism of nationalists.[113] Sri Krishna's play

---

[108] Ibid., pp. 128–33.   [109] Ibid., p. 132.   [110] Ibid., pp. 128–33.
[111] Ibid., p. 132.   [112] Ibid., p. 133.   [113] Ibid., pp. 133–5.

Khune Nahak and a play by another author entitled *Julmi Dayar* ('Dyer, the Oppressor') were both based on the Jallianwalabagh incident. At the same time, Sri Krishna wrote a series of alha songs, collectively called *Zulm ki Aag* ('The fire of tyranny'), on the theme of coercion and the arbitrary force of colonial rule. Sri Krishna also incorporated Bhagat Singh in his repertoire of plays and composed alhas on the theme of Non-Cooperation, called *Asahayog Chutney* ('The potent concoction of Non-Cooperation').[114] At a later stage, Sri Krishna's play *Ballia ke Sher* ('The lions of Ballia') held out the promise that the martyrdom and sacrifice of nationalists such as Chittu Pande of Ballia would one day eradicate oppression in an independent India.[115] Although nautankis did, thus, express nationalist sentiments, this was not undertaken widely or always overtly. This was largely because of the censorship that nautankis encountered as the most prominent form of popular entertainment.[116] Performances were at times terminated by police intervention, and nautanki chapbooks were banned and confiscated. Although direct expressions of nationalism were thus limited in nautanki, the metaphor of struggle against alien and unjust rulers was ever present. The plays thus allegorically expressed nationalist sentiments, and were at times used by the Congress for nationalist propaganda for mass mobilisation.[117]

The most crucial shift in nautankis in the 1920s and 1930s, however, related not so much to nationalism as to the expression of new social and political visions. It was from this period that the figure of the bandit hero, such as in the play *Sultana the Dacoit*, became prominent.[118] As Hansen has commented, the 'frequency and continued popularity' of these plays about social bandits 'make them noteworthy'.[119] These plays were based on the life of contemporary social bandits, who were portrayed as 'outlaws in the service of the poor',[120] redistributing the wealth of the rich to the deserving needy. Hansen interprets these plays based on real persons in terms of a process of 'myth in the making' and 'folklore visibly emanating from people's lives'.[121] This trend of dramatic glorification of heroes from real life in nautankis seems to have run parallel with contemporary processes of idolisation of local heroes

[114] *Jivan Parichay: Ek Jhanki*, pp. 4–5; Agarwal, *Sangit*, p. 131.
[115] Interview with Puran Chandra Mehrotra, son of Sri Krishna. A well-known line from the play *Ballia ke Sher* ran: *'Zulm zalim ka barbad ho jayega; jhanda ghar ghar tiranga lehrayega; ye watan apna azad ho jayega'* ('The tyranny of the tyrant will be destroyed; the tricolour flag will fly atop every home, our homeland will be independent').
[116] Hansen, *Grounds for Play*, p. 116; *Jivan Parichay: Ek Jhanki*, p. 5.
[117] Pandey, *Ascendancy*, p. 82.
[118] Hansen, *Grounds for Play*, pp. 135–43.
[119] Ibid., p. 135.   [120] Ibid., p. 98.   [121] Ibid., p. 136.

by popular acclaim. Chapter 6 discussed the custom of deification of heroic martyrs and the growing enthusiasm of the lower-caste poor in worshipping them as 'beers' at neighbourhood shrines in Benares. In the 1920s a new shrine was dedicated to the recently deceased 'Bachau Beer'. Bachau, in contemporary urban folklore, was described as an exceptionally brave and strong *ahir*. On one occasion when he was unarmed, he was set upon, vastly outnumbered, overpowered and killed by a group of armed high-caste landowners, who wanted to deprive him of his right to a plot of land.[122] The contemporaneity of the deification of Bachau and the appearance of the dacoit hero in nautanki is significant. Both addressed the questions of the right to property and control over assets or economic resources. The idealised and celebrated figures in both cases were drawn not only from real life but also from the ranks of the poor themselves. This suggests that in popular perception political and social initiatives of struggle were increasingly seen to rest with the poor themselves, and not simply vested in the figures of benevolent kings and nobles. On the one hand, this metaphorically signified the claims of the poor to exercise their own rights and their entitlement to power. On the other hand, this signalled a shift away from conceptions of rulership and political leadership based on paternalistic patriarchs and towards the 'common man'. In sum, this reflected the growing engagement of the poor in the public sphere. This ideal of the right of the common people to wield power was also expressed in the system of justice and order prevailing under the bandit hero, in contrast to the governing structures of the state or the weathy. It is not surprising that this range of ideas would come to the foreground of popular culture in a time of the extension of popular politics and mass mobilisation. Through political action and struggles, including nationalism, new conceptions of the polity and social order were clearly evolving amongst the poor, which the nautankis poignantly reflected.

The bandit hero, moreover, was no longer the patron, protector or benevolent guardian of the needy or the poor of an earlier conception. Instead, he was a redistributor, dealing with questions of wealth and power, embodying above all an ethos of egalitarianism, justice and social critique. Some of the key targets of attack in the plays were landlords and *seths* or moneylenders.[123] The plays also raised the issue of power as exercised through the law and the police. The bandit as an outlaw not only fled the arm of the law, but also set up a counter system of

---

[122] D. M. Coccari, 'The Bir Babas of Banaras and the Deified Dead', in A. Hiltebeitel (ed.), *Criminal Gods and Demon Devotees: Essays on the Guardians of Popular Hinduism*, Albany, 1989, pp. 251–69.
[123] Hansen, *Grounds for Play*, pp. 138, 141.

administration and justice.[124] A recurrent motif in the plays concerned the use of uniforms and arms by the bandit and his followers,[125] resonating with the spirit of the volunteer activities of nationalism. In this context, Hansen points out that the bandit plays are similar to the earlier plays of Rajput heroes for they 'dispute the hierarchical nature of society'. Yet their conception not only includes a critique of clan and caste view of hierarchy and difference, but 'exhibit[s] greater consciousness of both the class basis of economic privilege and the unrelenting arm of the law'.[126]

The nautankis then encapsulated a critique of the political system and the social order. They expressed the aspirations of the poor for power, a place in the political system and redistributive justice. The plays also suggest the ways in which the future nation and the national community were beginning to be envisaged by the poor. The desired polity was projected not so much in terms of paternalistic leaders of a Gandhian conception with a disciplined mass of followers or citizens, but increasingly in terms of a democratic society resting on redistribution and direct political participation. Many of these ideas echo the emerging preoccupations of popular politics as expressed through religious upsurge and nationalism, in particular the attempt by the poor to stake their own claim in the public sphere against social marginalisation and to stamp their presence both in the urban polity and in the wider democratic politics of the emerging nation. The growing stress on class, power and redistribution from the 1920s may also have related to the gradual dissemination of socialist ideas, including those of the Congress Socialist Party from the mid-1930s, which will be discussed below.

As seen in chapter 6, in the 1920s and 1930s increasing initiatives were mounted by middle-class nationalist or religious reformers to control and guide the entertainment habits and religious or cultural practices of the poor, including attempts to cleanse and purge nautanki of its supposed vulgarities. Nautanki had been singled out for purification, with a view to converting it to a more edifying form, which would be suitable for building the moral fibre of the citizens of the emerging nation.[127] Nautanki thus became grist to the mill of elite campaigns for moral and social uplift or reform of the lower classes. The emergence of nautanki as a key site of reformist action has been interpreted by Hansen as part and parcel of the wider drives for social improvement and reform of this period, and of the growing tension and rift between popular and elite cultural forms.[128] This history of control of lower-class practices and contest over rival modes of self-expression was certainly an important

---

[124] Ibid., pp. 137–9.   [125] Ibid., p. 138.   [126] Ibid., p. 136.
[127] Ibid., pp. 105–6.   [128] Ibid., pp. 105–6, 253–8.

element in the controversy over the unpalatable features of nautanki to middle-class sensibilities. The growing opposition to nautanki was also most likely to have been related to at least two other factors. First, the expression of potentially radical themes of social transformation, which were gradually becoming so important in nautanki, could render them suspect in the eyes of middle-class nationalists and also invite censorship by the state. Second, submerged in the narrative structures of nautanki were expressions of the political assertion of the poor, and as such the plays could become an important target for social control. It would, however, be misleading to assume that the political content of these plays signalled the inevitable march of the poor towards higher levels of class consciousness. These shifts in ideas related to the changing political practices of the time through which the poor gradually formulated new notions of ideal polity and society. The nautanki gave muted and partial expression to these conceptions.

Hansen has argued that, although nautankis expressed alternative, even radical, visions, ultimately they did not fully convey messages of emancipatory change.[129] She notes that, while the plays questioned power and hierarchy, the resolution of many of the plays ultimately restored the status quo, including, for instance, the capitulation of the bandit hero to the powers of the state.[130] The accepted social order was inverted only temporarily in the nautanki narratives. Hansen thus understands nautankis in terms of ritual inversion, which ultimately serves the functional purpose of reproducing social cohesion and the maintenance of order and hierarchy. However, rituals encapsulate a dialectic between the confirmation and the contestation of power.[131] They not only act to uphold the prevailing social hierarchy, but also help to interrogate it, as Hansen herself points out, as well as to envision alternatives.[132] From this perspective, it would be appropriate to view nautankis as expressing contested social and political ideals, despite the restrained radicalism of their narratives. Moreover, it is possible to speculate that the restoration of the status quo at the end of nautanki plays was probably not simply a mark of their watered-down radicalism, but might well have been because the plays had to contend with both reformist drives and censorship, and somehow had to devise means to survive within such constraints. After all, the nautankis were not minor underground activities that could operate at the edge of the political

---

129 Ibid., p. 117.   130 Ibid., pp. 140–3.
131 Nicholas B. Dirks, 'Ritual and Resistance: Subversion as a Social Fact', in D. Haynes and G. Prakash (eds.), *Contesting Power: Resistance and Everyday Social Relations in South Asia*, Oxford, 1991; 1st edn of the University of California Press, Berkeley, 1992, pp. 213–38.
132 Hansen, *Grounds for Play*, pp. 261–4.

world with their radical ideological beliefs. They were one of the most visible forms of public entertainment. This tended to stimulate the 'safe' strategy of muting or reining in their radical messages and falling back on 'conservative' resolutions. The authors or playwrights, while articulating popular aspirations and a critique of hierarchy and power, at the same time quite possibly exercised a degree of restraint to avoid both censorship and any political act of protest or resistance that direct emancipatory messages might encourage among the audience.

It has to be borne in mind in this context that, although the contested visions of nautankis thus frequently remained implicit in their narrative structures, they found fuller and freer expression through the character of the jester or the joker – *Ranga* or *Bidushak* – who was present in every play. The jester in nautanki drew upon the folk traditions of *bhand* (professional jester and clown) and *bahurupiya* (an expert in disguise), who were important figures in popular culture and often appeared in religious festivals such as the Ramlila processions.[133] The part of the Ranga or Bidushak in the nautanki plays was not pre-scripted. Their extempore performances were unstructured and not bound by either the artistic rules and conventions or the narrative structure of the plays. They thus had enormous latitude in improvising and innovating their own speeches and performance on the stage, and especially in invoking the present and contemporary issues by disrupting the narrative thread of the plays. As a result of the freedom and licence that they enjoyed, and under cover of being figures of ridicule and fun, they were able to subvert accepted norms and to deliver serious, trenchant social critique, usually through the media of jokes, scathing humour, absurd metaphors, wit and irony.[134] They usually appeared in the plays in the guises of the *Pissu* or personal servant, and of the *Munshiji* or clerk and assistant to businessmen and landlords. In both cases they were supposed to be close to people in high places and thus to have privileged access to the details of their personal lives and private practices. By revealing such 'inside' information, they ridiculed, insulted and undermined the authority of their social superiors. Pretending to be 'insiders', they also exposed the evil-doings of tyrannical policemen, corrupt officials, oppressive *chaudhuris* (headmen) in villages or unscrupulous businessmen and merchants. Through this, they highlighted and commented on the nature of oppression and injustice. A frequent refrain of the 'munshi' on stage was to ask for money from all the characters in the play. This

---

[133] Roshan Taki, 'Lakhnau ki Bhand Parampara', *Chayanat*, No. 21, April–June 1982, pp. 16–23.

[134] Dr Induja Awasthi, 'Hindi Paramparik Rangmanch mein Bidushak', *Chayanat*, No. 33, April–June 1985, pp. 13–19.

insistent attempt at extraction of money by the 'munshi', who is after all the assistant or representative of landlords or merchants, could point to economic exploitation. The significance of these jesters in the plays may, of course, be understood simply in terms of ritual transgression and temporary violation of accepted modes of behaviour. However, the very fact that the Ranga or Bidushak played such a pivotal role in nautankis with their social critique and questioning of power and authority also points to the central and growing significance for the poor of the social and political contestation that was developing through political action.

Religion and nationalism

The analysis of nautanki has, among other things, pointed to an enmeshing of religious and nationalist visions, and it is to this theme that this section now turns. The focus here is on the significance of religion for the participation of the poor in the nationalist movement from the period of the Civil Disobedience campaigns. The link between nationalism and religious ideology or identity has generated a substantial literature. As will be discussed further in this chapter, it is now well known that Congress campaigns relied extensively on Hindu religious imagery. Pandey has shown that Congress propaganda in UP from the 1930s increasingly displayed Hindu religious overtones. During the Civil Disobedience movement, the Congress frequently undertook its mobilisation drives at fairs and festivals, and pressed into action *sadhus* and ascetics.[135] In a somewhat different vein, historians have discussed the centrality of religious motifs, metaphors and ideologies in the reception of the nationalist message. Masselos has suggested that various traditions of religious processions and sacred public rituals provided the template for the structure of similar Congress events. Thus, previous religious experience conditioned the ways in which the masses related to Congress processions.[136] Ranajit Guha has argued that 'discrimination between purity and pollution', derived from Hindu religious conceptions, 'established a defining principle of nationalist conduct' in the Swadeshi and Non-Cooperation movements and that 'the ancient and conservative ideology of caste', in the form of social boycott, ostracism and caste sanctions, 'came to be grafted on a developing nationalism'.[137] Hardiman and Haynes, in particular, have

---

[135] Instances of Congress propaganda at Hindu fairs and festivals cited in Pandey, *Ascendancy*, pp. 82, 125.

[136] Masselos, 'Audiences, Actors and Congress Dramas', pp. 77–9, 82.

[137] R. Guha, 'Discipline and Mobilize', in P. Chatterjee and G. Pandey (eds.), *Subaltern Studies VII: Writings on South Asian History and Society*, Delhi, 1992, pp. 77–95.

explored the prominence of the idioms of renunciation, spiritualism and devotional Hinduism as the key to the success and potency of Gandhian nationalism, especially among peasants and commercial communities.[138] Haynes, in a detailed analysis, has drawn attention to a number of interconnected motifs of Hindu and Jain devotional provenance, in order to account for the dissemination of Gandhi's message in Surat.[139] The core sacred metaphors that Haynes identifies include duty; shame and honour; renunciation; penance; sacrifice and purity; and leadership and discipleship – all of which were further embellished with Hindu mythological motifs drawn from the epics. Haynes argues that the infusion of such 'potent indigenous vocabulary'[140] drawn from 'devotional Hinduism and mercantile prestige'[141] helped Gandhians to forge 'powerful psychic connections between critical indigenous values and the notion of nationalism',[142] and thus enlivened nationalism for the inhabitants of Surat. The motifs singled out by Haynes, however, are likely to have had only a sectional appeal, restricted largely to commercial communities and some segments of the urban middle classes with a tradition of Jain and Hindu devotionalism.

Other interpretations have been advanced to demonstrate the importance of religion in subaltern nationalism, notably by Pandey, Amin, Sarkar and Hardiman. They have argued, with varying emphases, that codes of religious conduct, belief in the magical powers of saints or notions of divine punishment and ritual obligations – all drawn from popular religious practices – provided familiarity and immediacy to the nationalist message for the subaltern classes.[143] Most recently, van der Veer has argued that a powerful conception of community in India had for long been in religious terms, thus contributing to the construction and imagination of the national community itself as a form of religious community. Thus it is not surprising, in van der Veer's view, that nationalism is overwhelmingly conceptualised through religion in the Indian subcontinent.[144]

Underlying all these interpretations is an assumption that the injection of religious imagery and ideas animates and augments the potency of nationalist messages and propaganda. Hindu values, rites and rituals are

[138] Hardiman, 'The Crisis of the Lesser Patidars', pp. 59–61; Haynes, *Rhetoric and Ritual*, pp. 220–37.
[139] Haynes, *Rhetoric and Ritual*, pp. 220–37.
[140] Ibid., p. 237.   [141] Ibid., p. 220.   [142] Ibid., p. 221.
[143] Pandey, 'Peasant Revolt and Indian Nationalism'; Amin, 'Gandhi as Mahatma'; Sarkar, *'Popular' Movements and 'Middle Class' Leadership in Late Colonial India*; Hardiman, *Devi*, p. 170; Sarkar, 'The Conditions and Nature of Subaltern Militancy', pp. 308–17.
[144] P. van der Veer, *Religious Nationalism: Hindus and Muslims in India*, Berkeley, 1994.

implicitly seen either to be a part of familiar everyday experience or to carry some intrinsic powerful meaning, whose presence inevitably lends significance to nationalism. Quite apart from the debatable 'essential' importance of religious conceptions in these perspectives, their efficacy in addressing the question of religion and nationalism for the urban poor in interwar UP seems particularly doubtful in the light of discussions in this book. Patterns of Hindu religious assertion as well as the key themes of nautanki indicate that saintliness, renunciation or quietist piety were not the most important religious concerns of the urban poor in the early twentieth century. These Gandhian motifs could scarcely have aroused much passion. The universality of appeal or acceptance of the concept of renunciation by Hindus of all castes and sects is, in any case, an arguable proposition. Most importantly, Hinduism itself was in a state of flux in the interwar period and a martial version was gaining currency, which was hardly likely to be compatible with the Gandhian devotional idiom and moral asceticism. Even the most resolutely devotional image of Ram, painted by Tulsidas, was in this period gradually metamorphosing into a fierce warrior figure. Clearly, the significance of religion in nationalism has to be approached through a history of religious change, rather than through 'traditional' facets of Hinduism. Equally importantly, it is necessary to address the implications for nationalism of the emergent and redefined Hindu religious identity of the poor, which, it has been seen, overlapped with a range of other identities to do with status, occupation or deprivation. How then is it possible to approach the issue of religion in the nationalist movement for the urban poor in UP in the 1930s? To answer this question, it is worthwhile to examine the religious metaphors being emphasised in nationalist propaganda and to analyse what those might have meant to the poor.

The Congress campaigns of the Civil Disobedience period largely targeted the Hindu population. With the increasing political alienation of the Muslim poor from the Congress in the 1920s,[145] the party could not hope for substantial success in gaining their support. The fact that Congress activists concentrated their campaigns mostly in the Hindu bazar areas, as seen above,[146] suggests that they directed their attention primarily at the Hindu bazar poor. Capitalising on the contemporary religious resurgence amongst the poor was a logical and expedient strategy. Political pragmatism demanded an emphasis on the version of Hinduism – militant and martial – that had gained public ascendance

---

[145] Discussed in chapters 6–7 above. See also Pandey, *Ascendancy*, pp. 114–27.
[146] See also ibid., p. 149.

from the 1920s, despite the importance of Gandhian devotionalism in the authorised discourse of the Congress high command. The use of religious motifs of an overtly martial nature would thus become prominent in Congress propaganda. This was, in no small measure, determined by the preferences and predilections of the bazar poor to which Congress activity responded. In addition, a large number of Congress activists were themselves involved with the Arya Samaj and the Hindu Sabha. Not surprisingly, therefore, it was the resurgent aggressive Hinduism, which these organisations favoured, that found prominence in the Congress campaigns of the 1930s. The newly emerging metaphor of religious warfare of the early twentieth century was thus at the heart of the Civil Disobedience campaigns in UP.

The invocation of the popular festival of Holi in nationalism provides an apt example of the nature of the linkages between nationalism and Hinduism that were being forged in the 1930s. That the Holi festival assumed importance in nationalist propaganda is in itself a significant fact. Holi, as shown in chapter 6, was the key festival of the bazar poor, and there was a steady expansion in the scale of celebration in the early twentieth century. It is perhaps not a coincidence that, even though Holi was not an important festival of the upper-caste Hindus who led the Congress organisation, they focused on this particular festival for popular mobilisation. How did they link nationalism with Holi? Holi had traditionally been celebrated as the festival of love, arising from its association with Lord Krishna, the great amorous figure of Indian sacred mythology. An editorial in the Kanpur newspaper *Vartman* referred to this spirit of love in merging Holi with nationalist celebrations. Holi, it was said, was a festival of love and amity when all animosities among Hindus were forgotten, and it was with this spirit of unity that all Hindus should join in the nationalist struggle against the British government.[147] Interestingly, the romantic love that Krishna represented was transmuted into a fraternal amity of all Hindus who must fight for nationalism. A new dimension of the festival was projected here in tune with the aim of the Hindu revivalist organisations to forge a unified Hindu community. It was not, however, love that found the most prominence in Holi in this period but, more crucially, the metaphor of sacred warfare, with which Lord Krishna is also associated. In his message in the religious text *Gita*, expounded at the Kurukshetra battlefield, Krishna convinced Arjun of the need for warfare, even against one's kinfolk, in order to adhere to one's *dharma* or righteous duty. It was urged that Holi be observed in this martial spirit

---

[147] *Vartman*, 15 March 1930, p. 2.

of Krishna at Kurukshetra, as well as of Rana Pratap at Haldighat, Padmini at Chittor and Kunwar Singh in 1857.[148] Not only was Krishna in the epic Kurukshetra war of the *Mahabharata* invoked in this case, but historical Hindu figures who fought either against Muslim emperors, such as Rana Pratap and Padmini, or against the British, such as Kunwar Singh, were absorbed in the same symbology of religious warfare. In the same vein, elsewhere the martial Krishna was privileged over the flautist lover: 'We are more in need of that Krishna who killed Kansa and who humiliated the enemies in the court of Duryodhan by showing his sword and chakra [discus]. Hindus! Change your views, worship the Krishna of sudharshan chakra [the sacred discus of Krishna] in place of the Krishna of the flute.'[149] A contemporary poem on Holi, entitled 'Invitation to War', went even further in rallying for battle: 'a new sort of Holi will come into being. We have to attain immortality in this ephemeral existence. We have to come to the battle-field; what is there to fear now?'[150] The vermilion hues of the festival of colour were invoked to conjure up images of blood-letting in battlefields. A journal article declared: 'he alone is a true kshattriya [warrior] who, seeing the suffering of the country, undertakes to celebrate Holi for the removal of those sufferings.'[151] All these views of Holi, expressed in nationalist, religious or caste journals and newspapers in 1930, empha-sised mainly one aspect of the festival to the exclusion of others, and largely an unorthodox or innovative one at that. The festival in this form was scarcely laden with familiar resonances. The propagandists here were, of course, drawing upon traditional figures and themes, but they gave them new orientations and built upon recent reconstructions of Holi in the process of the militant Hindu upsurge.

Martial themes drawn from the imagery of sacred warfare formed a recurrent motif in the Civil Disobedience movement, despite the simultaneous proclamation of non-violence. Indeed, the message of non-violence seems to have been modified and recast for popular consumption at the local level. Thus, for instance, following the police shooting and death of the extremely popular revolutionary-terrorist Chandrasekhar Azad, P. D. Tandon, a prominent Congress leader of the Province, explained to the audience at a Congress public meeting in Allahabad that Gandhi's message of non-violence had to be properly understood in relation to the self-sacrifice and heroism of the terrorists. He argued that non-violence in this case meant that it was better to die a

[148] *NNR*, No. 12/1930, p. 3, cites *Kshattriya Mitra*.
[149] *NNR*, No. 34/1930, pp. 2–3, cites *Krishna*.
[150] *NNR*, No. 20/1930, p. 3, cites *Anand*. The poem is by Kahan Chand Gautam.
[151] *NNR*, No. 12/1930, p. 3, cites *Kshattriya Mitra*.

brave death in violence than to run away with cowardice in non-violence, although he stressed at the same time the importance of maintaining non-violence in political action.[152] This exposition, however, points to overt acts of bravery and courage as supreme goals and coveted values, rather than non-violence, passivity and pacifism. Tandon was not publicly advocating revolutionary violence, but he did emphasise strength and heroism – the two key themes of martial Hindu resurgence. Non-violence seems to have been narrowly conceived to mean refraining from slaughter or murder and avoiding direct aggression, but incorporated valour, courage and a martial spirit, glossing over the fact that battles, even righteous ones, do inevitably entail fierce strife and bloodshed. On account of ambivalence of this kind in the message of the Congress and the need to modify it in the light of popular preferences, the Civil Disobedience and related campaigns in reality rang with the din of battle and were replete with the iconography of martial Hindu heroes and gods and celestial weaponry. The Kanpur newspaper *Aj*, on the occasion of independence day in 1930, exhorted all 'to take a vow to prove that they are worthy descendants of Krishna, Ashoka, Maharana Pratap, Shivaji, Maharaja Ranjit Singh, and innumerable other heroes who sacrificed their lives at the feet of the mother [India]'.[153] If the great pacifist Ashoka seems to be a misfit in this array of warlike heroes, it has to be borne in mind that, notwithstanding the Buddhist non-violence of his later years, he was a great warrior, conqueror and empire-builder in his early career. Moreover, in this late-colonial period, Ashoka and his pan-Indian empire were the emerging symbols of the historical unification of the Indian nation, leading to the inclusion of the Ashoka 'chakra' (wheel) in the national flag and the use of the Ashokan column in currency notes and as the official emblem of the independent Indian state. A pantheon of mythical and historical Hindu martial heroes and rulers was, in this way, publicly commemorated and valorised with a great deal of pomp and pageantry, especially through celebrations of their anniversaries. The birth anniversaries of Shivaji and of Rana Pratap, the Maratha and the Rajput rulers, respectively, who fought against the Mughal regime at different times, were given great prominence in the ritual calendar of the Congress and were, in particular, used as the occasion to promote wrestling and various martial arts.[154] In 1932, *Arya Mitra* not only urged processions, meetings and promotion of Khadi and temperance as part of Rana Pratap

[152] *PAI*, No. 9, 7 March 1931.
[153] *NNR*, No. 5/1930, p. 2.
[154] *PAI*, No. 24, 22 June 1929.

anniversary celebrations, but also encouraged pilgrimage to Haldighat, where the Rana had confronted Akbar's troops, and further argued: 'If we want to discard weakness, cultivate strength, discharge our duty towards our country and uplift ourselves, we should learn to accord due respect to Maharana Pratap, the guardian of liberty.'[155] During Shivaji day celebrations in 1930, Congress speakers in Benares dwelt on the fact that Gandhi started the Civil Disobedience movement on 12 March 1930, and Shivaji had launched his military campaigns against the Mughals on exactly the same day 300 years earlier in 1630.[156] Well-known mythological heroes and fighters, especially from the great Hindu epics, such as Bhima, Abhimanyu and Arjun, were also presented as role models. The Civil Disobedience freedom fighters were urged to 'display Arjun's skills in archery, Bhima's strength of arms and Abhimanyu's military strategy'.[157] This prompted the extensive formation of *dals* or volunteer corps named after these heroes, such as the Mahabir Dal and the Abhimanyu Dal, which marched in nationalist processions and toured the bazars.[158]

The imagery of warfare was further elaborated through the invocation of the powerful mythological weapons of divine heroes. Even the charkha (spinning wheel) was integrated into this armoury as an instrument of battle rather than as a symbol of constructive economic activity. A poem in praise of the charkha went thus: 'Thou art Kali's dagger, Parashuram's axe, thou art Mohan's discus which has destroyed the demons.'[159] Another poem from an earlier period in the 1920s had compared the power of the charkha with that of the discus (*chakra*) of Krishna and the thunderbolt (*bajra*) of Indra.[160] A contemporary nationalist khayal folk song similarly praised the *swarajya sankhya* or the conch of freedom, the conch being used both as a sacred horn and as a martial bugle; the charkha as chakra (discus); satyagraha as *gada* (club or mace); and *prem* or love, presumably love for the country, as *padma* or lotus – all of which are usually displayed in the various hands of the idols of the Hindu deity Vishnu.[161] A poem by Jai Narayan Jha 'Vinit', published in the Kanpur newspaper *Pratap* at the height of the Civil Disobedience movement, expressed the martial temper of the

---

[155] *NNR*, No. 23/1932, p. 3.
[156] *PAI*, No. 12, 29 March 1930.
[157] *NNR*, No. 7/1930, p. 1, cites *Ballia Gazette*.
[158] *PAI*, No. 34, 30 August 1930.
[159] *NNR*, No. 43/1930, p. 1, cites *Khandelwal*.
[160] Review of Hindi magazine *Volunteer* (Kanpur), No. 1, December 1924. Proscribed Publication, Accession No. 1870 (also held as Accession Nos. 1866, 1867), NAI. The original Hindi version of the poem is held as Accession No. 902.
[161] Sharma, 'Pandit Banarsidas Chaturvedi se Baatchit', p. 20.

movement in ringing tones and revealed some of the ambivalence of the non-violent message:[162]

> Hot ascetic
> youths are standing with the offering of
> life (in their hands). Make (them) worship the
> goddess of war; be prepared. Open the gate of
> the temple of war. May the effusions of
> the devotees fructify! Let these devotees
> under the impulse of devotion honour the
> goddess of war by means of cataclysmic
> songs (full) of bhairav (terrible) feelings and
> rudra (tempestuous) dance. Let us hear the
> shrill and interminable sounds of the weapons
> of war and the lute.

The propaganda of the Civil Disobedience years, conducted either directly by the Congress and/or by the nationalist media, clearly cast nationalism in terms of a religious war and extensively invoked the glory of past battles and heroes. In this, the nationalist campaign directly absorbed the imagery of militant Hinduism of the 1920s and 1930s. The army of Hinduism was now being invited to join the troops of the nation. From the perspective of the poor, martial Hinduism had been a mode of political assertion and the cultivation of a mighty and combative self-image. By analogy and extension, fighting the battle for the nation could refurbish and accentuate that self-image. It was the intermeshing of the messages of militant Hinduism and of nationalism that explains the potency of religion in popular nationalism. Religious imagery clearly animated nationalist mobilisation, although not because of the supposed inherent potency of its familiar or timeless meanings, but by association and interlinking with the powerful recent constructions of resurgent Hinduism of the 1920s. The mesh of interlocking images of both religious revival and nationalism, of course, featured well-known religious figures and myths, but the messages were far from familiar. The Civil Disobedience movement was launched at a conjuncture when popular Hinduism in north India was undergoing rapid and radical change, with martial militancy as its central motif. It is clearly this newly constructed version that the Congress promoted, driven in some measure by the pressures from below which demanded an aggressive, martial, combative and confident Hinduism, rather than a version stressing renunciation, piety, devotion, penance, self-purification, sacrifice and duty. In addition, the linking of resurgent Hinduism with

---

[162] *NNR*, No. 8/1930, p. 1, (translation of the poem cited in this report); for a similar poem from a Kanpur newspaper, see *NNR*, No. 9/1930, p. 1.

nationalism propelled the latter in more militant and activist directions, tending to override the messages of passive resistance or non-violence. Of course, a devotional idiom was also present in Congress propaganda, but this appears to be less prominent in UP than in Gujarat, as described by Haynes and Hardiman, and it appealed to a different constituency – mainly the commercial classes.

By identifying with the religious resurgence of the 1920s, the nationalist movement did not just draw in martial religion but also, by implication, absorbed many of the other meanings that religious change had carried for the poor. As discussed in chapter 6, Holi and Ramlila, the two festivals which became the staples of nationalist campaigns, both played a central role in the self-assertion of the poor and in expressing their identity as the deprived, but good, common people. Both festivals also expressed aspirations for an egalitarian and just social order. By association with Holi and Ramlila and with their mythological protagonists, Krishna and Ram, respectively, nationalism could also be conceived in terms of social liberation. Indeed, nationalist propaganda from the 1920s and more so in the 1930s did precisely that. The key figure of the Holi festival, Lord Krishna, was presented as the champion of the downtrodden, who disciplined and vanquished tyrants. One newspaper stated that Holi occurs each year 'to remind us of the power of our ancestors to humble the pride of oppressors'.[163] Holi was also projected as the occasion on which to abandon one's cowardice and slavishness and immerse oneself in the spirit of both religious zeal and nationalism.[164] In one case, drawing upon the mythological origins of Holi in the story of Prahlad, it was argued that just as the demon ruler Hiranyakashipu, who oppressed Prahlad, was destroyed as a consequence of the sufferings of Prahlad, so would British rule and its bureaucracy be destroyed by the satyagraha of the people.[165] The Janmastami festival, which commemorates the birth of Lord Krishna, was, on another occasion in Allahabad, turned into a nationalist celebration and Sri Krishna was extolled as the national hero who freed the country from oppression.[166] The Allahabad newspaper *Abhyudaya* argued that the misdeeds of the demon Hiranyakashipu were rampant in the country under British rule. It also compared Gandhi to Prahlad and stated that the celebration of Holi was a reminder to Indians to oppose tyranny.[167] On a similar note, another paper said 'it should be our duty

---

163 *NNR*, No. 9, 1926, p. 2, cites *Abhyudaya*.
164 Ibid.
165 *NNR*, No. 10/1923, p. 3.
166 *PAI*, No. 33, 26 August 1922.
167 *NNR*, No. 12/1930, p. 4.

to destroy the demonical slavery and to burn foreign cloth in Holi',[168] in keeping with the ritual burning of a straw effigy of the demoness Holika, who is seen as an evil instrument of oppression. In Lucknow, Holi and the launching of the Civil Disobedience movement were celebrated together on 15 March 1930 in the Aminuddaula Park, situated in the midst of the bazar area. A swadeshi fair was combined with the Holi fair, and Holika burning took the form of the burning of foreign cloth in the Aminabad bazar.[169] Two sets of imagery were brought together in these celebrations: the annihilation of evil signified by the burning of Holika merged into the destruction of foreign cloth, which symbolised the eradication of deprivation and tyranny. A poem from the 1920s, cited earlier, had already associated the charkha with the powerful, divine weapons of justice – the discus (chakra) of Krishna and the thunderbolt (bajra) of Indra, and by analogy praised the charkha not only as the instrument that would 'bring swaraj', but as the weapon that was 'the true friend of the oppressed and the poor'.[170] In Kanpur, magic lantern demonstrations organised by the labour organisation Mazdur Sabha used religious characters and brought out their contemporary relevance and meaning. In particular, reference to the mythical tyrant Raja Kansa, who persecuted the infant Krishna, formed the basis of an account of the British government and its oppressions.[171] It was through linkages and associations of this kind between nationalist messages and some of the emancipatory motifs of resurgent Hinduism that the radical political symbolism of nationalism was enhanced. This, in turn, expanded the possibility of the involvement of the poor in nationalism.

Three interlinked sets of factors played a significant role in the involvement of the bazar poor in nationalist action in the early 1930s. First, the programme of action of the Congress presented an opportunity to the poor to articulate their local conflicts. Secondly, and at the same time, the Congress forged an armoury of public political acts, which variously symbolised protest, defiance of authority and assertion of power or rights, all of which could be apprehended and deployed by the poor to express their own political concerns. In addition, the use of Hindu martial imagery by the Congress was a significant element. This facilitated the cross-linking of nationalism with the movements of religious resurgence. Nationalism then came to encapsulate the relevance and significance that the religious upsurge of the 1920s and 1930s carried for a large segment of the urban Hindu poor. Through its

---

[168] Ibid, cites *Anand.*
[169] *Vartman*, 16 March 1930, p. 1; also see *PAI*, No. 12, 29 March 1930.
[170] Review of Hindi magazine *Volunteer* (Kanpur), No. 1, December 1924.
[171] *PAI*, No. 29, 27 July 1929.

association with militant Hinduism, nationalism too could evolve as a form of self-assertion of the poor.

Crucially, however, the use of the Hindu martial metaphor excluded participation by the Muslim poor. While the Congress clearly succeeded in drawing in the support of the bazar poor, chapter 7 has shown that this generated extensive tensions in urban neighbourhoods between the Hindu and the Muslim poor, precipitating a number of communal clashes during the period of the Civil Disobedience movement. The untouchable poor too remained largely outside the purview of the nationalist campaigns. Some of the reasons for this have been discussed in chapter 5. In addition, the predominance of martial Hinduism in nationalist campaigns distanced them even further, for this was not compatible with the ideals of their *bhakti* devotional resurgence and Adi Hinduism. Notwithstanding this very critical exclusion of some sections of the poor, the Civil Disobedience movement involved a substantial section of the bazar poor, largely Hindu shudra groups. The analysis of forms of cultural performance has also suggested that, in the course of their political engagement in the 1920s and 1930s, popular aspirations were forged about a future nation and political culture which would be based on justice, egalitarianism and the participation of the poor common people.

The Civil Disobedience movement had provided a focus for the political action of the poor, but only temporarily. Directly related as the movement was to the agitational programme of the Congress, propaganda and political action both gradually abated after the termination of the campaign. Towards the end of 1932, the Congress began to concentrate less on mass demonstrations and more on the 'constructive programme' of promoting village industries, khaddar spinning, the uplift of harijans and social service. It was from the mid-1930s, with the emergence of the Congress Socialist Party (CSP) that the Congress would again provide a political platform for the poor. The rise of the CSP marked a change in the strategy for mass mobilisation in the Province and the emergence of a new rhetoric of nationalism. With these shifts in the Congress, the nature and forms of participation of the urban poor in nationalist politics were to undergo important transformations. The following chapter turns to these themes.

9   Congress socialist mobilisation

The emergence of the Congress Socialist Party (CSP) added a new edge and a different dimension to Congress nationalism from the mid-1930s. The CSP was formally inaugurated in May 1934 at Patna,[1] mainly by Congressmen who were sceptical about the efficacy of the Gandhian 'constructive programme' for mass mobilisation in the years after the Civil Disobedience movement. Explaining the reasons for the emergence of the party, Sampurnanand, a CSP leader of UP, wrote in his memoirs:

It was felt that the adoption of a socialist objective would rally the lower middle classes, the landless peasantry, the mill hands and other socially and economically backward classes to the ranks of the Congress in our final fight for freedom . . . people felt that somehow socialism would provide a break-through from the dead end which Congress strategy seemed to have reached.[2]

The CSP favoured an agitational programme to draw in the support of the masses by addressing social and economic issues. This was a counter to the 'constitutionalism' of the so-called 'right wing' of the Congress and their decision to participate in the legislatures, which was endorsed at the All India Congress Committee (AICC) session in May 1934. One of the declared aims of the CSP was 'to rescue the Congress from the hands of the right wing . . . and to carry on a constant propaganda for the exposure of the reactionary aims, policies and programme of the right wing group'.[3]

Although the rise of the CSP related partly to the discontent of a section of Congressmen with existing Congress policies, and partly to the ideological influences of communism and Bolshevism, its strategies were also conditioned by the need to contend with pressures from below and the groundswell that had become obvious during the Civil Disobedience movement, which the Congress had been unable to tap in the

[1] For the politics of the CSP, see B. R. Tomlinson, *The Indian National Congress and the Raj, 1929–1942: The Penultimate Phase*, London, 1976, chs. 2 and 3.
[2] Sampurnanand, *Memories and Reflections*, London, 1962, pp. 72–3.
[3] Quoted in Tomlinson, *Indian National Congress*, p. 51.

following years. It was evident to the emerging leaders of the CSP that if, either as the major nationalist party or as the future ruling party of the country, the Congress was to enjoy political legitimacy, authority and the right to hold sway over representative politics, it would be necessary not only to mobilise the masses but also to engage with some of the concrete and material concerns of the poor. Thus, a stated aim of the CSP was 'the establishment of a workers' society',[4] and at the Congress session of 1936 in Lucknow the socialist group moved a resolution to delineate more clearly the role of the 'masses', in order to 'enable the masses to appreciate what *swaraj* [self-rule] as conceived by the Congress will mean to them and to ensure that under swaraj they would be freed from economic exploitation'.[5] It was also clear that Congress politics would have to involve the participation of the 'masses' in more sustained ways, in addition to encouraging their episodic involvement during periods of active agitational campaigns. After the Civil Disobedience movement, popular political mobilisation largely ceased to occur within the ambit of the Congress, giving rise to an urgency among significant sections of Congressmen to institutionalise, centralise and organise popular political action under the umbrella of the party. This was necessary not only to strengthen the nationalist movement, but also, equally crucially, to consolidate the disparate popular political initiatives under direct Congress authority and discipline, in order to retain or establish control and direction over popular politics. In this context, socialism was seen to be an instrument which could link the Congress with the masses most effectively. The emergence of the CSP, based on these diverse political concerns, brought about a significant shift in nationalist discourse and forms of action, both of which would, in turn, have crucial implications for the politics of the poor.

In the deliberative bodies of the Congress at the national level, the CSP met with concerted opposition from the Gandhian 'right-wing' leadership and it was unable to persuade the Congress high command to adopt its programmes.[6] In particular, the 'right wing' refused to accept the plan of mobilising peasants and workers on the basis of economic demands, and prevented the CSP from introducing a system of functional representation of working-class groups in the Congress organisation.[7] The Congress Working Committee in 1934 rebuked the CSP for indulging in 'loose talk about confiscation of private property

[4] Cited in ibid.
[5] File No. 28/1936, AICC Papers, NML.
[6] Tomlinson, *Indian National Congress*, pp. 52–3; J. P. Haithcox, *Communism and Nationalism in India: M. N. Roy and Comintern Policy, 1920–1939*, Princeton, 1971, pp. 222–5.
[7] Tomlinson, *Indian National Congress*, p. 5.

and the necessity of class war', these ideas being 'contrary to the Congress creed of non-violence'.[8] Moreover, in opposition to the plans of the CSP, a 'constructive programme' was confirmed as the official strategy of the Congress, both at the Congress Working Committee meeting in June 1934 and at the October 1934 AICC session in Bombay.[9] The Congress central leadership also overruled the demands of the CSP to refrain from participation in legislatures. Instead, they adopted a parliamentary programme, partly in response to pressures from Indian business classes and partly to strengthen their own position within the Congress against the onslaught of the CSP.[10] The plans of the CSP being thus thwarted at the centre, the CSP leaders were forced to turn to the arena of provincial politics to translate their agitational programme into practice. While this was the case in several of the provinces of India, the impact of the rise of the CSP was especially decisive in UP. For this was one of the provinces where the socialists constituted a majority in the Congress organisation, and many of its leaders, who were already prominent figures in nationalist politics, including Nehru, were able effectively to change the direction of Congress policies and steer them leftward.

The first steps taken by the UPCSP towards the implementation of its programme were systematically to capture existing Congress committees at the provincial level, and to establish CSP organisations at the local village, town or *mohalla* (neighbourhood) levels. In May 1934, soon after the formation of the CSP, a police report noted that the CSP was strengthening itself through 'nuclei established at various centres' and was simultaneously beginning to reach out to the 'agricultural and industrial populations' by 'espousing their causes'.[11] The CSP earnestly set about organising its local bases, especially in the larger towns. In May 1934, a CSP unit was established in Benares, led by Sampurnanand, Sri Prakash, Tarapada Bhattacharya and Kamalapati Tripathi,[12] and the Congress organisation in the city soon came to be dominated by the socialists.[13] In June 1934, the Allahabad City Congress Committee was reorganised under the leadership of P. D. Tandon,[14] and in the August 1934 election CSP members captured most seats on

---

[8] Cited in Haithcox, *Communism and Nationalism*, p. 223.
[9] Cited in A. M. Zaidi and S. G. Zaidi (chief eds.), *The Encyclopaedia of the Indian National Congress*, Delhi, 1980, vol. 10, pp. 380–6, 395–6.
[10] Claude Markovits, *Indian Business and Nationalist Politics, 1931–1939: The Indigenous Capitalist Class and the Rise of the Congress Party*, Cambridge, 1985, pp. 101–4; Tomlinson, *Indian National Congress*, pp. 55–64.
[11] *PAI*, No. 19, May 1934.
[12] Ibid.; Sampurnanand, *Memories and Reflections*, pp. 73–4.
[13] *PAI*, No. 23, 16 June 1934.
[14] Ibid.

the Committee.[15] In Kanpur, a CSP unit had been inaugurated in June 1934 and at the September elections the CSP captured the local Congress Committee, under Ganga Sahai Chaube, Shibban Lal Saxena, Balkrishna Sharma, Chhail Behari Dixit and Hari Shankar Vidyarthi.[16] In Lucknow, the CSP had captured almost every seat on the City Congress Committee by July 1934.[17]

Simultaneously, the CSP began to establish its hold over the UP Provincial Congress Committee (UPPCC). Describing the proceedings of a meeting of the Executive Council of the UPPCC in June 1934, a police report commented that 'this meeting showed the way in which the socialist movement is gaining ground and how its adherents are rapidly absorbing positions from which they can dominate Congress policy'.[18] At this meeting, a National Service Board was elected to reorganise Congress volunteer corps in UP. Five out of the seven members of this Board were CSP members. A committee of twelve Congress leaders was also elected to supervise the revival of Congress organisations in the province. All except two of these twelve leaders belonged to the CSP. In August 1934, a publicity committee for the legislative election campaigns was set up by the UP Congress Parliamentary Sub-Committee, in which six out of ten members were socialists.[19] The preponderance of CSP members in these various Congress committees was reported to have led to a prominence of 'socialist' propaganda in the course of the party reorganisation and election campaigns.[20] By September 1934, the CSP had succeeded in capturing a majority of posts in the UPPCC Executive Committee. The president, Sri Prakash, all four vice-presidents, four of the six secretaries, and seven out of eleven members of the Executive Committee belonged to the CSP.[21] Twenty-six of the forty-six provincial representatives elected to the AICC in 1934 were also socialists.[22] Having thus captured the Congress machinery at both town and provincial levels, in December 1934 the CSP launched its programme to organise working-class groups. At a meeting of the UPPCC Executive Committee in that month, two committees were formed, consisting entirely of socialists, to report on possible strategies to enlist the support of the working

[15] *PAI*, No. 31, 11 August 1934.
[16] *PAI*, No. 24, 23 June 1934; No. 36, 15 September 1934.
[17] *PAI*, No. 29, 28 July 1934.
[18] *PAI*, No. 24, 23 June 1934.
[19] *PAI*, No. 31, 11 August 1934.
[20] *PAI*, No. 26, 7 July 1934.
[21] *PAI*, No. 37, 22 September 1934; also cited in G. Pandey, *The Ascendancy of the Congress in Uttar Pradesh, 1926–1934: A Study in Imperfect Mobilization*, Oxford, 1978, p. 71.
[22] *PAI*, No. 37, 22 September 1934.

classes.[23] The fact that this initiative emanated from the UPPCC Executive Council, rather than from the UPCSP Executive Committee, suggests that in the Province, by the end of 1934, the official Congress organisation and the CSP were scarcely distinguishable.

So far, the Congress had conducted its campaigns largely by stressing the misery and deprivation of the 'Indian people' in broad, general terms. Congress campaigns were based on the notions of injustice, oppression and exploitation in a generic way. The issue of class-specific poverty, deprivation or exclusion was not explicitly raised. The CSP, in its political rhetoric, began to shift away from the concept of an undifferentiated 'public' or 'people', and sought to hone it to identify specific groups: workers and peasants. The language of the 'people' was thus, fleshed out and elaborated, with the 'ordinary, common, poor people' – the *garib janata* – now being given more concrete identities in nationalist discourse. In addition to the political rituals and symbolic acts of protest through public demonstrations of an earlier period, the CSP was now eager to engage with the specific economic, social and political deprivation of the poorer classes. Even while still operating within the overall 'populist' framework of the Congress in the sense of invoking the 'people' as the rhetorical focus of propaganda, the CSP was more willing to take on board the concept of 'class', in its economic sense, in its political programme. Thus, the CSP sought to organise the poor on the basis of their workplace or economic grievances and demands, largely on the model of trade union activities. The party also addressed, both directly and extensively, a range of other material issues affecting the poor, including the problems of housing and access to local resources and infrastructure. In undertaking such political mobilisation, the CSP did not always directly or explicitly confront the colonial state, but was concerned to generate extensive political unrest at various levels, which would disrupt public order and ultimately undermine the stability, authority and legitimacy of the government.

With time, the CSP tended to become a focus of factional squabbles and of disgruntled groups in the Congress, many of whom were not of a socialist persuasion or held conflicting views about what socialism meant.[24] Nevertheless, the rise of the CSP was marked by an overall ideological emphasis on social change in the interests of the poor as the redefined aim of the nationalist movement, at least in political rhetoric. The difference between the CSP split and earlier factional rifts within the Congress, such as those involving Extremists, Moderates or Swarajists, was that, whereas these latter signified controversies over

[23] *PAI*, No. 48, 15 December 1934.
[24] Pandey, *Ascendancy*, p. 32; Tomlinson, *Indian National Congress*, pp. 51–2.

Congress policies and political strategies, the CSP split was also overlaid with an alternative ideology and definition of nationalism. As a consequence of this, seeking to enlist mass support in the towns in order to create a base for themselves within the Congress, the CSP cultivated a different style of politics, in both rhetoric and strategy.

The Congress socialist message

One of the most significant consequences of the rise of Congress socialism was the emergence of a new rhetoric of nationalism. In this, the social liberation of the masses was accorded central importance as the ultimate aim of the nationalist movement. Sri Prakash, a CSP leader of UP, in his welcome address to the Congress session at Lucknow in 1936, put forward the socialists' definition of nationalism:

The only person who I think matters, is that unknown but most important person – *the common man in field and factory, in the cottage and in the street*, on whom falls the heaviest load of life . . . It is no more possible to tolerate excessive wealth in the hands of a few on the one hand, and crushing poverty of the vast masses on the other; unlimited power for a handful and the condition of slaves for the rest. We definitely stand for an equitable distribution of work, wages and comfort for a society of freedom and of love.[25]

There are echoes here of Gandhi's humanitarian compassion and empathy for the common man, but with a difference. There is also an unequivocal rhetorical call to attempt to eradicate both poverty and the concentration of power, and to bring about 'equitable distribution of work, wages and comfort'. Freedom from British rule was projected as the means and the first step towards achieving this goal. Similar comments in the UP press of the mid- and late 1930s typify the preoccupations of the CSP and show how the CSP was trying to marry populism with a more class-based language in an attempt to direct popular political energies into nationalist, anti-British channels. The *Shakti* proclaimed that 'the Congress wants to provide clothing for *the naked*, food for *the hungry* and employment for *the unemployed*. But this purpose can be served only by wresting power from the foreign government and vesting it in the hands of the people.'[26] The newspaper *Sainik*, which had clear socialist leanings, featured on its red-coloured front page a flaming torch in a hand, and a poem by the well-known poet Agyeya, urging specifically '*the downtrodden Indians* to consume injustice

[25] Welcome Address by Sri Prakash at the AICC Session in Lucknow, 12 April 1936, cited in Zaidi and Zaidi (chief eds.), *Encyclopaedia of the Indian National Congress*, vol. 11, pp. 78–80, emphasis added.
[26] *NNR*, No. 3/1937, p. 1, emphasis added.

with the fire raging in their hearts and to make all sacrifice for freedom'.[27]

The rhetoric of social change and justice for the poor through nationalism and political freedom was extensively deployed by the CSP in its urban propaganda campaigns. CSP leaders and activists emphasised that the nationalist movement led by the Congress socialists was striving for the social emancipation of the 'common people', and they invited all to join in that struggle. Sampurnanand, addressing workers in the Kanpur bazars in November 1935, said that the source of the misery and poverty of the working classes lay in capitalism, which was introduced to India by British rule. Hence, he held, foreign rule must end and swaraj must come, when there would be no aggrandisement of one class against another.[28] At the same meeting, Santosh Chandra Kapoor echoed Sampurnanand's views and explained that the government and capitalists were united to oppress the 'poor workers'.[29] Nehru, addressing various groups of workers in Kanpur in 1936, similarly explained that the problems which the workers faced related to a universal problem of unemployment and poverty caused by capitalism and British rule; it was, therefore, necessary to fight for swaraj to bring about social justice.[30] In another speech, Nehru made the link between economic exploitation and British rule by calling the British government the 'greatest *bania*', invoking the most emotive and potent familiar symbol of exploitation, the figure of the merchant-moneylender.[31] In 1936, addressing a meeting of bazar labourers in Kanpur, he held out the promise of political participation and empowerment, alongside economic justice. He declared that 'the meaning of our nationalist struggle is that we can establish an independent country in which all of us will take part in the governance of the nation'.[32] Narendra Deva, a socialist leader, presided at an annual conference of the Kanpur Market Employees' Federation in 1938 and urged the workers to strengthen the nationalist struggle, stating that 'the Congress does not only aim to stop exploitation by foreigners, but also wants to eradicate all kinds of exploitation, even if the exploiters are inhabitants of our country'. He further declared in stirring words that 'linking the issue of the livelihood of the oppressed people with the issue of swaraj is our [i.e. Congress'] sacred duty . . . When we capture power, we can establish a new society

[27] Ibid., emphasis added.
[28] *PAI*, No. 47, 7 December 1935.
[29] Ibid.
[30] *PAI*, No. 36, 12 September 1936.
[31] *PAI*, No. 28, 24 July 1937.
[32] *Kanpur Bazar Karmchari Federation: Rajat Jayanti Smarika* (hereafter *Karmchari Smarika*), Kanpur, 1977, Part II, p. 4.

and economy in which the differences between the high and the low will be destroyed and every man will enjoy the fruits of his own labour.' He reminded the audience that 'when the new age [of independence] comes, all sorrow and misery of the exploited will come to an end'.[33] Yogesh Chatterjee at a meeting of Kanpur mill workers in 1938 asserted:

It is our belief that the road to revolutionary change and the road to independence are the same. Princes, rulers and *zamindars* [landowners] will, of course, be the enemies of independence, for they are happy in servitude. We [the CSP], however, want swarajya for the *garib* [deprived, poor]. Indeed, our ideal is to erase every trace of unemployment and *gulami* [dependence, social servitude] and to establish a socialist society.[34]

It is clear from the themes of these speeches that the CSP leaders attempted to postulate direct links between the nationalist movement and the struggle against garibi and gulami – the deprivation, servitude and powerlessness of the masses – primarily in two ways. Nehru, Sampurnanand and S. C. Kapoor solicited support for the nationalist movement on the ground that the termination of British rule would put an end to the poverty and political exclusion of the mass of the Indian people. Narendra Deva and Yogesh Chatterjee claimed that the nationalist movement would directly contend with the indigenous exploiters and address the question of livelihood, social justice and political enfranchisement for the poor. Redressing the plight of the poor was thus given a more central place in nationalist propaganda.

Congress socialism and workplace politics of the poor

The political initiative of the CSP in UP was not confined to the propagation of a radical, socialist ideology of nationalism, but included new forms of political mobilisation and activism. Without a programme of political action, the party could not expect to enlist popular support. To distinguish itself from the 'right wing', whom it blamed for failing to address the needs of the masses, it had to match its rhetoric with actual engagement in the political agitations of the poor. However, the CSP was not about to launch a political movement to bring about 'social revolution', notwithstanding its rhetoric. Although a grand vision of social change was projected, the actual political activities were largely anchored to local concerns of the workplace and the neighbourhood. The aim here was to give some tangible embodiment to the wider vision of change in locally meaningful ways. Confining political action to the

---

[33] Speech cited in ibid., Part II, p. 7; *Sangharsh*, 17 January 1938.
[34] *Samyavad*, 16 October 1938, p. 3, emphasis added.

workplace or neighbourhood, however, limited the possibility of achieving the wider political change and social revolution that the CSP orchestrated in its propaganda. This paradoxically, but probably intentionally on the CSP's part, served to undermine the radical, even revolutionary, political potential of the socialist message.

Still, the socialist message proved to be an extremely effective strategy for popular mobilisation. The CSP concentrated on organising various groups of the poor over specific issues in their localised contexts of work and everyday urban life. Such organisation was, however, often achieved outside the institutional framework of the Congress, and was not always envisaged as an integral element of nationalist mobilisation, as in the early 1930s. The CSP targeted specific occupational and neighbourhood groups, instead of relying on mass demonstrations, in striking contrast to the earlier period of the Civil Disobedience movement. CSP activists attempted to give a focus to local politics in the language of nationalism and socialism by promoting the formation of trade unions and neighbourhood organisations under the auspices of the party. In order to link these organisations with Congress units and activists at the local level, the CSP also introduced an amendment in the UP Congress Constitution in 1936, whereby 'stress was laid on [Congress] committees for as small areas as possible', which would be 'more in touch with their limited electorate in the mohalla than a large composite committee representing a big city.'[35] The CSP also sought to introduce a new style of political leadership. The ideal of Gandhian leadership was to cultivate an image of simplicity, social service and self-denial, with the hope of eliciting popular reverence. The CSP activists in comparison tried to project their own affinity with working-class lifestyles and a fraternal presence among the labouring population, often living among the poor in their neighbourhoods.[36] The CSP leaders may not quite have been the social bandit heroes, seen in the previous chapter, whom nautanki plays celebrated, but their activities related more directly to the everyday concerns of the poor than in an earlier era of Congress politics.

With a change in the strategy of political mobilisation and style of leadership, a middle tier of Congress activists, below the rank of the provincial leadership, gained greater prominence. An intermediate group of Congress leaders had already begun to emerge from the late 1920s.[37] This group now witnessed the entry of many new men and women into their ranks. Moreover, from the mid-1930s the CSP enlisted the help of the Communist Party of India (CPI), in a strategy to

[35] Reported in *Hindusthan Times*, 3 September 1936.
[36] Interview with Hajra Begum (Lucknow), a CSP/CPI activist of the 1930s.
[37] Pandey, *Ascendancy*, pp. 47–51.

create a 'united front' of 'left-wing' groups within the Congress, in order to strengthen their flank against the 'right' and to buttress their campaigns for mass mobilisation. Notwithstanding ideological differences between the two parties, the CPI joined the CSP on the basis of a shared programme to organise peasants and working-class groups. Such an alliance with the CSP provided a cover for the activities of the CPI, at a time when the party had been declared illegal by the government.[38] Though CSP and CPI activists came from middle-class professional backgrounds, some among them at this time also rose from the ranks of the poor. Suraj Prasad Awasthi, for instance, was initially a casual labourer in Kanpur, later worked in a mill and eventually became a full-time CSP activist and a trade union organiser.[39] Sudarshan Chakr, who followed his father as a mill worker, became a radical socialist activist.[40] Yogendranath Shukla, a shop employee in the Kanpur cloth market, was an active member of the CSP and organised a trade union of bazar workers.[41] People like Awasthi, Chakr and Shukla played a crucial role in CSP political organisations at the local level and served as crucial intermediaries to reach the poor.

The CSP and CPI activists forged links with various groups among the poor, who, at the time, had little sustained or direct contact with the Congress organisation, although some had been involved in the Civil Disobedience movement. Where organisations of urban labouring groups already existed, the socialists stepped in and facilitated strikes and agitations; in other cases they organised new unions. The ascendance of the CSP coincided with unprecedented political unrest at the workplace. Police and newspaper reports from 1934 onwards are replete with references to political agitation by numerous occupational groups, many of which were reported to have been aided by the CSP and CPI. Industrial action to claim higher pay and compensation for accidents and to prevent arbitrary dismissals occurred in the smaller mills of UP, such as the R. G. Cotton Mill and Upper India Cooper Paper Mill in Lucknow, in the Kashi Iron Foundry and the Benares Cotton Mill, in printing presses in Allahabad, and in various oil and flour mills.[42] CSP

[38] M. R. Masani, *The Communist Party in India: A Short History*, London, 1954, pp. 68–9.
[39] Interview with Suraj Prasad Awasthi, labour activist, in Kanpur; *Pandit Suraj Prasad Awasthi Abhinandan Granth* (Pandit Suraj Prasad Awasthi Felicitation Volume), Kanpur, 25 August 1986.
[40] Interview with Sudarshan Chakr, mill worker and labour activist, in Kanpur.
[41] *Karmchari Smarika*, Part III, pp. 3–4.
[42] *PAI*, No. 6, 16 February 1935; No. 9, 9 March 1935; No. 13, 4 April 1936; No. 12, 3 April 1937; No. 14, 17 April 1937; No. 32, 21 August 1937; No. 42, 30 October 1937; No. 1, 8 January 1938; No. 6, 12 February 1938; No. 1, 7 January 1939; No. 2, 14 January 1939; No. 5, 4 February 1939; *Samyavad*, 12 February 1939, p. 4, 20 August 1938, p. 3, 1 January 1939 p. 6, 5 February 1939, p. 7; Weekly Reviews of Labour

and CPI activists were involved in political action by municipal employees, such as untouchable sweepers and conservancy staff, as well as workers in the municipal electric power houses and water works, who were demanding higher pay and the abolition of the system of recruitment through *jamadars* (jobber or labour contractor), to whom the workers had to pay commission from their wages.[43] Railway coolies were organised by CSP workers over similar issues. CSP activists lent their support to *ekkawalas*, *tongawalas* and *thelawalas* against Municipal Boards for imposing high licensing fees, frequent and unjust fines, and police harassment.[44] Hawkers and petty shopkeepers similarly enjoyed the support of the CSP in protesting against local councils and the police for anti-encroachment drives, fines, bribery, high taxes and shop rents,[45] as well as against the wholesale merchants, who levied high rates of interest on credit purchase of goods.[46] CSP activists also worked among artisans and workers in small manufacturing units, such as embroiderers (*kamdani* and *zardozi* workers) in Lucknow, *bidi*, metal bucket and steel trunk workers in Allahabad, tailoring shop assistants (*darzis*) and hosiery workers in Kanpur, and bookbinders (*daftaris*), all of whom were demanding higher wages and prices for their finished products.[47] In Benares, in 1935, the CSP organised a *Bekar Sangh* (Union of the Unemployed).[48] Both the CSP and CPI were also involved in the trade union movement in the cotton textile industry in Kanpur. In many of these cases, the CSP supported the formation of volunteer corps of workers, which were often called the 'Red Army'. A pattern of political initiatives by the CSP becomes evident from these instances of labour unrest. The CSP, with the help of the CPI, promoted trade union organisations among various occupational groups and intervened in workplace politics, mainly by taking up economic demands as well as complaints and grievances against the local authorities and the police.

Situation, File Nos. 12/1/1939, 12/2/1939, 12/3/1939, 12/4/1939, Home Poll., GOI, NAI; File No. 6/1938–9, Department XXX, Labour Correspondence, Kanpur Collectorate, ERR.

[43] *PAI*, No. 19, 18 May 1935; No. 20, 25 May 1935; No. 34, 4 September 1937; No. 42, 30 October 1937; No. 7, 9 February 1938; No. 25, 28 June 1938; No. 32, 13 August 1938.

[44] *PAI*, No. 16, 1 May 1937; No. 22, 12 June 1937; No. 23, 19 June 1937; No. 32, 21 August 1937; No. 17, 30 April 1938; No. 25, 25 June 1938; No. 26, 2 July 1938; No. 32, 13 August 1938.

[45] *PAI*, No. 1, 9 January 1937; No. 22, 12 June 1937; No. 2, 14 January 1939.

[46] *PAI*, No. 36, 10 September 1936.

[47] *PAI*, No. 15, 24 April 1937; No. 16, 1 May 1937; No. 7, 12 February 1938; No. 9, 5 March 1938; No. 14, 9 April 1938; No. 26, 2 July 1938; *National Herald*, 12 September 1937; *Hindusthan Times*, 16 September 1938.

[48] *PAI*, No. 8, 2 March 1935.

Why did workplace politics link with nationalism from the perspective of the labouring poor? A discussion of the political action of bazar workers in Kanpur illustrates the nature of interconnections. The trade union movement in the bazars gained momentum from the mid-1930s. At the same time, bazar employees constituted an important source of support for the CSP. As the main locus of wholesale and retail trade and as the bulking centre of the province, Kanpur had by far the largest single agglomeration of shops and commercial establishments in UP, employing tens of thousands of workers in the mid-1930s, either as shop assistants and clerks or as manual labourers engaged in carting, loading, warehousing and transportation.[49] In the Kanpur bazars, a powerful labour union was formed in 1934 in the cloth market. This large market, primarily for the wholesale trade of mill-produced cloth, was especially vital in Kanpur for the presence of the textile industry in the city. Before 1934, a short-lived first bazar union had been organised in 1924 by local Congress leaders such as Ganesh Shankar Vidyarthi, but this organisation had gradually become defunct.[50] The union formed in 1934 not only proved to be more enduring (with a continued existence to the present), but also enjoyed extensive membership among workers in the cloth market in the 1930s. Articles on the history of the Cloth Market Employees' Union, published in the Silver Jubilee Souvenir of the Kanpur Market Employees' Federation in 1977, claimed that in the 1930s, out of a total of 8,000–10,000 workers in the Kanpur cloth market, 5,000 were members of the union, a large majority being *palledars* or manual labourers.[51] Workers in the cloth market had participated in Congress pickets of foreign cloth shops during the Civil Disobedience movement. The experience of being able to force merchants to stop the sale of foreign cloth through crowd demonstrations had revealed to the workers the possibility of challenging the merchants through collective action. In the wake of the Civil Disobedience movement, some employees in the cloth market formed the *Kapra Karmchari Mandal* (Union of Cloth Employees), on the initiative of Yogendra Nath Shukla, a shop assistant in Naughara, Generalganj. According to Ram Shankar Shukla, a union officer in 1977, the union from its early days represented both the relatively better-paid, non-manual workers – shop assistants and clerks – as well as the poorer manual labourers – the carters and hauliers (palledars), often described by the generic term

---

[49] *Karmchari Smarika*, Part II, p. 5. In the transcript of a speech by Narendra Deva in 1938 at a bazar workers' meeting, the number working in the central bazars in Kanpur is stated to be 20,000–25,000.

[50] 'Sanyukt prant mein mazdur andolan', *Mazdur Samachar* (Kanpur), 1, 1 June 1939, p. 5, Narayan Prasad Arora Papers, Printed Material, Serial No. 20, NML.

[51] *Karmchari Smarika*, Part II, p. 60; Part III, pp. 22, 70.

kahar or carrier. Shukla states that, in spite of status, caste and economic distinctions, all these groups participated in the union on the basis of their common social experience of being servile or *naukar* (literally, servant), at the beck and call of their masters, and their shared economic plight of indebtedness to their merchant employers.[52] The term '*karmchari*' (employee) rather than '*mazdur*' (labourer) in the name of the union, implying subordinate workers, encapsulated the experience of subservience that provided the basis of political unity for the formation of this union.

Immediately after the formation of the cloth workers' union in 1934, in November of that year, the palledars in the cloth market demanded higher wages, standardisation of wage rates in the bazars, shorter hours of work, weekly holidays and permanence of jobs.[53] A charter of demands was handed to the association of cloth merchants, the *Kapra Committee*, which overruled the demands. In response, on 12 November 1934 the palledars went on strike and picketed cloth shops to prevent the recruitment of substitute casual labourers. Being under a state of siege, perhaps reminiscent of the Civil Disobedience pickets, the employers, after only one day, agreed to a wage increase.[54] The remarkable success of the palledars' strike caused excitement elsewhere in the bazars and prompted the formation of several employees' unions between 1934 and 1936 at other markets in the city, including the grain, spice and iron markets. The various separate unions were federated in 1936 to form the *Sanjukta Bazar Karmchari Mandal* (Federation of Market Employees' Unions).[55]

The CSP established links with the various bazar unions from an early stage. The prominent CSP labour leaders of Kanpur, Raja Ram Shastri and Hariharnath Shastri, were closely associated with the unions and were honorary office bearers.[56] CSP leaders were active during the cloth market palledars' strike in 1934. Annual conferences of the various bazar karmchari unions, and subsequently of the Karmchari Federation, were held from 1935, at which CSP leaders were invited to speak.[57] At the first annual conference of the Cloth Employees' Union in 1935, an impressive pantheon of CSP leaders was present, including Sampurnanand, Balkrishna Sharma, Chhail Behari Dixit 'Kantak', Ganga Sahai Chaube, Ram Dulare Trivedi, Santosh Chandra Kapoor, Shibban Lal Saxena, Suraj Prasad Awasthi and Raja Ram Shastri. The proceedings

---

[52] Ram Shankar Shukla, 'Karmchari Sangathan aur Andolan Kyon?', *Karmchari Smarika*, editorial article.
[53] *Karmchari Smarika*, Part III, pp. 70–1.
[54] Ibid.   [55] Ibid., Part II, p. 7.
[56] Ibid., Part II, p. 15, Reminiscences of Raja Ram Shastri.
[57] Ibid., Part II, p. 61, Part III, p. 27.

of the annual Bazar Karmchari Federation conference of 1938 reveal the
nature and terms of the relationship between the CSP leaders and the
bazar workers. The conference, reported to have been attended by
5,000 bazar workers, was held in the Nachghar-Birhana Road area at
the heart of the Kanpur trading quarter, which was temporarily
renamed 'Lenin Nagar' for the duration of the conference.[58] Alongside
invoking Lenin as the symbol of socialism, the red flags of the CSP were
prominent. M. N. Roy, the communist leader, ceremonially unfurled
the red flag.[59] The CSP leader Narendra Deva, invited to deliver the
presidential address, declared that 'the oppressed are rising and challenging their oppressors', and assured the workers that 'your fight is being
fought on every side', especially by the CSP. He reiterated that the CSP
was mindful of the issue of livelihood of the 'oppressed people'.[60]
Spokespeople for the bazar karmcharis then declared their support for
the nationalist movement under CSP leadership as a means of bringing
about social justice. Simultaneously, they put forward their economic
grievances, along with a demand to pass a Shops and Commercial
Establishments Act in the UP legislature, stipulating the rights of bazar
workers, similar to the Factory Act for industrial labourers.[61] It appears
that the workers expected the CSP to fulfil its promises to further their
interests in return for political support. They sought to harness the
CSP's own rhetoric about justice for the poor to persuade the party to
introduce legislation through the Congress Ministry, which was in
power at the time.

The support extended by the bazar karmcharis to the CSP was thus
not simply a case of effective mobilisation of workers by the CSP
through populist rhetoric. Rather, the karmcharis appropriated the
rhetoric of the socialists for their own purposes, and deployed it to spur
on the leaders to further their own cause. It encompassed their attempt
to ensure the cooperation and protection of the CSP for greater political
clout and leverage in their workplace agitations. Identification with the
nationalist movement and the adoption of the language of socialism
enabled the bazar workers to legitimise their political militancy as well as
to mount resistance against the merchants and employers. For, while the
employers could silence trade union activities by dismissing workers or
refusing them credit, they were not always easily able to victimise those
who claimed their workplace politics to be part of 'nationalist' action

---

[58] Ibid., Part II, p. 20.
[59] *Sangharsh*, 17 January 1938, p. 15.
[60] Speech cited in *Karmchari Smarika*, Part II, pp. 5–7; *Sangharsh*, 17 January 1938.
[61] *Karmchari Smarika*, Part I, p. 2; *Sangharsh*, 17 January 1938.

and organisations, mainly for fear of opposition from Congressmen.[62] The workers thus projected themselves and their trade unions as nationalist to strengthen their own political action in the bazars. With the same aim, they formed their local organisations and volunteer units under the umbrella of the nationalist movement. 'Socialist' (*samyavadi*) and 'nationalist' volunteer corps were extensively organised by the bazar workers, such as the *Lal Fauj* or Red Army[63] and the *Samyavadi Fauj* or Socialist Army.[64] Several of these also began to overlap with the *Qaumi Sena Dal* (Nationalist Army), the volunteer corps organised by the CSP, which many workers joined.[65] These workers' volunteer organisations drew upon the developing tradition of *akharas*, *pahalwani* (body-building) and martial militancy in the bazars. If the karmchari unions enabled the labouring poor to articulate their identity as subordinate employees or 'servants', the volunteer organisations encapsulated their political assertion through the expression of physical or martial prowess within the ambit of nationalist and socialist politics.

It should be emphasised that the workers did not have a purely instrumental motivation in expressing their specific workplace demands in the language of nationalism. They also sought to carve a place for their own political action in the nationalist movement. Yogendra Nath Shukla, a leader of the Union of Cloth Employees, stated that their conference in 1938 'caused headache to the so-called Gandhibadi leaders of the Congress, who in the name of Gandhibad actually nursed capitalist notions'. For, he argued, the display of the red flag at the conference of the Karmchari Federation meant that the workers were claiming their rights in the bazar.[66] In this way, the power and legitimacy of the red flag was elevated over the tricolour flag of the Congress; political militancy inspired by the socialists was asserted against the conservatism or moderation of the 'Gandhibadis'; and, most importantly, a place for the socialist red flag, emblematic of workers' rights, was emphatically claimed within the nationalist movement. The bazar employees thus claimed rights and power for themselves through their trade unions, not only at the workplace, but more generally in the nationalist movement, and by implication ultimately in Indian polity and society. Congress socialist ideology enabled the workers to cultivate a vision of nationalism in terms of a wider and more fundamental political and social change. The crucial factor in the nationalist political

---

[62] Interviews, Dr Z. A. Ahmad (Lucknow), a CPI leader based mainly in Allahabad in the 1930s, and Devi Dutt Agnihotri, a CSP and trade union activist of Kanpur.
[63] *Samyavad*, 18 December 1938, p. 5; 25 December 1938, p. 4.
[64] Ibid., 12 February 1939, p.5.
[65] *Karmchari Smarika*, Part II, p. 29.
[66] *Karmchari Smarika*, Part III, p. 61, Reminiscences of Yogendra Nath Shukla.

action of the bazar workers, therefore, was the symbiosis between local and particular concerns, on the one hand, and the wider vision of social emancipation and political empowerment, on the other, even while actual action was rooted to the locality.

This dual dimension in the support of the bazar karmcharis for the nationalist movement was especially poignantly expressed by a spokesman of another occupational group in Kanpur. During a strike of the Tailors' Union in the Kanpur cloth market in 1937, Chhotelal Darzi, secretary of the union, issued an 'Appeal to the people of Kanpur' to support the tailors' cause. The appeal was published in the local newspaper, *Vartman*:

Please support us over the question of our right to our deserved daily bread [*ucheet roti*]. For, this is not a question involving only the darzis, but it is also the voice [*awaz*] of the millions of suffering labourers of our entire country . . . Today the Congress has taken up the cause of the workers and peasants, and therefore, it is our duty to fight our own battle for our daily bread and to strengthen their [i.e. the Congress'] hands.[67]

Chotelal Darzi's appeal clearly indicates that workplace political action was envisaged as a key element of the nationalist movement. Indeed, Chotelal considered workplace politics to be crucial in strengthening nationalism and achieving what was in his view the chief goal of the Congress, namely, advancing the cause of the workers and peasants. To him, the 'millions of suffering labourers' of the country were central to the project of nationalism, and hence fighting for his own 'daily bread' was not a narrow objective but constituted the core of Indian nationalism.

With such a perspective, the expression of nationalism through workplace organisation became increasingly widespread throughout the later 1930s among a range of labouring groups. At political demonstrations, the symbols of the trade union movement increasingly intermingled with nationalist ones. The socialist red flag, red shirts, the hammer and the sickle, the naming of places as 'Lenin Nagar' or celebrations of 'May Day' and 'Lenin Day' proliferated, together with the nationalist tricolour and observance of 'national' or 'independence' days.[68] Reports of agitation in the bazars indicate that most political events had a dual dimension: expressing support for nationalism and voicing specific demands of bazar workers. In September 1938, the *Bazar Karmchari Divas* (Bazar Workers' Day) was declared a holiday by the Karmchari Federation and all shops were closed. During a large procession slogans

[67] *Vartman*, 6 November 1937, p. 6.
[68] Ibid., 18 December 1938, p. 5.

were raised in support of the Bazar Karmchari Mandal, the CSP and the nationalist movement.[69] During the Independence Day celebrations of the Congress in February 1938, urban labouring groups were present in large numbers at meetings and demonstrations in the towns. In Allahabad, railway coolies, who at the time formed one of the most militant trade unions in the city, were especially prominent.[70] The May Day celebration of workers in Allahabad in 1937 served also as an occasion for anti-British demonstrations. The dominant theme of this May Day was the workers' struggle, not only against employers or capitalists, but also against their allies, the British government.[71] In all of these, workplace politics were located explicitly within a wider arena of political struggle. Trade unionism and nationalism were viewed by the workers as the twin planks of the same struggle, although nationalism presented a wider vision and promise and extended the meaning, scope and significance of trade union politics. Workplace politics were no longer about wresting a few economic concessions, although this remained important, but about eroding the broader basis of exploitation and oppression by integrating with the nationalist movement. As the Kanpur press workers declared in 1938: 'We have fully resolved to transform our degraded lives.'[72]

Such interconnections between nationalism and workplace politics were also evident in the case of the Kanpur textile mill workers. Nationalist politicians had been drawn into workplace politics in the mills from the early days of trade union organisation. The union of textile mill labourers in Kanpur – the Mazdur Sabha – was formed in 1919,[73] on the initiative of a group of workers in alliance with some local Congress leaders, who remained closely involved in the union throughout the 1920s and early 1930s.[74] During the first general strike of the textile industry in 1919, employers objected to the involvement of 'outside' activists in mill politics and refused to negotiate with nationalist leaders; the strike continued precisely against this stipulation by the mill owners.[75] Why were nationalist leaders drawn into labour politics and why did the workers attempt to operate within the framework of nationalist politics?

Congress leaders were experienced in the intricacies of institutional

---

[69] *Samyavad*, 2 October 1938, p. 3.
[70] *PAI*, No. 5, 5 February 1938.
[71] *PAI*, No. 17, 8 May 1937.
[72] *Samyavad*, 15 June 1938, p. 7.
[73] *RCLI*, III:I, p. 187, Memorandum of the Government of UP.
[74] Sudarshan Chakr, *Kanpur Mazdur Andolan ka Itihas*, Kanpur, 1986, pp. 14–15.
[75] Ibid., p. 11; Kedarnath Mehrotra, '"Ek Aur Surya": Pandit Surya Prasad Awasthi', in *Pandit Suraj Prasad Awasthi Abhinandan Granth*, p. 7.

politics and familiar with the rules and procedures of formal negotiation and labour legislation. This made them valuable allies in bargaining with employers and in representing workers in official circles. Presenting workplace struggles as part of a wider nationalist endeavour also enhanced the bargaining power of the workers. They could partake of both the ideological legitimacy and the political clout of the Congress. There were, however, other more compelling reasons than these obvious, instrumental ones for linking nationalism and workplace politics. In the early years of the twentieth century, the colonial state introduced a panoply of labour legislation, governing wages, working conditions and employment relations for workers in large factories.[76] At times, the government also intervened directly in mediating between workers and their employers. The Governor of UP, Sir Harcourt Butler, was himself involved in the settlement of the first general strike in the Kanpur mills in 1919.[77] The role of the government in labour issues was evidently critical. Nationalist politics provided one effective way for the workers to engage with this wider context of employment relations.[78] The importance of the colonial state in influencing workplace relations was obvious to the workers in another way. The use of physical force and coercion to maintain discipline at the workplace had been a central feature of employer–employee relations in Kanpur mills.[79] The imposition of fines, arbitrary dismissals, punitive forced idleness as well as physical and verbal abuse were integral aspects of the regime of workplace discipline.[80] This regime was, however, always open to resistance and contestation by the workers, either through 'everyday forms' of resistance[81] or through strikes, which inevitably reduced and undermined the effectiveness of employers' control. To buttress their limited disciplinary power and authority, employers frequently turned to the police and the law and order machinery of the colonial state, especially after

[76] R. K. Das, *Principles and Problems of Indian Labour Legislation*, Calcutta, 1938, pp. 5–50.
[77] Chakr, *Kanpur Mazdur Andolan*, pp. 12–13.
[78] For a discussion on the importance of the colonial state in working-class politics, on which the analysis here draws, see R. S. Chandavarkar, *The Origins of Industrial Capitalism in India: Business Strategies and the Working Classes in Bombay, 1900–1940*, Cambridge, 1994, pp. 408–11, 430.
[79] Chitra Joshi, 'The Formation of Work Culture: Industrial Labour in a North Indian City', *Purushartha*, 14, 1991, pp. 155–72.
[80] Ibid., pp. 156–60; Memorandum of the Mazdur Sabha, Kanpur, and Evidence of mill workers, especially Shivadhar and Zawar Husain, Proceedings dated 7 and 9 December 1937, Proceedings of Meetings of the Labour Inquiry Committee, Kanpur, (hereafter KLIC Proceedings), File No. 1145/1937, Box No. 418, Industries Department, GUP, UPSA.
[81] Joshi, 'Formation of Work Culture', pp. 155–72.

the First World War, when labour agitation gradually became wide-spread, beginning with the general strike in 1919.[82]

The most controversial deployment of the police related to the firing on workers of the Cawnpore Cotton Mills on 5 April 1924, which left six dead and fifty-eight injured.[83] In the following years the event assumed legendary notoriety amongst the town's workers, with the mill thenceforth coming to be known among them as the '*Khuni* (Mur-derous) Cotton Mill' and the dead remembered as the first martyrs to the workers' cause.[84] The shooting episode also provoked an indepen-dent, non-official enquiry by prominent public personalities of Kanpur, a number of whom were Congressmen. The enquiry committee re-soundingly condemned the intervention of the police in a dispute over bonus payments, which, the committee felt, could well have been settled by negotiations between the workers and mill management.[85] The report of the committee noted that in the textile industry 'as a rule the police is sent for by the mill managers when there is any trouble anticipated'.[86] They continued:

As soon as the police is indented for, the party against whose activities they are asked to take action is immediately convinced of the fact that the opposition party does not believe in its own power and in the reasonableness of its arguments to settle the matter by peaceful methods.[87]

Such involvement of the state in the workplace through the police was not only ubiquitous but also decisive. Manifestly, state repression and control severely restricted the possibility of resistance and negotiations at the workplace. In controlling political action by the workers against the mill owners, the arm of the state even reached beyond the immediate context of the factory and penetrated working-class neighbourhoods through various forms of surveillance, in particular by the Criminal Investigation Department, directed especially against militant workers.[88] The intervention of the police in labour politics became more pronounced in the 1930s, as labour unrest escalated when mill manage-ments sought to implement a range of measures of rationalisation, intensification, wage reduction and retrenchment, and simultaneously had to introduce a more stringent regime of discipline to enforce the

---

[82] *RCLI*, III:I, p. 191, Memorandum of the Government of UP.
[83] File (not numbered) on the Cawnpore Cotton Mill firing incident, 1924, Kanpur Collectorate, ERR; *Report of the Non-Official Enquiry Committee Regarding the Shooting of Mill Hands at the Cawnpore Cotton Mills Company, 1924*, Kanpur, 1924, p. 23, Narayan Prasad Arora Papers, Serial No. 10, Printed Material, NML.
[84] Chakr, *Kanpur Mazdur Andolan*, pp. 22–4; NNR, No. 15/1924, p. 4.
[85] *Report of the Non-Official Enquiry Committee Regarding the Shooting of Mill Hands at the Cawnpore Cotton Mills Company, 1924*.
[86] Ibid., p. 8.   [87] Ibid., pp. 8–9.
[88] Interview with Sudarshan Chakr, mill worker and labour activist, in Kanpur.

new policies in the face of workers' resistance.[89] Indeed, it was this discipline, often backed by police intervention, that to a large extent caused continuous labour unrest from 1936 to 1939. A secret memorandum by the Police Department noted that 'all the grievances are designed against enforcement of any form of discipline in the mills', and mentioned that a statement prepared by the Mazdur Sabha unleashed 'a tirade against "police excesses" in Cawnpore and arrests, lathi charges, and restraint orders, against workers and the Mazdur Sabha'.[90] Not surprisingly, labour politics encompassed the colonial state and assumed a nationalist orientation for this reason.

From the period of the depression, the economic policies of the colonial state also assumed increasing importance for the workers, faced with retrenchment, reduced work and declining wages.[91] The trade and tariff policies of the government in the early 1930s had implications for the cotton textile industry and these were extensively publicised by the nationalist press.[92] Importantly for Kanpur workers, these issues were widely aired in both the local nationalist press and the increasingly flourishing labour press.[93] The colonial state was directly implicated in shaping relations between capital and labour. This political message dovetailed with a more generalised one of earlier origin about the detrimental effects of colonialism on the labouring poor, which had been orchestrated initially during the Civil Disobedience movement and subsequently more strongly by the CSP. Similar political propaganda of the Islamic socialists, such as Hasrat Mohani and Azad Subhani, from an earlier period has been discussed in chapter 7. All of these interlinked developments powerfully drove the textile mill workers of Kanpur in the 1930s towards a wider arena of politics and to identify more closely with nationalism directed against the state. This was epitomised in their prominent involvement in a nationalist *hartal* (work stoppage) against the Government of India Act of 1935. This hartal, as recounted by Sudarshan Chakra, a mill worker and trade union activist, in his history

---

[89] *RCLI*, III:II, p. 219, Oral evidence of Mr W. G. Mackay, Chief Inspector of Factories, UP; Memorandum of the Mazdur Sabha, Kanpur, pp. 18, 37–42, and Evidence of Shivadar and Zawwar Hussain, mill workers, Proceedings dated 7 and 9 December 1937, KLIC Proceedings.

[90] Secret Memorandum, Intelligence Bureau, Home Department, File No. 12/1/38, Home Poll., GOI, NAI.

[91] Memorandum of the Mazdur Sabha, passim, and pp. 38–47, KLIC Proceedings; V. B. Karnik, *Strikes in India*, Bombay, 1967, p. 261.

[92] *Report of the Fact Finding Committee (Handloom and Mills), 1942* (Chairman P. J. Thomas) (Delhi, 1942), pp. 7–24; B. Chatterjee, 'The Political Economy of "Discriminating Protection": The case of Textiles in the 1920s', *IESHR*, 20, 3, 1983, pp. 265–6.

[93] Several labour newspapers were published in Kanpur in the 1930s. See Chakr, *Kanpur Mazdur Andolan*, pp. 38–47.

of the Kanpur labour movement, was perceived to be the first 'political' hartal of the workers,[94] as contrasted with workplace strikes. In Chakr's account, through this hartal, the workers overtly embraced the wider struggle against colonialism. A nationalist hartal was seen by the workers, explicitly for the first time, as an extension and integral part of their own political project. Nationalism in its socialist garb, for a time at least, provided the workers with a political platform from which to contend with the colonial state, and through the state, also with the employers. Equally importantly, the socialist rhetoric offered a plausible and powerful explanatory framework for their exploitation or repression, and provided an ideology and a plan of action for social and political change. As in the case of the bazar karmcharis and other groups of labour, the espousal of socialist nationalism by the mill workers was not just for strategic or instrumental reasons. The labour movement was conceived as a part of the wider struggle for nationalism and empowerment. In an article entitled 'It is in our own hands whether or not to bring about a revolution', which appeared in the socialist organ *Kranti*, Comrade Kashiram, a well-known working-class poet of Kanpur,[95] wrote: 'Today we are preparing for revolution. We want to wrest *our own* freedom – both economic and political.'[96] It was this promise of wresting power for themselves, and not just securing economic benefits or achieving political liberation from foreign rule, that led the workers to identify with the nationalist movement. As a poem in the labour paper *Mazdur* declared in 1937: 'The regime of misery will be replaced by happiness. The soul of man will be liberated.'[97] Sudarshan Chakr wrote a salutation to the Red Flag to express similar sentiments:

> May the red flag ever fly!
> May there be insatiable desire for sacrifice and unbounded courage.
> This flag was beloved by [sic] the Russians, who killed the oppressor
>   Czar.
> It has now come to India to make a settlement with the capitalists.
> Dear workers, come and gather under the flag, *teach the lesson of*
>   *socialism,*
> *create a strong and peaceful revolution, and destroy the unjust*
>   *government.*[98]

A flourishing working-class literature[99] of the period consistently expressed the idea that *azadi* (political liberation) and *kranti* (revolutionary social change) were integrally interlinked. This coupling of azadi and

---

[94] Ibid., p. 49.   [95] Ibid., p. 35.
[96] *Kranti* (monthly socialist journal, Kanpur), 1, 3 October 1939, p. 22, emphasis added.
[97] *NNR*, No. 49/1937, p. 2.
[98] Reported with translation of the poem in *PAI*, No. 14, 17 April 1937, emphasis added.
[99] Chakr, *Kanpur Mazdur Andolan*, pp. 35, 38–47.

kranti, while contributing to the support of mill workers for nationalism, did not, however, unambiguously amount to a harmonious relationship between the CSP and the workers, as will be seen later.

Congress socialism and the politics of the poor in the neighbourhood

Political action by various groups of the poor in urban neighbourhoods also came to be expressed in the language of nationalism. It has been seen that conflicts arising from local council policies fed into the Civil Disobedience movement and fuelled communal tensions. From the mid-1930s onwards, local issues began to affect CSP activities too. CSP leaders extended their support to the urban poor against local authorities and promoted the formation of mohalla organisations for protest. Newspapers in Kanpur, *Vartman* and *Pratap*, which had nationalist or CSP leanings, and *Samyavad*, the socialist trade union weekly, published regular columns on grievances related to local administration and government policies.[100] *Vartman*, for instance, reported in 1938 that unrest among the poor about housing had intensified against both the local authorities and the landlords. These agitations were against high house and shop rents, the lack of conservancy services for the poor and the policies of the Improvement Trust and the municipality, which dispossessed or targeted the poorer classes.[101] It was also stated in the report that CSP leaders in Kanpur were helping in these campaigns by organising town-wide processions and through newspaper appeals issued by various ward Congress committees.[102] *Pratap* reported that the Kanpur City Congress Committee was supporting the agitation for rent ceiling regulations and had organised meetings and processions in the city.[103] In Gwaltoli, a residential neighbourhood of mill workers and other urban labourers, the local CSP formed a twelve-member committee to enquire into living conditions in the *ahatas* (slums within walled compounds).[104] *Samyavad* reported that regular meetings were held in poorer residential areas, to demand better facilities for conservancy, water supply and lighting.[105]

Those who lived in these areas organised *Mazdur Mohal Committees* (Labourers' Neighbourhood Committees) or Ahata Committees. It is

---

[100] *Vartman* and *Pratap* published columns entitled '*Adikari dhyan de*' ('Officers Please Take Note'). A majority of the complaints that featured in these columns related to municipal administration and policing.
[101] *Vartman*, 28 July 1938, p. 6.   [102] Ibid.
[103] *Pratap*, 22 July 1938, p. 6.
[104] *Samyavad*, 22 January 1939, p. 5.
[105] Ibid., 4 December 1938, p. 7.

difficult to ascertain whether the CSP leaders took the initiative to form these committees, but it is clear that they stepped in to support them and indeed augmented the ability of these organisations to conduct and sustain their agitations. Moreover, many of the prominent local activists on Mohal Committees themselves joined the CSP. In 1938, *Samyavad* reported several public meetings of Mohal Committees, addressed by local residents and CSP leaders, which were held in Fazalganj, Darshanpurwa, Gwaltoli, Gadariyapurwa, Narayanpurwa, Purana Kanpur and other areas predominantly inhabited by the poorer sections of the urban population – casual labourers, mill hands, transport drivers, hawkers and vendors.[106] *Samyavad* also reported that at some of these Mohal Committee meetings it was resolved to have recourse to *satyagraha*, drawing upon a familiar nationalist form of protest, if the landlords continued to turn a deaf ear to demands for sanitary facilities and a lowering of rents or if the Improvement Trust refused to suspend slum demolition schemes in certain areas within these localities.[107] On one occasion, CSP activists, notably Raja Ram Shastri, met the landlord of an ahata in order to persuade him to reduce rents and to stop him from evicting tenants. On the refusal of the ahata owner to comply with these demands, the residents threatened to vacate the ahata *en masse* and to prevent the entry of new tenants. The CSP helped in this campaign by finding alternative accommodation in other ahatas for the protesting tenants.[108] The CSP also played a prominent part in an agitation against the Improvement Trust Scheme in Purana Kanpur (Old Cawnpore), which was a highly controversial issue in the late 1930s. The Old Cawnpore scheme was launched in 1936, under which the Improvement Trust planned to acquire a large area for bungalow construction. The area was inhabited by labourers, many of whom belonged to the lower castes. A Mazdur Mohal Committee was formed by residents to prevent the implementation of the scheme. The committee organised several meetings where CSP leaders, such as Hariharnath Shastri, denigrated the Improvement Trust for disregarding the housing needs of the labouring classes, and accused it of acting in concert with the British government.[109] Several 'mammoth meetings' on the Purana Kanpur issue were also organised by the CSP.[110] In all this, the CSP activists

---

[106] Ibid., 11 September 1938, p. 3; 24 September 1938, p. 3; 26 October 1938, p. 3; 13 November 1938, pp. 4, 8; 27 November 1938, p. 4; 4 December 1938, p. 7; 25 June 1939, p. 3.
[107] Ibid., 24 September 1938, p. 3.
[108] Ibid.   [109] Ibid.
[110] Reports of meetings in File No. 44/1936–37, Department XX, Police, Kanpur Collectorate, ERR; *Vartman*, 29 April 1938, p. 6; *Pratap*, 29 July 1938, p. 6, and 21 December 1938, p. 6.

cast themselves in the role of the champions and allies of the poor in securing vital urban services, basic infrastructural facilities, housing land and protection from rent extortion, all of which the state and the local government had failed to do. This helped CSP activists to gain legitimacy and authority as patrons, protectors and guardians of the poor.

The poor themselves often expressed their protest against the local authorities or landlords in the language of nationalism. In February 1939, the Mohal Committees in Fazalganj, Darshanpurwa, Narayanpurwa and Gadariyapurwa organised meetings to celebrate Independence Day, at which support for the nationalist movement and demands for municipal facilities in poorer neighbourhoods were simultaneously voiced.[111] An agitation in Kanpur in 1937–8 against the Factory Area scheme of the Improvement Trust provides an interesting illustration of how and why the poor linked their protests against urban local authorities with nationalism. The Trust planned to develop new factory sites on the periphery of the town, where some land was used for agricultural or farming purposes. The scheme included Narayanpur, where poorer people, including casual labourers from the city, lived as tenants on land owned by private landlords. They also cultivated crops and vegetables to supplement their incomes. When land was acquired from the landowners by the Improvement Trust to be handed over to factory owners, the resident tenants mounted a protest, which they projected as an agitation of the 'nationalist' poor. They argued that their protest against dispossession was a part of the wider nationalist struggle, for nationalism aimed at social justice for the poor. These views were expressed in a handwritten petition in Hindi, with signatures and thumb prints of Narayanpur residents. This petition, sent to Mrs Vijay Lakshmi Pandit, the Minister of Local Self-Government in the Congress Ministry, stated:

Since *we understand that the foremost aim of our Congress Government is to alleviate the hardships and gulami of the garib janata,* we take the courage to appeal to you to redress our plight . . . On 6 February 1938, several Congress leaders came to Gandhi Nagar in Kanpur for a political conference. At that time, we and our little children went to the railway station to receive them and we attended the meetings addressed by them in Coolie bazar and Nayaganj . . . There, Pantji [G. B. Pant, the Congress Premier of UP], in his speech, explained the duty of the Improvement Trust to the *jhopris* [temporary hutments, also used in the sense of 'humble dwellings'] of the poor. From this *we derived faith and hope, and believed that the nationalist Congress Ministry is engaged in alleviating the sorrow of the garib* . . . First the Trust took over our farm land and gave these away to rich people, whereby we became gulams [dependent or servile] for ever and we the poor are suffering now. In addition the Trust, as a venomous snake, has purchased land from zamindars, on which we reside as tenants. From this we now greatly fear that one day soon, the Trust would uproot us from our houses as well . . . and we will be shackled even further by the chains of gulami to the rich. Would *we, who believe in nationalism and justice*, have to see such a day of misery, even when our nationalist Congress Ministry is at the helm of affairs? We not only hope, but *firmly believe that our nationalist Ministry is mindful of the hardships of the poor and will soon save us from the injustice that threatens us.*[112]

This petition reveals two related reasons why the poorer tenants of Narayanpur invoked nationalism in their protest, which are similar to the ones that have been seen earlier in the case of workplace agitations. First, the arguments in this petition indicate that the rhetoric of nationalism was redirected towards the Congress leaders to urge them to intervene in local affairs on behalf of the tenants. The Narayanpur tenant-labourers demanded that the Congress should be 'mindful of the hardships of the poor' and should abide by its professed goal to 'save us from the injustice that threatens us', by influencing the Improvement Trust to redirect policies in favour of the tenants. Secondly, the petition also suggests that nationalism was seen as a means to 'alleviate the hardships and gulami of the garib janata', and hence the garib 'believe in nationalism and justice'. They expected the Congress and the nationalist government to protect them from being 'shackled even further by the chains of gulami'. Nationalism, with its specific connotation of social justice and deliverance of the poor from servitude, was the key theme invoked in local protests. The tenants interpreted the nationalist message of liberation from political subjection primarily in terms of a political project that would 'alleviate the hardships of gulami' or social subordination of the poor. They also directed the rhetoric of social justice at their leaders to demand that the latter safeguard the interests of the garib. Clearly, various groups of the poor were not simply responding passively to populist propaganda and rallying behind the Congress. Instead, they evolved a political ideology of rights and social justice, drawing upon Congress rhetoric. They also demanded, as a price for their support, that the leaders match their rhetoric of furthering the cause of the poor with action.

In a similar manner, hawkers of the Parade bazar and the Gandhi Nagar Congress Ward Committee, formed primarily by labourers who lived in that residential district, urged Nehru, at a meeting when he visited Kanpur in 1936, 'to point the way to break the chains of *slavery*

[112] Residents of Narayanpur to Mrs Vijay Lakshmi Pandit, Letter dated 29 March 1938, Kanpur Improvement Trust (KIT) File No. 81A/1938–39, Factory Area Scheme I, emphasis added.

and to end their poverty, humiliation and unemployment'.[113] Slavery here, like 'gulami' earlier, straddles both political and social subjection.

Once various groups of the poor began to undertake political action at the local level in this way in the language of nationalism and social justice, the process gained its own momentum. Any action by Congress leaders that seemed to be undermining the professed goal of improving the lot of the poor prompted the poor to distance themselves from the Congress. Instead, as will be seen later in this chapter, they tended to present themselves as the true nationalists, as opposed to the Congress Party. This trend was to be most prominent during the period of provincial autonomy, when the Congress Ministry in UP formed the government.

Class, religion and community in socialist politics and the Muslim poor

The CSP was concerned to distance itself from Congress mobilisation strategies of an earlier period, not only in making new overtures to the working classes, but also in avoiding religion as a rallying focus. Increasingly from this period, the CSP emphasised 'secularism' in public life more prominently. As Pandey has argued, while 'real' nationalism was projected as a struggle to achieve the 'common economic interests of the mass of the people', 'communalism', or the politics of religious community, was defined as antithetical to nationalism and outlawed as illegitimate.[114] The CSP thus attempted to privilege class and disregard community affiliation or religion in political mobilisation. However, in reality, this could not be avoided, and the earlier tendencies persisted.

While Hinduism did indeed feature much less in the CSP's propaganda, and the interlinking of religious festivals and political events was much less overt than in the early 1930s, this association could not be simply wished away. Owing to the interweaving of Congress nationalism with Hindu regeneration movements in the 1920s and early 1930s, the place of Hinduism in the Congress' political culture had become almost 'normalised' by this time. The singing of nationalist songs with a religious content, such as the anthem *Vandemataram* with its Sanskritised lyrics and Hindu imagery invoking the nation as the Mother Goddess, was not considered a subject of debate. This was a matter of everyday practice, as were physical culture, akharas and martial ceremonials of volunteer corps, which resonated with movements of Hindu revivification and unification. There is no evidence to suggest that the

---

[113] *PAI*, No. 36, 12 September 1936, emphasis added.
[114] Pandey, *Construction*, pp. 240–1, ch. 7 passim.

CSP found these controversial or tried to bring them into the domain of public discussion, let alone sought to reverse them. Indeed, the volunteer movement, with its strong links with Hindu militancy, militarism and physical culture, formed a central plank of the CSP's political initiative. The leading socialist P. D. Tandon, for instance, not only was a key person in the organisation of Congress volunteer corps in the late 1930s, but also spearheaded similar Hindu organisations, such as the Hind Raksha Dal. The history of the intermeshing of religious and nationalist iconography from the 1920s did not simply get spirited away by the assertion of a 'secularist', class-based rhetoric by the CSP leadership. On the contrary, class conflict itself was at times presented through a Hindu idiom, even by the most radical socialist labour activists.

Chitra Joshi has discussed the interesting case of a working-class socialist activist, poet and author of Kanpur, who assumed the name of Sudarshan Chakr.[115] The adoption of this pseudonym is significant, for it refers to the invincible weapon of Vishnu, deployed against evil and tyranny. Chakr wrote a major work in verse, entitled *Communist Katha*, on the history of the international communist movement and styled it on the *Ramayana*. The name of the piece was suggestive of religious discourses or *katha*, and the work consisted of seven chapters, as in the *Ramayana*. The chapter organisation similarly followed the *Ramayana* pattern of *kand* or episode and chapters were entitled 'Marx Kand', 'Rus [Russia] Kand', 'Chin [China] Kand' and so on. The metrical pattern too emulated the epic.[116] One of Chakr's poems, which elaborated the theme of the epic battle between the rich and the poor and the eventual triumph of justice, was called *Vishwamahabharata* or 'Worldly Mahabharata'. The poem, drawing upon the key message of the *Mahabharata*, pointed to the moral vindication of the good and the righteous, now shown to be the poor and the downtrodden. Joshi suggests that this trend of allegorical writing in Chakr and other contemporary authors derived from the hold of religion in the working-class mind. A more plausible explanation, however, would be that Chakr was influenced by and developed upon the recently emerging forces of religious resurgence from the 1920s, in which such religious deities and festivals as Ram and the Ramlila, Krishna and Holi, had been associated explicitly with political assertion and the expression of ideals of equality and a just polity. It should be stressed here that, in drawing upon religious imagery, Chakr was not seeking to promote Hinduism in any way, although some socialist leaders, such as Sampurnanand and P. D.

---

[115] C. Joshi, 'Bonds of Community, Ties of Religion: Kanpur Textile Workers in the Early Twentieth Century, *IESHR*, 22, 3, 1985, pp. 259–60.
[116] Ibid.

Tandon, did do so. Most CSP activists, even those committed to the advancement of Hindu religion, would not see themselves as anything but non-communal and 'secular' – in the sense of being non-discriminatory towards Muslims – and they certainly believed in the importance of class-based, not community-based, politics. Many like Chakr, who were avowedly 'secular' in the sense of being non-religious, and even atheistic, would find the suggestion that they harboured a religious consciousness absurd.[117] Rather, Chakr's case drives home the point that the recently constructed Hindu ideology and iconography, which overtly articulated emancipatory ideas during the 1920s and 1930s, were powerful forces, that he, or indeed the CSP, could not disregard. In fact, Chakr's writings show that the message of egalitarianism present in the religious resurgence of the 1920s and 1930s had become an integral aspect not only of nationalist politics but also of labour radicalism. Chakr did not invoke Hindu idioms in a religious mode, but reinterpreted and 'secularised' religious figures and texts in the light of the political concerns of the time. Thus, Ram and Krishna, overtly associated with egalitarianism from the 1920s, easily joined Lenin or Marx in Chakr's pantheon of venerated figures who stood for social justice and the downtrodden.[118] The moral message of the *Mahabharata* similarly assumed overt 'worldly' significance as the struggle between the rich and the poor. The problem with this conception of emancipatory ideas through Hindu religious metaphors, however, remained the lack of integration of Muslims on a common political platform, especially when a parallel ideology of Islamic socialism and anti-imperialism continued to be equally potent.

An important initiative by the CSP was to try to reverse the alienation of the Muslim poor from the Congress, which had become evident from the time of the Civil Disobedience movement.[119] This initiative became especially vigorous in the context of the Muslim Mass Contact Campaign, which was undertaken between 1937 and 1938 in the wake of the poor performance of the Congress among Muslim voters in the provincial elections.[120] The underpinning argument of the CSP in reaching out to the Muslim poor was that the leadership of the Muslim League were unable and unwilling to represent the interests of the poorer sections of the Muslim community. The latter could, therefore, be weaned over to the Congress by the adoption of policies that could be

[117] Interview with Sudarshan Chakr in Kanpur.
[118] Joshi, 'Bonds of community', pp. 259–60.
[119] Discussed in chapter 7.
[120] Mushirul Hasan, 'The Muslim Mass Contact Campaign', in R. Sisson and S. Wolpert (eds.), *Congress and Indian Nationalism: The Pre-Independence Phase*, Berkeley, 1988, pp. 198–222.

relevant to the Muslim poor. The increasing religious tensions from the 1920s as well as the growing distrust of the Congress on the part of the Muslim poor had, however, made it extremely difficult to organise them politically under the party's umbrella. The solution that was envisaged appears to have had two elements.[121] First, the Muslim poor were to be mobilised primarily in terms of their material grievances and local issues. Secondly, a group of militant Muslim communists and socialists, including Sajjad Zaheer, Dr Z. A. Ahmad, Dr K. M. Ashraf, Hajra Begum and Maulana Mohammad Mian Faruqi of Allahabad, specifically assumed responsibility for working with the Muslim poor. They were considered the successors to the earlier generation of Islamic socialists such as Hasrat Mohani and Azad Subhani, with the difference that they conceived socialism not through an Islamic metaphor of equity and redistribution, but more on materialist Marxist lines.[122] In keeping with the practice of some of the earlier Islamic socialists however, they targeted specific Muslim occupational groups and the predominantly Muslim workforces of particular industries, such as artisanal crafts and the bidi and steel trunk workshops in Allahabad. Their strategy was clearly successful, for a number of trade unions of Muslim workers were formed in this period under the auspices of the CSP.[123] A class-based message about capitalists and their exploitation of labour was prominent in these organisational efforts.[124]

In conjunction with this language of class, however, an argument about the specific and relatively greater deprivation of the Muslim poor as compared with other communities was also prominent, drawing upon earlier struggles against the decline and dispossession of Muslims. Moreover, an entirely class-oriented rhetoric, referring only to economic impoverishment, had its limitations, and other overlapping forms of social identities and political concerns required space. Agitation by Muslim occupational groups at their workplace in alliance with the CSP thus often linked with other forms of political action, including those concerned with 'community' issues or religion. Political developments in Allahabad provide an interesting example: workplace-based organisations and a range of other political initiatives accelerated among the Muslim poor from the mid-1930s. Communal tension escalated over Improvement Trust land acquisition policies, which sought to improve

[121] Interview with Hajra Begum (Lucknow), CSP/CPI activist of the 1930s.
[122] K. H. Ansari, *The Emergence of Socialist Thought among North Indian Muslims (1917–1947)*, Lahore, 1990, chs. 4, 5, 6.
[123] *PAI*, No. 16, 1 May 1937; *National Herald*, 12 September 1937; and *Hindusthan Times*, 16 September 1938; *PAI*, No. 14, 9 April 1938; No. 26, 2 July 1938.
[124] *PAI*, No. 14, 17 April 1937; No. 16, 1 May 1937; No. 20, 29 May 1937.

residential neighbourhoods of the Muslim poor. The political action and organisation of Muslim labourers at their workplace now overlapped with their political initiatives in urban neighbourhoods to reverse or stall municipal and Trust policies that threatened their housing or economic opportunities.[125] These initiatives also linked with the formation of local organisations for the defence or protection of the interests of the poorer Muslims. Religious meetings, mosque and shrines frequently provided the context for all these forms of organisation and propaganda. The notion of the endemic deprivation and dispossession of the poorer Muslims featured extensively. Maulana Mohammad Mian Faruqi and Maulana Shahid Fakhri of the town's two major sufi shrines led much of this activity. Both Fakhri and Faruqi, who were socialist in their political outlook, worked closely with the CSP, recruited members for the Congress from the local Muslim population and helped in the formation of neighbourhood or mohalla Congress Committees in Muslim localities.[126] CSP efforts to win over the Muslim poor to the Congress thus appear to have borne some fruit. However, a religious idiom as well as notions of Muslim victimhood and martyrdom were clearly significant even in the mobilisation drives of the CSP and its allies. The language of community thus had to be accommodated in CSP initiatives, notwithstanding their primary emphasis on class and their denial of the importance of religious identity or community, not least because these had come to be powerful forces in popular political action. Thus, in the CSP's political mobilisation, differences in caste and religion were often not transcended but incorporated. The languages of class and community coexisted, and labour organisations frequently occurred along sectarian lines.

That the CSP was able to achieve some following among the Muslim poor did not unambiguously settle the fraught question of their commitment to nationalism from the perspective of the Congress. Now that the Muslim poor associated themselves with the Congress in some respects, they could be seen to have metamorphosed smoothly into 'nationalist Muslims', which was equated with being 'Congress Muslims'.[127] However, the Congress was not the focus of nationalism among the Muslim poor, which continued to refer to the political and social decline of Islam and the Muslim community at the hands of western imperial powers, notably the British. Nationalism remained reliant on the

---

[125] *PAI*, No. 22, 12 June 1937.
[126] *PAI*, No. 23, 19 June 1937; No. 20, 29 May 1937.
[127] Mushirul Hasan, '"Congress Muslims" and Indian Nationalism: Dilemma and Decline, 1928–34', in J. Masselos (ed.), *Struggling and Ruling: The Indian National Congress, 1885–1985*, London, 1987, p. 105.

symbolism of dispossession and martyrdom, which had evolved from the turn of the century and had encompassed the Macchlibazar mosque controversy in Kanpur, the problem of sacred sites in the Middle East and the Khilafat issue as well as the question of *garha* (handwoven cloth) and the decay and decimation of Muslim artisanal communities. Importantly, anti-colonial political agitation involving these symbols and issues happened largely outside the confines of the Congress, or at best ran parallel to it, as in the case of the Khilafat movement.[128] Nationalism among the Muslim poor thus had other foci and expressions than the Congress, and, in the 1930s, the issues of Palestine and Shahidganj were powerful ones, alongside the continued importance of garha and the plight of the artisans.

Developments in Palestine,[129] orchestrated by Muslim propagandists and the press, provided an important symbolic orientation for the Muslim poor in the 1930s, both to express discontent at their own plight and to defy British imperialism world-wide. Allahabad was reported to have become a centre of the Palestine agitation, led by the local militant ulema Faruqi and Fakhri, with reinforcements from Hasrat Mohani and other socialists leaders such as Mohammad Ashraf and Sajjad Zaheer. Numerous meetings were organised at various mosques and shrines, often after prayers, which were attended by up to 3,000 people.[130] At one procession of 3,000 people, a large poster entitled '*Mazatun*' (Atrocities) was reported to have been displayed, which listed happenings in Palestine, such as curfews, a prohibition on congregations, the use of bombs and machine guns, the establishment of martial law, house searches, collective fines and the demolition of houses.[131] Many of these 'atrocities' were not far from the experience of the Muslim poor of Allahabad. The Palestine agitation now provided a focus for the renewed formation of local organisations in various mohallas, after the *tanzeem* period of the early 1930s. The stated aims and activities of these organisations ranged from bringing about reductions in house rents to holding garha bazars to forming volunteer corps.[132] The wider Palestine question assumed immediacy and relevance through its intermingling

[128] Pandey, *Ascendancy*, p. 36.
[129] Sandeep Chawla, 'The Palestine Issue in Indian Politics in the 1920s', in Mushirul Hasan (ed.), *Communal and Pan-Islamic Trends in Colonial India*, Delhi, 1985, pp. 43–58.
[130] *PAI*, No. 30, 1 August 1936, Supplement to the 'UP Police Abstract' No. 30, for week ending 25 July, Appendix No. 4; *PAI*, No. 31, 8 August 1936; No. 33, 22 August 1936.
[131] *PAI*, No. 31, 8 August 1936.
[132] *PAI*, No. 30, 1 August 1936, Supplement to the 'UP Police Abstract' No. 30, for week ending 25 July, Appendix No. 4; *PAI*, No. 31, 8 August 1936; No. 33, 22 August 1936.

with these local issues. Police reports noted both larger political events
and smaller processions and neighbourhood-based action, including in
the predominantly poorer neighbourhoods such as Bakshi Bazar. It was
reported that 'no respectable person of the mohalla' had joined in local
activities, much as in the days of tanzeem.[133] Similar developments were
noticed in Kanpur. One meeting in 1937 to protest against political
developments in Palestine was reported by the police to have been
attended by a large number of local mill workers and labourers,
including 'Red Army' volunteers of workers from the textile mills. At
this meeting, speeches by Mohammad Ashraf, the CPI leader who also
happened to be a Muslim, dealt with the oppression and violation of the
rights of the Palestinian people, whom he referred to as 'Comrades',
thus projecting them as united in a fraternity of suffering with the local
Muslim poor. Ashraf lamented the death and self-sacrifice of the
Palestinians in combating the imperialist onslaught and thus played
upon the potent imagery of martyrdom.[134] The intervention of the
British government in the Shahidganj mosque in the Punjab further
fanned the flames of perceptions of deprivation and martyrdom.[135] At
meetings and processions, once again, police reports noted the initiatives of the poor. One report emphasised that 'none of the prominent
members of the community attended' a prayer meeting of 800 at the
Jama Masjid in Allahabad on Shahidganj Day in September 1935.[136]
Another documented a prayer meeting on the same occasion at the
Kanpur Jama Masjid, followed by another meeting on the Parade
Ground, attended by 8,500 people, in which 'the distinctly enthusiastic
audience was composed chiefly of lower class Muhammadans'. Moreover, 'in the poorer quarters and along the procession route a number of
black flags were displayed'.[137]

What is significant in all these activities – ranging from the CSP-led
labour protests to neighbourhood organisations against Improvement
Trust policies to the Palestine or Shahidganj agitation – is the imagination of the specific deprivation of the Muslims, which animated the
nationalism and anti-colonialism of the Muslim poor. It was the CSP's
emphasis on this theme of deprivation and its leaders' attempts to
organise various groups of the Muslim poor to fight against it that had
briefly brought the poor close to the CSP in the mid-1930s. Equally
importantly, it was to be the Congress' apparent retraction from

[133] *PAI*, No. 33, 22 August 1936; No. 34, 29 August 1936.
[134] *PAI*, No. 36, 18 September 1937.
[135] *PAI*, No. 33, 22 August 1936; No 38, 28 September 1935.
[136] *PAI*, No. 38, 28 September 1935.
[137] Ibid.

precisely this commitment during the period of the Congress Ministry in 1937–9 which exercised a reverse pull. Although the CSP was actively organising labour from the mid-1930s, it will be seen that, during the period of provincial autonomy, the Congress government increasingly adopted a policy to curb and control labour unrest. Even the CSP gradually tempered its zeal and cast itself more in the role of arbiter between labour and capital, concentrating on the settlement and conciliation of workplace disputes, rather than spearheading industrial action. This had the effect not only of alienating labour, but also of turning Muslim workers away from the CSP. In Kanpur, for instance, the militant Muslim textile labourers began to reject the leadership of the CSP activists of the Mazdur Sabha by the late 1930s and turned to other political parties. This disillusionment with the CSP was possibly one of the reasons for the growth of influence of Islamic political parties in the early 1940s among the Kanpur workers.[138]

Moreover, during the Ministry, activities of Congress workers at the local level appeared to the Muslims to be reinforcing their deprivation, martyrdom and subordination once more, replicating developments during the Civil Disobedience period. The Congress at the time of the Ministry became concerned to elaborate a nationalist ritual of the state to demonstrate its newly established governmental power. Much of this found aggressive expression in the public arena in the locality, often by CSP activists. Through these initiatives, Congress workers were seeking to anchor the ministerial authority of the party in local practices, in an effort to undermine the symbols of the colonial state. Congress activists made it a point of honour to ensure the singing of *Vandemataram*, the staging of martial drills, the wearing of *khadi* and the Gandhi cap, as well as the regular hoisting of the tricolour flag, not only at Congress events but also at as many official ceremonies as possible, replacing, or at least establishing equivalence with, the Union Jack.[139] Similarly, Congress activists, and especially a nationalist volunteer movement, revived and reconstituted by the CSP, attempted to set up administrative units in the locality to bypass lower courts or other institutions of governance and sought to adjudicate in local disputes to enforce local order.[140] It was precisely these issues of the flag, nationalist dress and

---

[138] Joshi, 'Bonds of Community', pp. 276–7; Letter dated 1 November 1937, File No. 12/1/38, Home Poll., GOI, NAI; *NNR*, No. 22/1937, p. 8, reported that *Hamari Awaz*, 'a Muslim labour paper of Cawnpore', was growing suspicious of the Congress.

[139] G. Kudaisya, 'State Power and the Erosion of Colonial Authority in Uttar Pradesh, India, 1930–42', Ph.D. thesis, University of Cambridge, 1992, pp. 174–9.

[140] File No. G-5 (Part 4)/1940, AICC, NML; *PAI*, No. 33, 28 August 1937; No. 35, 11 September 1937; Quarterly Survey of Political and Constitutional Position in British India, Nos. 1–6, April 1937 to January 1939, File No. L/P&J/7/1813, GOI, IOR.

the volunteer corps that had been at the centre of the counter political assertion of the Muslim poor in the 1920s and 1930s. The green tanzeem flag had been unfurled in defiance of the nationalist tricolour; the Turkish cap had been donned as a mark of distinctive identity in contrast to the Gandhi cap; khadi had been resisted as a form of social and economic imposition on Muslim artisans; Muslim volunteer corps had been constituted to rival and resist the sway of the overlapping Congress and Hindu ones. Struggles to prevent Congress volunteers from imposing their will on Muslims and eliciting their compliance with nationalist action and events had been the driving force of much of the political action of the Muslim poor a few years earlier. The renewed assertion of Congress activists in the locality in the Ministry period rekindled the fears of domination and, indeed, magnified them, since to many Muslims these foreshadowed the 'Hindu Raj' and the possible oppression of minorities.

The apprehensions of the Muslim poor concerning Congress domination were further fuelled by a strident political campaign, led largely by the Muslim League, concerning the violation of the rights and interests of the Muslims by the Congress during the Ministry. The League expended a great deal of energy on local propaganda in the towns. In Allahabad, for instance, it condemned the Municipal Board for refusing grants-in-aid to institutions that were not willing to fly the tricolour flag. The League also issued leaflets asking Muslims to report cases of high-handedness or repression by Congress workers.[141] In addition to these local initiatives, two highly publicised reports were produced in this period under the auspices of the League, which came to be known as the Pirpur and the Fazlul Haq reports, after the names of the chief authors. The Pirpur report in particular described developments in several UP towns, including Allahabad, Kanpur and Benares, in detail to demonstrate that Muslims faced systematic discrimination, either directly at the hands of the Congress Ministry or by the local wings of the Congress, at which the Ministry connived. The report cited alleged instances of 'victimisation' of Muslims by Congress-dominated local authorities, violation of their religious rights, the perpetration of violence against them, as well as the tyranny of Congress workers and volunteers, who became laws unto themselves and foisted their own will on administrative and judicial processes.[142] With this renewed controversy about

---

[141] *PAI*, No. 9, 5 March 1938.
[142] *Report of the Enquiry Committee Appointed by the Council of the All India Muslim League to Enquire into Muslim Grievances in Congress Provinces, 1938* (President Raja Syed Mohamad Mahdi of Pirpur), published by the Secretary, All India Muslim League, 1938, passim and pp. 65–77.

the power and authority of the Congress over Muslims, the imagery of slavery and subjugation became as important in public discourse as in the days of Khilafat, though now not just in relation to British imperialism or capitalism but also with reference to the Congress.[143] It was within this context that there was a vigorous renewal of volunteer activities among the Muslim poor. Once more, competitive mobilisation between them and nationalist or Congress volunteers came to provide the context for a major spate of communal riots between 1937 and 1939.[144] If, in the past, the Congress had been rejected for furthering Hindu nationalism, it was now dreaded for potentially unleashing tyranny and injustice with the full authority of state power.

Thus, even though the Muslim poor seemed to have seen the CSP and its Muslim leaders as allies in their workplace struggles, yet in a broader framework of politics they remained highly suspicious of the Congress. As a CPI leader pointed out in his later reminiscences, Muslim workers took the view that, while they could identify with the CSP or the CPI as their union in the workplace, they did not consider the Congress as the party that represented them in the wider political arena.[145] Despite the efforts of the CSP, the Congress was not seen as the harbinger of emancipation for the Muslim poor. The notion of reversing deprivation was central to the politics of the Muslim poor, and hence it was the ability or commitment of leaders or political parties to achieve this goal that determined the nature and extent of support of the Muslim poor. This was why they did not embrace the Congress, and also why they refrained from resolutely and unequivocally turning towards the Muslim League. The poor remained, on the whole, wary of the Muslim League and suspected it of betraying their cause and representing only the interests of the upper classes and the privileged. The newspaper *Naqqara* voiced this sentiment when stating that to side with the Muslim League was tantamount to strengthening the chains of subjection.[146] Unwilling to rally behind either the Congress or the Muslim League fully, the Muslim poor remained imperfectly integrated into the mainstream of the party political structure of UP in the later 1930s. A substantial section, however, was inclined to support the Momin Conference, based as the party was on a notion of the historical decline of Muslim artisans and an ideology for their regeneration. In Allahabad and Kanpur, for instance, the Momin Conference developed

---

[143] *NNR*, No. 13/1937, pp. 3–5; No. 39/1937, p. 3.
[144] See, for instance, *PAI*s throughout 1937–9, which report developments strikingly similar to those from the mid-1920s to the early 1930s.
[145] Interview with Dr Z. A. Ahmad, CPI leader, in Lucknow.
[146] *NNR*, No. 22/1937, p. 8.

a large following in the 1930s,[147] and there were reports of clashes between Muslim League activists and Momin volunteers in Kanpur who refused to fall in line with the League.[148] However, the Momin Conference could not be the platform of political activity for all sections of the Muslim poor, based as the organisation was on the identity of ansari weavers. For some sections of the Muslim poor, then, in the specific context of the nationalist politics of the later 1930s, the existing constellation of political forces did not provide an adequate focus of nationalism for them, despite the brief and somewhat limited alliance with the CSP.

The parting of ways of the leaders and the led

In the late 1930s, the Congress not only failed to win back the support of the Muslim poor, but also gradually alienated large sections of the labouring poor (mostly Hindu) who had been drawn to the Congress with its new socialist orientation. The parting of the ways related to the growing political tensions during the years of the Congress Ministry, and led not only to the unpopularity of the Congress 'right wing' but also gradually to a disenchantment with the CSP, despite the fact that the CSP initially took up the cause of the poor against the 'right wing' and the Ministry. Various provincial Congress Ministries either came under the direct influence of, or faced subtle pressures from, the business classes and capitalists. These Ministries were also wary of the growing communist influence in workers' politics.[149] Thus, after a brief initial period of conciliatory policies towards labour, the UP Ministry gradually came to favour restraint in labour politics and proceeded to contain workplace unrest, armed with governmental power.[150] A section of Congressmen, including Gandhi, strongly deplored the militancy of the labouring classes for verging on 'violence'.[151] Moreover, having to contend with the problems of administration and of law and order, the Ministry increasingly used the police to control urban agitations.[152] The use of Section 144 of the Criminal Procedure Code to

---

[147] Interview with Habibur Rahman 'Betab' in Kanpur (office bearer and volunteer-activist of the Momin Conference in the 1930s); *PAI*, No. 7, 23 February 1935; No. 41, 23 October 1937. The Momin Conference has been discussed in chapter 7 above.

[148] *National Herald*, 8 September 1938; interview with Habibur Rahman 'Betab' in Kanpur.

[149] C. Markovits, 'Indian Business and the Congress Provincial Governments, 1937–39', *MAS*, 15, 3, 1981, pp. 487–526; Markovits, *Indian Business and Nationalist Politics, 1931–39*, pp. 150–78.

[150] V. B. Karnik, *Indian Trade Unions: A Survey*, Bombay, 1966, pp. 108–19.

[151] *Samyavad*, 1 September 1938, p. 2 (editorial article).

[152] See chapter 4 above.

prohibit strikes and pickets became more prominent. A government report commented in 1938 that the UP Congress was attempting to 'divest itself of the extremism which characterised the party before the responsibilities of administration were assumed' and that this had precipitated growing estrangement between the 'Congress right' and the 'extremer elements'.[153]

Faced with the Ministry's clearly unpopular policies, the CSP further boosted its campaign against the Congress 'right wing'. The provincial Ministry in 1937 was formed entirely by 'right-wing' Congressmen, and a majority of the Congress members of the legislature also belonged to the 'right wing'.[154] With the 'right wing' dominating the Congress legislative party and the CSP in control of the provincial Congress organisation, the cleavage between the CSP and the 'right wing' of the mid-1930s now coincided with a split between the parliamentary and the organisational wings of the Congress.[155] The battle lines were drawn even more clearly. Confronted with this situation, in order to strengthen its position and to extend its base of support, the CSP stepped up its bid for mass mobilisation. It became increasingly strident in its criticisms of the 'right wing' and the policies of the Ministry.

The CSP sought to portray itself as the 'true' Congress, mindful of the interests of the labouring classes, and accused the 'right wing' of reactionary tendencies and of perpetuating the repressive policies of the colonial state, in particular by deploying the argument of non-violence and peace. Narendra Deva wrote to Jawaharlal Nehru:

Truth and non-violence are noble ideas . . . It is extremely vulgar to press them in the service of a wrong cause . . . it sometimes so happens that *acts which were justified by the former governments in the name of law and order are today being defended in the name of truth and non-violence* . . . there is an attempt to suppress the rising tide of revolutionary conflict by some of our governments.[156]

Criticism of the government for clamping down on labour action was widely aired in some sections of the general press and in a flourishing labour press.[157] An article in the newspaper *Hamdam* succinctly summarised the range of issues that made the Congress Ministry a target of wrath:

Lathi-charge and firing on Kanpur mill-workers have opened the eyes of

---

[153] Quarterly Survey of Political and Constitutional Position in British India, No. 4, 1 May to 31 July 1938, File No. L/P&J/7/1813, GOI, IOR.
[154] Tomlinson, *Indian National Congress*, p. 93.
[155] Ibid.
[156] Narendra Deva to Jawaharlal Nehru, letter dated 10 December 1937, Jawaharlal Nehru Paper, Part I, Correspondence, vol. 54, Serial No. 3398, NML, emphasis added.
[157] See *NNR*, 1937 and 1938, passim, for extensive reports.

workers about the Congress. The hollowness of the promises of the Congress is now clear. The oppression of petty officials, and the aloofness between the government and the people have not abated in the least in the last nine months [even under a nationalist Congress government]. A regular crusade has started against newspapers [in the form of censorship or indirect pressure by the government]. . . . *The public now realises that the Congressmen are not the selfless and humble patriots that they posed to be. Power and wealth have spoilt the Congress Ministers* and they now believe more in violence [against workers, in particular] than in soul force. Section 144 and lathi-charges which the Congress once execrated are now its favourite weapons.[158]

CSP trade union papers, such as *Samyavad*, were especially scathing in their criticism of the Ministry for its tendency to silence political protests with police help. There were allegations that Congressmen who attempted to organise strikes were seen as the militant 'enemies' of the party and were being purged from the party.[159] CSP labour activists portrayed Congressmen who silenced the protests of the working classes as betraying the cause of 'true' nationalism. In view of this deviation from 'true' nationalism, editorial articles in *Samyavad* urged workers to participate in the nationalist movement with greater vigour, so that the Congress, and the nationalist movement it was leading, could be prevented from falling prey to the rich and to self-seeking leaders and corrupt *goondas*. The articles argued that the Congress in power was even averse to the struggle of the poor for their *roti* and *kapra* – the basic needs of food and clothing. The workers were, however, advised not to lose heart and distance themselves from the nationalist movement, for this would only help the rich to capture the Congress and to direct the nationalist movement in such a way that the poor would be deprived of their rights in independent India. Instead the workers should voice their condemnation of the Congress for acting on behalf of imperialists and capitalists, and thus restore the nationalist movement to its true and correct path. Indeed, the workers were urged to claim the Congress for themselves and wrest it away from the grip of the wealthy and the power-hungry.[160]

The tough approach of the Ministry towards labour unrest served to radicalise many sections of the poor, abetted by CSP propaganda. Labour militancy became more widespread precisely because the Ministry outlawed political action and failed to introduce promised labour legislation.[161] Developments in Benares provide an interesting and typical example. In 1937 and 1938, the CSP activist Shiv Pujan Tripathi

---

[158] *NNR*, No. 18/1938, p. 6, emphasis added.
[159] *Samyavad*, 18 June 1939, p. 1; 25 June 1939, pp. 2–3; 9 July 1939, p. 2.
[160] Ibid., 15 January 1939, p. 2; 18 June 1939, p. 1.
[161] Ibid., 18 June 1939, p. 1; 25 June 1939, pp. 2–3; 9 July 1939, p. 2.

and his colleagues Rustam Satin, Mohammad-uz-Zafar and Satyabrata Das Gupta had spearheaded the formation of at least eight trade unions in the town, involving the employees of the water works and the electric power house, municipal sweepers, ekka-tonga walas, railway coolies and workers at the Kashi Iron Foundry and the Benares Cotton Mill.[162] After several strikes by each of these groups, the district authorities anticipated a general strike in the town in February 1938 and declared prohibitory orders on labour agitations under Section 144, with the approval of the Ministry.[163] Shiv Pujan Tripathi and fifty-six workers from the Kashi Iron Foundry were arrested.[164] Labour militancy in Benares alarmed even a section of the CSP leadership in the town, including Sampurnanand. The Town Congress Committee appointed a labour committee to prevent a general strike and to settle labour disputes through arbitration.[165] However, the workers of the Iron Foundry refused to accept the terms suggested by this committee. Eventually a settlement was reached, but not before the workers denounced the Congress Ministry for undermining the cause of the labouring classes by letting the police loose on them. They rallied behind Shiv Pujan Tripathi, whom they claimed as their leader.[166] This impasse in Benares and unabated labour unrest eventually led to the expulsion of Tripathi and some of his colleagues from the Congress for indiscipline.[167] Tripathi, however, continued to enjoy the support of trade unions in the city, and the district authorities felt obliged to take him into custody on several occasions in order to prevent the impending strikes of water works and power house workers, railway coolies and ekka-tonga walas.[168]

By 1939, the Ministry's reliance on police action was common, and not only in Benares, thus eliciting ever greater discontent. In January–February 1939, for instance, labour agitations had assumed serious proportions in all four towns. In Kanpur, striking oil mill workers and thelawalas were prosecuted and arrested; and in Lucknow, workers in a cotton mill were arrested for picketing.[169] Soon afterwards, in July 1939, at a number of workers' meetings the Congress was condemned for this policy. In Benares, press workers tabled a resolution at a meeting that recent orders of the Congress government, directing police action

[162] *PAI*, No. 2, 15 January 1938; No. 4, 29 January 1938; No. 6, 12 February 1938.
[163] *PAI*, No. 7, 19 February 1938.
[164] *PAI*, No. 10, 12 March 1938.
[165] Ibid.
[166] *PAI*, No. 11, 19 March 1938.
[167] *PAI*, No. 45, 12 November 1938.
[168] *PAI*, No. 30, 29 July 1939; No. 31, 5 August 1939.
[169] *PAI*, No. 4, 28 January 1939; No. 8, 25 February 1939.

to be unleashed against workers who resorted to strikes and pickets, were against the avowed policy of the Congress.[170] In Allahabad, orders issued by the Congress Ministry that barred pickets at factory gates were similarly condemned at workers' meetings.[171] These developments ensured the estrangement of the urban labouring classes from the 'official' Congress, and the questions of who were the true nationalists and who had the right to rule came to occupy centre-stage.

Even though the CSP formed a focus for opposition against what it called 'reactionary' right-wing elements within the Congress, the CSP itself also gradually began to moderate its approach towards working-class agitation, when faced with overt militancy, as in the case of Benares mentioned above. While it continued to support some strikes, there was an increasing attempt to settle labour disputes through arbitration and conciliation.[172] The CSP began to act as a mediator between workers and employers and tended to concentrate more on labour administration than on facilitating strikes or agitations.[173] This culminated in the establishment of the Congress Labour Sub-committee in 1939. Its brief was to settle labour disputes within the framework of the regulatory regime of factory and labour legislation.[174] In this, the CSP increasingly fell out of step with communist labour leaders, who, in many cases, came to wrest the initiative in workplace politics from the CSP by the end of the 1930s. By the late 1930s, the 'left wing' within the Congress found itself out-manoeuvred by the Gandhian leadership and was required to make political compromises for fear of splitting the Congress and weakening the nationalist movement. Simultaneously, it increasingly parted company with the communists.[175] This considerable weakening of the Congress left was one reason why the CSP espoused increasing moderation in mobilising labour. However, the attempts of the CSP to direct protests and grievances into institutional channels were also largely because the party was gradually losing control over both militant labour politics and local agitations. Paradoxically though, this increasing moderation laid the CSP open to similar criticism to that which its leaders themselves had levelled at the Congress 'right wing'

[170] *PAI*, No. 27, 8 July 1939.
[171] *PAI*, No. 29, 22 July 1939.
[172] Evidence of Hariharnath Shastri, Proceedings dated 20 January 1938, KLIC Proceedings.
[173] For examples of CSP attempts to resolve labour disputes through official channels, see *Samyavad*, 1 September 1938; 8 September 1938, p. 4; 16 October 1938, p. 1; 23 October 1938, p. 2.
[174] 'Mazdur aur Congress', *Mazdur Samachar* (published by the Congress Labour Sub-Committee), 1, 1 June 1939, pp. 1–3. Narayan Prasad Arora Papers, Printed Material, Serial No. 20, NML.
[175] Haithcox, *Communism and Nationalism*, pp. 277–88.

and the Ministry. Gradually a rift opened between the CSP and sections of urban labour, reinforcing not only the slackening of control but also the escalation of political militancy on the part of the labouring poor. With increasing disillusionment, the CSP ceased to be seen as an ally in many cases. In the process, important definitions of legitimate leadership, and of 'them' and 'us', began to emerge among the poor.

The most spectacular falling-out between the CSP and the working classes happened in Kanpur in 1937, and the rift itself stimulated unprecedented militancy in the textile mills. Here the CSP, the Ministry and the Congress 'right wing' all faced the censure of the workers and only the CPI was able to maintain some influence. The worsening conditions of the workers during the depression and continued problems afterwards helped to set the stage for labour unrest, despite the growing prosperity of the mills.[176] However, the radicalisation of mill politics and the rift between workers and the nationalist leadership resulted more decisively from the changing political orientation of the Congress, including the CSP. Workplace organisation and agitation having been facilitated by CSP leaders, workers' expectations rose with the advent of the Congress Ministry about the possibility of an imminent reversal of their plight and the cutting down to size of the employers. Yet, quite the opposite happened. With the hope of change, in 1937, soon after the Congress came to power, the workers began to stage strikes, only to be met with restraint. During labour disputes and strikes in several mills in July and August 1937, police lathi charges, arrests of strikers and prohibitory orders on pickets were approved by the Congress Ministry. At workers' meetings throughout 1937, the Ministry was reminded of the Congress election manifesto, which had promised freedom of meetings, processions and associations. The use of Section 144 to ban agitations and to break up pickets was said to be against the principles of the Congress that Gandhi himself had enunciated. The Congress Ministry was accused of violating its own principles in order to protect the interests of the rich.[177] Indeed, it was argued that by imposing restrictions on labour action the government had espoused the cause of the factory owners.[178] It was also declared that the Congress Ministry could not be spared from attack if it extended police support to employers to prevent workers' agitations and continued the British

[176] For a discussion of labour unrest in Kanpur in 1937-8, see C. Joshi, 'Hope and Despair: Textile Workers in Kanpur in 1937-8 and the 1990s', in J. P. Parry, J. Breman and K. Kapadia (eds.), *The Worlds of Indian Industrial Labour*, New Delhi, 1999, pp. 171-203.

[177] *PAI*, No. 46, 27 November 1937; *NNR*, No. 49/1937, p. 1, cites *Pratap*, in which the declaration of Section 144 is condemned.

[178] *NNR*, No. 49/1937, p. 1, cites *Sainik*.

policy of repressing political action.[179] The radical labour paper *Lalj-handa*, supported by the communists, and the *Hindusthan* opposed government action against Kanpur workers, which they attributed to the 'united group of imperialists, capitalists and bureaucrats'.[180] The *Lalj-handa* held that 'Imperialism is today utilizing Congress Ministers for its own purposes.' Another article in the same paper declared: 'For the last fifteen months section 144 has been promulgated constantly in Cawn-pore for crushing the labour movement. We shall resist to the end attacks on our freedom and shall not rest until section 144 is withdrawn.'[181]

A key feature of industrial unrest in 1937 was the autonomous initiative and political militancy of workers, and the CSP's struggle to establish better control, or even to maintain its authority, over labour action. The industry experienced a spate of lightning strikes from July 1937. The CSP labour leaders failed to support these initiatives and they found themselves unable to exercise influence over workers through the Mazdur Sabha.[182] By August, an official report noted, 'the Em-ployers' Association received a message from the [trade union leaders of the] Mazdur Sabha that they had lost control of labour', who struck frequently, 'completely disregarding the ordinary rules of the Mazdur Sabha'.[183] These lightning strikes climaxed in a general strike in August, which was reported to have affected thirteen mills and 40,000 workers.[184] A police report remarked that during the general strike there had been a possibility that the workers would not even take counsel from the radical communist leadership to return to work,[185] let alone from the socialists, although the communists supported the general strike and thus enjoyed greater confidence among the workers than the CSP leaders did. The general strike was eventually called off as a result of the direct intervention of the provincial government, which promised to investigate and redress workers' grievances and instituted a formal enquiry into labour conditions, headed by the veteran Congress leader Babu Rajendra Prasad. The CSP leadership of the Mazdur Sabha, however, failed to re-establish effective control over labour action, not least because they had opposed the general strike, and the workers took the view that the leaders had undermined their interest in engineering a

[179] *PAI*, No. 49, 18 December 1937.
[180] *NNR*, No. 51/1937, p. 1.
[181] *NNR*, No. 49/1937, pp. 1–2, cites *Laljhanda*.
[182] Evidence of Hariharnath Shastri, Proceedings dated 20 January 1938. KLIC Proceedings; Report by J. Ramsay Scott regarding the labour trouble in Cawnpore, File No. 12/1/1938, Home Poll., GOI, NAI.
[183] Report by J. Ramsay Scott regarding the labour trouble in Cawnpore, File No. 12/1/1938.
[184] *PAI*, No. 32, 21 August 1937.
[185] *PAI*, No. 31, 14 August 1937.

compromise and suspending the strike.[186] Individual instances of work stoppage and of clashes with factory management continued despite the official truce after the general strike. The alienation of workers from the CSP and their independent action were largely the result of the moderation of the leaders and their advocacy against strikes, which was probably worsened by the fact that Nehru, at a meeting with the Employers' Association, accepted that 'no business or organisation could possibly be run successfully or profitably unless there was complete discipline within the organisation'. He also confirmed the right of the employers to appoint or dismiss their employees. By the end of September 1937, both the Mazdur Sabha and the City Congress Committee openly admitted that the lightning strikes continued against their advice and wishes.[187] The workers meanwhile prepared to stage further general strikes in the industry. The officials of the Mazdur Sabha, however, strongly appealed for circumspection.

In the face of the cautious and restrained policy of the Mazdur Sabha, workers' associations on the shop floor – the mill committees – had gradually seized the initiative. Mill committees had been formed from the mid-1930s not only in every mill but also in most departments of mills, often with communist support.[188] The Secretary of the Employers' Association of North India reported to the Kanpur Labour Inquiry Committee, which was formed at this time to investigate and bring about a solution to the labour impasse in Kanpur, that the lightning strikes had been engineered by mill committees, which 'appear to be a law unto themselves and over whom the Mazdur Sabha appears to have no control or authority whatsoever'.[189] The employers found it impossible to maintain order within the mills. The jobbers, who often served as the instruments of managerial control, were rendered largely powerless as workers repudiated their authority, with many of them frequently being beaten up.[190] The jobbers became largely ineffective in

---

[186] Joshi, 'Hope and Despair', pp. 175, 180.
[187] Report by J. Ramsay Scott regarding the labour trouble in Cawnpore, File No. 12/1/1938; Copy of letter dated 20 November 1937 from the Secretary, Employers' Association of North India, to Secretary, Labour Inquiry Committee, KLIC Proceedings.
[188] *Samyavad*, 29 January 1939, p. 4.
[189] Copy of letter dated 20 November 1937, from the Secretary, Employers' Association of North India, to Secretary, Labour Inquiry Committee; Evidence of Mr J. Tinker, assisted by Mr B. Shaw of Cawnpore Cotton Mills, Proceedings dated 8 December 1937; Evidence of Hariharnath Shastri, Proceedings dated 20 January 1938, KLIC Proceedings.
[190] Evidence of Mr J. Tinker, assisted by Mr B. Shaw of Cawnpore Cotton Mills, Proceedings dated 8 December 1937; Evidence of Mistry Abdul Latiff, Proceedings dated 10 December 1937, KLIC Proceedings. For the worker–jobber relationship in Kanpur, see Joshi, 'Formation of Work Culture', pp. 155–72.

containing militancy, which severely undermined discipline within the mills. An official report reflected the alarm of the employer, when it stated that 'a spirit of unrest prevailed and insubordinate and undisciplined incidents were the orders of the day. . . . The present great difficulty . . . is lack of discipline among workers.' The report expressed the view that the workers think 'that they can form mill committees by arbitrary methods and dictate the action of the management in the control of labour'.[191] Not surprisingly, the Employers' Association had to turn to the government to re-establish authority and strongly recommended official measures for the removal and outlawing of mill committees, for it felt 'it is impossible to maintain discipline and efficiency so long as these committees function'.[192] Inevitably, the state stepped in more decisively with its policing apparatus to restore order and discipline, revealing the Congress government to be complicit in suppressing labour.[193] The employers too reacted to the upsurge of militancy from the mill committees with victimisation and dismissals.[194] Labour newspapers claimed that the employers sought to chasten and penalise these dismissed workers even further by reporting them to the police, who then harassed or incarcerated them on concocted charges. That they had been dismissed and were unemployed was considered to be proof that they had 'bad livelihood' and earned their living through crime.[195] Moreover, hired toughs of the employers, in collusion with the police, were reported in labour newspapers to have beaten up militant workers.[196]

These strategies of employers and the state began to render organisation inside mills increasingly difficult, and mohal or neighbourhood committees as well as a volunteer corps, the well-known Red Army (Lal Fauj), were formed in working-class districts to supplement the mill committees.[197] According to one account, out of approximately 50,000 workers employed by the mills, 30,000 were members of the labour union, and 10,000 were directly involved in the Red Army. A Youth

[191] Report by J. Ramsay Scott regarding the labour trouble in Cawnpore, File No. 12/1/1938.
[192] Ibid.
[193] Complaints against police 'excesses' against labour were legion in Kanpur. Secret Memorandum, Intelligence Bureau, Home Department, File No. 12/1/38, Home Poll., GOI, NAI.
[194] Memoranda submitted to the Kanpur Labour Inquiry Committee by the Mazdur Sabha, dated 16 and 19 November 1937, regarding strikes at Elgin Mills, Cawnpore Cotton Mills and Lakshmi Ratan Cotton Mills and the lock-out at Maheshwari Devi Jute Mill, KLIC Proceedings.
[195] Samyavad, 16 July 1939, p. 3.
[196] Ibid., 1 January 1939, p. 3.
[197] Ibid., 5 February 1939, p. 4; 26 February 1939, p. 2.

Wing of the volunteer corps had also been organised under the leadership of a young boy who was popularly known as the Russi (Russian) captain.[198] These volunteer organisations built upon martial activities, akharas, pahalwani and the culture of physical prowess and manliness, described in chapters 6 and 7. The volunteer corps also derived inspiration and experience from the nationalist and religious volunteer movements. The Mazdur Sabha itself from its early days had its own akhara and gymnasium, as well as volunteer corps,[199] which the workers now vastly expanded. Based in the residential neighbourhoods, the mohal committees disseminated information and facilitated organisation. They also instituted networks of support and relief during strikes or for dismissed workers. Many of them also engaged in action over rent and neighbourhood sanitary infrastructure. The political radicalism of the mill and mohal committees and the Red Army kept Kanpur in a state of political instability for much of the Ministry period. Chakr, in his history of labour politics in Kanpur, sees this era as the pinnacle of achievement of 'Red Kanpur' and the heyday of workers' militancy.[200]

If the mill owners and managers were exercised by their inability to impose discipline, the mill and mohal committees and the Red Army too saw violating the order of mill managements and subverting their discipline as key elements in their political assertion. The staging of lightning strikes was one way of denying discipline. However, defiance was also expressed through a range of symbolic action within and outside the mills. Chakr's account of the labour movement highlights several such incidents as landmarks in the clash between capital and labour in Kanpur, in which the workers scored a victory. The mill authorities introduced a system of identity passes for workers to enter the mills in this period, in an attempt to keep out the more militant members of mill committees. The workers retaliated by tying their passes to their shoes and displaying the shoes when asked for the passes.[201] Other much celebrated occasions included the 'day of the red flag' (Lal jhanda divas) and the incident of the red shirt. In the first case, when some red flags were burnt by the mill authorities outside the gates of the Swadeshi Mills, the workers retaliated by hoisting the red flag on top of the highest tower, chimney or tank in every cotton mill in town.[202] Chakr commented on this event that the workers proved graphically that Kanpur was truly 'red' in its politics, and thus demonstrated that they had emphatically asserted their rights in the mills.[203]

[198] Chakr, Kanpur Mazdur Andolan, pp. 52–3, 61–71.
[199] Ibid., pp. 26, 105.   [200] Ibid., pp. 52–3.   [201] Ibid., p. 49.
[202] Samyavad, 25 December 1938, p. 5; Chakr, Kanpur Mazdur Andolan, pp. 62–3.
[203] Chakr, Kanpur Mazdur Andolan, p. 63.

The second incident unfolded after Illahi Baksh, a worker at the Elgin Mills, went to work wearing a red shirt and had his shirt torn off and was then dismissed from work. A meeting was convened in protest that weekend at the Parade Ground, where large vats of red dye were provided by the Mazdur Sabha and 20,000 workers dyed their shirts red. On the following day, nearly all workers turned up at work in red clothes, and vats of dye were again provided at all mill gates to facilitate this. The workers of the Elgin Mills also marched to work with Illahi Baksh, who was eventually reinstated in his job by the employers.[204] It is interesting that Chakr's history of the Kanpur labour struggle in the 1930s is narrated largely through these vignettes of symbolic triumph, rather than through a catalogue of concrete material gains.

Contestation and denial of authority and discipline, then, were central to the workers' perception of their struggle, through which they sought to etch their autonomous domain of political action and rights. Indeed, the denial of discipline encompassed not just the mill authorities or the strong arm of the state, but also the CSP labour leaders who sought to temper or regulate militancy and advised conciliation. This advice naturally rendered the CSP increasingly suspect in the eyes of the workers, despite the fact that the CSP did support the general strike that happened in 1938. Even after this event though, the socialists failed to regain the authority they had lost in 1937, and workers continued to challenge them. Thus, on one occasion in 1939, some workers refused to heed the CSP counsel to return to work because it would have constituted a capitulation to the employers. As a solution, the CSP advised that, in order to save face, the striking workers should resume work without seeking the 'forgiveness' of the employers or tendering their apologies (mafi), but merely express their 'regret' (afsos) to the employers.[205] Such semantic juggling could scarcely satisfy the workers. When, on another occasion, CSP leaders tried to convince workers at a public meeting that striking without proper organisation and funding would be ruinous, this was reported to have met with an extremely hostile reaction from the workers, who threatened never to follow the leaders again in staging strikes unless one was immediately announced.[206] Evidently, attempts by CSP leaders to establish control and discipline over labour politics was energetically contested. The only leaders who continued to have some limited clout were the militant communists, who were themselves increasingly inclined to diverge from

[204] Ibid., p. 60.
[205] Samyavad, 12 February 1939, p. 2.
[206] Ibid., 16 July 1939, p. 2.

the CSP by the end of the 1930s, and were more consistent in supporting labour radicalism.

The symbolic assertion of the supremacy of the 'red' in the mills was in no small measure directed against the nationalist Congress tricolour, as the workers set the pace of political developments and expressed their own power, outstripping the leaders. Significantly, similar dissent was expressed in the bazars in this period, as seen earlier in this chapter. Indeed, political militancy among the labouring poor in Kanpur was by no means confined to the mills, not least because the textile labour force was not a water-tight segment, but was characterised by movement to and from various other industries, large and small, as well as the trading and transport sectors. Political developments in the mills and other workplaces, such as the bazars, resonated with each other. As seen earlier, in the bazars too the colour red had been put forward as a deliberate challenge to the tricolour of the so-called moderate 'Gandhi-badis'. The CSP had taken nationalist mobilisation into the workplace, but then this sphere of politics itself became an arena for symbolic struggle over the nation and its colours – tricolour or red. The tricolour seemed to have come to represent the power of the government as embodied in the actions of the Congress Ministry and lost some of its emancipatory symbolism. In this way, a struggle over who has the authority to lead, and ultimately therefore over who should rule the nation, and on whose behalf, was implicitly emerging at the centre of the politics of the poor. The experience of political action and struggle, along with their triumphs and reversals, had brought these questions to the fore at this particular conjuncture in late-colonial India. With the Congress clearly destined to step into the shoes of the retreating colonial state, the contestation over order, control and discipline which had been emerging at the heart of urban politics from the early 1920s in caste, religious and nationalist action gradually came to a head by the end of the 1930s. At the heart of this political conflict lay the question of the place of the poor in the emerging democratic political order and the public sphere. All these political struggles found especially concerted expression in the late 1930s in the volunteer movement, which had emerged as the quintessential site of political action of the poor in the early twentieth century.

Struggle over the volunteer movement and claiming a space in the nation

According to the Governor of UP in 1938, 'the most disquieting feature at the moment is the movement to organise and train large bodies of

militant volunteers'.[207] Indeed, so important was the volunteer movement considered to be by the end of the 1930s, that the Government of
India found it necessary to produce regular reports on the subject.
Volunteer corps, organised by local activists in urban neighbourhoods
and workplaces, registered a phenomenal increase. The numbers involved are impossible to estimate accurately. Their dispersed, localised
and widespread nature permitted the collection only of imprecise
information and led to the production of widely divergent figures by
various official and non-official sources.[208] However, the magnitude of
the phenomenon was amply brought out impressionistically by a government report on the volunteer movement, which noted that UP was 'full
of mushroom organisations, created to meet the exigencies of the
moment . . . seldom properly organised or systematically developed,
without central control or financial backup . . . owing allegiance to
nobody'.[209] These volunteer organisations encompassed religious, nationalist and trade union interests, although these various elements
extensively overlapped with each other. In this expansion of the nationalist volunteer movement, the Congress socialists initially played a
significant role by vigorously promoting the formation of nationalist
volunteer corps from the mid-1930s. By the late 1930s, various groups
of the poor in the towns had entered these Congress volunteer corps in
large numbers. Soon, however, they came to dominate these volunteer
units, or had formed similar ones of their own. In Kanpur, for instance,
the bazar karmcharis had participated in the local units of the Qaumi
Sena Dal (National Army or Military Corps), the volunteer corps
sponsored by the CSP. However, other volunteer organisations, such as
the Karmchari Samyavadi Fauj (Employees' Socialist Army), Lal Fauj
(Red Army) and Samyavadi Sainik Dal (Socialist Army or Military
Corps), also appeared in the Kanpur bazars.[210] Workers in various small
mills and manufacturing workshops, as well as transport pliers and petty
traders, formed similar volunteer organisations, often entitled Sainik

[207] Governor's Situation Report, 22 November 1938, File No. L/P&J/5/265–266, GOI,
IOR.
[208] In 1939, the UP government estimated the number of 'nationalist' volunteers in the
province to be 18,000, while the number was reported to be nearly 45,000 at the end
of 1940. Volunteer Movement in India II & III, File No. 4/2/1939, Home Poll., GOI,
NAI; Quarterly Survey of Political and Constitutional Position in British India, No. 8,
1 May to 31 July 1939, File No. L/P&J/7/1815, GOI, IOR; Volunteer Movement in
India IV, File No. 4/1/40, Home Poll. (I), GOI, NAI.
[209] Quarterly Survey of Political and Constitutional Position in British India, No. 8.
[210] *Karmchari Smarika*, Part III, p. 29; *Samyavad*, 25 December 1938, p. 4; 12 February
1939, pp. 4–5.

Dal or Military Corps.[211] These organisations were not directly under the organisational control of the Congress, although they often involved Congressmen and CSP activists.

Volunteer corps, as seen in previous chapters, played a central role in the self-assertion of the poor and performed multiple functions. They staged drills, parades and processions. They helped mohalla people to deal with the law courts and government departments, as well as to mount defences against the police.[212] They organised pickets, strikes and agitations against the state, employers or municipal authorities. The volunteer corps also articulated the rivalries of competing groups of the poor in the urban neighbourhoods. At the local level, therefore, the volunteer organisations were grounded in the diverse conflicts at workplaces or in neighbourhoods. At the same time, and equally importantly, they served as vehicles for the political assertion and symbolic expression of power of the poor. All these factors had accorded a centrality to the volunteer movement in popular politics. The great spurt in the volunteer movement in the late 1930s to some extent indicated the further development of this process. However, it also owed a great deal to the reorientation in nationalist politics, notably the controversial policies of the Congress Ministry as well as the gradual taming of the CSP. At one obvious level, with the Ministry attempting to curb local agitation in the towns and the CSP gradually moderating its support for popular political action, the volunteer movement assumed greater significance among the poor as the vehicle through which to continue their political action in the locality in the face of waning support from the Congress.

There were, however, more compelling reasons. As seen earlier, the idea had gained popular currency in the late 1930s that the Congress, as a party holding governmental power, would ultimately be more inclined to enforce order and political stability with coercive power, even if that undermined its other stated goal of furthering the cause of the so-called 'common people'. The popular terms of political abuse used, for instance, by workers in Kanpur and mentioned in the labour paper *Samyavad* – 'netashahi' or 'goondashahi' (rule of the leaders and coercive rule of the thugs) – alluded precisely to these misgivings.[213] Such disillusionment fuelled the trend among the poor of forming local organisations and undertaking political action independently of the

---

[211] *Samyavad*, 29 January 1939, p. 7; No. 41, 15 October 1938; *PAI*, No. 3, 21 January 1939.

[212] Interim report of R. S. Pandit on Congress volunteer organisations, File No. 74/17/1940. Home Poll. (I), GOI, NAI.

[213] *Samyavad*, 9 October 1938, p. 2; 1 January 1939, p. 3; 15 January 1939, p. 2.

party by the late 1930s. By increasingly alienating the urban masses, the Congress paradoxically acted as a driving force in intensifying local-level political action among the poor, much of which was channelled into the volunteer corps. Moreover, as Pandey has argued, the Congress organisation had become increasingly tightly controlled from the 1930s,[214] and there was therefore little possibility of entering the organisation to contest power from within. The volunteer movement afforded greater opportunities for the poor to assume the political initiative, to forge an alternative site of nationalist action in defiance of the Congress as well as to attempt to force their will on the party through political militancy from outside. The phenomenal proliferation of the volunteer movement happened precisely at a time when the Congress' primary four-anna membership in UP collapsed from 1,472,456 in 1938–9 to 258,826 in 1940–1,[215] a staggering 70 per cent reduction in two years. Although a number of explanations for this depletion in the Congress ranks were put forward at the time and much caution was exercised in both official and Congress circles against hastily assuming that this indicated a loss of influence of the Congress, it seems an inescapable inference that a decline of this magnitude must have related to an erosion of the authority of the party, of which ample evidence has already been seen in this chapter.[216] This pronounced lack of enthusiasm in identifying with the Congress organisation, coupled with the mounting zeal in the volunteer movement, suggests that the volunteer movement was seen as the 'true' or 'real' repository of nationalism, in contrast to the netashahi of the Congress.

By the early 1940s, the volunteer movement was an important locus of popular politics in the towns. The government recognised its political importance and banned volunteer activities in August 1940, though the Congress Party was not outlawed. The announcement of the ban elicited a massive response. A rally of 25,000 people was promptly held in Kanpur.[217] This was followed by several demonstrations in all the towns[218] which took on rather menacing proportions, despite the fact that the Congress did not formally declare an agitation or issue any organisational directive to defy the ban. Moreover, when the Congress launched the individual satyagraha programme in October 1940, in which members of Congress Committees were to offer satyagraha

[214] Pandey, *Ascendancy*, pp. 43–5.
[215] Strength of the Indian national Congress (Primary members), 1939–41, File No. 4/7/41, Home Poll. (I), GOI, NAI; *PAI*, for week ending 24 January, dated 29 January 1941.
[216] Strength of the Indian national Congress (Primary members), 1939–41.
[217] *PAI*, No. 34, 24 August 1940.
[218] *PAI*, No. 36, 7 September 1940; No 37, 14 September 1940.

individually and court arrest by publicly pronouncing seditious anti-war slogans, but avoided mass demonstrations, it generated very little popular enthusiasm. Yet, precisely at that time, a steady flow of volunteers was maintained to violate the ban on the volunteer movement. Those involved in the latter were described in a police report as 'mostly persons of no importance',[219] who seemed to be offering themselves up as true patriots in competition with the official Congress Party approved satyagrahis.

In the mid-1930s, the Congress in UP, under the auspices of the CSP, had initially revived its efforts to promote the formation of Qaumi Sena Dal as bases for local social service, self-defence and 'parallel administration'. Soon, however, they were overtaken by the numerous organisations which had sprung up on local initiative, modelled on the Congress volunteer corps. Government reports on the volunteer movement in 1939 noted that 'the Congress volunteer corps still lacks central control and unity of effort'; 'they suffer from fissiparous tendencies' and 'lack of coordination'.[220] Other reports commented on 'unruly elements' and 'indiscipline' within the ranks of the Congress.[221] There is little doubt that the pace of the volunteer movement in the late 1930s was increasingly set by popular initiatives at the local level, with the gradual loss of direct control by the Congress Party, including that of the CSP. Not unexpectedly, the Congress leadership grew more and more apprehensive about the rising militancy of the volunteer movement by the late 1930s. The consternation of the provincial Congress leadership over the unregulated and unrestrained growth of volunteer activities precipitated several surveys, enquiries and reforms. In 1938, the provincial Volunteer Board of the UPPCC was given instructions to enforce discipline and to punish those who failed to fall into line with Congress directives, and hindered the regulated and orderly development of the volunteer movement.[222] A UP Congress Survey reported:

In 1939 it was realised that the aims and ideals of the Congress Qaumi Sena were not in line with the spirit of non-violence and service as desired. Moreover, military names, officers' titles and a lot of pomp and show had also begun to be introduced in our movement. We felt therefore that in order to inculcate a spirit of service and also to do away with militarism we should introduce changes.[223]

[219] *PAI*, No. 8, for week ending 14 February 1941.
[220] Volunteer Movement in India II & III, File No. 4/2/1939, Home Poll., GOI, NAI.
[221] Quarterly Survey of Political and Constitutional Position in British India, No. 7, 1 February to 31 April 1939, File No. L/P&J/7/1815, GOI, IOR.
[222] Answers to the questionnaire on the volunteer movement, by Jagdish Prasad, Secretary, Sewa Dal Office, UPPCC, File No. G-5 (Part 4)/1940, AICC Papers, NML.
[223] Ibid.

Accordingly, the Qaumi Sena Dal was renamed Qaumi Sewa Dal (National Service Corps) in 1939, changing the word *sena*, meaning army, to *sewa* or service. The office of the *Senapati* (Army Commander) as the leader of volunteer corps was also abolished.[224] It was envisaged that this change in nomenclature and divesting the volunteers of rituals and regalia emulated from the military and the police would transform the spirit and rationale of the volunteer movement, undermine militancy and foster greater discipline. The Sewa Dal was to be not only tamed and emasculated, but also 'depoliticised' by confining it to social service work, 'with absolute neutrality in Congress politics'. Its members were not supposed to engage in Congress elections or political pickets, and were to remain aloof from factional politics.[225]

This and other similar exercises of the late 1930s to regulate and control the volunteer movement clearly did not achieve the intended result. In the early 1940s, there was continued alarm among Congress leaders, including the socialists, at the autonomous development of volunteer organisations. Jawaharlal Nehru, in 1940, mentioned the development of two kinds of volunteer corps which called themselves 'nationalist' but were not directly organised or sponsored by the Congress: first, volunteer groups which consisted of Congressmen but were not officially under Congress control, and, second, those completely outside the Congress fold.[226] In view of the proliferation of such so-called 'nationalist' volunteer corps, Nehru advised an enquiry into the volunteer movement, in order 'to encourage the formation of volunteer organisations *within* the Congress'.[227] K. D. Malaviya, a member of the UP Congress Volunteer Board and responsible for guiding the volunteer movement, however, recommended a slightly different and more pragmatic course of action to assert control, specifically in urban areas where the proliferation was most noticeable. Malaviya advocated that the Congress, 'in special cases and in urban areas alone', should involve itself in volunteer activities that were taking place 'outside the Congress fold', for 'it is better that the lead of such non-Congress organisations may remain in Congress hands'.[228] An enquiry into the state of volunteer

---

224 Circular Bulletin of UPPCC, No. 2, May 1939, File No. P-20 (KW-1)/1939, AICC Papers, NML.

225 A note suggesting changes in the working of the Provincial National Service, File No. 64/1940, AICC, NML.

226 Note by Jawaharlal Nehru for R. S. Pandit on the enquiry into volunteer organisations of the Congress, dated 22 April 1940, Jawaharlal Nehru Papers, Part III, Writings and Speeches, Notes, Serial No. 179, NML.

227 Ibid., emphasis added.

228 'Suggestions for intensifying the volunteer movement' by K. D. Malaviya (n.d.). File on Volunteers and Qaumi Sewa Dal, Jawaharlal Nehru Papers, Part II, Subject File No. 56, NML.

organisations was also instituted in 1940 'to encourage volunteering along the right lines'.[229] One of the reasons for conducting this enquiry and for a subsequent Congress attempt to reorganise the volunteer corps in 1940 was the 'fear among Congress Committees and its members that the volunteer movement is gaining power and as such they look [at] it with misgivings'.[230] The fear was that the volunteer units were becoming more powerful and subverting or superseding the authority of the actual Congress Committees in the locality. It also appears that the enquiry into volunteer organisations was partly provoked by the fact that the volunteer movement had emerged as a focus of discontent against the Congress. For the enquiry was also aimed at curbing 'the spirit of indiscipline and erroneous notions of civil liberty and rights to criticise' which thrived among volunteer groups.[231] In response, the Congress had decided that 'rules for public court martial of the delinquent volunteers should be framed'.[232] In 1942, a UPPCC council resolution reiterated that disciplinary action would be taken against all those individuals and organisations that called themselves 'nationalists' but were 'pursuing policies which are diametrically opposed to the Congress policy and programme'.[233]

These developments had several implications and political significance. From the perspective of the leaders and urban elites, the volunteer movement brought to a head the problem of control and discipline of the poor not just within nationalist politics but in urban political life more broadly. Indeed, the controversy over disciplining the volunteer movement epitomised much of the elite efforts to reform, improve and control the political behaviour and culture of the urban poor that had characterised the interwar period. Moreover, the volunteer movement came to constitute a threat to the political authority of the Congress. The volunteer corps, by organising irrespective of the direction of the Congress and at times in defiance of it, challenged the supremacy of the Congress. The volunteers implicitly put themselves forward as the 'real' nationalists and 'true' patriots. That the volunteer organisations continued to call themselves 'nationalist' or 'socialist', in spite of an uneasy relationship with the Congress, points precisely to this process of political contestation. It suggests the refusal of the poor to abdicate from the public sphere in favour of the 'neta' or leaders of the Congress, now seen to be imposing 'netashahi' (rule of the leaders). It also points to the

[229] Volunteer Movement in India V, File No. 4/I/1940, Home Poll. (I), GOI, NAI.
[230] Answers to the questionnaire on the volunteer movement, by Jagdish Prasad.
[231] Reported in Volunteer Movement in India V, File No. 4/1/1940.
[232] Ibid.
[233] UPPCC Council Resolution, dated 4 February 1942. File No. P-22 (Part I)/1942, AICC Papers, NML.

will of the poor to claim for themselves the political language of the struggle against deprivation that underpinned socialist nationalism in the late 1930s. The struggle centring on volunteer activities thus epitomised the developing efforts of the poor throughout the interwar period to engage with wider political processes and for inclusion in the emerging democratic polity. It symbolised the contest between the leaders and the led over the nature of political authority, legitimacy and representation.

It would, however, be misleading to interpret this process of intense contestation in the late 1930s as the climax of an epic clash between the elites and subalterns, towards which the politics of the 1920s and 1930s were inevitably building up, culminating in a spectacular betrayal of the subalterns by the Congress. Rather this contestation was the very stuff of ongoing political relations between the elites and the poor in the interwar period, which briefly assumed accelerated force at the particular conjuncture of the heated political environment of the late 1930s and early 1940s with the possibility of independence appearing to be real, the Congress gradually ascending to state power and the socialist rhetoric of nationalism providing a radical rallying ideology for the poor. With the promise of change and emancipation, the poor, through their own 'nationalist' action, aimed to seize the political initiative, gain a voice in wider politics and exercise their power to force their will on the leaders. This contest between the leaders and the led, moreover, formed the central dimension of the politics of the urban poor in the interwar period, not only of nationalism but also of religious resurgence or caste-based action. Much of the energy of the politics among the poor had been devoted to establishing a political space for themselves in the public sphere, in resisting discipline and control, and in countering exclusion.

Nationalist political action of this nature by the poor, however, had limited transformative potential, with or without the attempts of the Congress organisation to contain their political radicalism. The language of social emancipation enabled the poor to formulate a broad general vision and an aspiration, but it did not help to envisage a systematic or specific political programme for social change. The nationalist political action of the poor therefore tended to remain focused on a struggle to make their mark in the public sphere. The attempt to achieve social change could not be translated into action because of this generality of the political vision and because the perspective of emancipatory change was clouded by the preoccupation with claiming the nationalist movement for themselves, especially through such means as the volunteer movement. Given that the volunteer movement and other socialist-oriented activities were rooted to the locality, and were fragmented and uncoordinated in their nature, the radical social vision could inform only these specific localised forms of political action. It did not develop into a broader political project or strategy for social change. Organisational weakness and diversity meant that such disparate action could not develop into a more sustained or effective political challenge to the elites. This then was not a simple question of the Congress betraying the subaltern classes. Rather, the nationalism of the poor was circumscribed by its specific localised organisational nature and by the constraints of political practice and the ideological limits of the period. Ultimately, from the perspective of the Congress, popular nationalism did not constitute an actual bid for power. It remained partly a symbolic challenge, signifying urges for popular democratic political participation, and largely a problem of control, order and discipline. In the years following independence, the Congress would proceed to neutralise precisely this problem by the limited integration of popular politics within the institutional framework of Indian democracy. The introduction of a universal franchise marked the attempt to institutionalise formal, procedural representative democracy as a periodic, controlled outlet for popular political energies through electoral mobilisation.

10   The politics of exclusion and the 'virtuous deprived'

The participation of the poor in caste, religious and nationalist politics and mass movements in late-colonial urban north India was fuelled by the intensification of class conflicts. The experience of exclusion and marginalisation, both discursive and material, that the urban poor faced in the interwar years exercised a defining influence on their politics and provided the motivating power. Social differences in the towns had become sharper and more pronounced between various groups of the poor, on the one hand, and the amorphous professional and commercial middle classes and the propertied, on the other. Insecure, impermanent and variable jobs and shelter, as well as poverty and indebtedness, of course, set the poor apart. While these potentially sowed the seeds of social contradiction, they did not in themselves contribute to class tensions. Social construction of the poor as dangerous and undesirable, and measures to discipline, segregate or improve them, served to crystallise class divisions and unleash social conflict. Local policy, policing, social and cultural reform initiatives, and attempts at political control, emanating either from the colonial state or from the Indian middle classes, were all based on the increasing identification and isolation of the urban poor as a separate social class laden with negative characteristics. Moreover, in the case of the untouchable or the Muslim poor, their caste status and religious affiliation further reinforced their stigmatisation and social exclusion by the urban upper and middle classes, who were predominantly higher-caste Hindu, and included orthodox commercial groups as employers of labour and as zealous promoters of Hindu revitalisation movements. All sections of the poor in varying degrees found themselves culturally and socially distanced, at times even physically segregated as the middle classes retreated into the safe havens of new urban residential areas. The poor were emphatically excluded from the self-definition of the 'respectable' middle classes, who increasingly withdrew from, or even outlawed, what they singled out as the practices and characteristics of the poor, in self-conscious contradistinction to their own supposedly superior, normative and respectable manners, morals and mores. The towns emerged as the sites of ever more intense struggle between lower-class self-expression and upper-class assertion of control in culture and politics. Implicitly or explicitly, the poor were denied a place in civic life and urban culture, and were seen as an impediment to progress and betterment of society. They came to be defined, both ideologically and in policy or political practice, as a 'problem' and, therefore, identified as the appropriate objects of moralising and discipline, of governance, and of uplift from deprivation. There was, however, a benign strand in attitudes towards the poor. Even while the poor were stigmatised, social reformers strove to assimilate and incorporate the lower orders into 'respectable' society. Similarly, political leaders in quest of mass support tried to carve out a place for the poor in their own constituencies. However, qualification for such inclusion required that the poor be first reformed, purified, improved and socialised into the norms of the 'superior classes' by the effacement of any distinctive practices or identity, and by the acceptance of discipline, control and orderly forms of political action. Thus, even the seemingly inclusive social uplift drives or Congress socialist mobilisation excluded and rejected the poor as they existed in reality. The poor were often held up as an abstract, idealised social group whose interests and concerns deserved to be represented and furthered by the elites and political leaders. Yet, in their supposedly unreformed and unruly state, the urban poor remained effectively excluded and disenfranchised in practice from the social and political order of the towns. While approaches to solving the 'problem' of the poor took diverse, even conflicting, forms, they were all anchored in the shared assumption that the poor were inferior, malefic and base. The overwhelming spirit of the period was to change the poor – their conditions, environment, character, behaviour, tastes, practices and activities.

Within this context of increasing class tensions, the politics of various groups of the poor, whether in the name of class, community or nation, related to an urgency to reverse or deny their exclusion and marginalisation, as well as to challenge or undermine the negative stereotypes applied to them. Their efforts at times took the form of overt resistance or protest, but often they endeavoured to contest their exclusion in symbolic ways or through the assertion of some distinctive forms of identity and practice, which were either historically derived, or newly constructed or, usually, an amalgam of both. The most powerful and quintessential expression of their imperative to resist exclusion lay in the formation of *akharas* and volunteer corps, both of which emerged at the heart of the politics of the poor in the interwar period, and spanned caste, religious, labour and nationalist politics. The volunteer corps emulated the rituals of power of the state through armed drills or parades, and they simultaneously marched across the urban terrain in the course of their processions, thus stamping their mark on urban space. The akharas, similarly, expressed an aspiration for might and power through physical culture and the display of arms, while they also registered a sense of territorial rootedness through their grounding in the neighbourhood. In response to marginalisation and exclusion, then, the poor, through the volunteer corps and the akharas, articulated the aspiration to define alternative or contested loci of power for themselves, and to lay claim to urban space, both tangibly and metaphorically, in order to imprint and inscribe a significant presence in the urban order.

The response of different sections of the poor to their marginalisation was, of course, not identical and took a variety of forms. Such diversity emanated, variously, from their location in particular segments of the urban labour market; their caste or religious position; their past traditions, ideological repertoire and history; and the nature of their appropriation of new ideas of class, community or nation as well as discourses of democratic politics. These diverse factors wrought their varied understanding of the nature and causes of exclusion, and, in turn, shaped the specific forms of their politics and identity. The untouchable poor, for instance, saw their low ritual status in the inegalitarian caste hierarchy as the most significant determinant of their experience of exclusion. They therefore asserted a heritage of religious devotionalism which levelled social and caste distinctions, and they claimed rights and power for themselves by presenting themselves as the Adi Hindu original inhabitants of India. Many poorer Muslims felt themselves marginalised in the towns largely owing to the loss of their status and importance as erstwhile artisans. They turned to a public display of piety and imagined a past golden age of social prominence as craftsmen, in order to express a sense of their historical importance in urban society. The predominantly lower-caste shudra manual labouring poor, being condemned as violent, unruly or prone to social and moral deficiency, found in martial religious militancy a means not only to dignify their physical labour but also to project their heroic qualities and to etch out a prominent place for themselves in urban society. A similar impulse brought them into the arena of nationalist politics in the 1930s. Public agitation against colonialism and Congress socialist activism provided them with the opportunity to affirm their entitlement to political enfranchisement, to contest authority and discipline, to envision a just and egalitarian social order, and to assert the centrality of their own role in nationalist politics and thus in the nation. All these various forms of politics of the poor were animated by their urge to defy exclusion and to entrench their presence in the public sphere.

The notion of being the 'excluded' emerged as a focal point in the self-perception of the poor. This identity of exclusion did not emerge spontaneously from their social experience, but developed in the course of their political engagement. As the poor asserted themselves through public religious rituals or the militant volunteer movement, they found themselves the objects of ever more resolute measures of control and discipline, which they then sought to resist more arduously. Through this ongoing contestation, the poor developed an identity of exclusion and an awareness of social rejection and denial of rights and entitlements. This was reflected, *inter alia*, in the popular *nautanki* urban folk plays of the 1920s and 1930s, in which the main characters gained their heroic status precisely because of their humble origin and their lack of access to power or wealth. Even when the protagonist was a king or a noble, he was either dispossessed from power or lacked a recognised place in the established hierarchies of clan or caste. Most importantly, popular heroes such as the social bandits were located entirely outside the pale of respectable society and polity, but they instituted just and equitable orders of their own. The nautanki plays were most often about the dispossessed, the outsiders and the outlaws, who succeeded in surmounting their predicament heroically.

Despite contesting exclusion, the political action of the poor did not necessarily have radical or emancipatory outcomes, nor did the poor always posit alternative conceptions of power. Their politics frequently harboured tendencies to replicate coercive forms of power, as did the volunteer corps in emulating the rituals of military might of the state or the akharas in cultivating martial strength. Not only did these unleash a propensity towards violence among the poor, they also failed to undermine the legitimacy of state-sponsored coercion, and even provoked a further elaboration of the repressive apparatus of the state. Thus, the efforts of the poor to contend with their exclusion gave an impetus not only to urban mass politics but also to mass violence. Moreover, the martial forms of self-assertion of the poor intrinsically valorised the supposed male virtues of physical strength and the superiority of male agency, thus privileging, in the public arena, a male-gendered expression of self-hood and a patriarchal conception of power. This reinforcement of patriarchy and the glorification of the male physique were decisive developments in this period, which have had long-term consequences. With hindsight, it may be postulated that the legacies were being harvested in the late-twentieth-century ascendance of a masculinist, macho and muscular religious fundamentalist nationalism.

While exclusion was one key motif in the politics of the poor, the other was the concept of deprivation of power. The poor's experience of scarcity, dispossession or subordination could generate an embryonic awareness of material and social deprivation. Translation of this experience into specific forms of identity required ideological mediation. The rudimentary, experiential awareness of deprivation crystallised into particular ideological formulations in the light of various political discourses of the period. The notion of deprivation came to be configured in a specific way, in terms of a lack of power and status, and not simply, or even primarily, material destitution. This particular conception arose, in no small measure, from the vastly magnified importance of the history of community under colonial rule and, especially, in the turbulent interwar years. A vast array of 'imagined' accounts of the past was produced by the ideologues of various caste and religious communities, many of which expounded the notion of their historical deprivation. Publicists of 'deprived' groups solicited special treatment from the government on the ground of their historically inherited disadvantages, which were argued to vitiate their present and jeopardise their future. In these accounts, importantly, the history of deprivation was seldom narrated in tales of progressive impoverishment, but rather in sagas of political dispossession, displacement from power, and loss of social status. The ubiquity of the metaphors of slavery, servility, dependence, subordination, subjugation and subjection in these histories of community, and also in nationalist rhetoric, expressed through the terms *dasata* and *gulami*, affirmed the definition of deprivation in the broader sense of social servitude and lack of political power, rather than in material terms alone.

Crucially, in the narratives of 'deprived' community, the extant state of deprivation was projected as a virtuous condition in which members of a particular community, suffering from historical and structural 'disadvantages' or 'backwardness', earned the right to special entitlements from the state. So the deprived people became the deserving, for they were the victims of historical wrong and inegalitarian social systems. They no longer remained inherently inferior or deficient; they now had a valid history, a plausible explanation for their plight and, also, a moral superiority. This particular construction of deprivation as powerlessness and the deprived as the 'good', not surprisingly, lent itself to elaboration in the politics of the poor. It provided them with ammunition to transcend their negative characterisations, valorise their own predicament, and morally tower over 'superiors'. Significantly, a substantial section of elites and middle classes and the state too accepted this deprived condition as deserving, in their professed commitment to uplift the 'depressed' or the 'backward' classes. This formulation of the deprived as virtuous thus in effect served to subvert the very legitimacy of those elite ideologies that sought to denigrate the poor and the lower orders. As a result, the poor extensively invoked the notion of deprivation as powerlessness with a historical explanation and as a virtuous state. Since this conception of deprivation was largely embedded in narratives of community, the idioms of caste and religion also assumed a particular potency in the politics of the poor. It was not the historical inheritance of community-based social conceptions among the subaltern classes, but the new histories of community that, by helping to elevate deprivation to a morally superior position, gave prominence to the language of community in the politics of the poor. In addition, the new discourses of community frequently set out to reclaim the supposedly lost heritage of past power, glory and heroism, and thus invested caste and religious ideologies with even greater potency in the politics of the poor. All these factors ensured that economic exploitation and impoverishment were not the only themes framing class identities. Of course, the experience of poverty in this period encompassed new forms of social and cultural subordination and exclusion. These too undermined the possibility of conceptualising class in material terms alone.

The term *garib janata*, meaning poor common people, emerged at the heart of political discourse in this period. For the poor, this appellation encapsulated precisely the conception of virtuous deprivation. 'Garib janata' referred to the morally superior, deserving, simple folk, who were excluded from power and denied their due. The importance of this self-definition of the poor has been seen for caste, religious and nationalist politics. Its characteristics were also the key traits of nautanki heroes, who had inner strength and virtue, moral authority and elevated stature, in contrast to those who exerted superiority by wielding outward forms of power and force. Similarly, the socialist labour paper *Samyavad* of Kanpur frequently juxtaposed good, poor, ordinary people against tyrannical, exploitative, corrupt, self-seeking leaders and elites. During workers' unrest in 1938 and 1939, the paper raged against the figures who featured in the political demonology of the workers.[1] They naturally included capitalist employers and their agents, stooges and toughs, including jobbers, who were all 'middlemen' or 'intermediary' figures acting on behalf of employers and government authorities. In addition, anger was vented at specific features of the political system. These included *goondashahi* – the regime of thugs, pointing to the coercive and armed imposition of state power, especially by the police;

---

[1] For instance, see *Samyavad*, 9 October 1938, p. 2; 1 January 1939, p. 3; 15 January 1939, p. 2.

sudharbadi netashahi – the rule of revisionist or conservative leaders who renege on the radical promise of upholding the interests of the poor; *nokarshahi* – bureaucratic rule and the government of 'servants' ('nokar' literally means servant); and, finally, *netashahi* or *netagiri* – domination by a professional political leadership committed only to self-interest, who claim to speak for the 'people' but in reality betray and marginalise them. The notions of 'them' and 'us' articulated through these terms did not primarily refer to economic exploitation, but addressed the questions of political morality, civic virtue and the legitimate authority of those who govern or lead. This is evident from the prominent use of the word *shahi*, referring variously to state power, rule, government, political regime and dominance. In essence, this political vocabulary questioned the extant coercive political system and unrepresentative leadership and so raised the issue of the rights and role of the poor in the emerging political order of late-colonial India. It directly engaged with the problems of political exclusion and the lack of power, rights and democratic participation. Not surprisingly, at this specific conjuncture of Indian history, the struggle for political inclusion and to claim the public sphere lay at the heart of the politics of the urban poor in all its forms, be it caste, religious or nationalist.

The rhetoric of the 'garib janata' was deployed, even coined as a potent political term, by the leaders themselves. In a period of expansion of representative politics and mass mobilisation, it was imperative to speak in the name of the common people. However, the development of the concept of deprivation was clearly a two-way process. The poor drew upon it for their own political action and so it proved to be an efficacious rallying instrument for political mobilisation, prompting the leaders to espouse it more zealously. However, while for the political leaders and propagandists it was largely a rhetorical device, among the poor it was central to their political awareness and action. The poor appropriated the rhetoric of the political elite for their own purposes, and then often turned it against the leaders. The identity of the poor thus was not easily or automatically subsumed under elite discourses of garib janata, as is evident from the stratified nature of and internal conflicts within caste assertion, religious resurgence or nationalist action. The alliance between the political leaders and the poorer sections in the towns remained fragile and unstable.

The language of the garib janata, while fuelling the political assertion of the poor, has also had some adverse implications for democratic politics. As an attractive refuge of leaders to prevent the withdrawal of popular support, it is prone to populist manipulation. Political regimes and parties in independent India have repeatedly invoked the garib janata in various forms, ranging from the campaign of *Garibi Hatao* (Eradicate Poverty) of the Congress Prime Minister Indira Gandhi in the early 1970s to the formation of numerous 'Janata' (people) parties in opposition to the Congress, some of which succeeded in ascending to state power from the late 1970s. The rhetoric of the garib janata, embodied in the inclusive political arguments of garibi hatao and mass empowerment, has provided the excuse to unleash populist electoral mobilisation, while in effect excluding the poor from political institutions and failing to reverse the structural conditions of their predicament. In this respect, the populist deployment and distortion of the concept of the deprived common poor people have circumscribed and constrained the transformative potentials of the politics of the poor. Most recently, the term 'janata' has appeared alone as the pivot of the majoritarian populism of the Bharatiya Janata Party, with the 'garib' (poor) increasingly jettisoned not only in discursive usage but also in policy formulations.

From the analysis of caste, religious and nationalist politics in this book, a common conception of 'class' identity, of what it entailed to be the poor in interwar urban UP, is identifiable. It included notions of exclusion and deprivation from power as well as aspirations for political participation and rights for a deserving, virtuous people. This particular conception of class, striking for its ubiquity in the variegated matrix of popular politics, was shared by many different groups of the poor. It did not, however, unify the poor in politics through an awareness of common interests and aims. This was partly because the self-image of being the poor was less strongly grounded in perceptions of the uniformity of the predicament of all poor people, and more clearly defined externally against those who were seen to wield power and authority illegitimately and to exercise domination wrongfully. Political divisions among the poor also arose partly because the notions of exclusion and deprivation were relational and situationally defined, not absolute. A diversity of groups of the poor could see themselves as the excluded, the deprived or the victims, not only in contrast to those who exercised power, but also in comparison with each other. Some saw themselves as more deprived than others; some were seen to be greater beneficiaries of the established order and power structure than others. Thus a section of the poor could easily exclude another group which was seen to be less deprived. By the same token, the poor at times acted in concert with leaders whom they saw to be the champions of the deprived and guided by political morality, but distanced themselves from the same leaders if they failed to further the interests of the poor. With a similar logic, the poor often allied with 'middlemen' such as jobbers when such 'intermediaries' appeared to be acting on their behalf. Thus, while the notion of virtuous deprivation underpinned the politics of the poor, the essentially relative nature of its conception helps to explain divisions among the poor. It is also important to recognise that the intensely conflictual situation in the towns drove political action by the poor in fiercely competitive and often violent directions, thus undermining the practical possibility of political solidarity. While the elites tended to see the poor as homogeneous, their policies and actions intensified material rivalries and scarcity among the poor, with the effect that the poor tended to turn against each other.

Although a conception of 'class' emerged among the urban poor in the interwar period, albeit with internal political divisions, it would be untenable to assume a historical teleology of the north Indian urban poor becoming and remaining aware of themselves as a 'class' from that period onwards. At the specific conjuncture of the 1920s and 1930s, when major urban social transformation coincided with the emergence of significant political movements and ideologies, the poor became engaged in political action in various ways, and through this process defined an identity for themselves as the excluded and the virtuous deprived. The crucial symbiosis of material conditions, discursive formations and political ferment fuelled political action by the poor and contributed to the development of particular political identities. Their identities would be recast and remoulded not only with changing social and economic contexts after the 1930s and 1940s, but also with new patterns of political contestation within the democratic polity of independent India, especially through elections. The interwar period marked a moment, not an end point, in the evolution of the political action and identities of the poor.

Political developments discussed in this book for the late-colonial period might provide clues to the long-term understanding of Indian politics and suggest questions and analytical frameworks to engage with political dynamics in post-colonial India. The questioning of the action of leaders and of the functioning of political institutions, which surfaced so powerfully among the poor in the formative phase of mass politics in the interwar years, suggests that the legitimacy of the independent Indian state – the pivot of the project of nation-building – was never successfully entrenched among the poor, thus leaving open a major axis of political conflict. The consequences of this for democratic participation, political conflict or violence in independent India are yet to be analysed. To consider some recent developments, it could be hypothesised that the historical importance of the notions of exclusion from and deprivation of power, especially by a coercive, bureaucratic state and corrupt leaders, may have primed the minds of at least some sections of the poor to embrace Hindu nationalism in the 1980s and 1990s, for it plays on the theme of the deprivation of the majority of the Indian people – the *bharatiya janata* – at the hands of a supposedly overbearing Indian state and its power-hungry, self-seeking leadership.

This book has examined the emergence of a casual, informal urban workforce in the interwar period, and illuminated its momentous political and social consequences in arenas far outside the workplace. On the one hand, the growing prominence of 'footloose labour' shaped elite self-construction and perceptions of the poor, influenced the social construction of poverty, and determined the contours of social relations, public policy and elite political practice. On the other hand, the vulnerability and insecurity of urban labour, and the relegation of the poor to the margins of urban society and polity, crucially configured their political ideology, identity and action in specific ways. The informal sector has proved to be remarkably resilient and of enduring importance in India, and it appears that economic liberalisation in recent years has accelerated the informalisation and casualisation of labour and reinforced the salience of the informal economy. Developments discussed in this book might point to fruitful lines of enquiry into the wider social and political impact of the persistence and expansion of an informal labour force.

This book has highlighted the significance of the social construction of the poor and poverty in shaping both public policy and political relations in late-colonial India. Very little is known, however, about contextual shifts in conceptions of poverty and the poor after independence, and the ways in which these might have determined policy formulation and implementation. Developmental initiatives and public policy are usually believed to originate in the rarefied domain of the Indian state and its administrative agencies, governed by 'expert' understanding of economic laws and models, and then implemented through a bureaucratic machinery. Even when the importance of social or political forces has been acknowledged, or political economy approaches have been adopted, analyses of public policy have focused largely on dominant elites and the counter-elite aspirants of upwardly mobile social segments. It has seldom been investigated whether, how and to what extent social and political relations between the poor and the dominant and propertied classes shape the preoccupations and nature of state policy. It has, similarly, not been systematically examined whether the exertions of the poor themselves – their social or political assertion – have any appreciable impact on public policy.

A related theme emerging from this book is the importance of the social conditions and actions of the poor in determining the self-constitution and political predilections of the elites. This remains an underdeveloped area of enquiry in contemporary Indian politics. Yet it can be postulated that the dynamics of Indian democracy, both at its inception and in its subsequent unfolding, cannot be understood without considering elite attitudes towards the poor, and without an understanding of the interface of elite and popular politics. The introduction of universal franchise as a key feature of Indian democracy after independence, at times construed as a 'gift' by the elite to the masses, could instead be argued to be related to a need to tame and contain the political energies of the poor that had been unleashed in the late-colonial period. Mass politics could be distracted from agitational and potentially socially disruptive forms and 'managed' through democratic institutionalisation by constraining political action within the straightjacket of electoral participation alone, coupled with ideological populism. In this way it was possible to keep the demotic element of Indian politics at bay, at least for a while after independence, by making rhetorical promises about eradicating poverty, and simultaneously allowing this element space in the periodic ritual of voting while seeking to define all other legitimate politics in terms of activity within formal institutional structures with elite monopoly. Controlled electoral mass mobilisation but continued substantive exclusion of the masses from the Congress organisation, the party political system and the institutions of governance would be the hallmarks of politics in early independent India. However, with the expansion of democratic activity, elite dominance came to be threatened once again by the political assertion of the poor and excluded groups. In turn, this led to attempts to consolidate elite politics through the concentration and centralisation of power within state structures and the erosion of democratic institutions and political practice. The extensive literature on the 'de-institutionalisation' of Indian politics, however, hardly pursues this line of enquiry. The history of the role of the poor in shaping politics and policy and of the struggle to control the masses in independent India remains to be written. The full potential of interpreting the evolution of Indian democratic politics through the analytical framework of class conflicts is yet to be realised.

Bibliography

MANUSCRIPT SOURCES

OFFICIAL

India Office Records, London (IOR):
Public and Judicial Papers (L/P&J series)
National Archives of India, New Delhi (NAI):
Proceedings and files of the Government of India (GOI): Home Department, Political Branch (Home Poll.)
Uttar Pradesh State Archives, Lucknow (UPSA):
Proceedings and files of the Government of the United Provinces of Agra and Oudh (GUP): General Administration (GAD), Police, Industries, Municipal and Public Health Departments
Criminal Investigation Department Office, Lucknow:
Weekly Police Abstracts of Intelligence of the Government of the United Provinces of Agra and Oudh (PAI) (weekly)
Allahabad Divisional Commissioner's Office Record Room:
Files of the General Administration (GAD), Municipal and Police Departments
English Record Room (ERR), District Collectorate, Benares, Kanpur, Lucknow:
Files of the Appropriation of Land, General Administration (GAD), Industries, Judicial, Municipal, Police, Public Works, and Revenue and Scarcity Departments
Lucknow Deputy Commissioner's Office Records, District Magistrate's Bungalow, Lucknow:
Files on the Shia-Sunni troubles in Lucknow
Municipal Board *(Nagar Mahapalika)* Record Rooms, Allahabad, Benares, Kanpur, Lucknow:
Annual administration reports, proceedings of meetings and municipal manuals
Improvement Trust (now called Development Authority) Record Rooms, Allahabad, Kanpur, Lucknow:
Annual administration reports and files on Improvement Trust schemes

NON-OFFICIAL

India Office Records, London (IOR):
    Waddell Papers, Indian Police Collection
National Archives of India (NAI):
    Proscribed Publications
Nehru Memorial Library, New Delhi (NML):
    All India Congress Committee (AICC) Papers
    Jawaharlal Nehru Papers
    Narayan Prasad Arora Papers
Northern India Employers' Association Record Room, Kanpur:
    Preliminary Draft of the Pro Forma Report on the Enquiry into Family
    Budgets and Housing Conditions of the Mill Workers at Cawnpore,
    1939–40 (prepared by the Bureau of Economic Intelligence, UP)

UNPUBLISHED DISSERTATIONS AND MANUSCRIPT ARTICLES

Banerjee, P. C., 'Labour and Industrial Housing in Cawnpore', D.Phil. thesis,
    Allahabad University, 1948.
Basu, S., 'Workers Politics in Bengal, 1890–1929: Mill Towns, Strikes and
    Nationalist Agitations', Ph.D. thesis, University of Cambridge, 1994.
    'Strikes and "Communal" Riots in Calcutta in the 1890s: Industrial Workers,
    Bhadralok Nationalist Leadership and the Colonial State', manuscript
    article.
Chand, Dr. P., 'Manav', 'Uttari Bharat ke Khayal-Lavni ka Sahityik Swarup',
    paper submitted to the U.P. Sangeet Natak Academy, for the Khayal-Lavni
    Festival, Firozabad, 30 September–2 October 1984.
Derbyshire, I. D., 'Opening up the Interior: The Impact of Railways on the
    North Indian Economy and Society, 1860–1914', Ph.D. thesis, University
    of Cambridge, 1985.
Dube, K. K., 'Use and Misuse of Land in the KAVAL Towns (Uttar Pradesh)',
    Ph.D. thesis, Benares Hindu University, 1966.
Dwivedi, R. L. 'Allahabad: A study in urban geography', D.Phil. thesis, Alla-
    habad University, 1958.
Faruqi, M. M., 'Biography of Maulana Vilayat Hussain', Urdu manuscript, n.d.
    (available at the Daira Shah Hujjatulla, Allahabad).
    'Mukhtasar Halat-e-Zindagi' (a brief autobiography), manuscript, n.d. (avail-
    able at the Daira Shah Hujjatulla, Allahabad).
Gooptu, N. 'The Political Culture of the Urban Poor: The United Provinces
    between the Two World Wars', Ph.D. thesis, University of Cambridge,
    1991.
Kudaisya, G., 'State Power and the Erosion of Colonial Authority in Uttar
    Pradesh, India, 1930–42', Ph.D. thesis, University of Cambridge, 1992.
Singh, A., 'Varanasi: A Study in Urban Sociology', Ph.D. thesis, Benares Hindu
    University, 1971.

PRINTED SOURCES

OFFICIAL PUBLICATIONS

Bureau of Economic Intelligence, U.P., Bulletin, No. 1, 1938, 'The Cawnpore Wholesale Clothing Trade' by C. Ackroyd and Devaraj.

Census of India, 1901, Volume XVI (Northwestern Provinces and Oudh), Part I (Report), Allahabad, 1902.

Census of India, 1911, Volume XV (United Provinces of Agra and Oudh), Part I (Report), Allahabad, 1912.

Census of India, 1921, Volume XVI (United Provinces), Parts I (Report) and II (Tables), Allahabad, 1923.

Census of India, 1931, Volume XVIII (United Provinces), Parts I (Report) and II (Tables), Allahabad, 1933.

Census of India, 1941, Volume V, Simla, 1942.

Census of India, 1951, Volume II, Part I-A (Report), Allahabad, 1953.

Department of Economics and Statistics, U.P., Bulletin, No. 3, 1937, 'Wages and Labour Conditions in Kanpur' by S. P. Saxena.

Department of Economics and Statistics, U.P., Bulletin, No. 20, undated, 'Directory of Certain Wholesale Agricultural Markets of U.P.'.

Department of Economics and Statistics, U.P., Bulletin, No. 21, 1951, 'Growth of Factories in U.P.' by R. C. Pande.

Department of Industries and Commerce, U.P., Bulletin, No. 2, New Series, 1939, 'Survey of the Hosiery Industry in U.P.' by R. C. Srivastava.

District Gazetteers:

Nevill, H. R. *Allahabad: A Gazetteer: Volume. XXIII of the District Gazetteers of the United Provinces of Agra and Oudh*, Allahabad, 1911.

Benares: A Gazetteer: Volume XXVI of the District Gazetteers of the United Provinces of Agra and Oudh, Allahabad, 1909.

Cawnpore: A Gazetteer: Volume XIX of the District Gazetteers of the United Provinces of Agra and Oudh, Allahabad, 1909.

Lucknow: A Gazetteer: Volume XXXVII of the District Gazetteers of the United Provinces of Agra and Oudh, Allahabad, 1909.

Uttar Pradesh District Gazetteers: Allahabad, Allahabad, 1968.

Indian Statutory Commission, Volume XVI, Selections from Memoranda and Oral Evidence by Non-officials (Part I), London, 1930.

Labour Investigation Committee, 'Report on an Enquiry into the Conditions of Labour in Tanneries and Leather Goods Factories', Delhi, 1946.

Memoranda of the U.P. Government Submitted to the All India National Planning Committee, 1939, Allahabad, 1940.

Mr. L. S. White's Report on the Incidents Which Occurred in Lucknow on 25–26 May 1930, Nainital, 1930.

Native Newspaper Reports of U.P., 1900–1939 (variously titled 'Selections from Indian-owned newspapers', 'Confidential selection from newspapers published in the U.P.', 'Note on the Press of U.P. of Agra and Oudh').

Parliamentary Papers, East India (Sanitary State of the Army), *Royal Commission on the Sanitary State of the Army in India*, Volume 7, Part I, Report, Session: 5 February to 28 July 1863, Volume XIX.

Parliamentary Papers, East India (Sanitary Measures). *Report on Sanitary Measures in India*, Session: 1911–12, Volume LXIII, Cd. 7113.

Report on Sanitary Measures in India, Session: 1912–13, Volume LXII, Cd. 6373.

Progress of Sanitary Measures in India, Session: 1912–13, Volume LXII, Cd. 6538.

Parliamentary Papers, East India (Cawnpore Riots), *Report of the Commission of Inquiry into the Communal Outbreak at Cawnpore and the Resolution of the Government of U.P.*, Session: 1930–1931, Volume XII, Cmd. 3891.

Recommendations of the Kanpur Improvement Committee, 1944, Volume II: Comments on the Recommendations of the Committee (Chairman, Edward Souter), Allahabad, 1945.

Report of the Benares Municipal Board Enquiry Committee, 1933, Allahabad, 1933.

Report of the Committee of Inquiry into Wages and Conditions of Labour in Cawnpore (Chairman, Dr. Rajendra Prasad), 1938; included in V. Chaudhary (ed.), *Dr. Rajendra Prasad: Correspondence and Select Documents. Volume Two: 1938*, Delhi, 1984.

Report of the Department of Industries, United Provinces, 1923–24 to 1939–40.

Report of the Director of Industries, United Provinces, 1921–22 to 1922–23.

Report of the Fact Finding Committee (Handloom and Mills), 1942 (Chairman, P. J. Thomas), Delhi, 1942.

Report of the Industrial Finance Committee, U.P. 1934 (Chairman, S. N. Pochkhanawala), Allahabad, 1935.

Report of the Industries Reorganisation Committee, U.P. 1932 (Chairman, J. P. Srivastava), Allahabad, 1934.

Report of the Local Self-Government Committee, 1938 (Chairman, A. G. Kher), Allahabad, 1939.

Report of the Lucknow Municipal Board Enquiry Committee, 1942, Allahabad, 1942.

Report of the Police Reorganisation Committee, U.P. 1947–48 (Chairman, Sita Ram), Allahabad, 1948.

Report of the Town Improvement Trusts Committee, 1924 (Chairman, S. H. Fremantle), Allahabad, 1924.

Report of the Town Improvement Trusts Committee, 1929 (Chairman, H. J. Crosthwaite), Allahabad, 1929.

Report of the Town Improvement Trusts Committee, 1935 (Chairman, J. F. Sale), Lucknow, 1936.

Report of the United Provinces Provincial Banking Enquiry Committee, 1929–30, vols. I (Report), II, III and IV (Evidence), Allahabad, 1930.

Report on Municipal Administration and Finances in the United Provinces, 1911–12 to 1939–40.

Report on the Administration of the Police of the United Provinces, 1920 to 1940.

Report on the Reorganisation of the U.P. Police Force, 1945 (Chairman, G. A. Pearce), Lucknow, 1945.

Royal Commission on Labour in India, Volume III (United Provinces and Central Provinces), Parts I (Written Evidence) and II (Oral Evidence), London, 1931.

Statistics of Factories Subject to the Indian Factories Act. For the Year Ending 31 December, 1931, Calcutta, 1932.

Statistics of Factories Subject to the Indian Factories Act. For the Year ending 31 December, 1938, Delhi, 1940.

The Municipal Manual: Laws, Rules and Instructions Relating to Municipal Administration in the United Provinces, Volume I: The Municipal Act and Rules, 1st edn, 4th reprint, corrected up to 31 December 1925, Allahabad, 1926; 1st edn, 9th reprint, corrected up to 30 June 1933, Allahabad, 1941.

The Trade and Industries Directory of the United Provinces, 1935, Kanpur, 1935.

United Provinces Municipalities Act, 1916 (Act II of 1916).

SOUVENIRS, PAMPHLETS AND (NON-OFFICIAL) REPORTS

Bharatiya Yadav Sangh: Rajat Jayanti Smarak Granth (Silver Jubilee Souvenir), Bombay, 1954.

Jivan Parichay: Ek Jhanki: Sangeet Natak Academy 1967–68 ke purashkar se vibhushit nautanki shiromani Pahalwan Sri Krishna Khattri, Kanpur, *vikrami samvat* 2025, c. A.D. 1968.

Kanpur Bazar Karmchari Federation: Rajat Jayanti Smarika (Silver Jubilee Souvenir, Kanpur), 1977.

Kapra Bazar Palledar Union: Rajat Jayanti Smarika (Silver Jubilee Souvenir), Kanpur, 1986.

Pandit Suraj Prasad Awasthi Abhinandan Granth (Pandit Suraj Prasad Awasthi Felicitation Volume), Kanpur, 25 August 1986.

Report of the Enquiry Committee Appointed by the Council of the All India Muslim League to Enquire into Muslim Grievances in Congress Provinces, 1938, (President Raja Syed Mohamad Mahdi of Pirpur), Published by the Secretary, All India Muslim League, 1938.

Report of the Non-Official Enquiry Committee Regarding the Shooting of Mill Hands at the Cawnpore Cotton Mills Company, 1924, Kanpur, 1924.

Smarika: Khayal-Lavni Samaroh (Souvenir of the Khayal-Lavni Festival), *Firozabad, 30 September–2 October 1984*, Sangeet Natak Academy, Kaiserbagh, Lucknow, 1984.

Smarika (Souvenir): *Pajawa Ramlila Committee, 1982*, Allahabad, 1982.

Smarika (Souvenir): *Sri Ramlila Committee, Daraganj, Prayag, 1979*, Allahabad, 1979.

Souvenir: Congress Centenary Celebration Organised by All India Momin Conference, New Delhi, 3–4 December 1984.

U.P. Depressed Classes League ki Teis Saal ki Report tatha Udyeshya, Karya Vivaran aur Appeal, Lucknow, 1935.

NEWSPAPERS AND JOURNALS

Abhyudaya (Allahabad)
Aj (Benares)
Hindusthan Times (Delhi)
Kranti (Kanpur)
Kalwar Kesri (Lucknow)
Kalwar Kshatriya Mitra (Allahabad)
National Herald (Lucknow)

Pratap (Kanpur)
Ranbheri (published by the Benares City Congress Committee)
Samyavad (Kanpur)
Sangharsh (Lucknow)
The Leader (Allahabad)
The Pioneer (Lucknow)
The Star (Allahabad)
Vartman (Kanpur)
Yadav (Benares)
Yadavesh (Benares)

ARTICLES AND BOOKS

Abhimanyu, M., *Ahir Vamsa Pradip*, Benares, *vikrami samvat* 1982, c. A.D. 1925.
    Yadukul Sarvasya, Benares, *vikramabda* 1985, c. A.D. 1928.
    Gop Jati Kshatriya Varna Mein Hai: Arthat Brahman Sammelan ke Anargal Pralap ka Muhtor Jawab, Benares, 1974, 4th edn.
Agarwal, R. N., *Sangit*, Delhi, 1976.
    'Nautanki ka Uday, Vikas aur Vartman Sthiti', *Chayanat*, 14, July–September 1990, pp. 23–8.
Agnihotri, V., *Housing Condition of Factory Workers in Kanpur*, Lucknow, 1954.
Ahmad, A., *Islamic Modernism in India and Pakistan, 1857–1964*, London, 1967.
Ahmad, I., *Ritual and Religion among Muslims in India*, Delhi, 1981.
Ahmed, R., *The Bengal Muslims, 1871–1906: A Quest for Identity*, Delhi, 1981.
Alter, J., *The Wrestler's Body: Identity and Ideology in North India*, Berkeley, 1992.
Ambedkar, B. R., *What the Congress and Gandhi Have Done to the Untouchables*, Bombay, 1945.
Amin, S., 'Gandhi as Mahatma: Gorakhpur District, Eastern U.P., 1921–2', in R. Guha (ed.), *Subaltern Studies III: Writings on South Asian History and Society*, Delhi, 1984, pp. 1–61.
    Event, Metaphor, Memory: Chauri Chaura, 1922–1992, Delhi, 1995.
Ansari, A. b. Y., *Hasrat Mohani: Ek Siyasi Diary*, Bombay, 1977.
Ansari, G., *Muslim Castes in Uttar Pradesh*, Lucknow, 1960.
Ansari, H. N., *The Momin–Congress Relation: A Socio-historical Analysis*, Patna, 1989.
Ansari, K. H., *The Emergence of Socialist Thought among North Indian Muslims (1917–1947)*, Lahore, 1990.
Arnold, D., 'The Armed Police and Colonial Rule in South India, 1914–1947', *Modern Asian Studies*, 11, 1, 1977, pp. 101–25.
    Police Power and Colonial Rule: Madras, 1859–1947, Delhi, 1986.
    'Touching the Body: Perspectives on the Indian Plague, 1896–1900', in R. Guha (ed.), *Subaltern Studies V: Writings on South Asian History and Society*, Delhi, 1987, pp. 55–90.
Arora, N. P., *Kanpur ke Prasidh Purush*, Kanpur, 1947.
    Pahalwani aur Pahalwan, Kanpur, 1948.
Arora, N. P. and Chaturvedi, N. C., *Kanpur ke Gata Pachas Varsh ki Rajnitik aur Sahityik Jhanki*, Kanpur, 1951.

Awasthi, I., 'Hindi Paramparik Rangmanch mein Bidushak', *Chayanat*, 33, April–June 1985, pp. 13–19.

Awasthi, R. K. (ed.), *Kranti ka Udghosh: Ganesh Shankar Vidyarthi ki kalam se*, Volume II, Kanpur, 1978.

Azhar, H. *Sheikh ul Isatazza: Maulana Gulam Yahiya Hazarwi*, Karachi, 1976–7.

Baker, C. J., 'Economic Reorganisation and the Slump in South and Southeast Asia', *Comparative Studies in Society and History*, 23, 3, 1981, pp. 325–49.

An Indian Rural Economy, 1880–1955: The Tamilnad Countryside, Oxford, 1984.

Bandhusamaj, Kanpur, *Hinduon ki Tez Talwar*, Kanpur, 1927.

Banerjee, S., *The Parlour and the Streets: Elite and Popular Culture in Nineteenth Century Calcutta*, Calcutta, 1989.

Barrier, N. G., *Roots of Communal Politics*, Columbia, Delhi, n.d.

Bayly, C. A., 'Local Control in Indian Towns: The Case of Allahabad, 1880–1920', *Modern Asian Studies*, 5, 4, 1971, pp. 289–311.

'Patrons and Politics in Northern India', *Modern Asian Studies*, 7, 3, 1973, pp. 349–88. (Also reprinted in J. Gallagher, G. Johnson and A. Seal (eds.), *Locality, Province and Nation: Essays on Indian Politics, 1870 to 1940*, Cambridge, 1973.)

The Local Roots of Indian Politics: Allahabad, 1880–1920, Oxford, 1975.

'The Small Town and Islamic Gentry in North India: The Case of Kara', in K. Ballhatchet and J. Harrison (eds.), *The City in South Asia: Pre-modern and Modern*, London, 1980, pp. 20–48.

Rulers, Townsmen and Bazaars: North Indian Society in the Age of British Expansion, 1770–1870, Cambridge, 1983; first paperback edn, 1988.

'The Origins of Swadeshi (Home Industry): Cloth and Indian Society, 1700–1930', in A. Appadurai (ed.), *The Social Life of Things: Commodities in Cultural Perspective*, Cambridge, 1986, pp. 285–321.

Indian Society and the Making of the British Empire: New Cambridge History of India: II.1, Cambridge, 1987.

'Rallying around the Subaltern', *Journal of Peasant Studies*, 16, 1, 1988, pp. 110–20.

Bayly, S. 'Caste and "Race" in the Colonial Ethnography of India', in P. Robb (ed.), *The Concept of Race in South Asia*, Delhi, 1995, pp. 164–218.

Berlanstein, L. R. (ed.), *Rethinking Labour History*, Urbana, 1993.

Berman, B. and Lonsdale, J., *Unhappy Valley: Conflict in Kenya and Africa: Book 2: Violence and Ethnicity*, London, 1992.

Boardman, P., *Patrick Geddes: Maker of the Future*, Chapel Hill, 1944.

The Worlds of Patrick Geddes: Biologist, Town Planner, Re-educator, Peace-warrior, London, 1978.

Bogle, L., *Town Planning in India*, London, 1929.

Brass, P., *Language, Religion and Politics in North India*, Cambridge, 1974.

Breman, J., 'A Dualistic Labour System?: A Critique of the "Informal Sector" Concept', *Economic and Political Weekly*, Part I, 27 November 1976, pp. 1870–6; Part II, 4 December 1976, pp. 1905–8; Part III, 11 December 1976, pp. 1939–44.

Beyond Patronage and Exploitation: Changing Agrarian Relations in South Gujarat, Delhi, 1993.

Footloose Labour: Working in India's Informal Economy, Cambridge, 1996.

Briggs, G. W., *The Chamars,* London, 1920.

Brown, J. M., 'War and the Colonial Relationship: Britain, India and the War of 1914–18', in M. R. D. Foot, (ed.), *War and Society: Historical Essays in Honour and Memory of J. R. Western, 1928–71,* London, 1973, pp. 85–106.

Calhoun, C., *The Question of Class Struggle: Social Foundations of Popular Radicalism during the Industrial Revolution,* Oxford, 1982.

Carroll, L., 'The Temperance Movement in India: Politics and Social Reform', *Modern Asian Studies,* 10, 3, 1976, pp. 417–47.

'Colonial Perceptions of Indian Society and the Emergence of Caste(s) Associations', *Journal of Asian Studies,* 37, 2, 1978, pp. 233–50.

Chakr, S., *Kanpur Mazdur Andolan ka Itihas,* Kanpur, 1986.

Chakrabarty, D., *Rethinking Working Class History: Bengal, 1890–1940,* Princeton, 1989.

'Communal Riots and Labour: Bengal's Jute Mill-hands in the 1890s', in V. Das (ed.), *Mirrors of Violence: Communities, Riots and Survivors in South Asia,* Delhi, 1990, pp. 146–84.

'Open Space/Public Place: Garbage, Modernity and India', *South Asia,* 14, 1, 1991, pp. 15–31.

Chandavarkar, R. S. 'Industrialization in India before 1947: Conventional Approaches and Alternative Perspectives', *Modern Asian Studies,* 19, 3, 1985, pp. 623–68.

The Origins of Industrial Capitalism in India: Business Strategies and the Working Classes in Bombay, 1900–1940, Cambridge, 1994.

Chandrasekhara, C. S., 'Kanpur: An Industrial Metropolis', in R. P. Misra (ed.), *Million Cities of India,* New Delhi, 1978, pp. 273–303.

Chartier, R., *Cultural History: Between Practices and Representations,* Oxford, 1988.

Chatterjee, A. C., *Notes on the Industries of the United Provinces,* Allahabad, 1908.

Chatterjee, B., 'The Political Economy of "Discriminating Protection": The Case of Textiles in the 1920s', *Indian Economic and Social History Review,* 20, 3, 1983, pp. 239–75.

Chatterjee, P., *Bengal, 1920–1947: The Land Question,* Calcutta, 1984.

The Nation and Its Fragments: Colonial and Post-Colonial Histories, Princeton, 1993.

Chaudhury, A. P., *Picchre tatha Dalit Barg ke Mahan Neta Rai Ram Charan ka Jivan Charit tatha Unke Sanshipta Karya,* Lucknow, 1973.

Chawla, S. 'The Palestine Issue in Indian Politics in the 1920s', in M. Hasan (ed.), *Communal and Pan-Islamic Trends in Colonial India,* Delhi, 1985, pp. 43–58.

Coccari, D. M., 'The Bir Babas of Banaras and the Deified Dead', in A. Hiltebeitel (ed.), *Criminal Gods and Demon Devotees: Essays on the Guardians of Popular Hinduism,* Albany, 1989, pp. 251–69.

'Protection and Identity: Banaras's Bir Babas as Neighbourhood Guardian Deities', in S. B. Freitag (ed.), *Culture and Power in Banaras: Community, Performance, and Environment, 1880–1980,* Berkeley, 1989, pp. 113–46.

Cohn, B., *An Anthropologist among Historians and Other Essays,* Delhi, 1990.

Cooper, F., 'Work, Class and Empire: An African Historian's Retrospective on E. P. Thompson', *Social History,* 20, 2, 1995, pp. 235–41.

Crooke, W., *An Introduction to the Popular Religion and Folklore of Northern India*, Allahabad, 1894.

The Tribes and Castes of the North-Western Provinces and Oudh, 4 vols., Calcutta, 1896.

(ed.), *Observations on the Mussulmauns of India by Mrs. Meer Hassan Ali*, Oxford, 1917.

Curry, J. C., *The Indian Police*, London, 1932.

Dalmia, V., *The Nationalization of Hindu Traditions: Bharatendu Harishchandra and Nineteenth-century Banaras*, Delhi, 1997.

Das, R. K., *Principles and Problems of Indian Labour Legislation*, Calcutta, 1938.

Dinkar, D. C., *Swatantrata Sangram mein Acchuton ka Yogdan*, Lucknow, 1986.

Dirks, N. B., 'Ritual and Resistance: Subversion as a Social Fact', in D. Haynes and G. Prakash (eds.), *Contesting Power: Resistance and Everyday Social Relations in South Asia*, Oxford, 1991, 1st edn of the University of California Press, Berkeley, 1992, pp. 213–38.

Eley, G. 'Edward Thompson, Social History and Political Culture: The Making of a Working Class Public, 1780–1850', in H. J. Kaye and K. McClelland (eds.), *E. P. Thompson: Critical Perspectives*, Cambridge, 1990, pp. 12–49.

Engineer, A. A. (ed.), *Communal Riots in Post-Independence India*, Delhi, 1984.

Fakhri, K. M., *Taskira Aulia*, Karachi, n.d. (c. 1976).

Faruqi, M. M. (compiler), *Sawane Hyat: Maulana Al-Haj Shahid-e-Ishq Shah Mohammad Hussain Rahamatullah Alay Allahabadi ma Adbiyat, Malfuzat, Maqtubat, Karamat*, Allahabad, c. 1933.

Faruqi, Z.-ul-H., *The Deoband School and the Demand for Pakistan*, London, 1963.

Flueckiger, J. B. 'Caste and Regional Variants in an Oral Epic Tradition', in S. H. Blackburn et al. (eds.), *Oral Epics in India*, Berkeley, 1989, pp. 33–54.

Freitag, S. B., '"Natural leaders", Administrators and Social Control: Communal Riots in the United Provinces, 1870–1925', *South Asia*, 1, 2 (New Series), 1978, pp. 27–41.

'Collective Crime and Authority in North India', in A. Yang (ed.), *Crime and Criminality in British India*, Tuscon, 1985, pp. 140–63.

Collective Action and Community: Public Arenas and the Emergence of Communalism in North India, Berkeley, 1989.

(ed.), *Culture and Power in Banaras: Community, Performance, and Environment, 1800–1980*, Berkeley, 1989.

'State and Community: Symbolic Popular Protest in Banaras's Public Arenas', in S. B. Freitag (ed.), *Culture and Power in Banaras: Community, Performance, and Environment, 1800–1980*, Berkeley, 1989, pp. 203–28.

'Enactments of Ram's Story and the Changing Nature of "the Public" in British India', *South Asia*, 14, 1, 1991, 63–90.

Fuller, C. J., *The Camphor Flame: Popular Hinduism and Society in India*, Princeton, 1992.

Ganju, S. 'The Muslims of Lucknow, 1919–1939', in K. Ballahatchet and J. Harrison (eds.), *The City in South Asia: Pre-modern and Modern*, London, 1980, pp. 279–98.

Geddes, P., *Cities in Evolution*, London, 1915, 2nd edn, 1949.

Ghai, R. K., *Shuddhi Movement in India*, Delhi, 1990.

Gilmartin, D., 'Democracy, Nationalism and the Public: A speculation on Colonial Muslim Politics', *South Asia*, 14, 1, 1991, pp. 123–40.

Gordon, R. A., 'The Hindu Mahasabha and the Indian National Congress, 1915 to 1926', *Modern Asian Studies*, 9, 2, 1975, pp. 145–203.

Gore, M., *The Social Context of an Ideology: Ambedkar's Political and Social Thought*, Delhi, 1993.

Griffiths, P., *To Guard My People: The History of the Indian Police*, London, 1971.

Guha, R., 'Dominance without Hegemony and Its Historiography', in R. Guha (ed.), *Subaltern Studies VI: Writings on South Asian History and Society*, Delhi, 1989, pp. 210–309.

'Discipline and Mobilize', in P. Chatterjee and G. Pandey (eds.), *Subaltern Studies VII: Writings on South Asian History and Society*, Delhi, 1992, pp. 69–120.

Gupta, R. B., *Labour and Housing in India*, Calcutta, 1930.

Gupta, S. L., *Pandit Madan Mohan Malaviya: A Socio-political Study*, Allahabad, 1978.

Haithcox, J. P., *Communism and Nationalism in India: M. N. Roy and Comintern Policy, 1920–1939*, Princeton, 1971.

Hansen, K., 'Sultana the Dacoit and Harishchandra: Two Popular Dramas of the Nautanki Tradition of North India', *Modern Asian Studies*, 17, 2, 1983, pp. 313–31.

'The Birth of Hindi Drama in Banaras, 1868–1885', in S. B. Freitag (ed.), *Culture and Power in Banaras: Community, Performance, and Environment, 1800–1980*, Berkeley, 1989, pp. 62–92.

Grounds for Play: The Nautanki Theatre of North India, Berkeley, 1992.

Hardiman, D., 'The Crisis of the Lesser Patidars: Peasant Agitations in the Kheda District, Gujarat, 1917–34', in D. A. Low (ed.), *Congress and the Raj: Facets of the Indian Struggle, 1917–47*, New Delhi, 1977, pp. 47–75.

Peasant Nationalists of Gujarat: Kheda District, 1917–34, Delhi, 1981.

The Coming of the Devi: Adivasi Assertion in Western India, Delhi, 1987.

Hardy, P., *The Muslims of British India*, Cambridge, 1972.

Harrison, J. B., 'Allahabad: A Sanitary History', in K. Ballhatchet and J. Harrison (eds.), *The City in South Asia: Pre-modern and Modern*, London, 1980, pp. 166–95.

Hasan, M., *Nationalism and Communal Politics in India, 1916–1928*, Delhi, 1979.

'"Congress Muslims" and Indian Nationalism: Dilemma and Decline, 1928–34,' in J. Masselos (ed.), *Struggling and Ruling: The Indian National Congress, 1885–1985*, London, 1987, pp. 102–30.

'The Muslim Mass Contacts Campaign: Analysis of a strategy of political mobilization', in R. Sisson and S. Wolpert (eds.), *Congress and Indian Nationalism: The Pre-Independence Phase*, Berkeley, 1988, pp. 198–222.

Hasan, S. M., *Aaqab Shah Badiuzzaman*, Lucknow, 1984.

Haynes, D., *Rhetoric and Ritual in Colonial India: The Shaping of a Public Culture in Surat City, 1852–1928*, Berkeley, 1991, Delhi, 1992.

Haynes, D. and Prakash, G., 'Introduction: The Entanglement of Power and Resistance', in D. Haynes and G. Prakash (eds.), *Contesting Power: Resistance and Everyday Relations in South Asia*, Oxford, 1991, 1st edn of the University of California Press, Berkeley, 1992, pp. 1–22.

Herklots, G. A. (ed.), *Qanoon-e-Islam or the Customs of the Mussulmans of India by Jaffur Shurreef*, Madras, 1895.

Himmelfarb, G., *The Idea of Poverty: England in the Early Industrial Age*, London, 1984.

Hollins, S. T., *No Ten Commandments: Life in the Indian Police*, London, 1954.

Holmstrom, M., *Industry and Inequality: The Social Anthropology of Indian Labour*, Cambridge, 1984.

Hussain, M. Z., *Kadeem Lucknow Ki Aakhri Bahar*, c. 1908; 2nd edn, Delhi, 1981.

Inden, R., *Imagining India*, Oxford, 1990.

Iyer, R. (ed.), *The Essential Writings of Mahatma Gandhi*, Delhi, 1990.

Jaffrelot, C. 'The Ideas of the Hindu Race in the Writings of Hindu Nationalist Ideologies in the 1920s and 30s: A Concept between Two Cultures', in P. Robb (ed.), *The Concept of Race in South Asia*, Delhi, 1995, pp. 327–54.
The Hindu Nationalist Movement and Indian Politics, 1925 to the 1990s, Delhi, 1996.

Jain, L. C., *Indigenous Banking in India*, London, 1929.

Jalal, A. and Seal, A. 'Alternative to Partition: Muslim Politics between the Wars', *Modern Asian Studies*, 15, 3, 1981, pp. 415–54. (Also reprinted in C. Baker, G. Johnson and A. Seal (eds.), *Power, Profit and Politics: Essays on Imperialism, Nationalism and Change in Twentieth-century India*, Cambridge, 1981).

Jeffries, C., *The Colonial Police*, London, 1952.

Jijnasu, C. P., *Bharatiya Maulik Samajvad: Srishti Aur Manav Samaj ka Vikas Athba 'Bharat ke Adi Nivasi' Granth ka Pratham Khand*, Lucknow, 1941.
Adi Hindu Andolan ka Prabartak Sri 108 Swami Acchutanand Harihar, Lucknow, 1968, 2nd edn.

Jones, K. W., *Arya Dharm: Hindu Consciousness in Nineteenth-century Punjab*, Delhi, 1976.
Socio-Religious Reform Movements in British India: New Cambridge History of India: III.1, Cambridge, 1989.

Jordens, J. T. F., 'Hindu Religious and Social Reform in British India', in A. L. Basham (ed.), *A Cultural History of India*, Oxford, 1975, pp. 365–82.
'Medieval Hindu Devotionalism', in A. L. Basham (ed.), *A Cultural History of India*, Oxford, 1975, pp. 266–80.

Joshi, B. R., *Democracy in Search of Equality: Untouchable Politics and Indian Social Change*, Delhi, 1982.

Joshi, C., 'Kanpur Textile Labour: Some Structural Features of Formative Years', *Economic and Political Weekly*, XVI, 44–46, Special Number, November 1981, pp. 1823–38.
'Bonds of Community, Ties of Religion: Kanpur Textile Workers in the Early Twentieth century', *Indian Economic and Social History Review*, 22, 3, 1985, pp. 251–80.
'The Formation of Work Culture: Industrial Labour in a North Indian City (1890s-1940s)', *Purusartha*, 1991, pp. 155–72.
'Hope and Despair: Textile Workers in Kanpur in 1937–8 and the 1990s', in

J. P. Parry, J. Breman and K. Kapadia (eds.), *The Worlds of Indian Industrial Labour*, New Delhi, 1999, pp. 171–203.

Joyce, P., *Visions of the People: Industrial England and the Question of Class, 1848–1914*, Cambridge, 1991.

(ed.), *Class: Oxford Reader*, Oxford, 1995.

'The End of Social History?', *Social History*, 20, 1, 1995, pp. 73–91.

Juergensmeyer, M., *Religion as Social Vision: The Movement against Untouchability in 20th-century Punjab*, Berkeley, 1982.

Karnik, V. B., *Indian Trade Unions: A Survey*, Bombay, 1966.

Strikes in India, Bombay, 1967.

Kaviraj, S., 'Filth and the "Public Sphere"', *Österreichische Zeitschrift für Soziologie*, 21, 2, 1996, pp. 36–65.

Kaye, H. J. and McClelland, K. (eds.), *E. P. Thompson: Critical Perspectives*, Cambridge, 1990.

Khare, R. S., *The Untouchable as Himself: Ideology, Identity and Pragmatism among the Lucknow Chamars*, Cambridge, 1984.

Khilnani, S., *The Idea of India*, London, 1997.

King, C., *One Language, Two Scripts: The Hindi Movement in Nineteenth-century North India*, Bombay, 1994.

Kitchen, P., *A Most Unsettling Person: An Introduction to the Ideas and Life of Patrick Geddes*, London, 1975.

Klein, I., 'Plague, Policy and Popular Unrest in British India', *Modern Asian Studies*, 22, 4, 1988, pp. 723–55.

Kolff, D. H. A., *Naukar, Rajput and Sepoy: The Ethnohistory of the Military Labour Market in Hindustan, 1450–1850*, Cambridge, 1990.

Kumar, N., *The Artisans of Banaras: Popular Culture and Identity, 1880–1986*, Princeton, 1988.

'The "Truth" about Muslims in Banaras: An Exploration in School Curricula and Popular Lore', *Social Analysis*, Special Issue on 'Person, Myth and Society in South Asian Islam' (P. Werbner, ed.), 28, July 1990, pp. 82–96.

'Class and Gender in the Ramlila', *Indian Economic and Social History Review*, 29, 1, 1992, pp. 37–56.

Lanchester, H. V., *Talks on Town Planning*, London, 1924.

The Art of Town Planning, London, 1925.

Lele, J. (ed.), *Tradition and Modernity in Bhakti Movements*, Leiden, 1981.

Lorenzen, D. N., 'The Kabir Panth and Social Protest', in K. Schomer and W. H. McLeod (eds.), *The Sants: Studies in a Devotional Tradition in India*, Delhi, 1987, pp. 281–303.

(ed.), *Bhakti Religion in North India: Community, Identity and Political Action*, New York, 1995.

Low, D. A., '"Civil Martial Law": The Government of India and the Civil Disobedience Movements, 1930–34', in D. A. Low (ed.), *Congress and the Raj: Facets of the Indian Struggle, 1917–47*, New Delhi, 1977, pp. 165–98.

Lubeck, P., *Islam and Urban Labor in Northern Nigeria: The Making of a Muslim Working Class*, Cambridge, 1986.

Lutgendorf, P., 'Interpreting Ramraj: Reflections on the "Ramayan", Bhakti and Hindu Nationalism', in D. N. Lorenzen (ed.), *Bhakti Religion in North India: Community, Identity and Political Action*, New York, 1995, pp. 253–87.

Lynch, O., *The Politics of Untouchability: Social Mobility and Social Change in a City of India*, New York, London, 1969.

McKibbin, R., *The Ideologies of Class: Social Relations in Britain, 1880–1950*, Oxford, 1990.

Mairet, P., *Pioneer of Sociology: The Life and Letters of Patrick Geddes*, London, 1957.

Marcus, S. L., 'The Rise of a Folk Music Genre: *Biraha*', in S. B. Freitag (ed.), *Culture and Power in Banaras: Community, performance, and environment, 1880–1980*, Berkeley, 1989, pp. 93–113.

Markovits, C., 'Indian Business and the Congress Provincial Governments 1937–39', *Modern Asian Studies*, 15, 3, 1981, pp. 487–526. (Also reprinted in C. Baker, G. Johnson and A. Seal (eds.), *Power, Profit and Politics: Essays on Imperialism, Nationalism and Change in Twentieth-Century India*, Cambridge, 1981.)

Indian Business and Nationalist Politics, 1931–1939: The Indigenous Capitalist Class and the Rise of the Congress Party, Cambridge, 1985.

Marriot, M., 'The Feast of Love', in M. Singer (ed.), *Krishna: Myths, Rites and Attitudes*, Honolulu, 1966, pp. 200–12.

Masani, M. R., *The Communist Party in India: A Short History*. (London, 1954).

Mason, P., *The Men Who Ruled India*, London, 1985.

Masselos, J., 'Audiences, Actors and Congress Dramas: Crowd Events in Bombay City in 1930', in J. Masselos (ed.), *Struggling and Ruling: The Indian National Congress, 1885–1985*, London, 1987, pp. 71–86.

Mazumdar, D. N., *Social Contours of an Industrial City: Social Survey of Kanpur, 1954–56*, Westport, Conn., 1960.

Mehra, S. P., *Cawnpore Civic Problems*, Kanpur, 1952.

Meller, H. E., 'Urbanization and the Introduction of Modern Town Planning Ideas in India, 1900–1925', in K. N. Chaudhuri and C. J. Dewey (eds.), *Economy and Society: Essays in Indian Economic and Social History*, Delhi, 1979, pp. 330–50.

Patrick Geddes: Social Evolutionist and City Planner, London, 1990.

Metcalf, B., *Islamic Revival in British India: Deoband, 1860–1900*, Princeton, 1982.

'Hakim Ajmal Khan: Rais of Delhi and Muslim Leader', in R. Frykenberg (ed.), *Delhi Through the Ages*, Delhi, 1986, pp. 299–315.

Perfecting Women: Maulana Ashraf Ali Thanawi's 'Bihishti Zewar': A Partial Translation with Commentary, Berkeley, 1990.

Minault, G., 'Urdu Political Poetry during the Khilafat Movement', *Modern Asian Studies*, 8, 4, 1974, pp. 459–71.

The Khilafat Movement: Religious Symbolism and Political Mobilization in India, New York, 1982.

'Some Reflections on Islamic Revivalism vs. Assimilation among Muslims in India', *Contributions to Indian Sociology* (n.s.), 18, 2, 1984, pp. 301–5.

Morris, M. D., *The Emergence of an Industrial Labour Force in India: A Study of the Bombay Cotton Mills, 1854–1947*, Berkeley, 1965.

Mujeeb, M., *The Indian Muslims*, London, 1967.

Mukerjee, R. and Singh, B., *Social Profiles of a Metropolis: Social and Economic Structure of Lucknow, Capital of Uttar Pradesh, 1954–56*, London, 1961.

Newman, R., *Workers and Unions in Bombay, 1918–29: A Study of Organisation in the Cotton Mills*, Canberra, 1981.

Niehoff, A. *Factory Workers in India*, Milwaukee, 1959.

O'Hanlon, R., 'Recovering the Subject: *Subaltern Studies* and the Histories of Resistance in Colonial South Asia', *Modern Asian Studies*, 22, 1, 1988, pp. 189–224.

Oldenburg, V. T., *The Making of Colonial Lucknow, 1856–1877*, Princeton, 1984.

Omvedt, G., *Dalits and the Democratic Revolution: Dr. Ambedkar and the Dalit Movement in Colonial India*, Delhi, 1994.

Dalit Visions, Delhi, 1995.

Page, D., *Prelude to Partition: The Indian Muslims and the Imperial System of Control, 1920–1932*, Delhi, 1982.

Pande, B. N., *Allahabad: Retrospect and Prospect*, Allahabad, 1955.

Pandey, G., 'A Rural Base for Congress: The United Provinces, 1920–40', in D. A. Low (ed.), *Congress and the Raj: Facets of the Indian Struggle 1917–47*, Delhi, 1977, pp. 199–223.

The Ascendancy of the Congress in Uttar Pradesh, 1926–34: A Study in Imperfect Mobilization, Delhi, 1978.

'Peasant Revolt and Indian Nationalism: The Peasant Movement in Awadh, 1919–22', in R. Guha (ed.), *Subaltern Studies I: Writings on South Asian History and Society*, Delhi, 1982, pp. 143–97.

'The Bigoted Julaha', *Economic and Political Weekly*, XVIII, 5, 29 January 1983, pp. PE19–28.

'Liberalism and the Study of Indian History: A Review of Writing on "Communalism"', *Economic and Political Weekly*, XVIII, 42, 15 October 1983, pp. 1789–91.

'Economic Dislocation in Nineteenth-century Eastern Uttar Pradesh: Some Implications of the Decline of Artisanal Industry in Colonial India', in P. Robb (ed.), *Rural South Asia: Linkages, Change and Development*, London, 1983, pp. 89–129.

The Construction of Communalism in Colonial North India, Delhi, 1990.

Pandey, S. M., *As Labour Organises: A Study of Unionism in the Kanpur Cotton Textile Industry*, Delhi, 1970.

The Hindi Oral Epic Canaini (The Tale of Lorik and Canda), Allahabad, 1982.

The Hindi Oral Epic Loriki (The Tale of Lorik and Canda), Allahabad, 1979.

Paribrajak, S., *Sangathan ka Bigul*, Dehradun, 1926.

Peabody, N., 'Inchoate in Kota?: Contesting Authority through a North Indian Pageant-play', *American Ethnologist*, 24, 3, 1997, pp. 559–84.

Pinch, W. R., *Peasants and Monks in British India*, Berkeley, 1996.

Pinney, C. 'The Nation (Un)Pictured: Chromolithography and "Popular" Politics in India, 1878–1995', *Critical Inquiry*, 23, 4, 1997, pp. 834–67.

Prasad, O., *Folk Music and Folk Dances of Banares*, Calcutta, 1987.

Prashad, V., 'Between Economism and Emancipation: Untouchables and Indian nationalism, 1920–1950', *Left History*, 3, 1, Spring/Summer, 1995, pp. 5–30.

Proccaci, G., 'Governing Poverty: Sources of the Social Question in Nineteenth-century France', in Jan Goldstein (ed.), *Foucault and the Writing of History*, Oxford, 1994, pp. 206–19.

Qureshi, I. H., *Ulema in Politics: A Study Relating to the Political Activities of the Ulema in the South Asian Subcontinent from 1536 to 1947*, Delhi, 1980.

Rajadhyaksha, A. and Willemen, P. (eds.), *Encyclopaedia of Indian Cinema*, Delhi, 1994.

Rao, M. S. A., *Social Movements and Social Transformation: A Study of Two Backward Classes Movements in India*, Delhi, 1979.

Robinson, F., *Separatism among Indian Muslims: The Politics of the United Provinces' Muslims, 1860–1923*, Cambridge, 1974.

'Professional Politicians in Muslim Politics, 1911–1923', in B. N. Pandey (ed.), *Leadership in South Asia*, New Delhi, 1977, pp. 372–94.

'Islam and Muslim Society in South Asia', *Contributions to Indian Sociology* (n.s.), 17, 2, 1983, pp. 185–203.

'The "Ulama" of Farangi Mahall and their *Adab*', in B. Metcalf (ed.), *The Place of Adab in South Asian Islam*, Berkeley, 1984, pp. 152–83.

'Ulema, Sufis and Colonial Rule in North India and Indonesia', in D. Kolff and C. Bayly (eds.), *Two Colonial Empires*, Dordrecht, 1986, pp. 9–34.

'Problems in the History of the Firangi Mahall Family of Learned and Holy Men', in N. J. Allen et al. (eds.), *Oxford University Papers on India: Volume I, Part 2*, Delhi, 1987, pp. 1–27.

'Religious Change and the Self in Muslim South Asia since 1800', *South Asia*, 20, 1, 1997, pp. 1–15.

Rothermund, D., *An Economic History of India: From Pre-colonial Times to 1991*, London, 1988, 2nd edn. 1993.

India in the Great Depression, 1929–39, Delhi, 1992.

Sadiq, M., *A History of Urdu Literature*, Delhi, 1984.

Sampurnanand, *Memories and Reflections*, London, 1962.

Saraswati, Swami N., *Lavni ka Itihas*, Kanpur, 1953.

Sarkar, S., *Modern India, 1885–1947*, Delhi, 1983.

'Popular' Movements and 'Middle Class' Leadership in Late Colonial India: Perspectives and Problems of a 'History from Below', Calcutta, 1983.

'The Conditions and Nature of Subaltern Militancy: Bengal from Swadeshi to Non-Cooperation, c. 1905–22', in R. Guha (ed.), *Subaltern Studies III: Writings on South Asian History and Society*, Delhi, 1984, pp. 271–320.

Writing Social History, Delhi, 1998.

Schaller, J., 'Sanskritization, Caste Uplift and Social Dissidence in the Sant Ravidas Panth', in D. N. Lorenzen (ed.), *Bhakti Religion in North India: Community, Identity and Political Action*, New York, 1995, pp. 105–16.

Schimmel, A., *Islam in the Indian Subcontinent*, Leiden, 1980.

Schomer, K., 'Paradigms for the Kaliyuga: The Heroes of the Alha Epic and Their Fate', in S. H. Blackburn et al. (eds.), *Oral Epics in India*, Berkeley, 1989, pp. 140–54.

Schomer, K. and McLeod, W. H. (eds.), *The Sants: Studies in a Devotional Tradition in India*, Delhi, 1987.

Seal, A., 'Imperialism and Nationalism in India', in J. Gallagher, G. Johnson and A. Seal (eds.), *Locality, Province and Nation: Essays on Indian Politics*,

1870–1940, Cambridge, 1973, pp. 1–27. Reprinted from *Modern Asian Studies*, 7, 3, 1973.

Searle-Chatterjee, M. ' "Wahabi" Sectarianism among Muslims of Banaras', *Contemporary South Asia*, 3, 2, 1994, pp. 83–95.

Sewell, W. H., *Work and Revolution in France: The Language of Labour from the Old Regime to 1848*, Cambridge, 1980.

Sharma, I. 'Varij', *Swang Nautanki*, Publications Division, Ministry of Information and Broadcasting, Government of India, 1984.

Shastri, R. S., *Bharatiya Varna Vyavastha mein Khatik Jati ki Utpatti Aur Uska Vikas*, Benares, 1975.

Shraddhanand, Swami, *Hindu Sangathan: Saviour of the Dying Race*, 1924.

Silberrad, C. A., *A Monograph on Cotton Fabrics Produced in the Northwestern Provinces and Oudh*, Allahabad, 1898.

Singh, Rajit, *Yaduvamsa Prakash*, Benares, 1983, revised edn.; first published c. 1925–6.

Singh, Rampravesh, 'Neeche se Upar ki Aur ki Gatishilata', *Ravidas* (Benares), *Praveshank* (introductory issue), 1, 24 February 1986, pp. 21–6.

Singh, R. L., *Banaras: A Study in Urban Geography*, Banaras, 1955.

Singh, U., *Allahabad: A Study in Urban Geography*, Varanasi, 1966.

Srinivas, M. N., *Caste in Modern India and other Essays*, Bombay, 1962; reprinted 1970.

Social Change in Modern India, Berkeley, 1968; Indian edn, Delhi, 1972.

Stedman Jones, G., *Outcast London: A Study in the Relationship between Classes in Victorian Society*, Oxford, 1971.

Languages of Class: Studies in English Working Class History, 1832–1982, Cambridge, 1983.

Steinberg, M., 'Culturally Speaking: Finding a Commons between Post-structuralism and the Thompsonian Perspective', *Social History*, 21, 2, 1996, pp. 193–214.

Stokes, E., *The Peasant and the Raj: Studies in Agrarian Society and Peasant Rebellion in Colonial India*, Cambridge, 1978, first paperback edn, 1980.

Swann, D. L., 'Nautanki', in F. P. Richmond, D. L. Swann and P. B. Zarilli (eds.), *Indian Theatre: Traditions of Performance*, Honolulu, 1990, pp. 249–74.

Taki, R., 'Lakhnau ki Bhand Parampara', *Chayanat*, 21, April–June 1982, pp. 16–23.

Tandon, H., *Prayagraj: Lala Manohardas ka Parivar*, Allahabad, 1993.

Tassey, G. de (trans. M. Waseem), *Muslim Festivals in India and Other Essays*, Delhi, 1995.

Thapar, R., *A History of India. Volume One: From the discovery of India to 1526*, London, 1966, reprinted 1987.

'The Theory of Aryan Race and India: History and Politics', *Social Scientist*, 24, 1–3, 1996, pp. 3–29.

Thomas, D. A., 'Lucknow and Kanpur, 1880–1920: Stagnation and development under the Raj', *South Asia*, 5, 2 (New Series), 1982, pp. 68–80.

Tinker, H., *The Foundations of Local Self-Government in India, Pakistan and Burma*, London, 1954.

Tiwari, S. G., *The Economic Prosperity of the United Provinces: A Study in the*

Provincial Income and its Distribution and Working Conditions, 1921–1939, Bombay, 1951.

Tomlinson, B. R., *The Indian National Congress and the Raj, 1929–1942: The Penultimate Phase,* London, 1976.

The Political Economy of the Raj, 1914–1947: The Economics of Decolonization in India, London, 1979.

The Economy of Modern India, 1860–1970: New Cambridge History of India, III:3, Cambridge, 1993.

Tripathi, L. K. and Arora, N. P., *Kanpur ka Itihas,* 2 vols., Kanpur, 1950.

Tripathi, P. G. 'Piyush', 'Lakhnau mein Khayalbaji aur Uski Parampara', *Chayanat,* 31–32, October 1984–May 1985, pp. 24–9.

Tyrwhitt, J. (ed.), *Patrick Geddes in India,* London, 1947.

Upadhyaya, G. (ed.), *Dalitoddhar,* Arya Samaj, Chowk, Prayag, 1941.

Vaudeville, C., 'Sant Mat: Santism as the Universal Path to Sanctity', in K. Schomer and W. H. McLeod (eds.), *The Sants: Studies in a Devotional Tradition in India,* Delhi, 1987, pp. 21–30.

Veer, P. van der, *Gods on Earth: The Management of Religious Experience and Identity in a North Indian Pilgrimage Centre,* London, 1988.

Religious Nationalism: Hindus and Muslims in India, Berkeley, 1994.

'The Politics of Devotion to Rama', in D. N. Lorenzen (ed.), *Bhakti Religion in North India: Community, Identity and Political Action,* New York, 1995, pp. 288–305.

Verma, K. K., *Changing Role of Caste Associations,* Delhi, 1979.

Wahab, M. J. A. et al., *Qulliat-e-Hasrat,* Karachi, 1976.

Washbrook, D., 'The Development of Caste Organisation in South India, 1880 to 1925', in C. Baker and D. Washbrook, *South India: Political Institutions and Political Change, 1880–1940,* Delhi, 1975, pp. 150–203.

Watt, C. A., 'Education for National Efficiency: Constructive Nationalism in North India, 1909–1916', *Modern Asian Studies,* 31, 2, 1997, pp. 339–74.

Yadav, B. P., *Ahir Jati Ke Niyamavali,* Benares, *Vikrami Samvat* 1984, c. 1927.

Zaidi, A. M. and Zaidi, S. G. (chief eds.), *The Encyclopaedia of the Indian National Congress,* vols. 10 and 11, Delhi, 1980.

Zelliot, E., 'Congress and the Untouchables, 1917–1950', in R. Sisson and S. Wolpert (eds.), *Congress and Indian Nationalism: The Pre-Independence Phase,* Berkeley, 1988, pp. 182–97.

Index

Other titles in the series

Lightning Source UK Ltd.
Milton Keynes UK
UKOW02f0851220816

281014UK00028B/179/P